A HISTORY OF ENGLISH LAW

A HISTORY OF ENGLISH LAW

IN SIXTEEN VOLUMES

For List of Volumes and Plan of the History, see p. x

A HISTORY
OF ENGLISH LAW

BY

SIR WILLIAM HOLDSWORTH

O.M., K.C., D.C.L., Hon.LL.D.

LATE VINERIAN PROFESSOR OF ENGLISH LAW IN THE UNIVERSITY OF OXFORD ; FELLOW
OF ALL SOULS COLLEGE, OXFORD ; HON. FELLOW OF ST. JOHN'S COLLEGE,
OXFORD ; FOREIGN ASSOCIATE OF THE ROYAL BELGIAN ACADEMY ;
FELLOW OF THE BRITISH ACADEMY ; BENCHER OF LINCOLN'S INN

VOLUME XI

*To say truth, although it is not necessary for counsel to know what the
history of a point is, but to know how it now stands resolved, yet it is a
wonderful accomplishment, and, without it, a lawyer cannot be accounted
learned in the law.* ROGER NORTH

LONDON
METHUEN & CO LTD
SWEET AND MAXWELL

Published by Methuen & Co Ltd
and Sweet & Maxwell Ltd
11 New Fetter Lane, London EC4

First published 1938
Reprinted 1966

Printed in Germany by
Nationales Druckhaus Berlin

TO

THE RIGHT HONOURABLE LORD WRIGHT OF DURLEY

LORD OF APPEAL IN ORDINARY

IN MEMORY OF THE DAYS WHEN HE AND THE AUTHOR

BOTH TAUGHT LAW

AT

LONDON UNIVERSITY

THIS WORK

IS

WITH HIS PERMISSION

DEDICATED

BY

HIS FORMER COLLEAGUE AND OLD FRIEND

PREFACE

IN the first and introductory volume, which contains Book I of this History, I have related the history of the Judicial System down to the passing of the Judicature Act in 1875. In the eight succeeding volumes, which contain Books II-IV, I have described the sources and influences which shaped the development of English law down to 1700, and I have related both the history of English public law during the same period, and also the history of the principal doctrines of English private law, in some cases to 1700 and in others down to the nineteenth century. These three succeeding volumes begin Book V, the last Book of this History, in which I propose to relate the history of English law from 1700 to 1875. They begin Part I of this Book, and they relate the history of public law, and of the sources and influences which shaped the development of English law, during the eighteenth century. If I continue to have sufficient health and leisure, I hope in a succeeding volume to complete Part I of this Book, and in Part II to complete the History in two more volumes by giving some account of the history of those doctrines of English law with which I have not fully dealt in the preceding volumes.

It may be thought that I have dealt with the legal history of the eighteenth century at too great a length. But there are several reasons why I have found it necessary to fill three bulky volumes. In the first place, this is the first complete legal history of the eighteenth century which has ever been written. In the second place, to make that history intelligible it has been necessary to deal somewhat more fully than in the preceding periods with the political background.

The Parliamentary history of this period, the history of the beginnings of the system of Cabinet government, the history and effects of the Act of Union with Scotland, the legislation as to Ireland, the beginnings of colonial constitutional law, and the legislation as to India, would not be intelligible without a full account of that background. In the third place, the growth of the colonies and the Indian Empire, the extension of the commerce and industry of Great Britain, and the demands of a more complex and a more civilized society, necessarily increase the complexity of the law both enacted and unenacted, and so make a more lengthy treatment of its history necessary. In the sphere of local government, for instance, and in the statutes relating to commerce and industry, the complexity caused by these demands is very obvious. Lastly, at several points, for instance, in my treatment of beginnings of bodies of local government law, of the royal prerogative, of the departments of the executive government, of the machinery of legislation, of private Acts of Parliament, of the legal profession, of case law, —I have found it necessary to go beyond the eighteenth century and to carry down the history of these topics to the nineteenth century. For this reason I think it will be possible to relate the rest of the history of public law and of the sources and influences which shaped the development of the law in a single volume.

I have to thank Dr. Hazel, the Principal of Jesus College, for his help in reading the proofs and for his suggestions and criticisms, and my son Mr. R. W. G. Holdsworth, Stowell Fellow and Tutor of University College, Oxford, for similar help. The indices and the lists of cases and statutes have been entrusted to the skilled hands of Mr. E. Potton, who prepared the consolidated index and the lists of cases and statutes to the preceding nine volumes.

ALL SOULS COLLEGE,
   January, 1937

PLAN OF THE HISTORY

CONTENTS

BOOK V (*Continued*)

PART I (*Continued*)

SOURCES AND GENERAL DEVELOPMENT

CHAPTER I

THE EIGHTEENTH CENTURY (*Continued*)

Public Law (Continued)

CHAPTER II

THE EIGHTEENTH CENTURY (*Continued*)

The Enacted Law

LIST OF CASES

LIST OF STATUTES

ERRATA

Page 29, line 19 :	*for* thay	*read* they
,, 38, ,, 23 :	,, possession	,, possessions
,, 50, ,, 18 :	,, hand	,, hands
,, 79, ,, 6 :	,, comtempt-	,, contempt-

BOOK V *(Continued)*

(1701-1875)

THE CENTURIES OF SETTLEMENT AND
REFORM

SOURCES AND GENERAL DEVELOPMENT
(*Continued*)

CHAPTER I

THE EIGHTEENTH CENTURY (*Continued*)

PUBLIC LAW (*Continued*)

VIII

GREAT BRITAIN AND IRELAND, THE COLONIES, AND INDIA[1]

"IT is a misrepresentation," says Seeley in his Lectures on *The Expansion of England*,[2] "to describe England in George III's reign as mainly occupied in resisting the encroachments of a somewhat narrow-minded King. We exaggerate the importance of these petty struggles. England was then engaged in other and vaster enterprises. She was not wholly occupied in doing over again what she had done before; she was also doing new and great things." In fact she was making Great Britain a world power, and, in consequence, English law one of the great legal systems of the world. The foundations had been laid in the Elizabethan age and in the seventeenth century.[3] At the very beginning of the eighteenth century the Act of Union between England and Scotland created Great Britain; and it was the creation of Great Britain which

---

[1] The Channel Islands, anciently part of the Duchy of Normandy, were, from the time of the Conquest, attached to England; and the Isle of Man, which was governed from 1405 to 1765 by the House of Stanley, came under the direct control of the Crown in the latter year; for these outlying possessions of the Crown see vol. i 520-522; the relation of the Channel islands and the Isle of Man to England was used, in the latter half of the eighteenth century, as an analogy in support of arguments as to the powers of the mother country over the colonies, below 122; we shall see that a similar use was made of the analogy of the Counties Palatine, below 118-119.

[2] At p. 120.   [3] Vol. ix 411.

was the condition precedent to the building, upon the Elizabethan and seventeenth-century foundations, of the structure of the Greater Britain.[1] The detailed history of the creation of Greater Britain falls outside the scope of purely legal history ; but the effects of its creation upon English law, public and private, fall within it. Of these effects I propose to say something in this section. But since the creation of Great Britain by the Act of Union was the condition precedent to the expansion of England, something must be said of the effects of the Act of Union upon the law of England and Scotland ; and since the relations between England and Ireland in this period, and still more in the following period, have had large effects upon the development of English constitutional law, something must be said of those relations. I shall therefore deal with the subject-matter of this section under the following heads : The Act of Union between England and Scotland and its Effects ; The Relations between England and Ireland ; The Western Expansion of England ; The Eastern Expansion of England ; The Legal Effects of these Expansions of England.

The Act of Union between England and Scotland and its Effects

I have already said something of the manner in which the Act of Union [2] was passed. We have seen that its enactment was due to the English and Scottish Whigs, assisted by some of the leaders of the Tories ; and that it was the necessary and logical result of the Revolution settlement, and the condition precedent for its permanence.[3] It was not, indeed, till Jacobitism had been finally suppressed after the rebellion of 1745, and till the legislation had been passed which made the Highlands an integral part of Great Britain,[4] that the union produced its full effects on the intellectual and commercial life of Scotland.[5] In 1766, Chatham, alluding to the services of the Highland regiments, said that it was indifferent to him " whether a man was rocked in his cradle on this or that side of the Tweed," and that he " sought for merit wherever it was to be found " ; [6] and in spite

---

[1] " The advantages gained by Scotland, though they turned out in the main a great benefit to the whole of Great Britain, were very considerable, and in fact in the course of less than fifty years created a kind of material and intellectual prosperity hitherto unknown in Scotland. Before the lapse of a century, i.e. before 1800, they had given to the whole of Great Britain a strength and wealth absolutely unknown before the Union, and also had laid the foundations of the present British Empire," Dicey and Rait, Thoughts on the Union between England and Scotland 242 ; " The Act of Union which created Great Britain laid the foundation of the British Empire," ibid 321 ; below 5 n. 4.

[2] 5, 6 Anne c. 8.   [3] Vol. x 41.   [4] Vol. x 78-81.
[5] Hume Brown, History of Scotland iii 333.
[6] Dicey and Rait, op. cit. 313-314.

of some animosity shown to Scotsmen after 1745 on account of the rebellion,[1] and at the beginning of George III's reign on account of the policy pursued by the King's favourite, the Marquis of Bute,[2] and in spite of some natural resentment on the part of Scottish writers at the abuse showered upon their nation,[3] the process of amalgamating the two nations proceeded steadily. During the second half of the eighteenth century the two nations began to draw together ; and, without sacrificing their peculiar social idiosyncrasies, intellectual outlook, and legal institutions, became in effect a united nation, both sections of which have contributed to the creation of that Greater Britain, which could not have been created without this collaboration.[4]

The achievement of these results was due partly to the skill with which the union was effected by the Act, and partly to the manner in which the provisions of the Act were applied in practice. The Act made the minimum of change in the institutions of the two countries, so that it was possible to adapt the working of the new Parliament of Great Britain to the exigencies of the law and conventions of the eighteenth-century English constitution, in such a way that leading Scotsmen took their fair share in the government of Great Britain, and the Scottish nation was educated in the conduct of Parliamentary government. Since both the provisions of the Act and the manner in which they were applied conduced to this result, I shall deal with the effects of the Act of Union under these two heads.

(1) *The direct effects of the Act.*

We must examine the direct effects of the Act (i) upon the Crown, (ii) upon Parliament, and (iii) upon the courts.

(i) The direct effects of the Act upon the Crown were slight, because the Crowns had been united since 1603. Since that date the Scottish King had ruled his Scottish kingdom from London. In 1607 James I had said to his English Parliament, " This I may say for Scotland, and may trewly vaunt it : here I sit and governe it with my pen ; I write and it is done ; and by a Clearke of the Councell I governe Scotland now—which others could

---

[1] Mathieson, The Awakening of Scotland 43-44 ; Lecky, History of England iii 219.

[2] Mathieson, op. cit. 44-46 ; Lecky, op. cit. iii 219-222.

[3] Dicey and Rait, op. cit. 312-313.

[4] Above 4 n. 1 ; " Across the ocean the Plantation trades brought wealth to the markets of Glasgow and Edinburgh, and opened a market to the manufactures of an industrial belt which has greatly increased the population of Scotland. The Scots on their side added strength to the Empire. Canada'owes much to them, first as factors and explorers for the Hudson's Bay Company, and afterwards as settlers in Ontario and the prairies. . . . Scottish names are prominent in the later history of British India, in the colonisation of Australia, New Zealand, and South Africa, and in the development of tropical dependencies," Camb. Col. Hist. i 266.

not doe by the sword." [1] We have seen that the union of the Crowns, by delivering the King of Scotland from the tyranny of powerful nobles and the preachers of the Presbyterian Kirk, gave him an authority which he had never had before.[2] The danger that, at the death of Anne, this union of the Crowns would come to an end, and the tension between the English and Scottish Parliaments at the beginning of the eighteenth century, which made this danger very real, united to set in motion the train of events that led to the passing of the Act of Union.[3] The English Parliament, by the Alien Act of 1705,[4] had made it plain that "there should either be a closer union between the two countries, or that the union of the Crowns, which had been treated as permanent since the accession of James to the Crown of England, should not be continued." [5] Fortunately for both countries the first alternative was chosen ; and the succession to the United Kingdom of Great Britain was settled in accordance with the English Act of Settlement.[6]

(ii) The direct effect of the Act upon Parliament was much more far-reaching. The separate Parliaments of England and Scotland disappeared, and, in their stead, was created the Parliament of Great Britain.[7] In this Parliament the peers of Scotland were represented in the House of Lords by sixteen of their number elected by them at the beginning of each Parliament.[8] These representative peers were to have all the privileges of Parliament to which peers of England or peers of Great Britain after the union were entitled.[9] The rest of the Scottish peers were to have all the privileges of peers of Great Britain " except the right and privilege of sitting in the House of Lords, and the privileges depending thereon, and particularly the right of sitting upon the trials of peers." [10] The commons of Scotland were to be represented by forty-five members, thirty to be chosen by the shires, and fifteen by the royal burghs.[11]

Immediately after the union the question arose whether a Scottish peer, who had been created a peer of Great Britain, had the right to a seat in the House of Lords. In 1709 the Duke of Queensberry, upon being created a peer of Great Britain with the title of Duke of Dover, had been allowed to sit in the House of Lords.[12] But in 1711, when the Duke of Hamilton was created a peer of Great Britain with the title of Duke of Brandon, the

---

[1] Works of James I 520-521.
[2] Vol. vi 8-9 ; Mathieson, The Awakening of Scotland 6-7.
[3] Dicey and Rait, op. cit. 160-179.   [4] 3, 4 Anne c. 7.
[5] Dicey and Rait, op. cit. 172.   [6] 5, 6 Anne c. 8, Art. 2.
[7] Ibid Art. 3.   [8] Arts. 22, 25.   [9] Art. 23.
[10] Ibid.   [11] Arts. 22, 25.
[12] Hume Brown, History of Scotland iii 148 ; The Duke of Queensberry and Dover's Case (1719) 1 P. Wms. 582.

House of Lords refused to allow him to take his seat. The House laid down the principle that a peerage of Great Britain conferred upon a peer of Scotland did not entitle that peer to a seat in the House of Lords.[1] The House adhered to this decision in 1719 in the case of the second Duke of Queensberry, in spite of the able argument of Peere Williams, based upon the words of the relevant articles of the Act of Union.[2] Probably the real reason for a decision, which had little or no legal reason to support it, was a fear that the government might create Scottish peers peers of Great Britain in sufficient numbers to give it a majority in the House.[3] Later in the century this decision was evaded by the device of making the eldest son of a Scottish peer a peer of Great Britain. He had thereby become a member of the House of Lords ; and his subsequent attainment of a Scottish peerage created no disability.[4] This device was rendered unnecessary in 1782, when the House of Lords, in accordance with the unanimous opinion of the judges, reversed its former decision, and held that the Act of Union did not exclude a Scottish peer who had been made a peer of Great Britain.[5] But this reversal of its former decision raised the question whether a representative peer, who was made a peer of Great Britain, could continue to sit as a representative peer. The House decided in 1787, in spite of Thurlow's opposition, that he could not.[6]

The Act of Union expressly ratified an Act of the Parliament of Scotland which prescribed the mode of electing the sixteen representative peers and the forty-five members of the House of Commons.[7] In the election of the representative peers all the peers of Scotland either in person or by proxy were entitled to a vote. In the election of the members of the House of Commons thirty were chosen by the shires, and fifteen were chosen by sixty-six burghs. Edinburgh had one representative, and fourteen groups of four or five of the other burghs—known as districts—each had one.[8] The Act of Union provided that members must have attained the age of twenty-one, and be Protestants ; and then it went on to enact that " none shall be capable to elect or be elected . . . except such as are now capable by the laws of this kingdom to elect or be elected as commissioners for shires or burghs to the Parliament of Scotland." Thus the

[1] Erskine May, Constitutional History i 286-287.

[2] 1 P. Wms. at pp. 583-591.

[3] Hume Brown, History of Scotland iii 149.

[4] Erskine May, Constitutional History i 287.   [5] Ibid.

[6] Ibid 287-288 ; Parlt. Hist. xxvi 596-607 ; till 1793 they were also disqualified from voting for the representative peers in accordance with a resolution of the House in 1709 ; but in 1793 this resolution was rescinded and all peers of Scotland were allowed to vote, Erskine May, op. cit. i 288-289.

[7] Art. 25.

[8] Mathieson, op. cit. 21 ; Dicey and Rait, op. cit. 290-291.

system in force in Scotland when the Act of Union was framed was perpetuated. Under that system the franchise was even more restricted and more anomalous than it was in England. In the shires it was feudal, depending in theory on the tenure of freehold land from the Crown. But it could be attached either to the land, if it was in the hands of the tenant from the Crown, or, if he had alienated it, to his superiority or lordship. Advantage was taken of this rule by landowners who wished to multiply votes which they could control. They parcelled their lands out into lots of sufficient value to attract the franchise, and conveyed these lots to trusted friends. The Crown granted charters to these persons, so that each became a tenant-in-chief. Then they conveyed the land back to the original owner, retaining only the superiority which gave the vote. The result was that many voters had no land at all.[1] Though attempts were made to suppress this practice, which at the end of the century had some success, these fictitious qualifications survived till 1832.[2] The result was that the franchise in the shires was ridiculously restricted. In 1790 it was reckoned that there were only 2665 voters, of whom 1318 were fictitious.[3] In the burghs the franchise was even more restricted. It was restricted to the burgh council, which was annually elected by the outgoing council. The council in each of the groups of burghs elected a delegate, and the delegates elected the member.[4] In 1832 the total burgh electorate numbered 1303.[5] Thus all Scottish members of the House of Commons were elected by some 4000 voters.

(iii) The Act of Union repealed all laws in both countries which were inconsistent with the Act.[6] But, subject thereto, all other laws were to remain in force, unless or until they were altered by the Parliament of Great Britain.[7] In particular the maintenance of the Scottish judicial system was guaranteed ; and its independence was safeguarded by the promise that, " no causes in Scotland be cognoscible by the courts of Chancery, Queen's Bench, Common Pleas, or any other court in Westminster Hall, and that the said courts, or any other of the like nature, after the Union, shall have no power to cognosce, review or alter

---

[1] Dicey and Rait, op. cit. 291 and App. A ; Mathieson, op. cit. 18-19.

[2] " From 1790 it became distinctly more difficult to create fictitious votes," Dicey and Rait, op. cit. 367 ; Mathieson, op. cit. 101.

[3] Ibid 20 ; Cockburn, Life of Lord Jeffrey, i 75 says, " there were probably not above 1500 or 2000 county electors in all Scotland ; a body not too large to be held, hope included, in Government's hands. . . . The election of either the town or the county member was a matter of such utter indifference to the people, that they often only knew of it by the ringing of a bell, or by seeing it mentioned next day in a newspaper."

[4] Mathieson, op. cit. 21.   [5] Ibid.

[6] Art. 25.   [7] Ibid 18 ; below 14.

the acts or sentences of the judicatures within Scotland, or stop the execution of the same." [1]   But the British House of Lords was not " a court in Westminster Hall," nor was it a court " of a like nature " with these courts.   The Act of Union therefore left open, and left open deliberately,[2] the question whether an appeal from the Scottish court of Session lay to the British House of Lords.[3]

In 1709, in the case of Greenshields, the House of Lords entertained an appeal from the court of Session, and in 1711 it reversed a decision of that court.[4]   The words of the Act of Union left it open to the House to hold that it had jurisdiction, if an appeal to the Scottish Parliament would have lain before the Act of Union.   But it was arguable that no appeal to Parliament was known to Scottish law, and that therefore no appeal from the Scottish courts would lie to the House of Lords.[5] Whether or not this argument was sound was a very doubtful question of Scots law ; [6] so that it was open to the House to decide it by holding that it had jurisdiction.   Whatever may be said about the correctness of this decision in point of law, there can be no question of its expediency.   In the first place it made for the efficiency of the Scottish bench.   Sir Walter Scott said of this right of appeal that " it was a privilege highly desirable for the subject, as the examination and occasional reversal of their sentences in Parliament might serve as a check upon the judges, which they greatly required at a time when they were much more distinguished for legal knowledge than for uprightness

---

[1] Art. 19 ; under the powers conferred by this Act, a court of Exchequer for Scotland was established by 6 Anne c. 26, the judges of which were to be either English barristers of five years' standing or members of the College of Advocates of the same standing ; the financial powers of the court were transferred to the Treasury in 1833, and the judicial powers were transferred to the court of Session in 1856, see Calendar of Inner Temple Records iv *iv ;* in 1807 the post of Chief Baron was described as a sinecure, Life of Lord Campbell i 199.

[2] " The 19th Article was read.   *Proposed* to ask the Judges the following question, Whether after the Union the House of Lords of Great Britain will have right to hear and determine causes which shall be brought before them by appeal, writ of error, or otherwise from Judicatories of Scotland, and whether the subjects of Scotland and whether the suitors of Scotland will have right to bring any such causes before the House of Lords of Great Britain to be heard and determined by them. The motion to ask this question was negatived and the Article agreed to," MSS. of the House of Lords (Hist. MSS. Com.) vii no. 2307.

[3] Dicey and Rait, op. cit. 192-193.

[4] Ibid 195 ; Trevelyan, England under Queen Anne iii 236-238 ; for an unsuccessful attempt to prove that there was a right of appeal in criminal cases see Calendar of Home Office Papers 1760-1765 614, 617, 618.

[5] Dicey and Rait, op. cit. 196-198.

[6] " At the time when the Commission was sitting, there existed a difference of opinion between a group of eminent Scottish lawyers and the Court of Session on the question how far there existed an appeal from the decisions of the Court to the Scottish Parliament," ibid 197-198.

and integrity." [1]   In 1830 it was said by a Scots lawyer that,

this appeal is in itself not merely expedient, but absolutely necessary.
It corrects error ; it excites attention ; it checks carelessness ; it ex-
poses extravagance. . . . Among all the persons who were examined
by the Commission of 1823, and amidst all the host of opinions that
were then given, there was no dissentient voice upon the subject.[2]

In the second place, it helped towards the unification of the law
of the two countries.   Dicey says : [3]

The decision in Greenshield's case did much towards securing the
same amount of religious toleration in Scotland as the Revolution of
1688 had practically established in England.   Experience shows further
that the existence of one Court of Appeal for the whole of the United
Kingdom has done a great deal towards establishing legal unity throughout every part of Great Britain, and this without destroying the different
character of English and of Scottish law in cases such as the law of
marriage, when the national feeling of each country has been opposed
to a unification of law where it runs against the popular sentiment
either of England or of Scotland.

But of the general effects of the Union upon English and
Scottish law I shall have more to say in the following section.[4]

(2) *The effects of the working of the Act.*

We must examine the effects of the working of the Act (i)
upon the constitutional relations, and (ii) upon the law, of the
two countries.

(i) In dealing with this subject we must remember three
things—the fact that before the Act of Union Scotland had
no constitutional tradition ; [5] the fact that the franchise in
Scotland was limited to very few persons ; [6] and the fact that
the working of the complex English constitution, to which the
Scottish representatives were introduced, depended upon a
series of conventions, centring round the system of representation
to the English House of Commons.   We have seen that these
conventions created a link between the divided powers of King
and Parliament, and between the divided powers of two Houses
of Parliament, and thus enabled these three partners, between
whom the power of the state were divided, to work together.[7]

The state of the Scottish representation made it easy for the
Crown to apply in Scotland the same means of influence that
it applied in England.   On the other hand, the Scottish members,
who were naturally not interested in purely English party
struggles, found it to their interest to support the government
of the day, which was always able and willing to reward support.

[1] Cited Dicey and Rait, op. cit. 199.
[2] Ed. Rev. li 138.   [3] Dicey and Rait, op. cit. 199.   [4] Below 14-20.
[5] Mathieson, The Awakening of Scotland 14-15 ; Dicey and Rait, op. cit. 70-78.
[6] Above 8.   [7] Vol. x 629-635.

The Scottish peers, in spite of occasional protests,[1] always complied with the directions of the Government, and elected as their sixteen representatives the " King's list." [2] The Scottish members of the House of Commons, though they sometimes showed independence on purely Scottish questions, almost invariably voted with the government.[3] Their point of view was expressed by Boswell of Auchinleck in 1782, when he said that, " as that man was esteemed the best sportsman that brought down the most birds, so was he the best representative that brought the best pensions and places to his countrymen." [4] The principal occasion on which they voted against the Government was at the close of Walpole's ministry.[5] But this is an exception of the rule-proving variety. Walpole was evidently about to fall, and the Scottish members wished to be on the winning side. James Oswald, for instance, who had been elected as the member for Kirkcaldy Burghs at the general election which preceded the fall of Walpole, had promised to support Walpole ; but he voted against him. When the friend, to whom he had given his promise, came to reproach him with his breach of faith, Oswald is said to have met him with these words : " You had like to have led me into a fine error. Did you not tell me Sir Robert would have the majority " ? [6] We could have no better illustration of the truth of Bagehot's statement that one of the greatest weaknesses of this system of influence was the fact that it failed to secure support for a minister just when he most needed it.[7]

The Scottish members were rewarded to an extent which, at the beginning of George III's reign, aroused much criticism, sometimes of an abusive kind. It was pointed out that Scotsmen filled all the official positions in their own country,[8] and many

---

[1] A debate in the House of Lords in 1734 shows that some of the peers resented this control, Parlt. Hist. ix 487-510 ; and in 1735 there were allegations of illegal and corrupt practices in the elections, ibid 759, 784 ; in 1770 it was found necessary to make modifications in the ministerial list, Walpole, Memoirs of George III iv 234 ; for a protest by the Duke of Buccleugh in 1774 see Calendar of Home Office Papers 1773-1775, 256, 257 ; in 1784 the peers made an unsuccessful stand against the mandates of the court, Walpole, Last Journals i 431.

[2] Meikle, Scotland and the French Revolution 12-13 ; Turberville, The House of Lords in the XVIIIth Century 159.

[3] Mathieson, op. cit. 22 ; Dicey and Rait, op. cit. 261-265, 292-293 ; Lecky, History of England ii 323-326.

[4] Benger, Memoirs of Mrs. E. Hamilton i 89, cited Meikle, Scotland and the French Revolution xviii-xix ; in 1784 Professor Laprade, Parliamentary Papers of John Robinson (R.H.S.) xiv-xv, says, " The case of Scotland was easy ; Henry Dundas was a party to the undertaking, and in most constituencies in that country Dundas was in a position to say, as Robinson quoted him as saying of the sitting member for Edinburgh, ' pro, or he will not come in ' " ; Dundas became Lord Advocate in 1775 and for nearly thirty years was the uncrowned King of Scotland, Hume Brown, History of Scotland iii 347.

[5] Mathieson, op. cit. 25-26.   [6] Ibid 32.

[7] Bagehot, Essays on Parliamentary Reform 157-158 ; vol. x 634-635.

[8] Dicey and Rait, op. cit. 312, 328-329.

to which Englishmen considered that they had a claim. And there is no doubt that the critics could make out a case. Mr. Mathieson says : [1]

In 1762 Bute was Prime Minister ; Mansfield was Lord Chief Justice ; Kinnoul had just retired with Newcastle from the Cabinet ; his brother, Hay Drummond, was Archbishop of York ; Oswald and Elliot were Lords of the Treasury ; Sir Andrew Mitchell, member for the Elgin Burghs, was British Ambassador at Berlin ; Colonel Graeme was the Queen's Private Secretary ; John Douglas, prominent in political controversy and a future bishop, was a Canon of Windsor ; Allan Ramsay was the painter, and Robert Adam the architect, in highest favour at Court.

Scotsmen were equally prominent in the army and navy. In 1762

Lord Loudoun commanded the British forces in Portugal ; General Murray, one of Wolfe's brigadiers, had succeeded that hero when he fell at the taking of Quebec ; Colonel Grant in Florida had just inflicted a severe defeat on the Cherokee Indians ; Lord Rollo as second-in-command was reducing the Windward Isles ; and in Bengal Major Hector Monro had begun the career of conquest which was to culminate in 1764 at Buxar. In two of these instances a Scottish General was assisted by a Scottish Commodore. The two frigates which brought relief to General Murray and averted the recapture of Quebec were commanded by Lord Colville of Culross ; and Sir James Douglas co-operated at sea with Lord Rollo in wresting Dominica from the French.

No doubt Scotsmen owed something to the constant support which the Scottish members of the House of Commons gave to the government. On the other hand, Scotsmen were obviously entitled to a share in the offices at the disposal of the Government of the United Kingdom ; and it is clear that a considerable number of these appointments was justified by the merit shown by the persons appointed.

In fact, it was the manner in which the Act of Union was worked by the Scottish and English statesmen during the eighteenth century which is the chief cause for its ultimate success. England and Scotland were, by their efforts, so thoroughly united that they were governed, not only by the same constitutional law, but also by the same constitutional conventions—in particular by that set of conventions which centred round the influence which the state of the representative system enabled the Crown to exert.[2] If, indeed, we look at the constitutional effects of the working of the Act through the spectacles of a Whig of 1832, we shall find much to condemn, and very little to praise. We shall find less to condemn if we look at the general effects of the Act from the point of view of the eighteenth

---

[1] Mathieson, op. cit. 46-47.   [2] Vol. x 629-635.

century.[1] The Act of Union introduced Scotland, as a partner with England, to a system of Parliamentary government.[2] Though its members were elected on a ridiculously narrow franchise, though they could nearly always be reckoned on to support the government of the day, they sometimes took an independent line on purely Scottish questions, they accustomed their nation to Parliamentary government, and their support of the government gave many Scotsmen the opportunity to serve the Crown in the civil service at home, abroad, in India, in the colonies, in the navy, and in the army. The working of the Act thus gave Scotsmen the opportunity to take their full share in the expansion of England ; whilst the freedom of trade which they had secured as the price of the Union [3] enabled them to share in the consequent expansion of trade and the development of many branches of industry.[4] At the same time some of the great Scottish landowners followed the example of the English landowners,[5] and effected great improvements in agriculture.[6] Throughout the country the level of civilization was raised, and Scotsmen won European reputations as economists, as historians, and as philosophers.[7] " Scotland—or at least lowland Scotland," says M. Halévy,[8] " was (in 1815) one of the most active centres of British civilization. Whether for agriculture or for manufactures the Lowlands could bear comparison with any English county. . . . At the Bar, in journalism, in letters the Scottish had won the first places."

We cannot wholly condemn the working of an Act which achieved such results as these, or the institutions which made these results possible. It is, I think, clear that the long result of the working of the Act in the eighteenth century was to give a political education to the nation, which enabled it to take its full share in the many fields of activity which were opening to Great Britain in that century ; and because the working of the Act of Union gave the nation this education, it enabled the

[1] See Dicey and Rait, op. cit. 292-294.

[2] " The parliamentary union of the kingdoms, both theoretically and in fact, was a very different thing from the subjection of Scotland to England. It was, as its very name proclaimed, a treaty whereby England and Scotland alike became members of the one State of Great Britain, wherein no doubt England was the predominant partner. But partnership made on fair terms is an essentially different thing from subjection or servitude," ibid 327-328 ; we shall see that England's relations with Ireland are a striking illustration of this difference, below 25-28.

[3] Mr. Hughes has pointed out, Studies in Administration and Finance 414-419, that with respect to the salt tax Scotland got much more favourable treatment than England, which the government did not dare to rectify for fear of diminishing its influence on the Scottish members of Parliament.

[4] Mathieson, op. cit. chap. vi ; Hume Brown, History of Scotland iii 358-359.

[5] Vol. x 624.   [6] Mathieson, op. cit. 284-285.

[7] Dicey and Rait, op. cit. 338-340 ; Hume Brown, History of Scotland iii 371-375 ; Mathieson, op. cit. 203-204.

[8] History of the English People in 1815 (English tr.) 104.

nation, at the end of this and at the beginning of the following century, to take its share in the various projects of reform which changed political, social, and industrial conditions were rendering necessary.[1] It enabled the nation to take in hand, in con-junction with the English reformers, the recasting of a repre-sentative system which had always been more anomalous than the English system, and had become even less suited than the English system to modern needs.[2] The fact that Scottish were thus able to combine with English reformers, is the best proof that by 1800 the working of the Act of Union had succeeded in making the British nationality created by it a real thing.

(ii) The effects of the working of the Act of Union upon the law of the two countries have been equally salutary.

The eighteenth article of the Act of Union drew a distinction between " the laws concerning public right, policy, and civil government," and the laws " which concern private right." The former " may be made the same throughout the whole United Kingdom " : the latter were not to be changed " except for evident utility of the subjects within Scotland." [3] The nineteenth article then went on to provide for the maintenance of the separate judicial system of Scotland. By these two articles of the Act of Union the differences between English and Scottish law and judicial institutions were preserved and per-petuated. These differences were very real, because they re-flected great differences in the history of the two systems of law, and great differences in the mental outlook of the lawyers of the two countries.[4]

The English legal system had been continuously developed, from the twelfth century onwards, on native lines. With some assistance from the Legislature, it had been developed mainly by the decisions of the courts, and, to a much smaller extent, by text-books, in which the results of those decisions had been summarized and co-ordinated. England had thus attained early in her history a native common law. But the attainment of a native system of law came late to Scotland. Lord Macmillan says : [5]

---

[1] Mathieson, op. cit. chap. iii ; Meikle, Scotland and the French Revolution, chaps. ii-v.

[2] Meikle, op. cit. 235-237.

[3] The judges, on being consulted by the House of Lords, gave it as their clear opinion that the Act in no way affected the law of England ; Holt C.J. said, " this incorporation cannot alter or repeal the laws of England ; laws are local and the Union cannot repeal them " ; Trevor C.J. said, " if I had thought this Union had or could destroy the laws of England, I would have proposed a remedy," MSS. of the House of Lords (Hist. MSS. Com.) vii no. 2307.

[4] The following paragraphs owe much to an address given by Lord Macmillan at the International Congress of Comparative Law at The Hague in August 1932, entitled " Scots Law as a Subject of Comparative Study " which has been published in L.Q.R. xlviii 477-487.   [5] Ibid 478

When she first began to emerge from the primitive tribal life of early times there was no body of generally accepted customs to form the foundation of a Scottish common law, and when she came to claim her place as a nation she found herself confronted with already formulated systems of law across the border in the neighbouring country of England, and across the seas among the politically advanced nations with which through alliances or trade connections she was brought into contact.

Therefore Scotland experienced, what many other countries of Europe in a like condition experienced, in the sixteenth century —a Reception of Roman Law.[1] Scotsmen studied their law in France, Germany, and more especially in Holland where the theological atmosphere was congenial.[2] The intellectual connection between the Dutch and the Scottish lawyers, which began in the sixteenth century, lasted throughout the seventeenth and eighteenth centuries [3]—" as late as 1833 there were still advocates in the Parliament House at Edinburgh who had studied at Leyden or Utrecht."[4]

The result was that the mind of the Scottish lawyer was formed on the logical and systematic principles of the Roman law, and the commentaries thereon of the famous Dutch lawyers.[5] " The formulary system and the fictions of the English common law, the outcome of pure empiricism, find no counterpart in the history of the law of Scotland. In Scotland the search was not for the appropriate form of writ, but for the legal principle involved."[6] In Scotland there have been three authoritative statements of Scots law in three successive centuries, which " follow closely the Roman philosophic model " : [7] in England

---

[1] For the sixteenth-century Reception of Roman Law and its effects in Scotland and on the different countries of Western Europe, see vol. iv 246-250.

[2] L.Q.R. xlviii 478 ; see Sources and Literature of Scots Law (Stair Soc.) i 232-234.

[3] Viscount Stair, the author of *The Institutions of the Law of Scotland*, fled to Leyden in 1682 to avoid a prosecution for refusal to comply with the Test Act ; " and among the many other Scottish lawyers who there imbibed their knowledge of the civil law I may mention Lord President Forbes (1685-1747), who proceeded to Leyden in 1705 and stayed there for nearly two years, attaining great proficiency as a civilian, and Lord President Dundas (1713-1787), who studied at Utrecht. Another Scottish judge, well known though less illustrious in the law, who crossed the sea in search of instruction, was Lord Monboddo, the eccentric precursor of Darwin, who spent three years at the University of Gröningen. I may conclude my list with the name of James Boswell, of the Scottish Bar, who on Friday, 5th August 1763, set out from London for the University of Utrecht," L.Q.R. xlviii 480.

[4] Ibid 481.

[5] In a catalogue of the Advocates Library in Edinburgh published in 1692 there are some 1,500 law books ; of these " there are only about thirty native law books, several of them still in manuscript, while London and Oxford contribute less than ninety. All the rest are continental treatises, and the publications of the press of Leyden are far the most numerous," ibid 483.

[6] Ibid 482 ; it is for this reason that, " if one excepts the period of the usurpation, there is no indication that English and Scots law made any kind of contact during the seventeenth century," Sources and Literature of Scots Law (Stair Soc.) i 217.

[7] L.Q.R. xlviii 483 ; they are Stair's Institutions of the Law of Scotland (1681), Erskine's Institute (1773), Bell's Principles (1829).

the statements of Bracton,[1] Coke,[2] and Blackstone [3] are not so complete, and their philosophy lacks the neatness of the philosophy of law books founded upon the Roman law. And so we get a contrast between the two rival ways of constructing a legal system—the logical and deductive Scottish method formed upon Roman models, and the empirical and inductive English method built up by decided cases on native lines.[4] It would not of course be true to say that the English lawyer had no logic. Logic he had—the system of special pleading was often dominated excessively by very pure and formal deductive logic. But his logic was always subordinated to the rules which he had inductively, and, to a large extent empirically, developed from decided cases.[5]

This contrast was taking shape in the sixteenth and seventeenth centuries when theology counted for much; and it was reflected in, and perhaps accentuated by, the very different intellectual outlook of the national churches of the two countries. The Calvinistic theology of the Scottish Presbyterian Church was completely logical. The theology taught by the English Church was a somewhat eclectic compromise. The difference in the theological outlook of the Scotsman and the Englishman matched the difference in his legal outlook.

We shall see that the most striking illustration of the fundamental difference between these two very different types of intellectual schools of legal thought is to be found in some of the decisions of Lord Mansfield.[6] Being a Scotsman, he had much of the mentality of a Scottish lawyer, and little of the unreasoning reverence of the English lawyer for the only system of law that he knew. For that reason he tried, without much success, to rationalize some of the settled rules of English law, which it was easier to explain historically than to justify logically. The heretical doctrines which he laid down on such topics as consideration, seisin and disseisin, the rule in *Shelley's Case*, and the relations of law and equity, are, as we shall see,[7] traceable to this fundamental difference in the mentality of the lawyers of the two nations.

Let us look at one or two of the concrete differences which existed between the Scottish and English legal systems. The main differences have been thus summarized by Mr. Brodie Innes:[8] First, the judicial systems of the two countries were different. This difference " accounts for all the differences in

---

[1] Vol. ii 236-286.   [2] Vol. v 456-490.   [3] Vol. xii 711-712, 731-736.
[4] " The contrast is that between the two main schools of legal thought, the logical and the empirical," L.Q.R. xlviii 483.
[5] See vol. ix 311-314.
[6] Vol. xii 556-557; and see vol. vii 19-20, 43-45 ; vol. viii 25-34.   [7] Vol. xii. 556.
[8] Comparative Principles of the Laws of England and Scotland 4.

procedure, in the nature and forms of legal remedies, in the classification of legal wrongs, in the terminology of wrongs and their remedies, also for the English division of common law and equity, which is a pure result of historic development, and which does not exist in Scotland." Secondly, England rejected Roman law from an early period, whilst in Scotland the influence of Roman law has always been marked. This difference "accounts for the large class of divergencies in questions of status, in rights in private relations, and in questions arising from the frequent occurrence in Scottish common law of the equitable maxims and principles considered in England the special prerogatives of the Court of Chancery "; and, it may be added, for the different development of the law of contract in the two countries. Thirdly, there was a difference in the development and application of feudal ideas in the law of property. The statute of Quia Emptores, which in 1290 abolished subinfeudation in England, did not apply to Scotland, so that the Scots law relating to the tenure of and estates in the land is essentially different from that of England.[1] Fourthly, there were differences resulting from the fact that, from an early date, Scotland had a system of registration of deeds. These two last differences are at the root of most of the differences between the laws of England and Scotland in the land law and the law of conveyancing.

It was inevitable that the working of the Act of Union should tend to modify some of these differences. First, when legislation was required on some new topic, and the problem to be solved was the same in both countries, a united Legislature necessarily made the same rule for the two countries. It is for this reason that in the most modern branches of the law there is the greatest uniformity. "Thus the law relating to patents, designs, copyright, trade marks, carriage, electricity supply, etc., is nearly identical in both countries."[2] Secondly, since it was after the passing of the Act of Union, and in consequence of its provisions, that Scotland became an important commercial country, it is not surprising to find that those branches of the law which govern commercial dealings are very similar. Thus the maritime law of the two countries—the law relating to such matters as shipping, charter-parties, and bills of lading—is practically identical.[3] On many topics of commercial law, such as the law of negotiable instruments,[4] and of companies, except the law as to the winding

---

[1] Encyclopædia of the Laws of Scotland, *sub voce* English Law in Scots Practice vi 164.

[2] Ibid 163 ; for the manner in which, and the conditions under which, the citation of English cases is permitted in Scots Law, see Sources and Literature of Scots Law (Stair Soc.) i 221-222.

[3] Encyclopædia of the Laws of Scotland vi 163, citing Clydesdale Bank v Walker and Bain [1926] S.C. at p. 82.

[4] Ibid vi 163, 190-191.

up of companies,[1] the laws of the two countries are very nearly the same ; and on other topics, such as partnership [2] and agency,[3] though there are important differences, there is a large amount of similarity. On the other hand, there are still important differences in the law as to sale of goods. These differences are due partly to the different development of the Scottish law of contract, and partly to the fact that certain topics, such as the topic of capacity to contract, are treated differently in the laws of the two countries. Thirdly, the fact that the final court of appeal is the same for both countries has made a bridge between the two systems. The working of such a court has made it necessary for a certain number of lawyers, both on the bench and at the bar, to acquire some knowledge of both systems, and thus to appreciate their differences and resemblances. These lawyers have been compelled to institute a comparison between the two systems of law, and, in a number of concrete cases, to find out what exactly the difference is, and what amount of under-lying similarity exists. Therefore the working of this court has helped towards a mutual understanding between the lawyers of the two countries. Above all it has helped, as a study of com-parative law always helps, to emancipate lawyers from an insular and unreasoning satisfaction with their own system, and thus to make them willing and able to apply to that system a sane criticism or an informed appreciation. " To learn another system of law," says Lord Macmillan,[4] " is like learning another language. It not only adds to one's knowledge but renders the system one already knows more intelligent and more vivid. A person who is bilingual is much better able to appreciate the merits of each of the languages he speaks, for each throws the other into relief."

As early as the middle of the eighteenth century the existence of this process of assimilation was becoming obvious. Bankton, in his *Institutes of the Laws of Scotland*, which was published in 1751, finds it necessary to compare the laws of England and Scotland. He tells us that Lord Stair, who published his *In-stitutes of the Law of Scotland* in 1681, had no need to make this comparison ; " but now, since the union of the two kingdoms, there is such an intercourse between the subjects of South and North Britain, that it must be of great moment that the laws of both be generally understood, and their agreement or diversity attended to ; so that people, in their mutual correspondence, may regulate themselves accordingly." [5]   Lord Kames also

---

[1] Encyclopædia of the Laws of Scotland vi 191-193.
[2] Ibid 176-179.   [3] Ibid 182-183.
[4] L.Q.R. xlviii 486 ; cp. Sources and Literature of Scots Law (Stair Soc.) 218-219.
[5] Cited L.Q.R. xlviii 484.

recommended the study of the differences and resemblances of
Scottish and English law, because, he said, " they have such resemblance as to bear a comparison almost in every branch ;
and they so far differ as to illustrate each other by their opposition." [1]

It would be a long and difficult task to state an account of
the mutual indebtedness of English and Scots law to one another ;
but, if it were skilfully stated, it would make a most interesting study in comparative law. If, in the eighteenth century,
English influence helped to abolish the use of torture,[2] if it
helped to get rid of the last remnants of servitude by the emancipation of the colliers and salters,[3] if it helped to build up a modern
system of commercial and maritime law,[4] Scotland had something
to give in return. Because Scots law was deeply influenced by
Roman law it was in much closer touch with continental legal
developments than English law.[5] For this reason it was saved
from some of the worst intricacies of the English land law,[6] and
from the failures of justice wrought by the writ system and the
resulting separation of the forms of action [7] and of the system of
special pleading.[8] Its closer touch with continental legal systems
gave it a law of bankruptcy which was much superior to that of
England ; [9] and some of its provisions were followed by English
legislators—it was said by a Scottish lawyer in 1830 that
" Thurlow, Loughborough, Eldon, Romilly, Abbot, and many
Parliamentary Commissions, have acknowledged their obligations
in the course of their reforms in commercial law to the bankrupt
law of this country." [10] Scots law never permitted a creditor
to arrest his debtor's person on mesne process as English law

---

[1] L.Q.R. xlviii 484-485.
[2] Hume Brown, History of Scotland iii 144 ; 7 Anne c. 21 § 5.
[3] Hume Brown, op. cit. iii 348-349 ; 15 George III c. 28 ; 39 George III c. 56.
[4] Above 17-18.
[5] " While the English, according to the image of Bacon, . . . were by their
exclusive addiction to their own ways, ' an island separated from other lands,'
we were ' a continent that joined them.' A residence at the great continental
schools of law, was, for centuries, an established part of the education, not only of
professional lawyers, but of liberally educated gentlemen. Hence our laws may be
said to have arisen under the tuition of all the jurists of Europe, who were appealed
to, freely and familiarly, both in Parliament and in our courts," Ed. Rev. li 125 ;
in 1775 Dr. Johnson wrote to Boswell, " I am going to write about the Americans.
If you have picked up any hints among your lawyers, who are great masters of the
law of nations . . . let me know," Boswell, Life of Johnson (ed. G. B. Hill) ii 292.
[6] Ed. Rev. li 128-130.
[7] For the abolition of the " pleadable brieve " in or about 1532 see Sources
and Literature of Scots Law (Stair Soc.) i 214.
[8] For the evils of special pleading see vol. ix 308-327 ; it was said, not unjustly,
by a Scottish lawyer in 1830 that enlightened jurists would see in it " incredible
intricacy, empirical inventions, circuitous remedies, unintelligible fictions," Ed.
Rev. li 136.
[9] For the defects of the English law see vol. i 471-473 ; vol. viii 243-245.
[10] Ed. Rev. li 131.

had done from the sixteenth century onwards.[1] Though in the
eighteenth century the system of trial by jury was not worked
so intelligently in Scotland as it was in England,[2] there were
other matters in which the law of Scotland was superior to that
of England.   In Scotland a prisoner was not refused the aid of
counsel ; [3] the institution of criminal proceedings was under the
supervision of a Public Prosecutor ; [4] and that scrupulous adherence to words and forms, which was for so long a blot on
English criminal procedure, was unknown.[5]

These are only a few illustrations of cases in which the two
systems of law had something to learn, and did learn, from one
another.   It is clear that the existence of these two systems has
helped the Legislature to reform the laws of both countries ;
and that it has helped both Scottish and English lawyers to a
better understanding of legal principles, by obliging them to
emancipate themselves from too exclusive a concentration on
the technicalities of their own systems.[6]   In conclusion we must
note another legal benefit which, in the eighteenth century,
England derived from the Union.   Just as Scotsmen made their
mark as public servants in many spheres of activity, so they
made their mark as English lawyers and judges.   Mansfield, who
was perhaps the greatest legal genius of the eighteenth century,[7]
Loughborough,[8] and Erskine, could never have made the great
contribution which they made to English law, if the way had
not been opened by the Act of Union.

We have seen that the passing of the Act of Union was due
to the fact that the happy moment was seized when, and when

---

[1] " I claimed a superiority for Scotland over England in one respect, that no
man can be arrested there for a debt merely because another swears it against him ;
but there must first be the judgment of a court of law ascertaining its justice ; and
that a seizure of the person, before judgment is obtained, can take place only if
his creditor should swear that he is about to fly from the country," Boswell, Life of
Johnson (ed. G. B. Hill) iii 77 ; for the English law see vol. viii 231-232 ; below
524-525, 595-597 ; Holdsworth, Charles Dickens as a Legal Historian 136-141.

[2] Until 1814 the jury's verdict must be given in writing in a fixed form ; this
document " was sealed, delivered in open court, and recorded, and it formed the
only attainable communication of the jury's opinion.   Except in the case of a few
extravagant clerical blunders, corrected by the *whole* jury on the *spot*, all errors . . .
remained incorrigibly part of the verdict ; and the court could not say a word,
but had only to receive and act upon the verdict as written," Ed. Rev. lxxxiii 199-
200 ; for the small importance of the jury in civil cases in Scotland see Sources and
Literature of Scots Law (Stair Soc.) i 222-224.

[3] Ed. Rev. lxxxiii 203.   [4] Ibid.

[5] Ibid ; for the exactitude of the English practice and its results see vol. iii
616-620.

[6] It was said in 1830 that the close connection between Scottish and continental
lawyers had kept open the minds of the Scottish lawyers—" technical forms, and
pre-established follies, seem, in all ages, to have opposed legal improvements as
sparingly in Scotland as in any kingdom in the world.   The opposite charge, of
an undue preference of novelty, has been oftener made against us, and perhaps with
greater justice," Ed. Rev. li 125.

[7] Vol. xii 464 seqq.   [8] Ibid 569-576.

alone, it was possible to pass it.[1]   We have seen that its success was due to the fact that the relations of the two nations were settled on a basis of a partnership, to which each made a substantial contribution, so that there was no taint of subordination in their relations.[2]   We shall now see that the history of failure, which marks the relations between England and Ireland in the eighteenth century, as much as the history of success marks the relations between England and Scotland, is due partly to the fact that opportunities were missed, partly to the fact that the accidents of history had made Ireland subordinate to England, and partly to the fact that this subordination made it impossible for Ireland to develop her resources and her laws on the lines needed to build up a united and a contented nation.

The Relations between England and Ireland [3]

During the latter part of the eighteenth century Irish politics began to influence the development of English public law ; and it is to the manner in which the Irish problem was then approached by English statesmen that we must look for the causes of that large influence which, in the following period, Ireland began to exercise upon the law and politics of England.   But, in order to understand the nature of the problem with which English statesmen were faced it is necessary to say a few words as to the condition of Ireland, and as to the relations between England and Ireland, at the beginning of the eighteenth century.

At the close of the Middle Ages English rule in Ireland was confined to the narrow limits of the Pale.[4]   In spite of the protests of the Irish Parliament, it had been held that the English Parliament could legislate for Ireland ;[5] and Poynings Act, passed by the Parliament of Drogheda in 1495, applied all statutes lately made in England to Ireland, and made the Irish Parliament completely subservient to the English government.   The causes for summoning a Parliament, and bills to be brought forward, must previously be certified to the King, and affirmed by the King and his Council in England.   Therefore all that the Irish Parliament could do was to accept or reject these bills. It could not originate any legislation.[6]   This Act was slightly modified by an Irish Act of Philip and Mary's reign, by which

---

[1] Vol. x 42.   [2] Above 13.

[3] In this short sketch I have relied mainly upon Lecky's very full and impartial History of Ireland in the Eighteenth Century.

[4] Hallam, C.H. iii 359-360 ; the Pale comprised the counties of Dublin, Louth, Kildare, and Meath, but " probably the real supremacy of the English laws was not established beyond the two first of these counties, from Dublin to Dundalk on the coast, and for about thirty miles inland."

[5] Berriedale Keith, The First British Empire 7 ; Y.B. 1 Hy. VII Mich. pl. 2.

[6] Hallam, C.H. iii 361-362.

the Irish Privy Council was empowered to send over bills while
the Irish Parliament was in session ; and, in the seventeenth
century, the Irish Parliament indirectly got a power to initiate·
legislation by sending heads of bills to the Irish Privy Council.[1]
In 1495 Poynings Act applied only to the Pale. It was not till
Elizabeth's reign that English rule and English law were extended
over the whole island. The establishment of that rule " brought
with it two new and lasting consequences, the proscription of
the Irish religion and the confiscation of the Irish soil." [2] The
proscription of the Irish religion and the confiscation of the
Irish soil led to further rebellions and further confiscations.
When William III finally defeated James II and his Catholic
supporters, the victorious Protestants thought it necessary to
fortify both their religion and their property by a penal code, the
object of which was not only to discourage the Catholic religion,
but to keep the Catholics both poor and depressed.[3] To effect
the latter object the code, in the first place, deprived Catholics
of all rights in public law.[4] In the second place, it made it
legally impossible for a Catholic to give his children a Catholic
education.[5] In the third place, in order to dissociate Catholics
from the land, it made it almost impossible for them to acquire
it. If they acquired it contrary to the law, any Protestant
informer, who could prove the facts, could deprive them of it.
If they inherited land a child who turned Protestant could deprive them of the control of it.[6] In the fourth place, they were
forbidden to possess arms, or a horse worth more than £5.[7] The
result was that, as Lecky says,[8] " in his own country the Catholic
was only recognised by law ' for repression and punishment.'
The Lord Chancellor Bowes and the Chief Justice Robinson both
distinctly laid down from the bench ' that the law does not
suffer any such person to exist as an Irish Roman Catholic.' "
The rulers of Ireland in the early years of the eighteenth century
repeatedly referred to the Catholics as " the common enemy." [9]

In fact the Roman Catholics, whom the law tried thus to
ignore, and against whom this code was directed, were the large
majority of the Irish nation ; and it was upon this ground that
the code was defended. The Protestants, it was said, were a
small minority. The title to their estates depended on recent
confiscations. Any relaxation of the code might lead to a
repetition of those Catholic risings and reprisals which the

---

[1] Hallam, C.H. iii 404-405 ; Lecky, op. cit. i 60-61.   [2] Ibid i 10.
[3] Speaking of these laws against the Roman Catholics, Burke says that " their
declared object was to reduce the Catholics of Ireland to a miserable populace,
without property, without estimation, without education," First Letter to Sir Hercules
Langrishe, Works (ed. Bohn) iii 300-301.

[4] Lecky, op. cit. i 145-146.   [5] Ibid 148-149.
[6] Ibid 150-156.   [7] Ibid 146.
[8] Ibid.   [9] Ibid 166.

seventeenth century had experienced.   The result was to establish a tyrannical dominant class, divided from the depressed
majority by religion and by the memory of recent confiscations.[1]
The code did not succeed in extinguishing Catholicism, and the
provisions of the code which were directed to this object gradually
ceased to be enforced.[2]   But they caused the Catholic population, who were the large majority of the Irish nation, to become "consummate adepts in the art of conspiracy and disguise."[3]   They caused the populace to regard the law, not as
a beneficent, but as a maleficent, agency;   and to look upon
illegal combinations and illegal violence as its sole protectors
against this maleficent agency.[4]   On the other hand, the code
did succeed in degrading and impoverishing the large majority
of the Irish nation.   "It was," said Burke in 1792,[5] "a machine
of wise and elaborate contrivance, and as well fitted for the
oppression, impoverishment, and degradation of a people, and
the debasement in them of human nature itself, as ever proceeded from the perverted ingenuity of man."

The larger landowners were generally absentees; and Swift
estimated that one-third of the rent of the country was remitted
to England.[6]   In fact the prevalence of absenteeism is shown by
the indignation of the large landowners at the proposal, which
was made in 1773,[7] to tax absentees.   These landowners let
their lands at moderate rents to middlemen, who sublet at an
increased rent; and "the process continued till there were three,
four, or even five persons between the landlord and the cultivator
of the soil."[8]   The result was that the Irish peasants were worse
off than any in Europe.[9]   They paid rents which were regulated

[1] "They divided the nation into two distinct bodies, without common interest,
sympathy, or connexion.   One of these bodies was to possess *all* the franchises, *all*
the property, *all* the education : the other was to be composed of drawers of water
and cutters of turf for them," Burke, First Letter to Sir Hercules Langrishe, Works
(ed. Bohn) iii 301 ; "Sure I am, that there have been thousands in Ireland, who
have never conversed with a Roman Catholic in their whole lives, unless they
happened to talk to their gardener's workmen, or to ask their way, when they had
lost it, in their sports," ibid 335 ; Lecky, op. cit. i 277-279.
    [2] Ibid 156-167.   [3] Ibid 167.   [4] Ibid 272-273.
    [5] First Letter to Sir Hercules Langrishe, Works (ed. Bohn) iii 343.
    [6] "One-third part of the rents of Ireland is spent in England ; which, with
the profit of employments, pensions, appeals, journeys of pleasure or health,
education at the inns of court and both universities, remittances at pleasure, the
pay of all superior officers in the army, and other incidents, will amount to a full
half of the income of the whole kingdom, all clear profit to England," A Short View
of the State of Ireland, Works (ed. 1768) iv 57 ; Lecky, op. cit. i 212-213.
    [7] Ibid ii 119-132 ; the project had been mooted early in the century, and Adam
Smith considered that such a tax would be just and expedient, ibid ii 119-120.
    [8] Ibid i 214.
    [9] "I would now expostulate a little with our country landlords ; who, by un-
measurable *screwing* and *racking* their tenants all over the kingdom, have already
reduced the miserable people to a worse condition than the peasants in France, or
the vassals in Germany and Poland," Swift, A Proposal for the Use of the Irish
Manufacture, Works (ed. 1768) iii 214.

only by competition between men who had no resource other than the land. They were obliged to pay tithes to an alien church. They paid dues to their own priests. Their landlords did nothing for them. Since they always lived on the edge of starvation, any failure of the harvest meant widespread famine.[1] Their position was aggravated in the earlier half of the eighteenth century by the wholsale conversion of arable into pasture.[2] Whole villages were turned adrift ; and no effective measures were taken, such as were taken in England by the Tudors in the sixteenth century, to regulate this process.[3] " Whoever travels this country," said Swift in 1720, " and observes the *face* of nature, or the *faces* and habits and dwellings of the *natives*, will hardly think himself in a land where *law, religion* or *common humanity* is professed." [4] It is not surprising that, in these circumstances, extensive agrarian disturbances from time to time broke out, and were with difficulty suppressed—the Whiteboys in 1762, the Oakboys in 1763, and the Steelboys in 1771. " The arts of conspiracy and disguise," and the necessity for resort to illegal combination and violence, which the provisions of the Catholic code had taught the Irish peasant, were applied with effect in these and later disturbances ; and, since the troubled course of Irish history has never suffered these lessons to be forgotten by Irishmen, many varieties of agitators in the nineteenth and twentieth centuries have turned to their own account that capacity for the planning of organized crime, which was the natural product of the long continuance of tyrannical laws and economic oppression.

The position of all classes of Irishmen was aggravated by the fact that both its agriculture and its commerce were regulated by English statutes in a purely selfish spirit. In 1666 and 1680 the importation into England of Irish cattle, meat, cheese, and butter was prohibited, because the landowners complained that the Irish competition lowered their rents.[5] In 1663,[6] 1670,[7] and 1696 [8] Ireland was excluded from the benefit of the Navigation Acts ; and the Act of 1696 provided that no goods should be imported directly from the colonies to Ireland.[9] The incipient wool

---

[1] Lecky, op. cit. i 184-188.

[2] Ibid 219-226 ; " This gave birth to that abominable race of graziers, who upon expiration of the farmers' leases were ready to engross great quantities of land. . . . Thus a vast tract of land, where twenty or thirty farmers lived, together with their cottagers and labourers in their several cabins, became all desolate, and easily managed by one or two herdsmen and their boys," Swift, An Answer to a Memorial, Works (ed. 1768) iv 62-63.

[3] Vol. iii 209-210 ; vol. iv 364-373.

[4] A Proposal for the Use of the Irish Manufacture, Works (ed. 1768) iii 215.

[5] 18 Charles II c. 2 § 1 ; 32 Charles II c. 2 § 2 ; Lecky, op. cit. i 173.

[6] 15 Charles II c. 7.   [7] 22, 23 Charles II c. 26 § 11.

[8] 7, 8 William III c. 22.

[9] § 14 ; see Camb. Col. Hist. i 279-281, 287-288.

manufacture of Ireland was crushed by the combined efforts of
the Irish and English Parliaments in 1698 and 1699, in response
to the demand of the English manufacturers.[1]   This was a fatal
blow to Irish commerce and agriculture.   " The relations between landlord and tenant were already harsh, strained, and unnatural, but they were fearfully aggravated when the destruction
of manufacturing industry threw the whole population for subsistence on the soil." [2]   No doubt the suppression of manufactures which might be dangerous competitors to those of England
was in accordance with the economic ideas of the day.[3]   But the
application of this policy to Ireland was, in the circumstances
of that country, peculiarly oppressive ; [4] and it was also peculiarly
foolish, because it destroyed the chance of the increase of the
Protestant population by the influx of artisans from England
and Scotland.[5]   This episode shows that it would have been to
the advantage of both countries if, at the beginning of the eighteenth century, a legislative union between them had been effected
on the same lines as the union between England and Scotland.
Such a union would have prevented England from interfering
with the development of Irish trade and industry, since freedom
of trade between the two countries would have been established.[6]
It would then have been welcomed by the Irish Parliament.
But it was prevented by the commercial jealousy of England ; [7]
and so one of the many opportunities of improving the relations
between England and Ireland, which occurred in the eighteenth
century, was missed.

Ireland was unable to resist this commercial oppression,
because its government was wholly in the hands of England.
There was, it is true, an Irish Parliament ; and, from the beginning of the eighteenth century, the insufficiency of the hereditary revenue made it necessary to summon Parliament every
second year.[8]   But we have seen that Poynings' Act, though
slightly modified by a later statute and by practice, had reduced
the Irish Parliament to a very subordinate position.[9]   It did not
possess the sole right of originating money bills.[10]   Its proposals
for legislation must be submitted first to the Irish Privy Council
which might suppress or alter them.   If it approved them it sent
them on to the English Privy Council, which again might suppress
or alter them.   The Irish Parliament, though it might reject,

---

[1] Lecky, op. cit. i 176-177 ; 10, 11 William III c. 10.
[2] Lecky, op. cit. i 180.   [3] Ibid i 188-189 ; below 412-418.
[4] " Ireland is the only kingdom I ever heard or read of, either in ancient or
modern story, which was denied the liberty of exporting their native commodities
and manufactures wherever they pleased, except to countries at war with their own
prince or state," Swift, A Short View of the State of Ireland, Works (ed. 1768) iv 56.
[5] Lecky, op. cit. i 189-190.   [6] Above 13.
[7] Lecky, op. cit. i 443-444.   [8] Ibid i 193-194.
[9] Above 21-22.   [10] Lecky, op. cit. i 194.

could not alter a bill returned from England as amended by the Irish and English Privy Councils.[1] The English Parliament could bind Ireland by its legislation ; and the English House of Lords was the final court of appeal from the Irish courts.[2] Until the Octennial Act of 1768 there was no Act limiting the duration of Parliament [3]—in George II's reign the same Parliament was in existence for thirty-three years.[4] Until 1780 the army in Ireland was governed by the English Mutiny Act ; and when, in 1780, Ireland insisted on passing its own Mutiny Act, the English government inserted an amendment which made it perpetual.[5] Until 1781 the Habeas Corpus Act did not apply to Ireland.[6] Until 1782 the judges held their places during pleasure,[7] and until 1793 there was no law which incapacitated placemen and pensioners from sitting in Parliament.[8] The state of the representation was such that the government could exercise a very large control over the composition of the House of Commons.[9] Catholics and nonconformists were excluded, so that the county electorate was very narrow ; and out of 300 members, 216 were elected by manors and boroughs. Of these 216 members " 176 according to the lowest estimate were elected by individual patrons, while very few of the remainder had really popular constituencies." [10] Many of the Irish peers were large borough owners, since peerages were frequently given to these borough owners in order to secure their support for the government.

We have seen that the condition of the Scottish representative system was quite as, if not more, anomalous than the Irish.[11] But there was this important difference between Scotland and Ireland : Scotland stood to England in the relation of a partner, so that the system of influence, by means of which the government secured the support of the Scottish members, benefited Scotsmen. They not only filled all the important governmental posts in their own country, but also very many governmental posts in the civil, naval, and military services of Great Britain.[12] Ireland, on the other hand, stood to England in the relation of a dependent, so that the system of influence, by means of which the government secured the support of the Irish members, benefited only the large borough proprietors. " Those who have the misfortune to be born here," said Swift, " have the

---

[1] Lecky, op. cit. ii 52.
[2] 6 George I c. 5 ; vol. i 371-372.
[3] Lecky, op. cit. ii 90-91.
[4] Ibid i 196.
[5] Ibid ii 254-259.
[6] Ibid i 196, ii 278.
[7] Ibid ii 315.
[8] Ibid iii 183-184.
[9] The government relied on " Undertakers," that is on " a few great personages who possessed an extraordinary parliamentary influence, and who ' undertook ' to carry the King's business through Parliament on condition of obtaining a large share of the disposal of patronage," ibid ii 54.
[10] Ibid i 195.
[11] Above 8.
[12] Above 11-12.

least title to any considerable employment ; to which they are seldom preferred, but upon a political consideration." [1] Except in the case of " persons preferred upon a political consideration," all the Irish patronage was used by the English ministers to strengthen their influence over the British Parliament, or to provide pensions for royal favourites who could not be so easily provided for in England.   Swift, in his fourth letter of a Drapier, said : [2]

All considerable offices for life here are possessed by those to whom the reversions were granted ; and these have been generally followers of the chief governors, or persons who had interest in the court of England : so the Lord Berkeley of Stratton holds that great office of master of the rolls ; the Lord Palmerston is first remembrancer, worth near £2000 per annum.   One Dodington, secretary to the Earl of Pembroke, begged the reversion of clerk of the pells worth £2500 a year, which he now enjoys by the death of Lord Newton.   Mr. South-well is secretary of state, and the Earl of Burlington Lord High Treasurer of Ireland by inheritance. . . . I say nothing of the under-treasurer-ship worth about £9000 a year, nor of the commissioners of the revenue four of whom generally live in England. . . . But the jest is, that I have known, upon occasion, some of these absent officers as keen against the interest of Ireland as if they had never been indebted to her for a single groat.

When Swift said that these were only a few amongst many instances he was perfectly accurate.   Both in the law and in the church all the considerable posts were occupied by English-men ; [3]   and many royal favourites,[4] relatives,[5] or mistresses [6] were endowed with grants of Irish lands or pensions charged on the Irish civil list.   Thus whereas in Scotland all those conventions of the constitution which centred round the manner in which Parliament was influenced, worked for the benefit of Scotsmen, because the relation of the two countries was a relation of part-nership, in Ireland they worked for the benefit of Englishmen, because the relation of the two countries was a relation of depend-ence.   Moreover, it is clear that this manner of disposing of the patronage of Ireland aggravated the economic evils from which the country was suffering, by increasing the already large drain

[1] A Short View of the State of Ireland, Works (ed. 1768) iv 57.
[2] Works iii 279-280.
[3] " In the legal profession every Chancellor till Fitz-Gibbon was an Englishman, and in the first years of the eighteenth century, every chief of the three law courts. In the Church every primate during the eighteenth century was English, as were also ten out of the eighteen archbishops of Dublin and Cashel, and a large proportion of the other bishops," Lecky, op. cit. i 198.
[4] William III gave Portland and Albermarle confiscated lands " exceeding an English county in extent," ibid.
[5] The Duke of St. Albans, the bastard son of Charles II, had an Irish pension of £800 a year, and the Queen Dowager of Prussia, the sister of George II, was similarly provided for, ibid 198, 199.
[6] E.g. Catherine Sedley, the Duchess of Kendal, the Countess of Darlington, and Madame de Walmoden, ibid.

of money from the country, which was caused by the prevalence of absenteeism amongst the great landowners.[1] It was not till the rise of a national feeling had made the management of the Irish Parliament more difficult, that there was any considerable increase in the number of Irishmen appointed to the Irish posts which were paid for by the Irish nation.

In spite of all the disabilities under which the Irish Parliament suffered, it did some useful work for Ireland. " Many measures of practical unobtrusive utility were passed, and a real check was put upon the extravagance of the executive." [2] And, though it represented but a small fraction of the nation, it was inevitable that it should resent the manner in which the British Parliament, in order to further its own commercial interests, prevented the commercial development of Ireland. In 1698 Molyneux had published an historical argument to prove that the Irish Parliament had always asserted, and ought to have, the same power to regulate Irish affairs, as the English Parliament had to regulate English affairs.[3] The book was condemned by the English House of Commons [4]; but the controversy as to the existence of the appellate jurisdiction of the English House of Lords, which arose in 1719 out of the case of *Annesley v. Sherlock*,[5] showed that a national resentment against English domination was growing. The affair of Wood's halfpence (1722-1723)[6] created a great outburst of national feeling, to which expression was given by Swift in his *Letters of a Drapier*. In his fourth letter he recalled Molyneux's arguments, and told the Irish people that they had been overborne by mere brute force.

It is true indeed, that within the memory of man the parliaments of England have sometimes assumed the power of binding this kingdom by laws enacted there ; wherein they were at first openly opposed (so far as truth, reason, and justice are capable of opposing) by the famous Mr. Molineux, an English gentleman born here, as well as by several of the greatest patriots, and best Whigs in England ; but the love and torrent of power prevailed. Indeed the arguments on both sides were invincible. For in reason, all government without the consent of the governed is slavery : but, in fact, ' eleven men well armed will certainly subdue one single man in his shirt.' [7]

He told them that " by the laws of God, of nature, of nations, and of your country, you are and ought to be as free a people

---

[1] Above 23 n. 6.   [2] Lecky, op. cit. i 313.
[3] Berriedale Keith, The First British Empire 7-8 ; Lecky, op. cit. i 443 ; Professor Schuyler, Parliament and the British Empire, chap. ii, has shown that Molyneux's argument, and the earlier argument of Darcy and of a book published in 1644, which were used by Molyneux, cannot be regarded as valid in law ; Mayart, a judge of the Common Pleas in Ireland, answered the book published in 1644, and, as Professor Schuyler says at p. 60, " historical scholarship has sustained Mayart's view."
[4] Lecky, op. cit. i 443.   [5] Ibid 447-448 ; vol. i 371-372.
[6] Lecky, op. cit. i 449 seqq.   [7] Works (ed. 1768) iii 285.

as your brethren in England." [1]   He appealed to their pride by telling them that the English,

> whose understandings are just upon a level with ours (which perhaps are none of the brightest), have a strong contempt for most nations, but especially for Ireland. They look upon us as a sort of savage Irish, whom our ancestors conquered several hundred years ago. And if I should describe the Britons to you as they were in Cæsar's time, when they ' painted their bodies and clothed themselves with the skins of beasts,' I should act fully as reasonably as they do. [2]

It was after this episode that all classes of Irishmen began to draw together, [3] and a formed opposition in the Irish Parliament began to appear. [4] The government found it more difficult and more expensive to manage Parliament—a fact which was shown by the increase in the price of boroughs in the middle of the century. [5] Protests were made against the notorious abuses of Irish patronage, and demands were made for the shortening of Parliament, and for a place bill. [6] At the beginning of George III's reign demands were also made for an Act for giving to the judges the same security of tenure as thay had in England, and for a Habeas Corpus Act. [7] Bowes, the Lord Chancellor, said in a letter to Dodington, " formerly Protestant or Papist were the key words ; they are now court or country, referring still to constitutional grievances . . . they have considered your House as the model, and in general think themselves injured in the instances in which theirs, upon the legal constitution, must differ." [8] But as yet the government was able, through the efforts of its " Undertakers," [9] to retain a majority in Parliament, and to stave off most of these demands, [10] The only victory won by the opposition was the passing of the Octennial Act in 1768. [11] It was the American war of independence which set in motion a train of causes which led to the attainment by the Irish Parliament of legislative independence.

The relations between Ireland and America had long been close. The troubled economic conditions of Ireland had caused successive waves of Irish emigrants to seek new homes in America.

---

[1] Works (ed. 1768) iii 286.   [2] Ibid 287.
[3] Boulter, the primate, said in 1724, " I find . . . that the people of every religion, country, and party here are alike set against Wood's halfpence, and that their agreement in this has had a most unhappy influence on the state of the nation by bringing on intimacies between Papists and Jacobites, and the Whigs, who before had no correspondence with them," Boulter's Letters i 8, cited Lecky, op. cit. i 458.
[4] Ibid 465.   [5] Ibid 467.
[6] Ibid 461, 467.   [7] Ibid ii 70.
[8] Ibid 54.   [9] Above 26 n. 9.
[10] In 1767 Camden, in a letter to Grafton, opposed the wish of the Lord-Lieutenant to give the Great Seal to an Irishman, on the ground that it would diminish the influence of the English government, see his letter cited Campbell, Chancellors v 269-270 ; his view, backed by Northington, prevailed, ibid 273.
[11] Lecky, op. cit. ii 90.

The suppression of the wool industry gave rise to one of these waves. The conversion of arable land into pasture, and the ejection of tenants which was its necessary result, gave rise to others.[1] Naturally, these emigrants, who had thus been compelled to leave their country, took the American side, and supplied the American army with some of its best troops.[2] The wisdom of the policy pursued with respect to Scotland and the folly of the policy pursued with respect to Ireland are illustrated by the fact that the emigrants to America from the Scottish Highlands were, for the most part, loyalist.[3] But, apart from these ties of relationship between Irishmen and Americans, which these waves of emigration had created and maintained, it was, from the first, clear to the opposition in the Irish Parliament that the cause for which the Americans were fighting was essentially the same as the cause which they were advocating. They were fighting to assert that legislative independence for which Molyneux and Swift had contended. Since, however, the opposition was in a minority in Parliament, Ireland was pledged to support England in the American war.[4] But the increased taxation caused by the war and by increases in the pension list, and the falling off of trade caused by the loss of the American, and later, of the French, markets, were fast reducing Ireland to bankruptcy. This was so obvious that in 1778, in spite of the protests of the English commercial men, some slight relaxations were made in the commercial code in favour of Ireland ;[5] and in the same year the progress towards the formation of an Irish nation was shown by important relaxations of the code of laws directed against the Catholics.[6] This relaxation was largely due to Grattan, who saw that the creation of a united nation was a condition precedent to the attainment of legislative independence. " The Irish Protestant," he said, " could never be free till the Irish Catholic had ceased to be a slave " ; " and as early as 1778 Charlemont attributed to the extraordinary eloquence and influence of Grattan a great part of the change which, on the Catholic question, had passed over the minds of Irish Protestants." [7]

[1] Lecky, op. cit. i 245-248, ii 51 ; in 1728 the prime serjeant and the attorney and solicitor-general of Ireland advised that a proclamation against emigration was valid, founding their opinion on 5 Richard II c. 2, vol. x 391 ; Acts of the Privy Council (Col. Series) vi 201 ; but in 1730 a bill which put obstacles in the way of emigration was said to lay an unreasonable restraint on the subject, and was vetoed in England, ibid iii 207-209.

[2] " They supplied some of the best soldiers of Washington. The famous Pennsylvanian line was mainly Irish, and Montgomery, who, having distinguished himself highly at the capture of Quebec, became one of the earliest of the American commanders in the War of Independence, was a native of Donegal," Lecky, op. cit. i 248.

[3] Camb. Hist. of the Empire i 266.　　　　　[4] Lecky, op. cit. ii 162-163.
[5] Ibid 177-180.　　　　[6] Ibid 213-217　　　　[7] Ibid 209.

The events which followed upon the intervention of France in the American war in 1778, showed that Grattan was right. In 1778 Ireland was unprotected. The navy was fully occupied, so that the country was open to invasion; and the greater part of the troops was serving abroad. The exigencies of national defence gave rise to the volunteer movement. It was essentially a national movement, in which both Catholics and Protestants took part; so that the volunteers were far more representative of Irish public opinion than the Irish Parliament. It soon appeared that public opinion was unanimous in demanding the abolition of the commercial restrictions and the grant of legislative independence. The abolition of the commercial restrictions was conceded in 1780.[1] But this was not enough. The volunteers were perfecting their organization, and they continued to demand legislative independence. In 1780 Grattan moved a series of resolutions in the House of Commons, which asserted that, while the Crowns of Great Britain and Ireland were indissolubly united, only the Parliament of Ireland could make laws for Ireland.[2] The resolutions were defeated; but early in 1782, at a meeting of the delegates of the Ulster volunteers at Dungannon, a resolution asserting the legislative independence of the Irish Parliament, and a resolution approving the relaxation of the laws against the Catholics, were unanimously carried.[3] As Grattan said shortly afterwards, when moving in the House of Commons a resolution asserting legislative independence, " it was impossible that England could safely refuse to the loyalty of Ireland the privilege she had offered to the arms of America." [4]

In fact the Americans had won both their own independence and the legislative independence of the Irish Parliament. In 1782 the Act of 1719, declaring the competence of the British Parliament to legislate for Ireland, and the right of the British House of Lords to hear appeals from Ireland, was repealed by the British Parliament.[5] At the same time Acts were passed by the Irish Parliament repealing the greater part of Poynings' Act, thereby abolishing the power of the Irish Privy Council to interfere with legislation; making the Irish House of Lords the final court of appeal for Ireland; limiting the duration of the Mutiny Act; and granting to the Catholics further relaxations of the penal code.[6] Since some constitutional lawyers held that the repeal of the Act of 1719 was not sufficient to establish the legislative independence of Ireland,[7] an Act was passed in 1783 [8] by

---

[1] Lecky, op. cit. ii 242.　　　　[2] Ibid 252-253.
[3] Ibid 282-285.　　　　[4] Ibid 286.
[5] 22 George III c. 53.　　　　[6] Lecky, op. cit. ii 315.
[7] It was said, with some reason, that the effect of the repeal of the Act of 1719 was merely to restore the law as it existed before the passing of that Act, so that it could be argued that the legislative control of the British Parliament still remained.
[8] 23 George III c. 28.

the British Parliament, renouncing all legislative and judicial powers over the Irish Parliament. Thus, though the Crowns of Great Britain and Ireland were still united, Ireland gained complete legislative and judicial independence. Two connected questions now arose—questions upon which the whole future of Ireland depended. First, what were to be the relations of the executive to the legislature under this new constitution ; and, secondly, how were the constitutional relations of the two countries to be regulated ?

Since the Crowns of England and Ireland were united, and since the Irish executive was appointed by the King on the advice of English ministers, it followed that the Irish Parliament had not got the same independent powers as the British Parliament, either in respect of legislation or in respect of its control over the executive. In England the royal veto on legislation had never been exercised since Anne's reign ; for it was hardly conceivable that a ministry which had allowed a bill to pass the two Houses, would allow the King to refuse his assent. But in Ireland the reasons which had made the royal veto practically obsolete in England did not apply. The King, on the advice of his English ministers, might refuse his assent to Irish bills sent over to England. In England Parliament could compel a change of ministers ; but in Ireland ministers were changed, not according to the exigencies of Irish, but of English party politics.[1] There was nothing approaching to the modern system of responsible government. Nor would such a system have then been possible ; for we have seen that in England the system of cabinet government was not fully developed ; [2] and responsible government is a copy of the fully developed system of cabinet government. In these circumstances it was easy to see that the maintenance of harmonious constitutional relations between the two countries was very difficult. Suppose the Irish Parliament disapproved of the policy of the Irish ministers, who represented the English government, and refused to pass the Mutiny Act or to vote supplies, or suppose that it chose to put a prohibitory tariff on English goods—in all these cases a very difficult situation would arise. At bottom the question came to this—how could the executive government ensure the co-operation of the Irish Parliament ? Now we have seen that, both in England and Ireland, the principal means relied upon in the eighteenth century for securing the harmonious working of the executive and Parliament, was that series of conventions which centred round the influence which the state of the representation made it possible for the King to exercise over Parliament.[3] We have seen that it

[1] Lecky, op. cit. ii 334-336.   [2] Vol. x 637-643.   [3] Vol. x 633-634.

was easier to influence the Irish Parliament in this way than the English Parliament.[1] It is not surprising therefore that a continued reliance upon this expedient should appear to English ministers the obvious solution of the difficulty.

But it soon appeared that this expedient, though it was easy and obvious, was a dangerous expedient. The Irish Parliament, as the episode of the volunteers showed, did not represent the Irish nation.[2] Inevitably the question of Parliamentary reform came to the front. A volunteer convention at Dublin in 1783 demanded a measure of Parliamentary reform ; and Flood moved for leave to bring in a bill for this purpose. Leave was refused ; and a similar bill was rejected on a second reading in 1784.[3] The government adopted and never departed from the policy advocated by Fitz-Gibbon, the Irish Chancellor—the policy of using corruption as the normal method of government.[4] It is not surprising, therefore, that, from 1784 onwards, " the conviction sank deeply into the minds of many that reform in Ireland could only be effected by revolution, and the rebellion of 1798 might be already foreseen." [5]

It was because the government was determined to rely upon its power to influence the Irish Parliament, as its main expedient for securing the harmonious working of executive and Parliament, that it set its face against all projects of Parliamentary reform ; [6] and it was for the same reason that it opposed legislation against the creation of offices and pensions, which would have made the exercise of that influence more difficult.[7] In 1793 the government was driven to give Catholics the vote ; but they refused to include in this concession a measure of Parliamentary reform, a measure giving the Catholics a right to sit in Parliament, and a measure for settling the franchise in such a way that the vote was given to persons with a substantial property qualification. The idea that the executive could not work harmoniously with Parliament, unless Parliament was elected in a manner which would enable the executive to influence it, was so ingrained in the minds of the statesmen of the

---

[1] Above 26.

[2] " To the pressure exerted by that body [the volunteers], it was said, Ireland ultimately owed her free trade, the concessions of 1782, and the final charter of 1783, and had Parliament been her sole representative, no one of these things would have been obtained," Lecky, op. cit. ii 345.

[3] Ibid 371-377.   [4] Ibid 420.   [5] Ibid 377.

[6] Camden said in 1784 that those who wished for Parliamentary reform at home could not logically refuse it to Ireland—" and yet their corrupt Parliament must be considered the only means we have left to preserve the union between the two countries," see his letter cited Campbell, Chancellors v 327 ; he added that " that argument will not bear the light, and no means ought in my opinion to be adopted too scandalous to be avowed" ; but the expedient was too obvious, and at that time too natural, not to be adopted, below 34-35.

[7] Lecky, op. cit. ii 429-430.

eighteenth century, that they steadily opposed the only measures which could have produced permanent harmony in the relations between England and Ireland. We shall see that, in the course of these controversies, both sides prayed in aid the obsolete idea that there were limitations upon the legislative competency of Parliament.

The effects of the Catholic code in depressing the largest section of the Irish people, the effects of the agrarian system, and the effects of the selfish commercial policy pursued by England, had combined to make the relations between England and Ireland difficult and delicate. But these difficulties might have been overcome if an attempt had been made to work the Irish constitution of 1782 in accordance with the views of the most enlightened Irish statesmen. If well-considered measures of Parliamentary reform and Catholic emancipation had been passed in the years which intervened between 1782 and the outbreak of the French Revolution, the strength of both Great Britain and Ireland would have been increased, the influence of the ideas of the French Revolution would have been comparatively innocuous, and a tradition of harmonious relations, on a basis of co-operation, might have been established between the two countries. "Reflect seriously," said Burke in 1792, "on the possible consequences of keeping in the heart of your country, a bank of discontent, every hour accumulating, upon which every description of seditious men may draw at pleasure." [1] If the problems arising out of the legislation of 1782 had been approached in this spirit, the later history of the relations of England and Ireland would have been very different.

But, then as now, politicians, who have lived their lives in the atmosphere of a particular set of ideas, can rarely emancipate themselves from the influence of those ideas—the idea of emancipation was to them an unpractical vision. Both English and Irish politicians had become so accustomed to think that Parliamentary government was impossible unless the executive had a large power of influencing Parliament, they had worked so long with a system which had produced tolerable results in England, that they could not see that it was dangerous to place their sole reliance upon it in the new situation which had arisen in Ireland as the result of the legislation of 1782. We have seen that Paley and others considered that one of the causes of the loss of the American colonies was the fact that the Crown did not possess the means of influencing the colonial assemblies, which it possessed of influencing the British Parliament.[2] Grattan said that, at the time of the American war of inde-

---

[1] First Letter to Sir Hercules Langrishe, Works (Bohn's ed.) iii 336.
[2] Vol. x 633.

pendence, many thought that Lord North ought to have complied with the demands of the colonial assemblies, and then built up within them a system of influence ; and he pointed out that this was the course which had been pursued in Ireland since 1782.[1] But politicians who reasoned in this way failed to see, as many politicians in many different times and in many different places have failed to see, that a set of political ideas or constitutional conventions which suit a particular people at a particular period, cannot be transplanted to, and applied in, a totally different environment. It was this blindness which was largely responsible for the failure of the eighteenth-century statesmen both in Ireland and America. It was because English statesmen learnt something from their failure in America that they were able to build up and retain a new Colonial empire.

Unfortunately the mistakes which they made in Ireland had more lasting effects upon the future development of English constitutional law than their mistakes in America. We shall see that Ireland and Irish politics began, in the following period, to influence England and English politics very much more directly than they influenced them in this period. But we shall see that it is to this period that we must look for the causes which determined the nature of that influence. It is partly for this reason that it has been necessary to say something of the relations between England and Ireland in the eighteenth century ; and partly also because they afford an instructive illustration of some of the weaknesses of the eighteenth-century constitution. For the latter reason they have, as we shall now see, some bearing upon the manner in which the legal and political problems, arising out of the colonial expansion of England in this century, were envisaged by English lawyers and statesmen.

The Western Expansion of England

The eighteenth century saw the disruption of the Old Colonial Empire, as the result of the American War of Independence. Its later years saw the beginnings of a New Colonial Empire, which has had a longer life than the old, because its founders had learned from the disruption of the old, and, as Sir Charles Lucas has said,[2] " turned from a narrow commercial view of imperial policy to a wider outlook." In order to understand these two different epochs of colonial expansion, and their bearings upon the development of English law, it is necessary, in the first place, to survey briefly the process of expansion. In the second place, we must look at the manner in which the different colonies were governed ; and, in the third place, at

---

[1] Lecky, op. cit. iv 186.   [2] Camb. Hist. of the Empire i 10.

their relations with Great Britain. Lastly, something must be said of the causes and effects of the American Revolution which caused the disruption of the Old Colonial Empire.

(1) *The process of expansion.*

At the beginning of the eighteenth century England had become one of the great colonizing powers ; and we have seen that, as the result of the Treaty of Utrecht, she became one of the most important of those powers.[1] We have seen, too, that, as the Dutch and Spanish powers declined, England and France became the two protagonists in the struggle for the control of the Eastern and Western worlds.[2] But, to understand the position which was created by the Treaty of Utrecht, and the sequence of events which flowed from it, it is necessary to say a few words as to the position which England had attained in these New Worlds at the beginning of the eighteenth century.

England had taken some small part in the western voyages of discovery at the end of the fifteenth and the beginning of the sixteenth centuries ;[3] and, in the age of Elizabeth, she had, together with the French and Dutch, contested the claims of Spain and Portugal to the monopoly of the right to trade and settle in the newly discovered countries in the East and West. Drake was the greatest of all the Elizabethan adventurers.[4] He dreamed of " a new England in the West and a vast empire in the East."[5] " In after years it was always recalled that the circumnavigator had staked out claims in advance of any but the Portuguese, and for more than a century the results of his work were the sheet anchor of our diplomacy in the East."[6]

To the age of the discoverers and adventurers there succeeded the age of the settlers. These settlements were often made by chartered companies, such as the East India Company and the Virginia Company ;[7] sometimes they were made by individuals like Penn, to whom the Crown granted a concession ;[8] and sometimes, as in the case of some of the New England settlements, they were the result of a desire to obtain a religious or a political freedom which could not be had in England.[9] There was a great diversity of origin and type in these English settlements overseas ; but except in the New England settlements, the predominant motive of their promotors was the opening up of profitable

---

[1] Vol. x 46.   [2] Ibid.
[3] For John Cabot's voyages see Camb. Hist. of the Empire i 26-27 ; for other voyages in Henry VIII's reign see ibid 28-29.
[4] Ibid 53-54 ; " that Spanish war is in fact the infancy of English foreign trade," Seeley, Expansion of England 111.
[5] Camb. Hist. of the Empire i 63.   [6] Ibid.
[7] For some of these companies see vol. viii 209.
[8] Camb. Hist. of the Empire i 254-255.   [9] Ibid 156-166.

trades. By the middle of the seventeenth century it was becoming apparent that the state must take measures to protect
these settlements, both against the Spanish claims to monopolize
the trade of the New World, and against French and Dutch
rivalry. It was soon seen that, for this purpose, two sets of
measures were necessary : first, the provision of a strong navy
to protect the trade for the sake of which most of these settlements had been made ; and, secondly, laws to encourage the
growth both of trade and sea-power. The establishment of a
strong navy under the Commonwealth, and the Commonwealth
Navigation Act, supplied these needs.[1]

The policy of the Commonwealth statesmen was continued
after the Restoration ; [2] and, under the later Stuart kings, the
English possessions overseas were enlarged and protected against
the rivalry both of the Dutch and the French.[3] Their growth was
helped by three sets of circumstances. First, their vitality was
superior to that of the Dutch and French settlements. As compared with the Dutch settlements, which were in very many cases
mere trading posts,[4] the English settlements were real settlements, the population of which increased, and expanded and over-
flowed into other settlements.[5] As compared with the French
settlements, there was far less state control. The troubled
domestic politics of the seventeenth century left England little
leisure to control her colonies, so that they were able to develop
very much on their own lines, and, consequently, possessed a
more vigorous and independent life than the French colonies.[6]
Secondly, since England was not so deeply immersed in the wars
of the Continent as Holland and France, she could pay more
attention to her navy, on which the protection of her colonies
in the last resort depended.[7] Thirdly, at the end of the seventeenth century, religious persecution led to the migration of
foreign Protestants, who proved to be very useful settlers both
from the military and the economic point of view.[8] The settlement of these Protestants in America was encouraged in the
eighteenth century, and stimulated the growth of the different
American colonies.[9]

---

[1] Vol. vi 316, 425 ; Camb. Hist. of the Empire i 133-135, 507.

[2] Vol. vi 316-319.   [3] Camb. Hist. of the Empire i 240-260, 508.

[4] Ibid 220-221.   [5] Ibid 249, 396-397.

[6] " The French settlements were more important, but they were dwarfed and
stunted by a restrictive and centralized, though not unskilful system of government ;
and when the Revolution involved the two nations in war, the superior force of the
English colonies was so manifest that William refused the offer of colonial neutrality
which had been made by Louis," Lecky, History of England ii 235 ; Camb. Hist.
of the Empire i 310-311.

[7] Ibid 509-510, 518 ; Seeley, Expansion of England 128.

[8] Acts of the Privy Council (Col. Series) ii *xxxvii*.

[9] Ibid 608-609, 614 ; iii 288-293, 547-551.

But the strong position held by Spain in South America and the West Indies, and the growth of the French settlements in North America, threatened both the Dutch and the English. At the end of the century, the imminent union of the Crowns of France and Spain threatened to shut out the Dutch and English from the commerce of the Eastern and Western worlds. It was a principal object of the partition treaties to guard against this danger; [1] and the decision of Louis XIV in 1700 to throw over the treaties was partly inspired by his wish to seize the opportunity to acquire for France the position of the leading colonial power, and the monopoly of commerce in the Eastern and Western worlds. [2] It was the fear that France would succeed in attaining these objects which helped to decide England to fight. [3]

The war of the Spanish Succession was waged mainly on the continent of Europe; and the fact that too exclusive attention was paid to campaigns on the Continent, and too little to the colonies, was made the subject of criticism at the beginning of Anne's reign, [4] and later by Swift in his *Conduct of the Allies*. [5] But, as Professor Trevelyan has shown, this criticism, however true it may have been of the later phases of the war, is not true of its earlier phases. It is clear that it was England's successes on the continent of Europe which won for her the very considerable increase in her colonial possession, and the valuable commercial concessions, which she secured by the Treaty of Utrecht. [6] We have seen that by that treaty England secured Gibraltar and Port Mahon which gave her the control of the Mediterranean, St. Christopher, Newfoundland, and Acadia, i.e. Nova Scotia; and that she also secured the Asiento, i.e. the right to supply the Spanish colonies with slaves, and the right to send an annual ship to the Spanish West Indies. [7]

At the peace of Utrecht the colonial possessions of Great

---

[1] Camb. Hist. of the Empire i 322-323.

[2] Ibid 323-324; Swift, Conduct of the Allies, Works (ed. 1768) ii 191.

[3] Camb. Hist. of the Empire i 518; Seeley, Expansion of England 130-131.

[4] G. M. Trevelyan, England under Queen Anne i 259.

[5] " I have sometimes wondered how it came to pass, that the style of *maritime powers*, by which our allies in a sort of contemptuous manner usually couple us with the Dutch, did never put us in mind of the sea; and while some politicians were showing us the way to Spain by Flanders, others to Savoy or Naples, that the West Indies should never come into their heads," Works (ed. 1768) ii 199.

[6] " Marlborough won Acadia and Newfoundland in Germany, and the Asiento on the plains of Ramilles. After the victories of 1704-1706 much of Swift's criticism begins to be true; but applied to the earlier stages of the war much of it is erroneous," Trevelyan, op. cit. i 260.

[7] Vol. x 46 n. 5; these concessions did not turn out to be very valuable; in 1750 claims under the Asiento concession, which concession had been handed over to the South Sea Company, were renounced for £100,000, Camb. Hist. of the Empire i 344; only eight annual ships started during the thirty years that the concession lasted, ibid i 338-339; it was disputes arising out of both these concessions which gave rise to the war with Spain in 1739, ibid i 338-343.

Britain in the Western World can be divided into three main groups. (i) The American group. This group comprised settlements round Hudson's Bay, Newfoundland, Nova Scotia, the New England provinces of Massachusetts, Connecticut and Rhode Island, New York, New Jersey, Pennsylvania, Virginia, Maryland, the Carolines, the Bermuda islands, to which was added in 1732 Oglethorpe's [1] new province of Georgia. Some of these colonies were becoming, and many had become, settled states, with vigorous and independent lives of their own ; [2] and some were already conducting an extensive trade, not only with the mother country, but with one another and with the West Indies.[3] (ii) The West Indian group. This group comprised Jamaica, the Barbadoes, the Leeward Islands, the Bahamas, and some settlements on the Mosquito Coast. They were the sources from which tropical products were supplied, of which the most important was coming to be sugar. Since they were cultivated mainly by slave labour they were important centres of the slave trade. (iii) The West African settlements. They comprised a fort on James Island and the mouth of the Gambia, and factories on that river and on the Gold Coast. It was from these that the supply of slaves was drawn, by means of which the West Indies and the southern provinces of America were cultivated.

During the greater part of the eighteenth century, the relative value of the colonies was determined almost solely by reference to their commercial value to the mother country. We shall see that, according to the mercantilist system, those colonies which produced commodities which could not be produced by the mother country were valued more highly than those which produced commodities similar to those produced at home.[4] It followed therefore that the West Indies and the southern states of America, which produced sugar, tobacco, and other tropical or sub-tropical products, were more highly valued than the northern American colonies, which produced commodities similar to those produced in England. It was from this point of view that Child described New England as " the most prejudicial plantation to this kingdom." [5] But the decline of the West Indies in the latter half of the eighteenth century,[6] and the growth of the American colonies, which created a demand for articles manufactured in Great Britain,[7] were causing the

---

[1] Horace Walpole tells us, Letters (ed. Toynbee) xiii 259, that at the age of 95 Oglethorpe had all his faculties, that his spirits were in " full bloom," and that at the age of 91 he had sent a challenge to a neighbour who had trespassed on his manor.

[2] Camb. History of the Empire i 377.

[3] Ibid 396.   [4] Below 81-82.

[5] A New Discourse of Trade 204, cited Camb. Hist. of the Empire i 572.

[6] Ibid 379.   [7] Ibid 589.

economists to revise their views as to the relative values of these two groups of colonies. The African settlements were regarded as essential to the prosperity of the trade, both of the mother country and of those colonies which were most valued, because they produced tropical or sub-tropical commodities. " Exports to Africa were largely paid for by the purchasers of slaves in the West Indies, and, in the circumstances, the contention that the institution of slavery was essential to the maintenance of the colonial system, could hardly be challenged." [1]

Thus, at the time when the Treaty of Utrecht was made, the colonial possessions of Great Britain in the Western world, and their economic relations to the mother country and to one another, were assuming their eighteenth-century form. As that century progressed, it became evident that Great Britain and France were the two great rivals for colonial pre-eminence in America, in the West Indies, on the West Coast of Africa, and, as we shall see later, in India. During the peaceful years which lasted till 1739, the settlements in the West Indies became prosperous, and the wealth and population of the settlements in America increased. Consequently both the commerce and shipping of England prospered. In 1739 London's shipping was double that of Amsterdam, and the growth of commerce caused English merchants to wish " to break through the irksome restraints of Spain on West India trade." [2] Disputes over the commercial concessions obtained from Spain forced Walpole to war with Spain in 1739; and that war was soon merged in the general European war of the Austrian Succession. In the course of that war the strength of the American colonies, and the efficiency of the navy, were illustrated by the capture of Louisbourg and Cape Breton.[3] At the peace of Aix-la-Chapelle (1748) these captures in America were restored in exchange for Madras. But the foundation of Halifax, in 1749,[4] kept the privateers of Louisbourg in check, and helped to protect Newfoundland, Nova Scotia, and the coast of New England.

The Treaty of Aix-la-Chapelle merely afforded a breathing space to Great Britain and France in their race for colonial supremacy.[5] France began to take measures to assert her

[1] Camb. Hist. of the Empire i 570-571.   [2] Ibid 524.

[3] " Some 4000 militia, chiefly from Massachusetts, very efficiently aided by the King's ships, captured Louisbourg, a fortress upon which the French were said to have spent a million sterling. Only eternity, urged a divine, would be long enough for the due thanksgiving," ibid 375.

[4] " This was the only English colony in America founded by direct government action. It prospered rapidly," ibid 393.

[5] " In the seven years' truce which preceded the Seven Years' War . . . France and Britain, intent on profit from overseas, moved towards their inevitable trial of strength," ibid 376.

supremacy in America, and war broke out in America in 1754-1755. So began the Seven Years' War.

From the first Pitt saw clearly that the great issue was in North America ; for Louis XV and La Pompadour that issue was secondary ; and not until too late did the one great Frenchman of that age (Choiseul) declare that the war in America and at sea was the true war.[1]

We have seen that Pitt's policy of supporting Prussia in Europe, and attacking France's colonies, was brilliantly successful.[2] The great accessions of territory which Great Britain won at the Treaty of Paris, like the great accessions she won at the Treaty of Utrecht,[3] were due in part to the manner in which the strength of France had been diverted to the European theatre of war.[4] But in the Seven Years' War Great Britain's main effort was directed to the colonies, and not, as in the war of the Spanish Succession, to Europe. Consequently her oversea gains were greater. Her commerce rapidly increased ; and at the end of the war she was supreme at sea.[5] The Treaty of Paris, which followed upon a series of successes which are unexampled in English history, marks the completion of the Old Colonial Empire. In the Western world Great Britain gained the whole of North America, France retaining only a share in the Newfoundland fisheries, and in fisheries in the Gulf of St. Lawrence. Spain ceded Florida, and acknowledged the right of the English to cut logwood in Honduras bay. In the West Indies England gained Grenada and the Grenadines, St. Vincent, Dominica, and Tobago. In Africa she retained Senegal. But she gave back to France Martinique, Guadeloupe, Marie Galante, St. Lucia, Belleisle, and Goree ; and to Spain, Cuba and Manila.

As at Utrecht, so at Paris, the advent to power of a minority determined to make peace prevented Great Britain from gaining all that she ought to have gained.[6]

There was hardly a clause in it which was not below what she might reasonably have expected. Every new acquisition which she obtained, and every conquest which she relinquished, was actually in her hands before the peace was signed.[7]

Pitt pointed out that the greatest defects of the treaty were, first, the fact that Great Britain sacrificed strategic security by the needless cessions which she made in the West Indies, and by the concessions which she made in respect of the Newfoundland fisheries ;[8] and, secondly, the fact that she sacrificed diplomatic security by the manner in which she abandoned her allies in

[1] Camb. Hist. of the Empire i 527.
[2] Vol. x 86.
[3] Vol. x 46 ; above 38.
[4] Ibid.
[5] Camb. Hist. of the Empire i 535.
[6] Vol. x 46, 90.
[7] Lecky, History of England iii 213.
[8] Vol. x 90.

Europe.[1] If she had retained Cuba or St. Lucia, it would not have been so easy for the French fleet to have assisted America in the war of independence; and if she had not abandoned her allies in Europe she would not have been left diplomatically isolated during that war.[2]

It is a curious reflection on the Peace of Paris that it was assailed by the greatest of all our colonial statesmen on the ground that it sacrificed British interests, both in the West Indies and in Germany, to those of the American mainland. Such a policy implied indeed an abiding trust in the loyalty of British settlers in North America. And the man who had this confidence, the man who cared nothing for Hanover, . . . who gambled on the loyalty of America was His Majesty King George III.[3]

The result of the American war of independence was the dismemberment of the Old Colonial Empire. The independence of the thirteen United States was recognized, and the Canadian frontier was resettled. France gained the two islands of St. Pierre and Miquelon as a protection for her Newfoundland fishing rights, and the islands of St. Lucia and Tobago. She restored to Great Britain Grenada and the Grenadines, St. Vincent, Dominica, St. Christopher, Nevis and Montserrat. In Africa France gained Goree and Senegal, and England retained Fort James and the river Gambia. Spain gained Minorca and Florida, but restored Providence, the Bahamas, and other British possessions.[4] In spite of the loss of the thirteen colonies, Great Britain still retained a considerable colonial empire; and already the way had been prepared for other acquisitions in other parts of the globe. Discoveries had been made in the South Seas in 1767-1769; [5] and Captain Cook's three voyages (1768-1771, 1772-1775, 1776-1779) " laid the foundation upon which every British colony in the Pacific, including British Columbia, was built." [6] The exploitation of these discoveries, and the gains made by Great Britain in the Napoleonic wars, raised up for her a New Colonial Empire, which has been more permanent than the old, because she has learned from past mistakes. Burke's great speeches on America, the results of the American war of independence, and the speeches of Burke and of the other managers of the impeachment of Warren Hastings, taught Great Britain that she must regard her colonies from a new point of view. These speeches and these events taught her that she must no longer regard the trade and patronage to be derived from her colonies, as more important than the colonies themselves; [7] and that she could not expect

---

[1] Camb. Hist. of the Empire i 506.   [2] Ibid.   [3] Ibid.
[4] Lecky, History of England v 186-188 ; Camb. Hist. of the Empire i 781.
[5] Ibid 535-536.   [6] Camb. Mod. Hist. xii 814.
[7] In 1782 it was enacted that the holders of patent offices in the colonies should only be tenable so long as the holder resided in the colony, and performed the duties of his office, and that they could be removed by the Governor for neglect of duty, 22 George III c. 75 ; vol. x 523.

to keep communities, which were rapidly growing to maturity, in a perpetual state of dependency upon herself. An account of her older ideas upon these matters, which led to her failure in America, and the beginnings of the new ideas, will be given in the two following sections.

(2) *The government of the colonies.*

Modern constitutional law divides colonies, from the point of view of their mode of acquisition, into settled colonies and conquered or ceded colonies ; and, from the point of view of their government, into Crown colonies, colonies having representative institutions without responsible government,[1] and colonies having responsible government. We shall see that the distinction between settled colonies, and conquered or ceded colonies, can be traced back to the constitutional controversies of the seventeenth century.[2] It was drawn by Holt, C.J., in the case of *Blankard v. Galdy* in 1694 ; [3] and it was elaborated by Lord Mansfield in the case of *Campbell v. Hall* in 1774.[4] But the distinctions drawn between colonies from the point of view of the form of their government, were not in the eighteenth century leading distinctions. In the first place, responsible government is the application of the modern system of cabinet government to the colonies ; and we have seen that, in the eighteenth century, that system was only in embryo in England, and that it did not assume its modern form till after 1832.[5] It was not till the last decade of the first half of the nineteenth century, that its application to the government of Canada introduced this new conception of responsible government into colonial constitutional law.[6] In the second place, although there were in fact certain possessions of the Crown, such as Gibraltar and Minorca, which were governed by the prerogative alone,[7] by far the largest number of the colonies possessed representative institutions, and were governed by a Governor, Council, and Assembly. For these reasons it was hardly possible, in the eighteenth century, to make the division of colonies based upon the form of their government a leading division. During the greater part of the eighteenth century the division between the colonies which would have come most naturally to constitutional lawyers, was a division based upon the source from which the authority of their governments emanated.

---

[1] Anson, The Crown (4th ed.) ii Pt. ii 63, 68-72, classes all colonies without responsible government as Crown colonies, and subdivides them as follows : Those having no legislative councils, those having legislative councils of which a minority is elected, those having elected legislatures but not responsible government.

[2] Below 233-235.   [3] Vol. vi 264 ; 2 Salk. 411.

[4] 20 S.T. 239 ; below 236-237.   [5] Vol. x 643.

[6] Anson, The Crown (3rd ed.) ii Pt. ii 69,

[7] Berriedale Keith, The First British Empire 170 ; below 65.

Was the colony chartered, proprietary, or royal ? This division between colonies was emphasized by Blackstone,[1] by Alleyne in his argument for the plaintiff in the case of *Campbell v. Hall*,[2] and by Lord Mansfield in 1766 in the debate on the American disturbances consequent upon the passing of the Stamp Act.[3]

We have seen that the origins of the different colonies were diverse ; but that, in most cases, their foundation was due to commercial or financial considerations.[4] Hence many colonies originated in grants made by royal charters to joint stock companies, or to individual proprietors.[5]. Variations upon these methods occurred when a chartered company, e.g. the New England Company, " let out to settlers portions of its territory. leaving the settlers to seek, if they thought fit, recognition from the Crown, or to carry on without such authority " ; [6] or when, as in the case of St. Christopher, land was occupied by a subject and then authority was got from the Crown to govern it.[7] But, in all these chartered and proprietary colonies, the characteristic feature was the fact that the governing body of the company created by the charter, or the proprietor, was the source from which the authority of the government of the colony directly emanated.[8] On the other hand, the Crown was the source from which the authority of the government in the royal colonies directly emanated. These royal colonies were, for the most part, a later growth, because it was " only after the preliminary work had been done at the expense of others that the Crown was prepared to take over the obligations as well as the privileges of government." [9] Virginia, after the forfeiture of its charter in 1624, was directly administered by the Crown, and thus became the first royal colony.[10]

At the end of the seventeenth century, much of the preliminary work of foundation had been done in the case of very many of the colonies ; the colonies themselves were becoming settled communities ; [11] and definite economic and political policies in relation to the colonies were making their appearance.[12] In these circumstances government by an independent chartered company or a proprietor was found to be inconvenient and

---

[1] Comm. i 108.   [2] (1774) 20 S.T. at pp. 273-274.

[3] " My lords, there are three sorts of colony in America : King's Provinces ; Proprietary Provinces, and Charter Provinces," Parlt. Hist. xvi 175.

[4] Above 36 ; Berriedale Keith, op. cit. 18 ; vol. viii 209.

[5] In these charters the power of the proprietor was sometimes modelled on those possessed by the bishop of Durham over his county Palatine ; this form was adopted in the grant of Newfoundland to Calvert in 1623—a precedent followed in the case of subsequent grants of Maryland, Carolina, and Maine, Berriedale Keith, op. cit. 39-40 ; such charters helped to suggest arguments, based on the position of the counties Palatine, as to the powers of Parliament over the colonies, below 118-119.

[6] Berriedale Keith, op. cit. 21.   [7] Ibid.

[8] Ibid 43.   [9] Ibid 21-22.   [10] Ibid 25.

[11] Vol. viii 210 and n. 4 ; below 59, 66-67.   [12] Vol. vi 319-323 ; below 81-84.

inappropriate. It is not surprising, therefore, that, at the end
of the seventeenth century, the number of colonies governed
directly by the Crown had increased.[1] In some cases, e.g. in
Massachusetts, the form of government was laid down in a
charter granted by the Crown,[2] and in other cases the colony
had no charter ; but in all these cases the Crown was the source
from which the authority of the government directly emanated.
During the eighteenth century the chartered and proprietary
colonies continued to diminish in number. The proprietors of
New Jersey surrendered their rights in 1702 ; [3] the proprietors
of the Carolinas, by an agreement which was embodied in a
statute, surrendered their charters in 1729 [4] ; and the new colony
of Georgia at the expiration of its charter in 1754, passed under
royal government.[5]

It was always possible to resume a charter for default or
neglect in the conduct of the government ; [6] and at the beginning of the eighteenth century the Board of Trade tried
to get rid of the proprietary and chartered governments, and
to establish royal governments in all the colonies. " We have
found by experience," it said in 1728, " that all proprietary
colonies, where the government is not in the Crown, are highly
detrimental to Your Majesty's service and to the welfare of
Great Britain " ; [7] and of the chartered colony of Connecticut
it said in 1730 :

The people of Connecticut have not for many years transmitted their
laws or any account of their public transactions. Their Governors,
whom they have a right to choose by their charter, ought always to be
approved by the King, but no presentation is ever made by them for
that purpose ; and they, though required by law to give bond to observe

---

[1] Professor Berriedale Keith, op. cit. 167, gives the following list of royal governments : Virginia since 1624, New Hampshire (1679-1680), New York (1685),
Jamaica (1655), Barbadoes (1663), the Leeward Islands (1671), Bermuda (1684),
Massachusetts (1691), New Jersey (1702).
[2] Ibid 142-147.   [3] Ibid 151-152.
[4] 2 George II c. 34 ; Acts of the Privy Council (Col. Series) iii 173-177;
Berriedale Keith, op. cit. 167-168.
[5] Ibid 170-171 ; Acts of the Privy Council (Col. Series) iv 123-128 ; Camb.
Hist. of the Empire i 395-396 ; see Chalmers, Opinions i 34-38, for the opinion of
Ryder and Murray on the King's right to receive the surrender of the charter of
Georgia.
[6] The law officers (Harcourt and Northey) said, following an earlier opinion of
Holt C.J., that " upon an extraordinary exigency happening, through the default
or neglect of a proprietor, or of those appointed by him, or their inability to protect
or defend the province . . . in times of war or imminent danger, your majesty may
constitute a governor for such province or colony, as well for the civil as military
head of government . . . with this addition only, that as to the civil government,
such governor is not to alter any of the rules of propriety (sic) or matters of proceeding in civil causes, established pursuant to the charters granted," Chalmers,
Opinions i 30-31.
[7] Acts of Privy Council (Col. Series) vi 197 ; cp. reports of the Board of Trade
in 1702, MSS. of the House of Lords (New Series) v 67, 75, 76, 77-78, 81 ; ibid
vi 99 (1704) ; ibid vii 295-296 (1707).

the Laws of Trade and Navigation, never comply therewith ; so that we have reason to believe they do carry on illegal commerce with impunity ; and in general we never hear from them, except when they stand in need of the countenance, the protection, or assistance of the Crown.[1]

But the Board of Trade did not succeed in inducing the government to accept this policy.[2] In Connecticut and Rhode Island the government was, to the end, administered under charters which gave these colonies a very large measure of independence.[3]

The executive and legislature were appointed by the voters. They chose their own governors, carried on illegal trade with impunity, and had no correspondence with the Government at home, except when they stood in need of assistance from the Crown.[4]

In Pennsylvania the proprietary government of Penn and his descendants, and in Maryland the proprietary government of the Calverts, continued, in spite of constant friction between the representatives of the proprietors and the assemblies,[5] which paralysed the government.[6] But, though all the colonies had not been reduced to one type, there was considerable similarity in the form of their government. In all these three types of colonies the powers of government were in the hands of a Governor, Council and Assembly.[7] There were variations in detail ; but this had come to be the normal form of colonial government in the eighteenth century—so normal that it was in many cases given to the new colonies in America and the West Indies acquired by cession or conquest.[8] I shall therefore describe, in

---

[1] Acts of the Privy Council (Col. Series) vi 215-216.

[2] The Board of Trade " aimed at a stricter control over the trade and development of the colonies, and the establishment of a homogeneous system of administration by converting all proprietary and chartered governments into Royal Provinces, governed directly by the Crown " ; but that policy was shelved by Walpole—" between 1700 and 1720 seven bills for the resumption of the charters were introduced into the House of Commons. They were rejected," Camb. Hist. of the Empire i 385.

[3] Berriedale Keith, op. cit. 99-101 ; in 1742 the position in Connecticut was described as follows : " This government is a sort of republic. They acknowledge the King of Great Britain for sovereign, but are not accountable to the Crown for any acts of government, legislative or administrative," ibid 176 ; the position was the same in Rhode Island.

[4] Camb. Hist. of the Empire i 386.

[5] Berriedale Keith, op. cit. 176-178.

[6] " Historically the utter failure of Pennsylvania and Maryland on the plea of disagreement with the proprietors, to make provision for defence, was largely the cause of the need for Imperial protection which led to Imperial taxation and American revolt, and this fact was in part at least due to the failure in this period to secure the extinction of proprietary rule and land-ownership," ibid 179.

[7] " By the beginning of the eighteenth century . . . a normal type of organisation, familiar to us as the ' old representative system,' became established. This system prevailed everywhere (except in Connecticut and Rhode Island . . .), for even in the proprietary colonies . . . conditions were essentially the same, the proprietor taking the place of the King," Camb. Hist. of the Empire i 409.

[8] Berriedale Keith, op. cit. 168-169.

the first place, this normal form of colonial government ; and, in the second place the variations from this normal form of government, which were necessitated by physical, geographical, or political conditions, or which, at the end of the century, were the result of the new position which had resulted from the conquest of the French possessions in Canada.

The normal form of colonial government.

We must consider first the constitution of the executive ; secondly, the constitution and powers of the Legislature ; and, thirdly the Judicial System.

(i) The constitution of the executive.

At the head of the executive government of the colony, and the principal link in the colony between it and the home government, was the Governor. He was appointed by order in Council on the recommendation of the Secretary of State,[1] and held office during the pleasure of the Crown.[2] Generally each colony had a separate Governor—earlier experiments of uniting two colonies under one Governor having been found to be unsatisfactory.[3] When the Governor arrived he read his commission, took the oaths of office, and administered the oaths to the members of his Council.[4] The Governor was not allowed to leave his colony without the consent of the Crown.[5] If he got leave of absence, or if he died, his authority devolved upon the Lieutenant-Governor or other person nominated by the Crown. If there was no person nominated, the Council or its senior member acted. But their authority was confined to necessary acts of

[1] " The normal procedure in the appointment of a Governor was for the Board of Trade to send to the Council a representation enclosing a draft commission. On the approval of this, one of the Secretaries of State was ordered to cause a warrant to be prepared for his Majesty's signature, in order to pass the commission under the Great Seal. Some time later a further representation, with two drafts of instructions, one general and one for trade, was submitted by the Board of Trade, and referred by the Council to a Committee ; on receiving their report, and after considering any proposed amendments, the Secretary of State was ordered to prepare the drafts for his Majesty's signature," Acts of the Privy Council (Col. Series) iii 813.

[2] Berriedale Keith, First British Empire 187 ; in the proprietary colonies, the proprietor appointed subject to the Crown's approval, ibid ; in the chartered colonies the governor was elected and the Crown's approval was not sought, ibid ; between 1752 and 1761 the recommendation came from the Board of Trade, ibid, and it would seem that this was also true at an earlier date, see last note.

[3] Ibid 189-190.

[4] Camb. Hist. of the Empire i 420 ; for the oath of office, as settled in 1676, see Acts of the Privy Council (Col. Series) i 664 ; ii 622.

[5] Ibid ii 12—an order of 1682 ; see ibid i 465 (leave of absence refused), 673 (leave of absence given), ii 496 (leave of absence extended) ; Berriedale Keith, op. cit. 190.

administration, pending the return of the Governor or the arrival of his successor.[1]

The powers and duties of the Governor were defined by his commission and his instructions.[2] The commission was a public document issued under the Great Seal. A new commission was issued whenever a Governor was appointed; but in the eighteenth century the form of the commission was to a large extent stereotyped; and since "government by Governor, Council, and Assembly, once conceded, could not be withdrawn by the King in Council, all that could be varied were minor details."[3] The commission gave to the Governor certain prerogative powers —executive, legislative, and judicial, and empowered him to act under any statutory powers conferred by the local Legislature,[4] which, if assented to by the Crown, might diminish his prerogative powers.[5] The instructions gave the Governor directions as to the use of the powers conferred by his commission. "Though legally the private orders of the King, they were in fact a composite draft, showing the handiwork of nearly every prominent official who had to do with the colonies."[6] They were passed by the Board of Trade, and grew more elaborate and more fixed as time went on. They were revised in 1752; but, unfortunately, this occasion was not taken advantage of to bring them into line with new needs and new aspirations of the colonies. To the end they ignored the fact that the colonies in the eighteenth century no longer occupied the same position of dependence upon the mother country as they had occupied in the seventeenth century.[7]

The powers and duties of the Governor were large and various. As the chief executive officer he owed many duties to the Crown—the duty to supervise other officials, to co-operate with the naval and military authorities, to assist the officers of the

---

[1] Berriedale Keith, op. cit. 190-191; cp. Acts of the Privy Council (Col. Series) iv 424-425.

[2] Berriedale Keith, op. cit. 179-182; Camb. Hist. of the Empire i 418-420; specimens of these instructions will be found in the Acts of the Privy Council (Colonial Series).

[3] Berriedale Keith, op. cit. 180.   [4] Ibid 181.

[5] His prerogative powers "might be limited indefinitely by statute duly assented to; thus the right of appointment might be taken away from the Governor or subjected to conditions; the control of military forces restricted or annihilated, and his financial powers reduced to nothing, while the legislature might determine its own existence and define its membership and franchise. Such measures might be refused assent or disallowed, but they were not invalid *per se*. . . . The Colonial Laws Validity Act, 1865, merely records standing doctrine when it by S. 5 asserts the inherent right of a representative legislature to change its constitution," ibid 181-182.

[6] Camb. Hist. of the Empire i 418-419; for some early sets of instructions see Acts of the Privy Council (Col. Series) i 127—Governor of Virginia, 1628, 355—Governor of the West Indies, 1663.

[7] Camb. Hist. of the Empire i 419-420.

customs, to perform certain duties under the Navigation and other Acts, to report fully on the condition of his colony, and to transmit the proceedings of, and laws passed by, the Assemblies.[1]

His powers were wide. With respect to legislation he could suggest to the Assembly any matter on which legislation was required; and his instructions often directed him to procure legislation on certain topics.[2] When a bill had been passed by the Assembly he could either assent to it, refuse his assent, or reserve it for the pleasure of the Crown.[3] Another course open to him was to refuse to assent to it, unless it contained a clause suspending its operation till it was confirmed by the Crown—a practice which aroused much opposition in the Assemblies.[4] The instructions given to the Governor as to the use of his power to assent to bills tended to grow more detailed; [5] and, as might be expected, these fetters on his discretion were often resented by the Assemblies.[6] Sometimes the Governor was compelled to assent, in spite of his instructions, by tacking the measure to a supply bill, or by making the grant of supply conditional on assent.[7] But, even if he assented to a bill, it might be disallowed by the Crown.[8] Matters which fell within the scope of the prerogative, e.g. the fees of offices, the creation of courts, or regulations in an emergency, could be dealt with by him by means of an ordinance without reference to the Assembly.[9]

The permanent revenues of the Crown were inconsiderable, so that the Crown was dependent on grants by the Assemblies for the greater part of the expenses of government.[10] The Assemblies were fully aware of the lever which this gave to them. They refused to make any but temporary grants,[11] they

[1] Berriedale Keith, op. cit. 197-198; in 1669 there was a complaint that Governors had not taken the oath required by the Navigation Act, Acts of the Privy Council (Col. Series) i 500; in 1663 Lord Willoughby of Parham, when he was made Governor of the West Indies, was instructed to see that all ships from other countries, which had not paid customs duties in England, paid duties on all the commodities which they imported, ibid 361.

[2] Berriedale Keith, op. cit. 242-243.

[3] Ibid 243; reservation was "a later device which was hit on as a means of saving the Governor from a decision which might prove inconvenient," ibid.

[4] Ibid.   [5] Ibid 244-245.   [6] Ibid 243.   [7] Ibid 245-246.

[8] Ibid 246; below 56.   [9] Ibid 246-247.

[10] For these revenues see ibid 213-214; for questions arising from such incidental sources of revenue as escheats, mines of gold and silver, quit rents, woods, treasure trove, see Chalmers, Opinions i 110-140; for the $4\frac{1}{2}$ per cent duty on exports from the Barbados and the Leeward Islands, voted in perpetuity for their government and defence, see Acts of the Privy Council (Col. Series) vi *xxi*; it is there pointed out that, "from 1698 to 1702 this was actually applied to the use of the Civil List in England, and, throughout the eighteenth century, assignments were made on this revenue in recognition of services which had nothing whatever to do with the West Indies"—a very sufficient justification for the refusal of the Assemblies to vote a permanent supply.

[11] Berriedale Keith, op. cit. 203-204; cp. Acts of the Privy Council (Col. Series) iii 49.

appropriated strictly the money granted,[1] and they insisted upon
vesting the money raised in their own nominees, who saw to it
that the money was spent as directed in the Appropriation Act.[2]
By pursuing this course, they conld exercise a stricter control
over the officials whom they paid than could the Governor.
Thus the Governor's control over finance came to be limited to
those items which did not depend upon grants by the Assembly.
For his expenditure of these revenues he must account to the
Crown. The Crown's agent for this purpose was the Auditor-
General, who had a deputy in the colony.[3] But even over this
expenditure the Assemblies had some control, since they were
allowed to inspect the Governor's accounts.[4]

The Governor was responsible for the defence of the colony.
He could muster and arm troops, and use them to repel invasion
or to put down rebellions.[5] In time of war he could exercise
martial law—a power which, as we have seen,[6] was in the eighteenth century by no means precisely defined. But here again
the Governor was very much in the hand of the Assembly. It
controlled finance, and it alone could pass the laws necessary
to preserve discipline amongst the troops.[7] In fact the Assemblies used their powers to usurp the functions of the executive, by
controlling the movements and the operations of the troops
which were raised. In 1756, during the French war, the Assemblies in many of the colonies tried to control the military
operations.[8] " There is much force," says Professor Berriedale
Keith, " in Chalmers's dictum : ' The King's representative acted
merely as the correspondent of his ministers ; the war was
conducted by committees of Assembly,' and, it may be added,
by no means well at that," [9] The Governor had also a commission from the Admiralty under which he could, *inter alia*,
establish and supervise admiralty courts, issue letters of marque,
and act against pirates.[10] He had no direct control over imperial forces sent to the colony, unless command over these
forces was specially conferred upon him.[11]

[1] Berriedale Keith, op. cit. 205-206; for a complaint of such action by the
Assembly of New York in 1719 see Calendar of Treasury Papers 1714-1719 462.

[2] Berriedale Keith, op. cit. 206-212 ; the Board of Trade said in 1731 that this
claim of the Assembly of Massachusetts to order payments, gave it a power " superior
to any which the British House of Commons lays claim to," and that, though empowered to raise money, its distribution is by its charter reserved to the Governor and
Council, Acts of the Privy Council (Col. Series) iii 327-328.

[3] Berriedale Keith, op. cit. 205.   [4] Ibid.

[5] Ibid 216.   [6] Vol. x 711.

[7] Berriedale Keith op. cit. 216-217 ; " in 1755 the Pennsylvanian Assembly
produced an Act which Dinwiddie of Virginia stigmatized as a joke on all military
affairs, and which was disallowed, as it allowed election of officers by ballot, and
provided no serious penalties for offences," ibid 217 ; cp. Acts of the Privy Council
(Col. Series) iv 337-339.

[8] Berriedale Keith, op. cit. 218-219.   [9] Ibid 219.

[10] Ibid 219.   [11] Ibid.

Foreign relations and questions of war and peace were outside the scope of a Governor's authority. But in America he had power to make treaties with the Indians, and even to make war upon them in an emergency.[1] Matters affecting different colonies were negotiated through their Governors ;[2] but both in respect to these matters, and in respect to commercial relations with the Indians, the influence of the Assemblies made itself felt.[3]

The Governor could exercise the prerogative of mercy ; but in cases of treason or murder he could only reprieve till the King's pleasure had been taken.[4] Legislation which attempted to encroach on this prerogative, by granting pardons or by rendering offences unpardonable, was disallowed.[5] The Governor had the power to grant charters of incorporation, to establish ports, and to grant the franchises of fair and ferry, and, with the advice of his Council, to make grants of land.[6] He had the custody and control of the Great Seal of the province.[7]

This summary of the Governor's powers shows that, as the connecting link in the colony between the colony and the home government, and as the head of the executive in the colony, he was as much the most important and essential part of the colonial executive government, as the Crown was of the executive government of Great Britain. Much therefore turned on the personality of the Governors. They were recruited partly from leading men in the colonies, partly from naval and military officers, and partly from " English members of the office-holding class at home, similar to those who were carrying on the real government of England herself."[8] On the whole they filled adequately the difficult position of agents of the Crown, representatives of their colonies, and mediators between the colonial policy of the Crown and the rising tide of nationalism in the colonies. Professor Andrews says that, of the two hundred and fifty governors who held office after 1685, a few were " greedy proconsuls," some were men of very mediocre powers, two were recalled on account of their misdeeds, two committed suicide ; but that " by far the greater number were men of honour, who did their best in an impossible situation." An impossible situation because " they stood for a different idea of government from that which was gradually shaping itself in America—government by royal grace and favour instead of government by consent of the governed—

---

[1] Berriedale Keith, op. cit. 220-221 ; for specimens of these treaties see Acts of the Privy Council (Col. Series) i 733—a treaty made in 1677 by the Lieutenant Governor of Virginia with certain Indian Princes.

[2] Berriedale Keith, op. cit. 221. [3] Ibid.

[4] Ibid 265 ; cp. Calendar of Home Office Papers 1770-1772, 447.

[5] Berriedale Keith, op. cit. 265-266.

[6] Ibid 215. [7] Ibid 214-215.

[8] Camb. Hist. of the Empire i 417.

and legally were obliged to direct their administration according to the wish and will of the executive authorities at home." [1]

The Governor was assisted in his executive duties by a Council, which, in addition to its executive powers, had also legislative and judicial powers.[2] The councillors were appointed by the Crown on the recommendation of the Board of Trade, from a list of names furnished by the Governor, who was directed to select leading inhabitants of the colony " of good life, well affected to the government, of good estates and abilities, and not necessitous people or much in debt." [3] The Governor could suspend a councillor, and report to the Crown, who usually removed a councillor if the Governor so desired.[4] In the eighteenth century the surveyor-general of customs and superintendents of Indian affairs were added to the Council.[5] The Governor could consult his Council on any executive matter, and on certain matters his instructions directed him to consult it, e.g. as to calling Assemblies and the establishment of courts of justice.[6] As we might expect, " the measure of control in fact exerted by the Council over the Governor depended on character and circumstances rather than formal law." [7]

The officials of the executive government fell into distinct classes. First, there were those appointed by the Crown and controlled by, and responsible only to, the Crown, or to the head of some department of the central government in England. Amongst these were the Governor himself, the deputy-auditor appointed by the auditor-general in England, the surveyor-general of woods, the surveyors of customs, the officers of the royal naval and military forces, the judges of the vice-admiralty courts, and the deputies of the Postmaster-General.[8] Secondly, there were officials appointed by the Crown by letters patent but subject to the control of the Governor, who could suspend, but could not remove them. These officers generally included the chief justice, the attorney-general, secretary, provost-marshal-general, surveyor-general, receiver-general.[9] Thirdly, there were officials appointed and removable by the Governor. The Assemblies often passed laws which limited the discretion of the Governor ; [10] and, as we have seen, they even went further and

---

[1] Camb. Hist. of the Empire i 417-418.
[2] Berriedale Keith, op. cit. 191, 193 ; below 53-54, 59.
[3] Acts of the Privy Council (Col. Series) iii 821 ; Camb. Hist. of the Empire i 420 ; Berriedale Keith, op. cit. 191-192.
[4] Ibid 192 ; " but in 1706 Cornbury was ordered peremptorily to replace Lewis Morris, and in 1719 Spotswood had to reinstate W. Byrd, and similar action occurred later, thus checking arbitrary power," ibid.
[5] Acts of the Privy Council (Col. Series) iii 382-383, 720 ; Berriedale Keith, op. cit. 193.
[6] Ibid 193-194.   [7] Ibid 195.
[8] Ibid 196.   [9] Ibid 195-196.   [10] Ibid 195.

encroached upon his powers by themselves appointing the officials
by whom taxing and other Acts were to be carried out.[1]

The Governors in the colonies, like the executive in England,
tried by the use of their patronage to influence the Assemblies;
and the Assemblies tried to counteract this influence by legislation similar to that passed in England after the fall of North's
ministry.[2]   But the fact that many of the most lucrative offices
were patent offices of a proprietary kind, granted by the Crown
to Englishmen as a reward for political services in England, and
exercised by the deputies of their holders in the colonies,[3] deprived the Governor of many opportunities which he would
otherwise have had of influencing his Assemblies.   These patent
offices also gave rise to many disputes between rival claimants to
them,[4] and led to disputes with the Assemblies, which tried by
legislation to diminish the profits of these officials.[5]   We have
seen that it was not till 1782 that it was enacted that the holders
of these offices must reside in the colonies, and faithfully discharge their duties.[6]   If the English government had not been
so eager to use its colonial patronage solely to improve its position
in the House of Commons, if it had realized the necessity of using
that patronage to control the Assemblies, it would have made
it more possible for the Governor to carry out the policy of maintaining and even increasing royal control over the colonies,
which his instructions directed him to pursue.   We shall now
see that, as the eighteenth century advanced, the growth in the
powers and independence of the Assemblies was making that
policy more and more impossible.

(ii) *The constitution and powers of the Legislature.*

Generally in the eighteenth century the Legislature consisted
of two Houses—the Council and an elected Assembly.

The Council was the same body as that which assisted the
Governor in his executive functions, and in some colonies, in
the early years of the eighteenth century, he presided over and

---

[1] Above 50.   [2] Below 55 ; vol. x 107.
[3] See Chalmers, Opinions i 143-144, for an opinion by Treby in 1689 that the
post of auditor of the Virginia revenue could be granted for life and could be performed by deputy ; for other cases of such posts in the colonies see Blankard v.
Galdy (1694) 4 Mod. 222, and R. v. Vaughan (1769) 4 Burr. 2494, cited vol. i
248 n. 4 ; Acts of the Privy Council (Col. Series) i 334—a grant for life of the office
of provost-marshal-general in the Barbados ; cp. ibid 727 for a rebuke to the
Governor of Jamaica for fining and imprisoning such an official ; in 1674 the Council
advised that no new offices of this kind should be created in Jamaica, ibid i 874 ;
Camb. Hist. of the Empire i 411 ; for the prevalence of these officials in England
see vol. x 501-503.
[4] Acts of the Privy Council (Col. Series) ii 83, 596, 660-664 ; iii 392 ; v 47-49.
[5] Ibid ii 528-531, 603-604 ; iii 418-419, 546-547, 741-742.
[6] 22 George III c. 75 ; above 42 n. 7.

voted in it.[1] But later the Council, when sitting as a branch of the Legislature, acquired its own President, who was the Lieutenant-Governor if he was a member.[2] The home government regarded it as equal in power to the Assembly.[3] This is not surprising, since the Council was expected to support the Governor in his efforts to give effect to the policy desired by the home government,[4] and councillors who supported the opposition were liable to dismissal, and were sometimes dismissed.[5] In these circumstances, it is not surprising that, early in the eighteenth century, the Assemblies, acting on the theory that they occupied the same position as the House of Commons, denied that the Councils had the power to originate and amend money bills, and even denied them the power to initiate legislation.[6] In spite of the protests of the Board of Trade, which were backed up by the lawyers, who denied the existence of any analogy to the English Parliament,[7] the Assemblies made good their claim. The result was that the Councils became comparatively unimportant branches of the Legislature.

Representing neither the colony nor the King, lacking both responsibility and executive authority, and exercising only a negative influence on the passage of laws, the colonial council was never able to grow into a constitutional body comparable with either the House of Lords or the Privy Council.[8]

[1] Berriedale Keith, op. cit. 231 ; in 1724-1725, West, the counsel to the Board of Trade, was of opinion that the Governor could not vote in the Council, when it was sitting as a branch of the Legislature, Chalmers, Opinions i 231 ; Acts of the Privy Council (Col. Series) iii 492-493.

[2] Berriedale Keith, op. cit. 231-232. [3] Below n 7.

[4] Thus in 1753 Popple, the Governor of Bermuda, maintained that " in the disputes between the Governor and the Assembly . . . the Governor is maintaining the rights of the Crown, and it is the duty of the Council to support him," Acts of the Privy Council (Col. Series) vi 320.

[5] Ibid ii 424-425 ; v 155 ; vi 102, 269 ; this state of affairs was criticized by Pownall ; he says, " it always struck me as a strange deviation [from the model of the British constitution] that the governor's council of state, although a distinct, and I had almost said, an incompatible, board, with the council, one branch of the legislature, is yet always constituted by the same persons, in general nominated and liable to be suspended by the governor," Administration of the Colonies (4th ed.) 115-116.

[6] Berriedale Keith, op. cit. 207-212, 232.

[7] Pratt, when Attorney-General, advising on the powers of the Council and Assembly of Maryland, said, with reference to the power of the Council to examine accounts, " The upper house . . . should take care how they admit encroachments of this kind, when they are supported by arguments drawn from the exercise of the like rights in the house of commons here. The constitutions of the two assemblies differ fundamentally in many respects ; our house of commons stands upon its own laws, the *lex parliamenti*, whereas assemblies in the colonies are regulated by their respective charters, usages, and the common law of England, and will never be allowed to assume those privileges, which the house of commons are entitled to justly here, upon principles that neither can nor must be applied to the assemblies of the colonies," Chalmers, Opinions i 263-264 ; it was on these grounds that the Privy Council decided that a colonial Assembly had not got the powers and privileges possessed by the House of Commons by virtue of the *lex et consuetudo Parliamenti*, below 57-58, 261-265.

[8] Camb. Hist. of the Empire i 421-422.

The Assembly was the elected body which represented the colony. The franchise, which could be settled either by the Governor or by Act of the Assembly, varied in the different colonies ; but in all there was a property qualification.[1] The qualifications for membership could be similarly determined ;[2] and the Assemblies, in order to diminish the influence of the Governors, passed legislation to disable office-holders, to which the Crown in many cases refused its consent.[3] The same two authorities could also settle the number and boundaries of the electoral districts.[4] Both upon this question, and upon the question of the duration of the Assembly, conflicts arose between it and the Crown.[5] In some cases the duration of the Assembly was fixed by legislative Act, but in many cases the Crown refused to assent to these Acts.[6] Subject to the restrictions, if any, contained in these Acts, the Governor could adjourn, prorogue, or dissolve the Assembly as he saw fit. His powers in these respects were the same as the powers of the Crown in relation to the Parliament of Great Britain ;[7] but it was the better opinion that, though the demise of the Crown dissolved the Assembly,[8] a change of Governor did not dissolve it.[9]

From the first the Crown regarded these Assemblies merely as subordinate law-making bodies.[10] In 1766 Lord Mansfield said that, in the royal provinces, they had merely the power " to make bye-laws for their interior government " ; that, in the proprietary provinces, they had by their charters merely " a subordinate power to make laws, so as the same were not contrary to the laws of England " ; and that the chartered colonies " were all on the same footing as are great corporations in London." [11] Three consequences followed from the subordinate

---

[1] Berriedale Keith, op. cit. 233.   [2] Ibid 233-234.
[3] Ibid 234.   [4] Ibid 234-236 ; Chalmers, Opinions i 271, 272.
[5] Berriedale Keith, op. cit. 235-237.

[6] Ibid 236-237 ; in 1738 Fane, counsel to the Board of Trade, advised the Board that an Act passed in New York limiting the duration of the Assembly to three years, and requiring a new Assembly to be called within six months of the dissolution of the old Assembly, was " a very high infringement upon the prerogative of the crown," and that consent to any such Act ought to be refused, Chalmers, Opinions i 188-189 ; see ibid 356 for a similar opinion on an Act which gave power to the Assembly to meet without the Crown's consent.

[7] Chalmers, Opinions i 231-237.

[8] Berriedale Keith, op. cit. 237 n. 3 ; Chalmers, op. cit. i 303-343 ; probably it was dissolved as from the time when notice was received of the demise, ibid 328 note.

[9] Ibid 244-259 ; it was pointed out, ibid 255-259, that a change of a Lord-Lieutenant did not dissolve the Irish Parliament.

[10] For attempts in the latter part of the seventeenth century, which failed, to subject the Jamaican and Virginian Assemblies to the restrictions of Poynings' Law, above 21-22, see Berriedale Keith, op. cit. 12-13, 82 ; Acts of the Privy Council (Col. Series) i 745 (1677), 763 (1678), 827 (1679).

[11] Parlt. Hist. xvi 175 ; for the effect of this view on colonial legislation see below 249 ; for its effect on later law, and the emergence of a somewhat different view see below 250-251.

character of the legislative powers of the Assemblies. First, no
Assembly could pass a statute which contravened a statute of the
British Parliament relating to the colony.[1] Secondly, though
within the colony Acts of the Assembly had the same force as
Acts of Parliament,[2] they had no extra-colonial effect.[3] It was
only the British Parliament which could legislate for the whole of
the Empire.[4] Thirdly, there were doubts as to the validity of a
colonial enactment which was repugnant to the principles of the
English common law.[5] This principle was enforced mainly by
the power of the Crown to disallow Acts which infringed it.
In the case of a chartered colony it was said that such an enactment went beyond the powers given by the charter.[6] In
the case of the royal colonies it was said that it was passed
contrary to the instructions given to the Governor.[7] The principle was also occasionally enforced by appeals to the courts to
declare such an enactment void.[8] And though there do not
appear to have been many cases in which this appeal was successful, the principle that such Acts could be declared judicially
to be void, remained as a theoretical and nebulous principle till
the Colonial Laws Validity Act of 1865.[9]

The manner in which the Board of Trade and the Privy
Council tried to give practical effect to the subordinate character
of colonial legislation has been admirably described by Professor
Andrews.[10] He says :

By successive instructions and by decisions of the Crown lawyers
or of the counsel to the Board of Trade, the Assembly was forbidden
to concern itself with any matters that lay outside the province it
represented, or which trespassed upon the prerogative of the King
or the powers of Parliament. It could not interfere in any way with
the laws of trade, or discriminate in favour of the colonists at the expense
of British merchants engaged in colonial trade. It could not pass
private Acts without a clause saving the rights of the Crown, bodies
politic and corporate, and all private persons, nor could it pass these
or other Acts, the nature of which was specified, without first obtaining

---

[1] Chalmers, Opinions i 344-348, 353-354 ; Berriedale Keith, op. cit. 251-252.
[2] Chalmers, Opinions ii 2 ; below 248.
[3] Ibid i 343-344 ; Acts of the Privy Council (Col. Series) iv 560 ; we have
seen that it was for that reason that the modern cases recognized that a colonial
naturalization Act could make a person a British subject only in that colony,
vol. ix 83.
[4] Lord Mansfield said, " The British legislature, as to the power of making laws,
represents the whole British empire, and has authority to bind every part and every
subject, without the least distinction, whether such subjects have a right to vote or
not, or whether the law binds places within the realm or without," Parlt. Hist. xvi
173.
[5] Chalmers, Opinions i 354 (Opinion of Yorke and Talbot 1730), 347 (Opinion
of Murray 1755) ; ii 31 (Opinion of Rawlin 1717).
[6] Berriedale Keith, op. cit. 249-251.   [7] Ibid 251, 252.
[8] Ibid 248-249, 252-253.
[9] 28, 29 Victoria c. 63 ; below 238.
[10] Camb. Hist. of the Empire i 423.

the King's consent or introducing a suspending clause binding the colony not to enforce the Act until the King's will were known. Thus the freedom of the Assembly was hedged in at many points by the instructions which the King sent to his Governor, and it was against the barriers which such instructions set up that the Assemblies in the royal colonies in the eighteenth century fought with all the resources in their possession.

In fact the Assemblies wholly denied the premises from which the Crown started. They considered themselves to be in the same position in their colonies as the House of Commons was in England.[1] The colonies of New England inherited the traditions of Parliamentary opposition to the Crown ; and their Assemblies naturally considered that they took the same position as the English Parliament.[2] This idea quickly spread to the Assemblies of other colonies ; [3] for a representative assembly, then as now, is as quick to claim powers and privileges as it is slow to learn how to use them wisely.

Just as the English Parliament, in the seventeenth century, became an effective instrument of opposition to the Crown by the use which it made of its rules of procedure and of its privileges,[4] and by the use which it made of its powers over finance ; [5] so the Assemblies in the eighteenth century asserted their claims to be something more than merely subordinate law-making bodies by exactly the same means.[6] The procedure of the Assembly depended upon the custom and usage of the particular Assembly,[7] which was based on that of the English Parliament [8] —though in many of the colonies it was far less elaborate ; [9] and, as in England, the Assembly elected its speaker subject to the Governor's confirmation, which was usually formal.[10] The Assembly claimed to possess as its undoubted right all the privileges of the House of Commons. These, it held, were a part of the *Lex Parliamenti*, and therefore a part of the common

---

[1] Berriedale Keith, op. cit. 129, 241 ; above 54 n. 7.

[2] " The English view was that the colony was in the position of a corporation, with powers therefore similar to those of a town council or any body constituted for a particular object. The colonists, on the other hand, from the first refused to accept this theory and maintained that their assemblies stood to them in the same position as did the Parliament of England to that country. This theory found its most complete and logical expression in Massachusetts," Egerton, The American Revolution 6-7.

[3] Ibid 8-10.   [4] Vol. vi 88-100.   [5] Ibid vi 81.

[6] Berriedale Keith, op. cit. 205-212, 240-242 ; Camb. Hist. of the Empire i 424-433.

[7] In 1755 Murray and Lloyd, the attorney and solicitor-general, said with reference to a privilege claimed by the Jamaica Assembly, " What the assembly claims seems analogous to the law and practice here ; but it does not from thence necessarily follow that it is, or ought to be, the law there ; that must depend upon their own constitution and usage," Chalmers, Opinions ii 3.

[8] Camb. Hist. of the Empire i 432.

[9] Berriedale Keith, op. cit. 241-242.   [10] Ibid 240.

law, which could not be taken away or diminished by the Crown.[1]
As in England, they used their privileges not only to discipline
their own members, but also to deal with outsiders who offended
their dignity,[2] and even to encroach on the jurisdiction of the
courts.[3]   As in England it was their powers over finance which
enabled the Assemblies to make good their claims as against
the Crown. They refused to vote a permanent revenue, or a
permanent salary to the Governor.[4] They strictly appropriated
the sums granted ; and they appointed their own officials to see
that the money was spent in accordance with law.[5] The successful assertion of these powers enabled the Assemblies to
encroach on the Governor's power to appoint officials,[6] and, by
the process of tacking or by bargaining for his assent to bills in
return for a supply, to encroach on his power to refuse to assent
to legislation.[7] They also evaded the consequence of a refusal
of the Crown to approve laws assented to by the Governor, by
passing temporary laws for short periods, and by re-enacting
disallowed Acts.[8] In 1755 the Board of Trade reported that
the Assembly of New York had by its Acts, and particularly
by temporary Acts for raising money, " taken to themselves,

[1] Berriedale Keith, op. cit. 241 ; below 261-262.
[2] Ibid ; this assumption of power was then and later held to be illegal,
below 261 n. 5 ; in 1713 the Jamaica Assembly claimed to be able to exempt its
members from all legal proceedings, Acts of the Privy Council (Col. Series) ii
670-671 ; ibid iv 399 ; in 1759 the Pennsylvania Assembly arrested a Mr. Smith
for libel and ordered the sheriff not to obey a writ of Habeas Corpus, ibid iv 384.
[3] In 1759 the Jamaica Assembly passed an Act to reverse a sentence of the
Jamaica Court, Acts of the Privy Council (Col. Series) iv 412-413.
[4] In 1704 and 1707 Massachusetts refused to vote a permanent salary to the
Governor, MSS. of the House of Lords (New Series) vi 98, vii 271-272 ; in 1729
the committee of the Privy Council reported, after hearing counsel for the Assembly
of Massachusetts on the question of voting a permanent salary for the Governor,
that " it appeared that the Point contended for, was to bring the Governor appointed
by Your Majesty over them, to a Dependence on their Good Will for his Subsistence,
which would manifestly tend to the lessening of his Authority, and consequently
of that Dependence which this Colony ought to have upon the Crown of Great
Britain," Acts of the Privy Council (Col. Series) iii 109 ; with this object the
Assemblies were ready to make presents to the Governor, and the home government objected to his receiving these presents, ibid ii 534 ; iii 239.
[5] Above 50.
[6] Above 52-53; in 1772 the Board of Trade reported that the Legislature of
Georgia " had of late fallen into a practice of passing laws, under the name of
ordinances, for the appointment of persons to various executive offices, appearing
to imply a claim in the Assembly to concur in the choice of such officers, thus im-
pairing the constitutional rights of the Crown," Acts of the Privy Council (Col.
Series) v 322.
[7] Berriedale Keith, op. cit. 245-246.
[8] Ibid 296-297 ; Acts of the Privy Council (Col. Series) iii 343 ; cp. Chalmers,
Opinions i 350-352, where Northey, the attorney-general, pointed out that the
practice of passing temporary laws in the royal colonies could be remedied by an
instruction to the Governor not to assent to them ; but that in the proprietary
colonies the only remedy was to pass an Act of Parliament forbidding the practice ;
an even more objectionable practice was the setting aside by a temporary Act, of
the provisions of a permanent Act, Acts of the Privy Council (Col. Series) iv 511.

not only the management and disposal of such Publick money, but have also wrested from Your Majesty's Governor, the nomination of all Officers of Government, the Custody and direction of the Public Military Stores, the mustering and regulating of troops raised for your Majesty's service, and in short almost every other executive part of Government." [1]

By these means the Assemblies had, by the middle of the eighteenth century, gained almost as important a position in relation to their colonies, as the House of Commons had gained in relation to Great Britain. They had become something very much more than subordinate law-making bodies, fettered by a Governor acting in accordance with the instructions which he had received from the Crown. It was for this reason that they refused to listen to any proposition that they should be taxed by Parliamentary requisition,[2] in spite of all the arguments (with which Adam Smith agreed) [3] that there was " no probability that the Parliamentary requisition would be unreasonable." By the middle of the eighteenth century it was becoming obvious that the future relations of Great Britain with the colonies would ultimately depend on the question whether the government would recognize the new position—whether they would recognize that the colonies, under the guidance of their Assemblies, were becoming mature political societies.

(iii) *The judicial system.*

The Governor, with the consent of his Council, could create courts of justice to administer the common law.[4] It was generally assumed in the eighteenth century that he could create courts of equity [5]—though the legality of the exercise of this power was perhaps more doubtful.[6] But the power to create courts was also claimed by the Assemblies ; and Acts were passed to establish new courts.[7] In some places the Governor, or the Governor and Council, acted as a court of Exchequer, as a court of probate, and as a court for matrimonial causes.[8] In many colonies the Governor and Council were the highest court of appeal in the colony ; [9] and sometimes the Governor or the Governor and Council sat as a court of Chancery, and administered an equitable jurisdiction.[10] But, as Pownall points out, the administration of equitable jurisdiction in this way was not

---

[1] Acts of the Privy Council (Col. Series) iv 247 ; cp. ibid 410-411 ; v 199, 304.
[2] Adam Smith, Wealth of Nations (Cannan's ed.) ii 121.
[3] Ibid 119.   [4] Berriedale Keith, op. cit. 255.
[5] Ibid ; Chalmers, Opinions i 182-183 ; below 266.
[6] Below 265-266.   [7] Berriedale Keith, op. cit. 255-256, 257.
[8] Ibid 256.   [9] Ibid 257.
[10] Pownall, Administration of the Colonies (4th ed.) 110.

satisfactory, and, on that account, had almost fallen into disuse.[1]

The admiralty jurisdiction in the colonies has a different history. The authorities from which the courts of admiralty derived their powers, the law which they administered, and the procedure which they used, put them outside the ordinary judicial system of the colonies.[2] In the earlier part of the seventeenth century, the need to protect trade and fishing rights had resulted in the creation of a vice-admiralty court in Newfoundland for their protection.[3] But little or no use was made of these and other charters which gave admiralty jurisdiction, and no system of admiralty courts was established.[4] In some colonies, indeed, the need for a court with an admiralty jurisdiction was becoming obvious. Boston was becoming a busy port, the trade of Maryland and Virginia was developing, and Bermuda was an important port of call. In all these colonies an incipient admiralty jurisdiction was developed.[5] But as yet it had not given rise to a distinct court, and "was grafted on to the existing judicial system." [6] It was not till after the Restoration that the need for a regular prize court, the need to suppress piracy, and the need to enforce the Acts of Trade, introduced a regular system of admiralty courts, which, after the Revolution, emanated from, and was dependent upon the English Admiralty.[7] By commission from the Lords of the Admiralty the Governor was given power to act as Vice-Admiral, and to appoint deputies to act as judges and officials of the vice-admiralty courts.[8] "In all twelve such courts were established, from New Hampshire and Massachusetts to Barbados." [9] They exercised the ordinary admiralty jurisdiction, jurisdiction over piracy conferred by a statute of 1700,[10] the jurisdiction conferred by the Acts of Trade,[11] and a jurisdiction over violations of an Act of 1722 relating to naval stores.[12]

---

[1] Pownall, Administration of the colonies (4th ed.) 110-111; he points out, ibid 111-112, that in the charter governments, where no provision was made for a court of Chancery, suitors had adopted the plan of petitioning the Legislature for relief—a practice which had very obvious abuses, below 96.

[2] Helen J. Crump, Colonial Admiralty Jurisdiction in the Seventeenth Century 2.
[3] Ibid 25, 27-29.   [4] Ibid 33-36.
[5] Ibid chaps. iii, iv, and v.   [6] Ibid 78, 91.
[7] Ibid 152; under James II the Irish and colonial Admiralties were separated from the English Admiralty, ibid 103-104; for admiralty jurisdiction in India see ibid chap. x; in 1703 Northey, the attorney-general, said that the general council of Rhode Island had no power to create a court of admiralty, and the colony was required to submit to the court created by the Lord High Admiral, Acts of the Privy Council (Col. Series) iii 38-39; Chalmers, Opinions ii 197.
[8] Berriedale Keith 261-262.   [9] Ibid 262.
[10] 11, 12 William III c. 7; for the admiralty jurisdiction in cases of piracy, and the jurisdiction under this Act to issue commissions directed to admirals, judges of vice-admiralty courts, and others, to try pirates, see West's Opinion of 1720, Chalmers, Opinions ii 202-205.
[11] 7, 8 William III c. 22; below 109-110.   [12] 8 George I c. 12.

It is not surprising that, in the course of the eighteenth century, the colonial admiralty courts became increasingly unpopular. They were under the direct control of the British government.[1] They acted by means of a procedure which was not that of the common law.[2] They enforced the hated Acts of Trade,[3] the Stamp Act, and other revenue Acts.[4] All these causes of unpopularity were combined with the traditional hostility of the common lawyers to the Admiralty, which was the legacy of the jurisdictional and constitutional controversies of the seventeenth century.[5] The Puritan colonists naturally adopted the view taken by their ancestors ; and in all the colonies the new causes of hostility to the Admiralty perpetuated and intensified the common law tradition. Therefore, just as in the seventeenth century, the jurisdiction of the English court of admiralty was crippled by writs of prohibition, so, in the eighteenth century, the jurisdiction of the colonial admiralty courts was attacked by the same weapon.[6] Since the unpopularity of these courts increased as the century proceeded, it is not surprising that the framers of the Declaration of Independence inserted amongst their grievances the extension of a jurisdiction which, without justification, they described as unwarrantable.[7]

The judges of the colonial courts were appointed by the Governor, but the King generally appointed the Chief Justice.[8] A judge could be removed by the Governor ; but the reason for his removal must be reported to the Board of Trade.[9] Burke's Act of 1782 empowered Governors to remove officers for absence from the colony or neglect of duty, and gave a right of appeal to the Privy Council.[10] This Act was held to apply to the judges.[11] Though this is not the most obvious interpretation of the Act, which seems to be aimed primarily at offices granted by letters patent, it accords with the view which had always

---

[1] H. J. Crump, op. cit. 131, 164.   [2] Ibid 130.   [3] Ibid 164.
[4] Berriedale Keith, op. cit. 342-345, 359 and n. 1.   [5] Vol. i 553-558.
[6] For a discussion of the question of prohibitions by West, the counsel to the Board of Trade, see Chalmers, Opinions ii 207-215 ; he said in effect that the common law courts in the colonies had the same power to issue prohibitions against the courts of admiralty as the common law courts in England ; for complaints of interferences by the Admiralty see Acts of the Privy Council (Col. Series) ii 726 ; iii 57, 272 ; Berriedale Keith, op. cit. 263-264.
[7] F. N. Thorpe, Federal and State Constitutions i 6, cited H. J. Crump, op. cit. 128 ; in the Declaration of Independence this grievance was alluded to in the clauses which complained that the Americans had been subjected to " a jurisdiction foreign to our constitution," and that they had been deprived in many cases of the benefits of trial by jury.
[8] Berriedale Keith, op. cit. 258-259 ; but in 1734 a Colonial Act empowering the Governor to appoint two assistant judges was disallowed as an infringement on the prerogative, Acts of the Privy Council (Col. Series) iii 410-412.
[9] Berriedale Keith, op. cit. 259.   [10] 22 George III c. 75 § 2.
[11] Willis v. Gibbs (1846) 5 Moo. P.C.C. 379 ; at p. 390 a case of 1829 was cited in which this interpretation had been put upon the statute.

been held by the Crown as to the tenure of the judicial office in the colonies. The Crown had always opposed the attempts made from time to time by the Assemblies to give the judges a tenure during good behaviour.[1] This was not unreasonable, since the judges were dependent on the Assemblies for their salaries, and there was reason to fear that, if they were given a tenure during good behaviour, they would become wholly dependent upon them. The Board of Trade pointed out in 1761 that in England the independence of the judges was guaranteed not only by the terms of their commission, but also by salaries sufficient to secure able lawyers ; that in the colonies no such salaries were provided, with the result that Governors had found it necessary to appoint men who accepted office

merely with a view to make it subservient to their own Private Interests and who, added to their Ignorance of the Law, have too frequently become the Partizans of a factious Assembly, upon whom they have been dependent for their support and who have withheld or enlarged that support according as the Conduct of the Judges was more or less favourable to their Interests.

To allow such men under such conditions to hold office during good behaviour would be " subversive of all true policy," and would tend " to lessen that just dependence which the Colonies ought to have upon the Government of the Mother Country." [2] But the latter result was one of the objects which the Assemblies had in view ; and the fact that the existing system might make the judges too dependent on the Governor was recognized by the Board of Trade in 1782, when it advised the Crown to assent to a Jamaica Act which retained the King's power to dismiss, but limited the Governor's power to dismiss, judges to a power, with the consent of the Council, to suspend.[3] " The real solution of permanent tenure and adequate salary appealed to neither party, for both desired to control the judiciary." [4]

The result was that an unfortunate tradition was established. As late as 1870 it was said by the President of the Council that " effective means ought to exist for the removal of colonial judges charged with grave misconduct, and that these means ought to be less cumbrous than those existing for the removal of one of her Majesty's judges in this country. The mode of procedure ought to be such as to protect judges against the party and personal feelings which sometimes sway colonial Legislatures,

[1] Chalmers, Opinions ii 105.
[2] Acts of the Privy Council (Col. Series) iv 499-500 ; cp. ibid 216-217, 505, 550-551 ; Lind was right when he said, in his *Answer to the Declaration of the American Congress* 46, that " it was the policy of the colonies to keep the Judges dependent on the deputies of the people for a temporary wretched and arbitrary support."
[3] Ibid v 504-505.
[4] Berriedale Keith, op. cit. 261.

and to ensure to the accused party a full and fair hearing before an impartial and elevated tribunal." [1] And this tradition was inherited by some of the States of the United States. Some of these States have failed to see that both a permanent tenure and an adequate salary are the two essential conditions precedent for securing a satisfactory bench of judges.

There is no doubt that the colonial courts were not very satisfactory tribunals. They suffered, Pownall says, from the defects which Hale had noted in the old county courts. The judges were often ignorant of law, " the various courts bred variety of law," and " all the business of moment was carried by parties and factions." [2] It is true that the Privy Council, in the exercise of its appellate jurisdiction, did its best to remedy these defects ; but Pownall rightly thought that this was not sufficient, and recommended " the establishment of a supreme court of appeal and equity, not confined to any one government, but circuiting through a certain district of governments." [3] Such a court, he thought

would become an established court of appeal and redress, would regulate all courts of law, so that they could not exceed their jurisdiction ; would have a general superintendency over all inferior courts ; would tend to establish some regularity, and introduce a conformity, not only amongst the courts themselves of the different colonies, but a conformity also to the courts of the mother country, in the construction and dispensation of law, . . . and would also maintain that dependency therein, which is the essence of colony administration.[4]

But this, like Pownall's other projects for putting the relations of the colonies and the mother country upon a more satisfactory footing,[5] failed to secure support.

Such, in very brief outline, was the normal form of colonial government during this period. It had both considerable merits and considerable defects. But before considering these merits and defects we must first glance at some of the variations from this normal form.

Variations from the normal form of colonial government.

Some of these variations are in the nature of survivals. We have seen that, for the most part, companies formed to colonize disappeared, when the colonies which they had founded became political societies.[6] The greatest exception was the East India

[1] A memorandum drawn up by the President of the Council at the request of Earl Granville, Secretary of the Colonial Department, and assented to by the Lords of the Council, 6 Moo. P.C.C. N.S. App. at p. 10.
[2] Administration of the Colonies (4th ed.) 106-110, citing Hale, History of the Common Law, chap. vii (6th ed.) at p. 169.
[3] Pownall, op. cit. 113-114.
[5] Below 78-79, 105-107.
[4] Ibid 114-115.
[6] Vol. viii 209-210.

Company, with which I shall deal later.[1] But, apart from the
East India Company, there were one or two exceptions. The
Hudson's Bay Company had obtained statutory authority for
the power given by its charter to make by-laws, and to the
Governors of its forts and plantations to punish crimes and
misdemeanours.[2] The validity of these powers was recognized
in 1849 ; and they were not abandoned till 1869.[3] The African
Company still continued to maintain its fortifications, in return
for which traders paid the company a 10 per cent. duty.[4] In
1750 a new company was set up,[5] to which the fortifications
were transferred in 1752.[6] To a committee of this company was
transferred the control of the fortifications,[7] and for their maintenance annual parliamentary grants were made.[8] But it had
no control over the traders, and no effort was made to establish
a civil government—though such government might have been
established under the powers given by the Act of 1750.[9] In
1764 the fort of Senegal and its dependencies were handed over to
the company ; [10] but in 1765 the Crown assumed jurisdiction over
all Senegal and its dependencies.[11] By Order in Council this
area was given the title of Senegambia, and was to be administered by a Governor and Council. To the Governor and Council
were given executive and legislative powers, and the administration of justice was entrusted to a Chief Justice. The government was financed from England.[12] In 1783 the greater part of
this dominion was ceded by the Treaty of Versailles, the Act of
1765 was repealed, and the African Company resumed control [13]—
" thus terminating ingloriously the life of the first Crown Colony
in West Africa " [14] In 1791 another company was created by
statute to trade with Africa, with power to acquire from the
Crown and the native princes the district of Sierra Leone.[15] It
had no exclusive right to trade,[16] and it was to last for thirty-
one years.[17] But in 1807 it was enacted that the territory acquired by the company should be vested in the Crown, and that
the company should come to an end in 1814.[18]

It was clear that to settlements in Africa the normal type of
colonial government could not be applied. An Assembly was
impossible because there was no large resident European population. The normal type of government was equally unsuited

[1] Below 139 seqq.   [2] Vol. viii 210 n. 7 ; Berriedale Keith, op. cit. 122.
[3] Ibid 123 ; vol. viii 210.   [4] Ibid 209-210.
[5] 23 George II c. 31.   [6] 25 George II c. 40 § 1.
[7] 23 George II c. 31 § 5.   [8] Berriedale Keith, op. cit. 391.
[9] Ibid 391-392.   [10] 4 George III c. 20.
[11] 5 George III c. 44 ; Berriedale Keith, op. cit. 392.   [12] Ibid 392-393.
[13] 23 George III c. 65 § 2.   [14] Berriedale Keith, op. cit. 394.
[15] 31 George III c. 55.   [16] § 45.
[17] § 48.   [18] 47 George III c. 44.

to naval and military stations such as Gibraltar and Minorca.[1] Similarly the conditions prevailing in French Canada, after its cession by the French, made it very inexpedient to attempt to introduce at once the normal type of colonial government. It is true that a proclamation of 1763 promised to introduce into Canada the normal type of government, and that some steps were taken to introduce it.[2] But it soon appeared that its introduction would be both dangerous and inexpedient.[3]

A solid mass of perhaps 60,000 French Roman Catholics confronted not more than 600 English, mainly very recent arrivals, for French Canada had been hostile to Protestants and English. Moreover, French policy had absolutely denied rights of self-government, and had habituated the people to obedience to orders from above, so that political capacity for elections, and membership of an Assembly . . . was lacking.[4]

For these reasons this project was abandoned, and a different form of government was introduced by the Quebec Act of 1774.[5] That Act vested the government in a Governor and Council, which had legislative power, but no power to impose taxes or customs duties.[6] Revenue was raised by a separate Revenue Act, which imposed duties on spirits and molasses, and continued the French territorial revenues.[7] The French law in civil matters was maintained ; but in criminal matters English law was substituted by reason of its greater " certainty and lenity." [8] Free exercise of the Roman Catholic religion was granted, and the priests were to enjoy " their accustomed dues and rights." [9] The boundaries of the province were to extend westward to the Ohio and Mississippi, and northward to the Hudson Bay territory. The province was also to include the territory under the government of Newfoundland.[10] But it was provided that the delimitation of these boundaries by the Act was not to affect the boundaries of any other province.[11]

The Whig party and the Americans denounced the Quebec Act, partly because it set up a despotic government, partly

[1] Berriedale Keith, op. cit. 170 and n. 1 ; in 1722 Raymond and Yorke reported upon the question of establishing a civil government at Gibraltar ; it appears that in 1720 a civil court with a summary jurisdiction in mercantile cases had been established, Chalmers, Opinions i 169-181.

[2] Berriedale Keith, op. cit. 386 ; cp. Camb. Hist. of the Empire vi 153-155.

[3] Ibid vi 153-156, 157-158.   [4] Berriedale Keith, op. cit. 387.

[5] 14 George III c. 83.   [6] §§ 12, 13.

[7] 14 George III c. 88.   [8] 14 George III c. 83 §§ 8 and 11.   [9] § 5.

[10] Newfoundland was for a long time merely a fishing station—in fact it was decided in 1676 to deport the settlers ; but this course was not taken ; and by the end of the century Newfoundland had become a colony of the normal type, see Camb. Hist. of the Empire vi chap. v ; " despite neglect, and sometimes in the face of positive hostility, a true colony had grown up, and henceforward its development became more normal, its peculiar amphibious character gradually passing away," ibid 145.

[11] §§ 1 and 2

because it gave toleration to the Roman Catholics, and partly because it extended this government to areas into which the American colonies would naturally expand.[1] But considering the imminent danger of a revolt of the American colonies, and considering the peculiar position of the French Canadians, the Act was a wise piece of statesmanship.[2] To have attempted to conciliate the Americans by settling the government of Canada according to their wishes, would not have secured their loyalty, so long as the more important causes of controversy remained open ;[3] and the pursuance of such a policy would almost certainly have entailed the loss of Canada. Moreover the Act shows that statesmen were beginning to free themselves from that narrow mercantile outlook on the colonies which had been prevalent all through the century, and were beginning to consider the problems of colonial government from the point of view of the position and needs of the colonies. Because the Act was partly inspired by this broader outlook it was eminently successful. During the war of independence Canada remained loyal, and defeated an attempted invasion by the Americans ;[4] and so the Act may be said to have saved Canada for the Crown. To very few Acts of Parliament can such beneficial and such far-reaching results be attributed. In 1791 the province of Quebec was divided into the two provinces of Upper and Lower Canada, and the normal type of colonial government was established.[5] Thus representative institutions were introduced into Canada, and the education of the Canadians in the art of self-government was begun.[6]

The history of this period shows that the normal type of colonial government had certain merits. It made the colonists self-reliant ; it gave them a political education ; and the protection afforded by the British army and navy saved them from the worst consequences of political inexperience during this period of education. Consequently the English colonies showed a capacity for expansion which was shown by the colonists of no other country—it was said that, in the eighteenth century, the population of the American colonies doubled itself every twenty years.[7] Consequently also the colonists tended to chafe at the

---

[1] Camb. Hist. of the Empire i 678, 708-709.

[2] Ibid ; I do not agree with Berriedale Keith's view, op. cit. 388, 389-390, that the Act was a nefarious scheme to introduce despotic government ; see Camb. Hist. of the Empire, vi 167-172 ; as Professor Burt says, ibid 172, " if the policy of 1763, instead of being abandoned, had been enforced and developed, it would have driven Canada into the American Revolution, or it would have created a new Ireland on the banks of the St. Lawrence."

[3] Below 102-107.   [4] Camb. Hist. of the Empire i 709.

[5] 31 George III c. 31 ; for an account of this Act see Col. Hist. of the Empire vi 198-200.

[6] Ibid 200.   [7] Col. Hist. of the Empire i 267.

position of subordination in which the home government desired
to keep them. They wished to share the political liberty which
had been won by the Revolution ; and the large powers possessed
by their Assemblies gave them abundant opportunities to make
this wish heard.[1] On the other hand, the disputes of the
Assemblies with their Governors, and the jealousy felt by the
colonies for one another, made the government of the colonies
weak and ineffective. The laws of trade were with difficulty
enforced ; and it was sometimes difficult to suppress riots,
because the executive had no means to pay for an efficient
police.[2] Even as against a foreign enemy it was difficult to
induce the colonies to combine ; and it was this difficulty in
securing any kind of combined action which for a long time
saved the French " from the normal outcome of numerical
inferiority." [3] During Pitt's decisive campaign, which expelled
the French from Canada, the colonies were often slow to help,
and their help was purchased by large subsidies.[4]

These effects, good and bad, of the working of the normal
type of colonial government were creating some very difficult
problems for the mother country. We have seen that the authorities in the mother country most immediately concerned with
the colonies, had some very definite and, unfortunately, some
very fixed, ideas as to the position which the colonies ought to
take in relation to the mother country, and as to the part,
political and economic, which they ought to play in the development of the British Empire ; [5] and that these definite and fixed
ideas were coming to be more and more opposed to the rising
tide of colonial aspiration for a larger independence and a
greater equality of status.[6] Burke realized the magnitude and
complexity of these problems. In 1769 he said : [7]

We have a great empire to rule, composed of a vast mass of
heterogeneous governments, all more or less free and popular in their
forms, all to be kept in peace, and kept out of conspiracy with one
another, all to be held in subordination to this country ; while the
spirit of an extensive, and intricate, and trading interest pervades
the whole, always qualifying, and often controlling, every general
idea of constitution and government. It is a great and difficult object ;
and I wish we may possess wisdom and temper enough to manage it
as we ought.

He was not the only statesman who realized the magnitude and
complexity of these problems. But there were many who were
more short-sighted. All this we shall see more clearly when we

---

[1] Camb. Hist. of the Empire i 436, 614.
[2] Berriedale Keith, op. cit. 212.
[3] Ibid.   [4] Ibid 329-330 ; below 92-93.
[5] Above 39, 55-57 ; below 81-83.   [6] Above 57 ; below 103-104.
[7] The Present State of the Nation, Works (Bohn's ed.) i 278.

have examined the nature of the relations of the colonies to Great Britain, and the manner in which the colonial problems, which resulted from these relations, were envisaged by the government.

(3) *The relation of the colonies to Great Britain.*

All parts of the colonial governments were in constant and intimate relations with the government of Great Britain. At the head of the colonial executives were the Governors, who represented the Crown, and through whom the policy desired by the home government was communicated to the colonies ; [1] and, in their capacity as representatives of the Crown, they were assisted by those of their officials who were appointed by the Crown and were immediately dependent upon it.[2] Other officials, who were appointed by, or who were for financial reasons more immediately dependent upon, the Assemblies [3] naturally tended to represent the colonial rather than the British point of view with respect to the relations of the colonies with Great Britain. The work of the colonial Legislatures was controlled by the power of the Crown to refuse its assent to their enactments ; and we shall see that the supervision exercised by the Crown was a strict supervision, designed to secure the commercial dependence of the colonies, the provision of an adequate system of defence, and the maintenance of the unity in fundamental principles of colonial and English law.[4] The work of the colonial courts was controlled by the appellate jurisdiction of the Privy Council.[5] Many different departments of the executive government of Great Britian, such as the Privy Council and its committee, the Secretaries of State, the Treasury, the Board of Trade, the Admiralty, and the departments responsible for the army, took their share in advising upon or controlling very many of the affairs of the colonies. Parliament could legislate for the colonies ; [6] and, since the Privy Council could in all cases give leave to appeal,[7] it had many opportunities to influence the law of the colonies by its decisions.

Of the work of the Privy Council as the final court of appeal from the colonies I have already spoken ; [8] and I shall have something to say later of the manner in which its decisions were helping to lay the foundations of colonial constitutional law.[9] At this point I shall say something, first, of the machinery through which the British government exercised a political control over the colonies, and of the modes in which they exercised that control ; and, secondly, of the policy pursued by the British government,

[1] Above 47-53.   [2] Above 52.   [3] Above 52-53.
[4] Below 84 seqq.   [5] Vol. i 517-518, 520-523.
[6] Above 56.   [7] Vol. i 522.
[8] Ibid 517-518, 520-523 .   [9] Below 229 seqq.

and its effects upon the relations of Great Britain and the
colonies.

Machinery and modes of control.

By far the most important parts of the machinery which
exercised a political control over the colonies were the Privy
Council, and the departments of the central government more
immediately concerned with particular sides of the colonial
government. There was not at this period any special department of the central government exclusively concerned with the
colonies. One or two officials in the departments more immediately concerned with the colonies were appointed to take
charge of particular items of colonial business ; but, " generally
speaking, no new machinery was set up for the supervision of the
colonies." [1] Colonial business was treated simply as a part of
the business of the executive government. Parliament played
a much less important part. It was concerned almost entirely
with the organization of the trade of the Empire and the consequent financial legislation ; and, though it had the power to
legislate for the internal affairs of the colonies, it rarely intervened in their affairs before 1765.[2] Occasionally, indeed, the
Privy Council threatened that, in case of the continued contumacy
of some colonial Assembly, it would invoke the legislative authority of Parliament.[3] But in the earlier half of the century
this authority was not invoked ; and we shall see that when the
growing tension between Great Britain and the American colonies
caused that threat to be carried out, the intervention of Parliament led quickly to the outbreak of war.[4] I shall therefore deal
first with the organs of the central government, because they
formed the most important part of the machinery through which
control was exercised over the colonies ; and, secondly, with
Parliament.

(i) During the seventeenth century the Privy Council was
the executive government of the state, and it exercised its
functions with respect to the colonies in different ways at
different periods. The seventeenth century was a century of

---

[1] Camb. Hist. of the Empire i 411.

[2] In 1757 the Board of Trade said that, " the intervention of Parliament in
the internal affairs of particular colonies has not been usual," Acts of the Privy
Council (Col. Series) vi 328.

[3] In 1726 the Board of Trade reported that, " if the people of New England
shall not comply with his Majesty's directions herein, we know no other method so
effectual to reduce them to compliance as to lay a state of that province before the
Parliament," Acts of the Privy Council (Col. Series) vi 162 ; for other instances
see ibid ii 641 (1711), 678 (1714) ; iii 472 (1735) ; for resolutions of the House of
Commons of 1733 and 1757 condemning the proceedings of colonial Assemblies see
ibid 630-631.

[4] Below 108-115.

experiment in this matter. In 1634 the Crown appointed a commission and a committee of the Council for Foreign Plantations. The commission and the committee were composed of the same persons, and to them were entrusted all matters relating to the government of the colonies.[1] This precedent was followed when a Council for Foreign Plantations was appointed in 1660 ; [2] but, whereas before the Great Rebellion the Crown had denied the right of Parliament to legislate for the colonies,[3] after the Restoration " the King participated the sovereignty of the colonies with the Parliament." [4] Together with a Council for Foreign Plantations, a Council for Trade was appointed, many of the members of which were also members of the Council for Foreign Plantations.[5] The function of these two Councils was advisory only, and they ceased to function in 1664.[6] But in 1668 an advisory Council for Trade, and in 1670 an advisory Council for the Colonies, were revived.[7] The latter Council became in 1672 the Council for Trade and Plantations.[8] But it was abolished in 1674, and its work was taken over by the committee of the Privy Council for Trade and Plantations.[9] This committee, because it was a committee of the Privy Council, was not a merely advisory body.[10] In 1688 it became a committee of the whole Privy Council.[11] After the Revolution the Privy Council and its committee continued to control the relations between Great Britain and the colonies.[12] They were assisted, after 1695,[13] by the Board of Trade and Plantations. That Board was created in May, 1696, and consisted of great officers of state, privy councillors and paid members who did the work.[14] It was at first treated as if it were a committee of the Privy Council. But, though its most important members were at first Privy Councillors, it always included members who were not Privy Councillors ; and under the Hanoverian Kings, when all the work of the Privy Council came to be done by its committee, the Board of Trade and Plantations came to be merely an advisory Board which reported to a committee of the Privy Council.[15] Therefore, in the eighteenth century the committee of the Privy Council, assisted by the Board of Trade and Plantations, was one of the principal organs through which the control of the central government was exercised over the colonists.

[1] Berriedale Keith, op. cit. 20-21 ; the commission is printed, Pownall, Administration of the Colonies (4th ed.) App. 67-73 ; it gave the commissioners wide powers to legislate for the colonies ; Acts of the Privy Council (Col. Series) i *xiii*.
[2] Berriedale Keith, op. cit. 59.
[3] Pownall, Administration of the Colonies (4th ed.) 48-49 ; below 233.
[4] Pownall, op. cit. 125.   [5] Berriedale Keith, op. cit. 59.
[6] Ibid.   [7] Ibid 60.   [8] Ibid.
[9] Ibid.   [10] Ibid 60-61.   [11] Ibid 61.   [12] Ibid 268.
[13] Ibid 268-269 ; cp. Pownall, Administration of the Colonies (4th ed.) 20-21.
[14] Berriedale Keith, op. cit. 273.   [15] Ibid 269, 274.

Its range of interest was a wide one. It received petitions and appeals from the colonies, of both a financial and a judicial nature ; confirmed or disallowed colonial laws ; placed its imprimatur on drafts of governors' commissions and instructions, approved appointments to colonial councils ; appointed commissioners of review in colonial boundary disputes ; exercised an ultimate authority in cases of controversy between governors and royal appointees in the colonies ; considered with care and concern the proper development of colonial resources ; sought to protect the Plantation trade, and endeavoured to meet as far as possible the demands of imperial defence.[1]

But we have seen that, in the course of the eighteenth century, the executive government of the state tended to be concentrated in the small committee of the King's servants which had come to be known as the cabinet ;[2] and that the real work of the executive government was done by the departments of the principal officers of state who were members of the cabinet.[3] Thus, during the eighteenth century, the political control over the colonies was tending to be engrossed by the Secretary of State, who was assisted by the Board of Trade and Plantations.

Appointments, defence of land and sea, finance as connected therewith, diplomatic issues and relations with Indians, and generally all political issues were his especial care ; but nothing was excluded from his sphere, and it rested vitally with him during the greater part of the life of the Board of Trade to decide the nature of its functions.[4]

Conversely the Board of Trade referred to him all matters which were brought before it which involved political issues.[5] The result of this development upon the committee of the Privy Council was to make its judicial functions more, and its political functions less, important. The committee acted with the Secretary of State, but the Secretary of State was its most important member ; and the Privy Council itself merely gave formal sanction, when this was necessary, to the decisions of the Secretary of State or the committee.[6]

The result of this development upon the Board of Trade was ultimately to reduce it to the state described by Burke in 1780—

a sort of temperate bed of influence ; a sort of gently ripening hot-house, where eight members of Parliament receive salaries of a thousand a year for a certain given time, in order to mature, at a proper season, a claim to two thousand, granted for doing less.[7]

But it was only after many vicissitudes that it was reduced to this condition. It began well ; but from 1714-1748 it declined,

---

[1] Camb. Hist. of the Empire i 412 ; cp. Thomson, Secretaries of State 1681-1782, 46, 54.
[2] Vol. x 472-475.
[3] Vol. x 473, 494-495.
[4] Berriedale Keith, op. cit. 271.
[5] Ibid.
[6] Ibid 270-273 ; Camb. Hist. of the Empire i 412-413 ; Acts of the Privy Council (Col. Series) iii *vii-ix.*
[7] Works (Bohn's ed.) ii 109.

and became inefficient. In 1748 Halifax was made its president, and he revived its powers, and recovered for it much of its former control, and its patronage. In 1752 governors were directed to correspond directly with it, and not with the Secretaries of State. But its patronage was taken away in 1761, and in 1766 the order of 1752 was revoked. These vacillations of policy were fatal to its efficiency ; [1] and when a third Secretary of State was appointed for the colonies in 1768 it rapidly sank to the position described by Burke,[2] and was abolished in 1782.[3] In the days when it was an active Board, it did good work in all spheres of colonial administration, more especially in the spheres of trade and legislation ; [4] and its standing counsel West (1718), Fane (1725), Lamb (1746), Jackson (1770) [5] played their part in moulding that part of constitutional law which relates to the colonies, by their advice on all matters legal, and more especially by their advice as to the sanctioning or disallowance of colonial legislation.[6] Its defenders in 1782 appealed to the two thousand three hundred folio volumes of its reports as evidence of its usefulness.[7] But they appealed in vain—and rightly, for its uselessness in its then form was admitted by Gibbon, one of its own members.[8]

The Secretary of State for the Colonies was also abolished in 1782 ; [9] and the work of the two surviving Secretaries of State was rearranged—the former Secretary of State for the Southern

[1] " From this jealousy and this struggle, this Board has been supposed to interfere at different times with every other office, while at one time it hath had the powers and held the post of a minister's office and at another hath become a mere committee inefficient as to execution, unattended as to reporting. The Colonies, and the officers of the Colonies, have one while been taught to look up to this Board as the minister for their affairs, and at another, have learned to hold it in that contempt which inefficiency gives ; which contempt, however, hath not always stopped them," Pownall, Administration of the Colonies (4th ed.) 26.

[2] Berriedale Keith, op. cit. 274-276 ; Acts of the Privy Council (Col. Series) iv *viii ;* see ibid v *xxix-xxx*, 3-4 for the order of 1766 directing governors to correspond with the Secretaries of State and not with the Board of Trade ; cp. Thomson, Secretaries of State 1681-1782, 47-64.

[3] 22 George III c. 82 § 1.

[4] This is clear from the many reports which are recorded in the Acts of the Privy Council (Col. Series) *passim ;* as Professor Andrews says, Camb. Hist. of the Empire i 414, " the Plantation Office was a workshop in which was prepared material for many important official documents. Large numbers of Orders in Council, royal warrants countersigned by the Secretary of State, the Treasury, and the Admiralty, and even occasional royal proclamations and Acts of Parliament found their origin in the activities of this office."

[5] Chalmers, Opinions of Eminent Lawyers i *xii-xiv.*

[6] Below 93-98.

[7] Mr. Eden " informed the committee, that the records consisted of upwards of 2300 volumes in folio, which he would be bold to say contained much important and interesting information. It was now, indeed, proposed to throw them into the flames, because the hon. gentleman who knew nothing of their contents and declined to be informed of them, presumed that they were no more than monuments of unprofitable labour," Parlt. Hist. xxi 234.

[8] Vol. x 467 n. 7.   [9] 22 George III c. 82 § 1.

Department becoming the Home Secretary with charge of Irish and colonial business, and the former Secretary of State for the Northern Department becoming Foreign Secretary.[1] Thus the principal bodies responsible for the colonies became the committee of the Privy Council and the Home Secretary. In 1786 the Board of Trade and Plantations was revived in the shape of a committee of the Council for Trade and Plantations which, in the nineteenth century, became the Board of Trade.[2]

The committee of the Privy Council, the Secretary of State, and their advisor, the Board of Trade and Plantations, were in close touch with each other,[3] and with other departments of the executive government. Of these departments the most important were the Treasury, the Commissioners of Customs, the Admiralty, and the War Office. In very many cases the committee of the Privy Council acted on the advice of these departments ; and in very many cases the reports of the Board of Trade and Plantations shaped the advice given by these departments.

The Treasury superintended the expenditure of all money voted by Parliament for colonial purposes, and money voted in the colonies for the King's service. It was thus interested in " many important colonial issues involving expenses incurred in this service." [4] It made payments for services rendered in relation to the colonies, such as the cost of special agents ; and it allocated Parliamentary grants for military aid in time of war. It also

drafted warrants and commissions touching salaries, contracts, grants, and remittances, prize money, transportation of convicts, and other matters relating or not relating to money, and in general controlled all payments by the Exchequer in peace and war.[5]

It was necessarily consulted whenever new revenue legislation which affected the colonies, or variations of the Acts of Trade, were proposed.[6]

The Commissioners of Customs were a subordinate department of the Treasury.[7] They controlled their own officers in the colonies till 1767, when a special Board of Commissioners of Customs for the American colonies, who were to be resident in

---

[1] Anson, The Crown (4th ed.) ii Pt. i 179.　　　　[2] Ibid 206.

[3] For the " course of office between the Secretary of State's office, the Council, and the Board of Trade," suggested in 1766, see Acts of the Privy Council (Col. Series) vi 437-438 ; business was facilitated by the fact that all these offices and the Treasury were housed in close proximity to one another, ibid *vi*.

[4] Camb. Hist. of the Empire i 415 ; see e.g. a Treasury memorandum of Oct. 4, 1765, on the state of the customs and the smallness of the revenue which resulted therefrom, Acts of the Privy Council (Col. Series) iv 569-572—a memorandum which is the prelude to the policy which led directly to the War of Independence, below 108.

[5] Camb. Hist. of the Empire i 415.

[6] Berriedale Keith, op. cit. 277-278.　　　　[7] Vol. x 490.

America, was created.[1] The Commissioners of Customs were responsible for the instructions given to Governors on trade matters, and they advised on colonial legislation affecting these matters. Their officers in the colonies could give them expert advice on many aspects of colonial administration.[2] Conversely, since the surveyors-general of customs were, after 1733, members of the colonial Councils,[3] they could give the Governor and Council expert advice upon the interpretation of the Acts of Trade and upon other points connected with the customs administration.[4] In theory the officers of the Commissioners of Customs should have kept a firm hand over the enforcement of the Acts of Trade.

But the service was far from ideally managed. The miserable practice of allowing the titular officers to act by deputies,[5] who were local men ill-remunerated and holders of as many other offices as they could engross, was responsible for the utterly slack performance of duty ; it was infinitely more popular and profitable to accept bribes to connive at illegal importations than to incur unpopularity and physical danger by insistence on laws which no colonials liked, and many Governors would not help to enforce. [6]

The Admiralty.—The control of the Admiralty over the colonies had two aspects—judicial and naval. We have seen that the judicial aspect was very important in connection with the Acts of Trade, and other revenue Acts ;[7] for, since the admiralty courts exercised their jurisdiction without a jury, it was easier to enforce these laws by their means. But, naturally, they were, for this reason, very unpopular tribunals. As we have seen, this cause for their unpopularity accentuated the traditional hostility of the common lawyers to the admiralty jurisdiction.[8] The naval aspect of the admiralty control over the colonies was important at all times, but more especially in times of war. Together with other departments connected with the navy, the admiralty was responsible *inter alia* for naval defence, for the transport of soldiers and Governors, for convoying merchant ships, and for the arrest of ships which infringed the Acts of Trade.[9]

The War Office.—The various departments which were responsible for the army and its equipment [10] were brought from time to time into contact with colonial administration. The Secretary of State was the chief authority, and he acted through

---

[1] Berriedale Keith, op. cit. 278 ; 7 George III c. 41.
[2] Berriedale Keith, op. cit. 278-279.
[3] Above 52.   [4] Berriedale Keith, op. cit. 280.
[5] A practice which was put an end to by statute in 1782, 22 George III c. 75.
[6] Berriedale Keith, op. cit. 280-281.
[7] Above 60-61 ; below 110.   [8] Above 61.
[9] Camb. Hist. of the Empire i 415.   [10] Vol. x 491-492.

the Treasury, the Ordnance Board, or the Secretary at War.[1]
On such questions as the despatch of troops, the grant of arms
or munitions, and the construction of defences, the authorities
responsible for the administration of the colonies were brought
into relation with the different departments which controlled
the army.[2] But, before 1756, neither the naval nor the military
defence of the colonies was efficient.[3] Both corruption and inter-
departmental jealousies prevented efficient action. It was not
till Pitt made the winning of colonial supremacy the main object
of England's effort in the Seven Years' War,[4] that the naval and
military authorities began to see that the naval and military prob
lems, which the winning of that supremacy involved, had become
matters of the first importance ; and it was not till that supremacy
was won that the problem of securing colonial co-operation for
the defence of the colonies, raised in a new form the whole question
of the relations of the colonies to the mother country.[5]

(ii) In the seventeenth century much the largest share of
the control over the colonies was taken by the Crown, and was
therefore exercised by the appropriate departments of the
executive government in the manner which has just been described. But even in the sixteenth and seventeenth centuries
Parliament had asserted its right to legislate for all the dominions of the Crown.[6] This state of affairs was not materially
altered by the Revolution, since Parliament was content to leave
the control of the colonies to the Crown. The one matter in
which Parliament made its control felt was in relation to revenue
and to the Acts of Trade.[7] We shall see that the Acts of Trade
were passed to settle the economic relations of the whole empire ;[8] and, because they were intended to bind all British subjects, it was only by Parliament that adequate provision could
be made. This fact is brought out very clearly by § 9 of the
Navigation Act of 1696, which declared to be null and void all
colonial legislation enacted or to be enacted which conflicted
with the present Act, or with any future Acts relating to the
Plantations.[9] As we have seen, the executive occasionally

---

[1] Berriedale Keith, op. cit. 282.   [2] Ibid.
[3] Camb. Hist. of the Empire i 417.
[4] Above 41.   [5] Below 107-108.
[6] Berriedale Keith, op. cit. 4-8 ; above 70 ; below 233.
[7] " It is characteristic of the period that, while there was a fair amount of Imperial
legislation regarding the colonies, it practically all dealt essentially with trade
questions," Berriedale Keith, op. cit. 299.
[8] Below 434-438.
[9] " And it is further enacted and declared by the Authority aforesaid, that all
Laws, By-laws, Usages, or Customs, at this time, or which hereafter shall be in
practice, or endeavoured or intended to be in force or practice, in any of the said
Plantations, which are in any wise repugnant to the before-mentioned Laws, or
any of them, or which are in any ways repugnant to this present Act, or to any other
Law hereafter to be made in this Kingdom, so far as such Laws shall relate to and
mention the said Plantations, are illegal, null, and void, to all Intents and Purposes
whatsoever," 7 and 8 William III c. 22 § 9.

threatened to invoke the overriding power of Parliament to reduce to submission a recalcitrant Assembly ; [1] but no such action was taken till the differences between the colonies and the mother country were becoming acute. We shall see that it was not till that dispute began to develop, that any suggestion was made that Parliament's right to legislate for the colonies was subject to any limitations.[2]

It is obvious that both the departments of the executive government which exercised control over the colonies, and the Legislature, must have some means of ascertaining the views of the colonies if they were to exercise their powers intelligently. These means were supplied partly by the colonial agents, and partly by a group of members of the House of Commons who were identified by birth, profession, trade, or occupation with the colonies.

The first instance of the appointment of a colonial agent comes from the year 1624, when an agent was appointed by Virginia.[3] The earliest agents were specially appointed for particular objects.[4] But their appointment had become so general after the Restoration, and their influence was so obvious, that, in the charter granted to Penn in 1681, a clause was inserted requiring him to keep such an agent in London.[5] Thus the way was paved for the permanent agencies of the eighteenth century. In some of the colonies agents were appointed and their salaries were provided by Acts of the Legislature ; and this course was favoured by the Board of Trade. It was favoured because an agent so appointed represented all parties in the colony.[6] But for this reason it did not always find favour with the Assemblies, who wished to have an agent who could voice their own point of view, and act on their instructions ; and the action taken by the Assemblies sometimes gave rise to disputes with the Board of Trade.[7] " Eventually in most of the colonies the

[1] Above 69.
[2] Below 121-123.
[3] Berriedale Keith, op. cit. 284 n. 2.
[4] Pol. Sci. Quart. xvi 24.
[5] Camb. Hist. of the Empire i 434 ; in 1711 Maryland had no agent, and the Board of Trade reported that " it be recommended to them to appoint some fit Person or Persons residing here to be Agent or Agents for that Province, who being fully empowered and instructed may from time to time, as occasion shall require, take care of and negotiate all such Matters as may concern the said Province," Acts of the Privy Council (Col. Series) ii 630-632.
[6] Berriedale Keith, op. cit. 285.
[7] Ibid 285-286 ; in 1769 Melville, the Governor of Grenada, contended that, since an Act was in force appointing an agent for the colony, the Assembly could not appoint another person to make complaints against him, Acts of the Privy Council (Col. Series) v 223 ; in 1770 Hutchinson, the Governor of Massachusetts, was instructed to withhold his assent to any vote to persons appointed to negotiate the affairs of the province, other than persons " appointed by some Concurrent Act of the whole Legislature "—an instruction inserted to stop the practice of the Council and Assembly each appointing its agent without the Governor's concurrence, ibid 264 ; for an account of the struggles of the assemblies to get control over the agents in the Southern American colonies see Pol. Sci. Quart. xxxv 372-392.

Assembly got control, and in some instances the Governor was obliged to have his own agent in addition to the official agent of the colony."[1] It was the duty of the agent not only to state the case for the colony when there was a specific colonial measure to be explained or defended, or a specific difference of opinion between the colony and the home authorities, but also to watch the course of business at home, and to be ready to intervene if measures contemplated either by the executive or by Parliament affected the interests of the colony.[2] " Just as the Governor was the representative of the Crown in the province to express its wishes and enforce its will, so was the colonial agent the mouthpiece of the provincial Legislature in England to plead its causes and express its purposes."[3] Thus he must be ready to explain and defend colonial legislation when the question of its disallowance or confirmation was before the Privy Council, he must advocate legislative or other measures which his colony wished to get carried, he must back the requests of the colony for munitions and other military assistance, he must be ready to give relevant information to the home government as to the conditions in or affairs of the colony whom he represented, he must watch the progress of legislation which affected his colony, and, if necessary, obtain the modifications desired by it.[4] The West Indian agencies were especially well organized ; and planters, merchants, and civil servants acted in this capacity.[5] Amongst the agents for the American colonies the two most famous are Burke who was agent for New York, and Franklin, who was agent first for Pennsylvania, and ultimately also for Georgia, Carolina, New Jersey, and the Massachusetts House of Assembly.[6]

Just as the West Indian agencies were the best organized, so the West Indies were the best represented in the House of Commons. In the second half of the eighteenth century there were a group of some forty members who had been born in the West Indies, or had held office there, or who were connected with them by birth or trade relations.[7] The Americans were much less directly represented in the House of Commons. In 1761 there was not a single American, and between 1763 and 1783 there were only five.[8] The reason is to be found partly in the fact that the owners of large West Indian estates often lived in England, and partly in the fact that their greater wealth enabled

---

[1] Camb. Hist. of the Empire i 434 ; cp. Pol. Sci. Quart. xvi 41-49.
[2] Ibid 32-38.   [3] Ibid 33.
[4] Berriedale Keith, op. cit. 285 ; for some illustrations see the account given by Namier, American Revolution 292-295, of the activities of Charles Garth, the agent for South Carolina, in respect of a bounty on colonial grown hemp, legislation as to colonial paper currency, and a clause in the Mutiny Bill of 1765 as to billeting soldiers in private houses.
[5] Berriedale Keith, op. cit. 285.   [6] Pol. Sci. Quart. xvi 40.
[7] Namier, The American Revolution 271-279.   [8] Ibid 267.

them to support the expense of a Parliamentary election.[1]   But, though there were very few Americans in the House of Commons, there were many members who had a considerable knowledge of American conditions.

There were, in the first place, the West Indians, themselves in a sense Colonials, and in close touch with North Americans.   Next there were a good many British merchants trading with America, and though only very few of them ever crossed the Atlantic, their knowledge of colonial affairs, and interest in them, were by no means negligible ; moreover these men, as a rule, entertained personal friendships and connexions with Americans.   Further, most naval officers, in the course of their professional duties, visited America, though more often Newfoundland, Nova Scotia, and the West Indian Islands, than the intervening continental Provinces ; and in the Seven Years' War, a certain number of army officers acquired personal knowledge of America, as during that time at least one-fifth of all the British infantry regiments crossed the Atlantic.   Lastly, there was a miscellaneous group of men interested in America, some of whom acted as agents, i.e. as quasi-representatives, for the American Colonies.[2]

Thus both the departments of the executive government which controlled the colonies, and Parliament, had some means of ascertaining the colonial point of view.   Unfortunately these means were not sufficient to enable either the executive government or Parliament to keep in sufficiently close touch with colonial public opinion to realize the dominant trend of that opinion as to the nature of the relations which should exist between Great Britain and the colonies.

It was pointed out by Thomas Pownall,[3] in his book on *The Administration of the Colonies*,[4] that the machinery of the executive government was so scattered amongst its different departments that it was difficult to establish " an effective administration for Colony affairs under any regular system of

---

[1] Namier, The American Revolution 269-270 ; Franklin in 1760 in his tract on *The Interest of Great Britain considered with regard to her Colonies*, Political Pieces (ed. 1779) 183-184 said, " Let it not be said we have no absentees from North America.   There are many to the writer's knowledge ; and if there are at present but few of them that distinguish themselves here by great expense, it is owing to the mediocrity of fortune among the inhabitants of the Northern colonies; and a more equal division of landed property, than in the West India Islands, so that there are as yet but few large estates" ; the strength of the West India interest was powerful enough to procure the rejection of many proposals to subject absentees to special taxation, see e.g. Acts of the Privy Council (Col. Series) iii 738-739.

[2] Namier, op. cit. 270-271.

[3] Pownall had served in the office of the Board of Trade, and had been Lieutenant-Governor of New Jersey, Governor of Massachusetts, and Governor of South Carolina.   From 1767-1774 he represented the Cornish borough of Tregony in the House of Commons.   He died in 1805.

[4] The first edition was published anonymously in 1764 ; the second edition, which was published under his name, came out in 1765 ; there was a third edition in 1766, a fourth in 1768 ; a fifth edition in two volumes appeared in 1774 and was reprinted in 1777.

policy." [1] There ought, he said, to be a single department responsible for the administration of the colonies.[2] The Board of Trade had been designed to supply this want, but it had failed to do so ; for there had been a series of struggles for power between the Board and the Secretary of State, which had ended in the Board becoming inefficient and even comtempt-ible.[3] The same result followed from the multiplicity of offices which handled colonial business.

While the military correspond with the Secretary of State, the civil in one part of their office with the Secretary of State, in another with the Board of Trade ; while the navy correspond in matters not merely naval with the Admiralty, while the engineers correspond with the Board of Ordnance, officers of the revenue with the several boards of that branch, and have no communication with the department which has, or ought to have, the general direction and administration of this great Atlantic and American, this great commercial interest—who is to collect, who does, or ever did collect into one view, all these matters of information and knowledge ?   What department ever had, or could have, such general direction of it, as to discuss, compare, rectify and regulate it to an official real use ?   In the first place, there was never yet any one department formed for this purpose ; and in the next, if there was, let any one acquainted with business dare to say, how any attempt of such department would operate on the jealousies of the others.[4]

The remedy was to establish a single directing department, which " must be sovereign and supreme as to everything relating to it ; or to speak plainly out, must be a secretary of state's office in itself." [5]   " If we mean to govern the Colonies we must previously form at home some practical and efficient adminis-tration for Colony affairs." [6]

The existing executive control was deficient because it was not centralized.   The control of Parliament was equally inefficient because it was not exercised, or exercised only at the direction of some department of the executive.   We have seen that the relations of the colonies with the mother country were mainly with the departments of the executive government.[7]   It was comparatively rarely that colonial affairs were discussed in the House of Commons ; and, if they were discussed, they did not arouse the interest which was aroused by more exciting domestic issues.   Moreover, since colonial affairs were more often than not brought before the House of Commons by a department of the executive government, and since the government could always be sure of a majority on questions which excited no keen public interest, the control exercised by the House of Commons did

---

[1] Administration of the Colonies (4th ed.) 24.   [2] Ibid 12-27.
[3] Above 71-72.   [4] Pownall, op. cit. 14.
[5] Ibid 14-15.   [6] Ibid 25.   [7] Above 69.

little to remedy the defects inherent in the system of executive control.[1]

These defects were creating a growing divergence between the British and the colonial theories as to the relations which should subsist between the colonies and the mother country, which was realized neither by the departments of the executive government nor by the House of Commons. No doubt the departments of the executive government listened to the arguments of the colonial agents, of merchants, and of other persons who appeared before them. But colonial agents were not always fully informed as to the feelings and wishes of the colonies which they represented ; [2] and, even if they were fully informed, their arguments made comparatively little impression upon departments which regarded adherence to departmental precedents and tradition as a matter of more importance than the ascertainment of those political conditions, and that trend of public opinion in the colonies which had given rise to the proposals and problems upon which they were asked to adjudicate. It is not surprising therefore that the political ideas of the colonies and the political ideas of the British government tended, during the eighteenth century, to diverge more and more widely. We shall now see that this growing divergence was caused mainly by the adherence of the British government to a theory of the relation of the colonies to the mother country, which was arousing a growing resentment in the colonies, because it was becoming wholly inapplicable to societies which had attained or were rapidly attaining political maturity.[3]

[1] Thus in 1733 the Council and Assembly of Massachusetts presented a petition to the House of Commons complaining of certain royal instructions to the Governor as to the issue of public money and as to the emission of bills of credit ; the House resolved that " the complaint contained in this memorial and petition is frivolous and groundless, an high insult upon his Majesty's government, and tending to shake off the dependency of the said colony upon this kingdom," Comm. Journals xxii 45 ; in 1740 a petition from Massachusetts as to the need for a new emission of paper currency met with no better success, and the House approved the royal instructions to governors not to assent to bills creating a paper currency, unless a clause were inserted in them suspending their operation till the King's pleasure was taken, ibid xxiii 527-528 ; in 1754 a petition from Massachusetts against extending the Mutiny Act to America was rejected, Parlt. Hist. xv 375-394 ; on the other hand, in 1749, the opposition of the American colonists to a bill prohibiting the issue of bills of credit caused it to be dropped, ibid xiv 563-564.

[2] " Sometimes the English agents appear to have made serious mistakes, arising from misapprehension and lack of information," Pol. Sci. Quart. xvi 33-34.

[3] " That the measures of 1765 and 1767 precipitated the crisis is obvious enough ; but that this crisis must sooner or later have come, unless Great Britain had altered her whole way of looking at the colonies, seems equally certain. . . . The American colonies were lost because the nature of the relation between the Mother Country and her colonies remained unsolved, and was, perhaps, at the time insoluble," Egerton, The American Revolution 4.

The policy of the British Government.

In the eighteenth century, as in the seventeenth century,[1] the colonies were regarded by the British government from a predominantly commercial point of view. " A great empire," said Adam Smith with some exaggeration, " has been established for the sole purpose of raising up a nation of customers who should be obliged to buy from the shops of our different producers all the goods with which these could supply them." [2] They were valued in proportion as they were commercially useful to the mother country ; and therefore their economic activities were so regulated that they conduced to her commercial prosperity. It necessarily followed that the colonies must be kept politically subordinate to the mother country, and that the activities of their governments must be so regulated that they in no way conflicted with her commercial interests. This commercial point of view, and its corollary, the political subordination of the colonies, are most clearly brought out, first by a statement of Martin Bladen, a member of the Board of Trade, which was written in 1726 ; secondly, by a statement of Davenant, who was inspector-general of imports and exports from 1705 to 1714 ; and, thirdly, by a statement of Thomas Pownall, the first edition of whose book on the administration of the colonies appeared in 1764.[3] Bladen wrote : [4]

Every act of a dependent provincial government ought to terminate in the advantage of the mother state unto whom it owes its being and protection in all its valuable privileges. Hence it follows that all advantageous projects or commercial gains in any colony which are truly prejudicial to and inconsistent with the interests of the mother state, must be understood to be illegal and the practice of them unwarrantable, because they contradict the end for which the colony had a being and are incompatible with the terms on which the people claim both privileges and protection. . . . For such is the end of colonies, and if this use cannot be made of them it will be much better for the state to be without them.

Davenant said : [5]

Colonies are a strength to their mother kingdom, while they are under good discipline, while they are strictly made to observe the fundamental laws of their original country, and while they are kept dependent on it.

[1] Vol. vi 320-323 ; cp. Lipson, Economic History of England iii 172-173—as he points out the Acts of Trade were founded on the conviction that " trade, as William Penn wrote, was the benefit England chiefly has by these colonies."

[2] Wealth of Nations (Cannan's ed.) ii 160 ; above 39.

[3] Above 78 n. 4.

[4] Egerton, The American Revolution 4-5, citing Col. Rec. of North Carolina. ii 626-627 ; these views correspond to the views expressed by Child in 1694 in his Discourse on Trade 194, cited vol. vi 320 n. 5.

[5] Camb. Hist. of the Empire i 619, citing Davenant, Works (1771) ii 10.

Pownall said that a nation, by establishing colonies, opened new channels of commerce, beneficial alike to the colonies themselves and to the mother country.[1] The mother country grants to her colonies privileges and protection, and has in return the " exclusive right to the external profits of their labour and to their custom." [2]

As it is the right, so it becomes the duty of the mother country to cultivate, to protect and govern the colonies : which nurture and government should precisely direct its care to two essential points : 1st that all the produce of the profits and manufactures of these colonies center finally in the mother country : and 2ndly, that the colonies continue to be the sole and proper customers of the mother country.[3]

The British government acted upon these principles right down to the American Revolution. In 1762 the Board of Trade said of a Jamaican Act, passed to regulate prize ships and goods, that such regulation was a matter of general trade policy ; and that therefore

this attempt of the Legislature of the Island of Jamaica to make Regulations in matters of General Policy in respect to the Commerce of your Majesty's Subjects by Acts the Operation of which are confined to that Island only, is such an Arrogant Assumption of Power as is not Warranted by the Constitution and which justly deserves the Severest Censure.[4]

In 1766 the committee of the Privy Council, in a report on certain Acts passed by the Legislature of Pennsylvania, stated that the general policy, which should be pursued by the Crown, was the policy " of not allowing the Legislatures in the American Colonies to pass Laws by which the Trade and Shipping of this Kingdom may be affected, either by being subjected to Duties and Taxes, or otherwise cramped or restrained." [5] In 1772 the Board of Trade adhered to the view, which was concurred in by Lord Hillsborough, the commander-in-chief in America, and by Sir James Wright, the Governor of Georgia, that it was neither commercially nor politically desirable to encourage the Western expansion of the colonies.[6] It was not commercially desirable because these colonies were so far inland that they " could supply no returns to pay for British manufactures, and would probably be led to manufacture for themselves, which experience shows

---

[1] Administration of the Colonies (4th ed.) 38-39.
[2] Ibid 39-40.   [3] Ibid 40.
[4] Acts of the Privy Council (Col. Series) iv 513 ; in 1763 a Massachusetts Act to incorporate the Society for Propagating Christian Knowledge among the Indians was disallowed, because " the operation of the Act . . . would extend beyond the limits of the Province itself," and because " so extensive a power given to one colony, may hereafter interfere with any general plan your Majesty may think it advisable to pursue for the management of Indian affairs in North America," ibid 559-560.
[5] Ibid 764.   [6] Ibid vi 512-518.

has constantly attended in a greater or lesser degree every inland settlement." [1]   It was not politically desirable because these
colonies were so far distant that they were beyond the reach
" of the exercise of that authority and jurisdiction which was
conceived to be necessary for the preservation of the colonies
in a due subordination to, and dependence upon, the mother
country." [2]

Blackstone's statement of the position of the colonies in
relation to the mother country represents very well the view
generally held on the eve of the American Revolution. He
admits that the colonists in a settled colony have the rights given
by the English laws then in force, but subject to the qualification
that only those laws apply which are applicable to their new
situation.[3]

What shall be admitted and what rejected, at what times and under
what restrictions, must, in case of dispute, be decided in the first
instance by their own provincial judicature, subject to the revision
and control of the king in council : the whole of their constitution
being also liable to be new-modelled and reformed by the general
superintending power of the legislature in the mother country.[4]

On the other hand, in conquered or ceded colonies, which have
laws of their own, the old laws remain till the King chooses to
change them. " The common law of England, as such, has no
allowance or authority there." [5] It is interesting to note that
Blackstone considered that most of the American colonies fell
into the class of conquered or ceded colonies, " being obtained in
the last century either by right of conquest and driving out the
natives (with what natural justice I shall not at present enquire)
or by treaties." [6] All colonies, whether settled or conquered,
were subject to the control of Parliament.[7]

It is in connection with the elaboration and the enforcement of
the Acts of Trade that the eighteenth-century policy of the commercial and political subordination of the colonies is most clearly
apparent. The pursuance of this policy involved two consequences. First, the colonies must be defended against their
European and their native enemies. Secondly, a strict supervision must be maintained over all the Acts of the colonial

---

[1] Acts of the Privy Council (Col. Series) vi 514.

[2] Ibid 512 ; the close relation between the commercial and the political argument was brought out by Lord Hillsborough, who said that " when all connection
upheld by commerce with the mother country shall cease, it may be expected that
an independency on her government will soon follow," ibid 515 ; and the danger
that the independence of the remote settlements would have bad effects upon the older
colonies was brought out by Sir James Wright, who said that these settlements would
be likely " to disturb government, and even give law to the other or first settled
part of country and throw everything into confusion," ibid 516.

[3] Comm. i 107 ; below 242, 243-244.   [4] Bl. Comm. i 107.
[5] Ibid ; below 245.   [6] Ibid 107-108.
[7] Ibid 108 ; below 233.

Legislature, and the royal assent must be refused to legislation which conflicted with the Acts of Trade or the policy which underlay them. This supervision was also directed to the prevention of the growth of great divergencies between the laws of the colonies and English law, to the prevention of legislation which was obviously impolitic, or which was unjust to individuals or classes of individuals, and to the correction of badly drafted Acts. Much of this supervision, which was exercised by the Council and the Board of Trade,[1] was beneficial to the colonists. It emphasized and rendered more permanent the advantages of the knowledge and civilization which they had brought with them ; [2] for it taught them how to establish and to maintain constitutional government upon a basis which was stable, because it was founded both upon principles of elementary justice, and upon a consistent set of legal principles. Similarly, the supervision of the British government over such matters as inter-colonial disputes, relations with the native races, and the conduct of Governors and other colonial officials, helped forward the development of the colonies. It was, in fact, a condition precedent to their rapid growth.

We shall be able to appreciate both the weak and the strong points of the policy of the British government if we look, first, at the elaboration and enforcement of the Acts of Trade ; secondly, at the care taken by the British government for the defence of the colonies ; thirdly, at the supervision which it exercised over colonial legislation ; and fourthly, at the supervision which it exercised in certain other matters.

(i) *The elaboration and enforcement of the Acts of Trade.*

We have seen that, as the result of the Navigation Acts of 1660, 1662 and 1663, no goods could be imported into England or the Plantations from countries in Asia, Africa, or America except in ships built and owned in England or the Plantations, of which the master and three-fourths of the crew were English subjects ; that certain enumerated commodities produced in the Plantations could be shipped only to other English Plantations or to England ; and that no commodities grown, produced,

---

[1] " The usual custom of the Privy Council, in dealing with Acts passed by colonial legislatures, was until May, 1696, to refer them to the Committee for foreign trade and plantations, and after that date to the Board of Trade, or in some cases to the Law Officers of the Crown, and to act in accordance with their report," Acts of the Privy Council (Col. Series) ii App. III p. 826.

[2] " The colonists carry out with them a knowledge of agriculture and of other useful arts, superior to what can grow up of its own accord in the course of many centuries among savage and barbarous nations. They carry out with them too the habit of subordination, some notion of the regular government which takes place in their own country, of the system of laws which supports it, and of a regular administration of justice," Adam Smith, Wealth of Nations (Cannan's ed.) ii 67.

or manufactured in Europe could be imported into the Plantations, unless shipped in England on a ship built and owned in England or in the Plantations, of which the master and three-fourths of the crew were English subjects.[1]   It was provided in 1779 that if goods produced in one country were manufactured in another, they could not be exported from the country where they were manufactured.   They could only be exported from the country where they were both produced and manufactured, or from the ports where that country's productions could only be or were usually shipped.[2]   We have seen that in 1695-1696 it was enacted that no goods should be imported into or exported out of any Plantation in Asia, Africa or America, or should be carried from one port in a Plantation to another, except in English or Plantation owned ships, manned as provided by the earlier Acts.[3]

These Acts had three main objects :   first, the encouragement of the navy and the mercantile marine ;   secondly, the encouragement of British manufactures ;   and thirdly, subject to the attainment of these two objects, the encouragement of the economic development of the colonies.

(a) The navy and the mercantile marine were encouraged by the monopoly of the carrying trade which the Acts attempted to secure for British ships.   We have seen that these provisions were approved by Adam Smith.[4]   We shall see that the shipping interest was also encouraged by the gift of bounties on the production of naval stores from America.[5]   Moreover, the obligation imposed by the Acts to ship the enumerated commodities to British ports made Great Britain a staple for these commodities, and thus gave British ships an opportunity to export these commodities to foreign countries.   At the same time the Acts compelled the colonies to import European commodities in British ships.

(b) But the chief object of imposing this obligation to send the enumerated commodities to Great Britain was to provide raw materials for British manufactures.   The list of these commodities was from time to time varied.   Commodities were sometimes added to the list,[6] and sometimes taken out of it.

[1] Vol. vi 316-317.
[2] 19 George III c. 48 § 1 ; in 1782 there was a slight relaxation—certain goods produced in Hungary or Germany could be shipped from the Austrian Netherlands, and goods produced or manufactured in other parts of Europe could be shipped in ships belonging to persons who were subject to the same sovereign as the country in which the goods were produced or manufactured, 22 George III c. 78.
[3] 7, 8 William III c. 22 ; 9 William III c. 42 ; vol. vi 317-318.
[4] Ibid 318 n. 6 ; Wealth of Nations (Cannan's ed.) i 428-429.
[5] 3, 4 Anne c. 10 ; 8 Anne c. 13 § 35 ; 9 Anne c. 17 ; 8 George I c. 12 ; below 397-398.
[6] 3, 4 Anne c. 5 § 12—rice and molasses ; 8 George I c. 15 § 24—furs ; c. 18 § 22—copper ore ; 4 George III c. 15 §§ 27 and 28—coffee, cocoanuts, silk, hides, iron, lumber.

Thus, in order to encourage the production of a particular commodity, an enumerated commodity was allowed to be exported directly to all foreign countries,[1] or, more generally, to certain foreign countries ;[2] and other encouragements were sometimes given.[3] But the principle of maintaining the list of enumerated commodities, which must be exported to Great Britain, was maintained. And, since the main object of the maintenance of the principle was to benefit British manufacturers, it followed that colonial manufactures, which competed with British manufactures, must be discouraged. We have seen that in 1698 the American colonies were forbidden to export their woollen manufactures to any place whatsoever.[4] In other words, they were allowed to manufacture for local needs only. In 1732 the export of hats from any of the American colonies was forbidden.[5] In 1750 a long dispute between the iron-masters and the manufacturers[6] was settled in favour of the latter. Bar iron was allowed to be imported from America to London duty free;[7] but all iron manufactures were forbidden. The erection of machinery for such manufactures was to be deemed a common nuisance, and governors, lieutenant-governors, and the commander-in-chief in any of the American colonies were to abate the nuisance when called upon to do so.[8]

Adam Smith condemned these Acts which suppressed American manufactures, on the ground that they were both unnecessary and impolitic. He denounced the prohibition of colonial manufactures as " a violation of the most sacred rights of mankind " ;[9] and he pointed out that it was really unnecessary :

Land is still so cheap, and, consequently, labour so dear among them, that they can import from the mother country, almost all the more refined or more advanced manufactures cheaper than they could make them for themselves. Though they had not, therefore, been prohibited from establishing such manufactures, yet in their present state of improvement, a regard to their own interest would probably have prevented them from doing so.[10]

[1] 12 George II c. 30—sugar.

[2] 3 George II c. 28—rice from Carolina was allowed to be exported to any European port south of Finisterre ; 8 George II c. 19—a similar provision as to rice from Georgia ; 5 George III c. 45 § 22—lumber.

[3] 19 George II c. 30—sailors employed in the sugar trade were exempted from impressment ; 33 George II c. 28—the duty on rum imported for the colonies was remitted on its export from England.

[4] Vol. vi 321 ; 10 William III c. 16 § 19.   [5] 5 George II c. 22.

[6] Lipson, Economic History of England iii 189-192 ; cp. Camb. Hist. of the Empire i 587-588.

[7] 23 George II c. 29 § 1 ; in 1757 it was allowed to be imported to any port in Great Britain, 30 George II c. 16 § 1.

[8] 23 George II c. 29 §§ 9 and 10.

[9] Wealth of Nations (Cannan's ed.) ii 83.

[10] Ibid 83-84 ; cp. ibid i 356-359 where he maintains the thesis that " according to the natural course of things the greater part of the capital of every growing society is first directed to agriculture, afterwards to manufactures, and last of all to foreign commerce."

Mr. Lipson agrees with this verdict.[1] On the other hand, it might be said that the colonists might, but for this legislation, have considered it to be for their interest to foster manufactures to compete with those of Great Britain ; that this might have diminished the sale of British manufactures ; and thus might have diminished a trade, the profits of which helped to defray the cost of the defence and the government of the colonies.[2]

(c) Subject to these limitations the colonies enjoyed considerably more freedom than the colonies of any other country ; and they were given very considerable economic advantages. Adam Smith pointed out that " in everything except their foreign trade, the liberty of the English colonists to manage their own affairs their own way is complete.   It is in every respect equal to that of their fellow citizens at home, and is secured in the same manner by an assembly of representatives of the people, who claim the sole right of imposing taxes for the support of the colony government." [3]   He pointed out also that the government of the British colonies was cheaper than that of any other nation.[4] We have seen that a large part of the cost of their defence, and a considerable part of the cost of their government was borne by Great Britain ; [5] and they were helped in other ways— statutes of 1710,[6] 1711,[7] and 1718 [8] gave a money grant to the inhabitants of St. Nevis and St. Christopher who had suffered losses owing to a French invasion.   Moreover " in the disposal of their surplus produce . . . the English colonies have been more favoured and have been allowed a more extensive market than those of any other European nation." [9]   On the export of some of their products a bounty was given.[10]   The growth of tobacco was suppressed in England in the interests of the colonies.[11] Their products were charged with a smaller import duty than the products of foreign countries.[12]   Till 1763 [13] the duties imposed on the import of foreign commodities to England were generally drawn back on their export to the colonies, so that the colonists

---

[1] Economic History of England iii 193-194.

[2] This argument was put forward by Gee, Trade and Navigation of Great Britain (1730) 79, cited Lipson, op. cit. iii 193.

[3] Wealth of Nations (Cannan's ed.) ii 86.

[4] " All the different civil authorities in North America, exclusive of those in Maryland and North Carolina . . . did not, before the commencement of the present disturbances, cost the inhabitants above £64,700 a year ; an ever memorable example at how small an expense three millions of people may not only be governed, but well governed," Wealth of Nations (Cannan's ed.) ii 75.

[5] Above 66-67.   [6] 9 Anne c. 23 § 88.   [7] 10 Anne c. 34.

[8] 5 George I c. 32.   [9] Wealth of Nations ii 76.

[10] Below 416, 417 ; see e.g. 9 George III c. 38—a bounty on raw silk from America.

[11] Vol. vi 322, 425.

[12] 5 George II c. 24 and 25 George II c. 35 § 1—coffee ; 6 George II c. 13— rum ; 23 George II c. 20—silk ; 23 George III c. 79—coffee ; cp. 21 George II c. 30 which encouraged the production of indigo ; Lipson, op. cit. iii 171-172.

[13] 4 George III c. 15 § 13.

could often buy them at a cheaper rate than Englishmen.[1]
Colonial shipping and shipbuilding profited by the Navigation
Acts ; [2] and the flourishing shipbuilding industry of the colonies
made it the more possible to mitigate the effects of these Acts by
extensive smuggling.   In these circumstances it is not surprising
to find that it is now generally agreed that it was not the Acts of
Trade which caused the American Revolution.[3]

In other ways also the commercial prosperity of the colonies
was assisted by the British Legislature.   An Act of 1710 established a general post office for all his Majesty's dominions,
and fixed the rates of postage.[4]   An Act of 1732 made the recovery of debts owing by American colonists more easy.[5]   An
Act of 1741 extended the Bubble Act to the American colonies.[6]
An Act of 1751 regulated paper bills of credit in New England,
and prevented them from being made legal tender for the payment of debts ; [7] and an Act of 1764 prevented paper bills of
credit, issued in any of the colonies, from being made legal tender
for the payment of debts.[8]   Of the wisdom of this legislation as
to paper money Adam Smith was quite convinced.[9]

Allowing the colony security to be perfectly good, a hundred pounds
payable fifteen years hence, for example, in a country where interest
is at six per cent., is worth little more than forty pounds ready
money. To oblige a creditor, therefore, to accept of this as full payment for a debt of a hundred pounds actually paid down in ready
money, was an act of such violent injustice as has scarce, perhaps,
been attempted by the government of any other country which pretended to be free.[10]

The policy which underlay these laws of trade was elaborated
by the Board of Trade and the Council ; and both these bodies
did their best to enforce it in the colonies, with all its implications.

---

[1] Wealth of Nations ii 85 ; see e.g. 21 George II c. 14—the export of tea to
Ireland and America freed from inland duties ; 33 George II c. 28 § 1—a drawback of
the duties on rum and spirits from America when exported.

[2] Vol. vi 322 ; cp. Lipson, op. cit. iii 179, 180.

[3] Ibid 194-196 ; below 105, 111-112.

[4] 9 Anne c. 10 ; in 1718 Virginia objected to the Act on the ground that Parliament was imposing a tax, but " the manifest advantage of the service seems to have
stifled serious objection," Berriedale Keith, op. cit. 303 ; Franklin, when examined
by the House of Commons in 1766, said that he did not consider the charge for
postage to be in the nature of a tax, but merely " a quantum meruit for a
service done," Political Pieces written by Franklin (ed. 1779) 278.

[5] 5 George II c. 7.

[6] 14 George II c. 37 ; for the Bubble Act (6 George I c. 18 §§ 18-22) see vol.
viii 219-221.

[7] 24 George II c. 53 ; the Act applied to Rhode Island, Providence, Connecticut,
Massachusetts Bay, and New Hampshire.

[8] 4 George III c. 34.

[9] " No law could be more equitable than the Act of Parliament so unjustly
complained of in the colonies, which declared that no paper currency to be emitted
there in time coming, should be a legal tender of payment," Wealth of Nations
(Cannan's ed.) i 310.

[10] Ibid 309 ; for other regulations as to paper currency see below 90-91.

This will be obvious if we look at one or two illustrations of the manner in which they approached any question which bore, however remotely,[1] on the policy of these laws. The imposition of import duties on British manufactures was regarded with suspicion,[2] and Governors were ordered not to assent to laws of this kind, or to any laws whereby the property of subjects or the trade or shipping of the kingdom might be affected, unless they contained a clause suspending their operation till the King's pleasure was taken ; [3] and in 1732 [4] and 1775 [5] the principle was asserted and insisted upon. On this principle tariff wars between the different colonies were stopped—they obviously interfered with the trade of British manufacturers.[6] On this principle also export duties on raw material were objected to—first because they increased the price which British manufacturers must pay, and secondly because they tended to give a preference to the manufacturers of the colony against those of Great Britain.[7]

The principle that colonial manufactures should be suppressed, and that the colonies should be mainly confined to the production of raw material, was very rigidly enforced.[8] Not only were all direct attempts to set up colonial manufactures prohibited, but also all projects which seemed likely indirectly to facilitate the setting up of manufactures. Thus, in 1766, the committee of the Council thought that the opening of coal mines should be discouraged, because it might easily lead to the setting up of factories for the working of iron ; [9] and in 1767 a Georgia Act, which encouraged settlers to come to Georgia, was disallowed, mainly because there was reason to fear that many of the settlers would be manufacturers.[10] One of the arguments for giving bounties upon the import of naval stores was

---

[1] Thus in 1718 a duty imposed by Jamaica on negroes landed by the South Sea Company for refreshment was objected to because it was offensive to the Company, and would have the effect of supporting Jamaica at the expense of the British trade," Acts of the Privy Council (Col. Series) ii 728.

[2] Ibid 740—an order to the Proprietors of Carolina to disallow an Act imposing a 10 p.c. duty on British manufactures.

[3] Ibid iii 63, 64, 71 (1724) ; 160-161 (1727).

[4] Ibid 348.

[5] Ibid v 408, where it was laid down by the Board of Trade that " the Legislative Authority of the Assemblies in Your Majesty's Colonies in America does not Extend beyond the imposing Taxes and Duties upon the Inhabitants of these Colonies," and " that all Laws Enacted by the Legislatures that operate to the Imposition of Duties upon Ships and Goods of the Merchants of this Kingdom or to prejudice or obstruct its Commerce, are not warranted by the Constitution."

[6] Berriedale Keith, op. cit. 294-295.   [7] Ibid 292.

[8] Acts of the Privy Council (Col. Series) v 37—a Virginia Act of 1766, which gave advantages to the exporters of dressed hides, was disallowed, as " every attempt . . . to check or interfere with the manufactures of this country ought in policy and reason to be discouraged " ; in 1772 a S. Carolina Act which gave a bounty on the export of linen manufactured in the colony was, for the same reason, disallowed, ibid 320.

[9] Ibid 19-20.   [10] Ibid 113.

that the bounties encouraged the production of raw material, and diverted attention from manufactures.[1]

Because the commercial value of the colonies was regarded as consisting in the fact that they were a source of supply of raw materials, and a market for British manufactures, colonial legislation which might affect adversely the British creditor was scrutinized with the greatest care, and the representations of the merchants in these matters were always listened to with the greatest attention.[2] Thus bankruptcy legislation, which gave opportunities for the evasion of debts, was several times rejected after hearing the objections of the merchants;[3] and it was their representations which secured the passing of the Act of 1764, which prevented the colonies from making their paper bills of credit legal tender for the payment of debts.[4] In fact, the policy to be adopted with regard to colonial legislation which set up a paper currency, was very difficult to decide. It was obvious that unrestricted issues depreciated the value of the currency, and that if the colony made this depreciated currency legal tender, the British creditor would suffer.[5] On the other hand, there were two reasons why a paper currency was badly needed in the colonies. In the first place, the colonies had no mints. In the second place, the balance of trade, as between them and Great Britain, was against them, and, owing to the operation of the Acts of Trade, must continue to be against them. Therefore specie was drawn out of the colony, so that, unless a paper currency was allowed, the colonists were deprived of a circulating medium.[6] The British government adopted the plan, approved of by Pownall,[7] of refusing to allow bills establishing a paper currency, unless they contained a suspending clause;[8] but of allowing issues provided that they were limited to the amount needed to supply a circulating medium, provided that full provision was made for refunding, provided that bills were of limited duration and were not reissued when retired, and provided that they were not made

---

[1] Acts of the Privy Council (Col. Series) vi 203-204.

[2] Below 107; in 1758 a Massachusetts Act was disallowed on the petition of the merchants trading there, and after hearing them and the agent for the colony, Acts of the Privy Council (Col. Series) iv 389.

[3] Last note; and see ibid 563—a Virginia Act of 1762.

[4] Above 88; Acts of the Privy Council (Col. Series) iv 623.

[5] Thus in 1724 merchants and traders to S. Carolina and traders in that province sent up a complaint against the Governor for allowing a law establishing a paper currency contrary to his instructions, ibid iii 81.

[6] " In Colonies, the essence of whose nature requires a progressive increase of settlements and trade, and yet who, from the balance of trade from the mother country being against them, must suffer a constantly decreasing quantity of silver money, a certain quantity of paper money is necessary," Pownall, Administration of the Colonies (4th ed.) 226-227.

[7] Ibid 227.

[8] Acts of the Privy Council (Col. Series) ii 510 (1706); ibid 739 (1720).

legal tender.[1]   The last requisite was the most important to the
British creditor; [2] and it was for that reason that it was, as we
have seen,[3] given statutory force.

On commercial questions, it was mainly in connection with
the Acts of Trade, and the commercial relations of the colonies
with Great Britain and foreign countries, that the British government exercised control.   Occasionally also it interfered with colonial laws passed to regulate internal trade.   Thus in 1684 a
Jamaica Act against engrossing and forestalling was disallowed
because it was " contrary to that freedom of trade which we
are willing to encourage amongst our subjects." [4]   In the latter
part of the eighteenth century the tendency of economic doctrine
to move in the direction of greater freedom of trade [5] is apparent
in the reasons given for the continued objections made to laws
against engrossing and forestalling,[6] and for disallowing laws
fixing the prices of provisions [7] and lowering the rate of interest.[8]
Thus in 1776 Mr. Jackson, the counsel to the Board of Trade,
said, with respect to a Montserrat Act to fix the price of provisions,[9]

that the experience of all ages has shown, that the price of provisions
can only be reduced by encreasing the plenty of them ; and this can
only be produced by encouragement ; that a price fixed above the
natural rate will be useless, a price equal to the natural rate impossible,
because the natural rate will frequently vary, and one below the
natural rate may operate to decrease the product, but can never
augment it, or lower the price, in-so-much as the amount of such a
regulation is in truth no more than that the commodity shall not be
consumed at all, unless at the rate fixed, not that any man shall produce
it and sell at the rate.

These objections to colonial statutes show that a belief in the
existence of natural laws which governed economic phenomena
was gaining strength ; and that this belief was making for a
relaxation of legal restrictions on trade.[10]   But those who made
use of these objections did not foresee that, in the not very distant future, this belief would gain such strength that it would

[1] Acts of the Privy Council (Col. Series) iii 56 (1723) ; iv 81-82 (1749), 414-
416 (1759) ; Berriedale Keith, op. cit. 293 ; it was pointed out in 1746 that the
making of these bills legal tender was contrary to the statute 6 Anne c. 30, which
fixed the rates for foreign coins in the American colonies.
[2] Pownall, op. cit. 228-230, 231-234.   [3] Above 88.
[4] Acts of the Privy Council (Col. Series) ii 833.   [5] Below 391.
[6] Acts of the Privy Council (Col. Series) v 508 (1781), where it was pointed out
that Parliament had in 1772 repealed the statutes against ingrossers and forestallers.
[7] Ibid 307 (1771).   [8] Ibid 406 (1775).   [9] Ibid 437-438.
[10] Thus, ibid v 406, Jackson recommended the disallowance of an Act to lower
the rate of interest on the ground that " it is either-useless or mischievous ; for,
if money abounds sufficiently in the province to induce possessors of it to lend at six
per cent. it will be lent at that rate, in case it does not, the only effect of the law
will be a prohibition on the lending at all to the manifest injury of the trade of the
colony, and the improvement of its lands."

subvert all those economic ideas upon which the Acts of Trade, and the resulting colonial policy of eighteenth-century statesmen, were founded.[1]

(ii) *The defence of the colonies.*

If the colonies were to be made commercially profitable to Great Britain, it is obvious that they must be defended ; and it was also obvious that the main burden of that defence must fall on Great Britain. She alone could supply the necessary munitions of war, because the Acts of Trade prevented the colonies from setting up the factories necessary for the supply of munitions ; she alone could supply men possessed of the necessary technical skill in land and sea warfare ; and she alone was in a position to direct the policy of the empire. In fact, just as she supplied the capital which fostered the economic development of the colonies, just as she supplied the brains which helped to put the development of the laws of the colonies on the right lines, so she supplied the munitions which were used in, and the brains which directed, the military operations needed to protect the colonists from their French, Spanish, and Indian enemies. Sometimes her efforts were backed up by the colonies.

If Massachusetts Bay haggled for nearly forty years before she paid for her supplies of powder, yet her sons died of fever before Carthagena in a quarrel which was none of hers, and under a New England colonel took Louisbourg on lines which in the second siege Amherst and Wolfe were fain to follow.[2]

Pitt, too, succeeded in inducing the colonists to spend their blood and their money in his campaign against Canada—though it is true that a large, though not perhaps a disproportionate, part of the expenses was paid by Great Britain.[3]

But more often the colonies showed a selfish particularism which led them to refuse to help their neighbours, and even to take adequate measures for the defence of their own borders.[4] At the Albany conference of 1754, Benjamin Franklin proposed

---

[1] Below 518. [2] Acts of the Privy Council (Col. Series) iii x.

[3] " The Crown was to provide arms, ammunition, tents, and provisions. The colonies were to raise, clothe, and pay the levies, but for this expense Pitt promised a parliamentary reimbursement, and this promise induced the colonists to make all the efforts that were required," Lecky, History of England ii 416 ; Burke, in his speech on American taxation (Works (Bohn's ed.) i 410-411) cites Governor Bernard for the proposition that the Americans had raised by loans and taxation as much as they were able, so that they " were not taxable objects."

[4] Above 67 ; below 111 ; in 1704 the Governor of New Hampshire and Massachusetts reported that " instead of receiving assistance from Rhode Island . . . that colony did harbour some hundreds of the young men fitted for service as well as seamen . . . so that if the war continue in these parts there will in a little time be few men fit to bear arms. . . . The like complaint was heard from Lord Cornbury, her Majesty's Governor of New York, relating to the colony of Connecticut," House of Lords MSS. (N.S.) vi 97.

a plan of union for defensive and other purposes of common interest to all the American colonies : there was to be a federal constitution, consisting of a General Council elected by the Colonial Assemblies, and a President appointed and paid by the Crown. The President and Council were to have power to direct all matters of defence, all Indian affairs, and all questions relating to unoccupied lands. Upon these matters they were to have power to legislate ; and to meet the expenses incurred, they were to have power to impose taxation.[1] The commissioners from the several states present consented to this plan, but none of the separate provinces would ratify it.[2] They were too jealous of one another, and too averse to sacrifice any iota of their autonomy. Even under the stress of Pontiac's rebellion in 1763 the different colonies refused to give efficient aid to one another.[3] It would seem that the colonies had come to believe that Great Britain could always be relied upon to defend them, and, as in the Seven Years' War, to pay the major part of the expense. And so they preferred to preserve their isolation, and to save the expense which the working of a federal scheme would have involved. If in the policy pursued in the administration of the Acts of Trade, and in the supervision of colonial legislation, the British government showed that it was oblivious of the new problems and the new needs of growing communities, these communities showed themselves equally oblivious of the responsibilities which maturity entails. If it was right that their subordination to Great Britain should be lessened, it was right that they should relieve Great Britain of some part of the charge for their defence.[4] But this aspect of the question was never fairly considered by the colonists. If it had been fairly considered the war of independence might have been averted ; for if " the colonies had really shouldered the burden of their defence, the experiment of taxing America need never have been tried." [5]

(iii) *The supervision exercised over colonial legislation.*

The maintenance of the Acts of Trade, and the commercial policy which underlay them, was by no means the only object which the British government had in view when it was called

---

[1] Political Pieces written by Franklin (1779) 85-119 ; Berriedale Keith, op. cit. 327-328.
[2] Ibid 328.   [3] Camb. Hist. of the Empire i 638-639.
[4] Adam Smith said in the last sentence of his Wealth of Nations (Cannan's ed.) ii 433, " If any of the provinces of the British empire cannot be made to contribute towards the support of the whole empire, it is surely time that Great Britain should free herself from the expense of defending those provinces in time of war, and of supporting any part of their civil or military establishments in time of peace, and endeavour to accommodate her future views and designs to the real mediocrity of her circumstances."
[5] Berriedale Keith, op. cit. 328 ; below 110.

upon to supervise colonial legislation. The major premise upon which the Acts of Trade, and the commercial policy which underlay them, depended, was the subordination of the colonies to Great Britain.[1] Acts which affected the prerogative, or conflicted with British statutes, were disallowed on the ground that they were contrary to this principle of subordination. Thus, in 1723, a Jamaica Act for the prevention of frauds and abuses in collecting the revenue, was disallowed, partly on the ground that it would " in a great measure take off the dependence of that island from the Crown of Great Britain, under which their government and laws have been and are established." [2] In the same year a Virginia Act was disallowed because it " weakens the process for the Crown in the recovery of forfeitures and arrears of quit rents." [3] In 1738 a New York Act for the frequent election of representatives, and the frequent meeting of the General Assembly, was disallowed, because it took away " the undoubted right which the Crown has always exercised of calling and continuing the Assembly of that Province at such times and so long as it has been thought necessary for the publick service." [4] In 1757 a Virginia Act, which established a town and a fair in Augusta county, was disallowed because the establishment of fairs was a part of the prerogative which was vested in the Governor.[5] In 1760 a Jamaica Act to ascertain the value of Spanish milled money was disallowed, because its provisions were " in their tendency highly injurious to the rights of individuals, introductory to fraud and usury, derogatory to your Majesty's royal prerogative, and repugnant to the true principles of the Act passed in the sixth year of Queen Ann, for ascertaining the rates of foreign coins in her Majesty's plantations in America." [6]

To secure the maintenance of this subordination of the colonies to Great Britain, it was necessary to take care that the Assemblies did not enact laws which conflicted with fundamental constitutional principles, or with the established principles of English law. Thus in 1766 a North Carolina Act, which empowered any person to kill those charged with felonies, if they did not surrender within a time fixed for their surrender, was disallowed because it was " contrary to the spirit and principle of the British laws " ; [7] and in 1722 another North Carolina Act for preventing tumults and riotous assemblies, which provided that, if persons presented for such crimes did not surrender

---

[1] Above 81-83. [2] Acts of the Privy Council (Col. Series) iii 49.
[3] Ibid 55. [4] Ibid 617.
[5] Ibid iv 138 ; cp. ibid v 163 (1768).
[6] Ibid iv 451 ; cp. ibid v 159-160 (1768) ; for other illustrations see Berriedale Keith, op. cit. 289.
[7] Acts of the Privy Council (Col. Series) v 38.

within sixty days, they were to be deemed to be guilty, and that
any one could kill such offender, was said to be " irreconcileable
to the principles of the constitution, depriving withal the Crown
of its prerogative of extending mercy to offenders, by committing
the execution of the law into the hands of the subject." [1]   In
1778 a Quebec ordinance as to the distribution of the estates of
persons who left the province without paying their debts was
disallowed because it was given a retrospective effect.[2]   In 1727
the Council recommended that a law of Connecticut, which
assimilated the law of intestate succession to realty to the law
of intestate succession to personalty, should be declared void
because it was contrary to the laws of England ; [3] and in 1729
a Virginia statute of limitations was disallowed because it was
contrary to James I's statute of limitations.[4]   In 1761 a Nova
Scotia Act was objected to because it allowed a divorce to be
obtained " not only for the usual causes of impotence, of kindred,
or of adultery, but also in the case of wilful desertion and withholding necessary maintenance for three years together." [5]

This policy of endeavouring to secure that colonial legislation conformed to constitutional principles, and that it did
not depart too widely from the principles of English law, had
both good and bad points.

Its good points were these :

First, as some of the instances given above show, it often
prevented flagrant injustice. In 1762 the Board of Trade
rightly stigmatized a Jamaica Act, which proposed to make it
a felony punishable with death without benefit of clergy, to
import sugar, rum, or molasses from a foreign colony contrary to
the Act of 1759, as a sanguinary clause, contrary to principles of
justice, equity, and reason [6]—though the Board was unfortunately
not accurate in its statement of law when it went on to say that
" punishment of death is by the laws of England applied only to
the most atrocious crimes, such as are destructive to society, and
subversive of government." [7]

Secondly, the Council was always very careful to see that
private Acts inflicted no injustice on individuals or classes of
individuals. Governors were instructed to see that persons
whose interests were affected, consented to, or at least were
notified of, the proposals in the Act ; to see that the rights of
the Crown or of persons or corporations not mentioned in the
Act were saved ; and to see that the Act had a clause suspending
its operation till King's assent was given.[8] There is much evidence

---

[1] Acts of the Privy Council (Col. Series) v 338.   [2] Ibid 458.
[3] Ibid iii 149.   [4] Ibid 227.   [5] Ibid iv 558.
[6] Ibid 519-520.   [7] See Bl. Comm. iv 18-19 ; below 562-563.
[8] Acts of the Privy Council (Col. Series) iv 449-450 ; Berriedale Keith, op. cit.
244-245, 291.

that these precautions were very necessary. There was a tendency to apply to the Legislature to settle by their action justiciable matters, which could only be fairly dealt with by the courts [1] —a practice which was no doubt fostered by the fact that the absence, in some of the New England colonies, of a court of Chancery, had led to the practice of petitioning the Legislature for equitable relief, which they gave by mere resolution, and to an extent beyond that ever attempted by a court of Chancery.[2] As might be expected, there are instances in which the Legislature intervened in a way which suggested sometimes a sinister influence, and sometimes a neglect of elementary justice. The following two instances show that the Crown's supervision was very necessary to guard against these perversions of legislative power : the first instance is an Act passed by the Assembly of Pennsylvania in 1755 " for the relief of George Croghan and William Trent for and during the space of ten years." [3] During that period it protected these two persons from all actions for debt. The committee of Council said :

This extraordinary indulgence is declared in the Act to have been granted on the petition of several, but not of the whole number of their creditors. On this partial application to the Assembly, the bill was brought into the House, and we find, by the Journal of that House, that it was read twice in the forenoon, never committeed, but passed in the afternoon of the same day.

The committee added that

to suffer the continuance of an Act so unjust and partial in its nature, passed so irregularly, and without the observance of any one of those rules which justice requires in all cases which affect private property would be a precedent of most dangerous consequence in the colonies.

The second instance is a Barbados Act of 1762 to render John Adams, Esqre, incapable of being elected a member of the General Assembly or of exercising any office in the island.[4] The committee of Council said that this Act

appears to be subversive of every principle of justice, it enacts a punishment for a crime *ex post facto*, and inflicts a second punishment upon a man for a misdemeanour after he had been tried before his country, found guilty, and suffered the punishment for the same.

---

[1] Thus in 1766 Sir Mathew Lamb said of a Massachusetts Act passed to enforce a contract that " it is a matter of right determinable in the courts of law there, and that the party aggrieved must seek for redress in such courts, when all the parties concerned will have an opportunity to make their defence, which it does not appear by this Act they have had," Acts of the Privy Council (Col. Series) v 31 (1766) ; for another instance see ibid v 151, 160, 161 (1768).

[2] Pownall, Administration of the Colonies (4th ed.) 111-112 ; apparently they even went to the length of " suspending public laws."

[3] Acts of the Privy Council (Col. Series) iv 341-342.

[4] Ibid iv 686.

Thirdly, other advantages which the colonies derived from the supervision of the British government were the encouragement which it gave to projects for the revision and restatement of their laws ; [1] and the criticism by skilled lawyers of the very rough drafting of some of these Acts. [2]   Thus, in 1723, a Jamaica Act which, *inter alia*, extended all the laws of England concerning the life, liberty, or property of the subject to Jamaica, and especially the Habeas Corpus Act, was disallowed, partly on the ground that the Act was so widely drawn that it would be very difficult to ascertain what laws were extended to Jamaica, with the result that the law would be wholly uncertain. [3]

The bad points of this system of supervision were due mainly to a failure to realize that a great many of the rules and principles of English law were ill adapted to colonial conditions, and that the colonial Assemblies were, in many cases, much better judges than the Board of Trade or the Council, of the expediency of modifying these rules and principles. [4]   Thus the ruling of the Privy Council in 1728, that a Connecticut law which abolished primogeniture was void, because it conflicted with the rules of English law, was so obviously unreasonable, that a contrary decision was reached in 1745. [5]   Similarly, it is difficult to see why the colonists should not have been allowed to pass Acts which modified the status of married women, [6] or Acts which set up local courts for the trial of petty civil cases ; [7] and it is impossible not to sympathize with the colonists, when their Acts to restrain the dumping of convicts upon them were disallowed, on the ground that they conflicted with an Act of Parliament. [8]   Nor does there seem to be any good ground for refusing to the colonial Assemblies the power, possessed by the British Parliament, of dissolving a marriage by legislative Act. [9] As in many other matters, so in this matter of the supervision of colonial legislation, the Board of Trade and the Council had come to be guided by a fixed set of principles, which they applied

[1] Acts of the Privy Council (Col. Series) iv 132 (1751) ; ibid 153 (1752).

[2] For instances of amendments made to improve Acts see ibid iii 719 (1745) ; ibid v 521 (1782), where it is pointed out that the word " not " was omitted in two places in a clause in the bill ; in one case the agent of the colony (Franklin) undertook that if the Act were allowed the Assembly would amend it in the way approved by the Council, ibid iv 442 (1760).

[3] Acts of the Privy Council (Col. Series) iii 47 ; cp. ibid v 161-162 (1768), 192 (1770).

[4] For the question how far colonial laws were void which were contrary to the English common law see above 56 ; below 238.

[5] Berriedale Keith, op. cit. 248-249.

[6] Acts of the Privy Council (Col. Series) iv 4 (1746), 489-490 (1761), 676 (1764).

[7] Berriedale Keith, op. cit. 257-258.

[8] Acts of the Privy Council (Col. Series) iii 162 (1731) ; Berriedale Keith, op. cit. 290.

[9] Acts of the Privy Council (Col. Series) v 361-366 (1773), 381 (1773), 395-396 (1774).

in accordance with a practice which tended to become very
rigid, and therefore more and more out of accord with the needs
of new and swiftly developing communities.

(iv) *The supervision exercised over other matters.*

There were several matters in respect of which the supervision exercised by the British government was of very considerable assistance to the political development of the colonies.

First, the different provinces in America were very separate
from one another in their origins, in their history, and, consequently, in social development and intellectual outlook. They
had, as Pownall said, no other principle of civil union than their
connection with Great Britain.[1] These diversities led to local
jealousies which made combination between them, even for
defensive purposes, very difficult to effect;[2] and to disputes
which might easily have led to inter-provincial wars, if the
British government had not been available to settle their disputes
by arbitration. Thus in 1709 there was a dispute between
Virginia and South Carolina, which arose out of the arrest of
Virginian traders for the non-payment of a duty imposed by
South Carolina upon the export of furs. The furs had been
bought from the Indians, and were merely being carried through
South Carolina on the way back to Virginia. The Council ordered
the discontinuance of this practice.[3] There were frequent
boundary disputes between different provinces which led to
murderous affrays. It was said in 1723 that a dispute of this
kind between Rhode Island and Connecticut had lasted for
sixty years, and that it might, " unless the royall authority
interfere, be perpetuall, to the great disturbance of the peace
of these colonys and to the utter discouragement of planting
and settling the lands in dispute."[4] In 1731 a dispute between
Maryland and Pennsylvania led to riots and murders on the
borders of the two provinces;[5] and there were similar disorders
in the middle of the century owing to a similar dispute between
New York and New Jersey.[6]

Secondly, the maintenance of peaceful relations with the
neighbouring Indian tribes was a condition precedent for securing

---

[1] " The different manner in which they are settled ; the different modes under
which they live ; the different forms of charters, grants, and frames of government
they possess ; the various principles of repulsion that these create ; the different
interests which they actuate ; the different religious interests by which they are
actuated ; the rivalship and jealousies which arise from hence ; and the impractica-
bility of reconciling and accommodating these incompatible ideas and claims, will
keep them for ever so, so long as the spirit of civil policy remains, and is exerted
to the forming and maintaining of this system of union," Administration of the
Colonies (4th ed.) 35-36.

[2] Above 67.   [3] Acts of the Privy Council (Col. Series) ii 610-613.
[4] Ibid iii 11.   [5] Ibid iii 337 ; vi 239-243.   [6] Ibid iv *xxx.*

the expansion, the commercial interests, and the defence of the
colonies, against the French and the Indian tribes who were
allied to the French.

While the Indian tribes were never treated as independent peoples,
but as subject to a British protectorate, every effort was devoted by
the Board, as representing the central and disinterested government,
to secure from relations with them the maximum security, and the
gradual advance of British settlement under conditions which would
secure co-operation rather than war.[1]

It is safe to say that, without the intervention of the British
government, these relations could not have been maintained ;
for their maintenance was no easy task.   In the first place,
since the British colonists were, and the French and Spanish
colonies were not, intent on making permanent settlements
which destroyed the Indian hunting grounds, the Indians were
more reluctant to ally themselves with the British.[2]   In the
second place, the misdeeds of the colonial traders, who dispossessed the Indians of their lands under cover of fraudulent purchases,[3] and of the provinces which encouraged settlements on
the Indian hunting grounds,[4] made the task of the British
government still more difficult.   That government did what it
could.   It listened to the complaints of the Indians, appointed
commissions to enquire into their complaints, and heard appeals
from the findings of the commissioners.[5]   It tried to enforce
fair dealings in the negotiations for concessions of land by means
of instructions, which it gave to Governors, not to allow the purchase of land from the Indians without licence ; [6] and it established a system of licensing traders to prevent the free supply
of rum to the Indians, and to stop the practices, facilitated by the
free supply of rum, by which the Indians were cheated out of
their land and the price of their furs.[7]   But for these measures
the Indian menace would have been much greater.   The colonists
themselves pursued no settled policy, and often did little or
nothing to enforce the laws against over-reaching the Indians
in the purchase of their lands, and in their commercial dealings
with them.   They were too apt to regard the Indians merely as

[1] Berriedale Keith, op. cit. 319 ; cp. Acts of the Privy Council (Col. Series) iv
xxiv-xxv.
[2] Pownall, Administration of the Colonies (4th ed.) App. 12-13 ; Berriedale
Keith, op. cit. 319.
[3] Pownall, op. cit. 261-262, 274-275.
[4] Acts of the Privy Council (Col. Series) iv 402, 403 (1759), 552-553 (1763) ;
cp. House of Lords MSS. (N.S.) vi 99 (1704)—complaints of Mohegan Indians
against Connecticut ; vii 304-308—exorbitant grants of land in the Mohawk country
which were revoked by the Assembly, and then the revoking Act was repealed.
[5] Acts of the Privy Council ii 459 (1704) ; iii 537 (1741).
[6] Ibid iv 283-284 (1755), 749 (1766).
[7] Berriedale Keith, op. cit. 334-335.

savages who had no rights, and with whom no faith need be kept.[1]
It would have been better for the colonists if they had co-operated
more loyally with the more humane and more far-seeing policy
of the home government. The fact that they failed to do so led
directly to the great Indian rising under Pontiac in 1763. We
shall see that the need for providing defence for the colonies
against such risings, and the unwillingness of the colonists to make
any satisfactory provision for their own defence, led to the determination of the home government to compel the colonists to
contribute to their own defence, and to those financial proposals
which were the immediate cause of the war of independence.[2]

Thirdly, the Council was always ready to investigate complaints against Governors, whether brought forward by individuals, or by councillors, or by the Assemblies. This supervision was probably far more effective in securing the colonists
from oppression by their Governors than the statute of 1700,
which provided that Governors, accused of oppression or of
crimes against the laws of England or the laws in force in their
governments, should be tried in the court of King's Bench; and
that, if they were found guilty, they should be liable to the same
punishments " as are usually inflicted for offences of like nature
committed here in England." [3] In many cases the complaints
were the echoes of local feuds; [4] and in some cases the accusations
against a Governor were based upon his pursuance of a policy
which he had been directed to pursue by the home government.[5]
In some cases the charges were frivolous.[6] But in other cases
there was substance in the charges, and then the Council gave
redress. Thus in 1709 three councillors, suspended by the
Governor, were restored, " on a representation from the Board
of Trade that if a Governor may suspend all who complain of

---

[1] In 1766 the Board of Trade enquired into an attack made by some frontier
settlers in Virginia upon a party of ten Cherokee Indians; it found that " the per-
petrators of these outrages have adopted an opinion, and declared it to be the principle upon which they act, that the killing a savage is an act for which no man ought
to suffer, and that these people have been encouraged by a promise of support from
a number of inhabitants of Pennsylvania adopting the same principles and of like
evil disposition with themselves," Acts of the Privy Council (Col. Series) iv 731.

[2] Berriedale Keith, op. cit. 335-337; below 110.

[3] 11, 12 William III c. 12; vol. vi 402.

[4] See e.g. the complaints against Melville, the Governor of Grenada, Acts of
the Privy Council (Col. Series) v 221-227 (1769-1770).

[5] Ibid iii 572 (1737)—complaints against Governor Johnson of N. Carolina;
ibid v 214 (1769)—complaints against Governor Bernard of Massachusetts.

[6] One of the complaints made in 1749 against Popple, the Governor of Bermuda,
was that he, " by his bad example, contrary to the express commands of Almighty
God, and to the great discouragement of virtue and religion, from time to time on
the Lord's Day, has by his great and open violation of the Articles of Religion and
in maintenance of irreligion and immorality, actually broke through all rules of
decency in disregard to the Lord's Day, played at cards and other games publicly
in the fields," ibid vi 277.

his conduct, no check on his administration will be left ";[1] and in 1739 the Governor of New Hampshire was found guilty of partiality and disobedience to instructions in proroguing the Assembly, so that they could not consider the findings of a commission appointed to settle a boundary dispute between that province and the province of Massachusetts Bay.[2] In all these cases the Council gave a very patient and thorough hearing to both parties to the dispute. There can be no doubt that the fact that such a tribunal was available, helped to settle local feuds, and thereby helped to make possible the constitutional government of these as yet rather primitive societies.

Fourthly we shall see that the appellate jurisdiction of the Council was helping to introduce a certain amount of uniformity in the fundamental legal principles which underlay the law in force in the colonies ;[3] and, in particular, that it helped to root these fundamental legal principles so firmly in America that they survived the war of independence.[4] Not only did the Council, by its decisions on matters of law, tend to keep the development of the law on the right lines, it also helped to keep the administration of justice pure. Thus in 1709 it removed from his office the chief judge of the court of Common Pleas of Barbados, because he had heard a case in which he himself was defendant.[5] That there was much need for a tribunal which could interfere to redress such miscarriages of justice is clear from Governor Pownall's testimony—" experience," he says,[6] " can well say, how powerfully, even in courts, the influence of the leaders of party have been felt in matters between individuals."

The policy pursued by the British government in all these matters conferred great benefits on the colonies, and helped them to grow to maturity more rapidly than would otherwise have been possible. The Acts of Trade probably assisted this development. It is true that Adam Smith considered that their economic effects were bad and dangerous,[7] and that Lecky considered that it was to the operation of these laws that the revolt of the American colonies were due.[8] But Adam Smith voiced the growing feeling in favour of greater freedom of trade ;[9]

[1] Acts of the Privy Council (Col. Series) ii 576 ; cp. ibid 786-787 for complaints against Lowther, Governor of the Barbados.
[2] Ibid iii 597.   [3] Below 230 seqq.   [4] Below 133-138.
[5] Acts of the Privy Council (Col. Series) ii 606-607 ; cp. ibid 344 (1699) for another similar case.
[6] Administration of the Colonies (4th ed.) 108.
[7] The Wealth of Nations Bk. iv chap. vii Pt. iii.
[8] " The political alienation which was the inevitable and most righteous consequence of these laws had already begun, and it is to the antagonism of interests thus created, much more than to the Stamp Act or to any isolated instances of misgovernment that the subsequent disruption must be ascribed," History of England ii 241.
[9] Below 392-393.

and Lecky wrote at a time when the superstitious belief in the absolute truth of the dogmas of free trade—dogmas which have done more permanent damage to British commerce and industry than the transient benefits which for a short period they conferred upon them—was as yet unshaken. The better opinion is that Burke was not far wrong when he said that, though these laws restrained colonial trade for the benefit of Great Britain, which thereby got a monopoly, yet these restraints were compensated for by the fact that " their monopolist happened to be one of the richest men in the world." His capital developed their fisheries, their shipbuilding, and their trade, with the result that their industry and commerce were able to get "far the start of the slow, languid operations of unassisted nature." [1] But for the naval and military help of Great Britain, it is difficult to see how the colonies could have made such rapid headway against their French, Spanish, and Indian enemies, and how they could have become mature political societies with established industries and an established commerce. Paine was absolutely wrong when he contended, in his pamphlet entitled *Common Sense*, that America owed nothing to Great Britain— though he was right when he contended that the policy suitable for infant states was not equally suitable for those states when they had grown to maturity.[2] Similarly, the supervision by Great Britain of colonial legislation, its intervention to stop inter-colonial disputes and to secure fair treatment for the Indians, its supervision over the conduct of Governors and other colonial officials, and its control over the administration of the law, helped to put and to keep the administration of the government of the colonies on the right lines.

The two great defects of this policy were, first, that it was too rigid in its application—it made no allowance for the political development of the colonies ; and, secondly, that it was too commercial in its outlook—the commercial interests of Great Britain rather than the needs and wishes of the colonies were all important.

(i) One example of the rigidity of the policy adopted by the British government in its regulation of colonial affairs is the

---

[1] Speech on American Taxation, Works (Bohn's ed.) i 403 ; Egerton, The American Revolution 48-51 ; vol. vi 321-323 ; below 105, 124 n. 1.

[2] " I have heard it asserted by some, that as America hath flourished under her former connection with Great Britain, that the same connection is necessary towards her future happiness. . . . Nothing can be more fallacious than this kind of argument. We may as well assert that because a child has thriven upon milk, that it is never to have meat, or that the first twenty years of our lives is to become a precedent for the next twenty. But even this is admitting more than is true, for I answer roundly, that America would have flourished as much, and probably much more, had no European power had anything to do with her," Common Sense (ed. 1776) 16.

manner in which it supervised colonial legislation.[1]   Other and
more important examples are to be found in the constant battles
which it waged with the Assemblies over such questions as the
voting and appropriation of supply, over the control of legislation by the Governor's instructions and by the prerogative of the
Crown, over the privileges of the Assemblies, over the appointment of officials, and over the tenure of the judges.[2]   In some
cases the home government was obliged to give way ; but it
never abandoned its fixed idea that the colonies must remain
politically subordinate ; [3] and, in the advice given by the Board
of Trade and in the resolutions of the Council, we can see too
great a desire to adhere to fixed precedents, and too little desire
to consider the actual conditions prevailing in the colonies, and
the state of public opinion to which those conditions were giving
rise.   Occasionally feelings rose so high that claims for independence from the control of the British government were made.   In
1747 Governor Clinton reported that the Assembly of New York
had assumed the right to be a branch of the supreme Legislature
of the kingdom, and had denied their dependence on Crown and
Parliament.[4]   In 1763 a Jamaica Act dealing with prize goods had
been disallowed on the advice of the Board of Trade, and the
Assembly had been advised to re-enact the Prize Act of 1756.
The Assembly refused to

admit the objection of the Lords Commissioners for Trade and
Plantations to that Act to carry any weight, as they are by no means
disposed to submit their sentiments to the determination of their
Lordships, nor ever will at any time suffer them in any respect to direct
or influence their proceedings by any proposition or decision whatever.[5]

It would not be true to say that there was as yet any general
desire for independence.   As yet the colonies were very separate
and very jealous of one another.[6]   But it would be true to say that
the policy of the government supplied causes of irritation, which
could easily be exploited, if ever a general desire for independence
should manifest itself.   It is true that the pursuance of this
policy was not dictated by a desire to tyrannize : it was due
largely to the fact that the government had not realized the
swiftness of the political development of the colonies.   To
Burke the colonies appeared more like " ancient nations grown
to perfection through a long series of fortunate events . . . than
the colonies of yesterday." [7]   Both English and American history
might have been very different if those who directed the policy

[1] Above 94-98.   [2] Above 50, 56-57, 58-59, 62 ; below 249-250, 261-262.
[3] Above 81-83.   [4] Acts of the Privy Council (Col. Series) vi 300.
[5] Ibid vi 350-351.   [6] Above 98.
    [7] Speech on American Taxation, Works (Bohn's ed.) i 403-404 ; here he was
in agreement with Paine, above 102 n. 2.

of the British government had possessed a fraction of Burke's historic insight.

(ii) The same qualities marked the commercial policy of the British government. The commercial interests of Great Britain were the first consideration ; and there is no doubt that the colonists had long chafed at the growing stringency of the retrictions imposed upon them by the Acts of Trade. As early as the latter part of the seventeenth century protests were made against them,[1] and officers who tried to enforce them were obstructed.[2] Early in the eighteenth century the Board of Trade complained that, in many of the American colonies and in the West Indies, they were disregarded.[3] There is no doubt also that the custom-house officers were guilty, sometimes of applying the law oppressively, and sometimes of conniving at its breach.[4] It was inevitable that as the century grew older, and as commercial conditions changed, these laws should grow more and more unpopular, because it was coming to be more and more evident that they were hindering, not only the commercial development of the colonies, but also the commercial development of the mother country. A petition from New York [5] complained that the law which compelled the colonies to send all their produce to Great Britain was hurtful, not only to the colonies, but also to Great Britain. Unless they could make money by sending their produce to foreign countries, they would be unable to purchase the commodities needed for their own subsistence and for their internal trade ; and, consequently, the demand for the manufactures of Great Britain must be lessened.

In fact, as Mr. Lipson has pointed out, the Acts of Trade "pursued divergent and incompatible aims," [6] which tended to become more divergent and more incompatible as the colonies came to maturity. A good illustration of this fact is the controversy which raged round the Molasses Act.[7] The northern colonies supplied the French and Dutch West Indies with fish and lumber, and took in return molasses from which they made rum. This was a profitable trade. It increased the prosperity of the colonies, and so made them the better able to buy British goods. But it was contrary to the interest of the British sugar colonies. A bill to prohibit the trade failed to pass in 1731 ; but in 1733

---

[1] Acts of the Privy Council (Col. Series) i 677-678—a complaint made in 1676 by the Assembly of Barbados.

[2] Ibid ii 28 (1682)—a letter complaining that Lord Baltimore had obstructed the revenue officers in Maryland;

[3] Ibid ii *xxii-xxiii ;* House of Lords MSS. (N.S.) v 70-71, 81 (1702) ; vii 249-250 (1707).

[4] Acts of the Privy Council (Col. Series) iv *xxi-xxii.*

[5] Cited in Pownall, Administration of the Colonies (4th ed.) 285-297

[6] Economic History of England iii 177.

[7] Ibid iii 177-179 ; 6 George II c. 13.

the Molasses Act imposed heavy duties on foreign molasses.[1]
In spite of petitions against it, the Act remained in force.   But
it was so generally disregarded that, in order to make smuggling
less profitable, the duties were halved in 1763,[2] and were still
further reduced in 1766.[3]

It is clear that the altered circumstances of the colonies
made a drastic revision of the Acts of Trade necessary.   Pownall
put the case for their revision very clearly.   He said : [4]

The laws of trade respecting America were framed and enacted
for *mere plantations*, tracts of foreign country, employed in raising
certain specified and enumerated commodities, solely for the use of
the trade and manufactures of the mother country—the purchase of
which the mother country appropriated to itself.   These laws considered these plantations as a kind of farms, which the mother country
had caused to be worked and cultured for its own use.   But the spirit
of commerce, operating on the nature and situation of these external
dominions, beyond what the mother country or the colonists themselves
ever thought of, planned, or even hoped for, has *wrought up these plantations to become objects of trade ;* has enlarged and combined the intercourse of the barter and exchange of their various produce, into a
very complex and extensive commercial interest. . . . If we are pre-
determined to carry into strict and literal execution the navigation
act and other laws respecting the plantation trade,—without reviewing
and considering what the very different circumstances of the colonies
now are . . . we must determine to reduce our colonies again to mere
plantations : we must either narrow the bottom of our commercial
interest to the model of our plantation laws, or we must enlarge the
spirit of our commercial laws to that latitude to which our commercial
interest does actually extend.   Thus stands the fact.   This is the
truth.   There is no other alternative.[5]

Burke was probably right when he said that, down to 1764,
there was no general wish to get rid of the Acts of Trade.[6]   But
it is clear, as Pownall pointed out, that there was an unanswerable case for their revision.   Obviously the fact that they remained unrevised supplied an ever-growing cause of irritation,
which could be easily exploited by those who were hostile to
the continuance of the control of the British government.

The fact that the growing tension between Great Britain and
her colonies was caused by ignorance of the actual conditions
prevailing there, and of the state of public opinion which those
new conditions had engendered, was realized by Pownall.   We
have seen that he advocated the creation of one central

---

[1] 6 George II c. 13 § 1.   [2] 4 George III c. 15 § 5.
[3] 6 George III c. 52 § 4.   [4] Op. cit. 282-284.
[5] Adam Smith, Wealth of Nations (Cannan's ed.) ii 106, substantially agreed
with these views ; he said, " some moderate and gradual relaxation of the laws which
give to Great Britain the exclusive trade to the colonies, till it is rendered in a great
measure free, seems to be the only expedient which can, in all future times, deliver
her from this danger " [the danger of an interruption of the colonial trade].
[6] Speech on American Taxation, Works (Bohn's ed.) i 403.

department for the management of colonial affairs, which could take a broad view of the problem of colonial administration.[1] He also advocated the adoption of a measure to ensure that this department should be informed of the conditions and aspirations of the colonists.　The government, he said,[2] ought to send out

some very considerable person, with a council to assist him, under a commission and instructions, to call a congress of commissioners from the several colonies.　He should have power and be instructed to call to his aid and assistance the governors, or any other of his Majesty's servants, as occasion should require.　By the representations and assistance of this congress and these persons, he should enquire into the *actual* state of the Crown's authority, as capable of being executed by the King, and by his governor, and other immediate executors of the Crown.

Amongst other things he should enquire into " the extent of the exercise and claim of the legislative powers " ; the state of the colonial laws ; the process and practice of the courts of judicature ; the state of commerce and the working of the Acts of Trade ; the state of the King's revenues, lands, naval stores, and military forces.　He should have power to settle intercolonial disputes, • more especially boundary disputes.　The report of this commission should be laid before the King in Council, and made the basis of a Parliamentary settlement of the relations between Great Britain and her colonies.

Pownall also advocated the project of creating a closer union between the colonies and Great Britain, by giving them the right to send representatives to Parliament.[3]　This project was in the air in the middle of the century ; it was favoured by Adam Smith ;[4]　and in 1754 Franklin was in favour of it, on condition that the Acts of Trade were repealed, " and British subjects on this side the water put, in those respects, on the same footing with those in Great Britain, till the new Parliament, representing the whole, shall think it for the interest of the whole to re-enact some or all of them." [5]　If Pownall's scheme of a central department for the management of colonial affairs had been adopted, if that department had been informed of the actual state of the colonies by means of his proposed commission, and if the colonies had been given representation in Parliament, the relations between Great Britain and her colonies might have been settled on a permanent and a satisfactory basis.　But under existing political conditions it was absurd to hope that these

[1] Above 79.　　　　　　　　　[2] Administration of the Colonies (4th ed.) 31-34.
[3] Op. cit. 141 seqq.
[4] Wealth of Nations (Cannan's ed.) ii 121-122, 123-124.
[5] Political Pieces written by Franklin (1779) 129.

far-reaching schemes would get a hearing.[1]   The existing departments which managed colonial affairs would certainly have
objected to a scheme which would have entailed the loss of their
power and patronage.   The merchants would have objected to
a revision of the Acts of Trade ;   and their opposition would
have been decisive, for, as Franklin truly said, the interests of
particular sets of artificers and traders were " more regarded
than all the colonies." [2]   The politicians would have objected
to a change in the representative system, which would have
disturbed the adjustment of that elaborate system of influence,
by means of which the composition of the House of Commons
was determined, and the relations between the two political
parties were settled.[3]   And so the existing system, with all those
causes of irritation, which were producing ever-increasing tension between Great Britain and her colonies, was allowed to
continue.   We shall now see that the changes in domestic
politics produced by the accession of George III, the changes
in colonial politics which were produced by the successful issue
of the Seven Years' War, and the policy pursued by Great Britain
as the result of these changes, made a conflict between Great
Britain and her American colonies inevitable.

(4) *The causes and effects of the American Revolution.*

The many causes which had long been making the colonies
dissatisfied with the existing relations between themselves and
Great Britain were intensified and aggravated by the new problems which arose after the Seven Years' War.   Victory had been
won ; but at a great cost.   Great Britain's debt had been doubled,
and the cost of naval and military defence was large.[4]   Neither
the Albany conference in 1754, nor the plan suggested by the
Board of Trade in the same year, had succeeded in producing
a scheme for a federal union to take over defence and Indian

---

[1] See Pownall, op. cit. 165-171, for some of the current British and American
objections.
[2] Political Pieces written by Franklin (1779) 129-130.
[3] Vol. x 577-580 ; Adam Smith tried to meet this objection by the argument that
" if the number of American representatives were to be in proportion to the produce
of American taxation, the number of people to be managed would increase exactly
in proportion to the means of managing them ; and the means of managing, to the
number of people to be managed.   The monarchical and democratical parts of the
constitution would, after the union, stand exactly in the same degree of relative force
with regard to one another as they had done before," Wealth of Nations (Cannan's
ed.) ii 124 ; but this view took too little account of the elaboration of the machinery
by which Parliament was managed and the relations of the two parties were settled ;
Mr. Namier's account of its intricacy makes it clear that neither of the parties would
have approved the intrusion of such a new and incalculable element as a set of representatives from America ; and in a later passage Adam Smith admits that the
obstacles to admitting American representatives to the British Parliament were
practically insurmountable, ibid ii 419.
[4] Berriedale Keith, op. cit. 338.

affairs ; [1] and Pontiac's rebellion in 1763 raised, in an acute form, the problems of trade relations with the Indians, and of colonial defence and the liability for its cost. The policy pursued by some of the colonies with respect to the Indians was the main cause of the rebellion ; and the colonies had been very backward in providing for their own defence. In fact, the main burden had fallen on the British regiments in America.[2] It was obvious that the colonies must be defended against the Indians ; it was obvious that a unified policy as to Indian affairs ought to be adopted ; it was obvious that since the colonies would not take united or effective action on either of these two matters, action must be taken by the British government ; it was obvious that such action would be costly. Who was to foot the bill ? British ministers were, with some reason, reluctant to add to the burden of the British taxpayer. Therefore the money must be raised somehow or other from America.

Unfortunately for Great Britain the King's chief minister in 1763 was George Grenville. He was acute and industrious, a good lawyer, well versed in the procedure of the House of Commons, and a capable and honest administrator. But his study of the law, and his immersion in the practical details of administration, had narrowed his mind.[3] As Burke said in his sketch of Grenville's character, the study of the law " is not apt, except in persons very happily born, to open and to liberalize the mind exactly in the same proportion " as it quickens and invigorates it ; and " men too much conversant in office, are rarely minds of remarkable enlargement." [4] Grenville had always seen in the Acts of Trade the principal means of securing the subordination of the colonies to Great Britain both politically and economically. These Acts were, as Burke said, " his idol." But it was obvious that the negligent and fraudulent administration of these Acts had made their evasion easy,[5] and that, if this evasion could be stopped, additional revenue could be got from the colonies, which could be applied to their defence. Therefore, in order to raise revenue for this purpose, he determined, in the first place, to amend the Acts of Trade, to enforce them with greater severity, and to use them to raise a revenue ; and, in the second place, to raise a revenue by direct taxation.

The principal Act by which it was sought to effect the first object was the Revenue Act of 1764.[6] That Act recited in its

---

[1] Berriedale Keith, op. cit; 327-329.
[2] Ibid 335-336 ; Camb. Hist. of the Empire i 638-639.
[3] Burke, Speech on American Taxation, Works (Bohn's ed.) i 406-407.
[4] Ibid 407.
[5] As to this see a Treasury memorial of 1763, Acts of the Privy Council (Col. Series) iv 569-572.
[6] 4 George III c. 15.

preamble that it was "expedient that new provisions and regulations should be established for improving the revenue of this kingdom, and securing the navigation and commerce between Great Britain and your Majesty's Dominions in America, which, by the peace, have been so happily enlarged." To effect these objects the Act made considerable rearrangements and alterations of duties,[1] added to the list of enumerated goods,[2] introduced measures to check the evasion of duties,[3] protected customs officers from actions for malicious prosecution whenever there was probable cause for the seizure of the goods,[4] and provided that penalties under the Act could be recovered, not only in the colonial courts of record, but also in the courts of Admiralty or Vice-Admiralty.[5]

There is no doubt that the administration of the Acts of Trade needed to be strengthened. One of the methods of strengthening them, adopted by the Act of 1764, had been suggested by the measures which had been taken during the war to suppress trading with the enemy. During the war many of the colonies had shown a signal absence of patriotism by continuing to trade with, or to assist trading with, the enemy; and the navy had been used to suppress that trade.[6] The navy did not cease to be used to prevent evasion of the Acts of Trade after the war. This practice was recognized by an Act of 1762, which also extended the hovering Acts to ships hovering on the coast of Ireland or any other of his Majesty's dominions.[7] Another method adopted to strengthen the administration of these Acts, was the more extensive use made of writs of assistance. These writs were issued by the court of Exchequer, and under their authority customs officers could call upon a public officer for assistance, and force an entry into houses, ships, or warehouses to search for uncustomed goods.[8] Moreover the whole system of administration was tightened up. In accordance with a Treasury report of 1763, new instructions as to their duties were issued to officers of the customs. They were required to go in person to their stations, to report as to the prevalence of illicit trade, and to suggest measures to suppress it. Naval and military officers were to protect and assist them; and a rearrangement of the courts of Admiralty in the colonies, recommended in the report,[9] was carried out in the following year.[10] But of all the different

---

[1] §§ 1-5.   [2] §§ 27, 28; for the "enumerated goods" see above 84, 85-86.
[3] §§ 23, 29, 30, 33, 35.   [4] § 46.   [5] § 41.
[6] Berriedale Keith, op. cit. 331-333.
[7] 3 George III c. 22 §§ 4 and 9.
[8] Berriedale Keith, op. cit. 135; Camb. Mod. Hist. vii 177-178; their legality was questioned in 1761 in Paxton's Case, but the Massachusetts court upheld it, ibid 177-180; this view of the law was confirmed by 7 George III c. 46 § 10 which declared their use to be legal, below 114 n. 1.
[9] Acts of the Privy Council (Col. Series) iv 569-572.   [10] Ibid iv 663-664.

methods adopted to strengthen the administration of the Acts, the most effective, and therefore the most disliked, was the extension given to the jurisdiction of the reorganized courts of admiralty and vice-admiralty. It was the most effective, because it deprived the defendant of the right to be tried by a jury which was almost certain to acquit him.

But these measures were not by themselves sufficient. The new duties provided by the Act, even after its administration had been thus strengthened, were not expected to raise more than £25,000 a year—"not a seventh of the cost of the army now to be kept in America." [1] It was necessary, therefore, to find some other expedient to raise money. Grenville told the agents for the colonies that he was prepared to raise this necessary revenue by a Stamp Act, and asked them to find out from their colonies whether they had any other suggestions to make as to methods for raising a revenue. [2] They made no suggestions "other than the idea of falling back on the outworn requisition system." [3] And so, after a year's delay, Grenville introduced his Stamp Act [4] in order to effect his second object—the raising of a revenue from America by direct taxation. The Act imposed duties on legal and commercial documents, newspapers, almanacs, pamphlets, cards, and dice; and, as in the case of the Revenue Act of 1764, it allowed penalties incurred under the Act to be sued for in the admiralty and vice-admiralty courts. [5] The Act passed by a majority of 156 votes (205-49) "almost without debate. Two or three members spoke against it, but without force or apparent interest, except a vehement harangue from Colonel Barré." [6] Petitions against the bill were presented by Connecticut, Rhode Island, Virginia, and Carolina, and also by the traders of Jamaica; but, though these petitions were recommended to the House by an order of the Council, the House refused to receive them. [7]

The extent and character of the opposition to the Act took the government by surprise. This fact is the best proof of that want of knowledge of the state of feeling in the American colonies to which Governor Pownall had called attention. [8] It is also the best proof of the wisdom of Walpole and other statesmen, who had steadily refused to consider the projects of taxing America, which had been put forward from time to time in the earlier part of the century. [9] No doubt Grenville, and others who thought with him, could make a good paper case. The

[1] Berriedale Keith, op. cit. 343.   [2] Camb. Hist. of the Empire i 645.

[3] Berriedale Keith, op. cit. 344.   [4] 5 George III c. 12.

[5] Berriedale Keith, op. cit. 344.   [6] Parlt. Hist. xvi 37-38.

[7] Ibid 40; the account given in the Parliamentary History is borne out by Burke's statement in his speech on American taxation, Works (Bohn's ed.) i 421.

[8] Above 105-106.   [9] Berriedale Keith, op. cit. 337-338.

American colonies must be defended. They would not vote money for their defence. It was unreasonable to expect the British taxpayer to shoulder the burden. But in fact it was a case which ignored all the realities of the position, because those who made it were ignorant of them. Both the British merchants and the British governments profited directly and indirectly from the working of the Acts of Trade ; and we have seen that some of these Acts pressed hardly on the colonists, and, from the point of view of both the British and the colonial merchant, needed revision.[1] But the government was ignorant both of the growing feeling in the colonies in favour of revision, and of the growing dissatisfaction with the extent and the kind of control exercised by these Acts over the colonies. The government ignored the fact that it was only the mutual jealousies of the colonies which prevented them from uniting to resist this control ; and therefore it did the very thing against which Governor Pownall had warned it—it supplied them with a principle of union.[2]   The Stamp Act Congress summoned by the Assembly of Massachusetts, which the representatives of nine colonies attended, is the most decisive proof of the folly of the British government, and was a clear sign that the old relations between Great Britain and her colonies could not continue on the old lines.[3]

Before the Stamp Act had actually come into force, Grenville had been succeeded by Rockingham. The House of Commons had been alarmed by the happenings in America, and tried to get some information of the state of feeling in America by an examination of Franklin at the Bar of the House.[4] He put the American case very ably. He tried to convince the House that America had, both in men and money, contributed her full share to her own defence. He admitted the legislative supremacy of Parliament. He admitted the right of Parliament to pass the Acts of Trade, and to regulate commerce by import and export duties. He said :

The sea is yours ; you maintain, by your fleet, the safety of navigation in it, and keep it clear of pirates ; you may have therefore a natural and equitable right to some toll or duty on merchandizes carried through that part of your dominions, towards defraying the expense you are at in ships to maintain the safety of that carriage.[5]

[1] Above 104-105.
[2] " And as it is not more necessary to preserve the several governments sub-ordinate in their respective orbs, than it is essential to the preservation of the whole empire to keep them disconnected and independent of each other, they must be guarded by this union against having or forming any principle of coherence with each other, above that whereby they cohere to this centre [Great Britain], the first mover," Pownall, Administration of the Colonies (4th ed.) 34-35 ; cp. ibid 93-94.
[3] Camb. Hist. of the Empire i 656.
[4] Parlt. Hist. xvi 137-160.   [5] Ibid 149.

But he made it quite clear that no colony could submit to any internal tax, and that only the repeal of the tax would restore America to its former obedience. Direct taxes, he said, had never been imposed on Ireland by the Parliament of Great Britain, and that Parliament had no more right to impose them on the colonies than they had on Ireland.[1] Franklin was not quite accurate when he said that, before 1763, the Americans "submitted willingly to the government of the Crown," and that they were governed "at the expense only of a little pen, ink and paper."[2] He exaggerated the willingness with which they complied with the Acts of Trade. But there is no doubt that he was accurate when he told the House of Commons that nothing would induce the Americans to submit to a direct internal tax ; that they did not otherwise dispute the sovereignty of Parliament ; and that therefore they would acquiesce in other exercises of the authority of the Parliament of Great Britain.

The House of Commons acted on this advice when it repealed the Stamp Act in 1766 ;[3] and, at the same time, passed an Act which, following the precedent of the Act passed in 1719 with reference to Ireland,[4] declared the right of Parliament to make laws for the colonies, and annulled all resolutions, votes, orders, and proceedings in any of the colonies, in which this right had been denied or questioned.[5] This action of the House of Commons got rid of the immediate cause which had made the differences between Great Britain and her colonies acute. But it did nothing to settle the larger causes of difference, which had been accumulating during the eighteenth century. Those causes of difference had now become more acute as the result of the Stamp Act agitation. The different colonies had found a bond of union. The whole question of Great Britain's powers of control over her colonies was being considered by many acute lawyers and politicians. It was inevitable, therefore, that many other constitutional questions, besides the right of Great Britain to impose direct taxation, should begin to be canvassed. It was clear that a militant party was forming which was inclined to advocate, if not independence, the greatest possible diminution of Great Britain's powers of control ; and it was also clear that the democratic atmosphere and conditions which prevailed in many of the colonies, would enable a militant minority to arouse the passions of the mob, and to use those passions to impose its will upon a comparatively lethargic majority. The situation was far more difficult and dangerous than anyone in England imagined ; and only the most consummate statesmanship could have found a peaceful conclusion.

[1] Parlt. Hist. xvi 156.
[2] Ibid 140-141.
[3] 6 George III c. 11.
[4] Above 31
[5] 6 George III c. 12.

The men in power were very ordinary politicians.   George III would tolerate no others ; and Chatham was disabled by illness. To some extent, it may be, they were misled by Franklin's insistence that, once the attempt to levy direct taxation was given up, the trouble would be over ; and that no American would object to recognizing the sovereignty of Parliament, or its right to impose customs duties.   There is no doubt that Chatham [1] and Burke [2] in 1774 exaggerated the effect upon America of the repeal of the Stamp Act.   It was forgotten that the general question of the right to tax had been raised ; and that the strict enforcement of the Acts of Trade, and the proceedings of the Admiralty and Vice-Admiralty courts, were causing increased irritation.   The ministers seem to have been ignorant of the fact that American opinion was now inclining to the view that, though it might be within the competence of Parliament to impose duties for the purpose of enforcing the Acts of Trade, it had no right to impose duties for the purpose of raising a revenue ; and that therefore the Revenue Act of 1764 and the later Acts, in so far as they were passed for the latter purpose, were so many infringements upon the constitutional rights of the colonies.[3]   It was because Charles Townshend, the chancellor of the exchequer, was ignorant of the real state of feeling in America, it was because he wished to please all parties in the House, that he thought that he could make use of the distinction between internal and external taxation, which had emerged during the discussions on the Stamp Act, and raise a revenue from America by import duties.[4]   He ridiculed the validity of the distinction ; but, since the Americans set such store by it, he was prepared to humour them, and raise his revenue in a way to which they had admitted they did not object.[5]   It was a scheme which was likely to commend itself to a clever House of Commons politician with great powers of speech and debate, but with no gifts of statesmanship ; [6] and, since it was advocated by a man who was a universal favourite, it was naturally adopted by a House, which was irritated by the

---

[1] Parlt. Hist. xvii 1353-1354.

[2] See Works (Bohn's ed.) i 423-424.

[3] See Camb. Mod. Hist. vii 204 ; cp. Burke, Speech on American Taxation, Works i 409, 431.

[4] Lecky, History of England iv 107-111 ; see Burke's sketch of Townshend's character in his speech on American Taxation, Works i 426-429.

[5] Lecky, op. cit. iv 110.

[6] " If mere cleverness were the criterion of statesmanship, Townshend is entitled to admiration.   The colonists were fairly caught in their own argument. The new taxes were external, and therefore admittedly constitutional," Camb. Hist. of the Empire i 664 ; of his wit, cleverness, and extraordinary debating power there can be no question, see the account given by Horace Walpole, Letters (ed. Toynbee) vii 105 note ; but, if Walpole is to be believed, he was so unprincipled that his dealings on the Stock Exchange in India stock determined his political conduct.

disobedience of New York to the clause in the Mutiny Act which required them to provide food and quarters for the troops, and by the growing disregard of the Americans for the authority of Parliament.

At the same time as the Act imposing import duties on tea, paper, red and white lead, painters' colours, and glass was passed,[1] another Act was passed to provide for " the more speedy and effectual collection " of these duties. This Act set up a separate Board of Customs, the members of which were to be resident in America.[2] A third Act suspended the legislative powers of the Assembly of New York till it had complied with the provisions of the Mutiny Act.[3]

Townshend's duties did not arouse so immediate and so universal a resistance as that aroused by the Stamp Act. But in the New England colonies, where the desire for independence was rapidly becoming stronger, they were fiercely opposed. It was contended, in effect, that, though Parliament might regulate trade, it had no right to interfere with the internal affairs of the colonies, and, more especially, that it had no right to pass Acts to raise revenue by any means. The claim of Parliament to exercise these powers was said to be contrary to the laws of nature, and an infringement of the rights of man.[4] Massachusetts was the centre of resistance ; and the riots, and the proceedings of the Boston town meeting, seemed to indicate so treasonable a tendency, that both Houses petitioned the King to issue a commission to bring the ringleaders to London, and try them under a statute of 1543-1544,[5] which provided for the trial of treasons committed outside the realm.[6] But it was becoming more and more obvious that it was not only Massachusetts that was prepared to resist any attempt by Parliament to impose any kind of taxation direct or indirect. Virginia protested both against taxation and against the project to try Americans in England.[7]

The American cause was most powerfully assisted by the futile policy of the ministry. Trade with America was dislocated ; and it was obvious that the duties could not be collected. There were only three possible policies—the policy of retaining the duties and collecting them by military force, the policy of simply repealing the duties, or the really statesmanlike policy of reviewing the whole question of the relation

[1] 7 George III c. 46 ; § 10 of the Act, in order to obviate the doubts which had arisen as to the legality of writs of assistance, declared that their use was legal, and permitted their issue by the supreme court of any colony ; coffee, cocoa, and tea exported to the colonies were freed from the duty they formerly paid on import into England, 7 George III c. 46 § 6 ; c. 56.

[2] Ibid c. 41. [3] Ibid c. 59.

[4] Camb. Hist. of the Empire i 665, citing John Dickinson's *Letters from a Farmer*.

[5] 35 Henry VIII c. 2 ; vol. iv 524. [6] Parlt. Hist. xvi 476-480.

[7] Camb. Hist. of the Empire i 668.

of the colonies to Great Britain in the light of actual conditions. None of the ministers saw the necessity for the third course ; and, instead of adopting either of the other two courses, they combined the disadvantages of both by repealing all the duties except the three-penny tax on tea, which they retained in order to assert the authority of Parliament. It was, as Burke called it " a tax of sophistry, a tax of pedantry, a tax of disputation, a tax of war and rebellion " ; [1] for " the repeal of the rest of Townshend's Act gave the agitators in America the stimulus of a triumph, and the retention of the tea tax left them with a grievance over a principle." [2] It was because this grievance was left, and because other long-standing differences between the Crown and the colonies, and more especially the differences arising out of the administration of the Acts of Trade, were left unremedied, that the militant minority, who now wished for independence, was able to get control.

Such incidents as the burning of H.M.S. Gaspée by the Rhode Islanders, Wedderburn's attack on Franklin for his conduct in the matter of the Whateley letters, [3] and the destruction of the tea in Boston harbour, exasperated public opinion in England. In 1774 Acts were passed closing the port of Boston, [4] providing that persons indicted for murder on account of their efforts to suppress riots in Boston should be tried in England, [5] and modifying the charter of Massachusetts. [6] Neither Chatham nor Burke could turn Parliament from the course upon which it had entered. The majority took the obvious and short-sighted view that only force could secure obedience, and the ministry were foolish enough to allow punitive measures to be passed without making any adequate preparations to enforce them. On the other hand, the militant party in Boston took measures to secure a united resistance by summoning a congress at Philadelphia, to which all the American colonies, except Canada, Florida, and Georgia, sent delegates. [7] That party soon got control of the congress, and, following the usual practice of militant democracies, it adopted the policy of intimidating those opponents whom it could not otherwise persuade. [8]

[1] Speech on American Taxation, Works i 391.
[2] Camb. Hist. of the Empire i 669.
[3] As late as Oct., 1775, Franklin wrote to Strahan, " send us over hither fair proposals of peace if you choose it, and nobody shall be more ready than myself to promote their acceptation ; for I make it a rule not to mix personal resentments with public business," Calendar of Home Office Papers 1773-1775, 437.
[4] 14 George III c. 19.   [5] Ibid c. 39.
[6] Ibid c. 45.   [7] Camb. Hist. of the Empire i 676.
[8] " American revolutionaries, like their French successors, quickly realised that the rights of man are not like the rains of Heaven which descend upon the just and the unjust, but that by some perhaps divine dispensation they are withheld from one's opponents. All over the country, but especially in New England, a reign of terror was being directed against supporters of the British government. Loyal farmers were tarred and feathered and driven off their lands," ibid i 677.

Such Acts of Congress as the Declaration of Rights, which demanded the repeal of no less than thirteen Acts of Parliament, and the adoption of an agreement to stop all commercial relations with Great Britain ; [1] such events as the setting up in Massachusetts of a provincial congress [2]—showed that separation was inevitable. Naturally anti-American opinion in England hardened. In 1775, in spite of Chatham's [3] and Burke's efforts to avert the coming conflict, Acts were passed to restrain the trade of the American colonies with Great Britain, Ireland, and the West Indies ; [4] and a last-minute offer by North to exempt any colony from taxation, which offered to vote an adequate sum for the support of its government, was rejected.[5] In April, 1775, the first skirmish in the now inevitable war was fought at Lexington, and it was followed in June by the battle of Bunker Hill. In 1776 the trenchant, one-sided, and largely a priori reasoning of Paine's timely pamphlet *Common Sense*, which demonstrated the futility of all appeals to constitutional law, coupled with the fact, which had been pointed out by Paine, that French aid could not be got unless a complete severance from Great Britain was made, produced the acceptance, on July 4, 1776, of the Declaration of Independence. But to appreciate the character of this document, its underlying theory, and the arguments by which that theory was supported, it is necessary to consider the arguments which Great Britain and her colonies had been using to support their claims.

The controversy between Great Britain and her colonies, like the controversy between Parliament and the Stuart kings, was cast into a legal mould. The events of, and the arguments used in, the earlier, were always present to the minds of the parties to the later, controversy. In fact there were many points of similarity between the two controversies, and there were also many points of difference.

Both controversies centred largely round fiscal questions, because in both cases fiscal difficulties had necessitated new methods of raising a revenue, the legality of which was asserted by one party and denied by the other. It is not therefore surprising to find that there was a striking similarity in some of the distinctions taken and the arguments used. The distinction taken in *Bates's Case* between a tax imposed for the

---

[1] Camb. Hist. of the Empire i 677-679.　　[2] Ibid i 679-680.

[3] For Chatham's speech on the motion to withdraw the troops from Boston see Parlt. Hist. xviii 149-155 ; for his bill for settling the American trouble see ibid xviii 198-203—it is doubtful whether at that date it would have been accepted by the Americans as a basis of negotiation.

[4] 15 George III cc. 10 and 18 ; 16 George III c. 5.

[5] Camb. Hist. of the Empire i 680; Burke denounced the offer as futile, Speech on Conciliation with America, Works i 454, 502-505.

regulation of trade and a tax imposed to raise a revenue,[1] was taken by both Franklin and Burke, and figured prominently in the American argument ; and in the eighteenth, as in the seventeenth century, the distinction was found to be useless in practice. Just as James I used the decision in *Bates's Case* to raise a revenue,[2] so Grenville used the machinery of the Acts of Trade. Again, in both controversies, it was not the amount of the taxation which was the burden of the complaint, but the principle involved in the imposition of any taxation, by the Crown in the earlier period, and by Parliament in the later. As Burke said,

> The feelings of the colonies were formerly the feelings of Great Britain. Their's were formerly the feelings of Mr. Hampden when called upon for the payment of twenty shillings. Would twenty shillings have ruined Mr. Hampden's fortune ? No ! but the payment of half twenty shillings, on the principles it was demanded, would have made him a slave.[3]

And the resemblances went deeper than the particular causes of controversy. Just as the Parliamentary opposition to the Stuarts was largely due to the fact that the Tudor despotism had done its work so well, that the country had become fitted to exercise the larger measure of liberty which it demanded ; [4] so the British control over the colonies had enabled them to become full-grown states, which naturally demanded a relaxation of that political and economic dependence which had been salutary and necessary when they were infant communities.[5] Just as the inability of the Stuarts to see that changed circumstances demanded a revision of the relations between Parliament and the Crown led to civil war ; so the inability of Great Britain to see that the changed political and economic conditions of the colonies demanded a revision of the relations between her and her colonies led to the war of independence.

There were also substantial differences between the two controversies. The fact that the eighteenth-century controversy was not, like the earlier controversy, a contest between the prerogative and Parliament, but a controversy between the King in Parliament and the colonies, made the legal arguments somewhat unreal. We have seen that, sometime before the controversy began to grow acute, the sovereignty of the King in Parliament had become a universally accepted legal doctrine.[6] But it was obviously very much more difficult to prove the legal incorrectness of the actions of an admittedly sovereign

[1] Vol. vi 43-45.   [2] Ibid vi 45-48.
[3] Speech on American Taxation, Works i 392 ; as Chatham said, " the spirit which now resists your taxation in America is the same which formerly opposed loans, benevolences, and ship-money in England," Parlt. Hist. xviii 154.
[4] Vol. vi 5-6, 14-15, 55, 58-66, 80.
[5] Above 102, 103.   [6] Vol. x 526-527, 530-531.

body, than to prove the legal incorrectness of the actions of a King whose prerogative powers were by no means clearly ascertained.   Partly for this reason, and partly because the contentions of the Americans altered in their character as the controversy proceeded, the legal arguments of the Americans were easily disposed of by their opponents.   Complaints of the way in which Parliament had exercised its authority—complaints, for instance, of the extended use made of writs of assistance, of the enlargement of the jurisdiction of the court of Admiralty, of the increased strictness of the Acts of Trade, of the prohibition of public meetings—might prove that Parliament had acted in an impolitic manner : they did not and could not prove that its actions were illegal.   Similarly, if the legislative authority of Parliament was admitted, as it was admitted in the earlier stages of the controversy, it was difficult to prove the illegality of a power to impose a tax.   It was difficult to escape from the force of Lord Mansfield's contention that, if the supreme legislative power over the colonies is in the British Parliament, there was no reason why the British Parliament could not impose a tax;[1] and that, if the chartered colonies were on the same footing as other corporations, and, like them, liable to have their charters forfeited for contraventions of their charters, there was a very good reason for contending that they could be taxed.   " Is it possible to suppose that a legislature can exist with a sole power of laying taxes, which legislature may be destroyed by a process in the courts of Chancery or King's Bench ? "[2]

It was to meet these objections that the Americans put forward three arguments.   One of these arguments was based upon the principles of the British constitution, a second upon the laws of nature, and a third upon a denial of the right of the British Parliament to legislate for the dominions of the Crown outside the realms of England and Scotland.

(i) It was argued that, according to the principles of the British constitution, there could be no taxation without representation.   In support of this argument the precedents of the county palatine of Chester and the principality of Wales were adduced.   These precedents, it was said, showed that communities were not taxed by Parliament so long as they were not represented.[3]   Moreover, it was pointed out that Ireland was taxed only by its own Parliament.[4]   Chatham, in 1760, made use

---

[1] " As a distinction has been taken between the power of laying taxes and making laws, I must declare, that after the most diligent searches on this head, I cannot find any distinction or difference whatever," Parlt. Hist. xvi 175.

[2] Ibid xvi 175-176 ; cp. also Lord Mansfield's speech in 1775, ibid xviii 269-271.

[3] Pownall, Administration of the Colonies (4th ed.) xxi-xxii, 56-60, 144-152, adopts and emphasises this argument.

[4] Franklin made this point in 1766, Parlt. Hist. xvi 156.

of the precedents of Chester, Durham, and Wales; and he maintained that those precedents proved, if any proof was necessary, the principle that taxation without representation was contrary to the principles of the constitution.[1] The reply given, that America was as much represented in the House of Commons as some of the larger towns which returned no members to Parliament, ignored the fact that some of the inhabitants of those towns had votes for the knight of the shire; [2] and the argument that America was "virtually" represented in the House of Commons, in the same way as many places and persons in England were "virtually" represented, ignored the common interest existing between English electors and non-electors, and the absence of this common interest between Englishmen and Americans. "Oppression of the colonies by taxation might be popular in England as giving ease to the people there." [3] We have seen that some suggestions were made that America should send representatives to the House of Commons; but that, for different reasons, that suggestion met with no favour from the leaders of either party to the controversy.[4] Though, politically, this was the strongest argument which the Americans produced, though it gained the support of Chatham and many others, legally it was difficult to support, partly because it was incompatible with the legislative sovereignty of Great Britain, and partly because it was admitted that, for the purpose of trade regulation, duties might be imposed.

(ii) The second argument used was an appeal to those laws of nature, which were incapable of being changed by a merely human legislator, and so were outside the range of Parliamentary sovereignty. There was much mediæval authority for the proposition that the law of nature, like the law of God, was part of the law of all Christian countries and therefore part of the law of England; and that it was superior in binding force to the merely human law of the state.[5] This mediæval theory appears in St. Germain's *Doctor and Student;* [6] and it was restated by Coke in *Calvin's Case.*[7] Locke had stated that there were certain

---

[1] " I come not here armed at all points, with law cases and acts of parliament, with the statute book doubled down in dogs ears, to defend the cause of liberty : if I had, I myself would have cited the two cases of Chester and Durham. I would have cited them to have shown that, even under any arbitrary reigns, parliaments were ashamed of taxing a people without their consent and allowed them representatives. Why did the gentleman confine himself to Chester and Durham ? He might have taken a higher example in Wales ; Wales, that never was taxed by parliament, till it was incorporated," Parlt. Hist. xvi 104.

[2] See McIlwain, The American Revolution 169-170.

[3] Camb. Mod. Hist. vii 194.   [4] Above 106-107.

[5] Vol. ii 443-444, 602-603.   [6] Vol. iv 279-280.

[7] " 2. For the laws : 1. That ligeance or obedience of the subject to the Sovereign is due by the law of nature : 2. That this law of nature is part of the laws of England : 3. That the law of nature was before any judicial or municipal law in the world : 4. That the law of nature is immutable, and cannot be changed," (1609) 7 Co. Rep. at f. 4b.

fundamental laws with which the Legislature ought to comply, and one of these laws was that taxes must not be raised " without the consent of the people given by themselves or their deputies." [1] We have seen that Blackstone agreed with Locke, that the principal aim of society was to protect the rights of man which had been given to them by that law of nature [2] which eighteenth-century thinkers had identified with the law of God ; [3] and that he had expressed views similar to those of St. Germain and Coke as to the incapacity of a merely human Legislature to infringe these laws.[4] It is not therefore surprising to find that, just as Chatham used arguments drawn from the cases of Chester and Wales to prove the thesis that taxation without representation was contrary to law,[5] so Camden used arguments drawn from the overriding law of nature. In 1766, in the debate on a resolution asserting the legislative sovereignty of Parliament over the American colonies, he said, " the omnipotence of the Legislature is a favourite doctrine, but there are some things they cannot do. They cannot enact anything against the divine law, and may forfeit their right. They cannot take away any man's private property without making him a compensation." [6] Later in the year, speaking on the declaratory bill, he said : " My position is this . . . taxation and representation are inseparable. This position is founded on the laws of nature ; it is more, it is itself an eternal law of nature." [7]

But we have seen that the recognition of the sovereignty of Parliament had destroyed the validity of these arguments.[8] They rested upon a political theory which the establishment of the modern state had rendered obsolete. We have seen that the view that courts could control Acts of Parliament and adjudge them to be void was never the accepted view of English lawyers [9]—as Otis found when he argued that if writs of assistance were sanctioned by statute, the statute would be void.[10] We have seen that the passages in Blackstone, which give countenance to the idea that there is an overriding law of nature, which all human Legislatures must obey, are contrary to other passages in which the sovereignty of Parliament is recognized.[11] We have seen also that, although there is no room for a sovereign in Locke's theory of government, the need for a sovereign was recognized at the end of the seventeenth century ; [12] and that Blackstone dissented from Locke's view that there is a right

---

[1] Two Treatises of Government Bk. ii § 142, cited vol. vi 286.
[2] Vol. x 528.   [3] Vol. x 8.
[4] Comm. i 41, 54, cited vol. x 529 nn. 8 and 9.   [5] Above 118-119.
[6] Parlt. Hist. xvi 168.   [7] Ibid 178.
[8] Vol. x 530.   [9] Vol. ii 442-443.
[10] Camb. Mod. Hist. vii 180.   [11] Vol. x 526-527.
[12] Vol. vi 279-280 ; vol. x 530.

to get rid of a government which fails to preserve those rights for the sake of which governments were created.[1] Moreover, as Professor McIlwain has pointed out,[2] arguments drawn from natural or fundamental law would not justify the claim put forward by the Americans in the later stages of the controversy, that they were totally exempt from the sovereignty of Parliament.

An opposition based on fundamental or natural law alone might properly be justified against *some* statutes of Parliament—the ones alone which infringed that law—but fundamental law provides no justification whatever for the total denial as made by the Congress of the whole legislative authority of Parliament over America.

An effective answer to this argument based on natural rights was made by Dr. Johnson in his tract entitled *Taxation no Tyranny*.[3] He pointed out that the claims of the Americans to an indefeasible right to life, liberty, and property, and their assertion that they had never ceded to any sovereign any control over this right, could not be disputed " while they speak as the naked sons of nature " ; [4] but that, when they went on to claim " all the rights, liberties, and immunities of free and natural-born subjects within the realm of England," " their boast of original rights is at an end—they are no longer in a state of nature." [5] They are ordinary British subjects, subject to the laws made by King in Parliament. And though an English colony " has very liberal powers of regulating its own manners and adjusting its own affairs," it is still subject, just as individual Englishmen are subject, to the sovereign power in the state.[6] And, once sovereignty is conceded, no reservations based on natural rights can be made.

In sovereignty there are no gradations. There may be limited royalty, there may be limited consulship ; but there can be no limited government. There must in every society be some power or other from which there is no appeal, which admits no restrictions, which pervades the whole mass of the community, regulates and adjusts all subordination, enacts laws or repeals them, erects or annuls judicatures, extends or contracts privileges, exempt itself from question or control, and bounded only by physical necessity.[7]

(iii) The third argument, which denied the rights of the British Parliament to legislate for the dominions of the Crown outside the realms of England and Scotland, met the objection based on the sovereignty of the King in Parliament, which was fatal to the other two arguments.[8] This claim was put forward

---

[1] Vol. x 528.   [2] The American Revolution 148-149.
[3] Works (ed. 1824) 167-216.   [4] At p. 186.
[5] At pp. 186-187.   [6] At pp. 179-180.   [7] At p. 180.
[8] " Of all the arguments urged by the Americans, one alone supports the whole of their claim to a right of exemption from parliamentary interference, the argument drawn from the constitutional relation of realm and dominions. . . . No arguments drawn from charters, or even from natural or fundamental law will sufficiently justify it," McIlwain, The American Revolution 148.

by the Assembly of Massachusetts in 1773,[1] and by the Continental Congress in 1774.[2]   In support of this argument considerable use was made of deductions drawn from the rule laid down in *Calvin's Case*, that allegiance was due to the natural person of the King.[3]   The allegiance of the colonists, it was said, was due to his natural person, not to him in his capacity of King of England.   That being so, the colonies were no more bound by the legislation of the British Parliament than Scotland was bound by the legislation of the English Parliament before the Act of Union.[4]   But this argument ignored the distinction, which was recognized by *Calvin's Case*,[5] and later in the case of *Craw v. Ramsey*,[6] between Ireland, the Channel Islands, the Isle of Man, Berwick, and " all the English plantations " on the one hand, and Scotland on the other.   The plantations were " dominions belonging to the Crown of England " : " Scotland was not a dominion belonging to the Crown of England, but to the King of England."   Over territories belonging to the Crown of England Parliament had legislative power : over territories belonging to the King of England it had not.[7]

It is true that James I had inclined to the view that the colonies ought to be ruled by the prerogative, and that Parliament ought not to interfere with their government.[8]   But this idea was repudiated by the Parliamentary leaders ;[9] and the events of the seventeenth century had established the sovereignty of the King in Parliament.   It had therefore become clear, as Lord Mansfield said in the case of *Campbell v. Hall*,[10] that even the large powers which the King had over conquered or ceded colonies, were " subordinate to his own authority, as a part of

---

[1] McIlwain, The American Revolution 122-137.

[2] Ibid 114-117 ; the Congress said, " that the foundation of English liberty, and of all free government, is a right in the people to participate in their legislative council ; and as the English colonists are not represented, and from their local and other circumstances, they cannot properly be represented in the British parliament, they are entitled to a free and exclusive power of legislation in their several provincial legislatures . . . in all cases of taxation and internal polity, subject only to the negative of the sovereign," ibid 115.

[3] Vol. ix 81-82.   [4] See McIlwain, The American Revolution 94-95.

[5] It was said that Ireland, being a conquered country, was bound by English Acts of Parliament, 7 Co. Rep. at f. 17b ; but that Scotland was governed by a distinct law, and had a distinct and separate Parliament, ibid at f. 15a.

[6] (1670) Vaughan 274.

[7] " Ireland differs from Scotland, in a common difference with Guernsey, Jersey, Isle of Man, Berwick, and all the English plantations, for that they are dominions belonging to the Crown of England, which Scotland is not. . . . A man born subject to one that is King of England, cannot inherit in England, for then the antenati in Scotland had inherited in England. . . . A subject born in any dominion belonging to the Crown of England is inheritable in England as well as native Englishmen," (1670) Vaughan at pp. 278, 279 ; cp. Campbell v. Hall (1774) 20 S.T. at p. 275.

[8] See Campbell v. Hall (1774) 20 S.T. at pp. 274-275 *per* Alleyn *arg.* ; cp. Berriedale Keith, op. cit. 9 ; below 233.

[9] 20 S.T. at p. 275.   [10] Ibid at p. 323.

the supreme Legislature in Parliament," and that he could make no laws " excepting from the authority of Parliament." In that case Wallace, the solicitor-general, who argued for the defendant, remarked upon the inconsistency of the plaintiff's argument with the American view that the English Parliament had no authority over the colonies.[1]

In fact the authority of Parliament over the colonies is supported by very many instances in which the English Parliament, or the Parliament of Great Britain, had exercised legislative power over Wales, the Channel Isles, the Isle of Man and the colonies.[2] We have seen that it was the better opinion that the English and later the British Parliament exercised this power over Ireland ; [3] and the evidence that it exercised a similar power over the colonies is so strong that it has generally been accepted as conclusive on both sides of the Atlantic.   The principal dissentient is Professor McIlwain.   In his book on *The American Revolution*, he has contended for the correctness of the view that the British Parliament had no right to legislate for the dominions of the Crown outside Great Britain.   His argument is to some extent in line with his argument as to the position and functions of Parliament, which he put forward in his book on *The High Court of Parliament*.   But we have seen that he adopts in that book a view as to the position of Parliament which exaggerates the mediæval elements contained in it, and unduly minimizes its position as the supreme legislative authority in the state, which it had attained in the latter part of the mediæval and in the Tudor period.[4] Similarly he adopts in his book on *The American Revolution* a view as to the legislative powers of Parliament over Ireland and the colonies, which negatives the distinction between dominions belonging to the Crown of England and dominions belonging to the King of England, and minimizes or explains away the many cases in which Parliament, from an early date, exercised legislative authority over Ireland and the colonies.   But both Professor Schuyler [5] and Professor Berriedale Keith [6] have shown so conclusively that Professor McIlwain's arguments cannot be supported that it is superfluous to add anything to their statements.

Although it was inevitable that the controversy between

---

[1] " And here I cannot help observing that it is a great change in the language of America to insist as they have done, and do, that the Parliament of England has no right to tax them, but that they derive their constitution from the king only : and now to say, in this cause, that the king has no power over them but as the head of the British constitution," ibid at p. 281 ; for the decision in this case see below 237-238.

[2] Schuyler, Parliament and the British Empire 8-34.

[3] Above 28 and n. 3.

[4] Vol. ii 434 nn. 4 and 5, 442 n. 1 ; vol. iv 183-187, 186 n. 4.

[5] Parliament and the British Empire chap. i.

[6] The First British Empire 380-383.

Great Britain and her colonies should be cast into a legal mould, it was unfortunate, because it obscured the substantial causes of those differences. Just as in the seventeenth century the legal form in which the issues between the Stuart kings and their Parliaments were stated, obscured the fact that the Tudor despotism had given so good a political education to the nation, that the time had come to revise the terms of the partnership between the Crown and Parliament, which had prevailed during the Tudor period ; so in the eighteenth century the legal form in which the issues between Great Britain and her colonies were stated obscured the fact that the protection, and the political and economic tutelage of Great Britain, during the seventeenth and early eighteenth centuries, had caused the colonies to come to political maturity so rapidly, that the time had come to revise the terms of the partnership between them and the mother country.[1] And the fact that the controversy was cast into this legal mould did more harm in the eighteenth than in the seventeenth century. In the seventeenth century the legal points at issue were less settled by authority, so that large play was left for considerations of expediency or public policy. In the eighteenth century the legal points at issue were settled by authority, so that less play was left for such considerations. It was more easy to prove that the legal arguments used by Americans were wrong ; and it was inevitable that those whose minds were narrowed by an exclusively legal outlook should regard this as decisive. It was inevitable also that many circumstances—the financial difficulties of Great Britain, the expense of defending the colonies, allegations that the colonies were not paying their fair share towards the cost of defence, evasions of the Acts of Trade, the turbulence of the colonial Assemblies—should create in the minds of many a prejudice against the colonies, and a willingness to press to the utmost the consequences of that legal sovereignty which the law gave to Great Britain.

No doubt there were some statesmen who refused to take the narrow legal point of view, who saw that the issue between Great Britain and her colonies was essentially a political question.

[1] Burke, in his speech on American Taxation, Works (Bohn's ed.) i 403-404, said " I never cast an eye on their flourishing commerce, and their cultivated and commodious life, but they seem to me rather ancient nations grown to perfection through a long series of fortunate events, and a train of successful industry, accumulating wealth in many centuries, than the colonies of yesterday ; than a set of miserable outcasts, a few years ago, not so much sent as thrown out, on the bleak and barren shore of a desolate wilderness, three thousand miles from all civilized intercourse" ; Camden said in 1774, " such [coercive] measures might be very properly exercised in the infancy of colonies, but that when they had acquired power by commerce, and strength by increase of numbers, it was wholly impolitic, if not dangerous, to compel them to submit to laws which tended to lay the least burden or restraint on that trade by which alone they existed," Parlt. Hist. xviii 36-37.

Walpole refused to consider a scheme for taxing the colonies ; [1]
and, if no project for a direct tax was sanctioned by the government till 1766, it was not for want of suggestions that such a
tax should be imposed [2]—there had always been persons who,
refusing to look beyond the narrow legal point of view, supposed that a reference to the sovereignty of Parliament was a
sufficient answer to colonial protests against particular exercises
of it.[3] But, till 1766, this attitude of mind had been kept in
check by more statesmanlike counsels. It was realized that the
Acts of Trade did confer great advantages on Great Britain,[4]
and it was realized that the colonies would not endure taxation
without representation. What was not realized was the strength
of the feeling against such taxation ; and the fact that, if it were
imposed, it would unite the colonies in an opposition which would
teach them their strength and necessitate a revision of their relations with Great Britain. All this was made very clear by the
disturbances which were caused by the enactment of the Stamp
Act. Chatham, in advocating the repeal of the Act, said, in
the debate on the Address, that the whole question of America
ought to be discussed,[5] and protested against treating the question of taxation as a dry legal question.[6] Governor Johnstone,
answering Mansfield's argument that right to tax and the right
to legislate could not be logically separated, pointed out that
" the various privileges which subsist in every free state are
hardly to be determined by any reasoning *a priori*." [7] Camden's

---

[1] Berriedale Keith, op. cit. 337.   [2] Ibid 337-338.

[3] In 1733 there was a debate on a petition of Rhode Island against the Sugar
Colony Bill ; a member said, " it has been the custom ever since the Revolution to
refuse receiving petitions against any duties to be laid on, and that without any distinction whether the duties to be laid on were for the raising of money or for the
regulation of trade : as our colonies are all a part of the people of Great Britain,
they are generally represented in this House as well as the rest of the people are,"
Parlt. Hist. viii 1264.

[4] This was Burke's argument ; he said, " all this was done by England,
whilst England pursued trade, and forgot revenue. You not only acquired commerce, but you actually created the very objects of trade in America ; and by that
creation you raised the trade of this kingdom at least fourfold. America had the
compensation of your capital which made her bear her servitude. She had another compensation which you are now going to take away from her. She had,
except the commercial restraint, every characteristic mark of a free people in all
her internal concerns," Works i 404 ; this was also Chatham's view ; he said that
from careful enquiries made while in office, he could say " that the profits to Great
Britain from the trade of the colonies, through all its branches, is two millions a
year. This is the fund that carried you triumphantly through the last war, the
estates that were rented at two thousand pounds a year, three score years ago, are
at three thousand pounds at present. Those estates sold then from fifteen to eighteen
years' purchase ; the same may be now sold for thirty. You owe this to America.
This is the price that America pays for your protection," Parlt. Hist. xvi 105-106.

[5] Ibid 98, 106.

[6] Ibid 104 ; in 1775 Chatham said, " as to the metaphysical refinements,
attempting to show that the Americans are equally free from obedience and commercial restraints, as from taxation for revenue, as being unrepresented here, I
pronounce them futile, frivolous, and groundless," Parlt. Hist. xviii 150-151.

[7] Ibid 62.

appeals to natural law show that he looked beyond legal technicalities.[1] But both Chatham and Camden were obliged, to some
extent, to treat the question from a legal point of view ; and
therefore neither could put it on its true ground. Neither could
base his case solely and squarely on the true political ground,
that changed circumstances had necessitated a revision of the
terms of the partnership between Great Britain and her colonies.

Pownall in his book on the colonies, had made all this very
clear ; and in Parliament he,[2] Burke,[3] and others [4] helped to
state the colonial case. But the unwise policy of the ministers
who succeeded Rockingham, the disturbances which followed in
America, the measures taken to deal with those disturbances,
the nature of the arguments used by American lawyers and
politicians, and the extending claims to autonomy which were
supported by those arguments—all hardened English public
opinion against the Americans, and prevented a statesmanlike
consideration of the American question in all its bearings—
political and economical as well as legal. Opinion was tending
in the direction of Mansfield's narrow view that either " the
supremacy of the British legislature must be complete, entire,
and unconditional ; or, on the other hand, the colonies must
be free and independent." [5] It was not till Burke's two great
speeches in 1774 [6] and 1775 [7] that the question in all its bearings
was at length stated in Parliament impartially and philosophically,
not as a legal question, but as a political problem, which demanded for its solution the application of considerations based
solely on statesmanship.

In those speeches Burke tried to make his audience realize
the real nature of the problem ; to teach them that it was only

[1] Above 120 ; cp. his remarks in 1775 when he said, " he would not enter into
the large field of discussion or collateral reasoning, applicable to the abstruse and
metaphysical distinctions necessary to the investigation of the omnipotence of Parliament ; but this he would venture to assert, that the natural right of mankind, and
the immutable laws of justice, were clearly in favour of the Americans," Parlt.
Hist. xviii 164.

[2] Parlt. Hist. xvi 331-341, 494-507, 610-622, 859-870 ; ibid xvii 1282-1286.

[3] Above 124, below 127-128.

[4] See e.g. Rockingham's speech in 1770, Parlt. Hist. xvi 1020-1022 ; he said
that the project of taxing America was, if not illegal, obviously injudicious—" while
they submitted to regulate their commerce by our discretion, they thought it hard
that their property should also be at our disposal " ; that they should have been
guilty of some excesses in opposing this taxation was not surprising ; " the mother
country herself upon particular occasions is not able to restrain the spirit of her own
populace, even when they have apparently less foundations for complaint. She
should consequently learn to make the same excuses for the Americans which she
requires for herself, and recollect that few popular insurrections have ever taken
place in an English government, without having a strong appearance of justice,
if they were not originally justified by the error of the governors."

[5] Parlt. Hist. xviii 269.

[6] Speech on American Taxation, Works (Bohn's ed.) i 382-437.

[7] Speech on Conciliation with America, ibid 450-512.

through an understanding of how the relations between Great
Britain and America had been shaped or had shaped themselves,
that the problem could be understood ; and to prove to them that
it was only by concessions to the colonies that their confidence
could be regained, and an harmonious partnership established
between the different members of the British Empire. He
brushed aside all the questions which had been raised as to
Great Britain's rights of sovereignty—" I do not enter into
these metaphysical distinctions ; I hate the very sound of them." [1]
" If that sovereignty and their freedom cannot be reconciled,
which will they take ? They will cast your sovereignty in your
face. Nobody will be argued into slavery." [2] To argue too
logically from speculative principles in political matters leads to
sophistries and absurdities ; and will very likely lead to dangerous
results. [3]

I can scarcely conceive anything more completely imprudent, than
for the head of the empire to insist, that if any privilege is pleaded
against his will, or his acts, his whole authority is denied. . . . Will
not this very soon teach the provinces to make no distinction on their
part ? Will it not teach them that the government, against which a
claim of liberty is tantamount to high treason, is a government to
which submission is equivalent to slavery ? It may not always be
quite convenient to impress dependent communities with such an
idea. [4]

He likewise brushed aside all questions of merely legal right.
The question of the legal right to tax raised " deep questions
where great names militate against each other ; where reason is
perplexed, and an appeal to authorities only thickens the confusion." [5] The question at issue was not the determination of
a point of law, but the restoration of tranquility. [6]

The only solution was to create an enduring partnership
between the colonies and Great Britain—" to admit the people
of our colonies into an interest in the constitution." [7] Force
was no solution. The rate of increase in their population ;

[1] Works i 432.   [2] Ibid 433.
[3] " It is a very great mistake to imagine that mankind follow up practically
any speculative principle either of government or of freedom, as far as it will go in
argument and logical illation. We Englishmen stop very short of the principles
upon which we support any given part of our constitution ; or even the whole of it
together," ibid i 500 ; this expressed an opinion held by many ; in Nov., 1775, an
American wrote, " *Declare you will not tax us.* I know you don't mean it, and
don't be too tenacious of words, to wit, a supremacy of Parliament in all cases ;
and the work will soon be done. Don't let us quarrel for the shadow and lose the
substance," Calendar of Home Office Papers 1773-1775, 481.
[4] Works i 476-477.   [5] Ibid 479.
[6] " I am not determining a point of law ; I am restoring tranquility ; and the
general character and situation of a people must determine what sort of government is fitted for them. That point nothing else can or ought to determine," ibid
i 480.
[7] Ibid.

their progress in commerce, and in agriculture ; their ingrained love of liberty fostered by the forms of their constitutions, by their laws and legal studies, and by their religion ; their distance —showed that force, even if successful, could have only a temporary effect, and that it would ruin the thing which was fought for.[1] It was impossible to use the weapons of the criminal law—" the thing seems a great deal too big for any ideas of jurisprudence. . . . I do not know the method of drawing up an indictment against a whole people." [2] The only method of conciliation was a readjustment of relations. The precedents of Wales, of Chester, and of Durham showed that when they were given the right of returning representatives to Parliament, and were thus admitted into partnership with England, all the old difficulties disappeared.[3] Distance, it is true, made the representation of America in Parliament impossible.[4] But another relationship was possible, based upon the freedom of the colonies in their internal concerns, coupled with the control of Parliament over matters which concerned the whole empire.

The parliament of Great Britain sits at the head of her extensive empire in two capacities : in one as the local legislature of this island . . . the other, and I think her nobler character, is what I call her imperial character ; in which . . . she superintends all the inferior legislatures, and guides and controls them all, without annihilating any. . . . It is necessary to coerce the negligent, to restrain the violent, and to aid the weak and deficient, by the overruling plenitude of her power. She is never to intrude into the place of others, whilst they are equal to the common ends of their institution.[5] . . . England is the head, but she is not the head and members too.[6]

The true bond of union was a partnership founded on " common names, kindred blood, similar privileges, and equal protection " —a participation in a common freedom.

Slavery they can have anywhere. It is a weed that grows in every soil. . . . Freedom they can have from none but you. This is the commodity of price, of which you have the monopoly. This is the true act of navigation, which binds to you the commerce of the colonies, and secures to you the wealth of the world.[7]

These principles, he said, will no doubt appear to be visionary theories to " the vulgar and the mechanical politician," to those who think that " nothing exists but what is gross and material " ; but not to those who have realized that " magnanimity in politics is not seldom the truest wisdom ; and a great empire and little minds go ill together." [8]

It is true that Burke's speeches ignored the fact that there was a growing tension between the colonies and Great Britain

[1] Works i 456-469. [2] Ibid 476. [3] Ibid 483-488.
[4] Ibid 488-489. [5] Ibid 434. [6] Ibid 501.
[7] Ibid 508. [8] Ibid 509.

before the project of taxing America matured.[1] It is true that, when they were spoken, the colonies would hardly have acquiesced in the position of authority which he claimed for the British Parliament. But they were the most statesmanlike pronouncement ever made in Parliament upon the principles which should guide the relations between a mother country and her colonies ; and there can be no doubt that they have played a large part in teaching future generations of Englishmen the right way of approaching this problem. To their teaching is due, at least in part, the avoidance of a disruption of the second British Empire which arose out of the ruins of the first. But, though their wisdom and eloquence have not been thrown away, they failed in their immediate object because they came too late. In 1774 the Continental Congress repudiated the sovereignty of Parliament ; war was begun in 1775 ; and in 1776 the Declaration of Independence was issued.

The Declaration begins with a dignified and appropriate preamble : " When in the course of human events it becomes necessary for one people to dissolve the political bands which have connected them with another, and to assume among the powers of the earth, the separate and equal station to which the Laws of Nature and of Nature's God entitle them, a decent respect to the opinions of mankind requires that they should declare the causes which compel them to the separation." It then sets out, first, the political theory which the states had adopted as the guide of their political action ; and, secondly, the concrete facts which, according to that political theory, justified their separation from Great Britain.

(i) The political theory of the states is contained in the following well-known passage in the Declaration :

We hold these truths to be self-evident, that all men are created equal, that they are endowed by their Creator with certain unalienable Rights, that among these are Life, Liberty, and the pursuit of Happiness. That to secure these rights, Governments are instituted among them, deriving their just powers from the consent of the governed. That whenever any Form of Government becomes destructive of these ends, it is the Right of the People to alter or to abolish it, and to institute a new Government, laying its foundation on such principles and organizing its powers in such form, as to them shall seem most likely to effect their Safety and Happiness.

Though the framers of the Declaration of Independence may have been principally inspired by Locke,[2] they projected his theories into societies very different from that aristocratic English society which had carried through the revolution of 1688, and in an intellectual environment very different from that of England at the end of the seventeenth century. Since society in

---

[1] Above 105-106.   [2] Above 119-121.

many of the American colonies, especially in the New England colonies, was democratic, and since it was by an appeal to the people at large, that support was won for the determination to become independent, the "self evident truths" of the Declaration of Independence had a connotation very different from that which they had in Locke's *Two Treatises of Government*. Theories as to the equality of men and their rights had a meaning for the Americans of 1776, who had learned from Rousseau and Paine as well as from Locke, very different from the meaning which they had for the Englishmen of 1688. The measure of this difference can best be seen from a comparison of Paine's *Common Sense* with Locke's *Two Treatises of Government*.

Paine's tract had an immense effect in putting an end to merely legal arguments, and in determining the Americans to declare for independence. In it the democratic elements in Locke's theory are emphasized ; and its method of reasoning displays the strong and weak points of the methods of reasoning employed by those new democratic forces which the American controversy was bringing to the front. It displays much acuteness in its analysis of existing conditions—the colonies had grown up,[1] any connection involving dependency upon Great Britain must be temporary,[2] the colonies were well able to protect themselves,[3] now was the time to declare for separation and independence.[4] It also displays much ingenuity in devising ways and means to effect the object aimed at—examples of this ingenuity are the suggested constitution of Congress,[5] the necessity for a declaration of independence if foreign help or mediation was to be secured,[6] the form which that declaration should take.[7] But it also displays some of the characteristic vices of democratic reasoning—much prejudice,[8] much shallow reasoning which is used to ridicule institutions and theories which are not understood,[9] conspicuous unfairness to opponents,[10] unscrupulousness in the use of any argument which seems likely to effect the object aimed at.[11] It would be unfair to compare Paine's essay to Burke's great speeches on America—Burke was unique in his power to give philosophical judgments on contemporary events, the truth of which posterity has ratified. But, compared with many of the speeches in the British Parliament, and with

[1] The London Reprint of 1776, at pp. 16, 22-23.
[2] At pp. 23, 25.   [3] At pp. 31-37.   [4] At pp. 15, 37.
[5] At pp. 27-29.   [6] At pp. 39-40.   [7] At p. 40.
[8] See the remarks about hereditary monarchy and aristocracy at pp. 4, 10-14.
[9] See the remarks on the theory that the English constitution is a union of three powers which check one another at pp. 4-7.
[10] See the remarks on those who still doubt the policy of separation at p. 20.
[11] For instance, the denial of all advantages in the British connection at pp. 18-19, and the assertion that Great Britain only protected America for her own selfish interests at pp. 16-17.

much that was written on the American side, Paine's essay is deficient in learning, in reasoning, and in appreciation of the nature of the opposing arguments.   It is reasoning of this kind which the growth of the democratic ideas of Paine, and the literal insistence on equality and the natural rights of man, has tended to make the prevalent mode of political reasoning, because it is only reasoning of this kind that the average electors and many of those whom they elect, can understand.

(ii) Having set out the political theory of the Americans, the Declaration goes on to state that " prudence will dictate that governments long established should not be changed for light and transient causes " ;   and then it proceeds to set out the causes which justified their determination to change their government.   Amongst these causes were the following :   The refusal of the King to assent to laws passed by the colonial Assemblies, and his direction to Governors to pass certain laws with a clause suspending their operation till his consent was given.   His refusal to allow an increase in number of representatives to correspond with the increase in the population of certain colonies.   His dissolution of Assemblies which did not comply with his wishes, and his failure to summon new Assemblies. His refusal to assent to laws establishing new courts, and his determination to keep the judges dependent upon his will.   The appointment of new officers " to harass our people and eat out our substance."   The maintenance of a standing army, which was made independent of, and superior to, the civil power.   His assertion of the legislative sovereignty of Parliament, and his assent to legislation passed by Parliament.   The quartering of troops in the colonies.   The imposition of taxes without the assent of the Assemblies.   The limitation of trial by jury.   The policy pursued with regard to the government of Canada.   A number of laws passed, and acts done, either to coerce the rebellious colonies, or in contemplation of the outbreak of the civil war, or in the course of the war after it had actually begun.

No one of the causes for separation assigned by the Declaration of Independence has any legal validity ; and some of the complaints as to acts done in the course of suppressing rebellion or of conducting the war are absurd.   Those who set out to answer the Declaration were able, either by using legal arguments, or by insisting upon the provocations given by the Americans, to present a case which, to the majority of Englishmen who had resolved upon war, seemed conclusive.[1]   But, when all deductions have been made, it is true to say that very many of the causes

[1] Perhaps the best of these answers is that written by John Lind, which was published in 1776.

set out in the Declaration do give a sufficient historical explanation of the reasons for separation.   These causes do set out with substantial truth all those causes of political disagreement between Great Britain and her colonies, which had been accumulating all through the eighteenth century, owing to the development of the colonies on the one hand, and, on the other, to the want of appreciation on the part of Great Britain of the existence and consequences of that development.   They prove the truth of the view set out by Pownall that the only means of relieving the existing tension, and of restoring cordial relations, were a thorough investigation of the state of colonial opinion and of the political and economic conditions and needs of the colonies, and a revision, in the light of that investigation, of the relations between Great Britain and her colonies.[1]

Great Britain, as the result of the war of independence, lost the greater part of her old colonial empire.   But though the greater part of her old empire was lost, its existence, its organization, and the rules of law to which it gave rise, have left deep marks upon the law of England and the United States, and upon the constitution of the United States.

First, it was through the foundation and growth of this empire in the West, and, as we shall see, through the foundation of another empire in the East,[2] that English law was ceasing to be an insular, and was beginning to become a world, system.   The loss of America necessarily caused a large diminution in the territory which owed allegiance to the British Crown, but it caused no diminution of the territory over which English law held sway.   Though the enmity resulting from the civil war caused some hesitation,[3] the fact that American lawyers had been trained in English law, the fact that it was by means of weapons provided from the armoury of English law that they had conducted their legal controversies with Great Britain, and, above all, the fact that Blackstone had summed up the principles of that law in a literary accurate and accessible form, combined to make it inevitable that the principles of English law should be the foundation of the law of the United States.[4]   This enlargement of the territory over which English law held sway, was necessarily followed by developments in many branches of that law.   The fact that English law was assuming a cosmopolitan character caused the rapid development

[1] Above 106.   [2] Below 139 seqq.
[3] Warren, History of the American Bar 225-228, 229-236.
[4] Some states—New York, New Jersey, Delaware, Maryland, Rhode Island, New Hampshire—expressly adopted in their constitutions such parts of the common law as were part of the law of the Colonies before 1775 or 1776 or the date of the state constitution, ibid 225.

of commercial and maritime law,[1] made it necessary for English lawyers to construct a system of prize law,[2] and to study closely developments in international law,[3] and emphasized the need for a system of private international law.[4]

Secondly, we shall see that it was during this period that the foundations of our colonial constitutional law were laid.[5] The many controversies which arose on constitutional questions within the different colonies, and the many controversies which arose out of the relationship of the colonies to Great Britain, gave rise to principles and rules which were the foundation upon which the judges and legislators of the nineteenth century built.

Thirdly, it was partly upon ideas derived from the legal and political relations between Great Britain and her colonies, and partly upon ideas derived from the British constitution of the eighteenth century, that the founders of the American constitution built. Therefore it would be true to say that the existence of the old colonial empire, its organization, and the rules of law to which it gave rise, have had an influence on the constitution of the United States as deep and as permanent as the influence which they have had on English law. Of this matter it is necessary at this point to speak a little more at length.

When the Americans had won the war of independence, it soon appeared that the loose confederation of the thirteen states was quite insufficient to supply the needs of a permanent national government for the United States. It appears from *The Federalist* that the same difficulties which had confronted Great Britain in her dealings with the colonies now confronted the congress of confederated states. Some national government was needed which could take the place formerly occupied by Great Britain, and deal authoritatively with such matters as foreign affairs,[6] national defence,[7] trade with the Indians,[8] commercial questions,[9] disputes between,[10] and disorders and factions in,[11] the several states, the enactment of legislation in one state directed against the inhabitants of another state,[12] the inconsiderate issue by particular states of bills of credit.[13] It was necessary to give the national government power to make and to enforce laws on matters which were within its cognizance throughout the Union, and to raise supplies throughout the

---

[1] Below 273; vol. xii 524-542.
[2] Vol. xii 693-694.
[3] Below 269; vol. xii 637-639.
[4] Below 269-273.
[5] Below 230 seqq.
[6] The Federalist nos. xi, xv, xlii.
[7] Ibid nos. xxii xli.
[8] Ibid no. xlii.
[9] Ibid.
[10] Ibid nos. vi, vii.
[11] Ibid nos. vii, x, xvi.
[12] Ibid nos. vii, xxii.
[13] Ibid no. xliii.

Union to enable it to fulfil its duties.[1] It was necessary to establish a court to interpret the laws made by the national government and to punish those who infringed them.[2]

In many cases Great Britain had, through her own officers, acted, not against the colonies, but against individuals in the colonies who had broken the law. This characteristic of the old control to which the colonies had been subjected was copied by the framers of the constitution ; and it was carried a great deal further. The immediate cause of the war of independence was the abandonment by Great Britain of her former practice of asking the colonial governments for pecuniary assistance, and the inauguration of the new practice of taxing the colonists directly. The framers of the constitution, taught by bitter experience,[3] saw that no national government could be effective unless it could act in all matters, including taxation, directly upon the individual citizen.[4]

The Government of the Union, like that of each State, must be able to address itself immediately to the hopes and fears of individuals ; and to attract to its support those passions which have the strongest influence upon the human heart. It must, in short, possess all the means, and have a right to resort to all the methods of executing the powers with which it is intrusted, that are possessed and exercised by the Governments of the particular States.[5]

It would thus seem that the need for a stronger federal government, the kind of powers which it was necessary to give to it, and the need to make those powers exercisable directly against the individual citizen and not indirectly through the government of his state, were caused by the passing of the control of the British government, and therefore were not wholly dissimilar in their ambit and in the manner of their exercise to that control.

Just as many of the powers which it was found necessary to give to the federal government were similar to the powers

----

[1] The Federalist nos. xvi, xxi.   [2] Ibid no. xxii.

[3] " Congress at this time scarcely possesses the means of keeping up the forms of administration, till the States can have time to agree upon a more substantial substitute for the present shadow of a Federal Government. . . . Each State, yielding to the persuasive voice of immediate interest or convenience, has successively withdrawn its support, till the frail and tottering edifice seems ready to fall upon our heads and to crush us beneath its ruins," The Federalist no. xv.

[4] " The great and radical vice in the construction of the existing Confederation is in the principle of legislation for states or governments, in their corporate or collective capacities, and as contra-distinguished from the individuals of which they consist. . . . Except as to the rule of apportionment, the United States have an indefinite discretion to make requisitions for men and money ; but they have no authority to raise either, by regulations extending to the individual citizens of America. The consequence of this is, that, though in theory their resolutions concerning those objects are laws, constitutionally binding on the members of the Union, yet in practice they are mere recommendations, which the States observe or disregard at their option," ibid.

[5] Ibid no. xvi.

formerly exercised by the British government, so the organization of the machinery of the federal government was, to a large
extent, inspired by that separation of the powers of government
which, as we have seen,[1] was a salient feature of the eighteenth-
century constitution.   The framers of the constitution were no
doubt inspired by Montesquieu.   But they pointed out that, in
practice, a complete separation was not possible ;[2] and that in
the British constitution " the Legislative, Executive and Judiciary departments are by no means totally separate and distinct
from each other."[3]   They concluded, therefore, that the object
to be aimed at was not complete separation, but so much separation as would prevent one department getting complete control
over another.[4]   The executive, judicial, and legislative departments of government must be, not necessarily completely separate, but substantially independent of each other ;[5] and the
danger of encroachments by the Legislature was recognized by
past experience to be the danger most to be feared.[6]   They saw
that the most effectual means of guarding against this danger
was to give " to those who administer each department the
necessary constitutional means and personal motives to resist encroachments of the others."[7]   Each department " must have a
will of its own."[8]   It is obvious that this interpretation of the
doctrine of the separation of powers approaches very closely
to the sense in which the powers were separated in the British
constitution ; for we have seen that the characteristic feature of
that constitution was, not complete separation, but the division
of the powers of government, both central and local, amongst a
number of autonomous units, all of which had some control over
or connection with the others, but none of which had complete
control over the others.[9]   It would seem therefore that the application of the doctrine of the separation of powers to the
different parts of the Federal constitution owed more to the
actual practice of the British constitution than to the theories
of Montesquieu ; and it is clear that the division of powers
between President, Senate and Congress, owed something to the
division of the powers of the central government in Great Britain

---

[1] Vol. x 714-716.

[2] " Experience has instructed us, that no skill in the science of Government
has yet been able to discriminate and define, with sufficient certainty, its three
great Provinces, the Legislative, Executive, and Judiciary ; or even the privileges
and powers of the different Legislative branches," The Federalist no. xxxvi.

[3] Ibid no. xlvi.   [4] Ibid.   [5] Ibid no. l.

[6] " In governments purely republican, this tendency is almost irresistible.   The
Representatives of the People in a popular Assembly seem sometimes to fancy
that they are the People themselves, and betray strong symptoms of impatience
and disgust at the least sign of opposition from any other quarter ; as if the exercise
of its rights, by either Executive or Judiciary, were a breach of their privilege, and
an outrage to their dignity," ibid no. lxx.

[7] Ibid no. l.   [8] Ibid.   [9] Vol. x 720-721.

between the King, the House of Lords and the House of Commons. Details were, of course, very different ; but both in the under-lying theory of divided powers, and in the scheme of division adopted, we can see a family likeness.

Perhaps the most characteristic feature of the constitution of the United States, and certainly the feature which has helped most efficiently to preserve its stability, was the creation of the Supreme Court of the United States. That court was given jurisdiction, *inter alia*, to safeguard the rights given by the constitution to the citizens ; to secure the observance of the law which fixed the boundaries both of the powers of the state and federal governments, and of the powers of the executive and legis-lative authorities in the state and federal governments ; and to maintain " the peace of the confederacy " by adjudicating in cases relating both to " the intercourse between the United States and foreign nations," and to the intercourse between the several states.[1] The establishment of this court with this juris-diction owes something, both to the supreme appellate juris-diction formerly exercised by the Privy Council, and to that idea of the rule of law which had been a characteristic feature of the English constitution from mediæval days.[2] Just as the ambit of the powers given to the federal government was suggested by the powers formerly exercised by the British government, so the ambit of the jurisdiction of the supreme court was suggested by the jurisdiction formerly exercised by the Privy Council. Just as the division of powers between King, Lords and Commons suggested the division of powers between President, Senate, and Congress, so the position of guardians of a supreme law, which the courts held in England,[3] suggested the creation of a Supreme Court to safeguard that law of the constitution which secured the rights of the citizen, and defined the boundaries of all the authorities between which the powers of the state were divided. And because the constitution of the United States, in which this old conception of the rule of law was applied, was a rigid and a federal constitution, that conception obtained a development and a practical importance, which it could never have obtained in a flexible and a unitary constitution ruled by a sovereign legislative body. The result is that the Supreme Court of the United States has been able to safeguard, more effectually than any other tribunal in the world, that supremacy of the law which the genius of Sir Edward Coke had made the most characteristic feature of the modern British constitution.[4]

Thus the American constitution was built up mainly by a skilful adaptation to a new situation of sound constitutional

[1] The Federalist nos. lxxviii, lxxx.   [2] Vol. x 647-649.
[3] Vol. x 416-417.   [4] Vol. v 428, 444, 454.

traditions, derived to some extent from the old relations formerly existing between Great Britain and her American colonies, and to a large extent from the British constitution. The political theory of the Declaration of Independence which dwelt upon the equality of men, their unalienable rights to life, liberty, and the pursuit of happiness, and their right to resist a tyrannical government, retired into the background. The founders of the American constitution recognized with Burke that such theories, however well they might be suited to a period of revolution, were of very little help in a period of reconstruction.[1] They therefore abandoned the democratic theories of Paine and Rousseau, and went for inspiration to that eighteenth-century British constitution of separated and balanced powers with which they were familiar. They were not inclined to entrust unfettered powers to a popularly elected Legislature; for they recognized that the usurpations of such a Legislature would lead to tyranny as quickly as usurpations by the Executive.[2] They were no believers in equalitarian theories; for they recognized that there was " a diversity in the faculties of men from which the rights of property originate," and that " the protection of these faculties is the first object of Government." [3] On the other hand, they saw that this diversity might lead to faction; and that if, in a popular government, a particular faction secured a majority, it was able " to sacrifice to its ruling passion or interest both the public good and the rights of other citizens." [4] They aimed, by means of the separation of the powers of government between the federal and state authorities, and between the legislative, executive, and judicial powers in the federal and state governments, "to secure the public good, and private rights, against the danger of such a faction, and at the same time to preserve the spirit and form of popular Government." [5]

The permanence of the constitution which they constructed is the measure of their success. Very many of the new constitutions constructed in the nineteenth century were inspired by those equalitarian theories of Paine and Rousseau, set forth in the Declaration of Independence, which the founders of the American constitution ignored; and a large number of them have been very transient phantoms. Maine's opinion that the

---

[1] " The pretended rights of these theorists are all extremes : and in proportion as they are metaphysically true, they are morally and politically false. The rights of man are in a sort of *middle*, incapable of definition, but not impossible to be discerned . . . I never liked this continued talk of resistance and revolution, or the practice of making the extreme medicine of the constitution its daily bread. It renders the habit of society dangerously valetudinary," The French Revolution, Works (Bohn's ed.) ii 335.

[2] The Federalist no. xlvii.
[3] Ibid no. x.
[4] Ibid.
[5] Ibid.

success and permanence of the work of the founders of the American constitution are due to the fact that they built upon the foundations of the eighteenth-century British constitution, and not upon the theories of Paine and Rousseau, is, I think, absolutely justified.[1] Because the founders of that constitution built on these sound lines, they constructed a constitution which contains a background of stable principles, derived from a long historical experience. For that reason there is a permanency in the political ideals of the United States, which is conspicuously absent in states the policy of which is at the mercy of a sovereign Legislature elected by universal suffrage.

Fourthly, the influence of English institutions and ideas is equally apparent in the constitution of some of the states of the United States. Bryce says : [2]

The State Constitutions are the oldest things in the political history of America, for they are the continuations and representatives of the royal colonial charters, whereby the earliest English settlements in America were created, and under which their several local governments were established. . . . When in 1776 the thirteen colonies threw off their allegiance to King George III, and declared themselves independent states, the colonial charter naturally became the State Constitution. In most cases it was remodelled, with large alterations, by the revolting colony. But in three States it was maintained unchanged (except, of course, so far as the Crown authority was concerned), viz. in Massachusetts till 1780, in Connecticut till 1818, and in Rhode Island till 1842.

Moreover there is no doubt that, when Massachusetts set up a new constitution in 1780, much of the old constitution was retained, and " profoundly influenced the Convention that prepared the Federal Constitution in 1787." [3]

Thus, in the formation both of the Federal Constitution and of the constitutions of the several states, history and precedent had far more influence than the new equalitarian democratic theories. But those theories had made their appearance, and could claim to have won their first victory when America gained her independence. The form which those theories were taking portended great changes in the future. But as yet they were a cloud no bigger than a man's hand upon the sky of eighteenth-century society. It was not till the coming of the

---

[1] " The Constitution of the United States is a modified version of the British Constitution ; but the British Constitution which served as its original was that which was in existence between 1760 and 1787. . . . When the American Constitution was framed, there was no such sacredness to be expected for it as before 1789 was supposed to attach to all parts of the British Constitution. There was every prospect of political mobility, if not of political disorder. The signal success of the Constitution of the United States in stemming these tendencies is, no doubt, owing in part to the great portion of British institutions which were preserved in it," Popular Government 253.

[2] The American Commonwealth (2nd ed.) i 427, 430.   [3] Ibid 429.

French Revolution, and the progress of the industrial revolution, that they began to threaten the existence of that society. It was not till then that we see the beginnings of the process which will substitute for the ordered aristocratic society of the eighteenth century, a democratic society based on an unreal equality ; and for the aristocratic constitution of the eighteenth century, which provided efficient safeguards for the varying liberties of different classes of society, a democratic constitution, which, in the course of its efforts to secure this unreal equality, has discarded very many of those eighteenth-century safeguards for the liberties of very many of its subjects.

But we must now turn from the Western colonies of Great Britain, and from the new political theories and constitutions which were arising in the Western world, to the empire which Great Britain was beginning to build up in the East, and to the very different set of legal and constitutional problems which were emerging as the result of the rise of that empire.

The Eastern Expansion of England

The continuous history of the Eastern expansion of England begins on December 31, 1600, when the first charter was granted to the old East India Company.[1]   Earlier companies had been formed to trade in Eastern lands—the Russia Company in 1553-1554, and the Levant Company in 1581.[2]   One of the objects of the latter company was to open up trade to India overland ; and some of its members were active in promoting the foundation of the East India Company.[3]   But the enterprise of the great Portuguese navigators had deflected the main channel of Eastern trade from the overland route and the Mediterranean to the sea route round the Cape of Good Hope and the Atlantic Ocean. And so " the causes which had destroyed the Italian merchant states were fatal to the Levant Company.   As the East India Company grew, the Levant Company dwindled, and in 1825 it was formally dissolved."[4]

The foundation of the East India Company, and the foundation two years later of a similar company in Holland, were due to the wish to wrest from Portugal, which was then subject to Spain, the monopoly of the Eastern trade which had been granted to her by the Bull of Alexander VI in 1493.[5]   Both companies were granted a monopoly of trade eastwards from a

---

[1] W. R. Scott, Joint Stock Companies ii 92 ; since these pages were written Professor Berriedale Keith has summarized the history of the Indian Empire in his Constitutional History of India 1600-1935.
[2] Vol. viii 209.   [3] Scott, op. cit. ii 89, 90-91.
[4] Ilbert, The Government of India (3rd ed.) 13.   [5] Ibid 4.

line drawn between the Cape of Good Hope and the Straits of Magellan. "The two charters may be regarded as the Protestant counter claims to the monopoly claimed under Pope Alexander's Bull."[1]

The duration of the East India Company's charter of 1600 was fifteen years, subject to the right of the Crown to give at any time two years' notice to determine it, if the company's trade did not appear to be profitable to the realm. If it appeared to be profitable, it could be renewed for another period of fifteen years.[2] The company was given power to hold courts, and to make " laws, constitutions, orders, and ordinances " for the good government of the company and its officials and servants ; and it could inflict punishment by imprisonment and fine for breach of its laws. But these laws and punishments must be reasonable and not contrary to the English common law or statutes. Those who infringed the company's monopoly were made liable to imprisonment and to forfeiture of their ships and goods. The government of the company was entrusted to twenty-four committees or directors.[3] Its members consisted of the persons who took shares in the first and subsequent voyages, and others who qualified by birth, service, or apprenticeship.[4]

James I renewed the company's charter in 1609 and made it perpetual, subject to the right of the Crown to determine it on three years' notice if its continuance appeared to be contrary to the national interest.[5] In 1615 the company was empowered to issue commissions authorizing the general in command of its ships to punish non-capital offences by martial law. In capital cases the accused must be tried by a jury.[6] Similar powers were given in 1623-1624 to the company's Presidents and other chief officials.[7]

We have seen that at first the East India Company was not a true joint stock company. The investor subscribed only for a particular voyage ; and the accounts of the different voyages were kept separately.[8] In 1613, however, capital was subscribed for four successive voyages, and this was known as the first joint stock.[9] Until 1657 capital continued to be subscribed for particular voyages or groups of voyages.[10] But in that year a permanent joint stock was formed.[11]

The voyages of the company in the early years of the seventeenth century were successful ;[12] and during the first twenty

[1] Ilbert, The Government of India (3rd ed.) 8.
[2] Scott, op. cit. ii 93.
[3] Ilbert, op. cit. 4-5.
[4] Berriedale Keith, Constitutional History of India 4.
[5] Ilbert, op. cit. 13-14.
[6] Ibid 14.
[7] Ibid.
[8] Vol. viii 206.
[9] Scott, op. cit. ii 101.
[10] Ibid 125-128.
[11] Ibid 128 seqq.
[12] Ibid 103.

years of that century factories had been established at Surat, Agra, Ahmedabad, and Broach, which were subject to the control of the President of the factory at Surat.[1] The fact that the Dutch Company was at this period vigorously fighting the Portuguese, helped the English Company to establish itself in the face of Portuguese opposition.[2] But the interests of the English and Dutch companies were conflicting ; and, though an agreement was come to in 1619, their rivalry continued, and all cooperation ceased after the massacre of Amboina, when ten members of the English factory at Amboina were put to death on a charge of conspiring to seize the fortress [3]—an outrage for which Cromwell secured compensation in 1654.[4] One result of this breach with the Dutch was the withdrawal of the company from the Eastern archipelago, and its concentration on India.[5]

The success of the company during this period led (i) to attacks upon its commercial monopoly in Parliament, and (ii) to infringements of that monopoly by the Crown. (i) The attacks made upon the company's monopoly in Parliament were part of the general agitation against monopolies, which marked the end of the sixteenth and the beginning of the seventeenth century.[6] But, in so far as these attacks were directed against the charters which gave a company a monopoly of foreign trade, they were not, either then or later in the century,[7] genuinely inspired, as their authors would have us believe, by a belief in the efficacy of freedom of trade ; for, as Professor Scott says,[8]

all through the seventeenth century the most powerful arguments against existing privileges were those of the would-be monopolist. It seems to have been recognised that a man was ' playing the game ' in condemning in unmeasured language the practice of exclusive trading grants ; and then, immediately he had fought his way within the charmed circle, to point out the evils of ' disorderly trading ' coupled with a petition for a more stringent monopoly.

It is therefore not surprising to find that these attacks did not succeed, either then [9] or later in the century,[10] in disproving the need for a centrally organized trade, if the English merchants were to be able to get privileges from the native princes, or to make headway against their foreign European rivals. It was for this reason that it was then, and continued to be, necessary to give a commercial monopoly to the company by whom the trade was organized.[11] (ii) There were one or two cases in which the Crown granted privileges to persons or companies which

---

[1] Camb. Hist. of the Empire iv 81.   [2] Ibid 82.
[3] Ibid 83-84.   [4] Ilbert, op. cit. 15.   [5] Ibid.
[6] Vol. iv 346-354 ; Scott, op. cit. i chap. vi ; ibid ii 101-103.
[7] Below 146.   [8] Op. cit. i 121.
[9] See Scott, op. cit. ii 105-106.   [10] Below 149.
[11] Vol. viii 210-211.

infringed the company's monopoly.[1] The most formidable of these privileged rivals was Courten's Association, of which Charles I was made a member, and in which Endymion Porter and Windebank, the secretary of state, were investors.[2] The company eventually came to terms with the transferees of the shares in this Association ; and in 1657 a new charter was granted to the company, " under which the rump of Courten's Association was united with the East India Company, and the different stocks of the company were united into a new joint stock." [3]

After the Restoration the company entered upon a period of commercial prosperity. This was due to the growing demand for its staple articles of trade—calicoes, tea, and coffee, and, in the last years of Charles II's reign, to the policy of Sir Josiah Child who allied himself with the court, and steadily supported the Crown.[4] As the result of the commercial prosperity of the company it was able to extend its settlements in India ; and, as the result of the favour of the Crown, its commercial monopoly was upheld, and the additional powers, needed to govern the settlements which it had acquired, were secured. Let us look at the progress made by the Company from these three points of view—the extension of its settlements, the maintenance of its commercial monopoly, and the extension of its political powers.

(i) The most considerable accession of territory was the acquisition in 1668, by a grant from the Crown, of the port and island of Bombay—a possession which had been acquired by Charles II as part of the dowry of his queen, Catherine of Braganza.[5] Its geographical position and fortifications made it a much more suitable centre for the trade of Western India than Surat, which was the original headquarters of this trade.[6] For the trade of Eastern India the most important centre was Madras. After the Restoration Fort St. George at Madras had become the headquarters of the company's factories on the east coast of India.[7] The headquarters of the trade of Bengal, Bihar, and Orissa at the time of the Restoration was Hugli ;[8] but from 1661 to 1681, and from 1684 to 1696, the factories of Bengal,

---

[1] Scott, op. cit. ii 98-99, 100.
[2] Ibid 112-114.   [3] Ilbert, op. cit. 15-16.
[4] Macaulay, Hist. of England chap. xviii, says, " when the Oxford Parliament had been dissolved, when many signs indicated that a strong reaction in favour of prerogative was at hand, when all the corporations which had incurred the royal displeasure were beginning to tremble for their franchises, a rapid and complete revolution took place at the India House. Child, who was then Governor, . . . separated himself from his old friends, excluded them from the direction, and negotiated a treaty of peace and of close alliance with the Court."
[5] Camb. Hist. of the Empire iv 100.   [6] Ibid 100-101.
[7] Ibid 103.   [8] Ibid 104.

Bihar, and Orissa were under the government of Fort St. George at Madras.[1] In the course of the century the importance of the Bengal factories increased. In 1690 the company had acquired a settlement at Sutanati at the mouth of the Ganges ; in 1696 a local rebellion gave an excuse for fortifying this factory ; and in 1698 the three villages of Sutanati, Calcutta, and Govindpur were rented by the company. " The fortified factory, which was named Fort William in honour of King William III, was made in 1700 the seat of a presidency, Sir Charles Eyre becoming the first president and governor of Fort William in Bengal." [2] Thus by the end of the century the company's factories were grouped round the three presidencies of Bombay, Fort St. George at Madras, and Fort William at Calcutta.

(ii) As in the preceding period,[3] the success of the company encouraged interlopers, who, in the name of free trade, wished to make use of the company's political position in India, and its organization of the Indian trade, without contributing to its cost. The dispute between Skinner and the East India Company, which led to a dispute between the two Houses of Parliament over the question whether the House of Lords had an original jurisdiction,[4] was caused by the activities of one of these interlopers.[5] All through the reign of Charles II those who supported them allied themselves with two sets of the company's opponents—those who opposed it because it exported silver to pay for its purchases in India, and those who opposed it because it imported fabrics which competed with the woollen and silk industries.[6] The legal question of the validity of the company's monopoly was settled in 1684 by the decision of the court of King's Bench in the case of *The East India Co. v. Sandys.*[7] We have seen that the decision given by Jeffreys, C.J., in favour of the company was both technically correct, and could be justified on grounds both of public policy and natural equity.[8] It is true that, after the Revolution, the Whig opponents of Sir Josiah Child induced the House of Commons to pass in 1693 a resolution " that all the subjects of England have equal right to trade to the East Indies unless prohibited by Act of Parliament." [9] But a resolution of the House of Commons cannot change the law ; and the law on this matter had been settled by the decision in the case of *The East India Co. v. Sandys.*[10] In fact, the need for a powerful company, with a monopoly which would enable it to regulate

---

[1] Camb. Hist. of the Empire iv 106, 108.
[3] Above 141.
[5] See Scott, op. cit. ii 150.
[7] 10 S.T. 371.
[9] Scott, op. cit. ii 159-160 ; cp. vol. i 572.

[2] Ibid 108.
[4] Vol. i 367-368.
[6] Ibid 135-138, 139-140.
[8] Vol. vi 326-327.
[10] 10 S.T. 371.

the East India trade, was so evident, that the new company incorporated under the Act of 1698 was given a monopoly similar to that of the old company;[1] and when the old and the new companies were amalgamated in 1709 the monopoly was continued.[2]

(iii) From the first it was obvious that a successful trade with India could not be conducted except through a company which had a political position sufficiently strong, first to obtain from the Mogul Emperor or his deputies permission to establish factories and to acquire trading privileges, and, secondly, to maintain a sufficient force to defend those factories and privileges if they were attacked. This was the substantial justification for the company's trading monopoly. But it was inevitable that the extension of its trade should entail an extension of its factories, and therefore a more elaborate governmental organization. If the company was to maintain its position as against the native princes and as against its European rivals, it must be given power to govern those territorial acquisitions which were necessary for the successful conduct of its trade, and to defend them against attack. These necessities are reflected in the large powers which were conferred on the company by the charters of Charles II and James II.

The charter of 1661[3] gave the company power to appoint governors and other officers for the government of their fortresses. The governor and council of each factory were given the power to exercise a criminal and civil jurisdiction in accordance with the rules of English law. The company was given power to make peace or war " with any people that are not Christians, in any places of their trade, as shall be for the most advantage and benefit of the said Governor and Company, and of their trade " ; and therefore power to maintain ships of war, armed forces, and fortifications. It was given power to seize unlicensed traders, and to punish its employées. If an employée appealed against his sentence, he was to be sent a prisoner to England, where his appeal was to be heard.

In 1668 Bombay was granted to the company. The charter, which made the grant, gave the company power to take into its service the King's officers and soldiers then in Bombay, who were willing to serve them.[4] It also gave the company power to make laws and ordinances for the good government of Bombay, to administer justice, and to take all necessary measures for its defence. The governor was given power to exercise martial law in cases of rebellion, mutiny, or sedition, and in cases of other

---

[1] Ilbert, op. cit. 28-29.   [2] Ibid 30.   [3] Ibid 16-17.
[4] Thus, says Professor Keith, " forming the nucleus of the Company's first European regiment, or Bombay Fusiliers," Constitutional History of India 10.

offences against military discipline.[1] In 1677 another charter
gave the company power to coin money at Bombay, which money
was to be current in India, but not in England.[2]

In 1683 a new charter gave the company a number of new
powers. It gave powers of making peace and war with the native
princes ; of raising and disciplining military forces ; of making
use, within the company's plantations forts and places, of
" the law called martial law for the defence of the said forts
places and plantations against any foreign invasion or domestic
insurrection or rebellion " ; and of establishing a court of Admiralty to determine maritime and mercantile causes according
to the rules of equity and good conscience, and according to
mercantile custom, by such procedure as the court might direct.
It was, however, provided that the power of exercising martial
law within the company's territories was subject to the Crown's
sovereign power " over all forts and places of habitation," and
to its power to make peace and war " when we shall be pleased
to interpose our royal authority thereon." [3] All these privileges
were renewed and enlarged by James II's charter in 1686, which,
inter alia, gave the company power to raise and discipline a naval
force, and to coin money in any of its settlements.[4] In 1687 it
was given power to establish by its charter a municipal corpora-
ion at Madras.[5]

In 1688-1689 two events interrupted the peaceful progress
which the company had been making since the Restoration.
Aurangzeb expelled the company's servants from Bengal,[6] and
the Revolution put the opponents of the company in England
into power. Peace was made with Aurangzeb in 1690 ; [7] but
the difficulties arising out of the new political situation in
England were not so easily settled. Child had identified the
company with the high Tory party, and had relied on the Crown
for protection and for the enlargement of its privileges. The
fact that the company had thus been identified with the high
Tories gave its opponents a strong political handle against it
of which they did not delay to take advantage. In 1691 a bill
was introduced into the House of Commons which proposed to
reform the constitution of the company, and incorporate in it
an association of its opponents, which was popularly known as

---

[1] Ilbert, op. cit. 18.   [2] Ibid 19.
[3] Ibid 19-20.   [4] Ibid 20-21.
[5] Ibid 21; the question whether this charter should pass under the great seal
or the company's seal was discussed at a cabinet council. The latter course was
adopted at the request of the company. The reason given by the governor of the
company was that no persons in India should be employed directly by the Crown,
" because the wind of extraordinary honour in their heads would probably render
them so haughty and over-bearing that the Company would be forced to remove
them," ibid.
[6] Camb. Hist. of the Empire iv 108.   [7] Ibid.

the "New Company." The reforms were aimed at getting rid of the predominating influence of Child and his friends. Though the bill was read a second time, the opposition of Child and the company wrecked this scheme.[1] But in 1693 the company failed to pay a tax of 5 per cent. on its stock, and thereby rendered its charters liable to be forfeited.[2]

After considerable controversy and much bribing of officials, Child obtained a new charter on October 7, 1693; but that charter bound the company to accept such alterations in its constitution as might be imposed by the Crown.[3] These alterations were made by two charters of November 11, 1693, and September 28, 1694.[4] The former charter was in reality a victory for Child, because it prevented his opponents from getting control over the company.[5] But, though the continuance of the company was secured, there was no security that its opponents might not succeed in inducing the Crown to incorporate a new company; and the action taken by the company in stopping a ship in the Thames, on the ground that it was freighted by interlopers who were intending to infringe the company's monopoly, raised a renewed agitation against the company's monopoly,[6] and produced the House of Common's resolution of 1693 in favour of freedom of trade to the East Indies [7]—a resolution which, as we have seen, was quite powerless to change the law laid down by the court of King's Bench in *The East India Co. v. Sandys*.[8] Helped by this agitation, which was used rather as a weapon against the company than because its users had any real belief in it, and under the pressure of the need to raise money for the war, it was determined to offer the monopoly of the East India trade "to any body of capitalists that would contribute most towards relieving the necessities of the State." [9] The company offered a loan of £700,000 at 4 per cent.; its opponents offered a loan of £2,000,000 at 8 per cent.; and their offer was accepted.[10]

But there were very considerable difficulties in producing a plan which would please all the opponents of the company. Some wanted a regulated company which would allow freedom of trade to all its members: others wanted a joint stock company after the pattern of the existing company.[11] The very ingenious plan produced by Montague, the Chancellor of the Exchequer, was designed to conciliate both those who believed in a reg-

---

[1] Ilbert, op. cit. 24.

[2] Scott, op. cit. ii 156; for a discussion of the reason for this failure to pay see ibid 157-158.

[3] Ilbert, op. cit. 25.   [4] Ibid.

[5] Scott, op. cit. ii 158.   [6] Ilbert, op. cit. 26.

[7] Above 143.   [8] 10 S.T. 371; above 143.

[9] Scott, op. cit. ii 163.   [10] Ibid 164.

[11] Macaulay, History of England chap. xxiii.

ulated, and those who believed in a joint stock, company.   Its
main features have been very clearly described by Macaulay.[1]

The lenders [of the £2,000,000] might be either individuals or corporations.   But they were all, individuals and corporations, to be
united in a new corporation, which was to be called the General Society.
Every member of the General Society, whether individual or corporation, might trade separately with India to an extent not exceeding the
amount which such member had advanced to the government.   But
all the members or any of them might, if they so saw fit, give up the
privilege of trading separately, and unite themselves under a royal
Charter for the purpose of trading in common.   Thus the General
Society was, by its original constitution, a regulated company ; but
it was provided that either the whole Society or any part of it might
become a joint stock company.

The Act of 1698, which gave effect to the arrangement, empowered the Crown to incorporate the subscribers to the loan
under the name of " The General Society," [2] and to incorporate
any section of these subscribers into a joint stock company.[3]
In pursuance of this power the Crown granted two charters—
one incorporating the General Society as a regulated company,
the other incorporating most of the subscribers to the General
Society as a joint stock company under the name of " The
English Company trading to the East Indies." [4]   The latter
company were given privileges similar to those of the old company, and it was provided that the privileges of the old company
should be continued, and should exist side by side with the
rights of the new company, till September 29, 1701 [5]—a period
which was prolonged by a private Act of 1700 to the time when
the whole of the loan of two million should be repaid.[6]

    In fact the old company was in a very strong position.
It had invested £315,000 in the new company, and they were
in possession of the factories and controlled the organization
of the Indian trade.[7]   The House of Commons might vote that
every Englishman had a right to trade to the East Indies ; but,
as Macaulay has said, " whatever respect might be paid to a
vote of the House of Commons by public functionaries in London,
such a vote was at Bombay or Calcutta much less regarded than
a private letter from Child ; and Child still continued to fight
the battle with unbroken spirit." [8]   And the hollowness of the
agitation in favour of free trade was as apparent at the end of

---

[1] Macaulay, History of England chap. xxiii
[2] 9, 10 William III c. 44 § 56.   [3] § 62.
[4] Ilbert, op. cit. 28 ; difficulties subsequently arose with the subscribers who
had remained outside the joint stock company, which were partly solved by the
company purchasing their stock, and partly by a power given by 6 Anne c. 17 § 7
to buy it up on three years' notice, Scott, op. cit. ii 191.
[5] Ilbert, op. cit. 28.   [6] 11, 12 William III c. 4.
[7] Ilbert, op. cit. 29.   [8] History of England, chap. xx.

the century as it was at the beginning; for the new company
was a monopolistic joint stock company of the same type as the
old.

It soon became apparent that an amalgamation of the two
companies was inevitable. "The old company had written to
its representatives abroad in this strain, even before the sub-
scription [for the two million loan] had been taken, while . . .
only two months after the charter of the new company had
been signed Papillon on its behalf proposed ' an accommodation '
with its rival." [1]   The inevitable amalgamation was effected in
1702.   By an indenture tripartite, to which the Queen and the
two companies were parties, it was provided that the shares of
the two companies in the two million loan should be equalized.
Neither company was to trade separately for the next seven years.
The trade was to be conducted by a committee of twenty-four
appointed in equal numbers from both companies.   At the end
of the seven years the old company was to surrender its charters,
and the new company was to continue its trade under its charter
of 1698.   Its name was to be henceforth " The United Company
of Merchants of England trading to the East Indies." [2]   It became
necessary to apply to Parliament to settle difficulties which
had arisen in working out this arrangement.   By an Act of 1707
the new company advanced a further sum of £1,200,000 without
interest, the privileges of the company were continued till 1728,
and Godolphin was empowered to settle all outstanding points
of difference between the two companies.[3]   He made his award
in 1708; [4]   in 1709 the old company surrendered its charters; [5]
and thus the new company's charter of 1698 " came to be, in
point of law, the root of all the powers and privileges of the
United Company, subject to the changes made by statute." [6]

At the end of the seventeenth century the company had
begun to be both a political society and a trading company.
This fact was emphasized by a resolution, " doubtless inspired, if
not penned, by Sir Josiah Child " in 1688.[7]   It runs as follows : [8]

The increase of our revenue is the subject of our care as much
as our trade ; 'tis that which must maintain our force when twenty
accidents may interrupt our trade ; 'tis that must make us a nation in
India ; without that we are but a great number of interlopers, united
by His Majesty's royal charter, fit only to trade when nobody of power
thinks it their interest to prevent us ; and upon this account it is that
the wise Dutch, in all their general advices that we have seen, write
ten paragraphs concerning their government, their civil and military
policy, warfare, and the increase of their revenues, for one paragraph
they write concerning trade.

[1] Scott, op. cit. ii 167.   [2] Ilbert, op. cit. 29-30.
[3] 6 Anne c. 17 ; Scott, op. cit. ii 191-192.
[4] Ibid 174.   [5] Ibid 177.   [6] Ilbert, op. cit. 30.
[7] Ibid 24.   [8] Cited ibid 23.

The policy outlined in this resolution was pursued all through the eighteenth century ; and the events of the eighteenth century ended by making the company first the chief of the ruling powers in India, and, ultimately, either the direct sovereign of large parts of India, or the paramount power over those parts of it which were still ruled by its native princes.

Down to the year 1765, when the company became in effect the rulers of Bengal, the company made steady progress both commercially and politically.

Commercially the company prospered. " The value of its imports rose from nearly £500,000 in 1708 to about £1,100,000 in 1748 ; while its exports increased from £576,000 (of which £375,000 was in bullion) in 1710, to £1,121,000 (including £816,000 in bullion) forty years later," [1] The dividends paid rose from 5 per cent. in 1708-1709 to 10 per cent. in 1711-1712.[2] They dropped to 8 per cent. in 1723, and to 7 per cent. in 1732. From 1745 to 1755 they rose again to 8 per cent.[3] In 1717 further privileges for Calcutta, Madras, and Bombay were secured from Delhi. All these three settlements grew in population and importance during the first half of the eighteenth century ; [4] and, as against the competition of European rivals, the company stood its ground successfully. Danish [5] and Swedish [6] companies gave little trouble ; and the Ostend East India Company, which seemed likely to be a serious competitor, was suppressed by diplomatic action. The treaty of 1731, by which England guaranteed the succession of Maria Theresa to the Austrian inheritance, provided for its suppression.[7]

Politically the company was aware of the necessity of maintaining the strength of its settlements, both in order to secure its position as against the native rulers, and to compete successfully with its European rivals. Though it often advised economy in expenditure on these settlements,[8] it was obliged to admit the necessity for expenditure.[9] For the same reason it was found necessary to get Parliament to give the company security for the continuance of its privileges, authority to deal with interlopers and other rivals, and additional powers to govern and administer justice in its settlements, and to provide for their defence. Parliament was willing to do all this—at a price.

---

[1] Camb. Hist. of the Empire iv 108. [2] Ibid 109.
[3] Ibid 111-112. [4] Ibid 112-113. [5] Ibid 114.
[6] Ibid 116. [7] Ibid 115. [8] Scott, op. cit. ii 198.
[9] Ibid 199 ; as Professor Scott says, " the court in London was forced to speak with two voices. It repeatedly ordered, in the most peremptory manner, that outlay on fortifications and buildings should be kept as low as possible. On the other hand, when the company suffered from attacks made upon its servants and was unable to obtain redress, it was forced reluctantly to authorize expenditure for the defence of the settlements."

First, in 1730, at the price of a loan to the state of £200,000 without interest, and a reduction of interest on previous loans from five to four per cent.,[1] the company got Parliament to prolong its privileges till 1769 ; and, in 1744, at the price of a loan of one million at three per cent., further to prolong its privileges to 1783.[2] The company also got further powers to deal with interlopers ; [3] and all attempts to support the Ostend Company were penalized.[4]

Secondly, additional powers were given to govern and administer justice in its settlements in India. Down to 1726 justice had been administered by courts which the company had been empowered by its charters to establish.[5] In Bombay the charter of 1668 authorized the establishment of a court, on English lines, to decide cases according to laws to be made by the company for the good government of the colony, which laws were to be consonant with reason, and not repugnant to the rules of English law.[6] The court, which was opened in 1672,[7] had a chequered history. It ceased to function during Keigwin's rebellion (1683-1684) ; it was re-opened in 1685 ; but it again ceased to function in 1690.[8] A charter of 1683 had authorized the establishment of a court of Admiralty ; and a court had been created in 1684 ; [9] but it, too, fell into abeyance in 1690.[10] In 1718 a new court of judicature was established, which functioned till 1728.[11] In Calcutta a court consisting of the governor and council was established in 1666.[12] In Madras a court, which possessed a general civil and criminal as well as an Admiralty jurisdiction, was established in 1686 ; [13] and in 1688 a mayor's court.[14] All these courts were set up by the company, and acted under its authority. A new charter of 1726 initiated a great change. It established " civil and military courts that derived their authority from the King instead of the Company." [15] Under this charter, and a charter of 1753,

[1] 3 George II c. 14.

[2] 17 George II c. 17 § 13 ; the total amount of the loans made by the Company to the State was, as the result of these transactions, £3,000,000 ; the interest on the earlier loans was reduced in 1750 from four to three and a half per cent. till 1755, and afterwards to three per cent., 23 George II c. 22 § 2.

[3] 5 George I c. 21 ; 7 George I St. 1 c. 21 ; 5 George II c. 29.

[4] 9 George I c. 26.

[5] On this subject see Charles Fawcett, The First Century of British Justice in India.

[6] Fawcett, op. cit. 6, 13 ; for the laws made by the Company see ibid 13-28.

[7] Ibid 52-55.   [8] Ibid 127-128, 157 seqq.

[9] Ibid 121-125.   [10] Ibid 157.   [11] Ibid 178.

[12] Ibid 201 ; both in Calcutta and Madras there were other courts which derived their authority from a delegation by Indian potentates to the Company, ibid 208-211.

[13] Ibid 202.

[14] Ibid ; it was set up as the necessary accompaniment to the municipal corporation which was established in that year.

[15] Ibid 214 ; for the reasons for this step see ibid 214-217 ; Berriedale Keith, op. cit. 17-18.

municipalities were created or reconstituted at Calcutta, Madras, and Bombay, and mayors' courts with civil and criminal jurisdiction were established.[1] " These courts," says Sir Charles Fawcett, " resulted in distinct progress in the administration of justice according to the principles and practice of the English courts of law.   They formed a useful link in the chain that led to the establishment of the improved courts of the nineteenth century." [2]

Thirdly, powers were given to take measures to protect the company's settlements against its European rivals, and against the native powers.   In 1748 the war with France had made it necessary for the company to establish an Indian army ; [3] and Acts of 1754 [4] and 1760 [5] applied to this army provisions corresponding to those contained in the English Mutiny Acts. A charter of 1757 granted to the company the moiety of the booty taken after Clive's victory at Plassey, which had been reserved to the Crown ; [6] and a charter of 1758 granted to the company all such booty taken after 1757, or which should hereafter be taken from any enemies of the company or the King ; provided that the booty was taken during hostilities begun by the company to recompense it for damage which it had suffered, or which it had reason to fear it would suffer, and provided it was taken in the course of hostilities carried on at the expense of the company. There was a saving of the Crown's prerogative in cases where the King's forces had co-operated with the company's forces, and for goods taken from the King's subjects.   The latter were to be restored on the payment of a reasonable salvage.   The charter also gave the company powers of ceding territory acquired from Indian Princes by treaty of peace ; but not territories acquired from a European power, without the licence of the Crown.[7]

The last two charters mark the opening of a new period in the history of the company—the period when it began to be the most powerful of all the competitors, Indian or European, for the sovereignty of India.   The victories of Clive and Lawrence in the Carnatic, culminating in Coote's victory at Wandiwash (1760), ruined the rising French empire in India, which Bussy and Dupleix had been building up during the previous fifteen years.[8]   Superior sea-power and superior finance had given Great

[1] Ilbert, op. cit. 31-32.
[2] Op. cit. 217 ; cp. Keith, op. cit. 43-49, 51 ; for the court of Cutchery and the Zamindari courts at Calcutta, which exercised the rights which the Company had as Zamindar of Sutanati, Govindpur, and Calcutta, see ibid 49-51.
[3] Ilbert, op. cit. 33.   [4] 27 George II c. 9.
[5] 1 George III c. 14.   [6] Ilbert, op. cit. 34-35.   [7] Ibid 35-36.
[8] Camb. Hist. of the Empire iv chap. vi.

Britain the victory over France in their struggle for the control of India.[1]   Clive's victory at Plassey (1757), Munro's victory at Buxar (1764), and the grant of the Diwani of Bengal,
Bihar, and Orissa, which Clive secured in 1765, made Great
Britain the strongest power in India.   These events made a
fundamental change in the position of the company ; and this
change set in motion a train of causes which, after some years of
controversy and experiment, ultimately gave to the government
of the British possessions in India the unique form which it retained till 1858.   These causes can be grouped under three main
heads :   (1) The inefficiency of the company's government ;
(2) The effects of this inefficiency upon the relations of the
company to the state ; and (3) The effects both of the inefficiency
of the company's government and of its relations to the state
upon its financial position.

(1) *The inefficiency of the company's government.*

The company's control over its settlements in India had
never been very strong or complete.   The directors did their
best.   They required reports and they scrutinized accounts.
They impressed upon their servants the need for economy, for
just treatment of the natives, and the diplomatic handling of
the situations created by native wars.[2]   But distance, and the
need to give large powers to meet emergencies, militated against
the establishment of a strict control ; and the effects of climate
and environment tended to lower moral standards.[3]   The effects
of this laxness of control was aggravated by four sets of circumstances.

First, though its charters had empowered the company to
set up a machinery of government in the three presidency towns
of Calcutta, Madras, and Bombay, both that machinery and the
machinery for the conduct of the Company's trade were not well
organized.   The combination of governmental and commercial
activities tended to render both ineffective in action ; and that
ineffectiveness was brought into striking relief by the great accession of political power which the victories of Clive and the
grant of the right of Diwani involved ; for those victories and
that grant had made the Company the *de facto* ruler of Bengal,
Bihar, and Orissa.   Hastings, speaking of the Calcutta council,
said : [4]

[1] Camb. Hist. of the Empire iv 164-165.   [2] Scott, op. cit. ii 197-198.
[3] " A particularly bad case happened at Bencoolen in 1710, where 2000 rupees
had been spent on liquor in six months, while timber and other stores were exposed
to the weather and allowed to rot.   To mark their displeasure, the directors sent
out a completely new staff from home, but seven years later a fresh remonstrance
was required," Scott, op. cit. ii 198.
[4] Cited by Stephen, Nuncomar and Impey i 14-15.

By the constitution of the Company the Council at large have the supreme authority in all matters which either come in the course of office before their notice, or of which they choose to take cognisance but as their power exists only while they sit in a body, so much of it is delegated to the governor, their president, as is supposed to be necessary for giving a continual currency to business, or for executing such of these functions as do not appertain to any distinct office of government. It is not easy to determine what points fall under this description. In effect, the governor is no more than any other individual of the Council, if the others choose to partake of his authority, although the responsibility of affairs seems to rest with him only. An opinion that he possesses something more, and a superior share of diligence or ability, may give him an influence in the administration which he wants constitutionally, but in the latter he may be exceeded by others, and the former must vanish when it is put to the test ; and whenever these cases happen, the government for want of a power to preside and rule it, must fall into anarchy. These indeed are the inevitable consequences of the ancient form of government which was instituted for the provision of the investment,[1] the sale of the Company's exported cargoes, and the despatch of their ships, being applied to the dominion of an extensive kingdom, the collection of a vast revenue, the command of armies, and the direction of a great political system, besides the additional charge devolved to their commercial department by its relation to the general trade of the country, and its effect on the public revenue.

So ineffective was the council that when reforms became imperative, it was in effect superseded by the appointment of Clive and a select committee.[2] Matters became even worse when, in 1772, the company resolved to " stand forth as Diwan," [3] that is to exercise through its own officials the authority of the Diwan. Hastings said in 1772 that

the new government of the Company consists of a confused mass of undigested materials as wild as chaos itself. The powers of government are ill-defined : the collection of the revenue, the provision of the investment ; the administration of justice (if it exists at all), the care of the police, are all huddled together, being exercised by the same hands, though most frequently the two latter offices are totally neglected for want of knowing when to have recourse for them.[4]

[1] At first the main business of the Company had consisted in trade—in import into and export from India. " The import had from early times consisted mainly of specie, so that the most burdensome duty of the Company's servants was the provision of the cargoes for England . . . in other words, the ' investment.' In the mid-eighteenth century . . . the main source from which the investment was provided—and the local expenses paid—was the territorial revenue of Bengal," Camb. Hist. of the Empire iv 438 ; cp. Ninth Report of the Committee of the House of Commons (1783), Burke, Works (Bohn's ed.) iv 31-33.

[2] Stephen, Nuncomar and Impey i 15.   [3] Ibid 11.

[4] Cited ibid 11-12 ; on another occasion Hastings said, " I found this government in possession of a great and rich dominion, and a wide political system which has been since greatly extended, without one rule of government, but what descended to it from its ancient commercial institutions," cited Camb. Hist. of the Empire iv 208.

Secondly, the organization of the government of the company in England was very defective. The directors of the company were elected annually, and were very much in the hands of the general court of proprietors, who thought mainly of their dividends.[1] The result was that the directors could exercise very little authority over their servants in India. These servants, as Clive pointed out in 1772,[2]

have never scrupled to set the orders of the court of directors at defiance, when it was to their interest to disobey them, and they have escaped punishment by means of the overawing interests of individuals at general courts. Thus have general courts co-operated with the court of directors in the mischiefs that have arisen in Bengal ; while annual contested elections have, in a manner, deprived the directors of the power of establishing any authority over their servants. The first half of the year is employed in freeing themselves from the obligations contracted by their last elections ; and the second half is wasted in incurring new obligations, and securing their election for the next year, by daily sacrifices of some interest of the Company The direction, notwithstanding all these manœuvres, has been so fluctuating and unsettled, that new and contradictory orders have been frequently sent out ; and the servants (who to say the truth have generally understood the interest of the Company much better than the directors) have in many instances followed their own opinions in opposition to theirs.

Thirdly, partly by reason of the meagre wages which the company paid its servants,[3] and partly by reason of the laxness of its control, it had never succeeded in preventing its servants from infringing its monopoly of trade. All its servants traded on their private account, because, unless they had done so, they could not have lived in India on their meagre wages. Sir William Foster, speaking of the end of the seventeenth century, says, " men went to the East to make money—for their meagre wages offered no temptation—and though some refrained from trenching upon their employers' monopolies, most had no scruple in taking advantage of every opportunity that presented itself." [4]

[1] Clive said in 1772 that it might have been expected that the directors and the court would have devised a scheme of government suitable to the empire which they had acquired ; but that they had behaved very differently—" they treated it rather as a South Sea bubble, than as anything solid and substantial : they thought of nothing but the present time, regardless of the future : they said, Let us get what we can to-day, let to-morrow take care of itself : they thought of nothing but the immediate division of the loaves and fishes : nay, so anxious were they to lay their hands upon some immediate advantage, that they actually went so far as to influence a parcel of temporary proprietors to bully the directors into their terms," Parlt. Hist. xvii 363-364.
[2] Ibid 365-366.
[3] Clive said in 1772 that " the salary of a counsellor is scarcely three hundred pounds per annum : and it is well known that he cannot live in that country for less than three thousand pounds. The same proportion holds among the other servants," ibid 338.
[4] Camb. Hist. of the Empire iv 94.

This was equally true in the eighteenth century;[1] and it is easy to see the enormous opportunities which the extension of the company's power throughout Bengal, Bihar, and Orissa gave to its servants. The military supremacy of the company gave its servants irresistible power; the company's machinery of government was powerless to restrain them; and so they made the most of their golden opportunity, as their predecessors had made the most of the much smaller opportunities open to them. As Burke truly said, the restrictions which the company attempted to impose could have little effect "whilst want and power were suffered to be united."[2] They not only carried on a greatly increased export trade, but they took the opportunity to assert the right, which they had always been prevented from exercising by the nawab of Bengal, of carrying on an internal trade free from all tolls.[3] Working in conjunction with native money-lenders, into whose power they had got, they used their rights most oppressively—forcing the inhabitants to buy their goods at exorbitant prices, and to sell at prices under the market rate.[4]

The effects upon the country of this assertion of the right of the servants of the company to conduct both internal and external trade were disastrous.

Whole districts which had once been populous and flourishing were at last utterly depopulated, and it was noticed that, on the appearance of a party of English merchants, the villages were at once deserted,

[1] Adam Smith said, Wealth of Nations (Cannan's ed.) ii 138, " Nothing can be more completely foolish than to expect that the clerks of a great counting house, at ten thousand miles distance, and consequently almost quite out of sight, should, upon a simple order from their master, give up once doing any sort of business upon their own account; abandon for ever all hope of making a fortune, of which they have the means in their hands; and content themselves with the moderate salaries which those masters allow them. . . . The servants naturally endeavour to establish the same monopoly in favour of their own private trade as of the public trade of the company."

[2] Ninth Report of the Select Committee of the House of Commons, Works (Bohn's ed.) iv 59.

[3] Camb. Hist. of the Empire iv 170-171.

[4] Clive described the process in 1772; he said, " Let us now take a view of one of these writers arrived in Bengal and not worth a groat. As soon as he lands a banyan, worth perhaps £100,000, desires he may have the honour of serving this young gentleman at 4s. 6d. a month. . . . The young man takes a walk about the town, he observes that other writers, arrived only a year before him, live in splendid apartments or have houses of their own, ride upon fine prancing Arabian horses, and in palanqueens and chaises; that they keep seraglios, make entertainments, and treat with champagne and claret. When he returns he tells the banyan what he has observed. The banyan assures him that he may soon arrive at the same good fortune; he furnishes him with money; he is then at his mercy. . . . He is in a state of dependence under the banyan, who commits such acts of violence and oppression, as his interest prompts him to, under the pretended sanction and authority of the Company's servant. Hence arises the clamour against the English gentlemen in India," Parlt. Hist. xvii 356; cp. Ninth Report of the Select Committee of the House of Commons, Burke, Works (Bohn's ed.) iv 57.

and the shops shut, and the roads thronged with panic-stricken fugitives.[1]

The reason why the assertion of these rights by the company's servants had these disastrous effects is clearly pointed out by Adam Smith.

The monopoly of the company can tend only to stunt the natural growth of that part of the surplus produce which, in the case of a free trade, would be exported to Europe. That of the servants tends to stunt the natural growth of every part of the produce in which they choose to deal; of what is destined for home consumption, as well as what is destined for exportation; and consequently to degrade the cultivation of the whole country, and to reduce the number of its inhabitants. It tends to reduce the quantity of every sort of produce, even that of the necessaries of life, whenever the servants of the country choose to deal in them, to what those servants can both afford to buy and expect to sell with such a profit as pleases them.[2]

There was considerable truth behind the magnificent rhetoric used by Burke in 1783 to describe the depredations of the company's servants upon the defenceless natives.[3]

Fourthly, since the servants of the company were in a position to give favours, they could easily increase their gains by the receipt of presents from the native authorities.

At every turn of the wheel, at every change in the system or personality of the Government, vast sums were drawn from the native treasury, and most steps of promotion were purchased by gifts to the English. A great part of these gifts, going to minor servants for procuring minor promotions have never been traced; but the Select Committee of 1773 published a detailed account of such sums as had been proved and acknowledged to have been distributed by the princes and other natives of Bengal from the year 1757 to 1766, both included. Omitting the great grant which had been made to Clive after the battle of Plassey, these sums amounted to no less than £5,940,498.[4]

[1] Lecky, History of England iv 264.
[2] Wealth of Nations (Cannan's ed.) ii 138-139.
[3] "Young men (boys almost) govern there, without society and without sympathy with the natives. They have no more social habits with the people, than if they still resided in England; nor, indeed, any species of intercourse but that which is necessary to making a sudden fortune, with a view to a remote settlement. Animated with all the avarice of age, and all the impetuosity of youth, they roll in one after another; wave after wave; and there is nothing before the eyes of the natives but an endless hopeless prospect of new flights of birds of prey and passage, with appetites continually renewing for a food that is continually wasting. . . . The cries of India are given to sea and winds to be blown about, in every breaking up of the monsoon, over a remote and unhearing ocean," Works (Bohn's ed.) ii 194-195; that "there is a large residuum of truth behind these burning words" is shown by Mr. Roberts, Camb. Hist. of the Empire iv 198; cp. Wealth of Nations ii 135-136.
[4] Lecky, History of England iv 266; Clive said in 1772 that, "from time immemorial it has been the custom of that country, for an inferior never to come into the presence of a superior without a present. It begins at the nabob, and ends at the lowest man that has an inferior. . . . I will take upon me to assert, that there has not been an officer commanding his Majesty's fleet; nor an officer commanding

" It is a very singular government," said Adam Smith,[1]
" in which every member of the administration wishes to get
out of the country, and consequently to have done with the
government as soon as he can." And yet that was literally the
case, for Clive said that the young servants of the company,
when they went out, calculated the period when they would
return with their fortunes made.[2] In these circumstances it is
not surprising to learn that Clive, when he returned to India
in 1765, found that the company had but few senior servants
left. " The secretary's department was in charge of a writer
of three years' standing, the accountant was a writer yet
younger than the secretary, while the paymaster of the army,
with balances of twenty lakhs in his hands for months together,
had also been a writer." [3]

The necessity of taking drastic measures to deal with this
situation had become so obvious, that Clive was sent back
to India in 1765 as governor and commander-in-chief in Bengal.
When he arrived he told the directors that " every spring of
government was smeared with corruption." [4] During his administration of eighteen months he accomplished much. The
most permanent part of his work was his settlement of the relations of the company with the native powers. It was a part
of that settlement that the company should have the Diwani of
Bengal, Orissa, and Bihar—an arrangement which gave the company " the full control of Bengal affairs without incurring the
inconvenience of formal and avowed dominion." [5] The less
permanent part of his work was his settlement with the servants of the company. The abuses arising from their private
trade and from their receipt of presents was obvious. The inadequacy of their pay was equally obvious. He tried, on the one
hand, to abolish private trade and to forbid presents, and, on
the other hand, to increase their pay by assigning to them a
share in the profits of the company's monopoly in the salt
trade. He effected these reforms in spite of the opposition of
the civil service, and in spite of a mutiny of the military officers.[6]
But the directors refused to ratify the arrangements which he

his Majesty's army ; not a governor, not a member of council, not any other person,
civil or military, in such a station as to have connection with the country government,
who has not received presents. With regard to Bengal they flow in abundance
indeed," Parlt. Hist. xvii 355.

[1] Wealth of Nations (Cannan's ed.) ii 140 ; cp. above 156 n. 3.
[2] Parlt. Hist. xvii 356.
[3] Camb. Hist. of the Empire iv 177-178 ; the writer was the lowest rank in
the company's service, next came the factor, then the junior merchant, then the
senior merchant, Ninth Report of the Committee of the House of Commons (1783)
Burke, Works iv 23.
[4] Lecky, Hist. of England iv 267.
[5] Camb. Hist. of the Empire iv 177 ; below 162, 231-232.
[6] Camb. Hist. of the Empire iv 177-180.

had made for increasing the pay of its servants from the salt monopoly, so that, when he left India, the old abuses revived.[1]

(2) *The results of the inefficiency of the company's government upon its relations to the state.*

The large opportunities for enrichment which were open to the servants of the company had resulted in an influx into England of newly rich men from India, who were soon nick-named "Nabobs." The newly rich are never popular—even in a democratic society. Much more were they distasteful to the aristocratic eighteenth-century society. They not only forced themselves on the attention of society in town and country, but, what was more serious, they forced themselves on the attention of the political world by the way in which they bought their way into the House of Commons.[2] This touched the political world in its tenderest spot; for these practices tended to upset the working of that delicately adjusted system of influence, by means of which the balance of the constitution was preserved.[3] The "Nabobs," being unattached to any particular party, and being desirous to gain the honours and decorations which would give them a place in society, naturally attached themselves to the growing party of the King's friends.[4] For all these reasons they were denounced by Chatham in 1770.[5] But here we are concerned with the effect which Clive's military successes and the consequent influx of "Nabobs" produced upon the company, and upon the relations of the company to the state.

The successes of the company's troops in India, and the great fortunes made by its servants, naturally led the share-

[1] Lecky, History of England iv 270-271; Lecky says that if " the lines of his policy had been steadily maintained, the affairs of the Company might never have passed under the hostile notice of Parliament" ; for Clive's account of this episode see Parlt. Hist. xvii 364-371.

[2] Erskine May, Constitutional History i 335-336.   [3] Vol. x 577-580.

[4] Erskine May, Constitutional Hist. i 336; Burke, in his speech on Fox's India Bill, said that these nabobs, needing protection, naturally attached themselves to ministers who could protect them—" when he comes to England he comes as to a prison or as to a sanctuary; and either is ready for him according to his demeanour. . . . That man's whole fortune . . . becomes an instrument of influence, without a shilling of charge to the civil list; and the influx of fortunes which stand in need of this protection is continual," Works ii 240 ; cp. a speech of T. Townshend in 1781, Parlt. Hist. xxii 334-335.

[5] " For some years past there has been an influx of wealth into this country, which has been attended with many fatal consequences, because it has not been the regular natural consequence of labour and industry. The riches of Asia have been poured in upon us, and have brought with them not only Asiatic luxury, but, I fear, Asiatic principles of government. Without connections, without any natural interest in the soil, the importers of foreign gold have forced their way into Parliament, by such a torrent of private corruption, as no private hereditary fortune could resist. . . . The corruption of the people is the great original cause of the discontent of the people themselves, of the enterprise of the Crown, and the notorious decay of the internal vigour of the constitution," ibid xvi 752.

holders of the company to conclude that its affairs were in a flourishing condition.

On the dispatch bearing the grant of the Diwani being read to the Court of Proprietors they began to clamour for an increase of dividend, and, in spite of the Company's debts and the opposition of the directors, they insisted on raising the dividend in 1766 from 6 to 10 per cent., and in 1767 to 12½ per cent.[1]

At the same time, the manner in which the company conducted its affairs at home and in India had begun to arouse criticism. There had been struggles between different parties in the company to gain control of it, and votes had been bought and sold.[2] Some rumours of the manner in which the servants of the company had made their money gave rise to well-founded suspicions as to the manner in which the company was using its political power in India. Moreover, the great accession of political power which the company had gained raised the important constitutional question of its right to the possession and exercise of this power. Did not such power, it was asked, vest in the Crown? Of this constitutional question I shall speak later.[3] At this point we must note another effect of this criticism. The necessity of reforming the constitution of the company, and the claims of the state to share in profits which it was supposed to be making, gave rise in 1766 to an enquiry into the state of the company.[4] As the result of that enquiry four Acts were passed in 1767, which were directed to reforming the company's constitution, and to securing some part of the profits of the company for the state.

The first Act made it necessary for a holder of stock to have held it for six months before he was qualified to vote in respect of it ; and prohibited the declaration of a dividend except at one of the half-yearly or quarterly courts, and at the distance of at least five months from the last declaration of a dividend.[5] The second Act regulated the procedure to be followed on the declaration of a dividend, and prohibited the company from declaring a larger dividend than 10 per cent. till the next session of Parliament.[6] The third Act reduced the tea duty on the company undertaking to make good the deficiency arising from

---

[1] Ilbert, Government of India 38.   [2] Ibid ; above 154.
[3] Below 230-232.   [4] Ilbert, op. cit. 38.
[5] 7 George III c. 48 ; the Preamble recites that " of late years a most unfair and mischievous practice has been introduced of splitting large quantities of stock, and making separate and temporary conveyances of the parts thereof, for the purpose of multiplying or making occasional votes immediately before the time of declaring a dividend, of choosing directors, or of deciding any other important question."
[6] Ibid 49 ; it should be noted that Lord Mansfield said that this restraint on the dividend was an unprecedented act of power, and an interference with rights of property, Parlt. Hist. xvi 351 note ; cp. Burke's views as to the absolute right of the Company to its territorial possessions, below 161.

the reduction.[1] The fourth Act provided that in consideration of the payment to the state of £400,000 for two years, " all the territorial acquisitions and revenues lately obtained in the East Indies shall remain in the possession of the United Company and their successors during the said term of two years." [2] In 1768 the restriction on the amount of the dividend which could be declared by the company was continued for a year.[3] In 1769 the agreement as to the payment of £400,000 a year in consideration of the recognition of the company's title to its territorial acquisitions was prolonged for five years ; the company was required to export a certain quantity of British goods ; and regulations were made as to the conditions under which the company could increase its dividend up to the limit of 12½ per cent.[4]

(3) *The effects both of the inefficiency of the company's government and of its relations to the state upon its financial position.*

It is clear from the proceedings of the company, and from this legislation, that everybody believed that the company was making very large profits. Down to 1772 dividends were declared at the rate of 12 and 12½ per cent. ; [5] and, at the same time, it was under a statutory obligation to pay a large subsidy to the state. But these appearances of prosperity were delusive. The wealth of the " Nabobs," so far from proving the capacity of the company to pay, really represented wealth which was, to a very large extent, subtracted from the coffers of the company—" whilst the servants of the company were amassing colossal fortunes, the company itself was advancing by rapid strides to bankruptcy." [6] The expenses of its government, and especially its military expenses, were very heavy ; in 1769 Hyder Ali inflicted a disastrous defeat on the company's forces in the Carnatic ; and in 1770 Bengal was devastated by a terrible famine.[7]

In 1772 the crisis came. The company tried to get Parliament to pass a bill to establish a new system of judicature in Bengal, to restrain the governor and council from trading, and to give the company a larger control over its servants. But the bill was thrown out.[8] The debates showed that an enquiry into the conduct of the company's affairs, and the doings of its servants was a necessary preliminary to legislation ; and so the House of Commons appointed a committee of enquiry.[9] Later in the year the company was obliged to confess that it

[1] 7 George III c. 56.
[2] Ibid c. 57.
[3] 8 George III c. 11.
[4] 9 George III c. 24.
[5] Ilbert, op. cit. 40.
[6] Ibid 39.
[7] Ibid 40.
[8] Parlt. Hist. xvii 327, and the account of the bill from the *Annual Register* there cited.
[9] Ilbert, op. cit. 40.

could not meet its obligations, and applied to the government for the loan of at least one million. Parliament's answer was the appointment of a new and secret committee of enquiry.[1] The first result of the deliberations of this committee was an Act suspending for six months the power of the company to appoint commissioners to regulate its affairs in its Presidencies.[2] In the following year two bills were proposed. They were vehemently opposed. One of their principal opponents was Burke, who argued that they were an attack on the chartered rights of the company, that the company had a clear right to its territorial possessions, and that its difficulties were mainly due to the exactions and the interferences of the Government.[3] But the need for reform was so obvious that they were carried by large majorities.[4]

One of these Acts dealt with the financial position of the company. A loan of £1,400,000 at 4 per cent. was granted to the company. The annual payment of £400,000 was remitted till their debt was discharged. Till then no dividend above 6 per cent. could be declared, and no dividend above 7 per cent. till the bond debts of the company were reduced to £1,500,000. Half-yearly accounts must be submitted to the Treasury. The company was disabled from accepting any bills drawn by its servants for an amount exceeding £300,000 a year, without the consent of the Treasury. British goods to a specified value must be annually exported by the company.[5] The other Act, generally known as The Regulating Act,[6] is, constitutionally, the most important. The deliberations of the secret committee had shown up some of the abuses of the company's government in India, and had made it plain that the company's political powers must be controlled by the State. The Act, therefore, created a partnership in the exercise of these political powers between the company and the state, and thus inaugurated that dual system of control under which India was governed till 1858. The passing of this Act marks, therefore, the beginning of the system under which a large part of our Indian Empire was acquired, under which it was governed, and under which its relations with the Indian States and their rulers were gradually settled.

The period inaugurated by this Act falls into two well-marked divisions—first the period from the passing of the Regulating Act in 1773 [7] to the passing of Pitt's Act for the government of India in 1784 ; [8] and, secondly, the period after 1784,

---

[1] Ilbert, op. cit. 40.   [2] 13 George III c. 9.
[3] Parlt. Hist. xvii 818-823, 834-835 ; Lecky, History of England iv 278-280.
[4] Ibid 281.   [5] 13 George III c. 64.   [6] Ibid c. 63.
[7] Ibid.   [8] 24 George III Sess. 2 c. 25.

when the system of government in India down to 1858 was settled, partly by later legislation, but mainly by the exercise of the powers conferred by the Act of 1784.[1]

The Indian problem which Parliament was called upon to face in 1773 was both new and difficult. In the first place, there was the difficulty of adapting British ideas of law and government to a country possessed of totally different ideas on these matters. This was then and always has been a difficult problem—a problem the difficulty of which has been materially increased in our own day by the wholly false assumption that there is in fact no such problem, and that British ideas of law and government can be transplanted *en bloc* to a country with a totally different past, and totally different moral and intellectual ideas.[2] In the second place, there was the difficulty arising out of the relations between the company and the state, and out of the different views which were held as to the rights of the company and the state to the company's territorial acquisitions.[3] On this matter three views were possible—first to leave the power of the company intact, secondly to take away from the company all its political powers and annex them to the state, or thirdly to create a partnership between the company and the state in respect of the company's political powers.[4] Having regard to the enormous abuses in the company's government previously known to exist,[5] and now proved by the enquiries of the select committee and the secret committee of the House of Commons,[6] the first course was impossible. The second course, which was favoured by Chatham,[7] would have been impolitic, partly because it would have run counter to those who saw in it an attack on proprietary rights granted by charters and sanctioned by Parliament,[8] and partly because annexation of the company's territorial possessions by the state " might be represented as sheer usurpation against the Moghul Empire, and Great Britain might be embroiled with the representatives of other European nations in the East." [9] The third course was therefore adopted. Having regard to the state of public opinion, it was the only possible course.

Both at this period and later the constitutional question

---

[1] Though the Act of 1784 had been almost wholly superseded by the Acts of 1793, 1813, and 1833, many of its provisions appeared in the later Acts, Ilbert, op. cit. 62 n. 1.

[2] Below 185-189.   [3] Above 157 ; below 231-232.

[4] Camb. Hist. of the Empire iv 183-184.

[5] Above 152-157 ; cp. Burgoyne's speech in 1772 on his motion for a select committee, Parlt. Hist. xvii 453-459.

[6] Camb. Hist. of the Empire iv 186-187, and the authorities there cited.

[7] Lecky, Hist. of England iii 397.   [8] Above 161.

[9] Camb. Hist. of the Empire iv 183.

of the government of India was bound up with the personal question of responsibility for past abuses.   The conduct of Clive had aroused almost as much feeling as the conduct of Warren Hastings was later to arouse.[1]   Both on the personal and on the constitutional question the House of Commons pursued a policy which was eminently judicious.

On the personal question the House passed· a resolution to the effect that Clive had, " through the influence of the powers with which he was intrusted, as a member of the select committee, and commander in chief of the British forces," possessed himself of sums of money amounting to £234,000.   But it refused to assent to the proposition that he had abused his powers ; and it did assent to the proposition that he had " at the same time rendered great and meritorious services to this country." [2]

On the constitutional question, the House resolved that " all acquisitions, made under the influence of a military force, or by treaty with foreign princes, do of right belong to the state " ;   that the appropriation of such acquisitions by persons in the civil or military service of the state was illegal ; and that such appropriation had been made by such persons in Bengal.[3]   These resolutions involved the acceptance of the principle that the state had the right to exercise control over the company's acquisitions in India.   But the principle was not pressed to its logical conclusion.   As Stephen has said, the provisions of the Regulating Act show " unwillingness to deal roughly with the theory of the East India Company " that Parliament had no right to interfere with its territorial acquisitions ; [4]   for those provisions established, not the complete control of the state, but a partnership in that control between the company and the state.   This will be obvious if we look at the objects of the Act, and the manner in which it attempted to effect them.

The three main objects of the Act were (1) the reform of the constitution of the company ;   (2) the reform of the company's government in India ;   and (3) the provision of remedies against illegalities and oppressions committed by the company's servants.

(1) The following were the principal reforms in the constitution of the company :   directors were to hold office for four years, a quarter of the board retiring annually.[5]   No person who had served the company in India was to be capable of election as a director until he had returned to England and had been resident there for two years.[6]   Collusive transfers

---

[1] Below 196-203.   [2] Parlt. Hist. xvii 881-882.
[3] Ibid 856, 870 ; cp. Berridale Keith, Constitutional History of India 20, 69, 70.
[4] Nuncomar and Impey i 14.
[5] 13 George III c. 63 § 1.   [6] § 2.

of stock for the purpose of creating votes were avoided and penalized, and stock-holders must have held their stock for twelve months before they were qualified to vote.[1] A holder of less than £1,000 of stock was not to have a vote.[2]

(2) The machinery of the company's government in India was recast, and rules were made for the conduct of the company's servants. The presidency of Fort William in Bengal was placed under the government of a governor-general and four councillors.[3] The Act appointed Warren Hastings as the first governor-general, and Clavering, Monson, Barwell, and Francis as the four councillors, all for five years.[4] They were not to be removable except by the King upon a representation made by the board of directors.[5] After the expiration of five years the directors could appoint and remove the governor-general and council.[6] The Act also specially saved the right of the company to appoint and control such other officers, agents, or factors as they saw fit.[7] To the governor-general and the four councillors was entrusted the civil and military government of the presidency of Fort William, and of the territorial possessions and revenues of the company in Bengal, Bihar, and Orissa, " during such time as they shall remain in the possession of the United Company."[8] If the governor-general and councillors were divided in opinion, the opinion of the majority was to prevail, and in case of an equal division the governor-general was to have a casting vote.[9] The governor-general and council were given a superintending and controlling power over the presidencies of Madras, Bombay, and Bencoolen.[10] Except in case of imminent necessity, and except in cases where direct orders had been sent from England, the subordinate presidencies were to have no power to make war or enter into treaties without the consent of the governor-general and council ; they were to obey the orders of the governor-general and council, and keep them informed of all matters "relating to the government revenues and interest " of the company.[11] Besides these powers of government in Bengal, and these powers of control over the other presidencies, the governor-general and council were given power to make regulations for the good order and government of all the company's settlements at Fort William and factories and places subordinate thereto,[12] But these regulations were

[1] § 3.   [2] Ibid.   [3] § 7.
[4] § 10.   [5] Ibid.   [6] Ibid.
[7] § 12.   [8] § 7.   [9] § 8.
[10] § 9 ; Bencoolen was in Sumatra, and was handed over to the Dutch in 1824 in exchange for " establishments on the continent of India and for the town and fort of Malacca and its dependencies . . . by 5 George IV c. 108," Ilbert, Government of India (3rd ed.) 45 n. 2.
[11] 13 George III c. 63 § 9.   [12] § 36.

not to be repugnant to the laws of the realm ; they must be registered in the supreme court " with the consent and approbation of the said court " ; [1] persons aggrieved by them, whether in India or England, could appeal to the King in Council against them ; they must be affixed in some conspicuous place in the India House ; [2] copies must be transmitted to the Secretary of State ; and the Crown could within two years disallow them.[3] Within the presidency of Fort William, and within the other settlements and factories subordinate thereto, the governor-general and council and the judges of the supreme court had the powers of justices of the peace.[4]

Liberal salaries were provided by the Act for the governor-general and council, and for the judges of the supreme court established by the Act, which were charged on the revenues of the company's territorial acquisitions in Bengal.[5] They and other servants of the company were expressly prohibited from accepting presents or from engaging in traffic on their own account.[6] It was also provided that none of his Majesty's subjects could take for loans of money or merchandize a higher rate of interest than 12 per cent.[7]

The relations of the governor-general and council to the company were similar to the relations of the subordinate presidencies to themselves—both sets of relations were dealt with in the same section of the Act.[8] They must obey the orders of the directors, and advise them upon all matters " relating to the government, commerce, revenues, or interest " of the company. The directors must, within fourteen days of the receipt of such letters of advice, transmit to the Treasury a copy of such parts of them as related to the revenue of the company, and to the Secretary of State a copy of such parts of them as related to the civil and military affairs and to the government of the company.[9]

(3) The Act contained a large number of important provisions designed to provide remedies against illegalities and oppressions committed by the company's servants. From the

---

[1] It would seem that the court could have refused to approve and therefore to register ; disputes upon this question did not arise, but it was probably because the court had this power that the governor-general and council did not attempt to decide by regulation the disputes which arose as to the jurisdiction of the court, below 186-189 ; in 1781 the governor-general and council acquired power to legislate in matters of revenue without reference to the supreme court, 21 George III c. 70 § 8 ; Ilbert, Government of India 59 ; the power of making regulations without the need for registration was extended by 37 George III c. 142 § 8 ; but the need for registration in the case of regulations intended to be operative in Calcutta, and also in the towns of Madras and Bombay, where supreme courts had been constituted, and not coming within the provisions of these two statutes lasted till 1833, 3, 4 William IV c. 85 § 45 ; below 224.

[2] 13 George III c. 63 § 36.   [3] § 37.
[4] § 38.   [5] § 21.   [6] §§ 23, 24, 27.
[7] § 30.   [8] § 9.   [9] Ibid.

beginning of the eighteenth century the Legislature had been conscious of the need to provide remedies against colonial governors who oppressed their subjects, or who broke the laws of England or of their colonies. We have seen that a statute of 1700 had enacted that governors accused of these offences could be tried by the court of King's Bench.[1] The provisions of this statute were extended in 1760 to the presidents and councils of the company's settlements in India.[2] But the evidence produced in 1772 to the committees of the House of Commons, showed that very much more elaborate provisions were required to meet the needs of the situation which existed in India. These provisions fell into two classes. First the provisions which established a supreme court and defined its jurisdiction ; and, secondly, the provisions which dealt with offences committed by the governor-general or his councillors, by the judges of the supreme court, and by other servants of the company.

(i) The Act provided that the Crown might by charter or letters patent establish a supreme court at Fort William, consisting of a chief justice and three other judges ;[3] the court was given

full power and authority to exercise and perform all civil, criminal, admiralty, and ecclesiastical jurisdiction, and to appoint clerks and other ministerial officers ; . . . and to form and establish such rules of practice, and such rules for the process of the said court, and to do all such other things as shall be found necessary for the administration of justice, and the due execution of all or any of the powers which, by the said charter shall or may be granted and committed to the said court.

The court was to be a court of record ; and it was to be a court of oyer and terminer and gaol delivery for the town of Calcutta, the factory of Fort William, and the factories subordinate thereto.[4] Its jurisdiction was to extend to all British subjects in Bengal, Bihar, and Orissa.[5] It could hear all complaints against British subjects for crimes and oppressions ; and these offences were to be tried by a jury of British subjects resident in Calcutta.[6] It could hear charges of breach of public trust, embezzlement, and frauds upon the company, made against the servants of the company.[7] It could hear all civil actions against British subjects, and against persons who, when the cause of action arose, were employed directly or indirectly by the company

[1] 11, 12 William III c. 12 ; vol. vi 402. [2] 1 George III c. 14 § 2.
[3] 13 George III c. 63 § 13 ; cp. Keith, op. cit. 73-75.
[4] Ibid. [5] § 14. [6] § 34.
[7] § 33 ; it was provided by § 35 that servants of the company, dismissed for misbehaviour, could not be reinstated without the consent of three-fourths of the directors and proprietors.

or by any of his Majesty's subjects.[1]   It could hear actions upon
contracts in writing brought by a British subject against a native
inhabitant of Bengal, Bihar, and Orissa, provided that the sum at
issue exceeded five hundred rupees, and provided that the contract contained a clause whereby the native agreed to submit to
the jurisdiction of the supreme court.[2]   A right of appeal from
the decisions of the supreme court was given to the King in
Council.[3]

The charter by which, in pursuance of these statutory powers,
the supreme court was established, was possibly drawn by
Impey, the first chief justice ; [4] but it was revised and settled
by Thurlow the attorney-general, Wedderburn the solicitor-
general, De Grey chief justice of the Common Pleas, and
Bathurst the Lord Chancellor.[5]   It defined the jurisdiction of the
court in accordance with the terms of the Act ; and empowered
the court to suspend the execution of capital sentences until the
King's pleasure was signified.[6]

The Act and the charter make it clear that the Legislature
intended to guard against the oppressions, of which the servants
of the company had been guilty, by giving to those aggrieved
thereby the benefit of the rule of law ; and that it intended
to make the rule of law effective by entrusting its administration
to a strong and independent court.   This intention must have
been obvious to those who drew the charter, and may well have
been stressed in the discussions which Impey had with those who
revised the draft.   If this is so, it will, as we shall see, go far to
explain the attitude which he adopted in the matters of dispute
which arose between the supreme court and the governor-general
and council.[7]   But the Legislature was aware that the supreme
court could not be so constituted that it was a complete safeguard
against oppression.   It was impossible to give it complete jurisdiction over the acts of the governor-general and council.   The
Act expressly provides that they were exempt from its criminal
jurisdiction except in cases of treason and felony,[8] and that they
should not be liable to be arrested upon any civil suit begun in
the court.[9]   Therefore it was necessary to make special provision
for offences committed both by the governor-general and his
councillors and by the judges of the court.

(ii) The Act, in the first place, provides generally that the
governor-general, and the president or governor and council

[1] § 14.
[2] § 16 ; such suits could be brought in the first instance before the supreme
court, or it could hear these suits on appeal from the provincial courts, ibid.
[3] § 18.
[4] Stephen, Nuncomar and Impey i 18, and Impey's statement to the House of
Commons in 1788, Parlt. Hist. xxvi 1354, cited ibid 17-18.
[5] Stephen, op. cit. i 17.   [6] Ibid 19.
[7] Below 186-189.   [8] 13 George III c. 63 § 15.   [9] § 17.

of any of the company's settlements, the judges of the supreme court or of any other court in any of the company's settlements, any other person in the military or civil employ of the company, and any of his Majesty's subjects in India, who commit any offence against the Act, or against another subject, or a native, "within their respective jurisdictions," and who have not been tried for the same offence in India, can be tried by the court of King's Bench.[1] In addition to any other punishment, the court could declare the offender incapable of serving the company in any capacity.[2] In the second place, to meet the difficulty of proving offences committed in India, the court of King's Bench was empowered to award writs of mandamus, requiring the judges of the supreme court, and of the mayor's courts at Madras, Bombay, and Bencoolen, to examine witnesses, and to transmit the record of the examination to it.[3] In the case of offences alleged against the judges of the supreme court the mandamus for the examination was to go to the governor-general and council.[4] In the case of proceedings in Parliament relative to offences committed in India, the Lord Chancellor or Speaker of the House of Commons could issue warrants to the governor-general and council, or to the judges of the supreme court or of the mayor's courts of Madras, Bombay, or Bencoolen, for the examination of witnesses.[5] Such proceedings in Parliament were not to be discontinued by a prorogation or a dissolution.[6]

The Regulating Act thus created a new machinery of central government for the settlements of the company in India, and for its territorial possessions in Bengal, Bihar, and Orissa; and this new machinery of government was responsible partly to the company and partly to the state. Thus a partnership in the government of India between the company and the state was created and the system of dual control was established. This new machinery, thus controlled, was superimposed on the existing, and as yet very rudimentary, machinery which the company had set up. In these circumstances, it was inevitable that the relations between the different parts of this new machinery, and its relations to the existing machinery of government, should cause difficulties. Both the new and the old machinery of government were in an experimental stage; and a scheme which embodied an attempt to rule a large territory by the joint efforts of a commercial company and the state, was a wholly new political experiment. The difficulties which were bound to

---

[1] § 39.   [2] Ibid.

[3] § 40 ; § 44 provided that, if the company or any other persons began any action or suit in law or equity in England, upon a cause of action or suit which had arisen in India, the court could require the supreme court, or the courts of Madras Bombay, or Bencoolen, to take the evidence of witnesses in India.

[4] § 41.   [5] § 42.   [6] § 43.

arise from these causes, were aggravated by the personal
enmities which arose between the governor-general and his
council ; and it is the personal element, thus introduced into
the political and constitutional controversies to which the
working of the Act gave rise, which invests these controversies
with their dramatic colour, and gives them their large effects
upon the fate of the principal actors, upon the course of the
Parliamentary controversies which they occasioned, and upon
the future government of India. Therefore to understand the
effects of this Act, and the difficulties which it caused, we must
look, first, at the existing machinery of law and government
for the company's possessions in India, and its modifications
by the government set up by the Act ; secondly, at the defects
in the Act ; and, thirdly, at the consequences which, directly
and indirectly, resulted from the personal enmities which arose
between the governor-general and his council.

(1) The man who began the long task of constructing a
machinery of law and government for the company's territorial
possessions of India was greatest of all Indian statesmen—
Warren Hastings. He had begun this work before the passing
of the Regulating Act. As governor-general under that Act he
continued it ; and, when he left India in 1785, he had laid the
foundations of the system of law and government upon which
Pitt's Act and later Acts [1] were built. While he was doing this
great constructive work, he was upholding the power of the
company, both as against its European rivals and as against the
native princes, so successfully that, when he returned to England,
Great Britain was rapidly becoming the paramount power in India.[2]
And he accomplished all this during the crisis of the American
war, when he could get no help from home. As Macaulay truly
says,[3] in these disastrous years " the only quarter of the world
in which Britain had lost nothing was the quarter in which her
interests had been committed to the care of Hastings." In
addition to these two great achievements, he had put the
finances of the company upon a sound basis ; [4] and, by his
encouragement of the study of the literature of the East, he had
made it possible for the servants of the company to acquire a
knowledge of Indian legal, political, and religious ideas, without
which the intelligent government of the company's possessions,
and intelligent and fruitful negotiation with the native princes,
would have been impossible.[5]

From the point of view of legal history it is with the first
of Hastings's achievements—the construction of a machinery

---

[1] Below 204-210.   [2] Below 177-179.
[3] Essay on Warren Hastings.
[4] Below 176 177.   [5] Below 175-176.

of law and government for the company's territorial possessions —that we are chiefly concerned. With his other achievements I shall only deal in so far as they bear upon his work in the sphere of public law.

Hastings first came to India in 1750 as a writer in the company's service. He fought as a volunteer under Clive; and Clive was so impressed by his ability, that he made him resident at the court of Meer Jaffir, whom he had made nawab of Bengal after the battle of Plassey. Hastings became a member of council at Calcutta in 1760, and supported Vansittart, the governor, against his corrupt council. He returned to England in 1764.[1] "It is certain that at this time he continued poor; and it is equally certain that by cruelty and dishonesty he might easily have become rich."[2] He gave evidence to the committee of the House of Commons which had been appointed in 1766; and the company was so impressed with his ability that in 1768 they appointed him second councillor in the Madras government. He showed such ability at Madras that in 1771 he was appointed governor at Bengal.[3] We have seen that in 1773 he was appointed governor-general by the Regulating Act.[4] He continued to be governor-general till he left India in 1785.

Since the company had resolved "to stand forth as Diwan," that is to administer their territorial possessions directly,[5] it fell to Hastings to devise the requisite machinery of law and government.

Until 1772 the company had exercised their rights of Diwani through native deputies, called naib diwans, controlled by supervisors appointed by the company.[6] This double government was ruining the country; and Hastings was ordered to put an end to it. This meant the construction of a wholly new system of government out of materials which he described as chaotic, and wholly unsuitable to the needs of a great province.[7] It meant, as he said, "implanting the authority of the Company, and the sovereignty of Great Britain, in the constitution of this country."[8]

The first step which was taken was the dismissal of the two naib diwans, Muhammad Reza Khan and Shitab Rai, and their prosecution for peculation. Both were acquitted, and it seems certain that the latter, at any rate, was not guilty.[9] In the proceedings against the former Hastings had obeyed the directors'

---

[1] G. W. Forrest, The Administration of Warren Hastings 1-2.
[2] Macaulay, Essay on Warren Hastings.   [3] Forrest, op. cit. 2-3.
[4] Above 164.   [5] Above 157.
[6] Camb. Hist. of the Empire iv 206.   [7] Above 153.
[8] Gleig, Memoirs of Hastings ii 30, cited Camb. Hist. of the Empire iv 209.
[9] Camb. Hist. of the Empire iv 209.

instructions to make use of Nundcoomar, whom he had met at Meer Jaffir's court, though he distrusted him.[1] Nundcoomar had hoped to supplant Muhammad Reza Khan. But Hastings had merely made use of him to facilitate the transfer of power from native to European hands ; and it was disappointment at failing to obtain what he expected which made him the bitter enemy of Hastings,[2] and led to a series of events which had a lasting effect upon Hastings' career and reputation.[3]

Having got rid of the naib diwans it was necessary to establish the new system. Hastings began by a measure of centralization. The Khalsa or treasury was moved from Moorshedabad to Calcutta. Thus all the governmental powers were centred in Calcutta, which became the capital of Bengal, and, as Hastings prophesied, the first city in Asia.[4] The whole council acted as a committee of revenue, and audited the accounts of the local authorities, assisted by an Indian officer called the rai raian. Its business was defined, and it was organized into departments.[5] In 1773 these duties were transferred to a committee of revenue, consisting of two members of the council, and three senior servants of the Company, assisted by the rai raian.[6] The committee was reorganized in 1781,[7] and further changes took place after the passing of Pitt's Act in 1786.[8]

It was a very much more difficult task to devise a method of settling the land revenue and a machinery for its collection. It was also a task of the first importance because the whole fabric of local government was largely dependent upon the measures which were taken.

The difficulties of this task were immense. All the necessary information was in the hands of the zamindars, who were agents for the collection of the revenue and had certain rights in the land, and the kanungos, who kept the records of dealings with the land and arrangements for the collection of the revenues.[9] With this exclusive knowledge the zamindars and the kanungos were naturally unwilling to part. The company's officers found that they were quite unable to ascertain " the difference between the sum received as land revenue by the government, and the sum actually paid by the ryot to the zamindar. This was the secret of the zamindar and kanungo which the company never fathomed." [10] The first attempts made by the government to settle the revenue were not very successful. The ignorance of

---

[1] Forrest, op. cit. 6-9 ; though he disliked Nundcoomar he pointed out that Meer Jaffir thought well of him, and that he had never been charged with infidelity to the sovereign to whom he owed allegiance, ibid 8.

[2] Ibid 10.　　　　　　　[3] Below 193-194.　　　　　　　[4] Forrest, op. cit. 11.
[5] Camb. Hist. of the Empire iv 416.　　　　　　　[6] Ibid 418.
[7] Ibid 427-429.　　　　　　　[8] Below 215.
[9] Camb. Hist. of the Empire iv 411 413.　　　　　　　[10] Ibid 413.

the government was aggravated by the disputes between Hastings
and the majority of the council appointed by the Regulating
Act—disputes which for a time delayed or rendered fruitless
many of Hasting's reforms in the machinery of law and government.[1] I do not propose to enter into the details of the different
schemes proposed by Hastings or by the council.[2] As in the case
of the organization of the central Treasury, so with the local
organization, it was a period of experiments. In 1772 the administration of the revenue was placed in the hands of the
company's collectors ; in 1773 it was turned over to provincial
councils ; in 1781 it was entrusted again to collectors. It was
not till 1786, after Pitt's Act, that a permanent system depending
on a responsible collector in each district was inaugurated.[3]
Thus the experiments tried during the administration of Hastings
failed to produce a permanent scheme. But, though they failed
to solve the problem, they prepared the way for its ultimate
solution. Hastings' experiments educated the men who went far
to solve the problem under his successors. Mr. Ramsbotham
says : [4]

The period 1765-1786 in the administration of the land revenues in
Bengal by the Company's servants is a record of progress from the
employment of untested theories to the establishment of an administration based on much solid knowledge. . . . The progress was largely
the result of unrecognized work by the district officers of the Company
in their own districts where, generally speaking, they laboured to
establish a just and humane collection of the land revenue. Their
advice, based on sound local knowledge, was too often rejected by
their official superiors in Calcutta, by whom, as well as by the Court
of Directors, they were regarded with suspicion and even hostility.
Their persistence had its reward : twenty years after the assumption
of the diwani the first sound and just administration of the land revenue
was established.

The machinery for the collection of revenue had always been
closely connected with the administration of justice [5]—we are
reminded of the same close connection which existed in England
in the Norman and Angevin period ; [6] and it long continued to

---

[1] Hastings wrote to the Directors in 1775, " I have seen all the labours of my
former Administration rendered abortive and my measures repealed for the sake of
condemning the principles on which they were formed," cited S. Weitzman, Warren
Hastings and Philip Francis 39, from Forrest, Selections from Letters, Despatches,
etc. ii 417 ; below 191-193.
[2] For details see Camb. Hist. of the Empire iv chap. xxv.
[3] Below 216.   [4] Camb. Hist. of the Empire iv 432.
[5] Shore, cited Camb. Hist. of the Empire iv 415, said, " it is impossible to draw
a line between the Revenue and Judicial Departments in such a manner as to
prevent their clashing : in this case either the Revenue must suffer or the administration of Justice be suspended. . . . It may be possible in course of time to induce
the natives to pay their rents with regularity and without compulsion, but this is
not the case at present."
[6] Vol. i 44.

be thus closely connected.[1] In the districts into which the country was divided for revenue purposes courts were set up, called courts of diwani adalat, with a civil and revenue jurisdiction.[2] The constitution of these courts varied from time to time with the different arrangements made for the collection of the revenue.[3] They were not very satisfactory courts when they were presided over by the members of the provincial councils ; and it was for that reason that in 1780 junior servants of the company were put at the head of new courts with a similar jurisdiction.[4] These courts were under the superintendence of the court of sadar diwani adalat, of which the governor-general and council were members.[5] This court, Hastings said in 1780,[6]

has been commonly, but erroneously, understood to be simply a Court of Appeals. Its province is, and necessarily must be, more extensive. It is not only to receive appeals from the decree of the inferior Courts in all causes exceeding a certain amount, but to receive and revise all the proceedings of the inferior Courts, to attend to their conduct, to remedy their defects, and generally to form such new regulations and checks as experience shall prove to be necessary to the purpose of their institution. Hitherto the Board has reserved this office to itself, but hath not yet entered into the execution of it, nor, I will venture to predict, will it ever with effect, though half of its time were devoted to this single department. Yet without the support and control of some powerful authority held over them, it is impossible for the Courts to subsist, but they must either sink into contempt, or be perverted into instruments of oppression.

It was in order to make the control of this court a reality, and to obviate the risk of the disputes which had recently taken place between the governor-general and council and the supreme court, that Hastings appointed Impey the judge of this court.[7] This was an expedient which had much to recommend it ; and it was in fact carried out eighty years later, when the supreme court and the sadar diwani adalat were united in the

---

[1] Macaulay, in his Notes on the Indian Penal Code, Works (Albany ed.) i 88-91, said that he and his colleagues had found it impossible to put into separate chapters contempts of courts, of revenue officers, and of the police—" The functions of Magistrate and Collector are very frequently united in the same person ; and that person is perpetually called upon, both as Magistrate and Collector, to perform acts which are judicial in their nature, to try offenders, and to decide litigated questions of civil right. While the division of labour between the different departments of the public service is so imperfect, it would be idle to make nice distinctions between those departments in the penal code."

[2] Camb. Hist. of the Empire iv 415.   [3] Ibid 418, 427-428.

[4] Stephen, Nuncomar and Impey ii 222-224.

[5] Camb. Hist. of the Empire iv 415 ; S. Weitzman. Warren Hastings and Philip Francis 61 ; it was for a time abolished when Francis and his party had the majority on the Council, ibid 64.

[6] Stephen, Nuncomar and Impey ii 225-226, citing Hastings' minute of Sept. 29 1780.

[7] Stephen, Nuncomar and Impey ii 226-228.

High Court.[1] But it did not then commend itself to Parliament which, in the Act of 1781, maintained the separation.[2]

For criminal cases there was another set of courts. "The head of the system was the Nawab Nazim, whom the Company kept up as a nominal subadar or governor under the nominal Emperor of Delhi."[3] Under him there were a series of criminal courts held by his deputies in Moorshedabad, his capital in Bengal.[4] In the country criminal justice was administered by the zamindars.[5] It was a system under which extortion and oppression were rampant. "The Nazims exacted what they could from the zamindars . . . whom they left at liberty to plunder all below."[6] In 1772 new courts were set up. In each district there was a court of faajari adalat staffed by Mahomedan judges and officials, who tried criminal cases in the presence of the collector, "whose duty it was to see that the trial was fairly conducted according to the law by which it professed to be guided."[7] From these courts appeal lay to the court of sadar nizamat adalat. This court was presided over by a Mahomedan judge; but the governor-general and council had powers of supervision. It administered Mahomedan law; but the governor-general assumed "a certain discretionary power in the interpretation of native practice when obscure or inhumane,"[8] which was virtually recognized as valid by the Regulating Act.[9]

Hastings was always anxious to strengthen the administration of the criminal law. In 1775 he introduced a new police system into Bengal.[10] But it did not work well. It was abolished in 1781, and the judges of the diwani adalat, collectors, and zamindars were given power to arrest dacoits, i.e. gang robbers, and those accused of crimes of violence.[11] In

---

[1] Ilbert, Government of India 55.

[2] 21 George III c. 70 § 8 ; below 189-190.

[3] Stephen, H.C.L. iii 285.   [4] Ibid 285-286.

[5] Ibid 286.   [6] Parlt. Papers 1812 vii 5.

[7] Stephen, H.C.L. iii 286-287 ; Camb. Hist. of the Empire iv 415.

[8] Weitzman, Warren Hastings and Philip Francis 61 ; while Francis's party had the majority on the council " it practically ceased to function," ibid.

[9] " The right existing in the government, to alter the Mahomeddan law, appears to have been virtually recognized in the Act of the 13 George III chap. 63 sect. 7, vesting in it authority for the ordering, managing and governing, ' in like manner and to all intents and purposes whatever, *as the same now are, or at any time heretofore might have been exercised* by the president and council in select committee' ; because it was *then* before the legislature, that the president and council *had* interposed, and altered the criminal law of the province in 1772," Parlt. Papers 1812 vii 40.

[10] " Native officers styled foujdars were appointed to the fourteen districts or local jurisdictions into which Bengal was divided, with an appropriate number of armed men, for the protection of the inhabitants, the detection and apprehension of public robbers, and for the transmission of intelligence to the presidency, of matters relating to the peace of the country," ibid 6.

[11] Ibid 9 ; Stephen, H.C.L. iii 287.

the same year Hastings established a separate department of the central government to which monthly reports of arrests and convictions were made.[1] But until the reforms of Cornwallis the police system, in the country at large, was in fact under the control of the zamindars.[2] Though Hastings' efforts to improve the administration of the criminal law were to a large extent fruitless while his opponents had the majority on the council, he had in the end a large measure of success. This was the opinion of a committee of the House of Commons in 1812,[3] and that opinion history has ratified. The company, says Mr. Ramsbotham,[4]

inherited from the Moghul government every evil that could afflict a political system : a disorganized and corrupt judicature and incompetent agents. Dacoity was rampant, and there was no ordinary security in the land. The new courts, although by no means perfect, brought great relief to the ryots and talukdars, and within a short time began to foster confidence in the Company's administration.

" For the first time within living memory," says Macaulay,[5] "the province was placed under a government strong enough to prevent others from robbing, and not inclined to play the robber itself." It is not surprising to find that this achievement was emphasized in many of the addresses which the natives of Bengal sent to Hastings on his departure from India.[6]

That Hastings' administration of justice, and his maintenance of law and order, were so successful, is partly due to the fact that he was as interested in the substantive law as in the machinery of justice. Outside the presidency towns, where English law prevailed, the natives were ruled by Hindu or Mahomedan law. Hastings had a digest of Hindu law prepared by ten pundits, and employed Nathaniel Halked to translate it.[7] He also had a translation made of a book of Mahomedan law, entitled the Hedaya, because, as he explained to the company, such a translation was necessary to the proper superintendence of the administration of criminal justice by the company's servants.[8] He established a college at Calcutta,

---

[1] Parlt. Papers 1812 vii 9-10.　　　　[2] Below 218.

[3] " An attentive consideration of the information which these documents afford has led your committee to believe that the administration of the British government proved at an early period of its introduction, beneficial to the natives of India residing under its protection," Parlt. Papers 1812 vii 10.

[4] Camb. Hist. of the Empire iv 416.

[5] Essay on Warren Hastings.　　　　[6] Below 179-180.

[7] D.N.B. sub voc. Hastings ;　Camb. Hist. of the Empire v 389-390.

[8] In a letter to the Directors of Feb. 21 1784 he said, " while the Mohammedan law is allowed to be the standard of the criminal jurisprudence of your dominion, under the control and inspection of your English servants, it seems indispensably necessary that judges of the courts should have a more familiar guide for their proceedings than the books of the Arabic tongue, of which few have opportunities of attaining a competent knowledge ; and as necessary that your servants should possess the means of consulting the principles on which those judgments are founded," Gleig, Memoirs of Warren Hastings iii 158-159.

in which Mahomedan students were instructed at the public expense in Mahomedan law and other subjects taught in Mahomedan schools.[1] A few years later a Sanscrit college was established at Benares by Duncan, the resident there, for the study of the laws, literature, and religion of the Hindus.[2] It is clear, therefore, that Hastings favoured the ideas of the party which came, in later years, to be known as the party of the Orientalists. That party favoured the policy of engrafting modern knowledge on the old system of Indian education, as contrasted with the English party which favoured the substitution for the old system of a purely English education.[3] We shall see that, when Impey was made judge of the sadar diwani adalat, he drew up a new code of procedure for that court, and that he thus became " the first of Indian codifiers."[4] Thus it was under the administration of Hastings that the different bodies of law, by which the natives were governed, began to be stated and systematically studied by natives and Englishmen, and that definite codes of procedure by means of which the law could be enforced began to be constructed. It was under his administration that the long process was begun of constructing from Indian and English materials a body of law, substantive and adjective, for all those parts of India which were under the direct rule of the company and the Crown.[5]

While Hastings, as a servant of the company and the Crown, was laying the foundations of the internal government of British India, as a servant of the company he was introducing reforms which restored its solvency.

In the first place, his administrative reforms, by purifying the administration, improved the territorial revenues of the company.[6] It is true that much remained to be done before the administration was entirely purified.[7] Appointments and promotions went by favour. " The relatives of directors expected special promotion without regard to seniority or talents."[8] The dissensions on the council made it necessary for Hastings to favour those who were willing to support him ;[9] and at the end of his administration there were too many servants of the company who were paid excessive salaries.[10] Thus the chief of the board which controlled the salt office had a salary of £18,480 a year.[11] Hastings himself was careless in his accounts ; and in spite of his own regulations his banyan farmed the revenue on a large scale.[12] But there is no doubt that Hastings himself

[1] Teignmouth, Memoirs of Sir William Jones 260 note.
[2] Camb. Hist. of the Empire v 96.
[3] Ibid 107.
[4] Below 222.   [5] Below 220-222.
[6] Below 172.
[7] Camb. Hist. of the Empire iv 210-212.
[8] Ibid 319.
[9] Ibid iv 212.
[10] Ibid 213.
[11] Ibid.
[12] Ibid 212-213.

was pure ; [1] and the fact that he could defend the large salaries
paid to the officials of the salt office, by proving that under his
new arrangement the company made a revenue of £540,000 a
year,[2] illustrates the extent to which his reforms improved the
financial position of the company. In the second place, his commercial reforms improved its revenues by increasing the prosperity
of its provinces. He abolished the use of the free pass, under
which the company's servants and their agents escaped customs
duties ; and he abolished the local custom houses in the zamin-
daris, and lowered the customs duties.[3] He stopped the practice
of forcing the weavers to work for the company and its servants
at fixed rates much under the market rates.

These measures restored, as he prophesied, the prosperity
of the country and therefore the prosperity of the company.[4]
By 1779 the company had repaid the £1,400,000 lent to it by
the state, and soon after it had reduced its bond debt to the
amount prescribed by the statute of 1773.[5] In 1791 Lushington,
the chairman of the court of directors, told the House of Commons
that " Bengal had for many years been in a very flourishing
state of improvement during all Mr. Hastings' administration.
When Mr. Hastings came to the government, the resources were
little more than three millions a year ; when he left it they
were more than five crores, an increase of about two millions a
year." [6]

As in the machinery of central government set up by the
Regulating Act,[7] so in the machinery of local government set up
by Hastings in the company's territorial possessions, we can
see the beginnings of the system which prevailed in British
India down to the abolition of the company's government in
1858. Similarly we can see in the work of the governor-general
and council, and in the work of the central courts English and
native, the beginnings of the different systems of law, substantive and adjective, by which in later days British India
will be ruled. But during the greater part of Hastings' administration there was war with the native princes, who were
assisted from 1778 to 1783 by the French. It is obvious that
Hastings could not have established this system of government
if he had not been able to defend his provinces against the
company's many enemies and keep them free from invasion.

The manner in which, by war and diplomacy, he attained
this result is the most spectacular and the most remarkable of

---

[1] This is admitted by Macaulay in his Essay on Hastings.
[2] Camb. Hist. of the Empire iv 213.   [3] Ibid 208-209.
[4] Forrest, The Administration of Warren Hastings 15-16.
[5] Ilbert, The Government of India 59 ; 19 George III c. 61 Preamble ; 13
George III c. 64 § 13.
[6] Parlt. Hist. xxviii 1259.   [7] Above 164-165.

all his achievements. His seizure of the French settlements in India,[1] his successes against the Marathas,[2] and his defeat of Hyder Ali in the Carnatic,[3] saved and secured the British dominions in India. His diplomatic dealings with the Indian princes and feudatories were all part of, and consequent upon, this need to defend his provinces against their enemies ; and they were as successful as his wars. Thus his dealings with the vizier of Oude, and the help which he gave him to conquer the Rohillas, were designed to give the company a secure frontier.[4] His dealings with Chayt Singh were designed to compel a feudatory, who owed services to the company, to perform those services at a time when the company's need was greatest.[5] His demands upon the Begums of Oude were justified, partly because they had abetted Chayt Singh's rebellion, and partly because they were possessed of money which belonged to the Nawab of Oude, who was a large debtor to the company.[6] It may be that the policy pursued in some of these cases was harsh and perhaps mistaken—though that was never proved. But there is no doubt that in all these cases it was a policy which, at a time of great danger, seemed best to the ablest man on the spot ; and there is no doubt that both in his wars and in his diplomacy Hastings was successful.

In spite of the utmost exertions both of European and Asiatic enemies the power of our country in the East had been greatly augmented. Benares was subjected : the Nabob Vizier reduced to vassalage. That our influence had been thus extended, nay, that Fort William and Fort St. George had not been occupied by hostile armies, was owing, if we may trust the general voice of the English in India, to the skill and resolution of Hastings.[7]

As the result of Hastings' successes in war and diplomacy it had become clear that Great Britain was in fact the paramount power in India. And so, just as we see in the government of that part of India over which the company ruled, some of the permanent features of the system of government which prevailed

---

[1] Forrest, op. cit. 153-160.

[2] Ibid 160-163 ; Camb. Hist. of the Empire iv 268, 269-271.

[3] Ibid 284-285 ; Forrest, op. cit. 232 seqq.

[4] Weitzman, Warren Hastings and Philip Francis 11 ; Professor Berriedale Keith takes the view that in this matter Hastings " is beyond excuse," op. cit. 68 ; and he is generally inclined to take a view of his conduct which more nearly accords with that of Macaulay than with other more recent authorities.

[5] This is the view taken by Forrest, Administration of Warren Hastings 190-210 ; but Mr. Roberts takes the view that Hastings' demands were excessive and that Chayt Singh never rebelled, though his troops mutinied on account of the way in which their master had been treated, Camb. Hist. of the Empire iv 295-299; cp. Berriedale Keith, op. cit. 83.

[6] Forrest, op. cit. 210-230 ; but cp. Camb. Hist. of the Empire iv 299-302, Berriedale Keith, op. cit. 83.

[7] Macaulay, Essay on Hastings.

till 1858 ; [1] so, in the relation of the company to the subordinate princes and feudatories, we see the beginnings of that distinction between British India and the Indian States which still prevails.[2] We see the causes at work which will eventually lead to a body of legal doctrine, which will define the rights, duties, and obligations of the Paramount Power and the Indian States.[3]

Hastings had hoped that Pitt's India Bill would have given him the powers which he needed to complete his work.[4] But Pitt's speech on the introduction of the bill showed him that this was not to be.[5] In fact " Pitt had learned the little he knew of Indian affairs from sources hostile to the governor-general." [6] And so Hastings was obliged to leave his work unfinished— " a great and weighty fabric of which all the parts were yet loose and destitute of the superior weight which was to give them their mutual support and their collateral weight." [7] But, though his work was unfinished, it was very permanent ; and in some cases, where his policy was reversed, it was later found necessary to return to it.[8] But perhaps the most striking testimony to the greatness of his achievements is to be found in the unanimous opinion of his contemporaries in India—English and native alike. They had seen and known him, and were eye-witnesses of the changes which he had wrought in the government of India and in the position of the company.

The natives were grateful to him for the manner in which he had kept the peace, put down oppression, and increased the prosperity of the provinces. The address of the inhabitants of

[1] Above 177.

[2] Burke said in 1783 that " the British dominion, either in the Company's name or in the names of princes absolutely dependent upon the Company, extends from the mountains that separate India from Tartary to Cape Comorin," Works (Bohn's ed.) ii 181 ; below 195-196.

[3] Below 228.

[4] On his voyage home he wrote, " yet may I feel a regret to see that hope which I had too fondly indulged, and which I had sustained during thirteen laboured years with a perseverance against a succession of difficulties which might have overcome the constancy of an abler mind, of being in some period of time, however remote, allowed to possess and exercise the full powers of my station, of which I had hitherto held little more than the name and responsibility ; and to see with it the belief, which I had as fondly indulged, that I should become the instrument of raising the British name, and the substantial worth of its possessions in India, to a degree of prosperity proportional to such a trust, both vanish in an instant, like the illusions of a dream," cited Forrest, The Administration of Warren Hastings 308-309.

[5] He wrote to Scott, " Mr. Pitt's introductory speech is a very unpleasant indication of his disposition towards me . . . it admits all the slanders which Mr. Fox and Mr. Burke rendered ineffectual by the personal rancour which they manifested in their first promulgation of them. It contains the same indiscriminate abuse of the Company's servants," cited Weitzman, Warren Hastings and Philip Francis 169.

[6] Ibid 164.

[7] Camb. Hist. of the Empire iv 214, citing Forrest, Selections from the Papers of Warren Hastings ii 64.

[8] Below 227, 228.

Moorshedabad, which is only one of many such addresses, runs as follows : [1]

The whole period of Mr. Hastings' residence in this country exhibited his good conduct towards the inhabitants. No oppression nor tyranny was admitted over anyone. He observed the rules of respect and attention to ancient families. He did not omit the performance of the duties of politeness and civility towards all men of rank and station when an interview took place with them. In affairs concerning the government and revenues, he was not covetous of other men's money and property ; he was not open to bribery. He restricted the farmers and officers in their oppressions in a manner that prevented them from exercising that tyranny which motives of self interest and private gain might instigate them to observe towards the ryots and helpless. He used great exertions to cultivate the country, to increase the agriculture and the revenues. He transacted the business of the country and the revenues without deceit, and with perfect propriety and rectitude. He respected the learned and wise men, and in order for the propagation of learning he built a college, and endowed it with a provision for the maintenance of students, in so much that thousands reaping the benefits thereof offer up their prayers for the prosperity of England and for the success of the Company.[2]

It is certain that these addresses were voluntarily offered ; [3] and the truth of their contents is confirmed by much independent evidence.[4] Some of the native princes were equally ready to testify to his justice and good faith ; and " we have the letters of two of the leading native sovereigns to his successor requesting to be treated by him as they were treated by Hastings." [5] Macaulay admits that the English in India were his enthusiastic admirers and advocates.[6] The united testimony of so many different classes of people, with so many different interests, is obviously wholly inconsistent with the charges which the Whig party brought against him on his return [7]—charges to which Macaulay, too loyal to his Whig predecessors, has unfortunately given the sanction of his great name.

Hastings summed up his own achievements in a paper which he read to the House of Lords in 1791 ; and, in the opinion of

---

[1] Cited Forrest, The Administration of Warren Hastings 313-314 ; Sir George Forrest has completely disposed of the suggestion made by Burke and Macaulay that these testimonials were not freely given, ibid 310-312.

[2] Burke in his speech on Fox's India Bill, Works ii 195, said, " England has erected no churches, no hospitals, no palaces, no schools ; England has built no bridges, made no high roads, cut no navigations, dug out no reservoirs. Every other conqueror of every other description has left some monument, either of state or beneficence, behind him. Were we to be driven out of India this day, nothing would remain to tell that it had been possessed during the inglorious period of our dominion, by anything better than the ourang-outang or the tiger " ; this was an exaggeration when it was uttered ; in fact Warren Hastings began the process of creating a system of law, and, by his political achievements, made it possible for his successors to create those monuments and public works which distinguish the English from any of the former conquerors of India.

[3] See above n. 1.   [4] Forrest, op. cit. 314-315.
[5] Ibid 315.   [6] Essay on Warren Hastings.   [7] Below 197.

Stephen, his summary is strictly true. Two passages, which I have taken from Stephen, are perhaps the best summary of the results of his policy, domestic and foreign.[1] The first passage runs as follows :

Every division of official business which now exists in Bengal, with only such exceptions as have been occasioned by the changes of authority enacted from home, are of my formation. The establishment formed for the administration of the revenue, the institution of the courts of civil and criminal justice in the province of Bengal and its immediate dependencies ; the form of government established for the province of Benares with all its dependent branches of revenue, commerce, judicature, and military defence ; the arrangements created for the subsidy and defence of the province of Oude, every other political connection and alliance of the government of Bengal were created by me.

The following is the second passage :

The valour of others acquired, I enlarged and gave shape and consistency to, the dominion which you hold there ; I preserved it ; I sent forth its armies with an effectual, but economical hand, through unknown and hostile regions to the support of your other possessions ; to the retrieval of one from degradation and dishonour ;[2] and of the other from utter loss and ruin. . . .[3] I gave you all, and you have rewarded me with confiscation, disgrace, and a life of impeachment.

Why then was a statesman to whom his country was indebted as deeply as she was indebted to Clive, whose misdeeds were trivial compared with those committed by Clive, rewarded by an impeachment ? The answer is to be found mainly in those personal enmities which arose between Hastings and some of the members of the council which had been appointed by the Regulating Act. But, to understand the full effects of these personal enmities, it is necessary to say something of the consequences of certain defects in that Act.

(2) It was said by Burke that the clauses of the Act, which changed the constitution of the company,[4] were defective in that they disfranchised the smaller proprietors.[5] He contended that they threw the control of the company into the hands of men who bought shares merely in order to get a control which would enable them to secure a share in the patronage of the company.[6] Many of these men were the former servants of the company, who were thus able to stop enquiry into their own misdeeds.[7]

---

[1] Stephen, Nuncomar and Impey i 25-26, citing History of the Trial of Warren Hastings iv 97-104.

[2] Bombay.   [3] Madras.   [4] Above 163-164.

[5] Ninth Report of the House of Commons Committee, Works iv 7.

[6] Ibid 6-7.

[7] " To add to the votes, which is adding to the power, in proportion to the wealth of men, whose very offences were supposed to consist in acts, which lead to the acquisition of enormous riches, appears by no means a well-considered method of checking rapacity and oppression," ibid 7.

The result, he said, had been that

the general court so composed has at length grown to such a degree of contempt both of its duty and of the permanent interest of the whole corporation, as to put itself in open defiance of the salutary admonitions of this House, given for the purpose of asserting and enforcing the legal authority of their own body over their own servants.[1]

Burke's criticism is coloured by the bias with which, under the influence of Francis, he approached all questions relating to India.[2] It is at least arguable that, if the court of proprietors were thus composed of men who knew India at first hand, it was likely to know much that the House of Commons did not know ; and that their action in preventing the recall of Hastings in 1782 [3] was a service to India, which justified the control which they were able to exercise over the company's policy.

The two chief defects in the machinery for the government of the company's territorial possessions were (i) the fact that the governor-general was not given the power to override the majority of his council ; [4] and (ii) the fact that the control of Calcutta over the other presidencies was too weak.[5] We have seen that a power of control was given in the matters of war and treaties, but that there were exceptions in cases of imminent necessity, and in cases where direct orders had been sent from England.[6] As Burke rightly said, " the first exception leaves it open to the subordinate to judge of the necessity of measures, which, when taken, bind or involve the superior : the second refers a question of peace or war to two jurisdictions, which may give different judgments." [7] We shall see that, owing to the personal enmity, which at once arose between Hastings and the majority of the council appointed by the Regulating Act,[8] it was the first of these defects which produced the most lasting effects upon the manner in which the Act worked, upon Warren Hastings himself, and upon the future government of India.

But the greatest defect in the Act was the position which it gave to the supreme court. Of this defect in the Act I must speak at greater length. Though, as we shall see, its worst consequences were remedied in 1781,[9] the difficulties to which it gave rise aggravated the enmity between Hastings and the majority of his council, and formed part of the charges made by the House of Commons against Hastings and against Impey, the chief justice.[10]

[1] Ninth Report of the House of Commons Committee, Works iv 7-8.
[2] Below 197.   [3] Camb. Hist. of the Empire iv 193-194.
[4] Ibid 190.   [5] Ibid 190-191.
[6] Above 164 ; 13 George III c. 63 § 9.
[7] Works iv 12-13.   [8] Below 190-192.
[9] Below 189.   [10] Below 193-194, 202.

It is, I think, obvious that the Legislature, when it constituted the supreme court, had in view two main objects.   The
first object was to provide a tribunal with a general common
law jurisdiction in civil and criminal cases for the town of
Calcutta, and with a jurisdiction over all persons in the provinces of Bengal, Bihar, and Orissa who were British subjects,
or who were employed directly or indirectly by the company.[1]
It was not intended to give the court a general jurisdiction
over natives outside Calcutta, except in cases where they were
employed directly or indirectly by the company or by any of
his Majesty's subjects, and except in certain civil cases where
the parties had agreed to submit to its jurisdiction.[2]   The second
object was to provide a remedy against that oppression of the
natives, of which it was clear that the servants of the company
had been guilty, from the time when it had, by the grant of the
Diwani, become the ruler of Bengal, Bihar, and Orissa.[3]   This
object the Act attempted to secure, by extending to the company's territories the principle of English law, that all the servants
of the state are personally responsible to the law for all unlawful acts committed by them or by their express authority.
With certain exceptions made in favour of the governor-general
and council,[4] all the servants of the company were to be answerable to the criminal and civil jurisdiction of the court for acts
which, by the rules of English law, would expose them to
criminal or civil liability.[5]

But the clauses by which the Legislature attempted to
attain these two objects were by no means clearly worded.

In the first place, the persons over whom the jurisdiction
of the court extended were by no means precisely defined.   It
was clear that it extended over persons employed by the
company, and over the inhabitants of Calcutta.   But it was by
no means clear to what other classes of persons (if any) it extended, because it was not clear what classes of persons were
included under the term, " British subjects," or " his Majesty's
subjects."   As Stephen says,[6] " in one sense the whole

---

[1] Above 166;   13 George III c. 63 § 14.
[2] Above 166-167 ;   13 George III c. 63 § 16.   [3] Above 167.
[4] Above 167 ;   13 George III c. 63 § 15.
[5] Above 167 ;   13 George III c. 63 §§ 14, 33.
[6] Nuncomar and Impey ii 126 ;   the difficulty of deciding who was and who was
not a British subject was clearly pointed out by Sir Charles Grey, the chief justice
of the supreme court, in 1829, Parlt. Papers 1831 vi 534-540 (App. V pp. 66-72) ;
cp. a letter of 1830 from the judges of the supreme court to the board of control,
ibid 599-600 (App. V 131-132) ;   thus enormous difficulties were caused in defining
the jurisdiction of the supreme court, since that court had jurisdiction over British
subjects, for, " by the obscurity in which the dominion of the Indian territories has
been left, and by the uncertain use of the term ' subjects' and ' British subjects,' the
very alphabet, or at least the elementary terms in which the limits of the jurisdiction must be expressed, have been made as it were a foreign tongue," ibid 541

population of Bengal, Bihar, and Orissa were British subjects. In another sense no one was a British subject who was not an Englishman born. In a third sense inhabitants of Calcutta might be regarded as British subjects, though the general population of Bengal were not." In fact, as Macaulay pointed out,[1] these difficulties arose because the company was for a long time in theory "under two masters"—the King of England and the great Mogul. " It was long considered as a wise policy to disguise the real power of the English under forms of vassalage and to leave to the Mogul and his Viceroys the empty honours of a sovereignty which was really held by the Company." It was a wise policy in India because it made the diplomatic relations of the company with the country powers easier,[2] and in England because it prevented the raising of some very fundamental constitutional questions.[3] And so although, by the beginning of the nineteenth century, it was clear that the natives of the company's territorial possessions had become British subjects, " it would be impossible to point out the particular time when they became so," [4] and it was still very difficult to say who was and who was not a British subject.[5] It is clear, however, that the native inhabitants of the company's territorial possessions were not British subjects when the Regulating Act was passed ; and for that reason the supreme court did not assume jurisdiction over Hindus and Mahomedans unless they were resident at Calcutta.[6] But it did assume jurisdiction over persons who were by birth British subjects, and over persons employed directly or indirectly by the company or by any of his Majesty's subjects.

In the second place, what was the extent of the jurisdiction given to the court over persons employed directly or indirectly by the company or by any of his Majesty's subjects ? Probably Stephen is right when he says that the framers of the Act intended to give the court a very wide jurisdiction to define and supervise the powers of the governmental authorities central and local—" such questions being raised from time to time by actions brought against servants of the Company, or against the Company itself, for acts done in their official capacity." [7] To give the court this jurisdiction would, it was thought, be the best security that could be devised against oppression :

(App. V 73) ; the real remedy for these difficulties was the amalgamation of the supreme court and the company's courts—a measure which was carried out in 1861 when the present chartered High Courts were created, 24, 25 Victoria c. 104 ; Ilbert, Legislative Methods and Forms 131.

[1] Notes on the Indian Penal Code, Works (Albany ed.) i 71-72.
[2] Below 231-232.   [3] Above 162 ; below 231-232.
[4] Macaulay, Notes on the Indian Penal Code, Works (Albany ed.) i 72.
[5] Above 183 n. 6.   [6] Stephen, Nuncomar and Impey ii 127-128.
[7] Ibid 130.

To protect the natives against oppression was the purpose for which, on many occasions, the Court was alleged to have been established, but, according to the whole order of ideas current in England in the eighteenth century, the only way of effectively preventing oppression was by subjecting every one to actions in the courts at Westminster for any illegal act which he might commit, especially if it were done in any official or public character.[1]

But this extension to a totally new environment of the English principle of ministerial responsibility of the servants of the government to the law, was made without any consideration of the problems, which an attempt to work it out in that environment was bound to cause. The application of the principle of ministerial responsibility of the servants of the government to the law, is hardly possible unless the state is governed by a uniform system of law, which is administered by courts which have been entrusted with the whole judicial power of a sovereign state. No one of these conditions prevailed in Bengal. There was no uniform system of law; and while the supreme court took its powers from Parliament and the Crown, the courts which administered justice to the natives took their powers from the authority exercised by the company by virtue of its Diwani. No clear settlement had as yet been arrived at as to the ambit of the authority of those rival sources of political power. This question had been a matter of acute political controversy which was as yet undetermined.[2] According to one view, the Crown was entitled to assume control over the territorial acquisitions of the company and to govern them in its name. According to the other view, the government of these acquisitions was still in theory vested in the Nawab and the Mogul Emperor. The company had merely acquired from these potentates certain privileges to govern in their names, which privileges were as much the private property of the company as any of its other possessions; so that any attempt by Parliament to interfere with their exercise was an unwarrantable invasion of its proprietary rights.[3] The Regulating Act had not attempted to decide between these rival theories.[4] It had handed over to the company the government of its territorial acquisitions; and then it had provided that the governor-general and council, set up by

---

[1] Nuncomar and Impey ii 130.   [2] Above 162, 184.

[3] " The East India Company . . . and its leading servants in India . . . were greatly disposed to regard the sovereignty of India as their own private property, and to resent all interference with it by Parliament as a wholly unwarrantable and tyrannical invasion of their rights. . . . The policy of Parliament was to assert the rights of the King of England and to establish in India institutions by which those rights might be maintained," Stephen, Nuncomar and Impey ii 125.

[4] " Like many later statutes the Regulating Act used language involving problems the solution of which was left to those who had to work it, because Parliament either from ignorance or from timidity, did not choose itself to solve, or even to study, them," ibid.

the Act, should have the same civil and military powers over those acquisitions as the authorities whom they had superseded.[1] But in these circumstances it might be, and it was, contended that the governor-general and council had all the powers formerly possessed by the native rulers whose deputies they in theory were ; and that since the exercise of these powers was not controlled by any law, they were not answerable to the jurisdiction of the supreme court for any acts done in pursuance of them. This, it might be contended, was a field into which English law and the court which administered it had no right to penetrate.[2] Moreover, it was clear that, if the governor-general and council were obliged to obey all the rules of English law, civil and criminal, in their conduct of the government, that government could not be conducted at all. The machinery by which they exercised the powers which they possessed as Diwan, would not work if this limitation was imposed upon them.[3] On the other hand, it was reasonably clear that it was exactly this limitation which Parliament, in its ignorance of the political condition of Bengal, had attempted to impose.[4]

In these circumstances it was inevitable that conflicts should arise between the governor-general and council and the supreme court. The former resented the control which its jurisdiction imposed on their activities : the latter regarded itself as a tribunal which must at all costs maintain its jurisdiction to protect the natives from oppression. Since it was staffed by English lawyers, its members could not help being influenced by the common law principle of the supremacy of law over all members of the state from the highest to the lowest ; and they naturally thought it their duty to interpret liberally those clauses of the Regulating Act which evidently contemplated that the court should apply this principle in order to prevent oppression.

In 1775, within a year after the establishment of the court, complaints were made by the council of the jurisdiction over revenue officers, which the court was assuming.[5] These complaints were evoked by one or two cases in which the court had interfered with the action of the government. For instance, in the case of *Commaul O Dien* the Court had ordered a person,

[1] 13 George III c. 63 § 7.
[2] " Whenever the Company found it convenient, they could play off the authority derived from the Mogul against the authority derived from British law, and justify under the one proceedings which it would have been difficult to justify under the other. In the one capacity the Company were the all-powerful agents of an irresponsible despot ; in the other they were tied and bound by the provisions of charters and Acts of Parliament. It was natural that the Company's servants should prefer to act in the former capacity," Ilbert, Government of India 51-52.
[3] See a minute of the majority of the council written in 1776, cited Stephen, op. cit. ii 138-141.
[4] Ibid 148.   [5] Ibid 133.

committed to prison for non-payment of taxes by the Calcutta
revenue council, to be released on bail; [1] and other cases had
arisen in which, by means of writs of habeas corpus and mandamus, the supreme court had exercised supervision over the
courts and servants of the company.[2] At the same time the
European residents in Calcutta complained that, owing to the
interference of the court, actions for assault and false imprisonment, arising out of arbitrary actions committed by the company's servants and other Europeans, were encouraged.[3] It
was for this reason that the Europeans petitioned Parliament
for the institution of trial by jury in all cases where they were
parties to an action.[4] On this petition, Rous, the standing
counsel of the company, made the comment, "admit the trial by
jury in civil cases and the oppressors themselves will decide
the degree of compensation for their own wrongs"; [5] and this
was substantially the view taken by Impey.[6]

Much the most important cause of conflict was the difference between the council and the court as to the extent of
their powers. This conflict gave rise to two important cases—
the Patna case and the Cossijurah case—both of which were
subsequently made the ground of the proposal to impeach
Impey.

The Patna case [7] arose out of an action for assault and false
imprisonment brought against three defendants. Two of these
defendants were officials of the provincial council of Patna, and
the third was a farmer of the revenue, and therefore a person
employed directly or indirectly by the company.[8] The court
held that the proceedings of the provincial council were irregular,
on the ground that the council had delegated the whole of its
duties of deciding cases to the two defendants. Because the
council only had a delegated authority, it could not delegate
that authority to others—*delegatus non potest delegare*.[9] These
two defendants were therefore held to be liable. The third
defendant was also held to be liable, since he had justified what
he had done by reason of the fact that he had acted under the
authority of the other two defendants, which authority they
had no power to give to him.[10] The case showed, as Stephen
says,[11] that "if the Patna Council was a fair specimen of the rest,
the Provincial Councils, considered as Courts of Justice, were
absolutely worthless, and that no system for the administration
of justice which deserved the name existed at that time out of
Calcutta." On the other hand it was contended with some force

[1] Stephen, op. cit. ii 134-135.   [2] Ibid 142.   [3] Ibid 205.
[4] Ibid.   [5] Ibid 206.   [6] Ibid 200-205.
[7] Ibid chap. xii.   [8] Ibid 169.   [9] Ibid 172.
[10] Ibid 170.   [11] Ibid 177-178.

that the pressure of business was such, that justice could not
be administered by these councils at all, unless this delegation
was permitted.[1] Moreover, it was said that, if every farmer of
the revenue was liable to have his actions controlled by the
supreme court; if at the suit of every plaintiff who had a
grievance against him he was liable to be arrested on mesne
process and sent to Calcutta; no revenue would ever be collected.[2]
No doubt all this was true; but it was the result of the clauses
of the Act, which set up an English court governed by the rules
of English law substantive and adjective, with a jurisdiction
over persons directly or indirectly employed by the company
or by any of his Majesty's subjects. " Parliament," as Stephen
says,[3] " was the real offender." That the decision was right
in law is shown by the fact that the company did not dare
to prosecute an appeal against it before the Privy Council,[4]
although it was granted by statute an extension of time for
its prosecution.[5]

The Cossijurah case [6] arose out of an action in the supreme
court for money lent, brought by the lender against the zamindar of Cossijurah. The plaintiff alleged that the defendant was
amenable to the jurisdiction of the supreme court because
he was employed to collect the revenue.[7] The defendant was
directed by the governor-general and council to pay no attention
to the process of the court. He resisted the sheriff; and, a
process of sequestration having been issued, the sheriff got together a force of fifty or sixty persons to execute it. Upon
hearing of this, the governor-general and council ordered a party
of soldiers to arrest the sheriff. Here again the company did not
dare to test the correctness of the supreme court's decisions by
an appeal to the Privy Council.[8]

Both these cases show that the governor-general and council
resented any interference by the supreme court, because " it
represented an authority which the Company's servants practically repudiated " [9]—the authority of English law. But it was
to support that authority that the supreme court was created.
Therefore it held, in accordance with well-ascertained principles of English law, that if a native of Bengal were sued, and
he contended that he was not amenable to the court's jurisdiction, he must appear and plead to it. If he proved that he
was not amenable to its jurisdiction, if, for instance, he was

---

[1] Stephen, op. cit. ii 181-182.   [2] Ibid 183.   [3] Ibid 192.
[4] Ibid 190-191.   [5] 21 George III c. 70 § 27.
[6] Stephen, Nuncomar and Impey chap. xiv.
[7] Impey carefully explained that the court never claimed jurisdiction over
zamindars as such, but " their character as zamindars will not exempt them from
the jurisdiction of the court if they be employed or be directly or indirectly in the
service of the East India Company or of any other British subject," ibid 214.
[8] Ibid 212, 218.   [9] Ibid 212.

a zamindar who was not employed directly or indirectly by the
company, the court would give judgment in his favour. But he
was not entitled to ignore the process of the court, and so make
himself a judge in his own case.[1]

These were the unfortunate results of the attempt by Parliament to apply, in a totally different political environment, the
English principle of the ministerial responsibility of the servants
of the government to the law. It is not unlike the modern
attempt to apply the modern theory of responsible government
to the government of India, in spite of the fact that the historical
antecedents and the political and social conditions of India
are totally different from those societies in which that theory of
government originated. This attempt has, in our own day,
produced as many difficulties as the attempt, in the eighteenth
century, to apply to the then existing conditions the English
theory of the responsibility of all the servants of the company
to the English law administered by English judges in the supreme
court. But eighteenth-century statesmen, unlike their successors
in the nineteenth and twentieth centuries, never allowed themselves to become the slaves of a political theory. They were
realists, they judged by results, and so they were ready to admit
that they had made mistakes. This admission was in effect made,
and the unfortunate quarrel between the governor-general and
council and the supreme court was ended, by an Act of 1781,[2]
which settled the points at issue in favour of the contentions of
the governor-general and council.

The Act provided that, except in the case of orders which
affected British subjects,[3] the governor-general and council
should not be liable to the jurisdiction of the supreme court
by reason of anything done or ordered by them in their public
capacity ; [4] and that such order should be a sufficient justification to persons who acted under it.[5] But the governor-general
and council and those acting under their orders could be made
liable for unlawful acts in the courts in England.[6] The supreme
court was to have no jurisdiction in revenue cases, or over acts
done in the course of its collection " according to the usage and
practice of the country or the regulations of the governor-general
and council." [7] Landowners and farmers of the land revenue
were not to be liable as such to the jurisdiction of the supreme
court.[8] Persons employed by the company, by the governor-
general and council, or by a British subject were to be liable to
the jurisdiction of the supreme court only in actions for wrongs
or trespasses ; [9] and the names of persons so employed were to

[1] Stephen, op. cit. ii 214-215.   [2] 21 George III c. 70.
[3] § 3.   [4] § 1.   [5] § 2.   [6] § 4.
[7] § 8.   [8] § 9.   [9] § 10.

be registered.[1] The supreme court's jurisdiction over all residents in Calcutta was confirmed; and it was provided that, in matters of contract and property, the court should apply, in case of the Mahomedans, Mahomedan law, in the case of the Hindus, Hindu law, and in cases where one of the parties was a Mahomedan and one a Hindu the law of the defendant.[2] The supreme court was also given power to make rules of procedure for the conduct of civil and criminal cases against the inhabitants of Bengal, Bihar, and Orissa.[3] The governor-general and council were recognized as the court of appeal from the provincial courts in civil cases. Their decision was final except in cases in which the amount at issue was £5,000 or upwards. In these cases there was an appeal to the Privy Council.[4] They were to have exclusive jurisdiction over all offences committed in the collection of the revenue;[5] and they could frame regulations for the provincial courts and councils.[6] The judges of these provincial courts were not to be liable to be sued in the supreme court for any judgment or order of their courts, and persons acting under orders of their courts were similarly protected.[7] Magistrates or other officers, if sued for corrupt practices, were not to be liable to arrest till notice of the cause of action had been served upon them, and they had declined to appear after such notice.[8] Finally, the governor-general and council were indemnified for their resistance to the process of the supreme court in the Cossijurah case.[9]

We must now consider the manner in which some of the defects in the Regulating Act were aggravated by the enmities which arose between Hastings and the majority of the council appointed by the Act, and the large effects which these enmities had both upon some of the principal actors and upon the future government of India.

(3) The Regulating Act nominated Hastings as governor-general, and Barwell, Monson, Clavering, and Philip Francis as his council.[10] Barwell [11] belonged to a family with an Indian

---

[1] §§ 11-16.   [2] § 17.

[3] § 19; the rules were to be sent to the secretary of state, and the Crown could approve, vary or refuse to assent to them, § 20.

[4] § 21.   [5] § 22.

[6] § 23; as in the case of rules made by the supreme court, they must be sent to the secretary of state for the King's approval, ibid.   [7] § 24.

[8] §§ 25, 26; as Stephen says, Nuncomar and Impey ii 145, the introduction of the law as to arrest on mesne process into India was "indefensible"; "the effect of it was that on an affidavit sworn behind his back, a man might be arrested at Dacca, for instance, or Patna, and brought to Calcutta there to be imprisoned at a distance of many hundred miles from his home, unless he could give bail for an action perhaps unjustly brought against him"; for the history of the law on this topic see vol. viii 230-232; vol. ix 250-251, 253-254; below 595-597.   [9] § 28.

[10] 13 George III c. 63 § 10; above 164.

[11] Stephen, Nuncomar and Impey i 31-32; Weitzman, Warren Hastings and Philip Francis 17-18; Camb. Hist. of the Empire iv 226-227.

tradition. His father had been governor of Bengal and a
director of the company ; and he had had experience in revenue
administration. He was accused in 1783 of oppression while in
charge of the company's factory at Dacca,[1] and of breaking the
rule which prohibited servants of the company from engaging
in private trade, by trading in salt under cover of native agents ;[2]
and his own admissions, and the fact that he made a large fortune,
lend some colour to the latter charge.[3] Before the changes introduced by the Regulating Act he had not been on friendly terms
with Hastings ; but the hostility of the other three councillors,
and the policy which, in entire ignorance of Indian problems,
they advocated, drew together the two men who had had Indian
experience. From the time when the schism on the council
became pronounced Barwell constantly supported Hastings.[4]
Monson was a soldier who had seen service in southern India ;
but he knew nothing of Bengal, and had had no administrative
experience.[5] Clavering was a soldier who knew nothing of
India. He had some Parliamentary influence, and was a favourite
of George III [6]—" a hasty violent person of no intrinsic importance." [7]

Philip Francis [8] was by far the most important of the four
councillors. He had been chief clerk in the War Office, and,
before his appointment as councillor, was an unknown man. But
he is strongly suspected of being the author of the Letters of
Junius ; and both his career in India, and the part which he
subsequently took in Indian affairs, lend colour to this suspicion.[9]
His knowledge of India was confined to the reports of the
Parliamentary committees of enquiry, and to conversations with
Clive. These sources of information had convinced him that
the abuses in India, which he had been sent out to correct,
were due to the conduct of the company's servants, and more
especially to Hastings ; and had led him to form some definite
conclusions as to the policy which ought to be pursued in order
to remedy those abuses. He was a clear and logical thinker,
capable of expressing his ideas tersely and logically, and a

---

[1] See Ninth Report of the Select Committee of the House of Commons, Burke,
Works iv 77-82.
[2] Ibid 110-117.   [3] Stephen, op. cit. i 31-32.
[4] Camb. Hist. of the Empire iv 226-227.
[5] Ibid 226 ; Weitzman, op. cit. 18.
[6] Ibid.   [7] Stephen, op. cit. i 31.
[8] Ibid 29-30 ; Weitzman, op. cit. 18-22.
[9] That Francis was Junius was firmly believed by Macaulay, and Miss
Weitzman's very able and interesting account of his relations with Hastings, of the
policy which he wished to pursue, and of the large part he took in the impeachment
of Hastings, seem to me to confirm this belief ; on the other hand, I do not think
that, after reading her book, anyone could agree with Macaulay in describing
Francis as " a man not destitute of real patriotism and magnanimity, a man whoso
vices were not of the sordid kind."

master of invective. He always professed to act from the
highest motives ; and his professions deceived many in his own
days and later.   In reality, his own advancement was his dominant
motive, and the supplanting of Hastings in the governorship
of Bengal was his objective.[1]   In the means which he used to
attain his ends, and to carry out a policy which was foolish
when it was not selfish,[2] he was utterly unscrupulous.   Stephen
says of his conduct in the case of Nundcoomar that it shows
that he was capable " not only of the faults of undying malig-
nity and ferocious cruelty, but also of falsehood, treachery and
calumny." [3]   This verdict has, I think, been proved by Miss
Weitzman to be true of his whole conduct in India, and of his
conduct after his return.   In India it was dominated by a desire
to supplant Hastings : in England by a desire to revenge himself on Hastings for the defeat which he had suffered at his
hands in India.

Such a man easily dominated such colleagues as Monson and
Clavering.   Francis had, while still in England, been of service
to Clavering.

The voyage out improved his opportunities.   For six months confined within the bounds of an Indiaman, the new councillors lived
in constant intercourse. . . . Francis, by a process of judicious flattery,
prepared the way for converting them into staunch adherents of his
own views, obsequious imitators of his temper, and pliant tools for
his schemes : in effect they became merely numerically important—
Francis had armed himself with three votes instead of one.[4]

The result was to reduce Hastings to impotence.   His foreign
policy was reversed, and the development of the reforms which
he was planning in the government of India was stopped.[5]
Francis and his party neglected no weapon, personal or political,
which they thought would be serviceable in their war against
him.[6]   The effect of such tactics upon the conduct of the government soon made itself felt.

The courts of justice scarcely functioned ; revenue collectors racked
the provinces ; bandits invaded the immediate outskirts of Calcutta,
while the Provincial Councils, infected with the spirit of discord that
pervaded the capital, suspended business, referring the most trivial
matters to the consideration of the Board.[7]

The board continued to meet ; but, said Hastings " the business of every department stands still," " and I sit in them all, a
passive spectator without the power of giving motion to your

---

[1] Camb. Hist. of the Empire iv 226.   [2] Below 195-196.
[3] Stephen, op. cit. i 30.   [4] Weitzman, op. cit. 22.
[5] Ibid 26-30, 31-32, 37-38, 64.   [6] Below 193 n. 6.
[7] Weitzman, op. cit. 38.

affairs or for any other purpose that I know but to be the butt of everlasting contumely." [1]

The best proof of the malevolent, cruel, and wholly unscrupulous way in which Francis conducted his feud with Hastings in India, and later in England, is to be found in the case of Nundcoomar. We have seen that Hastings, by order of the Directors, had made use of Nundcoomar in the prosecution of Mohammed Reza Khan and Shitah Rai ; [2] but that he had always distrusted him ; [3] and that Nundcoomar had been disappointed in his hope of succeeding to the post of naib diwan which these two men had formerly occupied.[4] The hostility of the majority of the council to Hastings, and their desire to get evidence against him which would justify that hostility, was Nundcoomar's opportunity. He used it to the full. In March 1775 Francis presented to the council a letter from Nundcoomar which contained charges of corruption against Hastings, which, for some months past, Nundcoomar had been elaborating in conjunction with Monson and Clavering.[5] Nundcoomar offered to appear before the council and substantiate his charges. Hastings refused to allow this, and dissolved the council. The majority then admitted Nundcoomar, heard his statement, and declared the charges proved.[6] Hastings then instituted a prosecution for conspiracy against Nundcoomar and a merchant named Fowke, who had been the intermediary between Nundcoomar and Monson and Clavering.[7] Shortly afterwards Nundcoomar was prosecuted for forgery by Mohun Persaud, tried, condemned to death, and executed.

Though he was encouraged by the majority of the council to expect that they would interpose in his favour,[8] they did nothing ; they refused to present Nundcoomar's petition to the governor-general and council ; [9] and Francis ignored an appeal

---

[1] Weitzman, op. cit. 39.   [2] Above 171.

[3] Above 171 ; cp. Stephen, op. cit. i 210-212, citing evidence given by Hastings.

[4] Above 171.   [5] Weitzman, op. cit. 34-35.

[6] Ibid 35 ; the situation which resulted was thus described by Hastings in a letter of March 25 1775 : " The trumpet has been sounded, and the whole host of informers will soon crowd to Calcutta with their complaints and ready depositions. Nuncomar holds his durbar in complete state, sends for zemindars and their vakeels, coaxing and threatening them for complaints, which no doubt he will get in abundance, besides what he forges for himself. The system which they have laid down for conducting their affairs is, as I am told, after this manner. The General rummages the Consultations for disputable matter with the aid of old Fowke. Colonel Monson receives, and, I have been assured, even descends to solicit, accusations. Francis writes," cited Stephen, op. cit. i 77.

[7] Weitzman, op. cit. 34 ; he was a friend of Clavering's, and Hastings' retrenchments had curtailed his trading privileges ; he had met Clavering on his arrival, and his information had confirmed in Clavering's mind, the suspicion of Hastings which Francis had implanted, ibid 23.

[8] See a passage in a letter written by Impey to Governor Johnstone in 1778, or 1779, cited Stephen, op. cit. i 257-258.

[9] Ibid i 233.

especially addressed to him.[1] When, after his execution, a
paper signed by Nundcoomar was presented to the board by
Clavering, who had received it the day before his execution,
it was on the motion of Francis ordered to be burnt by the
common hangman.[2] As Miss Weitzman says,[3]

> Nuncomar hanged would serve Francis's purpose to greater effect
> that Nuncomar alive. His death removed a dangerous and perjured
> witness, while the charge of having connived at it could be levelled
> at Hastings, who, Francis lost no time in insinuating, had succeeded
> with the aid of Impey in judicially murdering a troublesome witness.

The entire baselessness of this charge was proved by Impey to
the satisfaction of the House of Commons in 1788,[4] and by
Stephen to the satisfaction of all who have read the very elaborate
arguments of his book on *Nuncomar and Impey*. Since Francis's
own conduct in 1775 proves that he knew that the charge was
baseless, he stands convicted of conduct which is quite as morally
bad as that with which he charged Hastings and Impey.[5]

Francis was chiefly playing for his own hand. He wished to
supplant Hastings. It is true that he had a substantive policy
which he wished to substitute for that which Hastings was
pursuing. It is true that he believed in that policy. But it was
the policy of a mere theorist who knew little or nothing of
Indian conditions.[6] Hastings, who knew those conditions, was
trying to implement the company's resolve " to stand forth
as Diwan " by creating a machinery of government for its possessions in India. He was trying to pursue a policy with regard
to the native powers which would safeguard those possessions.
He was trying to render workable that partnership between the
state and the company, which the Regulating Act had set up.
Francis, on the other hand, had come to India with the precon-
ceived idea, first that British rule in India was *per se* a grievance,
and, secondly, that it was an obvious abuse that a trading com-

---

[1] Stephen, op. cit. i 235.   [2] Ibid 250.
[3] Warren Hastings and Philip Francis 36.
[4] Parlt. Hist. xxvi 1341 seqq.; below 202; but Professor Berriedale Keith,
Constitutional History of India 76-77 is not satisfied.
[5] " On the 1st August 1775, they had it in their power to save Nuncomar's life
by simply voting in their capacity of a majority of the Council, to send to the judges,
in the name of the Governor-General and Council, the letter which Farrer [Nund-
coomar's counsel] had drawn, with or without an addition as to Nuncomar's accusation of Hastings. If at that time they really did believe that he was an innocent
man on the point of being judicially murdered, they made themselves by their
conduct, accomplices in the murder, which they believed to be in course of being
committed . . . [Francis] could have no reason for believing in 1788 that
Nuncomar was judiciously murdered which he had not in 1775, yet in 1775 he might
have saved him by holding out his hand, or if he had not saved him, might, at all
events, have thrown upon the Supreme Court a far heavier responsibility than that
which rested on them as it was," Stephen, op. cit. i 233-234.
[6] For a very clear account of this policy see Weitzman, op. cit. chap. iii.

pany should exercise political power.[1] He wished, therefore, to abolish the political power of the company, and to vest the power in the Crown. He wished to see the Crown governing entirely through the native authorities. The declared policy of the company " to stand forth as Diwan " he regarded as a mistake. The policy of governing through the native authorities, under the supervision of the Crown, was, he considered, the right, and the only just, policy to pursue. In other words, he wished to apply to the company's territorial possessions a system somewhat similar to that which the Crown now adopts with regard to the Indian States, without any of the safeguards for good government in the States which the Crown now exacts. It followed that Hastings' judicial system must be got rid of, and that the administration of justice must be handed over to native officials. It followed also that Hastings' attempts to improve the revenue system were based on wholly wrong premises. Francis advocated a different system based on two entirely erroneous assumptions. In the first place, he assumed that these attempts were directed to the merely commercial object of extracting the highest possible revenue from Bengal without regard to the welfare of the inhabitants. In the second place, he invented a fancy picture of the constitution of the Mogul Empire, in which the zamindar was the owner of the soil, paying a fixed land tax, and governing his district, much as an English landowner and justice of the peace, governed his district. Therefore he wished to settle the revenue on the basis of a permanent settlement with the zamindars, who were to be given political power over their ryots.

Francis would thus have handed over the population of Bengal to the uncontrolled despotism of the native authorities. He would have denied to the English, not only the right to set up a stronger and a more enlightened government than any which would have been possible under native rule, but also the power to exercise adequate control over the effete native machinery of government. On similar principles he opposed the making of any alliances with the native states. " If the restriction of English influence was necessary in Bengal, all the more was this the case beyond the limits of the province." [2] On the other hand, Hastings saw that the best way of protecting the company's possessions was by a series of alliances with the

[1] That he had in 1783 converted Burke to this view is clear from Burke's speech on Fox's India Bill; in that speech Burke said " our Indian government is in its best state a grievance," Works (Bohn's ed.) ii 196; he adopted Francis' slander that Nundcoomar was hanged to save Hastings, ibid 231-232; and he inserted in it an elaborate panegyric on Francis, ibid 230-231.

[2] Weitzman, op. cit. 84; here again he had converted Burke to his views, see Burke's account of Hastings' dealings with the native states, in his speech on Fox's bill, Works ii 183-193—which is a travesty inspired by Francis.

native powers.   Only in this way could those possessions be protected easily and cheaply against the designs of the company's
native and European rivals.   Only in this way could the company
acquire that knowledge of Indian politics which was necessary for
the defence and protection of its possessions.[1]

If Francis had prevailed in his contest with Hastings there
would have been no British Empire of India.   Indeed it is quite
likely that the company might have lost all its possessions.
He was quite helpless when the government was called upon to
deal with the Marathas and with Hyder Ali.[2]   The burden of
the defence of India at that perilous time fell on Hastings alone ;
and the credit for the success of the measures taken is likewise
due to him alone.

Fortunately Monson's death in 1776 gave Hastings, by
virtue of his casting vote, a majority in the council.   He was
able to pursue his policy.   But in 1777 matters were again
thrown into confusion by the news that the directors had accepted Hastings' resignation.   Hastings had in 1775 given his
agent power to send in a resignation.   But he had afterwards
retracted this power.   He therefore denied that this acceptance
by the directors of his resignation was valid, and denied the
right of Clavering to act as governor-general.   Both sides
agreed to submit the dispute to the arbitration of the supreme
court, which decided in favour of Hastings.[3]   The final act
of the controversy between Hastings and Francis was the
famous duel in August 1780, in which Francis was wounded.
In December he left India, determined to carry on the struggle
against his victorious rival in England.

Before Francis left India he had begun to prepare for the
struggle.[4]   If he was Junius he was already an adept in the art
of stirring up opinion by anonymous writings : if he was not,
he used this weapon with a skill worthy of Junius.[5]   As the
result of his efforts the House of Commons had, before his return, been convinced that affairs in India were going badly ;
and many thought that the causes were the crimes and
folly of Hastings, and the incompetence of the company.[6]
In February 1781 a select committee had been appointed to
enquire into the administration of justice in India, and in April

---

[1] Weitzman, op. cit. 88-91.   [2] Ibid 114-128.
[3] Camb. Hist. of the Empire iv 228 ; it was with reference to this decision, and
not, as Macaulay thought, with reference to Nundcoomar's conviction, that Hastings
said that to Impey's support, " I was at one time indebted for the safety of my
fortune, honour and reputation," Stephen, op. cit. ii 43-45.
[4] Weitzman, op. cit. 134.
[5] " The manipulation of the anonymous press was the sharpest, deadliest
weapon in his possession, and he worked it with unparalleled success," ibid 134.
[6] Ibid 137.

of the same year a second committee had been appointed
to enquire into the causes of the war in the Carnatic.[1] When
Francis arrived in England, he found opinion upon the merits
of Hastings much divided both at the India House and in the
political world.[2] But he also found that he had gained one
convert to his views, whose support was destined to be of more
service to him in the conduct of his campaign, than all the
pamphlets and letters which he had written, and all the intrigues
which he had conducted.

Very shortly after his arrival in India, Francis had tried
to enlist the sympathy of Burke, by drawing lurid pictures of
the misery of Bengal under the rule of Hastings, and by constant
assertions that it was only by the adoption of his policy that
Bengal could be saved.[3] Unfortunately Burke's sympathy was
enlisted. He accepted all Francis's views as to the iniquities
of Hastings, and as to the right policy for India.[4] Therefore
Francis, on his return, found it easy to get the ear of the select
committee, of which Burke was one of the most important
members.[5] The reports of that committee, the ninth and
eleventh of which were drawn by Burke, were revised by Francis,
and were founded upon the evidence procured by Francis.[6]
They echoed his views ;[7] and they naturally influenced very
many of the leading statesmen of the day—among others
Dundas,[8] and, to some extent Pitt [9]—who were ignorant of the
way in which much of the evidence had been procured.

These reports, and the debates which they occasioned, showed
that there had been a curious reversal in the positions of some
of the leading actors in the drama. Burke had once been the
greatest upholder of the rights of the company, and the opponent of the view that the state had a right to interfere with
its chartered privileges.[10] He was now its fiercest opponent.
Wedderburn, who had been Clive's principal advocate in the
House of Commons, who had moved the resolution in which his
great services were recognized,[11] was a friend and correspondent
of Francis,[12] and, largely for that reason, so constant an opponent
of Hastings that, as Lord Chancellor, he voted in the minority
for his condemnation on some of the articles of his impeachment.[13]

---

[1] Weitzman, op. cit. 138.   [2] Ibid 139-141.
[3] Ibid 32-33.   [4] Above 194-196.
[5] He published the minutes of the council on the appointment of Impey to be
judge of the Sudder Diwani Adalat—" The select committee seized on the case.
Francis was the chief witness.   The Directors and the House of Commons denounced
the arrangement as a flagrant job.   Francis revived," Weitzman, op. cit. 142.
[6] Ibid 148.   [7] Ibid 146-147.
[8] Ibid 148-149.   [9] Ibid 186-187.
[10] Above 182.   [11] Above 163.
[12] Weitzman, op. cit. 155, 217, 277, 333.
[13] Camb. Hist. of the Empire iv 311.

But it was the winning of Burke's support which was the most important victory for the opponents of Hastings, because it meant the winning of the support of the Rockingham Whigs. Without that victory there would have been no impeachment; and, if there had been no impeachment, that strong Whig tradition of hostility to Hastings, which has done so much to affect the judgment of history, would never have been formed.[1]

The manner in which Francis presented the case against Hastings to Burke caught Burke on his weakest side. It appealed to two aspects of his character and intellect which were most calculated to mislead his judgment. In the first place, in his judgments on persons Burke was always apt to let his heart get the better of his head. If he thought that a person had served him he would go all lengths in his defence. The best illustration of this failing is the manner in which he defended the two rascals Powell and Bembridge, who were guilty of fraud, because they had helped him in working out his scheme of economic reform.[2] Another illustration is his well-known panegyric on Francis in his speech on Fox's bill in 1783.[3] He knew that he had owed much to Francis; and he failed to see that he owed so much that his judgment had been blinded. Conversely, if, as in the case of Hastings, he had come to the conclusion that a person was guilty, he let his imagination play upon his guilt. He embroidered it and exaggerated it, with the result that many have thought that his savage and sometimes grotesque denunciations of Hastings are evidence of a disordered mind. In the second place, Burke had an almost mystic reverence for old-established institutions, religious or political, which had made civilization possible.[4] He had never been to India. He knew nothing of the actual working of the religious and political institutions of India. He knew nothing of the enormous abuses and cruelties which they sanctioned. He knew nothing of the decadence into which they had sunk. He adopted all Francis's views as to the grievance of English rule in India,[5] as to the possibility of using Indian institutions as an instrument of government,[6] as to the iniquity of Hastings' attempts to reform them by a new system of government.[7] He therefore came easily to the conclusion that Hastings was a villain who, to gratify his own personal ambitions, and to secure gain for the company, was wantonly destroying an old and

---

[1] " It is rather like the tale of the house that Jack built. Because Burke believed Francis there was a trial of Hastings. Because James Mill believed Francis and Burke, there was a history of India coloured with their bias. Because Macaulay believed Francis, Burke, and Mill there was his famous essay on Warren Hastings," R. H. Murray, Edmund Burke 318.

[2] Vol. x 96 n. 5.   [3] Above 195 n. 1.   [4] Vol. x 93-94.
[5] Above 194.   [6] Above 195.   [7] Above 170-176.

respectable civilization together with the system of government which had created it ; [1] and that, to compass his ends, he was ready to commit any crime, and to sanction any cruelty and any oppression.

Burke naturally found it necessary to reconcile his new attitude to the company to the attitude which he had formerly taken up. The manner in which he did so in his speech on Fox's bill in 1783, shows his intellect at its strongest, just as the manner in which, in the select committee, he approached the enquiry into the conduct of Indian affairs, shows it at its weakest. He admitted that the company had chartered rights which were as sacred as rights of property ; but he went on to point out that all such rights were rights in the nature of a trust. Though they must not be wantonly interfered with,[2] they ought to be interfered with by Parliament if it could be shown that the trust had been abused [3]—by Parliament because that was the only body which could give due weight to political as well as to legal considerations.[4] And such considerations must be applied to the company, for it governed an empire " to which Great Britain is in comparison but a respectable province." " To leave these concerns without superior cognizance would be madness ; to leave them to be judged in the courts below, on the principles of a confined jurisprudence, would be folly." [5]

[1] " This multitude of men does not consist of an abject and barbarous populace . . . but a people for ages civilized and cultivated. . . . There, have been (and still the skeletons remain) princes once of great dignity, authority, and opulence. There, is to be found an ancient and venerable priesthood, the depository of their laws, learning, and history, the guides of the people whilst living, and their consolation in death ; a nobility of great antiquity and renown ; a multitude of cities, not exceeded in population and trade by those of the first class in Europe ; merchants and bankers, individual houses of whom have once vied in capital with the bank of England . . . ; millions of ingenious manufacturers and mechanics ; millions of the most diligent, and not the least intelligent, tillers of the earth," Speech on Fox's India Bill, Works ii 181-182.

[2] Ibid 177.

[3] " All political power which is set over men . . . ought to be in some way or other exercised ultimately for their benefit. If this is true with regard to every species of political dominion, and every species of commercial privilege . . . then such rights or privileges, or whatever else you choose to call them, are all in the strictest sense a *trust ;* and it is of the very essence of every trust to be rendered *accountable ;* and even totally to *cease,* when it substantially varies from the purposes for which alone it could have a lawful existence. This I conceive to be true of trusts of power vested in the highest hands, and of such as seem to hold of no human creature. But about the application of this principle to subordinate *derivative* trusts I do not see how a controversy can be maintained. To whom then would I make the East India Company accountable ? Why to Parliament . . . from which their trust was derived " ; ibid 178.

[4] " In every judgment given on a corporate right of great political importance, the policy and prudence make no small part of the question. To these considerations a court of law is not competent. . . . But Parliament can do what the courts neither can do nor ought to attempt. Parliament is competent to give due weight to all political considerations. It may modify, it may mitigate, and it may render perfectly secure, all that it does not think fit to take away," Burke, Works (Bohn's ed.) ii 269 *note.*

[5] Ibid 270 *note.*

The company had, in his opinion, abused its trust by the manner in which it had used its political power to oppress the natives. It was right therefore that its political power should, as it was proposed in Fox's bill, be taken away from it, and that it should be confined to its commercial activities.[1] The bill would thus rescue the natives from the oppression of the company and its servants, and would be a Magna Carta for the natives of India.[2]

During the troubled years which followed the death of Rockingham, Burke and Francis combined to accumulate their charges against Hastings.[3] They secured resolutions against Impey and Hastings in the House of Commons,[4] and they secured the support of the directors.[5] But the court of proprietors stood firm for Hastings, and overruled the directors.[6] It was unfortunate for Hastings that he was not as well served in the House of Commons as in the court of proprietors. His agent in the House of Commons, Major Scott, had abilities ; but he was not very judicious, and he was not in the first rank of debaters. Moreover, his speeches were discounted because he was regarded as being merely Hastings' advocate. He was quite incapable of representing Hastings' side of his case in the manner in which Wedderburn had represented Clive's.[7]

Although in 1783 Hastings' success against the Marathas had begun to turn opinion in his favour,[8] although the court of proprietors carried a vote of thanks to him,[9] although Mansfield and Thurlow warned Fox that he ought to go warily in Indian affairs, nothing could stop Burke.[10] Fox introduced his India Bill. Its defeat in the Lords at the bidding of the King,[11] the accession of Pitt to office, and his sweeping victory at the general election of 1784,[12] seemed to be a decisive defeat for Burke and Francis ; for Burke's party was now in a hopeless minority.

But, though Pitt exercised an infinitely more sane judgment on Indian affairs than Burke, he was not uninfluenced, as his India Bill showed,[13] by the findings of the Parliamentary committee.[14] Though there were a few who recognized the fact that

---

[1] " That the power, notoriously, grossly abused, has been bought from us, is very certain. But this circumstance which is urged against the bill, becomes an additional motive for our interference ; lest we should be thought to have sold the blood of millions of men, for the base consideration of money. We sold, I admit, all that we had to sell ; that is our authority, not our control. We had not a right to make a market of our duties," Burke, Works (Bohn's ed.) ii 178-179.

[2] " This bill, and those connected with it, are intended to form the *Magna Charta* of Hindostan," ibid 179.

[3] Weitzman, op. cit. 153.
[4] Ibid 148-149, 150.
[5] Ibid 151.
[6] Ibid 151-152.
[7] Above 197.
[8] Weitzman, op. cit. 155.
[9] Ibid 155-156.
[10] Ibid 156.
[11] Vol. x 111-112.
[12] Vol. x 112.
[13] Vol. x 122 ; below 204-210.
[14] Above 197.

those findings were prejudiced,[1] no one seems to have recognized the extent to which they had been inspired by the misrepresentations of Francis.   Although Pitt defended Hastings on the Rohilla charge, he felt that he could not wholly acquit him on the charges of oppression in connection with Chayt Sing [2] and the Begums.[3] He voted for an impeachment because, with some hesitation, he thought that there was a *prima facie* case.   His great mistake was allowing the opposition to have entire control of the impeachment.   That meant that its conduct was to a large extent entrusted to Burke and Francis ; and though, to their chagrin, the House refused to appoint Francis one of the managers of the impeachment,[4] he, its chief instigator, naturally continued to be their principal assistant.[5]   It is true that there would have been no impeachment if Francis had not converted Burke to his views ; [6] but it is also true that, because he succeeded in effecting this conversion, he must be regarded as its instigator ; and there is no doubt that, throughout its course he continued to be its moving spirit.[7]

The charges made against Hastings in connection with Nundcoomar logically involved the supplementary impeachment of Impey.   His impeachment was entrusted to Sir Gilbert Elliot.[8]   The articles of both impeachments were drawn by Burke and Francis.[9]   Their character, which supplies an indication of the manner in which the managers approached their task, has been justly denounced by Stephen.   He says : [10]

In his famous speech at Bristol, Burke declared himself to be incompetent to the task of preparing an indictment against a whole people.   He was certainly incompetent to draw an indictment against an individual, for it is impossible to imagine anything worse of their

[1] Governor Johnstone said in 1783 that he could not find out how the committee had proceeded ; and that " as a very near relative of his had been a member of the committee, he had applied to him to learn what had been the nature of the proceeding, upon which a report teeming with charges of so aggravated and heinous a nature had been founded.   His relation told him that he had early discovered so much heat and violence, so much passion and prejudice, in the majority of the members of the committee . . . that he had . . . determined to withdraw himself entirely from the committee, and never again attend their meetings," Parlt. Hist. xxiii 715-716 ; cp. ibid xxiv 187, where it was said that the reports of the select committee " carried on the very face of them the strongest marks of partiality."

[2] Ibid xxvi 110-111.   [3] Ibid 334-336.   [4] Ibid 1334.

[5] See the letter sent by the managers to Francis which is printed ibid 1334 *note*, which shows the extent to which they had relied, and continued to rely, upon him.

[6] Above 197.

[7] Weitzman, op. cit. 171 ; cp. R. H. Murray, Edmund Burke 319-322 ; in 1795 Sayer the caricaturist published a print called the " last scene of the managers' farce " ; in the print the face of Francis is peeping from behind a curtain—" the prompter, no character in the farce, but very useful behind the scenes," ibid 345.

[8] Parlt. Hist. xxvi 1018.

[9] Weitzman, op. cit. 181 ; Stephen, op. cit. ii 8 ; Miss Weitzman says that they were in the main the work of Francis ; but their style is reminiscent of Burke.

[10] Op. cit. ii 8-9.

kind than the articles which he preferred against Hastings and the articles preferred against Impey, which are in the same style, and presumably by the same author. . . . An accusation ought to state directly, unequivocally, and without going into either argument or evidence, that at such a time or place the person accused has done such and such things, thereby committing an offence against such and such a law. The articles of impeachment against both Hastings and Impey violated every one of these obvious rules. Instead of being short, full, pointed, and precise, they are bulky pamphlets sprinkled over with imitations of legal phraseology. They are full of invective, oratorical matter, needless recitals, arguments, statements of evidence —everything in fact which can possibly serve to make an accusation difficult to understand and to meet. They are, moreover, extremely tricky, being full of insinuations, and covering, by their profusion of irrelevant matter, the total and no doubt designed absence of averments essential to the conclusion which they are meant to support. In short, they are as shuffling and disingenuous in substance, as they are clumsy, awkward, and intricate in form.

Burke defended the number and minuteness of the charges by saying that he was trying to establish not one or two criminal acts, but " a general evil intention manifested through a long series and a great variety of acts." [1] But this affords no defence of the faulty draftsmanship of the articles, in which all these acts are set out and charged against the accused.

Impey's defence upon the charge of having conspired with Hastings to cause Nundcoomar to be prosecuted on a capital charge, and to refuse to respite him, was complete and conclusive.[2] It entirely convinced Pitt of the baselessness of the charge ; [3] and it is difficult to see how anyone who has read it can doubt either Impey's honesty or his ability.[4] The abandonment of Impey's impeachment foreshadowed the result of the impeachment of Hastings. The magnificent orations of Burke and Sheridan fitted in well enough with the rhetoric of the articles of impeachment. But, when the cold test of legal proof was applied to them, the charges withered. Hastings' counsel were some of the most distinguished lawyers of the day.[5] They took

[1] Burke's Correspondence iii 38, cited Weitzman, op. cit. 183.

[2] Above 193-194 ; Parlt. Hist. xxvi 1341-1446.

[3] " Mr. Pitt concluded with declaring, that, in no view could any corrupt motive be brought home to Sir Elijah Impey ; and that therefore he never voted from a more decided conviction of mind, that he should give his negative to the question," ibid xxvii 490.

[4] In Stephen's opinion the conduct of the trial was scrupulously fair ; on the question whether Impey ought to have used the power conferred on the supreme court by a clause in its charter, and respited Nundcoomar, his reason given in a letter to Governor Johnstone, cited Stephen, op. cit. i 257, seems conclusive ; he says, " had this criminal escaped, no force of argument, no future experience, would have prevailed on a single native to believe that the judges had not weighed gold against justice, and that it would ever preponderate "—in other words the reputation of the supreme court, and its possibility of usefulness were at stake ; cp. ibid ii 63-69 where the question of a respite is discussed.

[5] They were Law, afterwards Lord Ellenborough, Plumer, afterwards Master of the Rolls, and Dallas, afterwards Chief Justice of the Common Pleas.

advantage of all the procedural rules and all the rules of the
law of evidence which were at their disposal. Though the
adoption of this course dragged out the impeachment to an
interminable length, it made acquittal inevitable, both because
the flimsy character of the evidence upon which many of the
charges rested became increasingly obvious, and because public
opinion was turning in favour of Hastings. Before his final
acquittal very many realized the cruel injustice which the impeachment had inflicted upon a man who was, with the exception of Chatham, the ablest statesman of the eighteenth
century.[1]

Burke did not realize this—he complained of an Indian
influence, and of the lawyers' rules of evidence.[2] As the chances
of a condemnation grew more remote, his language increased in
violence, and brought down upon him the censure of the House
of Commons.[3] To the end he believed in the justice of his
cause.[4] So thoroughly was he convinced of it that Hastings'
acquittal in 1795 ended his Parliamentary career. The day
after the acquittal he left the House of Commons for ever.[5]
Francis, on the other hand, was under no illusions. "Hastings
has been impeached," he said, "and I have been condemned."[6]
This summed up the truth of the matter with an epigrammatic
force which Junius could not have surpassed.

Long before 1795 the troubled period in Indian constitutional
history, which the Regulating Act inaugurated, had closed. In
1784 Pitt's Act for the government of India had given to that
government the form which, in most essential points, it retained
till 1858.

Though the defeat of Fox's India Bill was due mainly to
English political conditions,[7] it was also due to some extent to
its provisions. The political powers of the company and its
patronage were in effect handed over to the seven commissioners
named in the Act, so that the constitution of the company was
radically altered.[8] The antagonism of the company was thereby
ensured, and that antagonism was the more bitter, because Fox
had not consulted the company before introducing his bill.[9]
This antagonism, coupled with Fox's unwise tactics, helped
George III and Pitt to win their sweeping victory at the general

---

[1] Stephen, op. cit. i 25 says, "if a man's ability is measured by a comparison
between his means of action and the results of his action, he must I think be regarded
as the ablest Englishman of eighteenth century"; and with this verdict Professor
Ramsey Muir agrees, see his Introduction to Miss Weitzman's book at p. xxviii.

[2] Parlt. Hist. xxviii 1233-1235.   [3] Ibid xxvii 1344-1422.
[4] Camb. Hist. of the Empire iv 311-312.   [5] Ibid 312.
[6] Cited by Miss Weitzman, op. cit. 195.   [7] Vol. x 111-112.
[8] Ilbert, Government of India 61.
[9] Camb. Hist. of the Empire iv 195-196.

election of 1784.[1] Pitt avoided Fox's errors. His Act maintained the partnership which already existed between the company and the state—though it increased the influence of the
state ; so that it maintained a continuity in the government of
the British possessions in India which Fox's bill would have destroyed. Moreover, Pitt took the company into his confidence—
" he had not dared," he said, " to digest a bill without consultation, which was to violate chartered rights sanctified by Parliamentary Acts." [2] Therefore the settlement made by his Act
was an agreed settlement.

We must consider, first, the provisions of the Act and the
eighteenth-century amendments of and additions to it ; and
secondly, the evolution of a government for India under the
guidance of this legislation.

(1) *The provisions of the Act and the eighteenth-century amendments and additions to it.*

Pitt's Act is the principal Act.[3] The amendments and
additions are comparatively unimportant. Even the Act of
1793,[4] which was passed on the occasion of the renewal of the
company's charter, made no important alterations. I shall
deal with this legislation under the following heads : (i) The
terms of the partnership between the company and the state ;
(ii) clauses relating to the government of India ; (iii) safeguards
against oppression by the company or its servants ; (iv) directions
as to the policy to be pursued in India.

(i) *The terms of the partnership between the company and the
state.*

The power to " superintend direct and control all acts
operations and concerns which in any wise relate to the civil
or military government or revenues of the British territorial
possessions in the East Indies," was vested in a board of control.[5]
This board was to consist of six privy councillors appointed
by the King, two of whom must be a secretary of state and the
chancellor of the exchequer.[6] Three were a quorum, and, in
the absence of the secretary of state and the chancellor of the

---

[1] Camb. Hist. of the Empire iv 200 ; vol. x 112.

[2] " He acknowledged himself to be so weak as to pay respect to the chartered
rights of men ; and that, in proposing a new system of government and regulation,
he did not disdain to consult with those, who, having the greatest stake in the matter
to be new-modelled, were likely to be the best capable of giving him advice. . . .
He had not dared to digest a bill without consultation, which was to violate chartered rights, sanctified by Parliamentary Acts," Parlt. Hist. xxiv 318-319.

[3] 24 George III Sess. 2 c. 25.   [4] 33 George III c. 52.

[5] 24 George III Sess. 2 c. 25 § 6.

[6] § 1 ; in 1793 it was provided that the two secretaries of state and the chancellor
of the exchequer must always be members, 33 George III c. 52 § 2.

exchequer, the senior of the four other commissioners was to be the president.[1] The president was to have a casting vote.[2] The office of commissioner was not to disqualify for a seat in Parliament.[3]

The members of the board of control were given access to all the papers of the company, to all resolutions and orders of the courts of directors and proprietors relating to the government and revenues of the company, to copies of dispatches received by the directors from India, and to copies of instructions relating to the government and revenues of India which the directors proposed to send to India.[4] The directors must obey the orders of the board with reference to the government and revenues of India.[5] If the directors did not send copies of their instructions to the board within fourteen days after being required to do so, the board could send their own instructions to the directors, who must transmit them to India ; unless, by reason of any representation made by the directors to the board, the board directed any alteration to be made.[6] If a difference of opinion arose between the board and the directors as to whether the instructions of the board related to the government or revenues of India, the directors could appeal to the King in council.[7]

The directors were required to appoint a secret committee of not more than three persons, to whom orders and instructions as to questions of war or peace with the native princes or the negotiation of treaties with them, which required secrecy, were to be sent for transmission.[8]

It was provided by the Act that the board was to have no power to appoint any of the servants of the company.[9] The directors, subject to the conditions laid down by the Act,[10] had the power to appoint all their servants civil and military ; but the Crown as well as the directors were given power to dismiss any of the servants of the company.[11] Except in the case of the governor-general, the governors of Madras and Bombay, and the commanders-in-chief, appointments must be made from amongst the covenanted servants of the company resident in India.[12] Power was also given to the directors to nominate persons to succeed in case there was a vacancy in the offices of governor-general, presidents of Madras and Bombay, commanders-in-chief, and members of council.[13] If the company failed to appoint within two months after a vacancy in these offices had

---

[1] 24 George III Sess. 2 c. 25 §§ 1-3.   [2] § 4.   [3] § 10.
[4] § 11.   [5] § 11.   [6] § 13.   [7] § 14.
[8] §§ 15, 16.   [9] § 17.   [10] Below 206.   [11] § 22.
[12] § 23 ; but if a covenanted servant were nominated to any of these posts he need not be resident in India, 26 George III c. 16 § 1.
[13] 24 George III Sess. 2 c. 25 § 26.

been notified to the directors, the Crown could appoint.[1] It was provided in 1786 that the King's approbation of these appointments should not be necessary.[2]

Orders of the directors approved by the board of control were not for the future to be rescinded or in any way affected by the court of proprietors.[3] This was a necessary consequence of the manner in which the Act had divided the control of the government of India between the state and the directors of the company.

(ii) *Clauses relating to the government of India.*

The government of Bengal was vested in the governor-general and three councillors.[4] The commander-in-chief was to have precedence next after the governor-general.[5] Similar provisions were made for the presidencies of Madras and Bombay.[6] In 1786 it was provided that the commander-in-chief was not to be a member of these councils unless specially appointed thereto, and the provision as to his precedence was therefore repealed.[7]

The governor-general and the presidents at Madras and Bombay were to have a casting vote.[8] In 1786 the governor-general or the presidents of the other provinces were empowered to override the majority of their councils.[9]

Whenever the members of any of the councils at Calcutta, Madras, or Bombay were reduced to two, including the governor-general or president, the senior person appointed by the directors to succeed in such an event, or the senior civil servant "on the spot," was to be called to the council till a successor was appointed by the directors.[10] No resignation of the offices of governor-general, president of Madras or Bombay, commander-in-chief, or councillor, was to be valid unless it was in writing and signed by the officer resigning.[11]

The governor-general and his council were given power

to superintend, control, and direct the several presidencies and governments now or hereafter to be created or established in the East Indies by the said United Company in all such points as relate to any transaction with the country powers, or to war or peace, or to the application of the revenues or forces of such presidencies and settle-

[1] § 25.   [2] 26 George III c. 25.
[3] 24 George III Sess. 2 c. 25 § 29.
[4] § 19.   [5] § 19.   [6] § 19.
[7] 26 George III c. 16 § 5 ; 33 George III c. 52 § 32 provided that, if made a member of council, he should have precedence next after the governor-general or governor.
[8] 24 George III Sess. 2 c. 25 § 21.
[9] 26 George III c. 16 § 4 ; 33 George III c. 52 §§ 47-51.
[10] 24 George III Sess. 2 c. 25 § 27 ; but 26 George III c. 16 § 3 repealed the provision that the senior civil servant on the spot should become a councillor.
[11] 24 George III Sess. 2 c. 25 § 28.

ments in time of war, or any such other points as shall, from time to time, be specially referred by the said court of directors of the said Company to their superintendence and control.[1]

Even if there was any doubt as to whether their orders referred to these matters they must be obeyed, unless contrary orders had been received from the directors or the secret committee, not then known to the governor-general and council.[2] Copies of these orders and of resolutions taken thereunder must be forthwith sent to the governor-general and council.[3] The governor-general and council were given power to suspend the presidents and councils of Madras and Bombay if they disobeyed their orders ; [4] and the latter were required to transmit to the governor-general and council copies of all their proceedings, material to be communicated to them, or which they required to be communicated.[5] In the councils of all the presidencies matters brought forward by the governor-general or the presidents were to have priority to all other business.[6]

The governor-general and the presidents of Madras and Bombay were given power to arrest persons suspected of

carrying on mediately or immediately any illicit correspondence, dangerous to the peace or safety of the settlement, or of the British possessions in India, with any of the princes, rajahs, zemindars, or other person or persons whomsoever having authority in India, or with the commanders governors or presidents of any factories established in the East Indies by any European power, contrary to the rules and orders of the said Company, or of the governor-general and council of Fort William aforesaid.

Provision was made for the examination of such persons, and for their trial in India or England.[7]

The Act directed the company to make a survey of all its establishments, civil and military, with a view to retrenchment. When the survey was complete, the company was required to present to Parliament, within fourteen days after the beginning of each session, lists of their employées together with the salaries and emoluments payable to them.[8] In future only so many persons were to be sent out from England as were needed to fill the vacancies notified by the officers of the company in India.[9] Promotions, civil and military, were to be made according to seniority of appointment, unless for urgent reasons, which must be stated on their minutes, the governor-general or the presidents and their councils saw fit to make an exception.[10] All appointments made otherwise than in accordance with this rule, whether by the directors or by the governments in India, were to be void.[11]

[1] § 31. [2] § 32. [3] § 32. [4] § 36.
[5] § 36. [6] § 33. [7] §§ 53, 54. [8] § 40.
[9] § 41. [10] § 42. [11] § 42.

Cadets sent out to India must be above the age of fifteen and under the age of twenty-two.[1] Servants of the company who returned to the United Kingdom, and who had been resident there or in any part of Europe for five years, were not to be capable of reappointment, unless either the board of control and the directors were satisfied that such residence was due to ill-health, or unless such servant's reappointment was sanctioned by a three-fourths majority of the court of proprietors.[2]

(iii) Safeguards against oppression by the company or its servants.

The safeguards provided by the Regulating Act[3] were strengthened and elaborated. British subjects, whether in the company's service or not, were declared to be amenable to the jurisdiction of competent courts in India and England for criminal offences committeed in native states, in the same way as if the offences had been committed in the company's territories.[4] The receipt of presents by any person in the service of the Crown or the company was to be deemed to be extortion and punishable as such.[5] Disobedience by servants of the company to the orders of the directors, except in cases where the servant could prove necessity, breaches of trust or duty, and the making of corrupt bargains with respect to any office or employment under the company, were to be deemed to be misdemeanours and punishable as such.[6] If a servant of the company were condemned and sentenced by any competent court in Great Britain or India, the company could not release or compound the sentence, or restore the servant.[7] All servants of the company, within two months after their return to Great Britain, must deliver on oath an inventory of all their property, specifying what parts of it were not acquired in consequence of their residence in India.[8] If it appeared to the court of Exchequer that there was reason to suspect the truth of the inventory the servant could, within three years, be examined on oath.[9] Default in delivering the inventory or in answering interrogatories, or untrue statements as to the amount of the property to the extent of £2,000, was punishable by the forfeiture of all the servant's property.[10] In 1786 these sections, which

---

[1] § 43.   [2] § 63.   [3] Above 165-168.

[4] 24 George III Sess. 2 c. 25 § 44; 26 George III c. 57 § 29 provided that such persons should be subject to the criminal jurisdiction of the courts of any of the British settlements in India for crimes committed in Asia, Africa, or America within the limits of the exclusive trade of the Company; whether or not they were committed against any of his Majesty's subjects.

[5] 24 George III Sess. 2 c. 25 § 45.   [6] §§ 49, 50.

[7] § 51.   [8] § 55.   [9] § 56.

[10] § 57; §§ 59 and 60 made provision for non-delivery of the inventory by reason of sickness, and § 61 provided for allowances to informers who made discovery of property not disclosed in the inventory.

required servants of the company to deliver an inventory, were repealed.[1]

Provisions were made for setting up a special tribunal for the trial of servants of the company accused of extortion. The House of Lords and the House of Commons were to choose panels of their members. These members must not be persons in the service of the Crown, members of the board of control, or directors of the company. From these panels four peers and six commoners, together with one judge from each of the three courts of common law, were to be selected to act as special commissioners to try charges of extortion or other misdemeanours. Seven commissioners, of whom one must be a judge, were to be a quorum.[2] Provision was made for the issue of writs of mandamus to the Indian courts to take evidence as to the matters in issue ; [3] and it was enacted that communications from India to the directors, and *vice versa*, sent in the usual course of correspondence and relating to the charge, should be admissible as evidence.[4] Prosecutions were made subject to a time limit of three years after the return of a servant of the company to England, or after he had delivered his inventory.[5] In 1786 these provisions were amended ; [6] but they have never been put into force.[7]

(iv) *Directions as to the policy to be pursued in India.*

On two matters the Act laid down principles as to the policy to be pursued by the company in India.

First, it was declared that " to pursue schemes of conquest and extension of dominion in India are measures repugnant to the wish, the honour and policy of this nation." [8] It was therefore enacted that, except in the case where hostilities against the British nation or the princes dependent upon or in alliance with them had begun or were imminent, the governor-general and council should have no power, without the express authority of the directors or the secret committee, to begin hostilities with, or to enter into any treaty for making war against, a native prince, or to make a treaty for guaranteeing the possessions of a native prince. Treaties with native princes must only be made in consideration of assistance to be given in a war begun or imminent ; and in all such cases full information as to the hostilities and treaties must be sent to the directors.[9] Except in cases of sudden emergency or imminent danger, the presidents of Madras and Bombay were forbidden to begin war or to make

---

[1] 26 George III c. 57 § 31.   [2] 24 George III Sess. 2 c. 25 §§ 64-77.
[3] §§ 78, 79.   [4] § 80.   [5] § 82.
[6] 26 George III c. 57 §§ 1-25.
[7] Ilbert, Government of India 66 n. 1.
[8] § 34.   [9] § 34.

treaties without the express orders of the governor-general and council, or the directors, or the secret committee. Any treaty which they made must, if possible, contain a clause which gave the governor-general and council power to reject or ratify it.[1]

Secondly, it was declared that " the principles of justice and the honour of this country " required that enquiry should be made into the complaints of native land-holders in the British territories in India, that they had been deprived of their lands and jurisdictions, or that the tributes, rents, and services exacted from them were excessive ; and that these complaints, if proved to be true, should be redressed. It was therefore enacted that such enquiry should be instituted ; and that there should be established " upon the principles of moderation and justice, according to the laws and constitution of India, the permanent rules by which their respective tributes, rents, and services, shall be in future rendered and paid to the said United Company." [2]

This legislation both regulated the machinery by which, and laid down the general principles according to which, the government of India was to be conducted. We must now examine the manner in which this machinery and these principles worked in practice and the way in which their working created a government for India.

(2) *The evolution of a government for India under the guidance of this legislation.*

We must consider, in the first place, the working of the partnership between the company and the state which this legislation had created, and, in the second place, the creation of the machinery of law and government in India.

(i) *The working of the partnership between the company and the state.*

The board of control, like other boards in other spheres of the executive government,[3] ceased to function in the manner contemplated by the Legislature, because its powers came to be vested in its president.[4] Its first president, Henry Dundas, was the real ruler of India. He was in the cabinet and the most trusted friend of Pitt. Having the support of the government, he did not hesitate to impose his will on the directors ; and at one time he seems to have contemplated taking all political power from the directors, leaving them only their control of the

---

[1] § 35.

[2] § 39 ; the persons complaining were described as " rajahs, zemindars, polyars, toloohdars and other native land holders."

[3] Vol. x 467, 488.   [4] Camb. Hist. of the Empire iv 314.

company's trade.   But this was too much like a reversion to
the policy of Fox's bill.   It aroused much hostility ; and the
Act of 1793 left the company with the powers which had been
secured to them by the Act of 1784.[1]   Later presidents were not
always cabinet ministers, and they did not exercise the same
control over the directors as Dundas had exercised.   In fact,
" each part of the Home Government could make the position
of the governor-general intolerable if it pleased." [2]   The result
was that questions of policy were settled on a basis of compromise.
It is true that in urgent cases the president could require the
secret committee to send off any dispatch that he wished.   But
generally the contents of dispatches were arranged after a discussion between the chairman of the directors and the president.[3]
The procedure was slow.[4]   But " this defect was largely neutral-
ized by the length of time that communications took to reach
India, and the large degree of discretion which the Indian
government necessarily enjoyed " ; [5]   and this procedure did
establish a definite link between the company and the government.   At the same time the powers which the government had
of acting through the secret committee ensured that on all
important questions of policy it could make its will prevail ; [6]
and the fact that the governor-general had been given increased
powers to overrule his council, and to control the subordinate
presidencies on both civil and military questions, made the
exercise of the government's control easier, and increased the
efficiency of the government of India.[7]

Both the exercise of this central control, and the efficiency
of the government of India, were increased by the manner in
which the Legislature had dealt with the abuses arising out of
the manner in which the company had appointed and promoted
its servants.   We have seen that, except in the case of the
highest officials, places must be filled from the ranks of the
covenanted service, from servants resident in India, and from

---

[1] Camb. Hist. of the Empire iv 314.   [2] Ibid 315.
[3] Similarly dispatches sent from India might be sent to the secret committee,
in which case they were only laid before the court of directors if the president so
desired, ibid.
[4] Mr. Dodwell thus describes the process : " Usually the chairman of the court
would informally propose a course of action to the president ; and the matter would
be discussed between them either in conversation or by private letters.   The
chairman would then informally propose a dispatch, which would be prepared at
the India House, and sent to the Board of Control with a mass of documentary
information on which the dispatch was founded.   This was technically called
a Previous Communication.   It was returned with approval or correction to the
Company, and after reconsideration sent a second time to Westminster, the document on this second submission being called a draft. . . . If the court concurred
with the amendments, the dispatch would then be sent off ; but if they did not, the
discussion might continue, in the last resort the board securing obedience by a
mandamus from the Court of King's Bench," ibid.
[5] Ibid 316.   [6] Ibid.   [7] Above 206.

servants belonging to the presidency where the vacancy occurred.[1]
This rule encouraged the formation of an expert and disciplined
civil service, imbued with a spirit of loyalty to their superiors in
India and England.

It was chiefly through the governor-general and, to a much
smaller extent, through the subordinate presidents, that the
control of the company and the state was exercised ; and the
governor-general and the subordinate presidents were able to
give effect to the policy which the company and the state desired,
because they controlled a trained and disciplined civil service,
and a trained and disciplined military force.   It was because the
governor-general and the subordinate presidents were the chief
connecting links between the home government and the government of India, that it gradually came to be the rule that the
governor-general, and later the presidents of the subordinate
governments, were not taken from the ranks of the covenanted
service.[2]   It was obviously desirable that such a post as governor-
general should be filled by a man of wider outlook than was
possible to those who had made their career in the company's
service.   Moreover, " their rank and standing secured for them
a more ready and willing obedience than the Company's servants
would have accorded to one of themselves " ; and " they carried
more weight, and their representations were treated with greater
respect by the home authorities than would have been the case
with the Company's servants." [3]   The same considerations applied, though much less decisively, to the appointments to the
presidencies of the subordinate governments.

The first of the governors-general of this new type was
Cornwallis.[4]   He was a soldier with no experience of India.   He
had failed in America, but his abilities were recognized by both
parties.   He was sent out to work Pitt's Act, and to carry out
the main object of that Act—the reform of the abuses of the
company's government of India.   That he succeeded so well was
due partly to the assistance of some of the able officials who had
been trained under Hastings—to men like Shore, James Grant,
Charles Grant, and Duncan ; [5] and partly to the fact that he
was able to build on the foundations which Hastings had laid.
" Every aspect of reform was foreshadowed in the work or in
the projects of Hastings, and hence the solidity of the work of
Cornwallis." [6]   To the consideration of his work we must now
turn.

[1] Above 205.
[2] Camb. Hist. of the Empire iv 320-321.
[3] Ibid 320.   [4] Ibid 434.
[5] For these distinguished civil servants see ibid 435-436.
[6] Ibid 437.

(ii) *The creation of the machinery of law and government in India.*

Before describing the manner in which Cornwallis created, from the more or less experimental work of his predecessors, a definite machinery of law and government for India, it is necessary to say a word of the commercial side of the company's organization, and of the manner in which it was affected by the great political position which the company had attained, and by the economic changes which were taking place at the end of the eighteenth century.

The East India Company was a trading company, and therefore its commercial activities were, for the first century and a half of its existence, its most important activities.   The political rights and privileges which it derived from its charters, or from the grants of Indian rulers, were comparatively unimportant, and were regarded as being merely incidental, though necessary, aids to the conduct of its trade.[1]   The victories of Clive and the successful administration of Hastings had changed the relative importance of the commercial and the political activities of the company.   But, notwithstanding this change, the commercial side of the company's activities was important throughout the eighteenth century, because, throughout that century, the company still retained its monopoly of trade, which it exercised with very little external interference.   The control of the company over the conduct of its commercial activities had been very little affected by the legislation which had given to the state a control over its political activities.

We have seen that, at the beginning of the century, the company's servants had bought cargoes of various commodities, such as wool, cotton, or indigo, and had paid for them mainly by specie exported from England ; that these cargoes were known as the investment ; and that, after the company had become in effect the rulers of Bengal, the investment was purchased out of the revenues of Bengal.[2]   The business of the investment was controlled by the company's board of trade, which had been reorganized in 1786, and subordinated to the governor-general and council.[3]   Cornwallis found that there was much fraud and negligence in the business of providing the investment. Some of the company's servants were dismissed, and in 1788 a new system was inaugurated.[4]   The commercial residents of the company arranged the contracts with the native manufacturers, supervised their performance, and saw to it that the workers were not oppressed.   They were paid by a commission on the

---

[1] Above 144-145, 149-157.
[2] Above 153 n. 1.
[3] Camb. Hist. of the Empire iv 438.
[4] Ibid 441.

goods which were supplied through them.[1] These reforms made by Cornwallis in the commercial department were among his " lasting achievements." [2]

These commercial activities were then of minor importance compared with the political activities of the company ; and, at the end of the century, it was clear that the privileges, upon which its commercial activities were based, would not last long. The ideas of Adam Smith and his school of political economy were in the ascendant ; and, according to those ideas, the commercial monopoly of the company was indefensible. " Such exclusive companies," said Adam Smith, " are nuisances in every respect ; always more or less inconvenient to the countries in which they are established ; and destructive to those who have the misfortune to fall under their government." [3] They were destructive to those who fell under their government, because their interest as merchants was directly opposite to their interest as sovereigns.[4] Since the legislation of the latter part of the eighteenth century had emphasized the position of the company as a sovereign, and put its powers as sovereign under the control of the state, it was clear that its interest as a merchant must sink into the background. When the company's charter was renewed in 1793, its monopoly had been attacked, and it had been compelled to allow private merchants to import and export a limited quantity of goods.[5] In 1813 the monopoly of the Indian trade was taken away from the company ; but it retained its monopoly of the China trade and the trade in tea.[6] In fact it was from the China trade that its chief commercial profits were derived ; [7] for " the application of machinery and power to the cotton manufacture and calico printing " was putting an end to the chief branch of its Indian trade—the export of cotton piece goods.[8] In 1833 all its commercial privileges were taken away.[9] The Charter Act of that year required the company " to close their commercial business and to wind up their affairs with all convenient speed. Their territorial and other debts were charged on the revenues of India, and they

---

[1] Camb. Hist. of the Empire iv 441-442.   [2] Ibid.
[3] Wealth of Nations (Cannan's ed.) ii 140.
[4] " It is the interest of the East India Company considered as sovereigns, that the European goods which are carried to their Indian dominions should be sold there as cheap as possible ; and that the Indian goods which are brought from thence should bring there as good a price, or should be sold there as dear as possible. But the reverse of this is their interest as merchants. As sovereigns, their interest is exactly the same with that of the country which they govern. As merchants, their interest is directly opposite to that interest," ibid 137.
[5] Camb. Hist. of the Empire iv 313 ;   33 George III c. 52 § 87.
[6] Ilbert, Government of India 75 ; 53 George III c. 155 § 6.
[7] Ilbert, op. cit. 73.
[8] Camb. Hist. of the Empire iv 313.
[9] 3, 4 William IV c. 85 §§ 3 and 4.

were to receive out of those revenues an annual dividend at the rate of £10 10s. per cent. on the whole amount of their capital stock (i.e. £630,000 a year), but this dividend was to be subject to redemption by Parliament on payment of £200 sterling for every £100 stock, and, for the purpose of that redemption, a sum of two million pounds was to be paid by the Company to the National Debt Commissioners and accumulated with compound interest until it reached the sum of twelve millions." [1]

During the remainder of its career the company was not a commercial society, but an anomalous political entity, closely connected with and controlled by the British government, through which Great Britain chose to govern India. We must now turn to this other and more important side of the company's activities, and examine the machinery of government which was set up in India by the joint efforts of the British government and the company.

Before Cornwallis came to India section 41 of the Act of 1784, which directed the company to make a survey of all its establishments,[2] had been put into force.[3] A special department of the central government had been entrusted with this work; and their survey of the establishments of the company had been completed in January 1789.[4] The work of the central government was divided into three main departments—the commercial department with which I have already dealt,[5] the public department which was concerned with matters of government—civil, military, and naval, and the revenue department. In all these departments reforms were made.

The treasury, the paymaster's office, and the accountant-general's office were all reformed; the duties of the *Khalsa* (the exchequer) defined; the establishment of the customs reduced. New regulations were presented for the postal service. A detailed examination was made of the inferior servants employed on the staffs of all the headquarters offices, and the whole system regulated. For each department a special list of rules for the conduct of business was drawn up. . . . The regulations on these matters were among the lasting achievements of Cornwallis. For, although the increase in business of later years necessitated further elaboration of the machinery, the later changes did not affect the main structure.[6]

This, as we shall now see, is also true of many of his other changes in the machinery of the government of India.

In the two closely allied departments of revenue and the administration of civil justice, the governorship of Hastings had, as we have seen,[7] been a time of experiment. The Act of

[1] Ilbert, op. cit. 82.
[2] Above 207.
[3] Camb. Hist. of the Empire iv 446.
[4] Ibid.
[5] Above 213-214.
[6] Camb. Hist. of the Empire iv 447.
[7] Above 172-174.

1784,[1] and the instructions given to Cornwallis,[2] showed that Parliament and the company both wished that a permanent settlement of the land revenue should be made. As a preparation for this a decennial settlement was undertaken in 1789, which was finished in 1793.[3] In 1793 the governor-general, acting under the orders of the company, declared this settlement perpetual.[4] This settlement of the land revenue was accompanied by reforms both in the machinery for its collection, and in the relation of that machinery to the machinery for the administration of civil justice.

When Cornwallis came to India the whole provincial administration centred round the collector. He was the collector of the revenue, judge of the court of diwani adalat and of the revenue court of mahal adalat, and superintendent of the police.[5] From the courts of diwani adalat there was an appeal to the court of sadr diwani adalat,[6] and from the court of mahal adalat to the board of revenue.[7] The company favoured this plan in 1786,[8] and Cornwallis had adhered to it down to his reform of 1793.[9] But two reasons convinced Cornwallis that it ought to be changed. In the first place, the whole system depended on the honesty and ability of the collector. Cornwallis wished to give the subjects of the company the security of " a system upheld by its inherent principles and not by the men who are occasionally to have the conduct of it." [10] He considered that the entrusting of judicial powers to the officers of the revenue tended to destroy confidence in the administration of the law. In the second place, the permanent settlement destroyed a principal reason for the old system. When the company became in effect the rulers of the country, its main object was to get a large revenue and a large investment. It knew nothing of systems of land-holding. If the farmers of the revenue " had been

[1] Above 210.
[2] Parlt. Papers 1812 vii 13 ; the directors, in fact, were tired of experiments and wanted some finality ; they wrote in 1786, " a steady adherence to almost any one system, attended with a watchful superintendence and control on behalf of you, our principal servants, to enforce the just and rigorous execution of it, and obviate defects as they may arise, is preferable to frequent changes, however attended with expectations of improvement," ibid 1810 v App. 12 p. 156.
[3] Ibid 1812 vii 18.
[4] See Cornwallis' proclamation to this effect cited ibid 21-22 ; Cornwallis favoured the measure (1) because he thought that it would stimulate industry and so increase the prosperity of the country, and (2) because it would leave officials more leisure to study the problems of administration, ibid 1810 v 173, 175 ; cp. Berriedale Keith, op. cit. 109.
[5] Parlt. Papers 1812 vii 30 ; the courts of mahal adalat had been created in 1790 to relieve the board of revenue in their task of hearing revenue appeals, Camb. Hist. of the Empire iv 444.
[6] Above 173.
[7] See Parlt. Papers 1810 v App. 9 p. 104 ; ibid 1812 vii 25.
[8] Ibid 30, 31.   [9] Camb. Hist. of the Empire iv 443-444.
[10] Parlt. Papers 1810 v 104.

restrained by prosecution in a judicial court, they would not have been able to realize what they had engaged to pay to the government." Therefore the government was " obliged to shut its eyes to what passed in the collection of the revenue, and to tolerate what it was not prepared to remedy." [1] The fixing of the revenue in perpetuity had changed the whole position, and had destroyed all the reasons for the continuance of the old system. [2]

It was for these reasons that Cornwallis took away all judicial power from the collectors and the board of revenue, and entrusted it to zillah or district courts. These courts were to have jurisdiction not only over the suits of private persons, but also over the collectors and other officers of the government. From these district courts appeals were to be brought to courts of appeal consisting of three judges, which were set up at Patna, Dacca, Moorshedabad, and in the vicinity of Calcutta ; [3] and from them to the court of sadr diwani adalat. [4]

These changes had been preceded by reforms in the administration of the criminal law. When Cornwallis came to India the collectors had certain magisterial powers ; but the provincial criminal courts were the courts of nizam adalat presided over by Mahomedan judges, from which appeal lay to the court of sadar nizamat adalat. [5] Cornwallis found that the organization of the criminal courts was very defective—" the most daring robberies and other enormities were," he said, " daily committed throughout the provinces." [6] He was convinced that no regulations for reform could be efficacious if " the execution of them depends on any native whatever." [7] He therefore instituted in 1790 courts of circuit, presided over by English judges assisted by Mahomedan assessors. They held a general gaol delivery every six months, and in capital cases their sentences must be confirmed by the nizamat adalat. That court was removed from Moorshedabad to Calcutta, [8] and was composed of the governor-general, and the members of his council, assisted by Indian assessors. [9]

When in 1793 the collectors were deprived of their judicial powers, opportunity was taken to link up the machinery of civil and criminal justice. Their magisterial functions were conferred on the judges of the zillah or district courts. [10] Serious cases were tried by the criminal courts, which were to be staffed

[1] Parlt. Papers 1810 v 111.   [2] Ibid 112-113.
[3] The City of Calcutta being under the jurisdiction of the supreme court, the provincial courts of appeal had no jurisdiction there, ibid 105.
[4] Ibid 104-105.   [5] Above 174.
[6] Minute of the governor-general of Feb. 11 1793, Parlt. Papers 1810 v 109.
[7] Camb. Hist. of the Empire iv 445, citing a minute of Dec. 3 1789.
[8] Parlt. Papers 1812 vii 14-15.
[9] Camb. Hist. of the Empire iv 445.
[10] Parlt. Papers 1812 vii 37-38.

by the same persons as those who staffed the provincial courts of appeal.[1] As circuit judges they were subordinate to the nizamat adalat.[2] Copies of the record of the trial, with the comments of the judge, were sent to the nizamat adalat,[3] and, after each circuit, the judges were required to make a general report to the same tribunal.[4]

This reform of the criminal courts was accompanied by the institution of a new police system. In 1791 Cornwallis had reorganized the police of Calcutta by creating superintendents of police, whose functions were confined to the maintenance of order and the arrest of suspected persons.[5] It was not till 1793 that a similar system was applied to the whole country. Until the reforms of 1793 the zamindars had been responsible for keeping the peace within their zamindaries. They were bound by the terms of the tenure of their estates to arrest criminals ; and if they failed to do so they were answerable to the injured person. If the zamindary was farmed the farmer came under the same liability.[6] But it was said by the governor-general in council in 1793 that this system was wholly ineffective, because it was notorious that the zamindars or their officers connived at or actually committed the crimes they were supposed to suppress.[7] Therefore to make the reforms in the administration of the criminal law effective it was necessary to introduce a new police system ; for

courts of Justice to try offenders, however well constituted, are comparatively of but little use towards deterring people from committing crimes, if, for want of local police establishments, robbers can commit excesses in the country, and reside with safety (as in many instances is the case at present) under the protection of the land holders.[8]

The police powers of the zamindars were taken away, and the whole country was divided into police districts of twenty square miles. To each district a certain number of police were attached. They were appointed by and were under the control of the magistrate,[9] who was, as we have seen, the judge of the zillah or district court.[10] Similar arrangements were made for policing the towns of Patna, Dacca, and Moorshedabad.[11]

---

[1] Parlt. Papers 1812 vii 39 ; ibid 1810 v 109, 114.
[2] Ibid 114.   [3] Ibid 1812 vii 42.
[4] " On the return of the judges from their circuit, they are required to make a report to the nizamat adalat, containing such observations as they have made during the circuit, touching the effects of the present system in the prevention and punishment of crimes, the state of the jails, the treatment and employment of the prisoners, and whatever matters appear to deserve the notice of the Court," ibid 42-43.
[5] Camb. Hist. of the Empire iv 452.
[6] Above 187, 188 ; Parlt. Papers 1810 v 105.
[7] Ibid.   [8] Ibid.   [9] Ibid 106.
[10] Ibid.   [11] Parlt. Papers 1812 vii 44.

These reforms in the machinery for the administration of civil and criminal justice were accompanied, first by rules for the regulation of the legal profession ; and, secondly, by provisions for the restatement and reform of the law, in which we can see the formation of those systems of Hindu and Mahomedan law which are administered in India to-day, and the beginnings of that introduction of the rules of English law, which will end in the construction of the Anglo-Indian codes.

(1) Cornwallis's minute of February 11, 1793, showed that the administration of justice was seriously impeded by the absence of a properly regulated legal profession. Suitors either appeared in person, or they appointed native pleaders or vakeels to plead their causes, or they appointed their own servants to act as their vakeels. The result of this system was that the administration of justice was seriously impeded.

The persons who practise as vakeels are generally of low character ; they have no reputation to lose by misconduct, and are often bribed by the opposite party to betray the cause of their constituent ; if detected in bad conduct in one court they can remove to another. They are generally ignorant of the Mahomedan and Hindoo law, and equally so of the British part of the judicial code of the country ; and consequently incapable of giving advice respecting a claim, or of urging the best arguments in support of the causes which they undertake.

Matters were even worse when suitors appointed their own servants to plead their causes.

Vakeels of this description, not being accustomed to plead in the courts of justice, are still more at a loss : unacquainted with the forms or practice of the court, their pleadings are generally diffuse, and often irrelevant ; they protract and prolong a suit with unnecessary exhibits, summon witnesses whose testimony is no use to their cause ; and are totally unacquainted with the manner of examining witnesses so as to draw forth the truth. To this ignorance of the vakeels is chiefly to be attributed the voluminous and irregular records of trials that are daily submitted to the Sudder Dewanny Adawlat.[1]

To remedy this state of affairs a certain number of vakeels were to be licensed, and they were to have the monopoly of practice in the courts. Of these one or more was to be appointed to represent the government. They were to take an oath to execute their duties faithfully, rules were to be made as to their qualifications, and provision was to be made for their education at the Mahomedan College at Calcutta and the Hindu College at Benares.[2]

Cornwallis was right in thinking that the institution of a regular and learned legal profession was a condition precedent to the formation of definite bodies of law adapted to the new constitution which the company was creating for its territorial possessions. But, as we shall now see, the creation of such bodies of law was a longer and a more difficult task than he realized.

(2) The law administered in Bengal consisted of (i) the rules of the English criminal law which were applied to European British subjects and to residents in Calcutta, and the other rules of English law which were applied to European British subjects; (ii) the codes of Hindu and Mahomedan law which were applied to Hindus and Mahomedans; and (iii) the growing mass of new laws applicable to the company's territorial possessions made by the regulations of the governor-general and council of Bengal, and by the regulations of the other presidencies. Of the second and third of these sources of law I must say a few words.

Hindu and Mahomedan Law.—We have seen that Warren Hastings had been impressed with the importance of making the study of Hindu and Mahomedan law possible, by the preparation of digests, and by procuring their translation into English.[1] The importance of proceeding with this work was made the more obvious by the clauses of the Act of 1781, which required the supreme court to decide controversies between Hindus or Mahomedans according to their laws.[2] In Sir William Jones [3] (1746-1794), who had been appointed a judge of the supreme court of Calcutta in 1783, the government had a man, who was better qualified than any other Englishman of his time, to undertake the task of compiling a digest of these laws.

Jones was a classical scholar, and so distinguished a student of oriental languages that he was elected a fellow of the Royal Society in 1772, and so distinguished a man of letters that in 1773 he was elected a member of the famous Literary Club, over which Dr. Johnson presided. He was called to the bar in 1774, and his *Essay on Bailments* gives him a place amongst famous legal authors.[4] His legal talents and his oriental learning made him so eminently fit for the post of a judge of the supreme court of Calcutta, that he was appointed to that office in 1783, in spite of his liberal opinions which had led him to oppose the American war of independence, and to write the "Dialogue between a Gentleman and a Farmer," which was the subject of the indictment in the *Dean of St. Asaph's Case.*[5] In India he founded and was the first president of the Asiatic Society. He

---

[1] Above 175-176.
[2] 21 George III c. 70 §§ 17, 18.
[3] Lord Teignmouth, Memoirs of Sir William Jones: D.N.B.; see also Mackinnon, Murder in the Temple 80-81.
[4] Vol. xii 393-394.
[5] R. v. Shipley (1784) 4 Dougl. 73; 21 S.T. 847; vol. x 675.

learned Sanscrit,[1] and wrote many tracts on different aspects of
the Indian languages, literature, and philosophy. As a judge
and a jurist he realized that a thorough knowledge of the native
systems of law was a condition precedent to the sound and
intelligent government of India; and that this knowledge
could only be got, if the native systems of law were restated in
a form which was intelligible to the Englishmen and natives
who were entrusted with their administration. In 1788 he
addressed a letter to Cornwallis in which he pointed out the
need for a complete digest of Hindu and Mahomedan law,[2]
" after the model of Justinian's inestimable pandects, compiled
by the most learned of native lawyers, with an accurate verbal
translation of it into English." He pointed out that, without
such a digest it was always possible that the judges might be
deceived by the native lawyers. He offered to superintend
the production of a work which he hoped would " give the natives
of these Indian provinces a permanent security for the due administration of justice among them." His offer was accepted
and the work was begun. He published a translation of the
Ordinances of Manu, a work on the Mahomedan law of intestacy,
and a work on the Mahomedan law of inheritance. But he
died in 1794, before the whole digest was completed.

The Regulations.—Though Jones's restatement of the native
systems of law was not completed, its incompleteness was
partially remedied by the regulations of the governor-general
and council of Bengal, and by the regulations made by the
other presidencies. These regulations had begun to supplement the two native codes of law, to introduce into them
Western ideas of justice, and thus to render them adequate to
meet the needs of the more advanced civilization which the
British government was introducing. That this work of reforming the law was speedily and efficiently done was due in
no small degree to some of Cornwallis's reforms. In order that
the experience gained by the judges might be utilized to suggest
reforms in the law, Cornwallis proposed that the various courts
should have power to suggest changes in the law.[3] In order
that the object of a new law might be better understood, it
was always to be prefaced by a preamble, in which the reasons
for its enactment were explained. These new laws were to be

---

[1] In 1785 he wrote, " I am proceeding slowly but surely . . . in the study of
Sanscrit; for I can no longer bear to be at the mercy of our pundits, who deal out
Hindu law as they please, and make it at reasonable rates, when they cannot find it
ready made," Teignmouth, Memoirs 264.
[2] Ibid 306-312.
[3] Parlt. Papers 1810 v 120-121 ; similarly Macaulay suggested in his Introductory Report on the Indian Penal Code, Works (Albany ed.) i 17-18 that judges
should report any doubts which had arisen on the construction of the code, and that
the highest judicial authorities should make periodical reports to the Legislature.

printed in English, Persian, and Bengali, bound up each year in a volume, and distributed to the courts and to officials. Collections of the existing regulations were to be similarly printed and bound up into volumes.[1] Two illustrations of the manner in which a new law for British India was thus built up are to be found in the law of civil procedure and in the criminal law.

One of the earliest and most beneficial of these regulations created a new code of civil procedure for the courts of diwani adalat. This code was drawn up by Impey after he had been made judge of the sadar diwani adalat and came into force in 1781. In 1812 it was said to be the " foundation of the rules now in force relative to the administration of civil justice." [2] It explained ambiguities, revoked obsolete or repugnant rules, prescribed a uniform set of rules and uniform fees for all these courts, and thus introduced a conformity in their practice and decisions.[3] The criminal law of the country was, as under the Mogul emperors, Mahomedan law.[4] But we have seen that the Legislature in 1773 had virtually recognized the power of the governor-general and council to alter the Mahomedan law ; [5] and the process of civilizing and humanizing its rules was begun after Cornwallis's changes in the machinery of its administration. Thus sentences of mutilation were changed for sentences of imprisonment and hard labour ; and the Hindu practice of infanticide was suppressed [6]—though no attempt was as yet made to put down the practice of suttee.[7] At the same time attempts were made to deal more effectually with such offences as perjury and forgery, and with dacoity or gang robbery.[8]

When Cornwallis left India in 1793, the enactment of definite codes of law for the whole of the British dominions in India was as yet far distant. But it was his work which eventually made the creation of such codes possible. His regulations of 1793 created the machinery and laid down the principles upon which the government of British India was conducted for many years to come.[9] The satisfaction of his contemporaries with the results which he had achieved is shown by two facts. In the first place, when the company's charter was renewed in 1793

[1] Parlt. Papers 1810 v 120-121.   [2] Ibid 1812 vii 9.

[3] The Preamble to the code cited ibid ; see Stephen, Nuncomar and Impey ii 245-247 ; Stephen says, " I should doubt whether anyone else then in India, except possibly Chambers, could have done it. It must have been an immense comfort and excellent guide to the new judges " ; it was revised in 1787.

[4] Parlt. Papers 1812 vii 39-40.   [5] Above 174 and n. 9.

[6] Parlt. Papers 1812 vii 40.

[7] " In regard to immolation in the various modes practised by self-devoted victims, who are invariably Hindoos, no further interference is permitted to take place, on the part of the magistrate, than may be necessary to ascertain from the party, that the resolution taken has been voluntary, and in no wise influenced by improper means," ibid 41.

[8] Ibid.   [9] Camb. Hist. of the Empire iv 452, 454-455.

very few changes were made by the Act [1] which renewed it. That Act for the most part codified the preceding legislation,[2] and the changes which it made were comparatively unimportant.[3] In the second place, the Bengal regulations were

introduced as the conquests of the Company increased the extent of their dominions into the greater part of upper India and in particular into what are now the North West Provinces. They were also introduced into Madras with few if any material variations ; and Supreme Courts similar in all respects to the Supreme Court of Calcutta were established in Madras in 1800 and in Bombay in 1823.[4]

These developments made the creation of a uniform body of law for British India possible. It was for this reason that the committee, which reported in 1812, was able to say that the English government in India was superior to its predecessor " in the vigour, the efficiency, and the *unity* of its authority, which neither acknowledges nor permits divided sovereignty, but keeps every other power in subordination to its own." [5]

By the beginning of the third decade of the nineteenth century the regulations had come to be the most important and the most bulky portion of the law. In some cases they had superseded the native codes of law. Thus in 1837 Macaulay said that " the penal law of Bombay is all contained in the Regulations, and is almost all to be found in one extensive Regulation." [6] But this method of modifying native law and of creating new law had defects, which became more serious as the law became more elaborate. What Stephen has said of the development of the criminal law is true also of the development of other branches of law :

It became necessary in many instances besides correcting the law to supply its defects, and for this purpose all sorts of expedients were devised. The law of England, instructions from the government, general ideas of justice, analogies, in short almost anything which occurred to those by whom the system was administered were resorted

---

[1] 33 George III c. 52.

[2] " It was a measure of consolidation, repealing several previous enactments, and runs to an enormous length, but the amendments made by it relate to matters of minor importance," Ilbert, Government of India 69.

[3] Some of the most important changes are summarized by Ilbert, op. cit. 69-70 as follows, " The two junior members of the Board of Control were no longer required to be Privy Councillors. Provision was made for the payment of the members and staff of the Board of Control out of Indian revenues. . . . Departure from India with intent to return to Europe was declared to vacate the office of governor-general, commander-in-chief, and certain other high offices. The procedure in the councils of the three presidencies was regulated, the powers of control exercised by the governor-general were emphasized and explained, and the power of the governor-general to overrule the majority of his council was repeated and extended to the Governors of Madras and Bombay. The governor-general, whilst visiting another presidency, was to supersede the governor, and might appoint a vice-president to act for him in his absence."

[4] Stephen, H.C.L. iii 295.   [5] Parlt. Papers 1812 vii 166.

[6] Introductory Report upon the Indian Penal Code, Works (Albany ed.) i 8.

to for that purpose. The result was a hopelessly confused, feeble, and indeterminate system of which no one could make anything at all.[1]

And these defects were aggravated by the fact that the presidencies of Bengal, Madras, and Bombay legislated independently. Though there was a certain amount of similarity in their governmental machinery and their rules of law, divergencies inevitably arose which caused injustice and inconvenience.[2] In 1833 measures were taken to remedy these defects.

First, by the Act of 1833 the governor-general of Bengal became the governor-general for India.[3] He was given power to legislate for the whole of India;[4] the requirement that regulations which were to be operative within the towns of Calcutta, Madras, and Bombay must be registered in their supreme courts, was abolished;[5] and the legislative powers of the other presidencies and governments were taken away.[6] In order that these legislative duties might be properly performed a legal member was added to the governor-general's council, who was only to be entitled to sit and vote at meetings of the council held for the making of laws and regulations.[7] The first legal member appointed under this section was Macaulay.

Secondly, provision was made for the creation of a uniform body of law for British India. Whitley Stokes tells us that the genesis of the measure adopted to effect this object is to be found in a correspondence which took place in 1829 between Sir Charles Metcalfe and the judges of Bengal.[8] This measure

---

[1] Stephen, H.C.L. iii 294; Macaulay said in his Introductory Report upon the Indian Penal Code, Works (Albany ed.) i 7 that "the penal law of Bengal and of the Madras Presidency is, in fact, Mahomedan law, which has gradually been distorted to such an extent as to deprive it of all title to the religious veneration of Mahomedans, yet which retains enough of its original peculiarities to perplex and encumber the administration of justice."

[2] For instances see Macaulay's Introductory Report on the Indian Penal Code, Works (Albany ed.) i 6-7.   [3] 3, 4 William IV c. 85 § 39.

[4] § 43; the Regulating Act, 13 George III c. 63 §§ 36, 37 gave the governor-general of Bengal power to legislate for Fort William and other factories subordinate thereto, but not for Bengal generally; but Cornwallis's regulations extended over the whole of Bengal, Bihar, and Orissa, and their validity is recognized by 37 George III c. 142 § 8, see Stephen, H.C.L. iii 298 n. 1; this gradual extension of the legislative authority of the British enactments corresponds with the gradual recognition of British sovereignty over the company's possessions.

[5] 3, 4 William IV c. 85 § 45; Macaulay in his speech on the government of India proved that this requirement was not necessary and might be mischievous; in fact it had become merely an historical survival of the attempt of eighteenth-century statesmen to secure good government by introducing into India the English conception of the rule of law, above 165, 185.

[6] § 59; Berriedale Keith, op. cit. 133-135.   [7] 3, 4 William IV c. 85 § 40.

[8] Whitley Stokes, The Anglo-Indian Codes i x; Metcalfe was a distinguished servant of the company who had served in many posts, and was provisional governor-general between the resignation of Lord Bentinck and the arrival of Lord Auckland; in 1829 he was a member of the governor-general's council; for the complexity of the law administered in the supreme court of Calcutta and the company's ourts, which those codes were intended to remedy, see Berriedale Keith, op. cit. 46-147.

is contained in § 53 of the Act of 1833.[1]   That section recites that
it is

> expedient that a general system of judicial establishments and police
> to which all persons whatsoever, as well Europeans as natives, may
> be subject, should be established . . . and that such laws as may
> be applicable in common to all classes, . . . due regard being had to
> the rights feelings and peculiar usages of the people, should be enacted,
> and that all laws and customs having the force of law . . . should be
> ascertained and consolidated, and as occasion may require amended.

The section then provides for the appointment of a Law Commission, with power to enquire into and to report upon courts,
police, judicial procedure, and civil and criminal law.   Four
commissioners were appointed of whom Macaulay was the most
eminent.[2]   They were instructed to settle the draft of an Indian
Penal Code ; and it is probable that in their instructions we can
trace the influence of Bentham exercised through his disciple
James Mill.[3]   That draft was mainly the work of Macaulay.[4]
Since it was the model which was adopted by those who later
constructed the Anglo-Indian Codes, in which the largest part
of Anglo-Indian law is contained, Macaulay may be regarded as
their parent.[5]   These codes are one of the most remarkable,
and will perhaps be the most lasting, of all the achievements of
British rule in India ; for, whatever happens to India, it is probable that the legal ideas introduced by the British Raj will be
permanent—even as the Roman legal ideas have been more
permanent than the Roman Empire.   " Nothing," as Lord
Bryce has said,[6] " clings to the soil more closely than a body of
civilized law once well planted."

[1] 3, 4 William IV c. 85.

[2] The others were J. M. Macleod, G. W. Anderson, and F. Millett.

[3] " James Mill was a devoted disciple of Bentham.   He was examiner of
Indian correspondence when Macaulay was sent out with instructions to draw up a
code or codes for British India ; and it is to the pen of James Mill that is attributed
by tradition the dispatch in which those instructions were emphasized and developed," Ilbert, Legislative Methods and Forms 126.

[4] Stephen, H.C.L. iii 299 ; both Stephen and Bryce regard it as Macaulay's
most remarkable achievement ;   Stephen, no mean judge of such work, thought it
to be Macaulay's most enduring title to fame—" the Penal Code has triumphantly
supported the test of experience for upwards of twenty-one years during which time
it has met with a degree of success which can hardly be ascribed to any other statute
of anything approaching to the same dimensions," ibid ; Bryce, Studies in History
and Jurisprudence i 127, says of it that it is " one of the noblest monuments of
Macaulay's genius " ;   after being revised, it became law in 1860, Ilbert, op. cit.
131 ; it was preceded by a code of civil procedure passed in 1859, and succeeded
by a code of criminal procedure passed in 1861, ibid.

[5] " The Penal Code was the first specimen of an entirely new and original method
of legislative expression.   It has been found of the greatest possible use in India,
and has been employed in all the most important acts passed since the Penal Code,"
Stephen, H.C.L. iii 302 ; for the later history of codification in India see Ilbert, op.
cit. 131-155.

[6] Studies in History and Jurisprudence i 141.

The result of all these developments has been that the law administered in British India is diverse in character. It consists partly of the Anglo-Indian codes, partly of Hindu, and partly of Mahomedan law ; and other native customs are also recognized. Sir Courtenay Ilbert sums the matter up as follows : [1]

The criminal law and the law of criminal and civil procedure are based wholly on English principles. So also, subject to some few exceptions, are the law of contract and the law of torts or civil wrongs. But within the domain of family law, including the greater part of the law of succession and inheritance, natives of India still retain their personal law, either modified or formulated, to some extent, by Anglo-Indian legislation. Hindus retain their law of marriage, of adoption, of the joint family, of partition, of succession. Mahomedans retain their law of marriage, of testamentary and intestate succession, and of *Wakf* or quasi-religious trusts. In the Madras presidency the legislature have dealt with, and to some extent recognized, the curious system of polyandry which prevails among the Nairs of Malabar. The law relating to the tenure of land in the different provinces of India is represented by enactments which are based on and supplemented by local usage.

The three makers of Great Britain's empire in India in the eighteenth century are Clive, Warren Hastings, and Cornwallis. The victories of Clive made the company a great territorial power in India. Warren Hastings not only made the company the strongest territorial power in India, he also began the long task of creating a strong and just government for the company's territorial possessions. Cornwallis continued his work. Under his rule some of the permanent features of the company's system of law and government began to take shape ; and " by his cleansing of the administrative system he established a lasting tradition." [2]

Of these three makers of Great Britain's empire in India Warren Hastings was the greatest. The company had resolved to " stand forth as Diwan " without realizing the difficulties involved in that resolve, or the political consequences which it entailed. Warren Hastings began the long task of putting that resolve into execution, by laying the foundations of an administrative system controlled by British covenanted servants of the company. Both he and Cornwallis realized that, unless this system was thus controlled, there was no hope of a just, honest, and efficient government.[3] It is true that the policy of Warren Hastings was not followed in its entirety by his successor.[4] The policy of a permanent land settlement, and the policy of

---

[1] Legislative Methods and Forms 168.
[2] Camb. Hist. of the Empire iv 461.
[3] Weitzman, Warren Hastings and Philip Francis 58-59 ; Camb. Hist. of the Empire iv 437.
[4] Weitzman, op. cit. 196-201.

non-intervention in the affairs of the native states—the policy " of the ring fence " as it has been called,[1] were policies which were advocated by his enemy Francis. But the fact that the first policy was not found to be wholly satisfactory and was not followed in all the later acquisitions of the company, and the fact that it was found necessary to abandon the second policy, are proofs of Hastings' statesmanship. His policy of organizing a system of education on an Indian basis, was abandoned in favour of the policy of substituting an English education, which should " form a class of persons Indian in blood and colour, but English in tastes, in opinion, in morals, and intellect." [2] But the results of this policy have not been wholly satisfactory. It is arguable that the educational results of the policy of engrafting new knowledge on a native stock would have produced better results.[3] In the most important matter of all—the construction of a system of law and government for India under British control—Hastings' policy was followed ; and the fact that it was followed successfully meant the creation of a British empire in India, a return to Hastings' policy with regard to the native states, and, consequently, the realization of his wish to make Great Britain the paramount power in India.[4]

Though these three great men had the largest share in constructing the British Empire in India, they never had an entirely free hand. They were controlled both by the company and by Parliament ; and, after 1784, by the King's ministers.[5] The legislation passed by Parliament, the debates in Parliament on Clive's conduct, and above all the impeachment of Warren Hastings, showed that Parliament realized its moral responsibility to the natives who had come under the company's government. And this responsibility was also realized both by Warren Hastings and by Cornwallis. But the problem of introducing into the government of an Eastern state English ideas of justice, and English securities against misgovernment, was a new problem, and, for that reason, a more difficult problem than any of the statesmen of the day at first realized. We have seen that one of the first devices employed—the establishment of a supreme

---

[1] Lee-Warner, The Protected Princes of India 56-57.

[2] Camb. Hist. of the Empire v 111.

[3] Sir Verney Lovett says, ibid 120, " A Hindu movement in Calcutta, due largely to the persevering efforts of the missionaries, combined with the general trend of political thought in England, with the eloquent pen of Macaulay, and with the inclinations of the governor-general, to produce the decision of 1835 which . . . broke violently with the past, took no account of the indigenous vernacular schools, or the importance of preserving as far as possible their self-supporting character, and encouraged tendencies which, as years went on, passed beyond control. The new policy was carried into effect in Bengal by a brilliant Whig politician who possessed no knowledge of the history of Indian thought, and no understanding of the Indian mind."

[4] Above 178, 195-196 ; Weitzman, op. cit. 87-89. [5] Above 204-205.

court with large powers over the acts of the officials of the government—was found to impede so seriously the conduct of the government, that it was necessary to curtail the jurisdiction of the court.[1] Later, Parliament saw that the best of all means for fulfilling the moral duty of Great Britain to India, was the establishment of an able and uncorruptible body of civil servants, through whom, or under whose supervision, the government was conducted. This was the policy pursued by Cornwallis ; and this policy was successful in introducing a better system of government than any that India had yet seen, and in educating those of the natives of India who, under the control and supervision of this civil service, took part in its conduct.

The statesmen of the eighteenth century were, as I have said, realists.[2] They could see when they had made mistakes ; and, since their vision was not blinded by political theories, they were able to take the obvious means to remedy their mistakes. The position which Great Britain had won in India proved that she was the strongest military power in India, and that she was equally superior in the arts of diplomacy and government. It was obvious, therefore, that the British servants of the company must rule. Nobody was foolish enough to contend, in the face of these obvious facts, that an Indian was as well fitted to rule as an Englishman ; or to suppose that a superficial education on European lines would immediately establish equality between the two races. And so, by a process of trial and error, a unique system of government was established in British India by the joint efforts of the company, the Crown, and Parliament, which was controlled by and responsible to all these three authorities.[3] Similarly, in later years, when the policy of " the ring fence " was abandoned, an equally unique relationship of paramountcy was gradually evolved between the British government and the Indian States.

The foundation of the British empire in India is one of the greatest achievements of the statesmen who made and worked the aristocratic eighteenth-century constitution. In its construction their genius for wise rule, which they had learned by long service in the central and local government of their own country, had full play. They worked hard to make themselves acquainted with the character and needs of a civilization, and of a set of religious, social, and economic conditions, very different

---

[1] Above 189.   [2] Above 189.

[3] " It is a very anomalous species of power and property which is held by the East India Company. Our English prerogative law does not furnish principles, much less precedents, by which it can be defined and adjusted. Nothing but the eminent dominion of Parliament over every British subject in every concern, and in every circumstance in which he is placed, can adjust this new intricate matter," Burke, Works (Bohn's ed.) ii 264 note.

from those of the Western world ; and they applied their knowledge to construct a system of law and government which would
not be out of harmony with Eastern needs and ideals, and yet
would introduce Western ideas of justice and efficiency.   It was
because they realized the deep differences between the Eastern
and Western worlds, and the consequent need to study the
Eastern phenomena, that they succeeded better in the East
than in the West.   We have seen that, in the West, similarities
in institutions law and mental outlook, blinded statesmen to the
consequences of the rapid growth of the American colonies ; so
that they failed to see that a reconsideration of their relations to the mother country, based upon a careful study of the
modern facts, was as necessary as was a careful study of Indian
facts for the creation of an administrative system for India.[1]
But both from success and failure valuable lessons had been
learned.   Those lessons had, as we have seen, borne fruit in the
creation either of interesting and important variations upon the
English system of government, or of new and original forms of
government.   We shall now see that they had also borne fruit
in the development of old, and in the evolution of new, principles
of constitutional law, and in other indirect, but no less important,
effects upon the whole body of English law.

The Legal Effects of these Expansions of England

In describing these expansions of England, and the creation
and working of the new governmental machinery which was
thereby rendered necessary, I have already dealt with many of
the legal effects which followed from them.   We have seen that
a direct consequence of these expansions of England was the
elaboration of old, and the evolution of new, rules of constitutional law ;   and that an indirect consequence was the introduction of leading English lawyers to new social and economic
needs and problems, and, in the East, to new systems of religion, philosophy, and law.   This indirect consequence broadened
the intellectual horizon of English lawyers, and so fitted them,
when they were called upon to act as Lord Chancellors, judges,
or counsel, to adapt the rules of English law to the new Imperial
position which Great Britain was winning in this century.

At this point I propose to say something, first of the beginnings of some of those leading principles of colonial constitutional law which made their appearance in this century ;
and, secondly, of some of the larger legal effects of these expansions of England upon English law as a whole.   The general
effect of these developments was to broaden and liberalize many

---

[1] Above 102-104, 105-106.

of the principles and rules of English law ; but they were broadened and liberalized by the evolutionary process of using old precedents and adapting them, wherever it was possible, to new needs. We have seen that the modern rules as to nationality and allegiance, which were laid down in *Calvin's Case*,[1] were justified by precedents drawn from that early mediæval period when the English kings were also continental rulers.[2] Similarly, analogies drawn from the relations of England with Scotland, Ireland, and the Palatinates, were often used to elucidate and to develop the new principles and rules which were being created as the result of the Western and Eastern expansions of Great Britain.[3]

(1) *Some principles of colonial constitutional law.*

Under this head I shall deal with the following topics : (i) The right of the Crown to territory conquered or settled by British subjects ; (ii) The distinction between settled and conquered colonies ; (iii) The systems of law in force in the colonies ; (iv) The prerogative rights of the Crown in the colonies ; (v) The position of the colonial governors ; (vi) The powers and the privileges of a colonial Legislature ; (vii) The colonial courts.

(i) *The right of the Crown to territory conquered or settled by British subjects.*

As early as 1647 it was argued before a Parliamentary committee that territory conquered by Englishmen became the King's territory, because Englishmen, wherever they were, owed allegiance to the King, and could not therefore acquire for themselves from the King's enemies ; and that territory acquired, not by conquest, but by settlement, vested in the King until he granted it away.[4] This argument seems to have been accepted in 1647. The analogy of chattels taken from an enemy makes it probable that this principle was then recognized, at any rate, as to territory acquired by conquest. We have seen that, according to Hale, the property of chattels taken from an enemy vested in the King, unless they had actually been taken in battle.[5] However that may be, it is clear that the Crown's proprietary right to territory acquired either by conquest or treaty of cession was recognized in the eighteenth century. In 1717 the law officers of the Crown said that

---

[1] (1609) 7 Co. Rep. 1.   [2] Vol. ix 76, 77-78, 81, 83, 84-86.
[3] Above 118-119, 122 ; below 234.
[4] Berriedale Keith, The First British Empire 10-11.
[5] Vol. vii 483 and n. 3.

a subject of the Crown could not make foreign acquisitions by conquest, but for the benefit of the Crown, and that the length of possession will be no bar to the Crown.[1]

In the case of *Campbell v. Hall* in 1774 Lord Mansfield pointed out that such territory was subject to the Crown's sovereignty :

A country conquered by the British arms becomes a dominion of the king in right of his Crown, and therefore necessarily subject to the legislative power of the Parliament of Great Britain.[2]

In the same case he laid it down that the Crown's sovereignty also extends to territory acquired by settlement, for " no colony can be settled without authority from the Crown." [3]   That this is the law to-day is recognized by the British Settlements Act 1887, which gives the Crown power to make laws and establish courts for British possessions acquired by British subjects otherwise than by cession or conquest, where no civilized government exists.[4]   The Crown also has proprietary rights over territory acquired by settlement till he has made a grant of those rights.[5] But though he has rights of sovereignty over all subjects, he has no proprietary rights over territory acquired by a subject from a foreign sovereign otherwise than by conquest or treaty of cession, or otherwise than by settlement.[6]

The general principle is and always has been undoubted. The only occasion upon which it might seem, at first sight, that any doubt was cast upon it, was in the course of the eighteenth century controversies as to the rights of the East India Company in their territorial acquisitions.   But the doubt then arose, not as to the general principle, but as to the manner in which, in the circumstances, it was politic to apply that principle to the facts.[7]   We have seen that in 1773 the House of Commons had quite clearly stated the principle that territorial acquisitions made by force of arms or as the result of a treaty belong to the state.[8]   The East India Company did not deny this principle ; but it contended that what it had acquired was proprietary rights and the privileges of the diwani over territory which was still subject to the native princes ; and this view seems to have been taken by the law officers of the Crown in 1757.[9]   We have

---

[1] Chalmers, Opinions of Eminent Lawyers i 41 ; for a similar statement in a petition of the African Company see Calendar of Treasury Papers 1714-1719 56.

[2] 20 S.T. at pp. 322-323.

[3] " All colonies have been established by grants from the Crown.   I do not mean it as material to this question, but that it should be understood no colony can be settled without authority from the Crown," ibid at p. 287.

[4] 50, 51 Victoria c. 54 Preamble and §§ 2 and 6.

[5] Berriedale Keith, The First British Empire 10-11.

[6] Berriedale Keith, A Constitutional History of India 20 ; below 232 n. 3.

[7] Above 162.   [8] Parlt. Hist. xvii 856, 870 ; above 163.

[9] Camb. Hist. of the Empire iv 593.

seen that the government did not decide definitely between these two opposing views ; but that it established a partnership with the East India Company in the exercise of its political powers,[1] in which it gradually came to be a more and more predominant partner.[2]   At the same time the growing decadence of the native princes, from whom in theory the East India Company held its powers, and the establishment of a stable and centralized government in the company's own territories, made it increasingly clear that the company had in fact acquired a large territory. It followed that it became increasingly clear that the general principle, which gave the Crown the right to territory acquired by its subjects, applied to the territorial acquisitions of the company, and that therefore the company exercised its political power over these territories as trustees for or as agents of the Crown.   That the British government was the real ruler of the company's territorial possessions was demonstrated in 1801 by Sir William Scott in the case of *The Indian Chief*,[3] and this fact was the foundation on which his decision was based ; and the Crown's sovereignty was clearly recognized in 1813.[4]   We have seen that, as the Crown's sovereignty gradually came to be recognized, it came, equally gradually, to be recognized that the native inhabitants of the territories ruled by the company were British subjects.[5]

(ii) *The distinction between settled and conquered colonies.*

In the course of the eighteenth century, the distinction between chartered proprietary and royal colonies [6] tended to become a less important distinction than that between settled and conquered colonies.   It was inevitable that the distinction between colonies, based upon the mode in which they had been founded, should tend to become less important, as they grew older, and as their institutions of government became more uniform ; and that the distinction between colonies, based

---

[1] Above 162.   [2] Above 204-205, 211-212.

[3] " Though the sovereignty of the Mogul is occasionally brought forward for purposes of policy, it hardly exists otherwise than as a phantom.   It is not applied in any way for the actual regulation of our establishments.   This country exercises the power of declaring war and peace, which is among the strongest marks of actual sovereignty ; and if the high, or as I might almost say, empyrean sovereignty of the Mogul is sometimes brought down from the clouds, as it were, for purposes of policy, it by no means interferes with that actual authority, which this country, and the East India Company, a creation of this country, exercises there with full effect," 3 C. Rob. at p. 31 ; he went on to point out that, in a treaty with America in 1794, and in the Act of 37 George III c. 117, the Company's possessions are described as British Territories, ibid at p. 32.

[4] " Nothing in this Act contained shall extend or be constructed to extend to prejudice or affect the undoubted sovereignty of the Crown of the United Kingdom of Great Britain and Ireland in and over the said territorial acquisitions," 53 George III c. 155 § 95.

[5] Above 183-184.   [6] Above 44.

upon the constitutional relations of a colony to the Crown and
Parliament, and upon the constitutional position of the colonists,
should tend to become more important. Moreover, this distinction between settled and conquered colonies became the
more important, not only because it affected the constitutional
position of the colony and the colonists, but also because it is,
as we shall see later,[1] closely related to the question of systems
of law in force in the colonies.

The roots of the distinction between settled and conquered
colonies can be traced back to the constitutional controversies
of the early years of the seventeenth century. James I held
the view that the colonies ought to be dependent solely on, and
controlled solely by, his prerogative ; and that therefore Parliament ought not to interfere in any way in their government.[2]
In 1621, when a bill for a freer liberty of fishing on the coasts of
Newfoundland, Virginia, and New England was before the House
of Commons, the King's secretary said that it was " not fit to
make any laws here for those countries which [are] not as yet
annexed to this Crown." [3]   But Brooke said that " we can
make laws here for Virginia, for if the King gives consent to the
bill passed here, and by the Lords, this will control the patent " ;
and he distinguished the case of a colony like Virginia, which
was annexed to the Crown (being holden, as another pointed
out, of the manor of East Greenwich), from foreign countries
like Gascony, which were outside the realm of England, and
therefore outside the jurisdiction of the English Parliament and
the English courts.[4]   This view commended itself to the House,
and the bill was committed.

It was clear therefore that colonies settled by Englishmen
were subject to the jurisdiction of Parliament. They were
not controlled exclusively by the prerogative ; and from this

[1] Below 240-248.
[2] Berriedale Keith, The First British Empire 9-10 ; Campbell v. Hall (1774)
20 S.T. at pp. 274-276 *per* Alleyne *arg.*
[3] Journals of the House of Commons i 591 ; Notestein, Commons Debates
1621 ii 321 ; v 98.
[4] Commons' Journals i 592 ; Notestein, op. cit. ii 321, iii 82, v 99 ; for the
distinction between countries dependent on the Crown and countries dependent on
the King personally see above 122 ; for the rule that the prerogative writs would
run to any part of the Crown's dominions see vol. i 226; R. v. Cowle (1759)
2 Burr. at pp. 855-856 ; Vaughan C.J., in Vaughan's Rep. at p. 402, thought that
a writ of error would also run to any part of the Crown's dominions, vol. i 226 n. 7 ;
but on this matter there were conflicting opinions, Com. Dig. *Pleader* 3 B. 3 ; the
question was discussed *in ex parte* Lees (1860) E.B. and E. 828, and in one case
a writ of error was issued to St. Helena, see *in re* Anderson (1861) 30 L.J.Q.B. at
p. 13, *per* Crompton J. ; but, in spite of these doubts, appeals from the colonies
were always brought to the Privy Council, vol. i 516-518 ; above 101 ; perhaps
this was due to the inadequacy of the writ of error, vol. i 213-215, 222-223, and the
superiority of the procedure by way of a rehearing which was the method used by
the Privy Council, and the court of Chancery; it was held in Fryer v. Bernard
(1724) 2 P. Wms. 262 that equity appeals lay only to the Privy Council.

premise it was easy to infer that the colonists had all the constitutional rights of Englishmen. We have seen that it had
been laid down as early as 1454 that the King, without Parliament, could not deprive his subjects of the benefit of the common
law.[1]   On the other hand, it was admitted that over conquered
colonies the King's prerogative was more extensive ; and that,
unless and until the King had given to their inhabitants the constitutional rights of Englishmen, he could govern them as he
pleased.   In 1554 it was said that, before the statute of 1536,[2]
which united Wales with England and gave to Welshmen all
the laws, rights, and privileges of Englishmen, the Prince or
King could legislate for Wales.[3]   That these conclusions had
been reached by the common lawyers at the beginning of the
seventeenth century is clear from Coke's statement in *Calvin's
Case*,[4] which runs as follows :

There is a diversity between a conquest of a kingdom of a Christian
King, and the conquest of a kingdom of an infidel ; for if a King
come to a Christian kingdom by conquest, seeing that he hath *vitae
et necis potestatem*, he may at his pleasure alter and change the
laws of that kingdom : but until he doth make an alteration of those
laws the ancient laws of that kingdom remain.   But if a Christian
King should conquer a kingdom of an infidel, and bring them under
his subjection, then *ipso facto* the laws of the infidel are abrogated for
that they be not only against Christianity, but against the law of God
and nature, contained in the decalogue ; and in that case, until certain
laws be established amongst them, the King by himself, and such
Judges as he shall appoint, shall judge them and their causes according
to natural equity, in such sort as Kings in ancient time did with their
kingdoms, before any certain municipal laws were given, as before
hath been said.   But if a King hath a kingdom by title of descent,
then seeing by the laws of that kingdom he doth inherit the kingdom,
he cannot change those laws of himself, without consent of Parliament.
Also if a King hath a Christian kingdom by conquest, as King Henry
the Second had Ireland, after King John had given unto them, being
under his obedience and subjection, the laws of England for the government of that country, no succeeding King could alter the same without
Parliament.

We shall see that Coke's distinction between Christian and
infidel countries was repudiated in the later cases [5]—in the
eighteenth century the English in India were applying to their
Indian subjects the laws of an infidel kingdom.[6]   It is not
therefore surprising to find that Lord Mansfield in 1774 told
counsel not to quote the distinction "for the honour of Lord

---

[1] Y.B. 32 Hy. VI Hil. pl. 13, cited vol. ix 78 n. 4.
[2] 27 Henry VIII c. 26 ; vol. i 123.
[3] Buckley v. Rice Thomas Plowden at p. 126.
[4] (1609) 7 Co, Rep. at f. 17b.
[5] Below 235, n. 1, 246.
[6] Above 220-221 ; below 240-241.

Coke." [1] But, omitting that distinction, which, we shall see, has survived in another form,[2] it is clear that the principles more fully expounded in the later cases, are implicit in Coke's statement. The King has full legislative power over conquered colonies. But if he ordains that such a colony shall be governed constitutionally, in accordance with the laws of England,[3] he can no longer alter those laws without the consent of Parliament —a rule which is based on the principle that the colonists have, as the result of such an ordinance, all the constitutional rights of Englishmen. Nothing is said in *Calvin's Case* about the extent of the King's prerogative, and the rights of the colonists, in settled colonies ; but it is reasonably clear from Coke's statement as to the rights of the King's subjects in a kingdom which the King has by title of descent,[4] and from what was said in the House of Commons in 1621,[5] that they were considered to have the constitutional rights of Englishmen.

In 1694, in the case of *Blankard v. Galdy*,[6] Holt, C.J., repeated in substance the rule laid down by Coke as to conquered colonies. But he modified Coke's statement as to the laws of infidel countries—" their laws do not entirely cease, but only such as are against the law of God " ;[7] and he stated explicitly the rule that in a settled colony " all laws in force in England are in force there." [8] This involved the proposition that the colonists in a settled colony had all the rights of Englishmen ; for, as was said in argument in the case of *Dutton v. Howell* in 1693,[9] when Englishmen with the King's consent settled in an uninhabited country,

the common law must be supposed their rule, as t'was their birthright, and 'tis the best, and so to be presumed their choice. . . . When they went thither, they no more abandoned the English laws, then they did their natural allegiance.[10]

[1] Campbell v. Hall(1774) 20 S.T. at p. 294 ; at p. 323 he speaks of " the absurd exception as to pagans in Calvin's case " ; but as late as 1766 the secretary of state wrote to the attorney-general to know if there was any foundation for the assertion made by a Mr. Brecknoch, that the King cannot by law receive an infidel ambassador, and that such an ambassador was not protected by the Act of Anne ; Brecknoch was obviously a fanatic—he talked of appealing to Magna Carta and the twenty-five barons, Calendar of Home Office Papers 1766-1769 62-63.

[2] Below 238-239, 246-247.

[3] Some parts of English law might be introduced without affecting the King's power or the status of the colony, see Stephen, Nuncomar and Impey ii 28 ; but this is not inconsistent, as Stephen thinks, with Coke's statement, for he speaks of the laws of England *"for the government of that country";* and it was a law of that description which was before the court in Campbell v. Hall, below 236-237.

[4] Above 234.   [5] Above 233.   [6] 1 Salk. 411 ; vol. vi 264.

[7] 1 Salk. 412 ; he agreed with Coke that " where the laws are rejected or silent, the conquered country shall be governed according to the rule of natural equity," ibid.

[8] Ibid 411.   [9] Shower, P.C. 24.

[10] At p. 32 ; as to the impossibility of depriving Englishmen of the benefit of the common law see above 234 n. 1 ; as to the impossibility of abandoning allegiance see vol. ix 78-79, 84 86.

In 1722 the Privy Council, in a judgment upon an appeal from the colonies, distinguished on these lines between conquered and settled colonies.[1] In 1704 Northey, the attorney-general, pointed out that the legislative power of the Crown over conquered colonies carried with it the power to levy a tax by virtue of the prerogative ; [2] and in 1724 Yorke and Wearg, the attorney and solicitor-general, said that the question whether the Crown could levy a tax in Jamaica depended on the question whether Jamaica " is now to be considered merely as a colony of English subjects, or as a conquered country." If it was to be considered a colony of English subjects it could not be taxed,

but by the Parliament of Great Britain, or by and with the consent of some representative body of the people of the island, properly assembled, by the authority of the Crown ; but, if it can now be considered as conquered country, in that case, we conceive they may be taxed by the authority of the Crown.[3]

Blackstone restates these principles. In the case of settled colonies " all the English laws then in being, which are the birthright of every subject, are immediately there in force." [4] But in conquered or ceded countries, that have already laws of their own, the King may indeed alter and change those laws ; [5] but till he does actually change them, the ancient laws of the country remain, unless such as are against the law of God, as in the case of an infidel country.[6]

These principles were finally stated in the case of *Campbell v. Hall* in 1774.[7] The facts of that case were as follows : The

[1] Anon. 2 P. Wms. 75 ; in 1704 the law officers advised that, in the part of St. Christopher conquered from the French, the Crown could by its prerogative levy the 4½ per cent. duties, MSS. of the House of Lords (Hist. MSS. Com.) vi no. 2057 p. 106.

[2] Chalmers, Opinions of Eminent Lawyers i 140-141.

[3] Ibid i 222-223 ; the opinion is calendared in Treasury Papers, 1720-1728 273.

[4] Comm. i 107.

[5] In 1767 Charles Yorke, the attorney-general, said that whether or not the Test Act was to be applied in the newly conquered French colonies was a question for the King's " political judgment," Calendar of Home Office Papers 1766-1769 152 ; later cases have settled that the Crown may signify a change in the law, not only by order in council, but also by any other means by which his pleasure is clearly intimated, Jephson v. Riera (1835) 3 Knapp. 130 ; Cameron v. Kyte (1835) 3 Knapp. 332.

[6] Comm. i 107 ; it is noteworthy that Blackstone put " our American plantations " into the class of conquered colonies, " being obtained in the last century either by right of conquest and driving out the natives (with what natural justice I shall not at present enquire) or by treaties. And therefore the common law of England, as such, has no allowance or authority there " ; probably he had in his mind the statement of Holt C.J. in Smith v. Brown (1707) 2 Salk. 666 that, as Virginia was a conquered country, the law is what the King pleases, so that slavery might well be a valid institution there, below 247 ; but it is curious that Blackstone, having said this, should not have gone on to say that in those colonies the main principles of the common law had been generally introduced, see Berriedale Keith, op. cit. 182-186.

[7] 20 S.T. 239.

island of Grenada was conquered in 1762, and finally ceded to
Great Britain in 1763. On October 7, 1763, the King issued a
proclamation, stating that he had given power to the governor,
so soon as the circumstances of the colony would admit, to call
a legislative assembly. On March 26, 1764, the King stated in
another proclamation that he had ordered a survey and a division
of the ceded islands, and invited persons to purchase land on
conditions therein specified. On April 9, 1764, Robert Melville
was by letters patent appointed governor, and he was given
authority to summon legislative assemblies as soon as the
circumstances of the island permitted. On July 20, 1764, a
duty of 4½ per cent. on goods exported from the island was
imposed by letters patent. The defendant Hall was the collector
of this duty. He levied the duty on the plaintiff Campbell.
Campbell, having paid this duty to Hall, brought an action of
indebitatus assumpsit against him to recover it.[1]   The jury
found a special verdict; and on this verdict the question of
law as to whether the duty had been validly levied, was argued.
After hearing three arguments, Lord Mansfield, C.J., held that
it was not validly levied. He held that, though the King had
power to levy such a duty by his prerogative in a conquered
colony, he had, by the grant of representative institutions,
put Grenada into the position of a settled colony; with the
result that such a duty could only be imposed either by an
Act of the Assembly or by Act of Parliament. He said:[2]

We think, by the two proclamations and the commission to governor
Melville, the king had immediately and irrevocably granted to all who
did or should inhabit . . . in the island of Grenada . . . that the
subordinate legislation over the island should be exercised by the
assembly with the governor and council, in like manner as in other
provinces under the king. And therefore, though the right of the
king to have levied taxes on a conquered country, subject to him in
right of his crown, was good . . .; yet, by the inadvertency of the
king's servants in the order in which the several instruments passed
the office, (for the patent of the 20th of July 1764, for raising the impost
stated, should have been first) the order is inverted, and the last we
think contrary to and a violation of the first; and therefore void.

Lord Mansfield's decision for the most part summed up the
pre-existing law, and settled definitely the principles of the

[1] Hall had retained the money, by the consent of the attorney-general, in order
that the question of law might be determined in this form of action, 20 S.T. at p. 320.
[2] 20 S.T. at p. 329; for an attack on this judgment by Mr. Baron Maseres in
the Canadian Freeholder see ibid 333-354; one ground of criticism was the theory
that the grant of representative institutions did not preclude the King from levying
the tax till the assembly met; and as it did not meet till 1765 the tax was validly
imposed; this is the only tenable ground of objection brought forward; for Baron
Maseres see vol. xii 398.

modern law.[1] But it also did a little more than this, in that it emphasized the rule that the King's power over conquered colonies " was subordinate to his own authority as a part of the supreme Legislature in Parliament," so that he could make no law " excepting from the laws of trade or authority of Parliament or privileges exclusive of his other subjects." [2] It was perhaps natural that the authority of Parliament should have been thus emphasized in 1774, for the Americans were denying that authority, and asserting that they owed allegiance only to the King.[3] On the other hand, the decision still left the law obscure on two points. In the first place it was said that the King could make no law for a conquered colony which was " contrary to fundamental principles." [4] This led to some uncertainty as to whether any given law made by the King for a conquered colony, or by the legislative assembly in a colony, was or was not valid; for it is clear that this limitation on the King's legislative power in the case of a conquered colony, was equally applicable to the legislative assembly of a settled colony. Both could only legislate subject to the authority of Parliament, and to conformity to the fundamental principles of English law.[5] It was not till 1865 [6] that it was enacted that a colonial law was not to be deemed void on the ground of repugnancy to the law of England, unless it was repugnant to an Act of Parliament or to an order or regulation having the force of an Act of Parliament, which extended to the colony. In the second place, though Coke's views as to the binding force of the laws in an infidel country were rejected, it was left uncertain how far the principle laid down by Holt, C.J.,[7] and Blackstone,[8] that laws repugnant to the laws of God cease to have validity, is operative. Probably it would be true to say that the principle still operates to render void laws which are wholly contrary to the moral ideas of a Christian people. It is on this ground that such practices as suttee or infanticide, which are sanctioned by Hindu law, have been made illegal in India.[9] And although Coke's dicta in *Calvin's Case* were rightly repudiated

---

[1] For an application of these principles see *in re* Lord Bishop of Natal (1864-1865) 3 Moo. P.C. N.S. at p. 148, where the Privy Council said : " We apprehend it to be clear, upon principle, that after the establishment of an independent Legislature in the Settlements of the Cape of Good Hope and Natal, there was no power in the Crown by virtue of its Prerogative . . . to establish a Metropolitan See or Province, or to create an Ecclesiastical Corporation whose *status*, rights, and authority the Colony could be required to recognise. After a Colony or settlement has received legislative institutions, the Crown . . . stands in the same relation to that Colony or Settlement as it does to the United Kingdom."

[2] 20 S.T. at p. 323.

[3] Above 121-123 ; Blackstone also states explicitly, Comm. i 108, that the colonies are subject to the control of Parliament.

[4] 20 S.T. at p. 323.   [5] Below 246, 250.

[6] 28, 29 Victoria c. 63 §§ 2 and 3 (Colonial Laws Validity Act).

[7] Above 235.   [8] Above 236.   [9] Above 174 n. 9.

in the eighteenth century, we have seen that the process by which
civilized bodies of law were constructed in British India by the
regulations of the governor-general and council, was not wholly
unlike the process outlined by Coke [1] and Holt.[2] " The King
by himself and such judges as he shall appoint " did judge
to a large extent " according to natural equity, in such sort as
Kings in ancient time did with their kingdoms, before any certain
municipal laws were given." [3]

It was pointed out in the case of *Freeman v. Fairlie*,[4] that
generally the distinction between conquered and settled colonies
corresponded to a distinction between countries in which there
were, and countries in which there were not, settled institutions
at the time of their acquisition.   In the former case there was
generally an established *lex loci* : in the latter case there was
not, so that English law necessarily applied.[5] But it was also
pointed out that the distinction between conquered and settled
colonies, whether or not it was based on the presence or absence
of an established *lex loci*, did not apply to India :

The acquired territory was not newly discovered or inhabited, but
well peopled, and by a civilized race, governed by long established
laws, to which they were much attached, and which it would have
been highly inconvenient and dangerous immediately to change.   On
the other hand those laws were so interwoven with, and dependent on,
their religious institutions, as Mahomedans and Pagans, that a great
part of them cannot possibly be applied to the government of a Christian
people. . . . Some new course was to be taken in this peculiar case ;
and the course actually taken seems to have been, to treat the case,
in a great measure, like that of a new discovered country for the
government of the Company's servants, and other British or Christian
settlers using the laws of the mother country, as far as they were
capable of being applied for that purpose, and leaving the Mahomedan
and Gentoo inhabitants to their own laws and customs.[6]

But this question of the laws applied in India more properly belongs to another problem, which is closely connected with this

---

[1] Above 234.   [2] Above 235 n. 7.
[3] 7 Co. Rep. at f. 17b.   [4] (1828) 1 Moo. Ind. App. 305.
[5] " The reason why the rules are laid in books of authority, with reference to
the distinction between new-discovered countries, on the one hand, and ceded or
conquered countries on the other, may be found, I conceive, in the fact that this
distinction had always, or almost always, practically corresponded with that between
the absence or existence of a *lex loci*, by which the British settlers might, without
inconvenience, for a time, be governed," ibid at pp. 324-325.
[6] Ibid at p. 325 ; Lord Lyndhurst L.C. at p. 343 said : " I think it clear that
those persons who there established themselves, carried with them the English law.
It does not appear . . . that the English law was established there, in the first
instance, by any proclamation or charter : but it is probable that the English carried
with them, and acted upon the law of England from the necessity of their situation ;
because the two systems of law, which at that time existed there—the Mahomedan
and Hindoo laws—were so blended with the particular religions of the two descriptions of persons, as to render it almost impossible for that law to have been
adopted by the English settlers."

distinction between settled and conquered colonies—the question of the systems of law in force in the colonies : to the consideration of this problem we must now turn.

(iii) *The systems of law in force in the colonies.*

The question of what system of law prevails in any particular colony depends generally upon the question whether it is a settled or a conquered or ceded colony. We shall see that, in the case of a settled colony, the settlers are governed by the laws of England so far as they are applicable to their new situation ; [1] and that in the case of a conquered or ceded colony the original systems of law remain until they are changed by the conqueror or the sovereign to whom the cession has been made, unless those laws are wholly repugnant to the political or moral ideas of the new sovereign.[2] But, just as India falls outside this distinction, and cannot be classed as either a settled or a conquered colony, so the systems of law prevailing there were determined by the peculiar circumstances of India, and the peculiar manner in which the British empire in India was established. As we have seen, India was treated as a settled colony in so far as the British and European settlers were concerned, so that they were governed so far as possible by English law ; and as a conquered or ceded colony in so far as the native inhabitants were concerned, so that they were governed by their native systems of law.[3]

The reason for this peculiarity, which was found in other Eastern countries where Europeans had settled,[4] was explained by Sir William Scott in a famous passage in his judgment in the case of *The Indian Chief :* [5]

Wherever even a mere factory is founded in the eastern parts of the world, European persons trading under the shelter and protection of those establishments, are conceived to take their national character from that association under which they live and carry on their commerce. It is a rule of the law of nations, applying peculiarly to those countries, and is different from what prevails ordinarily in Europe and the western parts of the world, in which men take their present national character from the general character of the country in which they are resident ; and this distinction arises from the nature and habit of the countries : In the western parts of the world alien merchants mix in the society of the natives ; access and intermixture are permitted ; and they become incorporated to almost the full extent. But in the East, from the oldest times, an immiscible character has been kept up ; foreigners are not admitted into the general body and mass of the society of the nation ; they continue strangers and sojourners as all their fathers were—*Doris amara suam non intermiscuit*

---

[1] Below 241-242.   [2] Below 245, 246-247.   [3] Above 220.
[4] The Indian Chief (1801) 3 C. Rob. at pp. 29-31—citing the cases of Turkey, China, and Cochin.
[5] Ibid at pp. 28-29.

undam; not acquiring any national character under the general sovereignty of the country, and not trading under any recognised authority of their own original country, they have been held to derive their present character from that of the association or factory, under whose protection they live and carry on their trade.

It followed that, though European settlers might be governed by English law, the natives of India were not so governed. To them "European laws and usages are as little suited as the laws of the Mahomedans and Hindoos are suited to Europeans." [1] On this ground it was held in 1863 that the English law as to *felo de se*, and the rule that the chattels of a suicide were forfeited to the Crown, did not apply to a Hindu. [2] As we have seen, it is only gradually and partially that a common law for the whole of British India, applicable both to Europeans and natives, has been established. [3]

In the British possessions, other than those possessions or settlements in India and other Eastern countries, the question what system of law prevails, depends, as I have said, [4] on the question whether a colony is a settled colony, or a conquered or ceded colony. I must therefore deal separately with these two classes of colonies; and then consider the question of the effect of legislation enacted by the colonial legislative authorities, and the systems of law in force in the colonies.

Settled Colonies.

From the seventeenth century onwards, there is clear authority for the proposition that the settlers in an uninhabited country, or in a country inhabited only by barbarous tribes, carry with them their own legal system. We have seen that this principle was probably accepted in the early part of the seventeenth century. [5] It was stated by Holt, C.J., in 1694, [6] by West, the counsel to the Board of Trade, in 1720, [7] by the Privy Council in 1722, [8] and by Blackstone. [9] It has frequently been repeated and acted upon in modern cases. [10] But it is subject to two qualifications:

[1] Advocate-General of Bengal v. Ranee Surnomoye Dossee (1863) 2 Moo. P.C. N.S. at p. 60.

[2] Ibid 22.   [3] Above 222-257.   [4] Above 240.

[5] Above 233-234.   [6] Blankard v. Galdy 2 Salk. 411.

[7] " The common law of England is the common law of the plantations. . . . Let an Englishman go where he will, he carries as much of law and liberty with him, as the nature of things will bear," Chalmers, Opinions of Eminent Lawyers i 194-195 ; and see a similar opinion by Pratt and Yorke, ibid 195.

[8] " If there be a new and uninhabited country found out by English subjects, as the law is the birth-right of every subject, so, wherever they go, they carry their laws with them, and therefore such new found country is to be governed by the laws of England," 2 P. Wms. 75.

[9] Comm. i 107.

[10] The Falkland Islands Co. v. the Queen (1863) 2 Moo. P.C. N.S. 266, 273 ; cp. Kielley v. Carson (1841-1842) 4 Moo. P.C. at pp. 84-85.

(*a*) The colonists take with them the English law in force at the time when the colony was settled ; but only such parts of it as are adapted to their new situation. Blackstone says : [1]

Such colonists carry with them only so much of English law, as is applicable to their own situation and the condition of an infant colony ; such, for instance, as the general rules of inheritance, and of protection from personal injuries. The artificial refinements and distinctions incident to the property of a great and commercial people, the laws of police and revenue (such especially as are enforced by penalties) the mode of maintenance for the established clergy, the jurisdiction of spiritual courts,[2] and a multitude of other provisions, are neither necessary nor convenient for them, and therefore are not in force. What shall be admitted and what rejected, at what times, and under what restrictions, must, in case of dispute, be decided in the first instance by their own provincial judicature, subject to the revision and control of the king in council.

This qualification, though vague, has, as Lord Blackburn said, sound sense in it ; [3] it has been approved in modern cases ; [4] and we shall see that it applies also to those conquered or ceded colonies into which English law has been introduced—[5] it has been held, for instance, that the rule against perpetuities is applicable both in settled [6] and in conquered or ceded colonies.[7] But, as we shall now see, its chief applications, in the case of settled colonies, have been in relation to statute law.

(*b*) The law which the settlers take with them is the English law, both enacted and unenacted, at the date when they made

[1] Comm. i 107.

[2] In 1725 Yorke and Wearg gave it as their opinion that in New England there was no regular establishment of a national or provincial church so as to warrant the holding of convocations or synods of the clergy ; but that the royal supremacy in ecclesiastical affairs, being a part of the prerogative, was operative in the colonies, so that synods could not be held without royal licence, Chalmers, op. cit. i 12 ; in 1764 Sir James Marriott pointed out that the commission given by George I to the Bishop of London, to act in all respects by his commissaries as diocesan of the colonies, was personal, and was never obeyed, nor held to be sufficient, Forsyth, Leading Cases, 44-45 ; in *in re* the Lord Bishop of Natal (1864) 3 Moo. P.C. N.S. at p. 153, it was held that the ecclesiastical law of England is not part of the law of England carried with them by the settlers in a new colony ; see Forsyth, op. cit. 57 ; Lord Ellenborough C.J.'s statement to the contrary in R. v. Brampton (1808) 10 East. at p. 288 is clearly not law, see Forsyth, op. cit. 18 ; in Long v. the Bishop of Cape Town (1863) 1 Moo. P.C. N.S. at p. 437 Sir Hugh Cairns *arg.* pointed out that the effect of 16 Charles I c. 2, and 13 Charles II c. 12, was to deprive the Crown of the power to create new ecclesiastical jurisdictions by letters patent ; the result is that such courts can only be created by the legislative authority in a colony, see *in re* the Lord Bishop of Natal at pp. 151-152 ; Berriedale Keith, The First British Empire 222.

[3] The Lauderdale Peerage (1885) 10 A.C. at p. 745.

[4] See Cooper v. Stuart (1889) 14 A.C. at pp. 291-292, where the Privy Council, after approving Blackstone's statement, said, " if the learned author had written at a later date he would probably have added that, as the population, wealth, and commerce of the colony increase, many rules and principles of English law, which were unsuitable to its infancy, will gradually be attracted to it ; and that the power of remodelling its laws belongs also to the colonial legislature."

[5] Below 247-248.   [6] Cooper v. Stuart (1889) 14 A.C. at p 293.

[7] Yeap Cheah Neo v. Ong Cheng Neo (1875) L.R. 6 P.C. 381.

their settlement.[1] Statutes passed subsequently do not bind
them, unless there are express words in the statute making it
binding upon the colonies or a particular colony ; [2] or unless
there are words in an Act which introduces English law, stating
that the law as at a particular date is to be introduced ; [3] or,
probably, unless by usage a subsequent statute has been adopted.[4]
That this principle was well established in the eighteenth
century is shown by one of the points which arose on the trial
of Nundcoomar.[5]   The legality of his trial and sentence depended
upon the date of the introduction of the English statutes as to
forgery into Calcutta.   Were they introduced " in 1661 by the
letters patent of Charles II ? or in 1726 by the letters patent by
which the mayor's court was established ? or by the letters
patent of 1753, which were issued when the patent of 1726 was
surrendered ? or in 1774 by the charter of the supreme court ? " [6]
If English law had been introduced in 1661 or 1726, Nundcoomar
ought not to have been indicted under a statute of 1752.   But if
English law could be regarded as reintroduced in 1753 and 1774,
he could properly be indicted under this statute.   It was held
by Impey and the other judges of the supreme court that English law had been re-introduced in 1753 and 1774,[7] and with this
view Stephen agrees.[8]

But this principle was subject to the same qualification as
that which applied to the unenacted law—the statute must be
adapted to the new situation in which the colonists found themselves.   Thus in *R. v. Vaughan* [9] Lord Mansfield, C.J., held that
statutes of Richard II's and Edward VI's reigns as to the sale of
offices, did not extend to Jamaica :

[1] West said in 1720, " all statutes, in affirmance of the common law, passed in
England antecedent to the settlement of any colony, are in force in that colony, unless
there is some private Act to the contrary ; though no statutes made since those
settlements are then in force, unless the colonies are particularly mentioned,"
Chalmers, Opinions ii 202 ; cp. the opinion of Yorke and Wearg given in 1724,
ibid i 220-221 ; The Lauderdale Peerage (1885) 10 A.C. at p. 745 *per* Lord
Blackburn.

[2] Last note.

[3] For instances see Tarring, Law Relating to the Colonies (2nd ed.) 6-7.

[4] In 1724 Yorke and Wearg included in the laws binding on the colony " such
parts of the common or statute law of England as have by long usage and general
acquiescence been received and acted under, though without any particular law of
the country for that purpose," Chalmers, Opinions i 220 ; in 1729 Yorke said that
statutes made since the settlement would not bind " unless they have been introduced and declared to be laws by some act of assembly of the province or have been
received there by long uninterrupted usage or practice, which may import a tacit
consent . . . that they should have the force of a law there " ; the efficacy of usage
to introduce an Act is recognized by 25 George II c. 6 § 10 ; Professor Berriedale
Keith, however, First British Empire 184, would limit the efficacy of usage merely
to supplying evidence that the statute law existing at the date of the settlement is
adapted to local conditions.

[5] Above 193.   [6] Stephen, Nuncomar and Impey ii 29.

[7] Ibid 19.   [8] Ibid 29-30.

[9] (1769) 4 Burr. 2494.

If Jamaica was considered as a conquest, they could retain their old laws, till the conqueror had thought fit to alter them. If it is considered as a colony (which it ought to be, the old inhabitants having left the island) then these statutes are positive regulations of police, not adapted to the circumstances of a new colony ; and therefore no part of that law of England which every colony, from necessity, is supposed to carry with them at their first plantation.[1]

On the same principle it has been held that George II's statute of charitable uses was not applicable to New South Wales ; [2] that the provisions of the statute of Frauds as to devises did not apply to the Barbadoes ; [3] and that the statute as to charitable uses did not apply to St. Nevis.[4] As Lord Campbell said in the case of *Whicker v. Hume*,[5] it is often a very difficult question to decide what statutes comply with the test of adaptability to the situation, and what do not. He had no difficulty in deciding that the provisions of George II's statute of charitable uses showed that it could not possibly apply to New South Wales. But there are early instances in which different courts took opposite views as to the adaptability of any given statute or line of statutes. In 1676 and 1720 it was said that the jurisdiction of the court of Admiralty in Jamaica was restricted by two statutes of Richard II and Henry IV's reigns. But other authorities in 1676 took the opposite view.[6] In Maryland there was a ten years' controversy (1722-1732) as to whether the whole of English law enacted and unenacted applied to the colony ; [7] in many of the colonies there was much controversy as to whether the Habeas Corpus Act of 1679, and all the provisions of the Bill of Rights and the Act of Settlement were applicable.[8] Many of these cases were evoked and coloured by the political and constitutional controversies of the period.[9] They were not merely dry questions of law. The purely legal test of the applicability of a statute, hinted at by Lord Mansfield in the case of *R. v. Vaughan*, is now recognized as the right test.[10] Is the law a law " of local policy adapted solely to the country in which it was made ? " ; or is it a general regulation which it is possible and reasonable to apply to any country governed by English law ? [11]

---

[1] (1769) 4 Burr. at p. 2500.
[2] Whicker v. Hume (1858) 7 H.L.C. 124 at p. 161.
[3] Anon. (1722) 2 P. Wms. 75.
[4] Campbell v. Hall (1774) 20 S.T. at p. 289.
[5] 7 H.L.C. at p. 161.
[6] Berriedale Keith, op. cit. 186.
[7] Ibid 185.   [8] Ibid 184-185.
[9] Above 62.   [10] Above n. 1.
[11] " Whether the statute of Mortmain be in force in the island of Grenada, will, as it seems to me, depend on this consideration—whether it be a law of local policy adapted solely to the country in which it was made, or a general regulation of property equally applicable to any country in which it is by the rules of English law that property is governed," Attorney-General v. Stewart (1817) 2 Mer. at pp. 160-161.

Conquered colonies.

The law in force in a conquered or ceded colony remains till it is altered by the conqueror or by the sovereign to whom the cession is made.[1] It is this principle which accounts for the large variety of laws which prevail in different parts of the British Empire. Thus the old French law prevails in Canada ; Roman Dutch law prevails in Ceylon, the Union of South Africa, Southern Rhodesia, and British Guiana ; and Spanish law in Trinidad. But the Crown can alter the law at its pleasure, subject, however, to the rule that, if it grants to its new subjects the constitutional privileges of Englishmen, it cannot withdraw the grant, and reassume its power to legislate without the consent of Parliament.[2] But it should be noted that this difference between the systems of law prevailing in different colonies, makes it untrue to say that a grant of these constitutional privileges puts a conquered or a ceded colony into exactly the same position as a settled colony. In a settled colony the law in force is the common law of England : in a conquered or ceded colony it is the law in force when those constitutional privileges were granted. The difference would be apparent if a conquered or ceded colony surrendered its constitution to the Crown.[3] It would in that case revert to the position which it held before the constitution was granted. But if a settled colony surrendered its constitution it would still be governed by the common law, and, for this reason, the powers of the Crown would be very much more limited.

As in the case of settled colonies, these general principles are subject to qualifications.

(a) It was pointed out by Lord Stowell in the case of *Ruding v. Smith* [4] that

no small portion of the ancient law is unavoidably superseded. . . . The allegiance of the subjects, and all the law that relates to it —the administration of the law in the sovereign and appellate jurisdictions—and all the laws connected with the exercise of the sovereign authority—must undergo alterations adapted to the change.

He pointed out that the case before the court, which concerned the validity of a marriage in the Cape of Good Hope at the time when the Dutch ceded it to England, furnished an instance of the application of this principle. According to the law then in force, dispensations from the requirement that banns must be

---

[1] Calvin's Case (1609) 7 Co. Rep. at p. 17b ; Blankard v. Galdy (1694) 4 Mod. at p. 225 ; Campbell v. Hall (1774) 20 S.T. at p. 323.

[2] Above 237.

[3] For such surrenders see Anson, The Crown (4th ed.) ii Pt. 65 ; how far these surrenders are valid without the consent of Parliament is perhaps doubtful, see 39, 40 Victoria c. 47 Preamble.

[4] (1821) 2 Hagg. Con. at p. 382.

published must be got from the states of Holland. That requirement, as Lord Stowell said, " could not be continued during the existence of the war, and the extinction or suspension of the sovereignty of Holland." [1]

(b) Lord Mansfield said in the case of *Campbell v. Hall*, that the Crown could make no laws contrary to fundamental principles.[2] By that he probably meant that he could make no laws which shocked the moral sense of Englishmen of the day ; and this clearly carried with it the consequence that he could not permit any such laws to remain. Thus, in the case of *Fabrigas v. Mostyn*,[3] the defendant Mostyn, the governor of Minorca, was condemned to pay heavy damages because, in his treatment of the plaintiff, he had infringed this principle. He had first imprisoned him, and then confined him on board ship with a view to banishing him to Carthagena. De Grey, C.J., said : [4]

I do believe Mr. Mostyn was led into this under the old practice of the island of Minorca, by which it was usual to banish : I suppose the old Minorquins thought fit to advise him to this measure. But the governor knew he could no more imprison him for a twelve-month, than he could inflict the torture ; yet the torture as well as banishment, was the old law of Minorca, which fell of course when Minorca came into our possession. Every English governor knew he could not inflict the torture ; the constitution of the country put an end to this idea.

This principle is necessarily somewhat vague.[5] What will be regarded as contrary to the moral sense of the nation varies from age to age. We have seen that Coke thought that all the laws of an infidel state were abrogated because they were contrary to the truths of Christianity and to the laws of God and of nature ; [6] but that this sweeping statement was condemned by Lord Mansfield.[7] We, at the present day, would say that laws which legalized the institution of slavery would *ipso facto* cease,

---

[1] (1821) 2 Hagg. Con. at p. 383 ; in that case Lord Stowell said that the old laws remain and govern the relations of the old inhabitants, but not " the separate transactions of the British conquerors" ; but, as Tarring says, Law Relating to the Colonies (2nd ed.) 20, this is stated too broadly, and is inconsistent with the law as laid down by Lord Mansfield C.J. in Campbell v. Hall (1774) 20 S.T. at p. 323 ; below 248.

[2] 20 S.T. at p. 323.   [3] (1773) 20 S.T. 81.

[4] 20 S.T. at p. 181 ; cp. The Case of Thomas Picton, governor of Trinidad, who was tried for causing torture to be inflicted (1807) 30 S.T. 225 ; at pp. 742-743 Lord Ellenborough C.J. said, " The laws that are repugnant to the rights of the conquering state cease of course " : on which Nolan *arg.* replied : " That position carried to its proper extent is all for which it is necessary that I should contend. By the laws respecting religion in the very country from which this island has been conquered, an heretic is to be burned ; and by the laws of the same country, any person converting a Roman Catholic to the Protestant religion might be burned likewise. If therefore the chaplain of one of his Majesty's regiments had converted this poor girl to the Protestant faith, General Picton would have had a right, nay it would have been his duty, to have burned this reverend person upon the principle for which his counsel must contend to-day."

[5] See ibid at pp. 944-945.   [6] Above 234.   [7] Above 234-235.

if a country, where this institution was legal, was conquered by, or ceded to, us. But that was certainly not the view taken by lawyers in the seventeenth and eighteenth centuries. It was not till 1771 that it was finally decided that English law will not recognize the institution of slavery, so that a slave brought to England at once becomes a free man.[1] As Blackstone said, many of the American colonies were conquered colonies; [2] and therefore though many of the rules of English law were introduced, the Crown could, without any objection, permit the institution of slavery to remain. In the case of *Smith v. Brown* [3] Holt, C.J., after holding that *indebitatus assumpsit* would not lie for the sale of a negro " in parochia Beatae Mariae in Warda de Cheape," because as soon as a slave comes to England he becomes free, said : " You should have averred in the declaration that the sale was in Virginia, and, by the laws of that country, negroes are saleable ; for the laws of England do not extend to Virginia, being a conquered country their law is what the King pleases." [4]

(c) If the Crown made English law the law of a conquered or ceded colony, the question which of the rules of law enacted and unenacted were applicable, was answered in the same way as it was answered in settled colonies.[5] Only those rules of law were introduced which were applicable to the situation of the colony. Thus, we have seen that the Crown contended, with some reason, that the clause of the Act of Settlement relative to the tenure of the judicial office, was not applicable to the situation of the American colonies ; [6] and in modern times there are many instances of the application of this principle. In 1817 it was held that George II's statute of charitable uses did not apply to Grenada ; [7] and in 1806 that Lord Hardwicke's Marriage Act did not apply to India.[8] In 1836 it was held that the rule of English law that aliens could not acquire or hold real property had not been introduced into India ; [9] and in 1876 it

---

[1] Sommersett's Case (1771-1772) 20 S.T. 1 ; vol. iii 507-508 ; vol. x 658 ; E. Fiddes, Lord Mansfield and the Sommersett Case L.Q.R. l 499-511 gives a good account of the conflicting opinions of the judges and other lawyers before 1771, and of Lord Mansfield's fluctuations of opinion ; it may be true that Lord Mansfield's decision was, not that the slave was free, but that the master could not forcibly remove him from England, op. cit. 499, The King v. Inhabitants of Thames Ditton (1785) 4 Dougl. at p. 301 ; but his decision involved the consequence which Blackstone had previously drawn, Comm. i 424, that " the law will protect him in the enjoyment of his person and his property," so that in effect he was free, as Blackstone said, ibid 425 ; the fact that he might be obliged to serve his master was no proof that he was not free ; for that was an obligation to which an apprentice was subject ; therefore though Lord Mansfield put this limited construction on his own decision, the popular view of its consequences is substantially correct.

[2] Comm. i 107-108 ; above 236 n. 6.   [3] (1707) 2 Salk. 666.
[4] Ibid.   [5] Above 242-244.   [6] Above 62.
[7] Attorney-General v. Stewart, 2 Mer. 143.
[8] Latour v. Teesdale 8 Taunt. 830.
[9] Mayor of Lyons v. The East India Co. 1 Moo. P.C. 175 at pp. 276-283.

was held that the English law as to maintenance and champerty had not been introduced in their entirety into India.[1] On the other hand, it was held in 1835 that the English law as to dower had been introduced into Gibraltar ; [2] and in 1875 that the rule against perpetuities had been introduced into Penang.[3]

(d) Though the Crown has power to legislate for a conquered or ceded colony, the Crown's legislative power is subordinate to the legislative power of Parliament. We have seen that Lord Mansfield emphasized the fact that it was " a power subordinate to his own authority as a part of the Supreme Legislature in Parliament." [4] Therefore statutes passed by Parliament, which expressly or by implication refer to all the dominions of the Crown, override laws made by the sole authority of the Crown. Thus, as Lord Mansfield pointed out in the case of *Campbell v. Hall*, the laws of trade applied to all colonies settled or conquered.[5]

Colonial legislation and systems of law in the colonies.

The law in force in a colony bound all the inhabitants thereof and residents therein, as fully as English law bound all residents in England.

The law and legislation of every dominion equally affects all persons and property within the limits thereof, and is the true rule for the decision of all questions which arise there : whoever purchases, sues, or lives there, puts himself under the laws of the place, and in the situation of its inhabitants. An Englishman in Minorca or the Isle of Man, or the plantations, has no distinct right from the natives while he continues there.[6]

But this assumes that the legislation is valid legislation ; and since the colonial legislatures were not sovereign legislative bodies, it might well be that a given piece of legislation was for one reason or another not valid. We must therefore consider the different limitations upon the powers of colonial legislatures which, at different periods, might invalidate their enactments.

Two different views have been taken of the position of the colonial legislative Assemblies, and, consequently, of their legislative powers. The first view, which was the dominant view during the eighteenth century, emphasizes the limitations upon their powers. The second view, which is a modification of the earlier view adopted in the nineteenth century, emphasizes their position as autonomous bodies, with a right to act independently within the limits of their powers.

[1] Ram Coomar Coondoo v. Chunder Canto Mookerjee 2 A.C. 186 at pp. 209-210.
[2] Jephson v. Riera 3 Knapp. 130.
[3] Yeap Cheah Neo v. Ong Cheng Neo L.R. 6 P.C. 381.
[4] Campbell v. Hall (1774) 20 S.T. at p. 323 ; above 238.
[5] 20 S.T. at p. 323.   [6] Campbell v. Hall (1774) 20 S.T. at p. 323.

(a) We have seen that Lord Mansfield regarded the Assemblies in the royal colonies as very subordinate legislative bodies, having in effect only a power to make by-laws for their own territory ; and that he equated the powers of these Assemblies in the chartered colonies with the powers of other corporations, such as the corporation of London.[1] We have seen that three consequences followed from this view of the legislative powers of the colonial Assemblies. First, they could pass no Act which contravened a statute of the British Parliament which related to the colony ; secondly, their Acts had no extra-colonial effect ; and, thirdly, there were doubts as to the validity of colonial Acts which were repugnant to the principles of the common law.[2] The subordinate character of the legislation of a colonial Assembly was emphasized in 1707 by Harcourt, the attorney-general, when he said of an Act of recognition, passed by the Maryland Assembly on the accession of Anne, that

although the said Act be an instance of the fidelity of the inhabitants of this province, yet in regard the said province is entirely dependent on the crown of England, and no such law has been thought proper to pass in England. . . . I humbly conceive such a law was improper to be passed by the assembly in this province.[3]

In 1717, Rawlin, the attorney-general of the Barbadoes, emphasized the limitations on the legislative powers of the colonial Assemblies ; [4] and both in the eighteenth and in the nineteenth centuries, the lawyers have denied to colonial Assemblies those peculiar powers and privileges which the House of Commons possess by virtue of the *Lex Parliamenti*.[5]

This view of the extent of the legislative powers of colonial Assemblies left its mark on modern law. No Act of a colonial Assembly could contravene an Act of the British Parliament which applied to that colony,[6] and no Act of a colonial Assembly could have an extra-colonial effect.[7] But this view has been considerably modified by the adoption of another view, which emphasizes the autonomous character and the independent powers of these Assemblies.

[1] Above 55. [2] Above 56.
[3] Chalmers, Opinions i 343.
[4] " It cannot be granted them, that they are capable to enact, at their will and pleasure, what they think fit. For they cannot, by a law, alter the common law of England, and the settled course of proceedings thereon, they cannot change the common securities of the kingdom. They cannot enact anything against her majesty's prerogative. They cannot take away, by any act they can establish, any authority vested in the governor by her majesty's commission, with many other things, too many here to be enumerated, and they cannot pretend to have an equal power with the parliament of England," ibid ii 31.
[5] Above 57-58 ; below 261-264.
[6] See above 248 ; below 251.
[7] Above 56 ; cp. Low v. Routledge (1865) 1 Ch. App. at p. 47 ; Macleod v. Attorney-General for New South Wales [1891] A.C. 455.

(b) In 1713 Robert Raymond, the attorney-general, said that an Act of the Assembly has the same force " as an Act of Parliament here "—a dictum which seems to emphasize the independent legislative powers of the Assemblies.[1] Pownall, in his book on *The Administration of the Colonies*, contested Mansfield's view that the colonies were on the same subordinate footing " as our great corporations in London." He said that they were on a very different footing, because, like the counties palatine, they possessed the *jura regalia ;* and he pointed out that some of them were actually given the same powers as the counties palatine.[2] This view naturally gathered weight when, after the American war of independence, the control of the British government over colonial legislation was relaxed.[3] In fact there are one or two instances in which, on grounds of expediency, Acts which were repugnant to the principles of English law, and even Acts which had an extra-colonial effect, were allowed to become law.[4] It is not surprising therefore that, in the course of the nineteenth century, a new emphasis should be laid upon the independence of the legislative powers of colonial Assemblies. In the first place, we have seen that in 1865 the Colonial Laws Validity Act got rid of the idea that a colonial law could be declared to be invalid on the ground of repugnancy to the laws of England.[5] In the second place, in 1841-1842 the Privy Council said that a colonial Assembly had an authority " subordinate indeed to that of Parliament, but supreme within the limits of the colony, for the government of its inhabitants " ; [6] and in 1878 it laid it down that an Indian Legislature, when acting within the limits of its powers, " is not in any sense an agent or delegate of the Imperial Parliament, but has, and was intended to have, plenary powers of legislation, as large, and of the same nature, as those of Parliament itself." [7] In 1883 it was said that provincial Legislatures " are in no sense delegates of or acting under any mandate from the Imperial Parliament," so that, like the Imperial Parliament, they could delegate authority to bodies of their own creation ; [8] and this principle was again affirmed in 1885.[9] It follows, therefore, that

if what has been done is legislation, within the general scope of the affirmative words which give the power, and if it violates no express condition or restriction by which the power is limited (in which category

[1] Chalmers, Opinions ii 2.
[2] Administration of the Colonies (4th ed.) 56.　　　　[3] Above 42-43.
[4] Berriedale Keith, The First British Empire 253-254.
[5] 28, 29 Victoria c. 63 ; above 238.
[6] Kielley v. Carson, 4 Moo. P.C. at p. 85.
[7] The Queen v. Burah (1878) 3 A.C. at p. 904.
[8] Hodge v. The Queen (1883) 9 A.C. at p. 132.
[9] Powell v. Apollo Candle Co. (1885) 10 A.C. at p. 290.

would, of course, be included any Act of the Imperial Parliament at variance with it), it is not for any Court of Justice to inquire further, or to enlarge constructively those conditions and restrictions.[1]

Therefore the only two restrictions which remained were the two perfectly definite restrictions—first, that colonial legislation is not valid if it conflicts with an Act of Parliament applicable to the colony, so that the powers of a colonial Legislature were limited by the provisions of the Act of Parliament by which its powers were conferred upon it ; and, secondly, that colonial legislation could not have an extra-colonial effect.

There are many diverse systems of law in force in the different countries which compose the British Empire, because these different countries have been acquired in different ways and have had different histories.[2] Moreover, differences in their local needs and circumstances have necessarily caused differences in their enacted laws. But though there are many diversities in the laws prevailing in different parts of the British Empire, there is also a certain unity, which has been produced by the fact that these laws have been administered by lawyers and statesmen whose legal and political ideas have been formed by the principles and rules of English law. There has therefore been an infiltration of these principles and rules into all the different parts of the British Empire. The Anglo-Indian codes are the most striking instances of this infiltration ; [3] and the causes which led to their enactment have operated in other places. In other places besides India, there has been a tendency to fill up gaps by borrowing from English law.[4] It was in fact inevitable that the expansion of English law should accompany the expansion of Great Britain ; for England was the dominant partner in the United Kingdom, and played the largest part in the creation of the British Empire.

Having considered the differences between settled and conquered colonies, and the systems of law prevailing in those colonies, we must now consider some of the rules of law which define or regulate the powers and duties of the persons or bodies through which their government is carried on.

(iv) *The prerogative rights of the Crown in the colonies.*

The colonies were annexed to the Crown of Great Britain, and the colonists were British subjects. Hence the Crown had the same prerogatives in the colonies as it had in Great Britain.

---

[1] The Queen v. Burah (1878) 3 A.C. at p. 905.
[2] Above 245.   [3] Above 225, 226.
[4] See above 17-18 for the influence of English upon Scots law ; for the reception of English law in the colonies governed by Roman-Dutch law, see Lee, Roman Dutch Law (2nd ed.) 22-23.

Thus we hear of the King's rights to royal mines,[1] to escheats,[2] to *bona vacantia*,[3] to the chattels of felons,[4] to treasure trove,[5] and to royal fish ;[6] and the grant of some of these rights to the founders of some of these colonies sometimes raised questions as to the interpretation of these grants, and as to the power of the Crown to make them,[7] which kept alive these recondite topics of Crown law. Similarly, in relation to the colonies, other parts of the prerogative, which were becoming obsolete in England, make their appearance. Thus the prerogative of the Crown in relation to the coinage,[8] and its prerogative to prevent its subjects from leaving the realm,[9] or to recall its subjects from foreign countries,[10] were occasionally considered.

Other prerogatives of greater importance, which were wholly obsolete in England, were of considerable importance in relation to the colonies. Thus, in a newly settled country, the Crown's power to create institutions of government was obviously a prerogative of great practical importance. In 1752 Ryder and Murray, the attorney and solicitor-general, said that, on the surrender of their powers by the trustees for Georgia, the Crown could by proclamation establish a government for Georgia, by authorizing the existing magistrates and officials to continue to exercise their offices.[11] In 1842 the Privy Council said that in a settled colony the Crown had the right of establishing courts of justice and a national assembly.[12] It was said in 1723 [13] and 1747 [14] that the Crown could make and alter rules as to the constituencies which returned members to the colonial assemblies ; and, in 1753,[15] that any such changes ought to be made by the Crown, and not by an Act of the Assembly, in order to preserve the King's prerogative.

It was in relation to the colonies that the application and extent of other parts of the prerogative were discussed. We

---

[1] Chalmers, Opinions i 120 (1723).   [2] Ibid 121-122.
[3] Ibid 131 (1736-1737).   [4] Ibid 153-154 (1727).
[5] Ibid 131 (1736-1737).   [6] Ibid 131-132 (1713).
[7] Ibid 153-155 (1727).   [8] Ibid ii 322 (1705) ; vol. x 407-411.
[9] Chalmers, Opinions ii 254-255 (1788) ; vol. x 390-392.
[10] Chalmers, Opinions ii 261 (1731) ; vol. x 390-391.
[11] Chalmers, Opinions i 187-188.
[12] Kielley v. Carson 4 Moo. P.C. at p. 85 ; in 1753 Ryder and Murray advised the Crown not to assent to a Jamaica Act appointing commissioners of *nisi prius* and extending the jurisdiction of justices of the peace, because it was " so great an encroachment upon the royal prerogative, to which the creating and establishing courts of justice belongs," Chalmers, op. cit. ii 106-107 ; for limitations upon the Crown's powers in the establishment of courts of justice see below 265-267.
[13] Chalmers, op. cit. i 268-269.   [14] Ibid 271-276.
[15] " Though it may not be advisable for the Crown to impeach rights heretofore granted and enjoyed, we think, as the province grows more peopled and cultivated, the king may erect towns and counties, and give them the privilege of chusing representatives ; and to preserve the king's prerogative, we think it ought rather to be done, in this way. than by act of assembly," ibid 294.

have seen that the recognition of the independence of the United States raised an important question as to the nationality of the inhabitants of the ceded territory.[1]   The question of the extent of the treaty making power of the Crown was raised and discussed in connection with the colonies.   An opinion upon a colonial case clearly lays down the rule that the Crown, by an exercise of its treaty making power, cannot affect the legal rights of its subjects, because the law cannot be changed by the prerogative ; [2] and other opinions discuss the question as to the extent of the Crown's power to cede territory by treaty,[3] and to proceed criminally against those who break treaties.[4]   Similarly we shall now see that the implications of, and the limitations upon, the principle of ministerial responsibility, were very fully worked out by a series of cases which settled the legal position of the colonial governor and his subordinate officials.

(v) *The position of the colonial governor.*

In general the position of the colonial governor is the same as that of any other servant of the Crown.[5]   This will be apparent if we look, first, at his liability to criminal, and, secondly, at his liability to civil, proceedings, for acts done by him as governor.

Criminal liability.

" Great Britain," says Kenny,[6] " like France and the United States, prefers, in nearly all cases, to adhere to the principle that crimes are local matters, to be dealt with where they are committed."   But from time to time exceptions to this rule have been made by statute.   We have seen that a statute of 1541-1542 made provision for the trial at any place in the kingdom of persons accused of having committed treason or murder anywhere in the King's dominions ; [7] and that a statute of 1543-1544 made provision for the trial in England of treasons committed abroad.[8]   In 1802 Governor Wall was tried and found guilty of murder by a commission of oyer and terminer issued under the statute of 1541-1542.[9]   We have seen that there was considerable doubt as to whether this statute, so far as it applied to treason, had not been repealed by a statute of 1554.[10]   But,

---

[1] Vol. ix 87.

[2] Chalmers, op. cit. ii 339-342 (1728) ; ibid 243-244 (1764).

[3] Ibid 405, 448-449.   [4] Ibid 328-329 (1677).

[5] For the position of the servants of the Crown see vol. x 650-658.

[6] Outlines of Criminal Law (ed. 1904) 413.

[7] 33 Henry VIII c. 23 ; vol. iv 523-524 ; it should have been stated at p. 524 that the statute applied to crimes committed within the realm " or other the King's dominions."

[8] 35 Henry VIII c. 2.   [9] 28 S.T. 51.   [10] Vol. iv 524 and n. 6.

so far as it applied to murder, it was admitted that it remained
in force,[1] till it was repealed in 1828.[2] We have seen that in
1700 an Act was passed to provide for the trial and punishment
in England of governors who were proved to be guilty of oppressing their subjects, or of breaking the laws of England or their
own colonies.[3] Since it was then supposed that a governor was
not amenable either criminally or civilly to the jurisdiction of
the courts of his colony,[4] this was a very necessary enactment ;
and since it was not possible, except under statutory powers,
to try a person in any place other than the place where he was
accused of committing a crime,[5] it is not at all surprising to read
in the preamble to that statute, that governors did not consider
themselves " punishable here nor accountable for such crimes and
offences to any person within their respective governments."
This Act was supplemented in 1802 by an extension of its provisions to persons in the civil and military service of the Crown
out of Great Britain, who were accused of committing any crime,
misdemeanour or offence in the execution of their service.[6]
But this Act, unlike the Act of 1700, applied to misdemeanours
only and not to felonies.[7] The Act also made provision for the
issue of writs of mandamus, directed to the courts or the governor
of the country where the offence was committed, in order to
obtain evidence.[8] We have seen that other statutes made provision for the trial of criminal offences committed by the officials
of the East India Company.[9] It was under the Act of 1802 that
General Picton was tried in 1804.[10]

Civil liability.

In respect of civil liability the difficulties as to venue, which
were felt in respect of criminal liability, did not as a rule arise,
because the actions by which this liability was enforced were
generally transitory actions.[11] From a very early date it was
recognized that a governor could be made liable in a common
law action for torts committed by him. This principle was

---

[1] Forsyth, Cases in Constitutional Law 168.
[2] 9 George IV c. 31 § 1.
[3] 11 William III c. 12 ; vol. vi 402.
[4] Below 257.　　　　　　　　　　　　　　　[5] Above 253.
[6] 42 George III c. 85.
[7] R. v. Shawe (1816) 5 M. and S. 403 ; the Act provided for the prosecution
of the offences mentioned therein by way of information as well as by way of indictment ; this conclusively showed that it applied to misdemeanours only and not
to felonies, see at p. 405 *per* Lord Ellenborough C.J. ; for the procedure by way
of information see vol. ix 241-244.
[8] 42 George III c. 85 §§ 2 and 4.
[9] Above 165-166, 167-168, 208-209.　　　[10] 30 S.T. 225.
[11] For the difference between local and transitory actions, and manner in which
the common law courts assumed jurisdiction over acts done abroad where the action
was transitory see vol. v 118, 140-142.

assumed in 1693 in the case of *Dutton v. Howell,* in which an action
for false imprisonment was brought against the governor of the
Barbadoes ; [1] and there were several other cases in which this
liability was asserted in the eighteenth century.[2]

The whole question was considered by De Grey, C.J., and by
Lord Mansfield, C.J., in 1773 in the case of *Fabrigas v. Mostyn.*[3]
This was an action for assault and false imprisonment brought
by the plaintiff, an inhabitant of Minorca, against the defendant,
the governor of Minorca. The defendant justified his action
by the allegation that the plantiff was endeavouring to create
a mutiny amongst the inhabitants ; but he failed to prove his
allegation. The jury found against the defendant, and awarded
the plaintiff £3,000 damages. The court of Common Pleas having refused a motion for a new trial, the case was taken by
a writ of error to the court of King's Bench, where the judgment
was affirmed. Both the Chief Justices emphasized the rule that
a governor is simply one of the King's servants invested with
powers limited by his commission.[4] It followed that he was
liable to be sued if he inflicted damage upon one of his subjects
by breaking the law, or by exceeding the powers with which he
was invested. On this matter the following eloquent passage
from Lord Mansfield's judgment sums up the result of the authorities, and lays down the law for the future : [5]

To make questions upon matters of settled law, when there have
been a number of actions determined, which it never entered into a
man's head to dispute—to lay down in an English court of justice such
monstrous propositions as that a governor, acting by virtue of letters
patent under the great seal, can do what he pleases ; that he is accountable only to God and his own conscience—and to maintain here that
every governor in every place can act absolutely ; that he may spoil,
plunder, affect their bodies and their liberty, and is accountable to
nobody—is a doctrine not to be maintained. . . . The king in council
has no jurisdiction of this matter.[6] . . . They cannot give damages,

---

[1] Shower P.C. 24.

[2] Several of these cases are cited by Lord Mansfield C.J. in his judgment on
Fabrigas v. Mostyn (1773) 20 S.T. at pp. 234, 237-238.

[3] 20 S.T. 81.

[4] " In the island the governor is the king's servant : his commission is from the
king, and he is to execute the power he is invested with under that commission, which
is to execute the laws of Minorca under such regulations as the king shall make in
council," 20 S.T. at p. 178 *per* De Grey C.J. " The first point I shall begin with is
the sacredness of the person of the governor. Why, if that was true, and if the law
was so, he must plead it. This is an action of false imprisonment : *prima facie,*
the Court has jurisdiction. If he was guilty of the fact he must show a special matter
that he did this by a proper authority. What is his proper authority ? The king's
commission to make him a governor. Why then, he must certainly plead it," ibid
at pp. 228-229 per Lord Mansfield C.J.

[5] Ibid at pp. 231-232.

[6] This followed from Lord Mansfield's view that a governor could not be sued
in the courts of his colony, below 257 ; but now that this view is overruled, below 258)
it is obvious that the Privy Council has jurisdiction to hear such a case on appeal
from the colonial courts.

they cannot give reparation, they cannot banish, they cannot hold plea in any way. Wherever complaints have been before the king in council, it has been with a view to remove the governor. . . . But . . . suppose his government is at an end, and that he is in England, they have no jurisdiction to make reparation to the party injured. . . . How can the arguments be supported, that, in an empire as extended as this, every governor in every colony and every province belonging to the Crown of Great Britain, shall be absolutely despotic, and can no more be called in question than the king of France ? and this after there have been multitudes of actions in all our memories against governors, and nobody has been ingenious enough to whisper them, that they were not amenable.

This case and the later cases in effect lay down the following rules : First, if the act of a governor is authorized by the terms of his commission, and it is an act which the Crown had power to authorize, it can give rise to no cause of action. As Lord Mansfield said in the case of *Fabrigas v. Mostyn*,[1]

if the justification had been proved, perhaps the Court would have been of an opinion that it was a sufficient answer, and he might have moved in arrest of judgment afterwards, and taken the opinion of the Court.

Secondly, if the act, though authorized by the governor's commission, is one which the Crown had no power to authorise, the governor will be liable like any other servant of the Crown in such a case.[2] The Privy Council pointed out in the case of *Hill v. Bigge* that we must not forget, " in reference to the position of the supreme power in the state, that by our law and constitution it is not in the Sovereign, but in Parliament." [3] The authority of the Crown is no justification for a breach of the law.[4] Thirdly, if the governor does an act wholly outside the scope of his commission which injures another, he is liable. This principle, which was laid down in the case of *Fabrigas v. Mostyn*,[5] has been emphasized in many subsequent cases. Perhaps the clearest statement is contained in the judgment of Parke, B., in the case of *Cameron v. Kyte*.[6] He said :

If a Governor had by virtue of his appointment, the whole sovereignty of the Colony delegated to him as a Viceroy, and represented the King in the government of that Colony, there would be good reason to contend that an act of sovereignty done by him would be valid and obligatory upon the subject living within his government, provided the act would be valid if done by the Sovereign himself. . . . But if the Governor be an officer, merely with a limited authority from the Crown, his assumption of an act of sovereign power, out of the limits of the authority so given to him, would be purely void, and the Courts

---

[1] (1773) 20 S.T. at p. 230.   [2] Vol. x 651-652.
[3] (1841) 3 Moo. P.C. at p. 477 ; cp. Cameron v. Kyte (1835) 3 Knapp. at p. 343, cited below n. 6.
[4] Vol. x 651-652.   [5] (1773) 20 S.T. 81.
[6] (1835) 3 Knapp. at pp. 343-344.

of the Colony over which he presided could not give it any legal effect. We think that the office of Governor is of the latter description, for no authority or dictum has been cited before us to show that a Governor can be considered as having delegation of the whole Royal power, in any colony, as between him and the subject, when it is not expressly given by his commission.

The case of *Fabrigas v. Mostyn* [1] shows that the law as to the legal position of the governor was then, for the most part, settled in its final form. But there was one point in which the law there laid down has been overruled by the later cases. That case, and all the cases there cited, appear to have been cases in which the governor was sued in the courts of this country. That this was so was sometimes due to the fact that, in the place where it was alleged that the tort had been committed, there was no settled court of justice. Lord Mansfield gave two instances of cases of that sort in his judgment in the case of *Fabrigas v. Mostyn*.[2] But it was also due to the belief that a governor held, in relation to the courts of his colony, a position similar to that held by the King in relation to the English courts. It was thought that he was in the nature of a viceroy, and that therefore he could not be made either criminally or civilly liable in those courts.[3]

The reasons why this belief was held are clearly stated in Lord Mansfield's judgment. He said : [4]

A governor is in the nature of a viceroy, and, of necessity, part of the privileges of the king are communicated to him during the time of his government. No criminal prosecution lies against him, and no civil action will lie against him ; because, what would the consequence be ? Why, if a civil action lies against him, and a judgment obtained for damages, he might be taken up and put in prison on a Capias ; and therefore, locally, during the time of his government, the courts in the island cannot hold plea against him.

There was also another reason for this rule, which was deduced from old precedents relating to the Isle of Man and Wales and from the analogy of the proprietary colonies in America. That reason is as follows : The charge against the governor in this case was a charge of abusing the authority given to him by the King's letters patent. But even

if everything within a dominion is triable by the courts within that dominion, yet the consequence of the king's letters patent, which gives the power must be tried here ; for nothing concerning the seigniory

---

[1] (1773) 20 S.T. 81.
[2] An action for acts done on the coast of Nova Scotia, and another for acts done on the coast of Labrador, 20 S.T. at pp. 237-238.
[3] Thus it was said in the argument for the plaintiff in the case of Dutton v. Howell (1693) Shower P.C. at p. 27, that " no man will pretend that an action can lie against the chief Governor or Lieutenant of Ireland or Scotland ; and by the same reason it ought not in this case."
[4] 20 S.T. at p. 229.

can be tried in the place where it is. In the proprietary governments in America, they cannot try any question concerning the seigniory, in their own courts ; and therefore, though questions concerning lands in the isle of Man are triable in the courts of the Isle of Man, yet wherever there is a question concerning the seigniory, it must be tried in some courts in England. It was so held by the chief justice and many of the judges in the reign of Queen Elizabeth, upon a question arising concerning the seigniory of the Isle of Man. Or whenever there is a question between two provinces in America, it must be tried in England by analogy to what was done with respect to the seigniories in Wales being tried in English counties ; so that emphatically the governor must be tried in England, to see whether he has exercised legally and properly that authority given him by the king's letters patent, or whether he has abused that authority, contrary to the law of England, which governs the letters patent by which he is appointed.[1]

That these views were then generally held is shown by the legislation as to India. We have seen that the extent to which the governor-general of Bengal was to be amenable to the jurisdiction of the supreme court, which was set up by the statute of 1773, was very carefully regulated.[2] It is therefore obvious that the Legislature must have supposed that, unless this jurisdiction had been specially given, the governor-general was not amenable to any court in India. But these views were logically inconsistent with the principle that a governor is in the same position as an ordinary servant of the Crown, possessed only of such powers as the Crown may choose to give him.[3] Moreover, as was pointed out by the Privy Council in the case of *Hill v. Bigge*, Lord Mansfield's assertion that, if a governor could be sued in his own courts, he could be arrested on a *Ca. Sa.*, was not correct ; for peers and members of Parliament were protected by their privileges from arrest, but not from the liability to be sued.[4] For these reasons Lord Mansfield's dictum on this question was overruled, and it was held that a governor is liable to be sued either in the courts of his own colony or in the English courts.[5]

But the Irish courts continued to refuse to follow this reasoning, and continued to apply to the Lord-Lieutenant the rule laid down by Lord Mansfield. The earliest of these cases was decided long before the case of *Hill v. Bigge*. But the later cases were decided after that case ; and they follow the earliest Irish case, and not the later decisions of the Privy Council.

The earliest Irish case, in which this question arose, was the case of *Tandy v. The Earl of Westmoreland* in 1792.[6] It was held in that case that the Lord-Lieutenant of Ireland was not liable to be sued in the Irish courts for any act done by him in his public

[1] 20 S.T. at p. 230.
[2] Above 167.
[3] Above 253.
[4] (1841) 3 Moo. P.C. at p. 480.
[5] Hill v. Bigge (1841) 3 Moo. P.C. 465.
[6] 27 S.T. 1246.

capacity. The authority of this case was questioned by the Privy Council in the case of *Hill v. Bigge.*[1] But in two subsequent cases in the Irish courts the case of *Tandy v. The Earl of Westmoreland* was followed ; and the case of *Hill v. Bigge* was distinguished on the ground that the cause of action in that case was a private debt, and not an act done by the governor in his public capacity.[2] But if once it is admitted that a governor is liable to be sued in the courts of his colony, the distinction between acts done by a governor in his private and in his public capacity becomes meaningless. No servant of the Crown can commit a tort in his public capacity. If he commits a tort with the authority of the Crown, he is personally liable in his private capacity ;[3] and *a fortiori* the same result follows if he commits a tort which has not been authorized.[4] It follows, therefore, that the courts must be competent to enquire whether the acts complained of are in fact torts, or whether they are lawful acts which have been duly authorized. Otherwise it is not possible to ascertain whether they are lawful acts done by the official in his public capacity, or wrongful acts, which because they are wrongful acts, he has necessarily committed in his private capacity. It is therefore the duty of the court to hear the case, in order to ascertain the legality of the acts done. For the liability of the governor turns upon the legality of the acts done, and not upon the capacity in which the governor assumed to do them.[5] That this is the law is clear from the cases of *Cameron v. Kyte*[6] and *Musgrave v. Pulido*,[7] in both of which a governor was sued successfully in the courts of his colony for acts done in his public capacity. It may

---

[1] (1841) 3 Moo. P.C. at p. 480.

[2] Luby v. Lord Wodehouse (1865) 17 Ir. C.L.R. 618 ; Sullivan v. Earl Spencer (1872) L.R. Ir. Rep. C.L. 173.

[3] Above 254-256. [4] Above 256.

[5] In the case of Musgrave v. Pulido (1879) 5 A.C. at pp. 107-108 the Privy Council said : " The defendant has sought to strengthen his claim of privilege by averring in his plea, that the acts complained of were done by him ' as Governor,' and as ' acts of state.' . . . It appears to their Lordships that if the Governor cannot claim exemption from being sued in the Courts of the colony in which he holds that office, as a personal privilege, simply from his being Governor, and is obliged to go further, his plea must then show by proper and sufficient averments that the acts complained of were acts of state policy within the limits of his commission, and were done by him as the servant of the Crown, so as to be, as they are sometimes shortly termed, acts of state. A plea, however, disclosing these facts would raise more than a question of personal exemption from being sued, and would afford an answer to the action, not only in the Courts of the colony, but in all Courts ; and therefore it would seem to be a consequence of the decision in *Hill v. Bigge* that the question of personal privilege cannot practically arise, being merged in the larger one, whether the facts pleaded show that the acts complained of were really such acts of state as are not cognizable by any municipal court."

[6] (1835) 3 Knapp, 332—an unauthorized reduction by the governor of Berbice of the commission payable to the vendue master.

[7] (1879) 5 A.C. 102—the detention by the governor of Jamaica of a ship in the port of Kingston.

therefore be doubted whether, if these Irish cases had been carried
to the House of Lords, they would have been upheld. However
that may be, it is true to say that the only cases in which the
rule laid down by Lord Mansfield has been followed is the case
of the Lord-Lieutenant of Ireland ; and, to a modified extent,
and, by virtue of express statutory provision, the cases of the
Viceroy of India, and the governors of Bengal, Madras, and
Bombay, and the members of their councils.[1]

(vi) *The powers and the privileges of a colonial Legislature.*

I have already described the constitutional position of the
colonial Assemblies, and said something of the powers and
privileges which they claimed and actually exercised.[2] We
have seen that both in their relations to the Crown, and in
the extent of their powers and their privileges, they claimed
to hold in their colonies the same position as that held by the
House of Commons in Great Britain.[3] No doubt, in some
respects, the Crown had similar prerogatives and they had
similar powers and privileges. Thus the Crown, through the
governor, could exercise its prerogative of proroguing or dissolving the Assemblies in the same way as it exercised this prerogative in respect of the Parliament of Great Britain ;[4] and
an Assembly was dissolved by the demise of the Crown so soon
as notice of the demise was received in the colony.[5] But in
other cases the Crown claimed a more extensive prerogative.
Thus its prerogative to create new constituencies, which was
obsolete in England, was regarded as still subsisting in the
colonies.[6] Similarly the Assemblies had a control over finance
which was very similar to that exercised by the House of Commons ;[7] and, in spite of the protests of the British government,
they succeeded in eliminating the control of the legislative
Councils, in much the same way as the House of Commons had
succeeded in eliminating the control of the House of Lords.[8]
On the other hand, we have seen that their legislative powers
were very much smaller than those of the House of Commons.[9]
We have seen that in the eighteenth century they were regarded
as very subordinate law-making bodies ;[10] and that it was not
till the nineteenth century that it was recognized that, as the
supreme Legislatures of their colonies, they held a more independent position.[11]

---

[1] Ilbert, the Government of India (3rd ed.) 154, 275-276.
[2] Above 55-59.   [3] Above 57.
[4] Above 55 ; Chalmers, Opinions i 232.
[5] Above 55; Berriedale Keith, The First British Empire 237 n. 3.
[6] Chalmers, op. cit. i 267-269, 271-272 ; above 252.
[7] Above 58.   [8] Above 54.   [9] Above 55-56.
[10] Ibid.   [11] Above 250-251.

In fact, all through the eighteenth century, the lawyers denied that the Assemblies could be equated with the House of Commons ; and therefore they denied that they had that peculiar set of powers and privileges which was summed up in the phrase *Lex et Consuetudo Parliamenti*. In most respects the Assemblies gradually attained, in the course of the nineteenth century, to that amount of equality with the House of Commons which they had claimed to possess all through the eighteenth century. Subject to the right of the Parliament of Great Britain to legislate for the colonies [1]—a right which all through the nineteenth century was becoming more and more shadowy—the Assemblies came to be recognized as the supreme legislative authorities within their own colonies. But the denial to the colonial Assemblies of the powers and privileges possessed by the House of Commons by virtue of the *Lex et Consuetudo Parliamenti* had a more permanent legal result. It drastically curtailed the privileges of the colonial Assemblies.

We have seen that the Assemblies claimed all the powers and privileges possessed by the House of Commons by virtue of the *Lex et Consuetudo Parliamenti*.[2] This claim was always denied by the law officers of the Crown and by the British government. We have seen that it was denied by Sir Charles Pratt when he was attorney-general ;[3] and in 1759 the law officers said that the privilege of committing for contempt, which belonged to the House of Commons, " ought never to be suffered in these inferior Assemblies in America who must not be compared either in power or privileges to the Commons of Great Britain." [4] The same view was expressed by the law officers in 1772, in their advice upon a case in which the Assembly of St. Christopher seems to have acted in a very arbitrary manner under colour of privilege.[5] In fact the substantial justification for the denial to these Assemblies of the privileges of the House of Commons,

[1] Above 248. [2] Above 57-58. [3] Above 54 n. 7.
[4] Acts of Privy Council (Col. Series) iv 384.
[5] The law Officers said that from the *ex parte* information given to them the House " seems to have corrupted its own constitution, by affecting a power which they have not, analogous, and coequal to that of the House of Commons in Great Britain" ; *inter alia* they had voted that no member of Council should vote for members of the Assembly, they had declared a seat in the Assembly to be vacated and ordered a new writ to be issued, they had punished absent members and strangers, and they had declared their own privileges and enforced them by punishment ; " these pretensions they have carried to such an excess as to imprison seven gentlemen of their own body, one of whom has lost his life by their violence, and when they sued out writs of habeas corpus returnable before the governor, and other such writs returnable before the court of King's Bench and Common Pleas, the prisoners were not only denied redress in both places, but the counsel who argued for them were imprisoned by the Assembly as for a contempt of their House, and when actions at law were brought for such imprisonment in the court of King's Bench and Common Pleas, the Assembly took upon itself to command the judges of that court to order a discontinuance of such actions with costs to be paid by the plaintiffs," ibid v 278.

was the unfair and often tyrannical manner in which the Assemblies tried to exercise them. Lyttelton, the governor of Jamaica, wrote in 1765 : [1]

The present discontents could not have been prevented, unless I would have sacrificed the most essential duties of my station both civil and judicial to pretensions as boundless as they appeared to me to be illegal, and have suffered the Assemblies, under a notion of Parliamentary powers inherent in them, to treat the king's instructions with contempt, and to exercise a tyranny as oppressive to individuals in obstructing the course of public justice and restraining the liberty of their persons by commitments for pretended breach of privileges, as the authority they have assumed is dangerous to the Crown.

But the reason why the law on this subject laid down in the eighteenth century was approved by nineteenth-century cases, was not the fact that it was based upon this substantial justification, but the fact that it was based on a sound legal reason. It seemed indeed at one time that, just as a fuller recognition was given by the nineteenth-century cases to the legislative powers of the colonial Assemblies,[2] so a closer approximation between their privileges and the privileges of the House of Commons would be made. In the case of *Beaumont v. Barrett* [3] it was laid down by the Privy Council that, since the legislative Assembly was no mere corporation with a power to make by-laws, but the supreme legislative Assembly of Jamaica, it had an inherent power of punishing contempts ; that the contempts which it could punish were not merely those which directly obstructed its proceedings, but those which had a tendency indirectly to produce such an obstruction ; and that this power was analogous to the power possessed by courts of record.[4] But this case was not followed. It was pointed out by the Privy Council in the case of *Kielley v. Carson* [5] that the only privilege given to a legislative Assembly by the common law, was a power to protect itself from all impediments to the due course of its proceedings, and to take what measures were necessary to secure the free exercise of its legislative functions ; and that this common law power did not give it the right to punish contempts which did not obstruct its proceedings. It did not therefore give it the right to punish a person who had used insulting language to a member of the Assembly ; for the possession of such a right was not necessary to enable it to perform its legislative functions. The fact that the House of Commons possessed this power to punish for contempt did not show that it was a power which necessarily belonged to a legislative Assembly ; for the House of Commons

[1] Acts of the Privy Council (Col. Series) vi 402.   [2] Above 250-251.
[3] (1836) 1 Moo. P.C. 59.   [4] At p. 76.
[5] (1842) 4 Moo. P.C. 63 ; Baron Parke delivered the opinion of the Privy Council both in this case and in the case of Beaumont v. Barrett.

possessed it, not because it was a legislative Assembly, but by virtue of the *Lex et Consuetudo Parliamenti*. Nor could it be said to be incident to a legislative Assembly by analogy to the powers possessed by a court of record.[1]

This Assembly is no Court of Record, nor has it any judicial functions whatever ; and it is to be remarked that all those bodies which possess powers of adjudication upon, and punishing in a summary manner, contempts of their authority, have judicial functions, and exercise this as incident to those which they possess, except only the House of Commons whose authority in that respect rests upon ancient usage.[2]

The principles laid down in this case have been accepted in later cases. In the case of *Fenton v. Hampton* [3] it was held that a select committee of the legislative Assembly of Van Dieman's Land could not commit for contempt a witness who had refused to appear before it. In the case of *Doyle v. Falconer* [4] it was held that an Assembly could not commit a member for a contempt committed in the presence of the Assembly. The following passage explains very clearly the distinction drawn in the case of *Kielley v. Carson* between the common law powers belonging to all legislative Assemblies by the common law, and the additional powers belonging to the House of Commons, which these legislative Assemblies do not possess :

The learned Counsel for the Appellants invoked the principles of the Common Law, and as it must be conceded that the Common Law sanctions the exercise of the prerogative by which an Assembly has been created, the principle of the Common Law, which is embodied in the maxim, *Quando lex aliquid concedit, concedere videtur et illud, sine quo res ipsa esse non potest*, applies to the body so created. The question, therefore, is reduced to this : Is the power to punish and commit for contempts committed in its presence one necessary to the existence of such a body as the Assembly of *Dominica*, and the proper exercise of the functions which it is intended to execute ? It is necessary to distinguish between a power to punish for a contempt, which is a judicial power, and a power to remove any obstruction offered to the deliberations or proper action of a Legislative body during its sitting, which last power is necessary for self-preservation. If a member of a Colonial House of Assembly is guilty of disorderly conduct in the House whilst sitting, he may be removed, or excluded for a time, or even expelled ; but there is a great difference between such powers and the judicial power of inflicting a penal sentence for the offence. The right to remove for self-security is one thing, the right to inflict punishment is another. The former is, in their Lordship's judgment, all that is warranted by the legal maxim that has been cited, but the latter is not its legitimate consequence. To the question, therefore, on which this case depends, their Lordships must answer in the negative.

[1] 4 Moo. P.C. at pp. 88-89.
[2] Ibid at p. 90.   [3] (1858) 11 Moo. P.C. 347.
[4] (1866) L.R. 1 P.C. 328 ; cp. Barton v. Taylor (1886) 11 A.C. at pp. 203-205.

If the good sense and conduct of the members of Colonial Legislatures prove, as in the present case, insufficient to secure order and decency of debate, the law would sanction the use of that degree of force which might be necessary to remove the person offending from the place of meeting, and to keep him excluded. The same rule would apply, *a fortiori*, to obstructions caused by any person not a member. And whenever the violation of order amounts to a breach of the peace, or other legal offence, recourse may be had to the ordinary tribunals.[1]

We have seen that one of the grounds of the decision in the case of *Beaumont v. Barrett*, for allowing a legislative Assembly these extended powers, was the fact that it was the supreme Legislature of the colony.[2] There is something to be said for this argument. It may well be that such an Assembly requires a more efficient protection than that afforded by the rules of the common law, and that it ought to have at least the protection given to all inferior courts of record.[3] Though this argument did not prevail in the case of *Doyle v. Falconer*, it has in some cases prevailed with the Legislature ; and, though a wider power to commit for contempt may be dangerous to the liberty of the subject,[4] it has been given to the colonial Assemblies in all the larger dominions.[5] The earliest Assembly to get this power was the legislative Assembly of Victoria. An Act of 1855 gave it the power to define its powers and privileges, provided that those powers and privileges should not exceed those enjoyed by the House of Commons and its members.[6] The Assembly, by virtue of these powers, passed an Act giving it the same powers and privileges as those enjoyed by the House of Commons and its members.[7] It was held that this Act gave it the power to commit for contempt a person who had libelled a member ; [8] and, in a later case, that it had also the power of deciding for itself whether or not a contempt had been committed ; so that a return to a writ of *habeas corpus* that a person had been committed for contempt, without specifying in what the contempt consisted,

---

[1] At p. 340.   [2] Above 262.

[3] See Doyle v. Falconer (1866) L.R. 1 P.C. at p. 341.

[4] Ibid.

[5] It has been given to the Dominion and the Provinces of Canada ; to the Commonwealth of Australia, and to Victoria, Western Australia, and South Australia ; to the Transvaal, the Orange River Colony, and Natal ; " and to every colony whose Legislature comprises a legislative body of which one half is elected by the inhabitants of the colony," Halsbury, Laws of England (1st ed.) x 536-537, (2nd ed.) xi 88-89, 186.

[6] " It shall be lawful for the Legislature of Victoria, by any Act or Acts to define the privileges, immunities, and powers to be held, enjoyed, and exercised by the Council and Assembly, and by the members thereof respectively ; provided, that no such privileges, immunities, and powers shall exceed those now held, enjoyed and exercised by the Commons House of Parliament or the Members thereof," 18, 19 Victoria c. 55, Schedule I § 35.

[7] 20 Victoria no. 1 ; Tarring, Law Relating to the Colonies (2nd ed.) 140.

[8] Dill v. Murphy (1864) 1 Moo. P C. N.S. 487.

was a good return.[1] The acquisition of these privileges involved the disappearance of the last remnant of the eighteenth-century view as to the very subordinate character of colonial legislative Assemblies.

(vii) *The colonial courts.*

I have described the organization of the courts in the colonies [2] and India,[3] and given some account of their jurisdiction. At this point it is only necessary to say something of the extent of the Crown's prerogative to create courts of justice, and of the powers of these courts to punish contempts.

Blackstone states generally that the King " has alone the right of erecting courts of judicature." [4] But this general statement is misleading, since it is now well established that the King by his prerogative can only create courts to proceed according to the course of the common law ; and that the creation of courts with any wider jurisdiction must be sanctioned by the Legislature.[5] This limitation upon the prerogative has old roots. It is due historically to the campaigns which Coke waged, in the sixteenth and seventeenth centuries, against all those rival courts which administered a jurisdiction outside of, and differing from, the common law.[6] He maintained that no new court with a jurisdiction which was not a common law jurisdiction could be created by the prerogative ; and that courts with a jurisdiction which was not a common law jurisdiction could be created only by prescription or by the authority of Parliament.[7]

The fact that Blackstone omits to state this limitation upon the prerogative is probably due to the fact that, when he wrote, its extent was by no means clear. We have seen that courts

---

[1] The Speaker of the Legislative Assembly of Victoria v. Glass (1871) L.R. 3 P.C. 560, at pp. 572-573 ; for the privilege of committing for contempt enjoyed by the House of Commons see Burdett v. Abbott (1811) 14 East 1 at p. 150 ; the Case of the Sheriff of Middlesex (1840) 11 Ad. and E. 273 ; vol. i 393-394 ; vol. vi 272.

[2] Above 59-63.   [3] Above 166, 173, 216-218.
[4] Comm. i 267.   [5] Below 266-267.
[6] Vol. i 414-415, 510-514, 553-554 ; vol. v 429, 432, 470.
[7] " Herein three things are to be observed. 1. That this new court [the court of Wards and Liveries] could not be created without an act of parliament. 2. That when a new court is created, it is necessary that the jurisdiction and authority of the court be certainly set down. 3. That the court can have no other jurisdiction, than is expressed in the creation, for this new court cannot prescribe," Coke, Fourth Instit. 200 ; " the king cannot make any Commission to hear and determine any matter of equity, but matters of equity ought to be determined in the Court of Chancery," ibid 213, citing a resolution of the Lord Chancellor, Dodderidge and Winch J.J. in 1614 ; " a Commission without an Act of Parliament cannot raise a court of equity," ibid 242 ; for this there was some mediæval authority, see vol. i 169 n. 1, and Hale, H.C.L. (6th ed.) 30 there cited.

of Admiralty had been introduced into the colonies,[1] and that
their introduction had been sanctioned and extended by the
Legislature, which used them to enforce the Acts of Trade.[2]
It seems to have been thought, in spite of Coke's express words,
and in spite of Comyns's endorsement of Coke's views,[3] that a
court of equity could be set up in the colonies by the prerogative ; [4]
and it is certain that courts of equity,[5] and other courts with a
jurisdiction other than a common law jurisdiction,[6] were so
created. On the other hand, it was clear that the system of
ecclesiastical courts and ecclesiastical law which prevailed in
England was not in force in the colonies ; [7] and we have seen
that the lawyers and the Crown always denied that the colonial
Assemblies had the privileges and jurisdiction possessed by the
House of Commons by virtue of *Lex et Consuetudo Parliamenti*.[8]
When, as in India, courts were created, the jurisdiction of which
differed from that of an ordinary common law court, the sanction
of the Legislature was obtained.[9]

It is clear that there were doubts as to the extent of the prerogative. Colonial practice and legal theory were to some extent
divergent ; and it was not till the nineteenth century that the
law on this matter was settled in accordance with the principles
laid down by Coke. In 1827 the law officers expressed doubts
whether the Crown by its prerogative could create in Upper
Canada a court with an equitable jurisdiction.[10] In 1865 it was
held that it could not create a court with ecclesiastical jurisdiction ; [11] and in its decision the Privy Council laid down the
law in accordance with Coke's views. " It is a settled constitutional principle or rule of law," it said, " that, although the

---

[1] Above 60-61.   [2] Above 110.

[3] " The king, by his prerogative, may make what courts for the administration
of the common law, and in what places he pleases. But the king cannot erect a
court of chancery or conscience, for the common law is the inheritance of the subject," Digest *Praerogative* D. 28.

[4] In 1703 Northey, the attorney-general, said that the charter of Massachusetts,
which gave the General Court power to create courts to hear criminal and civil
pleas, did not exclude the Crown's prerogative " to erect a court of equity in the
said province, as by her royal authority they are created in other her majesty's plantations " ; and that the General Assembly could not under its charter erect such a
court, Chalmers, Opinions i 182-183.

[5] Berriedale Keith, the First British Empire 255.

[6] In 1720 a mercantile court was created at Gibraltar with a summary jurisdiction, because a court " erected after the manner practised according to the common law in Great Britain, or in imitation thereof, or such as are established in his
majesty's colonies abroad, would be very dilatory and expensive, and consequently
not well adapted to the decision of transitory or mercantile disputes in a free port,"
Chalmers, Opinions i 173-175 ; no legal objection was raised by the law officers,
Robert Raymond and Philip Yorke, ibid 180-181.

[7] Berriedale Keith, op. cit. 222 ; Chalmers, opinions i 4-14 ; above 242.

[8] Above 261-262.

[9] Above 166 ; cp. Forsyth, Cases on Constitutional Law 187.

[10] Forsyth, op. cit. 173-174.

[11] *In re* Lord Bishop of Natal (1865) 3 Moo. P.C. N.S. at p. 152.

Crown may by its prerogative establish courts to proceed according to the Common Law, yet that it cannot create any new court to administer any other law." [1]

It is clear that a court of record in the colonies, whether created by the prerogative or otherwise, has the power inherent in all courts of record of committing for contempt ; [2] and if a contempt has been committed, and the guilty person has been punished by the appropriate punishment of fine and imprisonment or either, the Privy Council will not entertain an appeal.[3] But if an inappropriate punishment has been inflicted, as for instance disbarring or striking off the rolls, the Privy Council will interfere ; [4] and also if it appears that no contempt has been committed.[5] Moreover the Privy Council will interfere if the question is referred to it by the Crown [6] under § 4 of the Act of 1833.[7]

This short summary of some of the leading principles of colonial constitutional law shows that the foundations of this branch of English public law had been laid in this period. That they had been so laid was the direct legal effect of the expansions of Great Britain in the East and in the West. In conclusion we must glance briefly at some of the larger and more indirect legal effects of these expansions.

(2) *The larger legal effects of these expansions of England.*

We have seen that the expansion of Great Britain had brought about an expansion of English law ; and that, though there were many diversities in the laws which governed the different colonies and dependencies, the fact that these colonies and dependencies were administered by Englishmen, and the fact that their courts were staffed by English lawyers, tended to introduce into all of them English legal ideas and principles.[8] And so, with the growth of the British Empire, these ideas and principles began to make their influence felt in many parts of the world. We must now turn to the other side of the picture, and examine the effects upon English law of this geographical extension of its influence. We shall see that this extension has helped to develop many branches of English law by the process of elaborating old and introducing new principles. With the history of some of these

---

[1] *In re* Lord Bishop of Natal (1865) 3 Moo. P.C. N.S. at p. 152.

[2] Rainy v. the Justices of Sierra Leone (1852-1853) 8 Moo. P.C. 47 ; McDermott v. Beaumont and Beete (1868) L.R. 2 P.C. 341.

[3] Last Note.

[4] Smith v. the Justices of Sierra Leone (1841) 3 Moo. P.C. 361.

[5] McLeod v. St. Aubyn [1899] A.C. 549.

[6] *In re* the Bahama Islands [1893] A.C. 138 ; cp. Rainy v. the Justices of Sierra Leone (1452-1453) 8 Moo. P.C., at p. 55.

[7] 3 & 4 William IV c. 41 ; vol. i 524.　　　　[8] Above 251.

principles I shall deal later. At this point I can only survey rapidly some of the branches of English law which began to be developed in the eighteenth century as the result of this expansion of Great Britain.

In the sphere of *Public Law* such fundamental constitutional ideas as the rule of law and the doctrine of ministerial responsibility were elaborated by their application to colonial conditions. We have seen that a series of cases, which arose out of the activities of colonial governors and officials, added to the law upon such matters as the liability of the servants of the Crown for their wrongful acts,[1] and the legal position of the Crown and its servants in relation to contracts and other lawful acts done by them as agents of the Crown.[2] Similarly, cases arising in the colonies illustrated the application of, and so helped to give precision to, some of the prerogatives of the Crown. Thus the rule that any exercise of the treaty-making power of the Crown which involves an alteration of law needs the sanction of Parliament was stated and applied in cases which were concerned with colonial trade ;[3] and the vexed question of the extent of the prerogative right to cede territory by treaty was raised and discussed with reference to the events which led to the recognition of the independence of the United States, and the accompanying cession of territory.[4] Such half-obsolete prerogatives as the power of the Crown to forbid its subjects to leave the country, or to recall its absent subjects to England, were considered in connection with difficulties which arose out of the regulation of colonial trade.[5] The Crown's prerogatives in relation to the constitution of colonial Assemblies,[6] and in relation to colonial legislation,[7] kept alive, in relation to the colonies, prerogatives which were obsolete in England ; and the discussion of the claims of these Assemblies to have all the privileges which the House of Commons possessed by virtue of the *Lex et Consuetudo Parliamenti*, helped to elucidate the nature of these privileges, and the extent of the privileges of the Assemblies, to which this *Lex et Consuetudo* did not apply.[8] The extent of the Crown's prerogative to create courts of justice was elucidated by cases which arose in relation to the exercise of this prerogative in the colonies.[9]

---

[1] Above 253-260.　　　　　　　　　　　　　　　　[2] Vol. x 652-655.

[3] Chalmers, Opinions ii 243-244—an opinion given in 1764 to the effect that a treaty with France respecting the Newfoundland fisheries could not be carried into effect because it was contrary to 10, 11 William III c. 25 ; ibid ii 341-342—an opinion of 1728 as to the interpretation of a treaty made in 1686 between England and France.

[4] Ibid ii 403-408, 445-499; the nineteenth-century developments of the law on this matter will be discussed in a later chapter.

[5] Ibid ii 246-247, 363-364.　　　　　　　　　　　[6] Above 252.

[7] Above 93-95.　　　　　[8] Above 261-264.　　　　　[9] Above 265-267.

In those branches of the law which are on the borderline between *Constitutional Law* and *International Law* the colonial contribution was considerable. It was in connection with the cession of Surinam to the Dutch in 1667, that we get the earliest recognition of the principle that the stipulations of a treaty bind the contracting states, but give no rights to the subjects of those states, enforceable in municipal courts. The statement of De Witt, the correctness of which Sir William Temple admitted, is thus summarized by Temple : [1]

That which my Lord de Witt insists upon, and principally contends for, is, that after the said cession, or reliction of the sovereignty of the place to any state is past, the dispensing of that justice, due to the said inhabitants, by virtue of any former treaty, or articles of surrender, doth, not only singly, but exclusively belong to the right of the said state, who is the present possessor of the said place, as an inseparable branch, or part of the sovereignty ; and that there lieth neither any right of appeal in the inhabitants of the said places so surrendered, nor so much as right of mediation or inter-cession,[2] and much less of judgment and arbitration in him that was the former sovereign ; although the present sovereign of the said places should either fail of observing the said articles, or should do any injury to the said inhabitants ; and, therefore, though the English at Surinam have several undeniable rights, which do belong to them, by virtue of the articles made by them, at the surrender of the said place, and such as they may in justice expect to be made good to them ; the judgment, nevertheless, of the rights, with the due dispensing and administering of them, is, since the general articles of peace, so much, and so exclusively the right of the states-general, as the said English neither can, may, nor of right ought to apply themselves to any other than the said states-general, for the making good of them.

It was in connection with the recognition of the independence of the United States, that the question of the effect of a cession of territory upon the allegiance of the former subjects of Great Britain, and the application to such a situation of the maxim *nemo potest exuere patriam*, were discussed.[3] Similarly, it is clear from that discussion that the conception of commercial domicil, and the difference between that conception and the conception of allegiance, was beginning to be perceived.[4] As we have seen, the courts had, at the end of this and the beginning of the following century, laid the foundations of the modern law upon this topic, in the cases which had arisen out of the activities of alien enemies resident in this country by the licence of the Crown, and of British subjects resident and trading in an enemy country.[5]

That branch of law which is known as *Private International Law* or the *Conflict of Laws* has, for the most part, been created

---

[1] Chalmers, Opinions ii 498-499.
[2] This denial of the right of remonstrance if the treaty be broken is not correct.
[3] Vol. ix 86-87.   [4] Chalmers, Opinions ii 457-458, 462.
[5] Vol. ix 99-103.

by the courts in the course of the nineteenth and twentieth centuries ;[1] and therefore I shall deal with its history in a later chapter. But during this century we can see the beginnings of some of the topics which fall within it ; and one of these topics—the effect of foreign judgments—was attracting considerable attention. The fact that this topic was beginning to attract attention was due partly to the growth of the colonies, and partly to the growth of Great Britain's foreign trade, which was fostered by the growth of the colonies. Many of the early cases upon this branch of the law arose out of the judgments of colonial courts ; and the others arose out of the commercial activities of Englishmen. A rapid glance at one or two of these cases will show us that the law was then in an inchoate stage, but that some of the principles recognized to-day were beginning to emerge.

First, the English courts refused to recognize a judgment unless it was the judgment of a regular court of judicature. Lord Mansfield refused to recognize the jurisdiction of a so-called court held by the Marshals of France, which put pressure on gamblers who delayed to pay their losses ;[2] and Lord Hardwicke refused to pay attention to the sentence of a French commissary court on the ground that it was " of a political nature."[3]

Secondly, both Lord Hardwicke and Lord Mansfield were of opinion that the English courts could not be used to enforce the penal or the revenue laws of a foreign country. Thus, Lord Hardwicke held in 1734 that the English courts could pay no attention to a Portuguese law which made the export of gold unlawful.[4] He said :[5]

The carrying on of a trade prohibited by the laws of England is of material consequence, and it is said that the parties in that case shall receive no relief, as they are both participes criminis, and therefore the law will not give one any remedy against the other. But if it shall be laid down, that because goods are prohibited to be exported by the laws of any foreign country from whence they are brought, therefore the parties shall have no remedy or action here, it would cut off all benefit of such trade from this kingdom, which would be of

---

[1] Dicey said in 1896 : " This branch of law has been created within little more than a century by a series of judicial decisions, and is now, to the great benefit of the public, year by year extended and developed through the legislative activity of our judges," Conflict of Laws (1st ed.) Preface; as Cheshire points out, Private International Law 41-42, the beginnings of the modern English system owe most to Story's Commentaries which were published in 1834.

[2] Robinson v. Bland (1760) 2 Burr. at p. 1080, where he pointed out that " the Parliament of Paris would pay no regard to their judgment " ; Wilmot J. called it " a wild illegal fantastical court of honour."

[3] Gage v. Bulkeley (1744) 3 Atk. 215.

[4] Boucher v. Lawson (1734) Cases t. Hardwicke 85.

[5] At p. 89 ; cp. Folliott v. Ogden (1789) 1 H.Bl. at p. 135 where Lord Loughborough C.J. said, " the penal laws of foreign countries are strictly local and affect nothing more than they can reach."

very bad consequence to the principal and most beneficial branches of our trade ; nor does it ever seem to have been admitted.

This statement is accepted to-day as good law, in all cases where the law imposes a penalty recoverable at the suit of the state.[1] It was on this principle that Lord Mansfield laid it down more than once that " one nation does not take notice of the revenue laws of another " [2]—a principle which has been applied in a modern case to the revenue laws of a Dominion.[3]

Thirdly, the law distinguished between judgments *in rem* and judgments *in personam*. The clearest statement of that distinction is contained in the judgment of Blackburn J., in 1870, in the case of *Castrique v. Imrie ;* [4] but the distinction and its consequences were recognized in the eighteenth century. The rule that the sentence of a foreign court of Admiralty condemning a ship as prize, was conclusive as against all the world, was laid down in 1682, in the case of *Hughes v. Cornelius ;* [5] and it was repeatedly recognized in the eighteenth century.[6] In 1678 Lord Nottingham recognized the conclusive effect of a foreign decree dissolving a marriage between two foreigners, who were the subjects of the state when the decree was made.[7] But we shall now see that the effect to be given to a foreign judgment *in personam* was not as yet clearly ascertained.

Fourthly, it was held in 1705 by Cowper, L.K., that a foreign judgment *in personam*, not being the judgment of a court of record, created only a simple contract debt ; [8] and that rule was treated as settled law by Lord Mansfield in 1778 in the case of *Walker v. Witter*.[9] This conclusion was based upon the fact that

---

[1] Huntingdon v. Attrill [1893] A.C. at pp. 156-158.

[2] Planche v. Fletcher (1779) 1 Dougl. at p. 253 ; cp. Holman v. Johnson (1775) 1 Cowp. at p. 343.

[3] Municipal Council of Sydney v. Bull [1909] 1 K.B. 7.

[4] " When a tribunal, no matter whether in England or a foreign country, has to determine between two parties, and between them only, the decision of that tribunal, though in general binding between the parties and privies, does not affect the rights of third parties " ; but " when the tribunal has jurisdiction to determine not merely on the rights of the parties, but also on the disposition of the thing, and does in the exercise of that jurisdiction direct that the thing, and not merely the interest of any particular party in it, be sold or transferred, the case is very different," (1870) L.R. 4 H. of L. at pp. 427, 428 ; the case is very different because the sale or transfer, and therefore the title of the purchaser or transferee, is held to be valid by the courts of all countries as against all the world.

[5] 2 Shower K.B. 232.

[6] See e.g. Bernardi v. Motteux (1781) 1 Dougl. at p. 581 *per* Lord Mansfield C.J. ; Geyer v. Aquilar (1798) 7 T.R. at p. 696 *per* Lord Kenyon C.J.

[7] *Ex parte* Cottington 2 Swanst. 326 ; cp. Roach v. Garvan (1748) 1 Ves. Sen. at p. 159 where Lord Hardwicke said, speaking of the validity of a marriage, " it has been argued to be valid from being established by the sentence of a court in France, having proper jurisdiction. And it is true, that if so, it is conclusive, whether in a foreign court or not, from the law of nations in such cases : otherwise the rights of mankind would be very precarious and uncertain."

[8] Dupleix v. De Roven 2 Vern. 540.

[9] 1 Dougl. at p. 5.

the very technical qualities of a court of record [1] were not attributable to foreign courts, and not even to all English courts.[2] It followed that there was no merger of the original cause of action in the judgment ; [3] so that it was open to the party who had recovered judgment, either to bring an action of *indebitatus assumpsit* upon the judgment, or to sue upon the original cause of action.[4] Moreover it was recognized that, if the judgment was not a final judgment, the plaintiff could only pursue the latter course.[5] *A fortiori*, the fact that proceedings had been begun in England, and not further prosecuted, could be no bar to the institution of proceedings in another jurisdiction.[6]

It was also recognized at the beginning of the nineteenth century that it was only if the judgment was for an ascertained sum that an action could be brought upon it.[7] Probably this was always the law, since the action of debt, which was the appropriate action on a foreign judgment, and the action of *indebitatus assumpsit* which had taken the place of the action of debt,[8] lay only for an ascertained sum.[9] Though this rule may have originated in the technical requirements of the action of debt it was a rule which was convenient and even essential ; for the courts could no more have enforced a foreign judgment for an uncertain amount, than a judgment which was not a final judgment ; [10] and it would be obviously impossible to enforce any judgment other than a judgment to pay money.

But there was one very fundamental question upon which the lawyers had not as yet made up their minds. What was the principle upon which a foreign judgment *in personam* gave rise to a cause of action ? According to one view the judgment was merely prima facie evidence of the original cause of action, so that in an action on the judgment it was possible to question the findings both of law and fact on which the judgment was based, and thus, in effect, to retry the case. According to the

---

[1] Vol. v 157-160.

[2] In Walker v. Witter 1 Dougl. at p. 6, Lord Mansfield C.J. said, " The difficulty in the case had arisen from not fixing accurately what a court of record is in the eye of the law. That description is confined properly to certain courts in England, and their judgments cannot be controverted. Foreign courts, and courts in England not of record, have not that privilege."

[3] Walker v. Witter (1778) 1 Dougl. at p. 5 ; Galbraith v. Neville (1789) 1 Dougl. at p. 5 *note* per Buller J. ; Hall v. Odber (1809) 11 East at pp. 126-127 *per* Bayley J. ; Smith v. Nicolls (1839) 5 Bing. N.C. at p. 221.

[4] See Smith v. Nicolls (1839) 5 Bing. N.C. at p. 221.

[5] Plummer v. Woodburne (1825) 4 B and C. at p. 637 *per* Bayley J. ; cp. Nouvion v. Freeman (1889) 15 A.C. 1.

[6] Bayley v. Edwards (1792) 3 Swanst. 703 ; cp. Mutrie v. Binney (1887) 35 C.D. at pp. 619-620.

[7] Sadler v. Robins (1808) 1 Camp. 253 ; cp. Henderson v. Henderson (1844) 6 Q.B. at pp. 297-298.

[8] Vol. iii 442-444.

[9] Ibid 423 ; Ames, Lectures in Legal History 89-90.   [10] Above n. 5.

other view, the findings of fact and law contained in the judgment conclusively bound the parties, so that a defendant, when sued on the judgment, could not defend the action unless he could show that for some reason he was not bound by the judgment. Since it was not till 1851 that the second view was definitely accepted by the courts,[1] the history of this conflict must be dealt with in a later chapter. At this point I need only say that the solution ultimately reached was due in part to the fact that the consequences of holding that a colonial judgment was merely prima facie evidence of the original cause of action were obviously inconvenient; for, if it were possible in an action on a colonial judgment to enter into the merits of the case, and so, in effect to retry it, a conflict might easily arise between the court which retried the case and the Privy Council, if the parties to the original action appealed.[2] It is clear that this consideration weighed with the court which, in 1851, settled this long controverted question; so that I think it is clear that, both during the eighteenth and the nineteenth centuries, it was the problems arising out of the enforcement of colonial judgments, which helped to settle this difficult branch of Private International Law.

In the sphere of *Private Law* the commercial developments which were fostered by colonial trade were the direct cause of the elaboration of those principles of commercial and maritime law which had begun to be incorporated into the body of English law in the preceding period.[3] Indirectly these developments of commercial and maritime law produced developments, statutory and otherwise, in many different branches of English law. Of this we shall meet many instances in later chapters of this history. At this point two instances will suffice. In *Zenger's Case* in 1735 the jury, as in the later English cases,[4] refused to follow the court's direction that the criminality of a libel was a matter of law for the court, and, in defiance of the court's direction, acquitted the prisoner.[5] In the case of *Penn v. Lord Baltimore*,[6] which was a suit in equity arising out of an agreement for the settlement of the boundaries of Maryland and Pennsylvania, we get a clear

---

[1] Bank of Australasia v. Nias 16 Q.B. 717; Lord Campbell C.J. at p. 735 said, " The dicta against retrying the cause are quite as strong as those in favour of this proceeding; and being left without any express decision, . . . we must look to principle and expediency."

[2] " Before the Judicial Committee, the judges there presiding would fairly examine the judgment, and only set it aside if it was unjust. But, though perfectly regular and just, it may be set aside if the same questions are again to be submitted to a jury," ibid at p. 736.

[3] Vol. viii chap. iv.   [4] Vol. x 689.

[5] Berriedale Keith, The First British Empire 229-230.

[6] (1750) 1 Ves. Sen. 444.

statement of the principle that equity acts *in personam*,[1] and an example of the most important class of cases—cases concerning foreign land—in which that principle has been applied in the modern system of equity. We have seen that some of the Acts passed by the colonial Assemblies attempted reforms in the law which were negatived by the Crown because they appeared to be too revolutionary ; but that they foreshadow statutory changes which have later been made in England.[2]

With these effects of the expansion of Great Britain upon the development of different branches of English law, enacted and unenacted, I shall deal in more detail both in the two following chapters, and in later chapters, of this History. But, before I turn to the history of the different branches of English law in the eighteenth century, I must sum up the merits and defects of this complex system of English public law which the eighteenth-century lawyers and statesmen had evolved.

IX

The Merits and Defects of the Eighteenth-Century Constitution

On the Continent as in England, the political and religious controversies of the sixteenth and the first half of the seventeenth centuries had resulted in the creation of stable governments in the principal states of Europe ; and, except in England, the form of that government was autocratic monarchy. In England alone the monarch's powers had been limited and subjected to the rule of law. The result was that England had acquired a form of government and a system of law which were unique, because in both the government and the law of England mediæval and modern elements had met and blended. From this blend there had emerged a constitution in which the two Houses of Parliament had the predominating influence, and in which all the members of the state, except the King, and all the institutions of government, including the prerogative itself, were subject to a supreme law. Could a modern state be governed by a constitution of this kind ? Foreign observers, who, at the end of the seventeenth century, looked at English politics from the point of view of the troubled history of that century,

---

[1] Lord Hardwicke said at pp. 446-447 : " It is certain that the original jurisdiction in cases of this kind relating to boundaries between provinces, the dominion and proprietary government, is in the King and council." . . . But," The conscience of the party was bound by this agreement ; and being within the jurisdiction of this court, which acts *in personam*, the court may properly decree it as an agreement, if a foundation for it " ; vol. xii 264-265.

[2] Above 95, 97.

were very sceptical.[1] But the eighteenth century silenced these sceptics. England was successfully governed under the constitution which she had acquired as the result of the Great Rebellion and the Revolution ; and, as we have seen, its merits attracted the notice of many continental thinkers, who chafed under the restrictions and abuses of autocratic rule.

That England was thus successfully governed during the eighteenth century by its very unique machinery of government was, I think, mainly due to the fact that its autonomous units were, to a very large extent, staffed by men of many different classes, who served for the most part voluntarily and generally gratuitously. Privy councillors and members of the two Houses of Parliament ; the peers who held the great offices of state and the lord lieutenancies of the counties ; the country gentlemen who, as justices of the peace, ruled the counties ; the mayors, alderman, and governing bodies of the larger cities ; the humbler classes who were compelled to serve as officials of hundreds or parishes ; those who were compelled to serve on grand or petty juries—were all taught something of government in very various spheres by the part which they took in it. Thus the nation acquired a political sense—a lesson which can never be learned from those books of theory from which many of the leaders or would-be leaders of a democracy imagine that they can get a political education. There can be no doubt that it was the acquisition of this political sense which fitted the nation for liberty by teaching it that, because rights and duties are correlative terms, all classes must give services to the state which were proportionate to the rights and privileges which their rank or status conferred upon them. It was because Englishmen had received this political education, it was because the opposing principles of authority and liberty were more skilfully blended in the eighteenth-century constitution than they had ever been before or have ever been since, that Englishmen were able to work successfully the complex machinery of government, and to found many colonies, and an Indian Empire. It is the secret of England's most important achievements in this century.

Because in this century both Houses of Parliament contained very many men of property and ability, who had had this political education, the advantages conferred upon the country by Parliamentary government largely out-weighed its disadvantages. Those advantages and disadvantages can be summed up as follows:

First, the fact that in normal times the Crown and the members of the House of Lords were, to a large extent, able to control

[1] Vol. vi 300, and the references there cited.

the elections to the House of Commons, and the fact that members of the House of Lords filled the most important ministerial posts, gave continuity both to the domestic and foreign policy of state, and a very definite and a very important constitutional position to the House of Lords.[1] Though it was, as a House, the weaker of the two Houses,[2] it had a very distinct part to play in the eighteenth-century constitution ; and nobody thought of questioning its right to exercise freely the powers which enabled it to play that part.[3] All through the century, by virtue both of its powers as a House and by virtue of the position and the talents of individual peers, it acted as the balance weight of the constitution which helped the complex machinery of government, central and local, to run steadily.[4]

Secondly, though the elections to the House of Commons were, to a large extent, controlled in normal times by the Crown and by members of the House of Lords, the existence of an elected and representative House gave to the nation, in times of political excitement, a chance, denied to the other nations of Europe, of expressing its will.[5] Moreover, the fact that the King and his ministers were obliged to explain and justify their policy to this assembly, ensured some measure of ability in those ministers. Rule by royal favourites without ability was impossible.[6] Having regard to the King's dislike of the elder Pitt, it is difficult to see how he could have risen to power under an autocracy ; and if he had not risen to power the history of England and of the world would have been very different.

Thirdly, by reason of the control which the House of Commons exercised over finance, the government of England was economical and financially sound. " Great nations," Adam Smith truly said,[7] " are never impoverished by private, though they sometimes are by public, prodigality and misconduct " ; and he admitted that, in spite of its defects, the fiscal system of Great Britain was " as good and better than most of our neighbours," and a great deal better than that of France.[8]

---

[1] Vol. x 576, 579-580, 613.   [2] Ibid 618-619.
[3] Ibid 614-617.   [4] Ibid.
[5] " The present representation, after all these deductions . . . is still in such a degree popular ; or rather the representatives are so connected with the mass of the community, by a society of interests and passions, that the will of the people when it is determined, permanent, and general, almost always at length prevails," Paley, Principles of Moral and Political Philosophy (2nd ed.) 490, Bk. vi c. 7.
[6] " The King's choice of his ministers is controlled by the obligation he is under of appointing those men to offices in the state who are found capable of managing the affairs of his government, with the two houses of parliament. Which consideration imposes such a necessity upon the crown, as hath in a great measure subdued the influence of favouritism ; in so much, that it is become no uncommon spectacle in this country to see men promoted by the King to the highest offices . . . who have been distinguished by their opposition to his personal inclinations," ibid 480.
[7] Wealth of Nations (Cannan's ed.) i 324.   [8] Ibid ii 383, 389.

No doubt this economy had its weak side. The executive government was feeble. We have seen that it had at its disposal no adequate police force, with the result that lawlessness was rife, and riots were with difficulty quelled.[1] We have seen, too, that both the state of the prisons [2] and the state of the highways [3] were a disgrace. In many of the government offices sinecure places and an obsolete procedure prevented efficiency.[4] In fact, the eighteenth century was weak where the twentieth century is strong, and vice versa. The eighteenth-century machinery of executive government was very feeble : the twentieth-century machinery is very efficient. But the eighteenth century was strong in its finance and in its capacity to follow a steady foreign, and a steady economic, policy ; and because its statesmen had vision and capacity to follow the vision, they raised Great Britain to the first rank amongst the states of Europe and won India and the greater part of the overseas Dominions. Our democratic governments of the twentieth century are weak in their finance and are unable to pursue a steady policy ; for they depend for power on an electorate, a large proportion of whom are mainly preoccupied with the question what comforts and amenities they can induce the state to provide gratuitously for its members. In this age of machinery we are too apt to forget that the character and abilities of the men who work the machinery are more important than the machinery. The men who worked the faulty machinery of the eighteenth-century constitution were no political theorists, but practical men who had learned from that constitution a political sense. And so they accomplished results which political theorists, possessed of the most perfect machinery, have never achieved. " Men talk of patriarchal systems," said Horace Walpole, speaking of the constitutional controversies with America,[5] " and original compacts. Necessity and accident formed all systems, and men were governed long before they reasoned." This is as true of the speculations of to-day as of the speculations of the eighteenth century. But it is easier to secure a trial of some of the speculative schemes of to-day—generally at a vast expense ; for modern politicians have forgotten Paley's aphorism that " the courage of a statesman should resemble that of a commander, who, however regardless of personal danger, never forgets that, with his own, he commits the lives and fortunes of a multitude ; and who does not consider it as any proof of zeal or valour, to stake the safety of *other* men upon the success of a perilous or desperate enterprise." [6] It is well to remember that, in the eighteenth century, when speculative schemes were

[1] Vol. x 144.
[2] Ibid 181-183.
[3] Ibid 207, 210.
[4] Ibid 501-503, 506-509.
[5] Memoirs of George III ii 74.
[6] Op. cit. 469.

less readily taken up, the cheapness of the government enabled commerce and industry to expand, and capital to accumulate. And so, when the great engineering and scientific discoveries of the latter part of the century were made, it was possible to exploit them to the utmost.

Fourthly, the great majority of Englishmen were contented with their form of government. A large number were proud of it. George III in 1778 spoke of the " beauty, excellence, and perfection of the British Constitution as by Law Established " ; [1] and Lord Chesterfield [2] said that " England was the only monarchy in the world that can properly be said to have a constitution, for the people's rights and liberties are secured by laws." Burke echoed the sentiments of very many when, in his *Appeal from the New to the Old Whigs*, he compared the English constitution to one of those great artistic or literary masterpieces which all the learned world admires ; and said of it that, if we find ourselves unable to admire it, we should " rather believe that we are dull, than that the rest of the world has been imposed on," and, consequently, that " we ought to understand it according to our measure ; and to venerate when we are not able presently to comprehend." [3] Horace Walpole prayed " that, with all its deficiencies, we may preserve our mixed government." [4] Even Bentham in his younger days said of it that it was " the finest and most excellent with all its imperfections of any the world ever saw yet." [5] And there was some reason for this contentment and this pride. The wealth of the nation was increasing ; and the fact that its strength was in no way diminished, is shown by the fact that, at the beginning of the following century, it emerged successful from the ordeal of one of those great wars which, every century since 1588, England has fought to preserve the balance of power in Europe.

But, fifthly, this contentment and this pride were apt to degenerate into an attitude of complacent satisfaction with things established which blinded statesmen to the real character of the problems, domestic and foreign, which they were called upon to solve ; and that attitude was apt to lead to the pursuit of policies which were marked by insular and class selfishness and intolerance—to a pursuit of policies which were rarely illumined by great ideas. Chatham's policy was illumined by great ideas. [6] But he stood apart from all the statesmen of the

---

[1] Fortescue, Papers of George III iv 220-221.
[2] Letters ii 2.   [3] Works (Bohn's ed.) iii 114.
[4] Memoirs of George III iii 179 ; in 1782 he wrote that America was the " only country that ever had an opportunity of choosing its constitution at once ; it may take the best one that ever was, ours, and correct its defects," Letters (ed. Toynbee) xii 204.
[5] A Comment on the Commentaries 211.   [6] Vol. x 84-86.

day in his range of vision. The policy pursued with regard to Ireland was selfish and intolerant ; [1] and the policy pursued with regard to America was remarkable for the manner in which, in spite of the warnings of Burke and Chatham, a large question was approached in a spirit of pettifogging legality.[2] Chatham had won " a great empire," but a large part of it was lost when that Empire fell under the control of " little minds." These defects began to be apparent at the end of the century. The spirit of complacent satisfaction with things established did not provide an ideal approach for the right understanding of those new ideas and those new social and economic conditions, which, at the end of the century, were undermining the spiritual and material foundations of the static eighteenth-century political society. We shall see that grave mistakes were made in the handling of some of these new social and economic problems. These mistakes were caused partly by the defective machinery of the eighteenth-century constitution, partly by a lack of knowledge of and sympathy with the misery which the Industrial Revolution was causing amongst the humbler classes of society, but chiefly by the surrender of the Legislature to the theories of the economists, who preached the doctrine that all social and economic ills would be cured by *laissez faire*.[3] We shall see that the mishandling of these social and economic problems was beginning to create class antagonisms which were unknown in the eighteenth century ; and that Adam Smith, Bentham, and Paine were beginning to teach men to approach the law and constitution of England from a point of view which was the exact opposite to that of Blackstone and Burke. Whether or not the younger Pitt could have led the country to adapt gradually the eighteenth-century institutions to the new conditions, even as the Tudors had adapted mediæval institutions to modern needs, is an interesting speculation. He never had the chance. The outbreak of the French Revolution, and the animosities which it engendered, stopped all chance of gradual reform and adaptation. Then came the Napoleonic wars, and for many years the energies of the nation were concentrated on a struggle for existence.

The policies pursued with regard to Ireland [4] and America,[5] and the failure to realize the nature of the social and economic problems which the Industrial Revolution was beginning to set to the state,[6] were the three great political mistakes of the statesmen of the eighteenth century. Their combined effect was the disappearance of the former complacent satisfaction with English institutions and English law, and the substitution

[1] Above 22-25, 27.　　[2] Above 113-114, 118, 124-128.　　[3] Below 517-518.
[4] Above 22-25, 33-35.　　[5] Above 113-114, 118.　　[6] Below 498.

of a critical attitude and a demand for reforms. But though serious mistakes had been made, though there was much in the eighteenth-century constitution and eighteenth-century law which was unsuited to the new social and economic conditions, the many strong and good points in the eighteenth-century constitutional law and statesmanship enabled Great Britain to found a new colonial empire in place of her lost American colonies ; and though the Irish problem continued to baffle British statesmanship,[1] the flexibility of the constitution enabled the changes demanded by new social and economic conditions to be made gradually by way of reform, and not suddenly and violently by way of revolution. All this we shall see in the chapters which relate the history of the public law of the following period. In the meantime we must turn to the history of other branches of the law of the eighteenth century.

[1] Vol. x 20-21, 22 ; above 35.

CHAPTER II

THE EIGHTEENTH CENTURY (*Continued*)

THE ENACTED LAW

WE have seen that after the Great Rebellion it was recognized that Parliament was the sole legislative authority in the state,[1] and that the operative force of royal proclamations was confined within the limits laid down by Coke in *The Case of Proclamations*.[2] This ruling in effect confined their operative force to the sphere of executive government, so that a statute passed by Parliament was the only means of making even the smallest modification in the law. The Revolution put the finishing touch to this development by finally divesting the prerogative of the supra-legal sanctity which the royalists had claimed for it.[3] It was clear that a King who reigned by a Parliamentary title, whose prerogative was limited by the law, who had lost all power to suspend or dispense with statutes, could not claim any supra-legal power to legislate. Therefore, except in respect of colonies acquired by conquest or cession,[4] proclamations issued by the King by virtue of his prerogative have ceased to be legislative, and have become purely executive, acts, operative only in respect of those matters which by the law of the constitution, the King has power to regulate by virtue of his prerogative. We have seen that this principle was so well established that, in 1766, ministers who had inadvertently issued a proclamation which contravened the law, were obliged to protect themselves by an Act of Indemnity.[5]

It is true that the matters which the Crown was able to regulate by its prerogative were numerous ; it is true that the Crown could and did by proclamation " admonish its subjects that they keep the laws " ;[6] it is true that the Crown could take measures to enforce the provisions of statutes, and could by proclamation inform its subjects of the measures which it

---

[1] Vol. vi 303.   [2] (1611) 12 Co. Rep. 74 ; vol. iv 296-297.
[3] Vol. vi 230-231.   [4] Above 234-237.
[5] Vol. x 365 ; 7 George III c. 7.
[6] Case of Proclamations (1611) 12 Co. Rep. at p. 75.

proposed to take for that purpose; [1] it is true that, for all these reasons, proclamations still occupy an important place in the machinery of government. They still illustrate many sides of the national life, and therefore throw some sidelights on legal developments. More especially they illustrate the development of international law ; [2] for it was in the sphere of foreign affairs that the Crown's prerogative was most unfettered, and there fore it was in that sphere that much could still be effected by proclamations. But, though proclamations cannot be neglected by the legal historian, they have definitely ceased to be a part of the enacted law of England ; so that their influence on the development of the law must be dealt with in connection with the particular branches of the law—mainly public law [3] and international law [4]—which have been affected by them.

The supreme legislative authority of Parliament has affected what may be called the prerogative power to legislate in two opposite directions.

In the first place, many matters which were formerly regulated by the prerogative have come to be regulated by statutes. Matters so regulated, to the extent to which this regulation extends, pass from the sphere of the prerogative, because, having become part of the general body of English law, they cannot be altered by the prerogative. Thus the statutes which, in the eighteenth and later centuries, regulated the coinage,[5] the army,[6] the conditions under which an alien accused of some crime could be extradited,[7] the conditions under which the Crown could take land for the defence of the realm [8]—have all operated to curtail the sphere of the prerogative. In the case of *The Attorney-General v. De Keyser's Royal Hotel* Lord Dunedin, after stating the rule that the Crown is not bound by a statute unless it is specially provided in the statute that it shall be so bound, said : [9]

---

[1] For instances see vol. vi 303 nn. 4 and 5 ; cp. 25 George III c. 51 § 5.
[2] Vol. xii 637-639. [3] Vol. x 240, 368, 374; above 234, 237.
[4] Vol. xii 637-639. [5] Vol. x 407-410. [6] Ibid 378-380.
[7] Ibid 398-400.

[8] These Acts begin in 1708, 7 Anne c. 26 ; at first they were passed to enable the Crown to acquire particular pieces of land ; general temporary Acts authorizing the acquisition of land were passed in 1798, 38 George III c. 27, and in 1803, 43 George III c. 55 ; and permanent Acts were passed in 1804 and 1842, 44 George III c. 95, 5, 6 Victoria c. 94 ; of these Acts Lord Moulton said in The Attorney-General v. De Keyser's Royal Hotel [1920] A.C. at p. 550, "these Acts commence in 1708 and occur at intervals up to 1842. At first they related only to land for fortifications mentioned in the Act, but later they became more general in their character, and authorized the Crown to select suitable land and acquire it. In all cases compensation was given to the owners for the land taken . . . the Defence Act 1842 repealed all such existing Acts, and laid down general provisions which have regulated since that time the procedure for the acquisition by the Crown of land for such purposes."

[9] [1920] A.C. at p. 526.

None the less it is equally certain that if the whole ground of something which could be done by the prerogative is covered by the statute, it is the statute that rules. On this point I think the observation of the learned Master of the Rolls is unanswerable. He says : " What use would there be in imposing limitations, if the Crown could at its pleasure disregard them and fall back on prerogative ? " The prerogative is defined by a learned writer as " the residue of discretionary or arbitrary authority which at any given time is legally left in the hands of the Crown." In as much as the Crown is a party to every Act of Parliament it is logical enough to consider that when the Act deals with something which before the Act could be effected by the prerogative, and specially empowers the Crown to do the same thing, but subject to conditions, the Crown assents to that, and by that Act, to the prerogative being curtailed.

The operation of the principle thus stated by Lord Dunedin has, in effect, been curtailing the sphere of the prerogative from the beginning of the eighteenth century down to modern times.

But, in the second place, the same power which has curtailed the sphere of the prerogative, has in other directions extended the power of the Crown or its servants. Throughout the course of English history, but more especially during the nineteenth and twentieth centuries, the Legislature has given extended powers to the Crown or its servants to legislate. Of the use made by the Legislature of this expedient during the eighteenth century, and at earlier periods, I must, at this point, say something.

During the course of the nineteenth and twentieth centuries the Legislature has given large powers to the Crown or its servants to make rules, orders, or regulations of a legislative character.[1] At the present day these rules, orders, or regulations cover all and more than all of the sphere occupied by proclamations in the Tudor and early Stuart period.[2] But in the eighteenth century the jealousy of the prerogative felt by Parliament prevented the Legislature from making any large additions to the powers—legislative or otherwise—of the Crown or its servants. The memory of the constitutional controversies of the seventeenth century still exercised a great influence over the minds of statesmen ; the Whig party, which was predominant till 1760, were traditionally opposed to any extension of the prerogative ; and George III, and the new Tory party which he created, found that they could effect their objects more easily and with less

[1] C. T. Carr, Delegated Legislation 1-18.
[2] " In mere bulk the child now dwarfs the parent. Last year (1920), while 82 Acts of Parliament were placed on the statute book, more than ten times as many " Statutory Rules and Orders " of a public character were officially registered under the Rules Publication Act. The annual volume of public general statutes for 1920 occupied less than 600 pages ; the two volumes of statutory rules and orders for the same period occupy about five times as many. This excess in mere point of bulk of delegated legislation over direct legislation has been visible for nearly thirty years," ibid 2 ; and this does not complete the tale, for not all delegated legislation is published under the Rules Publication Act. ibid n. 1.

odium by their influence over the Legislature.[1] It is true that
statutes, especially financial statutes, gave the Crown powers to
take the means necessary to create machinery for their enforcement ; [2] and to that extent they enlarged the powers of the
Crown.   But neither in the eighteenth nor in earlier centuries are
there many instances in which the Crown was given a statutory
power to make regulations of a legislative kind binding upon all
its subjects.   A short survey of the legislation of the eighteenth
and earlier centuries will make this clear.[3]

The chief if not the only clear instances in which, before
the eighteenth century, the Crown was given a wide power to
make regulations of a legislative kind are, first a statute concerning the Staple (1385), secondly Henry VIII's statute of Sewers
(1531), thirdly Henry VIII's statute of Proclamations (1539),
and fourthly Henry VIII's statute of Wales (1542-1543).

The statute of the Staple [4] provided that the staple should be
held in England, but left it to the King's council to provide for
the places at which, and the times during which, it was to be
held, and for its due ordering and government.   It then enacted
that the provisions made by the council were to have legislative
force.[5]   This is a strong instance of the delegation of legislative
power to the Crown ; but it should be noted that the statute
was passed at a time when the legislative procedure of Parliament
was not fixed in its final form, and when the King was still regarded as playing the most important part in the enactment of
statutes.[6]   We have seen that it was not till the fifteenth century
that the Commons claimed to be as well assentors to as petitioners
for legislation.[7]   The statute of Sewers [8] gives the commissioners
wide legislative powers, as well as taxing and judicial powers.

---

[1] Vol. x 101.

[2] Thus the Acts relating to customs and excise gave the commissioners of
customs and excise powers which Blackstone said " increased to a very formidable
height" their power over the property of the people, Comm. iv 281 ; these powers
provoked Dr. Johnson's definition in his Dictionary of the term " Excise" cited
vol. x 454 n. 8 ; that definition might have exposed him to a prosecution had not
Murray, the attorney-general, advised that a prosecution would be imprudent, Boswell,
Life of Johnson (ed. 1811) i 269 n. 5 ; these Acts aroused considerable opposition
in Parliament, see Parlt. Hist. xxvi 117-120, xxviii 231-232, 748-749 ; it should be
noted that they restricted the right of the subject to appeal to the courts, by writ of
certiorari, against the decision of the commissioners, R. v. Whitehead (1780) 2
Dougl. 549.

[3] On this matter see Report of Committee on Ministers' Powers 1932,
Cmd. 4060, 10-15.

[4] It is not included in the Record Commission Ed. of the Statutes, but is to be
found in R.P. iii 204, and it is cited Stubbs, C.H. ii 641 n. 1.

[5] Quod Stapula teneatur in Anglia ; sed in quibus erit locis, et quando incipiet,
ac de modo et forma regiminis et gubernationis ejusdem, ordinabitur postmodum
per consilium domini regis, auctoritate parliamenti ; et quod id quod per dictum
consilium in hac parte fuerit ordinatum, virtutem parliamenti habeat et vigorem."

[6] Vol. ii 436-439.   [7] Ibid 439.

[8] 23 Henry VIII c. 5 § 2 ; vol. x 203.

Their acts and ordinances were to be in force while their commission lasted; but if they were certified into the Chancery and given the royal assent, they were to be in force permanently.[1] We have seen that Henry VIII's statute of Proclamations [2] gave the Crown a power to issue proclamations having the force of law, but that it provided that the common law, statute law, and rights of property could not be affected by these proclamations. We have seen that a clause in the statute of Wales [3] gave the King power to make laws for Wales which were to have the same effect as if they had been made by the authority of Parliament.[4]

The statute of Proclamations was repealed in 1547,[5] and the clause of the statute of Wales in 1624.[6] The staple towns and staple courts had disappeared by the beginning of the seventeenth century.[7] Thus at the beginning of the eighteenth century there were very few instances in which the Crown or the servants of the Crown had a statutory power to legislate. Nor were such powers given extensively in the eighteenth century. Apart from the powers given to the commissioners of excise,[8] the chief instance of the gift of such a power is to be found in the Mutiny Act of 1717.[9] That Act empowered the Crown to make articles of war for the government of its troops both within the kingdoms of Great Britain and Ireland and beyond the seas. But the extent of the power given aroused opposition; [10] and in 1749 its scope was cut down by the proviso that no persons within the kingdoms of Great Britain and Ireland could be adjudged, by virtue of the articles of war, to suffer any punishment extending to life or limb, unless their crimes had been made so punishable by the Mutiny Act.[11]

[1] §§ 16, 17.   [2] 31 Henry VIII c. 8 ; vol. iv 102-104.
[3] 34, 35 Henry VIII c. 26 § 59 ; vol. iv 38.
[4] It was enacted by this clause that the laws made by the King for Wales " shalbe of as good strengthe vertue and effecte as if they had been hadde and made by authoritie of Parliament" ; two statutes of 1536 and 1547, 28 Henry VIII c. 17 and 1 Edward VI c. 11, gave power to the successors of Henry VIII and Edward VI, if they succeeded to the throne while still under age, to repeal, on the attainment of the age of twenty-four, statutes made between their accession to the throne and the attainment of that age ; this was then regarded, not as the grant of a power to legislate, but as an application of the mediæval doctrine, known as the demurrer of the parol, vol. iii 513-514, that an infant's position must not be prejudiced by acts done during his minority ; this doctrine had, from the time of Henry III, been applied to the King, P. and M. H.E.L. (1st ed.) i 507 ; vol. iii 464 n. 6 ; for in the Middle Ages the doctrines that the King could do no wrong, and could not be affected by the disabilities of minority, were not then recognized, vol. iii 464-466 ; the two statutes of 1536 and 1547 were repealed in 1751, 24 George II c. 24 § 23.
[5] 1 Edward VI c. 12 § 4.   [6] 21 James I c. 10
[7] Malynes, Lex Mercatoria 135, cited vol. i 570.
[8] Vol. x 454, and n. 9.
[9] 3 George I c. 2 ; cp. Maitland, Constitutional History 449.
[10] Vol. x 379-380 ; Report of Committee on Ministers' Powers 1932, Cmd. 4060, 12.
[11] 22 George II c. 5 § 57.

There are very few other instances in which the Crown or its servants were given by Parliament a delegated power to legislate.[1] It is true that some of the autonomous bodies, through which the local government was conducted, were occasionally given,[2] but more often assumed, this power.[3] It is true that the departments of the central government, the courts, and Parliament, assumed power to make rules for the discipline of their members, for the better ordering of their business, and for carrying out the statutory duties which were imposed upon them;[4] and it was seldom that a statute expressly conferred upon them powers to do any acts necessary for the carrying out of the duties imposed upon them by the statute.[5] It is true that the power to make rules assumed by some of these autonomous bodies is similar to the delegated powers to legislate given by modern statutes—for instance the power assumed by the courts in the eighteenth and earlier centuries to make rules of procedure now rests upon the statutory basis of the Judicature Acts.[6] But when all deductions have been made, it would be true to say that, in the eighteenth century, nearly all of the legislative work of the state was done by Parliament. Nothing which involved a change in the law, however trifling, could be effected except by an Act of Parliament; and since the Crown had ceased to possess any suspending or dispensing power,[7] it was necessary to invoke the authority of Parliament not only to suspend the operation of the ordinary law in a time of emergency,[8] but also to dispense with the ordinary law in favour of individuals in cases where the strictness of its rules worked inconvenience or injustice.[9]

It was inevitable in these circumstances that the methods and forms of Parliamentary legislation should be elaborated. It is in this elaboration, which was going on all through the eighteenth century, that we can see the beginnings of some of the familiar features of our modern statute book. Therefore I shall, in the first place, say something of the formalities of legislation; and, in the second place, I shall deal with the contribution made by the eighteenth-century statutes to legal development.

---

[1] One instance is a statute of 1785 which gave the commissioners for stamp duties the power to make regulations for securing the duties imposed on post horses and carriages, 25 George III c. 51 § 51; another instance is the permission given to the Crown by 31 George III c. 30 § 14 to allow, by orders in council, corn to be exported, notwithstanding the provisions of that Act.

[2] One instance is the power given to quarter sessions by 31 George II c. 29 § 14 to settle the jurisdictional areas for the setting of the assize of bread.

[3] Vol. x 234-235.   [4] Ibid 221.   [5] 25 George III c. 51 § 5.

[6] 39, 40 Victoria c. 59 § 17; 44, 45 Victoria c. 68 § 19; 57, 58 Victoria c. 16 § 4; 15, 16 George V c. 49 § 99.

[7] Vol. vi 240-241.

[8] E.g. to suspend the Habeas Corpus Act.   [9] Below 624.

I

THE FORMALITIES OF LEGISLATION

A very cursory glance at the contents of the statute book of the eighteenth century shows us that there were substantial differences between different classes of statutes. Some were obviously public and general : others were obviously local or personal. It was inevitable that differences should arise in the procedure adopted by Parliament for dealing with the bills presented to it for public, local, or personal objects ; and that the statutes into which these bills were converted should be treated, in some respects, differently. It is for this reason that we begin to see in the eighteenth century the beginnings of modern classification of the statutes and modern methods of publishing them, and the beginnings of the modern differences between public and private bill procedure. Moreover, we begin to get more precise information, than in earlier periods of history, as to the manner in which these bills were drafted. I shall therefore deal with this topic under the following heads : The classification and publication of the statutes ; the process of making statutes ; and the drafting of legislative proposals.

The Classification and Publication of the Statutes

These two topics are, and, throughout their history, have been, closely related. I propose to state briefly the existing rules as to these two matters, and then to give a short sketch of the stages by which these rules have been reached.

In 1868 statutes were divided into three classes : (1) Public General Acts ; (2) Local Acts ; and (3) Private Acts.[1] These three classes are distinguished by the different type used in numbering their chapters.[2] The local Acts of each session, including those passed as public Acts but treated as local, are printed at the end of each session in separate volumes. The private Acts are not always printed ; but a list of these Acts is printed in the table of local and private Acts appended to the annual volumes of the public general Acts.[3] From 1887 the public general statutes for the year are printed annually in an octavo volume which is edited by an official paid by the Treasury.[4]

---

[1] Ilbert, Legislative Methods and Forms 26, 64.

[2] " Public General Acts have their chapters in Arabic characters (62 and 63 Vict. No. 10) ; Local Acts in small Roman numerals (62 and 63 Vict. No. x) ; Private Acts (if printed) in italicized Arabic figures (62 and 63 Vict. No. *10*)," ibid 27.

[3] Ibid.

[4] Ibid 26 ; before 1887 the annual statutes were printed in different forms and at different prices, ibid ; below 319-320.

Each volume contains the public general Acts, a table of the titles of these Acts arranged chronologically in the order in which they received the royal assent, a table showing the effect of these Acts on preceding public general Acts, a table of the local and private Acts including public Acts of a local character, and since 1925, the measures passed by the National Assembly of the Church of England which have received the royal assent.[1] Each volume also contains indices to the public general Acts, and the church assembly Measures, and to the local and private Acts.

The stages by which this modern system of the classification and publication of the statutes has been reached can be divided roughly into the following periods: (1) the position down to 1539; (2) developments from 1539 to 1797; and (3) the development of the modern system.

(1) *The position down to* 1539.

At a time when all statutes were made by the King on the petition either of Parliament, or of private persons or bodies of persons,[2] there was not and could not be any distinction between public and private Acts of Parliament. We have seen that, during the fourteenth century, enactments made on the petition of Parliament were separated from enactments made by the Crown without such petition; and that it was only the former which were regarded as Acts of Parliament.[3] But so long as all Acts of Parliament were made by the King on the petition of Parliament, the distinction between public and private Acts could not easily emerge. All Acts began by a petition, and all were enacted by the King.[4] It was the introduction, in the fifteenth century, of the new system of legislation by bill, and the recognition of the fact that statutes were enacted by the authority, not of the King alone, but of the King in Parliament,[5] which gave precision and technical form to a distinction, which must always have existed in substance—the distinction between those petitions which asked for some general law which affected the whole community, and those petitions which asked for a law which affected only a particular person or community or locality.

[1] This is the result of § 4 of the Church of England Assembly (Powers) Act 1919, 9, 10 George V c. 76, under which Measures submitted by the Legislative Committee of the Church Assembly and reported to Parliament by the Ecclesiastical Committee (which is a committee of the two Houses of Parliament), are to be laid before Parliament; on a resolution of both Houses to that effect, they are to be laid before the King; on his assent being given they are to have the same effect as an Act of Parliament.

[2] Vol. ii 436.

[3] Ibid 437; for the gradual evolution of the idea that a statute is a legislative act assented to by King and Parliament see Richardson and Sayles, the Early Statutes L.Q.R. l 555-563.

[4] Vol. ii 438-439.   [5] Ibid 439-440.

From the latter part of the fifteenth century onwards, general laws which affected the whole community were made by bill, and ceased to be initiated by petition.[1] On the other hand, laws which affected only a particular person or community or locality —laws which created something in the nature of a privilegium— continued to be and still are initiated by petition.[2] Thus arose the origin of the distinction between public and general, and private Acts of Parliament. In the case of public Acts the procedure by petition has disappeared; but, as Palgrave said in 1833,[3] " private Acts have arisen out of the old course; all the private Acts are only the ancient petitions in a new shape. . . . The practice of our modern Parliament in passing private Bills . . . are exactly the old remnants of the old petitions for redress when the ordinary courts could not grant relief."

Thus, by the end of the fifteenth century the two forms of enactment were distinct; and, since the formal distinction corresponded to a substantial difference, technical differences between the two classes of enactment soon began to appear. These differences can be summarized as follows :

First by 1509,[4] and probably earlier,[5] it was recognized that the proper form of royal assent to a public Act was " Le Roy le veult," whilst the proper form of assent to a private Act was " Soit fait comme il est desiré." Secondly, in the middle of the fifteenth century a public Act was always enrolled, but a private Act was not enrolled except at the request of the promoters of the Act.[6] In 1483 the practice changed. We have seen that from that date all Acts were for a short time enrolled.[7] In 1539 the

---

[1] " Both (public and private bills) had their rise in the ancient petitions to the Crown for redress of public or private grievances. All trace of this origin has disappeared from public bills, which are now introduced without question in the Lords, and by leave of the House, at the instance of any member in the Commons. . . . Petitions against public bills are the only survival of the old form," Clifford, History of Private Bill Legislation i 270 and n. 4.

[2] " Private bills, with some exceptions, can only be brought into either House upon petition from the promoters, and thus retain traces of an ancient form which has in their case survived for well nigh six hundred years," ibid i 270.

[3] Parlt. Papers 1833 xii 174.

[4] Clifford, op. cit. i 311 says, " the existing forms are authoritatively declared in the Lords' Journals for 1509 and again in 1597 "; in 1706-1707 a bill was introduced to substitute equivalent English formulæ for the French formulæ, but though it was read a second time and committed, it failed to pass, MSS. of the House of Lords (Hist. MSS. Com.) vii no. 2365.

[5] An Act of 1504 appears on the Parliament rolls with the form of assent proper for a private bill; this is run through with a pen, and the form of assent proper for a public bill is inserted, Clifford, op. cit. i 313; Statutes (Rec. Com.) i *lxxi*.

[6] In Y.B. 33 Hy. VI Pasch. pl. 8, Kirkby, the clerk of the Parliament rolls, said that if the King and Lords agreed to a bill sent up by the Commons, it was handed over to the clerk of the Parliament to be enrolled, " et si soit un common bill il sera enrolle et enacte : mes si soit un particular bill, il ne sera enrolle, mes sera file sur le filace, et est assez bien : mes si la party veut suir pur l'entre pour estre le mieux sure, il purroit estre enrolle etc."

[7] Vol. ii 426 and n. 6.

distinction between public and private Acts is specifically stated on the rolls ; [1] and this specific statement was of great assistance to those who published collected editions of public Acts, because they were able to separate these Acts from private Acts.[2] We have seen that from 1593 to 1758 only the titles of private Acts were enrolled ; [3] and that after 1758 even their titles ceased to appear.[4] From 1593 their text is to be found only in the series of original Acts in the Parliament Office.[5] If it was necessary to give evidence of their existence they were certified into Chancery by the clerk of the Parliament in answer to a writ issued for that purpose.[6] Thirdly, in the latter part of the fifteenth century it was a well-established rule that a public Act need not be specially pleaded, but that a private Act must be specially pleaded.[7] Fourthly, by the end of the fifteenth century differences were arising as to the methods by which public and private Acts were promulgated and published. We shall now see that these differences as to promulgation and publication accentuated the distinction between these two classes of Acts, and gave rise to other formal differences between them.

Though it was said in 1366 that publication was not needed to give a statute validity,[8] it is obvious that some form of publica-

[1] Statutes (Rec. Com.) i *lxvi*.

[2] Previously the publishers of these editions had treated the Acts published in the sessional publications of the statutes, below 291, as public Acts, and all others as private ; by so doing they were led into error, since some of the Acts not printed in these publications were public Acts, see the Preface to vol. iii of the Rec. Com. Ed. of the statutes ; thus 5 Henry VIII c. 5, " an Act concerning the grant of the King's general pardon is rightly printed as a public Act, but 7 Henry VIII c. 5, which is also an Act concerning the King's general pardon, is classed as a private Act ; it is not till after 1539, and in consequence of the specific statement on the roll, that this confusion began to be cleared up ; but this was merely a formal distinction ; and it was not till later that the substantial distinctions were evolved ; for some time, therefore, the classification is not always consistent, e.g. 32 Henry VIII c. 11, the Act for the attainder of Thomas Cromwell, is classified as a private Act, but 33 Henry VIII c. 26, an Act to avoid certain conveyances made by Sir John Shelton is classified as a public Act ; and local Acts are classified sometimes as private and sometimes as public on no ascertainable principle ; it is not till the following period that the rules laid down by the courts and by the two Houses of Parliament gradually drew the modern substantial distinctions between the two classes of Act, below 294-301.

[3] Vol. ii 426 n. 6 ; from 1583 to 1593 the enrolment of private Acts was intermittent.

[4] Ibid.   [5] For this series see vol. ii 426.

[6] Statutes (Rec. Com.) i *lxii ;* in order to make this cumbrous procedure unnecessary some local and personal Acts provided that they should be printed by the King's Printer, and that a copy so printed should be evidence, ibid ; below 298.

[7] " En Bank le Roy en le case de Seignior *Say* vers ceux de Nottingham fuit tenus que un act de Parliament que touts corporations et licences grauntes per le Roy Henry etc. serront voide, que ils covient estre pledes, et le Court n'est tenus d'aver conusance de eux, nient pluis que un particular act, pur un particular person. . . . Ou un act est general que extende a chescun home, ceo ne besoigne d'estre plede, car il est general et commen ley etc.," Y.B. 13 Ed. IV Pasch. pl. 4.

[8] Y.B. 39 Ed. III Pasch. pl. 7 *per* Thorpe C.J., cited vol. ii 436 n. 5 ; that the mediæval methods of publication were not effective is shown by the ignorance of pleaders and judges as to their wording, Plucknett, Statutes and their Interpretation 103-112.

tion was very necessary. The official measures [1] taken to secure publication before the introduction of printing, are thus described by the Record Commissioners : [2]

The publication of the statutes of England was made by means of exemplifications thereof, sent to the sheriffs, under the great seal, out of Chancery, with writs annexed, requiring the proclamation and publication of the same by them, and sometimes also directing copies to be made and distributed, and the sheriffs to return what was done by them thereupon. The earliest statutes were published in this manner ; as appears not only by copies of the writs subjoined to the records and manuscripts of the respective statutes of the thirteenth century, but also by original writs still preserved in the Tower of London.

Moreover, copies of the statutes enrolled in the Chancery, certified under the great seal, were sent to the three common law courts with orders to those courts to enroll and enforce them.[3] Collected editions of the statutes began to be printed in 1482 or 1483 ; [4] and the regular publication of the statutes of each session begins in 1484.[5] Of the earlier collected editions of the statutes down to the end of the seventeenth century I have already given some account.[6] The sessional publication of the statutes was, no doubt, from the first, made by printers authorized by the Crown, and afterwards by the official known as the King's Printer ; [7] but " no perfect series of these sessional publications has yet been collected together ; and of some few years no printed copy is now known to exist." [8]

---

[1] For other unofficial means of diffusing a knowledge of the statutes see vol. ii 436 n. 4.

[2] Statutes (Rec. Com.) i *xlv*, and the references cited in n. 1 ; ibid App. H. 1 ; vol. ii 436 ; L.Q.R. l 546-548 ; Coke says, Second Instit. 526, that " before printing and till the reign of H. 7 statutes were ingrossed in parchment and by the King's writ proclaimed by the sherife of every county : this was the ancient law of England, that the King's commandments issued, and were published in form of writs " ; cp. also Fourth Instit. 26 ; in the case of proclamations the old system lasted much longer ; in 1796 a committee of the House of Commons reported that writs under the great seal were issued to the sheriffs and others commanding them to publish the proclamation set out in the schedule to the writ ; fourteen copies of the proclamation were sent which were directed to be set up in public places, Reports from Committees of the House of Commons xiv 121.

[3] Y.B. 8 Ed. II (S.S.) *xvii*.

[4] Statutes (Rec. Com.) i App. A ; vol. iv 308.

[5] Statutes (Rec. Com.) i *xlv*, and App. B ; " These publications, from 1 Ric. III to 3 Car. I inclusive, contain the body of the statute as made in each session ; the several Acts or Chapters thereof, being distinguished by numbers and titles. From 16 Car. I they consist of the several Acts of the session ; each being printed separately, but paged progressively, from the beginning to the end of Session," ibid *lvi*.

[6] Vol. iv 308-310 ; vol. vi 312-313.

[7] Professor Winfield, Chief Sources of English Legal History 91 n. 3, says that the " first traceable King's Printer is William Faques (*circa* 1504) who describes himself on the title page of his books as " Regius Impressor." Richard Pynson succeeded him in 1518, and published the first book issued " cum privilegio " ; but the earlier sessional publications may well have had some sort of royal sanction ; for the King's Printer and the history of his connection with the publication of the statutes see below 302-303.

[8] Statutes (Rec. Com.) i *lvi*.

We shall see that in later centuries the King's Printer, besides printing the statutes from the ingrossed text of the original Acts,[1] did a certain amount of editorial work.[2] At this point, and from the point of view of the distinction between public and private Acts, the important matter to note is the fact that the King's Printer did not include private Acts, nor indeed all public Acts,[3] in his sessional publication of the statutes. At first private Acts were not mentioned in his sessional publication ; but after 1571 their titles were printed.[4]

The Record Commissioners in their edition of the statutes took 1539—the date at which the distinction between public and private Acts is specifically stated on the rolls [5]—as the date from which they ceased to print the private Acts *in extenso*.[6] Their action emphasized the fact that, by that date, the distinction between the two classes of Acts was formally established. But we have seen that, though the formal distinction between them was established, the substantial distinctions had not yet been elaborated.[7] We must now trace the history of the process by which these distinctions were so developed and elaborated by the courts and by Parliament, that they became the centre of a mass of technical rules, which were neither very clear nor very consistent.

(2) *Developments from 1539 to 1797.*

We have seen that by the year 1539 some of the technical differences between a public and general Act and a private or particular Act were already recognized. A private Act must be specially pleaded by a litigant who wished to rely upon it,[8] it was not printed by the King's Printer,[9] it was initiated by the petition of the persons or bodies who promoted it,[10] and the King gave his assent to it in a form of words which differed from the form in which he gave his assent to a public bill.[11] But what was the substantial difference between the two forms of Act ? There is I think no doubt that Blackstone's statement of this difference is as applicable to the sixteenth as to the eighteenth century. It is as follows : [12]

---

[1] Since the original rolls suffered from being sent to the printer, the Commons in 1662 sent a message to the Lords asking that " the original rolls of Acts of Parliament be kept in the office, and not delivered to the printer, but that true copies be delivered to him from the roll, fairly written and carefully examined and attested," Statutes (Rec. Com.) i *xlv* n. 5.

[2] Below 303-304.
[3] Above 290 n. 2.
[4] Statutes (Rec. Com.) i *lvi*.
[5] Above 289-290.
[6] Statutes (Rec. Com.) i *xxxiii*.
[7] Above 290 n. 2.
[8] Above 290.
[9] Above n. 3.
[10] Above 289.
[11] Above 289.
[12] Comm. i 85-86.

Statutes are either *general* or *special, public* or *private*. A general or public Act is an universal rule, that regards the whole community ; and of this the courts of law are bound to take notice judicially and *ex officio ;* without the statute being particularly pleaded, or formally set forth by the party who claims an advantage under it. Special or private acts are rather exceptions than rules, being those which only operate upon particular persons or private concerns . . . and of these (which are not promulgated with the same notoriety as the former) the judges are not bound to take notice, unless they be formally shewn and pleaded.

But though it is comparatively easy to draw a theoretical distinction of this kind, it is not so easy to apply it in practice ; and the difficulty was increased when the ingenuity of hostile litigants in the courts, and the pecuniary interests of the officials of both Houses of Parliament, combined to prevent the impartial application of this theoretical distinction to Acts which were on the border line between public and private. In fact there are many such border line Acts. In Parliament to-day there is a class of " hybrid bills " ; [1] and the courts have been obliged to recognize that an Act may be public in respect to some of its clauses, and private in respect to others.[2]

In these circumstances it was inevitable that the technical differences between public and private Acts, which were beginning to be apparent at the beginning of the sixteenth century, should be developed. They were developed on different lines by the courts and by Parliament, in such a way that it sometimes seems that the substantial difference in principle, upon which all these technical distinctions were founded, was almost submerged.

The committee of the House of Commons, which reported in 1796,[3] pointed out that the meaning attached in the language of the law to the terms " Public and Private Acts," differed from the meaning attached to these terms in the language of Parliament. In the language of the law public and general Acts, of which the courts took judicial notice, were Acts concerning the King, the Queen, and the Prince, Acts concerning all persons of a class such as all the clergy or all the sheriffs, Acts concerning trade in general or all persons pursuing a particular trade, Acts concerning all persons generally, although they related to a particular matter ; but private Acts, which must be specially pleaded, were Acts concerning only a particular species, thing,

[1] " When a public Bill affects private interests in such a manner that if it were a private Bill the Standing Orders would require notices to be given, it is called a hybrid Bill, and the practice is to refer the Bill to the examiners of Standing Orders like a private Bill, and to make the Bill proceed in nearly the same way as if it were a private Bill," Ilbert, Legislative Methods and Forms 29 ; for the quasi-judicial procedure used in the passing of private bills see below 324-351.

[2] Below 294.

[3] Reports from Committees of the House of Commons, xiv 122 *note*, cited Ilbert, Legislative Methods and Forms 48 n. 3.

or person, such as Acts relating to the bishops only or to the toleration of dissenters, or Acts concerning a particular place. In the language of Parliament a public or general Act was an Act upon which no fees were payable to the officers of either House, whilst a private Act was an Act upon which fees were payable; and some Acts, though local or personal, were accounted as public by virtue of a special clause to that effect in the Act. I must now trace the steps by which these results had been attained. I shall deal with the evolution first of the legal, and secondly of the Parliamentary, distinctions.

The legal distinctions.

It is clear from Coke's report of *Holland's Case* [1] that the application of the distinction between general and particular statutes had given rise to a mass of detailed rules which were not altogether rational or easy to comprehend. Coke tells us that an Act concerning the whole spirituality was a general Act, but that an Act concerning only the bishops was a particular Act; that an Act concerning the sheriffs or other of the King's officers was a general Act, but an Act concerning sheriffs only was a particular Act. So "an Act concerning all the nobility or Lords of Parliament or all the bishops of England, or all corporations made by King H. 6, are special and particular Acts"; and "Acts of Parliament concerning mysteries or trades are General Acts, but an Act of Parliament concerning the trade of grocery is a Special Act." An Act dealing with a particular writ is a general Act because it affects all persons who use that writ. On the other hand, Acts which concern "singular things as any particular manor or house etc., or all manors houses etc., which are in one or sundry particular towns, or in one or divers particular counties," are particular Acts. "But of every Act (although the matter thereof concerns *individua* or singular things) yet if they touch the King" they are general Acts, "for every subject has interest in the King as head of the commonwealth"; and the same is true of Acts which concern the Queen or the Prince of Wales. [2] Later cases added further distinctions which made it still more difficult to draw the line. Acts, as to some of their clauses, might be general, and as to others particular. [3] A particular Act might be accounted as

---

[1] (1597) 4 Co. Rep. at ff. 76a-77a; see also Dive v. Manningham (1551) Plowden at p. 65.

[2] Willion v. Berkley (1561) Plowden at p. 231; the Prince's Case (1606) 8 Co. Rep. at f. 28a.

[3] Case of University of Oxford (1614) 10 Co. Rep. 53b, at f. 57b; cp. Anon (1699) 12 Mod. 249 where Holt C.J. said, "an Act of Parliament concerning the revenue of the King is a public law; but it may be private in respect to some clauses in it relating to a private person"; see also the note to R. v. Inhabitants of Milton (1843) 1 Car. and Kir. 59; in fact the very miscellaneous character of the contents of some of the statutes made this rule very necessary, below 373.

general if it imposed a forfeiture to the Crown for its breach,[1]
or if its provisions had been recognized as general by a public
Act.[2] An Act which, according to the principles laid down by
Coke, ought to have been accounted as a particular Act, was,
in at least one case, held to be a general Act on grounds of convenience ; [3] and the views of the judges as to where the line ought
to be drawn have varied at different periods.[4] It is obvious,
therefore, that, by the end of the eighteenth century, it was often
a difficult matter to determine whether any given Act or part of
an Act was private or public ; and yet, as we shall now see, it
was often of the first importance to litigants to determine this
question. The reasons why it was important can be summarized
as follows :

In the first place, there was the pleading difference, which
goes back to the period of the Year Books.[5] It was not necessary
to plead a public Act because the judges must take judicial notice
of it : it was necessary to plead a private Act, and its existence
as pleaded was " tried by the record upon *nul tiel record* pleaded." [6]
The substantial reason for drawing this distinction was stated
by Coke [7] and Hale [8] to be that, in the case of many of the older
statutes no record was extant,

nor yet any other written evidence of the same, but what is in a manner
only traditional ; as, namely ancient and modern books of pleadings,
and the common received opinion and reputation, and the approbation
of the judges learned in the laws.[9]

If proof by the record had been insisted upon then old statutes
would have ceased to be binding. This reasoning did not apply
to private Acts which must, as we have seen,[10] be strictly proved
by the record.

---

[1] R. v. Buggs (1695) Skin. at p. 429.

[2] Thus there was considerable conflict of opinion as to whether the statute of
23 Henry VI c. 9 as to the taking of bail by sheriffs was a public Act ; but it was held
in Samuel v. Evans (1788) 2 T.R. 569 that, whatever doubts there may formerly have
been, they had been set at rest by 4 Anne c. 16 § 20, which had recognized its public
character.

[3] In Jones v. Axen (1697) 1 Ld. Raym. 119 at p. 120, an Act for the discharge
of poor prisoners was held to be a public Act, " 1. because all the people of England
may be concerned as creditors to these poor prisoners. 2. It is an Act of charity
and therefore ought to have a more candid interpretation. 3. It is an Act too long
and difficult to be pleaded at large, so that it would put these poor people to a greater
expence than they can bear, to plead it specially."

[4] See the arguments in Samuel v. Evans (1788) 2 T.R. 569 ; in Jones v. Axen
(1697) 1 Ld. Raym. at p. 120 Treby C.J. said that " if the Act concerning the bishops
were to be adjudged now, it would be adjudged a general Act."

[5] Above 290.

[6] " The judges and courts of justice are, *ex officio*, bound to take notice of
public acts of parliament, and whether they are truly pleaded or not ;—and therefore
they are the triers of them. But it is otherwise of *private* acts of parliament, for
they may be put in issue and tried by the record upon *nul tiel record* pleaded,
unless they are produced exemplified," Hale, Hist. Com. Law (6th ed.) 15-16.

[7] The Prince's Case (1606) 8 Co. Rep. at f. 28a.

[8] Hist. Com. Law 15, 19-20.

[9] Ibid 15.   [10] Above 290 and n. 6.

In the second place, this difference in the mode of pleading and proving public and private Acts gave rise to many consequential differences in some of the other rules of pleading. Thus, if an action were brought on a public Act, the plaintiff must set out the facts and say that his action was brought for acts done *contra formam statuti ;* [1] but a private Act must be recited in the pleading, and the court would only take notice of so much of it as was recited.[2] If the subject matter of an Act, whether public or private, were mis-recited the error was fatal ; but there were differences, according as the Act was public or private, in the manner in which the opposing party could take advantage of the mistake. In the case of a public Act the misrecital was, as in the case of other faults of pleading, ground for a general demurrer, a motion in arrest of judgment, or a writ of error.[3] In the case of a private Act the misrecital could only be taken advantage of by a plea of *nul tiel record*,[4] or by proving the variance and demurring or moving in arrest of judgment,[5] " for the court cannot in any other manner inform itself of its contents, and therefore till the contrary is shewn must take the Act to be as it is recited." [6]

In the third place, the manner in which a private Act was interpreted differed from the manner in which a public Act was interpreted. A public Act binds all persons who are affected by it ; but a private Act never binds any except the persons mentioned therein. In the case of *Lucy v. Levington* Hale, C.B., said : [7]

Every man is so far party to a private Act of Parliament as not to gainsay it, but not so as to give up his interest ; 'tis the great question in *Barrington's Case*.[8] The matter of the Act there directs it to be between the forresters and the proprietors of the soil ; and therefore it shall not extend to the commoners to take away their common. Suppose an Act says, whereas there is a controversy concerning land between A and B 'tis enacted, that A shall enjoy it. This does not bind others, tho' there be no saving, because it was only intended to end the difference between the two.

[1] Comyns' Digest, *Action on Statute* H ; cp. Lee v. Clarke (1802) 2 East at p. 340 *per* Lawrence J.
[2] Lord Cromwell's Case (1578) 4 Co. Rep. at ff. 12b-13a ; Holby v. Bray (1668) 1 Sid. 356 ; in Platt v. Hill (1699) 1 Ld. Raym. at p. 382 Holt C.J. said, in answer to an exception that a statute had been mis-recited in a plea, " this being a private Act, the Court must take it to be as it is pleaded, unless the plaintiff denies it, as he might by pleading *nul tiel record*, or by alleging that it is farther enacted, etc., and then if it is material he shall take advantage of it."
[3] See e.g. Partridge v. Strange (1553) Plowden at p. 84—count abated for misrecital of a statute ; Mills v. Wilkins (1702) 6 Mod. 62—demurrer upheld ; R. v. Marsack (1796) 6 T.R. 771—motion in arrest of judgment ; there was a good deal of discussion as to what amount of variance was fatal, see Creswick v. Rooksby (1613) 2 Buls. at p. 48 ; R. v. Marsack at pp. 775-776 ; Boyce v. Whitaker (1779) 1 Dougl. at p. 97 ; even an agreement of the parties to waive the misrecital was inoperative—the court must award a repleader, Love v. Wotton (1591) Cro. Eliza. 245 ; see vol. ix 278 and n. 7.
[4] Platt v. Hill (1699) 1 Ld. Raym. at p. 382, cited above n 2.
[5] Ibid ; R. v. Wilde (1672) 1 Lev. 296.
[6] Note G. to Holland's Case (1597) 4 Co. Rep. at f. 77a.
[7] (1671) 1 Ventr. at p. 176.   [8] (1611) 8 Co. Rep. 136b.

It appears from *Barrington's Case* that this was then a well-established principle, and it has always been observed.[1] It follows that the provisions of a private Act, which confer benefits upon the persons to whom it applies, are strictly construed—otherwise the rights of third persons might be affected. As Lord Esher, M.R., once said : [2]

In the case of a public Act you construe it keeping in view the fact that it must be taken to have been passed for the public advantage, and you apply certain fixed canons to its construction. In the case of a private Act, which is obtained by persons for their own benefit, you construe more strictly provisions which they allege to be in their favour, because the persons who obtain a private Act ought to take care, that it is so worded that that which they desire to obtain for themselves is plainly stated in it.

We shall see later that the very peculiar process by which private Acts were made induced the courts to treat them differently in several other respects from public Acts.[3]

The difficulties placed in the way of litigants by the hazy character of the distinction between public and private Acts, and by the legal consequences which flowed therefrom, were increased, first, by the action of the courts in admitting various exceptions to its principles ; and, secondly, by the action of Parliament and the interpretation put by the courts on that action.

First, though it was generally true that public Acts will be judicially noticed and that private Acts must be pleaded, there were exceptions to both branches of the rule. After some conflict of opinion, the courts held that a statute of limitations must be pleaded ; [4] and though an Act of general pardon is a public Act which need not be pleaded,[5] yet Coke notes that " in these days the general pardons have so many qualifications and exceptions of offences and things, and of persons also, that the court cannot take notice of them, neither can the party take benefit or advantage thereof, unless he plead it." [6] There were also a few cases in which the necessity of pleading a private Act was dispensed with. If to an action for anything done under

---

[1] 8 Co. Rep. at f. 138a ; Coke cites a case of Henry VII's reign, and Boswel's Case in Curia Wardorum of 1584, " where it was resolved that when an Act makes a conveyance good against the King, or any other person or persons in certain, it shall not take away the right of any other, although there be not any saving in the Act" ; cp. Bl. Comm. ii 345.

[2] Altrincham Union v. Cheshire Lines Committee (1885) 15 Q.B.D. at p. 603.

[3] Below 354-364.

[4] Puckle v. Moor (1672) 1 Ventr. 191 ; Gould v. Johnson (1702) 2 Ld. Raym. 838.

[5] Third Instit. 234.

[6] Ibid ; in Ingram v. Foot (1702) 1 Ld. Raym. at p. 709 Holt C.J. said that the court was not bound to take notice of an Act of Pardon unless so directed by the Act and that therefore the Act ought to be pleaded.

the Act the defendant was allowed to plead the general issue, he need not plead the Act, but could prove its provisions as evidence to support his plea ; [1] and, as we have seen, if a private Act had been recognized as a public Act, it took effect as a public Act.[2]

Secondly, in order to relieve persons from the necessity of proving and specially pleading a private Act, Parliament sometimes provided either that the Act was to be deemed to be a public Act and judicially noticed as such, or that copies printed by the King's Printer could be put in as evidence of it. Both these provisions were restrictively construed by the courts. The provision that the Act was to be deemed to be a public Act was held to apply only to methods of pleading and proof.[3] The provision did not give it all the characteristics of a public Act—in particular, like any other private Act, it could not affect the rights of third persons not mentioned in the Act.[4] The provision that a copy of the Act should be printed by the King's Printer, and that it could be put in as evidence, only made it possible for a person relying upon the Act to use the copy as evidence : it did not enable the opposite party to rely on an objection founded on the copy of the Act, if it had not been put in as evidence by his opponent.[5]

We shall now see that the Parliamentary distinctions drawn between public and private bills were as elaborate and confused as the legal distinction.

The Parliamentary distinctions.

The three main Parliamentary distinctions between a public and a private bill were, first, the fact that a private bill was initiated by the petition of its promoters,[6] secondly, the fact that fees were payable upon it,[7] and thirdly, the fact that the royal assent was given in a special form.[8] It was the second of these distinctions which had the most important effect upon the Parliamentary distinction between a public and a private bill.

We shall see that the officials of the Houses of Parliament, like the officials of the courts of common law and equity,[9] were, till the beginning of the nineteenth century, paid by fees upon the work which they did.[10] Of these fees by far the largest part

---

[1] Dwarris, Treatise on Statutes (2nd ed.) 470. [2] Above 295.
[3] See Beaumont v. Mountain (1834) 10 Bing. 405.
[4] Hesse v. Stevenson (1803) 3 B. and P. at p. 578 ; Brett v. Beales (1829) Moo. and Malk. at p. 425.
[5] Greswolde v. Kemp (1842) Car. and Marsh. 635 ; to obviate the necessity of proving that the Act had been printed by the King's Printer it was sometimes provided that such proof should not be necessary, see Woodward v. Cotton (1834) 1 C.M. and R. 44.
[6] Above 289. [7] Above 294. [8] Above 289.
[9] Vol. i 255-256, 424-425. [10] Below 337-340.

was derived from private bill legislation; and at the end of the eighteenth, and during the first part of the nineteenth century, they formed the largest part of the incomes of the officials of the two Houses.

As early as 1607 there is evidence that the Speaker was careful to see that his fees and the fees of the other officers of the House on private bills were paid;[1] and, by the middle of the century, the officers of the House of Commons had invented a system by which more than one fee was charged on the same bill.[2] In 1649 a table of fees authorized the clerk to take a fee from every person taking a benefit under any private bill or proviso thereto;[3] and these exactions were largely increased in the eighteenth century. Inclosure Acts, where many interests were concerned, carried enormous fees in addition to all the other costs; and, just as suits in equity swallowed up in costs the whole amount of the property about which the litigation arose,[4] so "instances are numerous in which the cost of an Inclosure Act was barely paid by the sale of all the land inclosed."[5] Whenever legislation seemed likely to affect the fees of the officials there were loud protests. In 1709 they protested because a general naturalization Act had deprived them of their fees on naturalization bills, and because a standing order as to printing private bills had deprived them of their fees for making copies of the bill.[6] But, in fact and in practice, the officials had very little cause to complain. In the course of the eighteenth century they found no difficulty in increasing their fees, and getting the Houses to sanction their usurpations.[7]

In these circumstances it was to the interest of the officials to enlarge as much as they could the definition of a private bill. No doubt they were helped by the confused character of the definitions accepted in the law courts; but they were also helped

[1] "After much delay in a bill for repairing highways in Sussex, Surrey, and Kent, a member moved that it might have some expedition. . . . Mr. Speaker answered 'that the Bill was long and of much labour to the clerk; that it was followed and pressed as a public Bill, but was indeed, by all former precedents, to be accounted and taken as a private Bill, being only for three shires; yet no fees were paid for it to the officers, nor any man took care to answer them.' Thereupon the House ordered 'that the ordinary duties should be performed, or else there should be no further proceeding in the Bill,'" Clifford, History of Private Bill Legislation ii 722; in 1621 a member said, "Theise private bills benefitt yow Mr. Speaker," Notestein, Commons Debates 279; in 1751 a Standing Order provided that "no bill or clause for the particular interest or benefit of any person or persons, county or counties, corporation or corporations, or body or bodies of people shall be read a second time unless fees be paid for the same," Parlt. Papers 1830 xxx 161-162.
[2] Clifford, op. cit. ii 722-723.   [3] Ibid.   [4] Vol. ix 374.
[5] Clifford, op. cit. ii 733; for this reason it was provided in 1801 that, if the extent of the land to be inclosed did not exceed three hundred acres, only a single fee was to be charged, and if it did not exceed one hundred acres only a half fee, Parlt. Papers 1810 ii 219.
[6] Clifford, op. cit. ii 724-725.   [7] Ibid 728-730; below 338-339.

by the vagueness of the rules of the two Houses ; and still more
by their own ingenuity. In the first half of the eighteenth
century, says Clifford,[1] " measures which would now undoubtedly
be classed as of a public character had been gradually made to
pay toll " ; and Hatsell gives a long list of such cases.[2] The
House of Commons tried to draw a clear line of distinction in
1751.[3] Bills for the particular interest of counties or corporations,
or persons or bodies of persons, were to be classed as private bills
for the purpose of the payment of fees ; and fees must be paid
for every enacting clause in a bill, whether public or private,
which was for the benefit of any of these particular interests.
Bills relating to counties, corporations, or bodies of persons were
" double bills," that is they paid double fees ; but if more than
three such bodies were concerned in the bill each body only
paid a single fee. Every distinct provision for a county, corporation, person, or body of persons carried a fee, and likewise
every provision for a distinct interest, estate, or matter.[4] The
House of Commons no doubt intended to put a limit upon the
power of the officials of the House to extend arbitrarily the
categories of bills which carried fees, and the amount of those
fees ; but the officials had little difficulty in getting round its
resolutions. A striking instance of their success is the fact that
in 1788 fees were charged upon a bill for consolidating the laws
relating to the export of wool.[5]

It is thus obvious that the lawyers and the officials had
combined to obscure the classification of Acts of Parliament.
An Act might be private in the eyes of the law for some purposes and public for others. It might be private in respect of
some of its clauses and public in respect of others. It might
have begun by being private, and have become public by being
recognized in a public Act. On the other hand, many Acts
stated to be public from the point of view of judicial notice,
were regarded by the courts as private from other points of
view, and from all points of view by the officials of the two
Houses of Parliament ; and many Acts regarded as private by
these officials must have been regarded as public by the courts.
In these circumstances the work of authors who published editions of the public statutes was difficult. It would have been
still more difficult if they had not been assisted by the work

[1] History of Private Bill Legislation ii 730.
[2] Precedents ii 268-269 (at pp. 209-210 of the 1st ed.), cited Clifford, op. cit.
ii 730-731.
[3] Hatsell, op. cit. (1st ed.) ii 211.
[4] These Orders are printed in Parlt. Papers 1830 xxx 161-162.
[5] Clifford, op. cit. ii 731 ; the officials could always get the last word if the
Speaker agreed with them, as he generally did, because he could hold back the bill
till the fees were paid ; for a case where he adopted that course in 1782 see Hatsell,
op. cit. (1st ed.) ii 211-212 note.

done by the King's Printer upon sessional volumes of the statutes which were issued by him.[1] We must now consider, first, the rights and duties of the King's Printer in relation to the publication of the statutes ; and secondly the nature of his services in relation to that publication.

The rights and duties of the King's Printer.

We have seen that in the sixteenth and seventeenth centuries the Crown was accustomed to issue letters patent giving to a person or persons the monopoly of printing certain books ; and that these monopoly patents were exempted from the operation of James I's statute which regulated the conditions under which patents of monopoly could be granted by the Crown.[2] During the latter part of the seventeenth century it was thought by some that the Crown could only exercise this right in respect of books in which it had a copyright ; [3] and the arguments used in cases which turned on the validity of these patents give colour to this view.[4] But down to the Revolution the courts were easily persuaded to extend on very flimsy grounds the Crown's right to copyright in many classes of books.[5] Some of these decisions were set right in the eighteenth century ; and it was settled that the Crown had no right to grant these patent rights except in respect of books in which it had copyright.[6] It was clear, however, that in respect of some classes of books the Crown had a copyright, and that, in respect of them it could grant patents

[1] Above 292. [2] Vol. vi 365-366.
[3] In The Company of Stationers v. Seymour (1677) 1 Mod. at p. 257 Pemberton *arg.* said, " when Sir Orlando Bridgman was chief justice in this Court, there was a question raised concerning the validity of a grant of the sole printing of any particular book, with a prohibition to all others to print the same, how far it should stand good against them that claim a property in the copy, paramount to the King's grant ; and opinions were divided upon the point."
[4] Vol. vi 373-374. [5] Ibid.
[6] It would seem from the MS. report of The Stationers' Company v. Partridge (1709), cited by Lord Mansfield C.J. in Millar v. Taylor (1769) 4 Burr at p. 2403 that Powell J. thought that the Crown could not grant such a patent to print a book unless it could show that it had copyright in the book ; in fact the question whether the Crown could grant an exclusive right to print almanacs, which was the point at issue, was argued on the basis of the possession by the Crown of a copyright in almanacs ; Lord Hardwicke accepted this view of the law in 1752, see 4 Burr. at pp. 2328-2329 *per* Willes J., and so did Lord Mansfield C.J. ibid at p. 2404 ; on this ground the court of Common Pleas in 1775 (De Grey C.J., Gould, Blackstone, and Nares J.J.) certified the court of Chancery that the Crown could not grant the Stationers' Company an exclusive right to print almanacs, The Stationers' Company v. Carnan 2 W. Black. 1004. But it had long been supposed that the grant of this right, which had been enjoyed by the company and the two universities, was valid ; in consequence of this decision 21 George III c. 56 § 10 provided that £500 a year should be paid to each of the two universities out of the duty on almanacs, to compensate them for the loss of the £500 a year which they had received from the company in return for their assignment to the company of their right to print almanacs, 2 W. Black at p. 1009 n. (*k*).

giving the sole right to print. Amongst these publications were the statutes and the abridgments of the statutes.[1]

By a succession of letters patent beginning with the year 1547, the King had granted to various persons the office of King's Printer, with the sole right to print the statutes,[2] and, later, the abridgments of the statutes.[3] This grant did not prevent the Crown from granting a concurrent right to others; and it in fact granted concurrent rights to the Universities of Oxford and Cambridge. Necessarily friction was caused between the King's Printer and the Universities, and also between the Stationers' Company, to whom grants of the sole right of printing other books had been made,[4] and the Universities. Charles I's charter to the University of Oxford in 1636 decided these differences in favour of the University, and gave it the right to print the statutes and all other books.[5] But the root of the old controversies remained, because, after the Revolution, and especially after the expiration of the licensing Act, the extent of the King's prerogative to make these grants, and therefore the validity of the different grants which he had made to the King's Printer and to the two Universities, was by no means clear. Differences turning upon this question arose between the King's Printer and the University of Cambridge in the first half of the eighteenth century, and came to a head in 1758.[6] In that year the case of *Basket v. The University of Cambridge* decided that royal grants of Henry VIII and Charles I to the University to print all books, gave it an authority, concurrent with the authority of the King's Printer, to print the statutes and the abridgments thereof.[7]

[1] "Acts of Parliament are the works of the Legislature : and the publication of them has always belonged to the King, the executive part, and as the head and Sovereign," Millar v. Taylor (1769) 4 Burr. at p. 2404 *per* Lord Mansfield C.J.
[2] An account of these patents is given in Basket v. The University of Cambridge (1758) 1 W. Black at pp. 105-107.
[3] The first mention of Abridgments was in 1589 in the grant to Roland Barker, ibid 106
[4] Vol. vi 366.
[5] The charter is printed in Bodleian Quarterly Record vii 73-94 ; see pp. 89-92 for the university privileges in the matter of printing ; the Stationers' Company and the King's Printer contended that the licence given by earlier letters patent to the University to print " omnimodos libros *publice non prohibitos* " prevented it from publishing books which the Crown had given the company or the King's Printer the sole right to print, e.g. the statutes ; the charter decides that this interpretation is wrong, ibid at p. 90.
[6] The case of Basket v. The University of Cambridge arose out of a case stated by the court of Chancery in 1743, but it " lay dormant for many years," 1 W. Bl. at p. 105.
[7] Ibid at pp. 121-122 ; a similar privilege was enjoyed by Oxford University, see Universities of Oxford and Cambridge v. Richardson (1802) 6 Ves. 689 ; Charles I's charter of 1636 empowered the University to print all manner of books, The Bodleian Quarterly Record vii 89-92 ; cp. The Oxford University Press 1468-1926 11.

There was thus no doubt as to the validity of these patents to the Universities and to the King's Printer ; [1] and the King's Printer exploited his privileges. We shall see that Viner, before he could print his Abridgment, was obliged to come to terms with the patentees possessing the exclusive rights to print the statutes enjoyed by the King's Printer. [2] The University of Cambridge made some use of its victory over the King's Printer when it published Pickering's edition of the statutes. [3] But it never competed with the King's Printer in the publication of the sessional editions of the statutes ; and, after the publication of Pickering's edition, it ceased to publish any of the statutes. Oxford University never seems to have made any use of its right to print statutes or abridgments of the statutes. [4] The King's Printer thus got a monopoly of the right to print the statutes ; [5] and we shall now see that the manner in which he exercised it facilitated the publication, in an intelligible form, of editions of the public and general statutes.

The services rendered by the King's Printer in relation to the publication of the statutes.

We have seen that the King's Printer had drawn a distinction between public and private Acts ; that at first he had not printed the private Acts ; and that, from 1571, he had printed only their titles. [6] But if local or personal Acts (other than Road Acts which from 1753 were separately printed) [7] were deemed to be public, either by virtue of a special clause in the Act or by usage, or if they were directed to be printed by the King's Printer, they were printed by him. [8] So numerous were these Acts that they filled more than double the space occupied by the public and general Acts. [9] The King's Printer also printed abstracts of the statutes published by him, which were of no great value, and added tables of the titles of the public and private statutes. [10] These Acts when printed by the King's

---

[1] In the report of the House of Commons committee of 1831-1832 on the King's Printers' patents there is a copy of the patent to Eyre & Spottiswood granted in 1830, Parlt. Papers 1831-1832 xviii 192-194 ; at that time it had become the practice to insert in the patent a clause to the effect that the prices charged must be such as appeared to the Lords of the Treasury to be reasonable, ibid 178.

[2] Vol. xii 165.　　　　　　　　　　　　　　　　　　[3] Below 306.

[4] A committee of the House of Commons reported in 1835 that the Universities had a right concurrent with the right of the King's Printer, but that they had not for many years availed themselves of it, Parlt. Papers 1835 xviii 164 ; see also Lord Eldon's statement to the same effect in Universities of Oxford and Cambridge v. Richardson (1802) 6 Ves. at p. 710.

[5] Parlt. Papers 1835 xviii 165.　　　　　　　　　　[6] Above 292.

[7] F. H. Spencer, Municipal Origins 48 n.

[8] Reports from Committees of the House of Commons xiv 119.

[9] Ibid 122 ; in 1793 the King's Printer published two thick folio volumes which together contained 3936 pages, ibid 35 n. (*d*).

[10] Ibid 119.

Printer were distributed at the public cost to members of Parliament, the Privy Council, and some of the officers of state. In all a little over eleven hundred copies were thus distributed.[1]

It was easy for the King's Printer to see which Acts were in form public and which were private ; and in his sessional publications he drew a distinction between them, which must have been of considerable service to the editors of collected editions of the public and general statutes. Whereas on the Parliament roll the statutes public and private were numbered in a continuous series, the King's Printer divided the public from the private Acts, and numbered each series separately.[2] He also helped the compilers of these editions of the statutes by other kinds of editorial work. He numbered the sections of the statutes, inserted marginal abstracts, and punctuated the text.[3] It followed that the division into sections, the marginal notes, and the punctuation, were due to the work done by the King's Printer, and rested on his authority alone ;[4] and the title also was no part of the Act.[5] But it was a work which it was absolutely necessary that some one should do. Without it the statutes would have been very difficult to understand and to cite ; and the work of the authors who compiled collected editions of the statutes for the use of the legal profession would have been very laborious, and probably very unsatisfactory. Of the collected editions and of the abridgments of the statutes which appeared in the eighteenth century I must now say something.

I have given some account of the collections of the statutes published in the seventeenth century.[6] The principal editions of the statutes published in the eighteenth century were as follows :

(i) In 1735 serjeant Hawkins published in six folio volumes an edition of the statutes from Henry III to 7 George II.[7] It contains

---

[1] Reports from Committees of the House of Commons xiv 120.
[2] Ibid 38. [3] Ibid.
[4] Ibid ; Bentham, in his tract on Nomography or the Art of Inditing Laws, Works iii 250, criticized, with some reason, this state of things ; he says, " an Act of Parliament repels the dividing line of the arithmetician with no less horror than the accursed soil sown with salt rejects the plough and yields no fruit " ; but, " the licentiousness of the press has divided it into parts called sections ; and to each of these sections this same licentiousness has gone so far as to affix a different number ; but in the manuscript, on which alone has been imprinted the touch of the legislative sceptre, this conceit has no mark to give warrant or allowance to it. Number it has none—division it has none " ; in a book by Rayner, entitled Readings on Statutes xv (see vol. xii 402) it is said that Worrall, the book-seller, first suggested numbering the Acts by chapters, and had hard work to get the King's Printer to adopt this expedient.
[5] Attorney-General v. Lord Weymouth (1743) Amb. at pp. 22-23 *per* Lord Hardwicke.
[6] Vol. vi 312-313.
[7] Statutes (Rec. Com.) i *xxiii-xxiv ;* for Hawkins see vol. xii 361.

The Latin and French texts of most of the statutes to 8 Edw. IV with translations of such as had been before translated, and as appeared to him to be in force and use : Of some of these statutes a translation only is given, without the original text : Of the statutes and parts of statutes considered by him as obsolete, or which are expired or repealed, the original text is given without a translation, and occasionally an abridgment without either the text or translation. . . . He gives the text (of the early statutes) from the statute rolls in the Tower, from ancient manuscripts, or from Coke's Second Institute ; all in many instances varying from the earliest printed editions.

In an Appendix to the last volume he inserted the text of various ancient statutes which had been omitted or given only in translation in the body of the work, " together with some ancient records of statutes omitted in the statute roll, but entered in other Parliamentary records." He deliberately retained the old translation, and made no attempt to correct mistakes of the existence of which he was fully conscious ; [1] and the same course was substantially followed by compilers of the other eighteenth-century editions of the statutes.[2] That translation is in substance the translation printed in Pulton's edition of the statutes ; [3] and it is very unsatisfactory. In the first place, there were many errors which were left uncorrected, and remained uncorrected. In the second place, the translation had been sometimes altered by Pulton and other editors to suit the text as taken from the record, and sometimes allowed to remain in its original state. The result was that it corresponded neither with the record nor with the old printed editions.

Throughout the whole translation sentences are frequently inserted or omitted, contrary to the authority of the Latin or French text, as given from the record or manuscript in the opposite column of the book ; and the translation, thus varying from the text of the record or manuscript, is sometimes consistent with, and sometimes contrary to the old printed copies, which are not at all noticed.[4]

[1] Hawkins says in his Preface, " it was proposed to make a new translation of the French and Latin statutes, and it must be owned that there are some mistakes in the old translation, but it having, by its long use, obtained a kind of prescriptive authority, and seeming for the most part to have been done with greater learning and accuracy than can be expected from any modern hand, willing to undertake a work of such difficulty, and it being easy for the reader to correct the mistakes in it by the help of the original, it was judged most proper to retain it," cited Statutes (Rec. Com.) i *xxiv.*

[2] Ibid.   [3] For this edition see vol. iv 309-310.

[4] Statutes (Rec. Com.) i *xxiv-xxv ;* " corrections, comparatively very few in number, were silently made in the progress of the editions called Pulton's and Keble's. Those made from time to time in Rastell's English collection were numerous and important, but they have not been fully adopted in any edition of the statutes at large. The suggestions of corrections by notes in the margin in Cay's edition are very rare, comparatively with the numerous errors actually existing ; but the number of these suggestions was somewhat increased in the edition by Ruffhead, though not to any considerable extent. The like observations apply to Pickering's edition," ibid *xxv.*

(ii) Cay's edition of the statutes in six folio volumes down to 30 George II was published in 1758—the year after the death of its editor.[1] It follows much the same plan as the edition of Hawkins; but it has some additions. Some of the mediæval statutes omitted by Hawkins were inserted, and other omitted statutes were inserted from the earlier printed editions and from the Parliament Rolls.[2] Like Hawkins, he deliberately declined to amend the errors of the translation which he used.[3]

(iii) Ruffhead [4] (1723-1769) published between 1762 and 1765 an edition of the statutes down to 4 George III in nine quarto volumes. It contains all Cay's matter; and, in an Appendix to the ninth volume, some additional Acts of Henry VII's and later reigns are introduced. This additional matter was taken from the records and from the early printed editions.[5]

(iv) Between 1762 and 1766 Danby Pickering [6] published at the Cambridge University Press an edition of the statutes down to 1 George III in twenty-three octavo volumes. It also contains all Cay's matter with additions from the early printed editions, and other sources. There is an appendix to the twenty-third volume which contains some of the same matter as is contained in Ruffhead's appendix.[7]

All these editions were continued by subsequent volumes, which contained the statutes printed in subsequent years.

The Record Commissioners point out that the additional matter introduced into these editions is not important, and that some of the documents introduced are not entitled to the character of statutes.[8]

---

[1] Cay was born in 1700 and died in 1757; he was called to the Bar by Gray's Inn in 1724, and became a bencher in 1748; he was steward and judge of the Marshalsea, and a member of the Society of Antiquaries, D.N.B.; Pension Book, Gray's Inn ii 257; for his work on the abridgments of the statutes see below 307-308.

[2] Statutes (Rec. Com.) i *xxiv*.

[3] " It has often been desired that a new translation should be made, but as this has been used for some ages, not only by the public in general, but even by the Parliament, and many statutes are recited in subsequent Acts in the words of this translation, it seems to be too much authenticated for an editor to presume to reject it," ibid.

[4] Ruffhead was the son of Owen Ruffhead, baker to George I. When he was a child, his father bought him a lottery ticket which drew a prize of £500, and the father spent the money on his son's education. He was called to the Bar in 1747, and got a practice as a consultant and framer of bills for Parliament. In addition to his work on the statutes he undertook, at the request of Bishop Warburton, a critical biography of Pope. He also published a new edition of Jacob's Law Dictionary, D.N.B.

[5] Statutes (Rec. Com.) i *xxiv*.

[6] Pickering was called to the Bar by Gray's Inn in 1741. He edited the original five volumes of the Modern Reports (Wallace, the Reporters 350) and Finch's Law (vol. v 399 and n. 3), D.N.B.; vol. xii 80-81.

[7] Statutes (Rec. Com.) i *xxiv*.

[8] Ibid.

It is evident also that Ruffhead and Pickering took, each, advantage of the circumstance of their editions being in the course of publication during the same period, and that, in the insertion of new matters, they by turns borrowed from each other.[1]

At the beginning of the eighteenth century the two chief abridgments of the statutes were those of Rastell[2] and Wingate.[3] Wingate's abridgment, first published in 1642, was, as we have seen, continued by Hughes and Manby in 1663, 1670, and 1675.[4] After the Revolution it was continued by Joseph Washington, and later by Henry Boult.[5] At some time before 1720 the work of Wingate, Washington, and Boult was consolidated into an abridgment of the statute law in four volumes, which was continued by supplemental volumes down to 1735.[6] Some of these volumes were, it is said, edited by Nelson,[7] who, besides publishing reports,[8] probably published in 1723 a book of " Readings upon the Statute Law Alphabetically Digested." [9] In 1713 and 1719 two abridgments of the statute law were published by Giles Jacob,[10] the author of the Law Dictionary.[11]

It was because these abridgments were not adequate to the needs of the profession that John Cay[12] in 1739 published his " Abridgment of the Public Statutes in force and use from Magna Charta in the ninth year of King Henry III to the eleventh year of his present Majesty King George II inclusive." Cay had had some experience of the work of abridging statutes, since he was a son-in-law of Henry Boult, and had helped Joseph Washington to edit some of his supplements to Wingate's abridgment.[13] He said that Rastell's method of abridgment was " too large to be followed when the statutes grew more voluminous " ; and that Wingate, in abridging Rastell, was rather too brief.[14] Moreover Wingate's work, having been continued by many hands, was not composed according to a consistent method, so that it was not always easy to discern the title under which any particular statute was placed.[15] Cay attempted in his abridgment to

---

[1] Statutes (Rec. Com.) i *xxiv*.
[2] Vol. iv 311-312 ; J. D. Cowley, A Bibliography of Abridgments (S.S.) xxxii-xxxiv.
[3] Vol. iv 313 ; J. D. Cowley, op. cit. xxxv.   [4] Vol. iv 313.
[5] J. D. Cowley, op. cit. xxxv-xxxvi.   [6] Ibid xxxvi.
[7] " There is no evidence to connect the name of any particular writer with either the consolidation or the supplements beyond the tradition enshrined in the trade catalogues to the effect that William Nelson participated in the compilation of some of the supplements to Wingate," ibid.
[8] Vol. vi 556, 562, 617 ; vol. xii 109.
[9] J. D. Cowley, op. cit. xxxvii ; cp. vol. xii 175-176.
[10] The first was " A Review of the Statutes both Ancient and Modern," published in 1713 ; the second was " The Statute Law Commonplaced," published in 1719, ibid xxxvi-xxxvii ; for Giles Jacob see vol. vi 555-556.
[11] Vol. xii 176.   [12] For John Cay see above 306 n. 1.
[13] J. D. Cowley, op. cit. xxxviii.
[14] Preface to the Abridgment.   [15] Ibid.

remedy these defects ; and, in order to enable the reader to discover the head under which he might expect to find the statute which he wished to consult, he carefully explained the analytical method which he had followed in selecting the titles under which the statutes were abridged.[1] Cay's work supplied the need for an up-to-date abridgment. A second edition, edited by his son Henry Boult Cay,[2] appeared in 1762 ; and it was continued by annual abstracts of the statutes down to 1795.[3]

At the end of the eighteenth century the increase in the number and size of the statutes made the work of preparing an abridgment more and more difficult. Only one later abridgment, entitled " A Compendious Digest of the Statute Law," was compiled by T. W. Williams and published in 1787.[4] It was enlarged and continued to 1812.[5] We shall now see that abridgments of the statutes became less necessary as the result of improvements made during the nineteenth century in the classification and in the arrangements for the publication of the statutes.

Daines Barrington, in his *Observations on the Statutes*, which was first published in 1766,[6] had commented upon the defects of the statute book.[7] He pointed out that it contained obsolete and sometimes dangerous laws ;[8] and that there was much need for Acts to consolidate various statutes dealing with the same topic. He suggested that a standing commission of two or more barristers should be appointed, to report to the Lord Chancellor, the Master of the Rolls, and the judges the measures

---

[1] " It is very difficult to mark out an analytical method of ranging the several titles of the statute law; as so little has been done this way before, and as there are many titles which may be placed under different general heads for different reasons : but as it may be of service to assist in the consulting of this abridgment, I shall endeavour to do it as well as I can, though in a very imperfect manner "—then follows his analysis, Cay, Abridgment Preface.

[2] He published his father's edition of the statutes after his death ; he died in 1795, D.N.B.

[3] " Cay's *Abridgment* maintained its popularity throughout the century, and according to the older authorities was continued by annual abstracts of statutes until 35 George III," J. D. Cowley, op. cit. xxxviii.

[4] Ibid ; an attempt to compile an abridgment was made by Timothy Cunningham in 1762, but the project was abandoned after the publication of the first volume, ibid.

[5] Ibid.   [6] For this book see vol. xii 400-402.

[7] (1st ed.) App. 339-340 ; at some period between 1702 and 1710 one John Cressett had petitioned the Crown that he might be employed to review the statute and common laws, and to separate what was valuable "from the rubbish they almost lay buried under," with a view to their amendment, Calendar of Treasury Papers, 1702-1707 98.

[8] Thus, 25 Henry VIII c. 13 made it an offence to keep more than 2000 sheep, see vol. iv 365, and though " the greatest part of most of the Welsh counties is fit for nothing else," yet " there was an indictment in Cardiganshire within these six years " on this statute ; also a son had within the last eight years prosecuted his mother on the statutes of Elizabeth's reign which penalized those who did not go to church.

of reform which ought to be adopted, and to draft the measures necessary for this purpose. But nothing was then done.[1] It was not till 1796 that the House of Commons took the first step towards reform by appointing a committee to enquire into the temporary and expiring laws ; and, later, as a result of the report of this committee, a committee to consider the most effectual means for promulgating the statutes. This committee was directed to consider the parts of the report of the committee upon temporary and expiring laws which were relevant to their enquiry.

The first committee reported that there was no authentic and entire publication of the statutes in existence, that the matter of the statutes was sometimes discordant, sometimes obsolete, and sometimes perplexed, and that the style in which many of the statutes were composed was often verbose, tautologous, and obscure.[2] It found that much confusion was caused by the omission of Parliament to state clearly the duration of an Act which was intended to be temporary ; [3] and that

the variety of periods prescribed for the duration of each statute, is such that caprice herself seems to have exercised her full dominion, and displayed her uncontrolled powers over different clauses of the same law. . . . And the numberless continuances of statutes still remaining temporary in form, though permanent in their principle, strongly claim the attention of Parliament, as contributing to add complication to a labyrinth already too intricate.[4]

The committee therefore recommended the preparation of a complete and authentic edition of the statutes, which should be the basis of a revision of the statute book.[5]

The second committee recommended that the number of copies of the public general Acts distributed at the public cost [6] should be increased ; [7] that the number of public local Acts so distributed should be diminished ; [8] and that the printing of abstracts of the local Acts should be discontinued.[9] It further

---

[1] For an earlier committee to revise the criminal laws which effected hardly anything see below 579.

[2] " It appears to your committeee that there is no authentic and entire publication of the statutes ; that a very considerable number of statutes, as well as clauses and sentences of statutes, which are upon the original rolls, never have been printed at all ; that many, which are printed as statutes, do not exist upon record ; or have not properly the form or force of statutes ; and that the statute law has through a series of six centuries, accumulated at length to a most voluminous mass, which is rapidly increasing, and has been more than doubled in bulk within the last fifty years. . . . Your committee cannot but observe the matter of it to be in many places discordant, in other places obsolete ; in others perplexed by its miscellaneous composition of incongruities ; and that its style is for the most part verbose, tautologous, and obscure," Reports from Committees of the House of Commons xiv 34-35.

[3] Ibid 37.   [4] Ibid.

[5] Ibid 36-37.   [6] Above 304.

[7] Reports from Committees of the House of Commons xiv 138.

[8] Ibid 122-123.   [9] Ibid.

recommended that private Acts, which, the committee said, amounted during the reign of George III " to nearly one half of the whole mass of statutes produced in each session of Parliament," should be printed ; that part of the cost should be borne by their promoters ; and that, as compensation for this additional charge, the King's Printer's copies of private Acts should be admissible in evidence.[1] The committee emphasized the need for a general index to the statutes ; [2] and stated that

The particular requisites with which each bill ought to be introduced into Parliament, such as the numerical distinction of its sections, their marginal abstract and their punctuation ; the form of title which should be afterwards prefixed to bills . . . and the number which should be finally marked on each roll . . . should be settled by resolutions or standing orders adapted to those purposes.[3]

As we shall now see, the recommendations made by this committee foreshadow many of the measures directed to the simplification of the statute book, and to a more convenient classification and publication of statutes, which have been carried out in the nineteenth century. They were the first step towards the introduction of the modern rules upon these matters.

(3) The development of the modern system.

In relating the history of the process by which the modern system of classifying and publishing the statutes has been reached, I must deal first with the many important measures which were taken in the nineteenth century for the simplifying of the statute book. These measures were the necessary pre-requisites for the establishment of the modern system, and explain its characteristics. They can be summed up under the following heads : first, the preparation of a complete and authentic edition of the statutes ; secondly, the preparation of a revised edition of the statutes ; thirdly, measures of consolidation and codification ; and fourthly, the preparation of an adequate index to the statutes.

The preparation of a complete and authentic edition of the statutes.

In 1800 a Select Committee of the House of Commons reported inter alia that a complete and authoritative edition of

---

[1] Reports from Committees of the House of Commons xiv 124-125, 149 ; the committee was careful to see that the officials of the Parliament Office did not lose by the change—it was suggested that a fee should be charged for the examination of the print by the roll, so as to compensate for the loss of profits on office copies of these Acts ; for the fees charged by the officers of the two Houses see above 298-300.

[2] Reports from Committees of the House of Commons xiv 125.

[3] Ibid 126 ; but, in spite of these recommendations, John Church, the superintendent of the Stationery Office, said in 1831 that the examination and promulgation of Acts of Parliament were duties which were still left to the King's Printer, Parlt. Papers 1831-1832 xviii 142.

the statutes ought to be published.[1] This report led to the appointment of the first Record Commission ; and the commissioners at their first meeting resolved to prepare such an edition of the statutes. I have already said something of their edition of the English statutes, which contains the statutes down to 1713—the last year of Anne's reign.[2] It appeared in nine large folio volumes between the years 1810 and 1822. A parallel edition of the Scottish statutes was begun in 1807. Volumes 2-11, containing the statutes between the years 1424 and 1707, were published between 1814 and 1824 ; and the first volume, containing statutes of an earlier date, was published in 1844.[3] A folio edition of the Irish statutes, printed by the King's Printer in Ireland, appeared in 1762, in pursuance of an order made by Lord Halifax, then Lord-Lieutenant of Ireland.[4]

There is no doubt that the Record Commissioners' edition of the English statutes was an improvement upon all the previous editions. But modern historical scholars have shown that it is by no means perfect. It has been pointed out [5] that no attempt is made to estimate the value of some of the manuscripts used ; that the dating of the statutes is faulty—to one of the statutes a date is assigned for which there is no evidence, and another is said to be undated though the date appears on its face ; and, above all, that no attempt is made to use the evidence afforded by the records as to the instruments which should be included in the statute book.[6] Messrs. Richardson and Sayles say : [7]

Highly as the editors regarded manuscript evidence, they had a greater regard for the printed word : for, as they envisaged their task, they were concerned with finding support for the received text rather than with constructing an historically faithful text. Their work reflects the labours of compilers in the closing years of the thirteenth and the early years of the fourteenth centuries, compilers working obscurely without official authority and with no precise standard of textual integrity. . . . The editors deliberately put aside the inconvenient bulk of instruments which had, with great care and diligence, been collected from record sources for their consideration, and confined themselves to the contents of the statute roll and of the early printed editions which had the authority of generally received tradition. Their recourse to manuscripts, while it resulted in some redistribution of the material between dated statutes and statutes of uncertain date, left the work of the early compilers substantially as the editors found it. They did not conceive it their duty to analyse the early collections in

---

[1] Ilbert, Legislative Methods and Forms 21.
[2] Vol. ii 428-429 ; Ilbert, op. cit. 21-23.
[3] Ibid 23.   [4] Ibid.
[5] T. F. T. Plucknett, Statutes and their Interpretation in the first half of the Fourteenth Century chap. ii.
[6] See as to this and other matters, two articles on the Early Statutes by H. G. Richardson and G. Sayles, L.Q.R. l 201, 540.
[7] L.Q.R. l 569-570.

order to determine their primitive constituents, nor to establish and date the original texts that lay behind those collections, nor to introduce into the canon legislative instruments which Edwardian compilers had excluded or overlooked, or which had not found their way into the manuscripts used for the early printed editions.

Thus the old error of regarding the so-called statutes of uncertain date as coming from the last year of Edward II's reign —an error which arose from the accident of the chronological order in which the early printed editions of the statutes had been published [1]—was perpetuated by the Commissioners. And as it was with the text so it was with the translations of the text. Professor Plucknett has pointed out [2] that in nearly all cases they come from Cay's version of 1751, or older versions ; that, consequently, the translation is not necessarily a translation of the text which accompanies it ; and that, if the translation was erroneous, corrections were seldom made, and then only in footnotes. No doubt the achievement of the Record Commissioners was considerable. [3] But there is much force in the plea, which has been recently put forward, for " an edition of the early statutes on historical principles." [4]

We have seen that the Record Commissioners disclaimed any adjudication upon the authority of the instruments which they inserted into their collection ; but that the fact that an instrument finds a place in their collection raises a presumption in favour of its authority. [5] The Interpretation Act 1889 [6] recognizes this fact by enacting that, in Acts passed after January 1, 1890, references to Acts previously passed shall, unless a contrary intention appears, be taken to refer to the version of the statutes included in any revised edition of the statutes purporting to be printed by authority ; but that, in the case of statutes not so included and passed before the reign of George I, such references shall be taken to refer to the Record Commissioners' edition. In other cases such references are to refer to copies of statutes printed by the King's Printer, or under the authority of His Majesty's Stationery Office. [7] It is clear that

---

[1] Vol. ii 222-223 ; these so-called statutes come chiefly from the reigns of Henry III and Edward I, and some have no claim to be regarded as statutes, being, as Maitland has said, a sort of apocrypha to the statute book, ibid ; Maitland, Collected Papers ii 39 n. 1.

[2] Op. cit. 14-15.

[3] " The early twentieth century plumes itself too much on meticulous accuracy in some small fields of research to sympathize with the partial success of the early nineteenth century in far wider regions," Winfield, Chief Sources of English Legal History 92.

[4] L.Q.R. 1 569.   [5] Vol. ii 428.

[6] 52, 53 Victoria c. 63 § 35, 2.

[7] " Where any Act passed after the commencement of this Act contains such reference as aforesaid, the reference shall, unless a contrary intention appears, be read as referring, in the case of statutes included in any revised edition of the statutes, purporting to be printed by authority, to that edition, and in the case of statutes not

this enactment does not guarantee the authenticity of everything which is contained in the Record Commissioners' edition
of the statutes; so that it would not prevent the courts from
giving effect to another version of an old statute, if the text
given in the Record Commission's edition was proved to be
erroneous.[1]

The Record Commissioners' edition of the statutes was more
complete and authentic than any previous edition—so far as
it went. But it went no further than the end of Anne's reign;
and because it was a complete edition it contained all the
statutes both repealed and unrepealed. There was no attempt
to indicate which of the statutes were in force and which were
not. This was a very difficult task; but, after a long series
of experiments and suggestions, the task of eliminating obsolete matter from the statute book, and of producing a revised
edition of the statutes, was carried out in the latter half of the
nineteenth century.

The preparation of a revised edition of the statutes.

During the whole of the nineteenth century many different
measures were proposed for the purgation of the statute book,
and the production of a revised edition of the statutes. These
proposals sometimes originated from individuals, but generally
from the many commissions and committees which were from
time to time appointed to consider the problem of the statute
book. The history of these proposals will, I think, be more
intelligible if, by way of preface, I state shortly and in chronological order the steps taken by the government to deal with
the problem.[2]

In 1806 the Public Record Commission resolved that Francis
Hargrave should be asked to " report on the best mode of
reducing the statute law into a smaller compass and more
systematic form." His memorandum on this subject inspired
a resolution of the House of Commons in 1816, to the effect
that a digest of the statutes ought to be made, and that an
eminent lawyer with a staff of twenty clerks should be com-
missioned to do the work.[3] In 1833 Lord Chancellor Brougham

---

so included, and passed before the reign of King George the First, to the edition
prepared under the direction of the Record Commission; and in other cases to the
copies of the statutes purporting to be printed by the Queen's Printer, or under the
superintendence or authority of His Majesty's Stationery Office."

[1] Professor Winfield, op. cit. 92-93, thinks that this section of the Interpretation
Act may " put the courts in an awkward position," since it made this edition
" authoritative with respect to Acts of Parliament passed subsequently to the Interpretation Act itself "; I do not think that this section which deals only with the
method of citing and referring to statutes, can have this effect.

[2] My account is based upon Ilbert's lucid statement in his Legislative Methods
and Forms 50-76.   [3] Ilbert, op. cit. 50.

appointed a royal commission to prepare two statutes dealing with the criminal law—one dealing with the enacted, and the other with the unenacted, law ; and to enquire into the expediency of consolidating other branches of English Law.[1] This commission was dissolved in 1845 ; and in the same year another commission was appointed to consider the expediency of consolidating the whole or part of the criminal law.[2] In 1853 Lord Cranworth appointed a board to carry out a revision of the statute law. But the members of the board differed as to the manner in which this revision should take place,[3] and it was superseded in 1854 by a strong statute law commission.[4] This commission came to an end in 1859. In 1866 Lord Westbury appointed a royal commission to

inquire into the expediency of a digest of law, and the best means of accomplishing that object, and of otherwise exhibiting in a compendious and accessible form the law as embodied in judicial decisions.

But this ambitious scheme came to nothing.[5] In 1867 Lord Cairns suggested to Lord Chelmsford, then Lord Chancellor, that it would be desirable to prepare an index and chronological table to the statutes ; and this suggestion was adopted.[6] In 1868 Lord Cairns, who had become Lord Chancellor, initiated the project for a revised edition of the statutes, and the establishment of the statute law committee, which continues to supervise statute law revision and other matters connected with the statutes.[7]

This half-century of active discussion produced many plans for the improvement of the statute law—measures of consolidation and codification,[8] measures to improve the drafting of the statutes,[9] and measures to provide an adequate index to the statute law.[10] As the result of this discussion steps have been taken to effect all these objects, which have greatly improved the statute book. With these projects I shall deal later. At this point I must consider the measures taken for the revision of the statute book.

Projects for the revision of the statute book bulked large in all the proposals for the improvement of statute law made

---

[1] Ilbert, op. cit. 51.   [2] Ibid 52.   [3] Ibid 53-55.
[4] It consisted of the following persons : Lord Cranworth (Chancellor), Lord Lyndhurst, Lord Brougham, Lord Wrottesley, Lord Campbell (Lord Chief Justice), Sir John Jervis (C.J. of C.P.), Sir F. Pollock (Chief Baron), Baron Parke, Mr. Moncrieff (Lord Advocate), Mr. Spencer Walpole, Mr. Joseph Napier, Vice-Chancellor Page-Wood, Sir A. Cockburn (Attorney-General), Sir R. Bethell (Solicitor-General), Mr. Brewster (Attorney-General for Ireland) Mr. Keogh (Solicitor-General for Ireland), Mr. James Crawford (Solicitor-General for Scotland), and Mr. Bellenden Ker, Mr. Walter Coulson, Sir Fitzroy Kelly, and others who were subsequently added, ibid 55-56.
[5] Ibid 61 n. 1, 127.   [6] Ibid 63-64.   [7] Ibid 65-66.
[8] Below 315-318.   [9] Below 380-387.   [10] Below 318-320.

during the nineteenth century.   The first practical step to effect this object was taken by the statute law commission of 1854. The first Statute Law Revision Act, which was passed in 1856, was based on the recommendations of this commission.[1]   It repealed 120 obsolete statutes.   A register of statutes, showing how far each was in force, which had been prepared by order of this commission,[2] was the basis of the second Statute Law Revision Act, which was passed in 1861.[3]   It disposed of 900 obsolete statutes passed between 1770 and 1853.   A third Statute Law Revision Act was passed in 1863.[4]   It

expurgated the Statute Book from the twentieth year of Henry III to the first year of James II.   It has been taken as the model of all subsequent Statute Law Revision Acts, and in particular contains the elaborate and extensive saving clause embodied in each of these Acts.[5]

It was these Statute Law Revision Acts, and other Acts which repealed obsolete law,[6] which made it possible to produce a revised edition of the public and general statutes.   The first edition of the revised statutes was published between the years 1870 and 1878.[7]   The complete collection of the statutes occupied one hundred and eighteen volumes : in the revised edition all the statutes in force down to 1878 were published in eighteen volumes.[8]   In 1888 the first volume of a second edition was produced based on later Statute Law Revision Acts.[9]

Measures of consolidation and codification.

The House of Commons Committee of 1796 had recommended the consolidation of statutes dealing with particular parts of the law.[10]   During the first thirty years of the nineteenth century progress was made in consolidating the statutes relating to the slave trade, to the customs and excise, and to certain branches of the criminal law.[11]   The commission of 1833 was directed in the first place to consider measures for the consolidation of the criminal law.[12]   But neither the reports made by this commission, nor the reports made by the commission of 1845, resulted in legislation ; [13] and attempts made in 1852 and 1853 to codify

---

[1] 19, 20 Victoria c. 64 ; Ilbert, op. cit. 57-58.   [2] Ibid 59.
[3] 24, 25 Victoria c. 101 ; Ilbert, op. cit. 60.
[4] 26, 27 Victoria c. 125 ; this and the preceding Act were drawn by Messrs. Reilly and Wood, who had prepared the register of statutes referred to above ; Sir Hugh Cairns praised their accuracy and intelligence and pointed out that whereas about £50,000 had been spent on the statute law commissioners, these two Acts had been compiled for the sum of between £3000 and £4000, Ilbert, op. cit. 60, 62.
[5] Ibid 62.   [6] Ibid.   [7] Ibid 24, 66.
[8] Ibid 25.   [9] Ibid 70.
[10] Reports of Committees of the House of Commons xiv 37.
[11] Ilbert, op. cit. 50-51.   [12] Ibid 51.   [13] Ibid 52.

the criminal law failed.[1] The statute law commission of 1854 prepared a number of consolidation bills. But these bills failed to pass;[2] and the expense of preparing these abortive bills roused considerable criticism in the House of Commons.[3] At length, in 1861, seven criminal law consolidation bills, which were due to the work of the commissions of 1833 and 1845, were enacted.[4] The need for consolidating statutes was emphasized by a select committee of the House of Commons in 1875;[5] and since the establishment of the statute law committee in 1868,[6] and the office of Parliamentary Counsel to the Treasury in 1869,[7] numerous consolidation Acts have been passed.[8] One example, which I have already noticed, is the Public Authorities Protection Act of 1893.[9] Another is the Merchant Shipping Act of 1894, which contains seven hundred and forty-eight clauses and twenty-two schedules.[10]

The work of codifying the law has made less progress than the work of consolidating the statutes. The two processes of codification and consolidation are distinct. Codification " means an orderly and authoritative statement of the leading rules of law on a given subject, whether those rules are to be found in statute law or in common law."[11] It was an expedient which was Bentham's great panacea for reforming the law; and it was he who invented the word and introduced the idea to lawyers.[12] Many of the Whigs who came into power in 1832 had learned from Bentham and his school; so that it is not surprising that the royal commission appointed by Brougham in 1833 was directed to consider both measures of codification and measures of consolidation.[13]

We have seen that it was from this date that the policy of codification was begun in India;[14] and it was largely inspired by Bentham.

James Mill was a devoted disciple of Bentham. He was examiner of Indian correspondence when Macaulay was sent out with instructions to draw up a code or codes for British India; and it is to the pen of James Mill that is attributed by tradition the dispatch in which those instructions were emphasized and developed.[15]

---

[1] Ilbert, op. cit. 53.   [2] Ibid 59.   [3] Ibid 58.

[4] Ibid 60; 24, 25 Victoria cc. 94-100 mainly drafted by Mr. Graves.

[5] Ilbert, op. cit. 68; for the manner in which consolidation bills are now drafted, and the difficulties in making a good consolidation bill, see Graham-Harrison, Criticisms of the Statute Book, Journal of the Soc. of Public Teachers of Law 1935 21-25.

[6] Above 314.   [7] Below 381-382.

[8] Between 1870 and 1934 109 consolidation bills have been passed, Graham Harrison, op. cit. 24.

[9] 56, 57 Victoria c. 61; vol. x 157.

[10] 57, 58 Victoria c. 60.

[11] Ilbert, op. cit. 128.   [12] Ibid 122.   [13] Above 313-314.

[14] Above 225.   [15] Ilbert, op. cit. 126.

But, though the policy of codification has been successfully followed in India, because in the circumstances of that country it was eminently desirable and practically possible, it made little progress in England in the first three-quarters of the nineteenth century. In India it was necessary to make new law on a large scale to meet the needs of the new civilization which British rule was introducing ; and, since much of this law was administered by unprofessional magistrates to comparatively primitive peoples, and sometimes to barbarous tribes, it was necessary that it should be stated shortly and simply.[1] Conditions were far otherwise in England. It was much more difficult to codify an elaborate body of law which had had a long and a continuous history. And since this body of law was, in spite of the criticism of the Benthamites, regarded by very many as a possession of which the nation was as proud as it was of that constitution which was to a large extent its product, it was politically very difficult to carry any measure of codification. And so it happened that the policy of consolidating the statutes bore very much more fruit than the policy of codifying the law. Bills for the codification of the whole or parts of the criminal law failed to pass in 1846 and 1854 ;[2] and the royal commission appointed in 1866 to enquire into expediency of a digest of the law failed to effect anything.[3] A more serious attempt at codification was made some ten years later. Sir James FitzJames Stephen attempted to do for England what he had done for India. But his codes of the law of evidence, and his criminal codes, failed to pass.[4] This failure " gave a check to the cause of codification in England." [5] It was not till the last years of the nineteenth century that any codifying Acts were passed. The first—the Bills of Exchange Act—was passed in 1882.[6] It was followed by the Partnership Act 1890,[7] the Sale of Goods Act 1893,[8] the Perjury Act 1911, the Forgery Act 1913, and the Larceny Act 1916.

Bentham, as Sir Courtenay Ilbert has said, demonstrated the utility of codification ;[9] and though experience has shown that a complete code " which shall absolve from the necessity of researches into the case law or statute law of the past, which

[1] Above 221-222.
[2] Ilbert, op. cit. 52, 53.
[3] Above 314.
[4] Ilbert, op. cit. 127-128.
[5] Ibid 128.
[6] 45, 46 Victoria c. 61.
[7] 53, 54 Victoria c. 39.
[8] 56, 57 Victoria c. 71.
[9] " ' Bentham,' wrote J. S. Mill in 1838, ' demonstrated the necessity and practicability of codification, or the conversion of all law into a written or systematically arranged code.' In truth, he demonstrated neither the one nor the other. What he did was to set up an ideal towards which legislation should tend, an ideal which has been materially modified by subsequent reflection and experience, but which has profoundly influenced the thought and action of lawyers and legislators since his time. He has not shown the necessity, but he has shown the utility, of codification," op. cit. 125.

shall preclude the judicial development of law in the future, and which shall provide a simple rule applicable to every case with which the practical man may have to deal," [1] is impossible, yet he did much indirectly to bring about reforms which have made a partial measure of codification possible. It is due to his influence that those measures of revision and consolidation, which have done so much to clarify the statute book, have been passed ; [2] and we shall see that the measures which have been taken to improve the drafting of statutes owe something to his teaching.[3] Moreover, it is largely due to his teaching that the substance as well as the form of the law has been rationalized ; and it is due partly to this rationalization, and partly to the rise of an adequate system of legal education,[4] that there has been an improvement in legal literature, which has had a large effect in elucidating and clarifying the whole body of the law. Though Sir James Stephen's criminal codes failed to pass into law,[5] they were the parents of his digests of the criminal law and criminal procedure, which were the best statements of the modern law on these subjects that had yet appeared ; and, as Sir Courtenay Ilbert has said, " a good text book has often been the foundation of a code, and in the meantime is not a bad substitute." [6] That this is true is shown by the three measures of codification which passed in the last years of the nineteenth century. The Bills of Exchange Act 1882, and the Sale of Goods Act 1893, were founded on digests of these branches of the law which had been written by M. D. Chalmers ; and the Partnership Act 1890, on a digest of this branch of the law which had been written by Sir Frederick Pollock.[7]

The preparation of an adequate index to the statutes.

The want of an adequate index to the statutes was noticed by the House of Commons committee which reported in 1796.[8]

---

[1] Ilbert, op. cit. 125.   [2] Above 314-315, 316.   [3] Below 375-376.

[4] This fact was very clearly shown by Dicey in his valedictory lecture on Blackstone's Commentaries, Camb. Law Journal iv 303-307.

[5] Above 317.   [6] Legislative Methods and Forms 162.

[7] " The popularization of legal ideas has stimulated the effort to reduce the rules of English law to such a body of principles as is to be found in Stephen's *Digest of the Criminal Law*, or Chalmers' *Digest of the Law of Bills of Exchange ;* and these unauthorized digests, some of which have already passed into Acts of Parliament, are laying the foundation of a complete code of the law of England," Dicey, Blackstone's Commentaries, Camb. Law Journal iv 307.

[8] Reports of Committees of the House of Commons xiv 125 ; above 310 ; Mr. Cowley, A Bibliography of Abridgments (S.S.) xxxviii-xxxix, says, " The indexes, were very infrequent up to 1800 ; two had appeared in the sixteenth century, one in 1553 printed by Berthelet, and one probably in 1570 printed by Tottell ; the next was that ascribed to Jacob published in 1716 ; and finally an index carried down to 10 George III was issued in 1772 by Owen Ruffhead, editor of the statutes at large. Tables had of course been included in editions of the statutes by Pulton and others, and Cay's edition of the statutes at large was fully indexed in 1739 " ; for Ashe's Tables to the statutes which had been equitably interpreted see vol. iv 312.

Indices to the statutes at large had appeared in the course of the nineteenth century ; [1] but it was not till 1867 that the task of compiling an official index and chronological table to the statutes was taken in hand. That it was then taken in hand was due to Lord Cairns. We have seen that he suggested to the Lord Chancellor the preparation of an index and a chronological table. [2] This index and table were prepared under the direction of the committee to whom the Lord Chancellor had referred Lord Cairns's proposal, [3] and the first edition was published in 1870. [4] The index and table are now published periodically, and have been improved in the successive editions. [5]

These changes have gradually produced the modern system of classifying and publishing the statutes. In pursuance of the recommendations of the House of Commons committee of 1796, [6] the statutes were classified in three classes : (1) Public General Acts ; (2) Local and Personal Acts declared public and to be judicially noticed ; (3) Private and Personal Acts. [7] The first two classes were to be printed in separate volumes, and their chapters were to be separately numbered. The last class was not to be printed. [8] A new classification was adopted in 1814, which was due to the resolution of the Houses come to in 1801. [9] The statutes were to be divided into the following four classes : (1) Public General Acts ; (2) Local and Personal Acts declared to be public and to be judicially noticed ; (3) Private Acts printed by the King's Printer, copies of which could be given in evidence ; and (4) Private Acts not so printed. [10] In 1857 it was enacted that all Acts were to be judicially noticed unless there was a clause to the contrary in the Act. [11] But Acts were still classed as public and general, or local and personal, according as they originated in public or private bills. [12] This was an artificial distinction ; and in 1868 the modern classification into Public General, Local, and Personal Acts was initiated. [13]

Down to year 1887 the statutes published by the King's Printer were published in different forms and at different prices. [14] The committee appointed by Lord Chelmsford in 1867

---

[1] Cowley, op. cit. xxxix. [2] Above 314.
[3] Ilbert, op. cit. 63-64. [4] Ibid 66. [5] Ibid 67.
[6] Reports of Committees of the House of Commons xiv 122-123.
[7] Ilbert, op. cit. 49-50, citing Commons' Journals lii 45.
[8] Ilbert, op. cit. 49-50.
[9] Parlt. Papers 1831-1832 xviii 216 ; the resolution was that private Acts were to be printed, if the parties consented, at their expense ; in return copies of the Acts so printed were to be admissible in evidence.
[10] Ilbert, op. cit. 50.
[11] 13, 14 Victoria c. 21 § 7, replaced by § 9 of the Interpretation Act 1889, 52, 53 Victoria c. 63.
[12] Above 289 ; Ilbert, op. cit. 28.
[13] Above 287. [14] Ilbert, op. cit. 64.

recommended that they should be published in octavo only.[1] This recommendation was carried out when the existing edition of the annual statutes was first published in 1887, edited, as we have seen, by an officer paid by the Treasury.[2]

We must now revert to the eighteenth century and examine the process by which the statutes were then made.

The Process of Making Statutes

The main outlines of Parliamentary procedure, and therefore of the procedure on public bills and money bills, had been settled before the beginning of the eighteenth century.[3] As Porritt says,[4]

the last House of Commons which met in the old chapel of S. Stephen's —that of the parliament in existence at the time of the fire of 1834— was following in its main lines the procedure which the Journals show to have been in use when, in 1547, the House migrated from the Chapter House of Westminster Abbey to the famous chapel which Edward VI then assigned to the Commons for their meeting place. First reading, second reading, reference to committee, third reading, the stages of a bill in the House of Commons as we know them to-day were the steps in procedure when the House first met in S. Stephen's, and the Journals now printed were begun on the 8th November in the first year of Edward VI.

We have seen that that procedure was for historical reasons a procedure of opposition, and that it was, consequently, a procedure which gave a minority in opposition great powers to criticize and delay.[5] We have seen that it was the existence of these powers which, in spite of all the defects of the representative system, made Parliament a body which represented faithfully the feelings and wishes of the nation, and so made the Parliamentary government of the eighteenth century a form of government which was on the whole successful and respected.[6] But we have seen also that this characteristic of Parliamentary procedure was emphasized by the elaboration of the rules of procedure which took place in the eighteenth century.[7]

One illustration of this elaboration in the process of legislation is the number of divisions which might be demanded upon the passage of any bill through the House of Commons. The Speaker, Shaw Lefevre, told a committee of the House of

[1] Ilbert, op. cit. 64 ; this recommendation had been made as early as 1835, Parlt. Papers 1835 xviii 131.

[2] Above 287.

[3] Vol. x 532-533 ; see vol. ii 431-434 ; vol. iv 175-178 ; vol. vi 88-92, 254-256 ; in 1732 Pulteney said, " by the ancient orders and methods of proceeding in this House, nothing relating to the raising of money or taxing the people can properly be brought before us, till it has gone regularly through the Committee of Ways and Means," Parlt. Hist. viii 1014.

[4] The Unreformed House of Commons i 528 ; and see vol. x 532-533.

[5] Ibid 536.　　　　[6] Ibid 537-538.　　　　[7] Ibid 533.

Commons in 1848 that eighteen different questions must be put, on each of which a division might be challenged, in order to pass a bill through the House. These eighteen questions were as follows : [1]

(1) That leave be given to bring in the bill.[2] (2) That this bill be read a first time. (3) That the bill be read a second time on (a named day). (4) That this bill be now read a second time. (5) That this bill be committed on (a named day). (6) That this bill be committed. (7) That the Speaker do now leave the chair. Then after it has passed through the committee : (8) That the report be received on (a named day). (9) That this report be now received. (10) That this report be now read. (11) That these amendments be now read a second time. (12) That the House agree with their committee in the said amendments. (13) That this bill be engrossed. (14) That this bill be read a third time on (a named day). (15) That this bill be now read a third time. (16) That this bill do pass. (17) That this be the title to the bill. (18) That Messrs. A. and B. do carry this bill to the Lords.

And it should be noted, first, that these eighteen questions were in addition to the infinite number of questions which might arise in the discussion of the bill in committee ; and, secondly, that these eighteen questions were " merely the normal skeleton of the discussion of a bill, irrespective of all the conceivable variations of subsidiary motions, instructions, and motions for adjournment." [3]

Another illustration of the unnecessary formalities which had grown up around the process of legislation, is to be found in some of the methods of communication between the two Houses. Two of the masters in Chancery were employed in carrying bills and messages from the House of Lords to the House of Commons ; and the House of Lords would not receive a bill from the Commons if it was brought up by less than eight members.[4] If several bills were brought up the Lord Chancellor would not receive them all together. Each must be brought up separately, and on each occasion the Lord Chancellor must walk from the woolsack to the bar to receive them. On one occasion, when fifty-one bills were brought up to the Lords, it was calculated that the Lord Chancellor had walked 1,670 yards before they were all received ; and the time taken was forty-four minutes—though " he had walked as quickly as possible." The origin of this time-wasting practice is curious and characteristic. The Lord Chancellor used to get a fee of ten guineas for each bill he received, and so he must earn his money.[5]

[1] Cited Redlich, The Procedure of the House of Commons i 65 n. 1.
[2] If the bill was already prepared it was brought in ; if not, the House ordered a member or members to prepare and bring it in ; and this was regarded in 1733 as the ordinary and regular procedure, Parlt. Hist. viii 1183-1184.
[3] Redlich, op. cit. i 64-65.
[4] Parlt. Papers 1847 xii 621-622—the evidence of Nassau W. Senior.
[5] Ibid 619.

Modern politicians and publicists, who, in this mechanical age, are apt to stress unduly the importance of efficient machinery, and to neglect the much greater importance of the personal qualities of the men who work the machinery, naturally wonder how, under these conditions, any legislation at all was possible. That it was possible was due, as we haveseen, partly to the static character of eighteenth-century politics, and partly to the homogeneous character of the governing class who composed the Legislature.[1] Both parties agreed that the King's government must be carried on ; and both parties agreed that the forms of the House, which secured the adequate consideration of legislative proposals, must be preserved.[2] And so, while there was plenty of reasoned criticism, and much intelligent opposition, no one thought of using the forms of the House for purposes of obstruction.[3] That criticism was the more intelligent, and that opposition was the more reasoned, because the task of criticizing and opposing was left mainly to the leaders of the principal parties in the House. Lord Balfour, in 1902, said of eighteenth-century politics that " the difficulty was not to check the flow of oratory, but to make it flow at all ; " and that in consequence those who made the rules of procedure " exhausted their ingenuity in finding opportunities for gentlemen to speak, and offering them temptations to air their opinions, or to deal with the case of their constituents." [4]

The result was that the legislative, as well as all the other business of the House of Commons, was, in spite of this cumbrous procedure, dispatched without difficulty. Gladstone said in 1882 : [5]

I well remember in my boyhood, when sitting in the gallery of the House which was burnt down, that the same things used to take place as now take place in the other House of Parliament, namely, that between 6 and 7 o'clock the House, as a matter of course, had disposed of its business and was permitted to adjourn.

But, in the nineteenth century, the growing complexity of the problems of government, which was caused partly by the industrial revolution, partly by the expansion of trade which came in its train, and partly by the political development of the

[1] Vol. x 536-537.
[2] Charles James Fox said in 1787 that " no part of the constitution had been more tenaciously preserved than the forms by which all laws were enacted " ; that the forms of passing bills were very deliberate, and might by some be considered to be tedious ; but that the reason was " to give Parliament so many different opportunities of considering the tendency of the measure before they finally gave it their concurrence. This caution was therefore exceedingly wise ; for nothing required more deliberation than laws enacted for the welfare, protection, and government of the people," Parlt. Hist. xxvi 659-660.
[3] Vol. x 537.
[4] Cited Redlich, op. cit. i 64.
[5] Redlich, op. cit. i xix.

overseas dominions, made the task of the Legislature far more difficult and more intricate.[1] The advent of the Irish members after the Act of Union in 1800 added a considerable element of loquacity; and in the course of the first thirty years of the nineteenth century an increased number of English and Scottish members of the House of Commons became more earnest and more vocal.[2] All the causes making for the increase of the business of the House of Commons were intensified after 1832, so that, in the course of the next forty years, it was becoming obvious that the old procedure was quite unsuited to modern conditions.[3] When, in the last quarter of that century, a section of the Irish members set out deliberately to wreck the procedural machinery of the House of Commons, by making use of its forms for the purpose of obstruction, it became necessary to make radical reforms in that procedure. The reforms which were made in the last quarter of the nineteenth and in the first years of the twentieth century, have substituted for the old procedure " the new procedure under which the House of Commons now conducts its business." [4]

In the eighteenth century these developments were still in the distant future. Throughout that century the process of legislation, so far as concerns the enactment of public and general statutes, was in essentials the procedure of the seventeenth century. But, in the procedure used to pass private bills into law, there were great developments both in the House of Commons and the House of Lords. The result of these developments was that a private bill procedure was gradually evolved, which was and is a unique example of a procedure which combines judicial and legislative characteristics. It was largely due to this procedure that it was possible, by means of private Acts of Parliament, to try experimentally new devices both for correcting the deficiencies of the law public and private, and for supplementing the machinery of government; and that, as the

[1] " There was then [in the eighteenth century] no constant stream of reforms on a large scale, there were no bills with hundreds of clauses and countless technical details of a contentious character. Domestic legislation for the whole of the period of parliamentary conservatism was confined to small alterations in administrative law, to special and local enactments. The centre of gravity of the action of the House of Commons lay in the region of foreign and colonial policy, and the financial measures rendered necessary by the decisions on such subjects. The manifold forms of financial discussion furnished the framework into which the members of the House could insert the motions which arose out of the political situation or party tactics," Redlich, op. cit. i 66.

[2] " The old Tory Sir Robert Inglis, in one of his speeches on the Reform Bill (1831) said : ' Formerly very few members were wont to address the House; now the speaking members are probably not less than four hundred.' And of the Irish members not four of the hundred were wholly silent," Redlich, op. cit.i 68 n. 1, citing Townsend, History of the House of Commons ii 390.

[3] Ibid 73-132.   [4] Ibid Part ii chaps. ii-iv.

result of these experiments, it was possible to introduce wholly new ideas into English law. In fact, the number and variety of the private Acts of Parliament, which were passed in the eighteenth century, went far to supplement the comparatively small number and limited range of the public and general Acts. I have already said something of this phenomenon in the sphere of local government.[1] We shall see that it is equally true of other branches of English law.[2] But at this point I am concerned, not with the subject-matter of this legislation, but with the procedure by which it was brought into being. We shall see that the evolution of this procedure has created a piece of political machinery which is capable of being turned to very various uses, and that it is as original as many of the other institutions of English law public and private—as original for instance, as the jury or the trust.

We have seen that Parliament in the mediæval period was, like most other mediæval governing bodies, regarded as a court; [3] but that, in the course of the fifteenth and sixteenth centuries, it had developed legislative and other powers which differentiated it from all other courts.[4] When associated with the King it had become " the great corporation or body politic of the kingdom "; [5] and its two Houses had acquired powers which were different in kind from those of any other court. Coke recognized this fact when, as Speaker, he told the House of Commons in 1592-1593 that it was " not a court alone." [6] But, though the two Houses had come to differ so markedly from any other court, yet they still retained so many of the characteristics of a court that all the writers of the sixteenth century could speak of Parliament as a court ; and they still retain so many of these characteristics that we are conscious of no anachronism when we speak of the High Court of Parliament.[7] It is true that the judicial aspect of the House of Commons is not so obvious as the judicial aspect of the House of Lords. But the House of Commons has a judicial aspect. Some of its privileges, for instance, and some of the modes used to enforce them, recall it.[8] But it is chiefly recalled by the procedure which it has evolved to deal with private bills. That procedure combines the ideas of the early mediæval period, when Parliament was regarded more especially as a court and its

---

[1] Vol. x 188-195.   [2] Below 619-626.
[3] Vol. i 352 ; vol. ii 434 and n. 4.
[4] Ibid 431-434 ; vol. iv 174-184.
[5] Coke, Fourth Instit. 2, cited vol. iv 184.
[6] D'Ewes' Journal 515, cited vol. iv 184.
[7] Ibid 182-183.   [8] Ibid 183 and n. 2 ; vol. vi 268-272.

decisions as the judgments of a court,[1] and the ideas of the late fifteenth and sixteenth centuries, when it had become a legislative body and its decisions took shape in statutes.[2] It is because Parliament, when it became a Legislature, never wholly ceased to be a court, it is because in this, as in so many other parts of our public law, mediæval ideas survived, that it has been possible to evolve gradually a piece of constitutional machinery, which could never have been devised by a person who was constructing a code of constitutional law on logical *a priori* principles.

A Private Act of Parliament is as truly a legislative Act as a Public and General Act. Whether an Act has been promoted by a private person or a body of persons, or whether it has been promoted by the ministers of the Crown or by a private member in the interests of the whole community, it is an Act of the sovereign Legislature and a part of the law of the land. But the process of passing a legislative proposal of the former kind differs in many essential points from the process of passing a legislative proposal of the latter kind. In the case of a private bill some stages of the process are of a very distinctly judicial character ; and it is the elaboration of these judicial character-istics which has resulted in the evolution of a unique method of using the legislative power of the state.[3] It is a method which combines the power to act freely in the interests of the state which is possessed by the legislator, with the duty to weigh the com-parative merits of the cases of the promoters and opposers which is imposed upon the judge. No doubt the extent and character of the legislative and the judicial elements differ in different kinds of private bills. In the estate bills, which were common in the eighteenth century,[4] the judicial characteristics largely predominated : in such bills as town improvement bills,[5] turn-pike bills,[6] or inclosure bills,[7] there was a larger legislative element, because considerations of public policy bulked larger. But in all these bills there was an admixture of legislative and judicial aspects, which demanded a procedure which could give due weight to both of them.

It is not difficult to see why this is so. A private bill pro-moted by a person or a body of persons asks for a *privilegium* —for something which the ordinary law of the land denies or forbids. The promoters appeal to the Legislature to give them this *privilegium*, either because the law leads to manifest hardship

---

[1] Y.B. 7 Hy. VII Trin. pl. 1 p. 15, cited vol. ii 434 n. 4 ; vol. iv 183 n. 3.
[2] Y.BB. 8 Hy. IV Mich. pl. 13 p. 13, 4 Hy. VII Trin. pl. 6, cited vol. ii 434 n. 4 ; vol. iv 185-186.
[3] Below 326-351.
[4] Below 619-621.
[5] Vol. x 214-219 ; below 625-626.
[6] Vol. x 207-210.
[7] Vol. ii 60-61 ; below 455 457, 625.

in a particular case, or because some new need has arisen which
cannot be satisfied in the existing state of the law, or because
some new idea or new invention cannot be exploited without the
gift of extraordinary powers. The Legislature can give these
powers because it is sovereign ; and, in coming to a decision
whether to give or to refuse them, it must take into account
those considerations of public policy which are peculiarly within
its province. And so the debate upon a private bill must have
its legislative aspect. On the other hand, because the promoters
of a private bill are asking for a *privilegium*, they must assign
reasons for their request, and they must prove the truth
of those reasons. Moreover, it is not improbable that the advantages sought by the promoters may infringe the rights of
other persons. Since these rights are given to these persons by
the law, they are entitled to ask that their rights shall be protected, or, if it is decided that they must be infringed, to ask for
compensation for the infringement. For all these reasons the
debate upon a private bill has a well-marked judicial aspect,
and the contents of the bill must, in very many cases, reflect the
judgment which is passed upon the conflicting claims of its promoters and opposers.

From an early period this dual character of private bill legislation has been emphasized. Its legislative character has always
been marked ; but its judicial character has been its distinguishing feature ; and the history of private bill procedure has
been, in the main, the history of the strengthening of this feature.
I propose to consider, first, the evolution of the judicial aspects
of private bill legislation ; secondly, its legislative aspects ;
and, thirdly, the manner in which the courts have regarded the
statutes enacted by means of this mixed legislative and judicial
procedure.

(I) *The judicial aspects of private bill legislation.*

In the eighteenth century there were three stages in which
the judicial aspect of private bill legislation was prominent—
the proceedings on the petition for the bill, on the second reading,
and on the committee stage. So prominent was this judicial
aspect that the procedure naturally assumed certain of the other
characteristics of the judicial procedure of the time. Thus just
as the procedure of the courts suffered from many defects, so
the procedure of the two Houses had defects which caused undue
delays and expense, and, what was more serious, prevented Parliament, in some cases, from giving a truly judicial consideration
to the problems which called for that kind of consideration.
Therefore at the end of the century we can see the beginnings of

changes which will remedy these defects, and will provide a machinery which will strengthen the judicial character of the procedure of the two Houses. I shall deal therefore with this topic under the following heads : The three stages at which the judicial aspect of private bill legislation was prominent ; other judicial characteristics of the procedure of private bill legislation ; the strengthening of the judicial aspects of private bill legislation.

The three stages at which the judicial aspect of private bill legislation was prominent.

(i) We have seen that all bills originally began by petition ; but that, while public bills had ceased to be begun in this way in the latter part of the fifteenth century, private bills have never ceased to be initiated by petition.[1] The proceedings on the petition for a private bill are therefore the first stage of such a bill ; and, though the form of the proceedings has changed from time to time, these proceedings have never ceased to have a judicial character.

From the year 1278, if not before, the House of Lords, at the beginning of each session, appointed certain persons to be the receivers and triers of petitions.[2] In the mediæval period the receivers of petitions were the masters in Chancery,[3] and later some of the judges were joined with them.[4] The triers of petitions were lords of Parliament, and sometimes persons, like the judges, who were summoned to the House by writs of assistance.[5] In practice the judges, though generally only nominated as receivers of petitions, acted as triers ; [6] and in 1705 the House of Lords made an order that all petitions for private bills should be referred to two judges, who were to summon the parties concerned in the bill, and make a report to the House on the bill.[7] But it would seem that in practice this examination by the judges was confined to estate bills,[8] long before it was expressly so confined

[1] Above 289.
[2] Clifford, History of Private Bill Legislation i 271 ; cp. vol. i 354.
[3] Clifford, op. cit. i 271 ; for the masters in Chancery see vol. i 416-418.
[4] Clifford, op. cit. i 271.
[5] Ibid ; the triers could call upon the King's serjeants to help them to deal with English petitions, the Justice and Treasurer of Ireland to help them to deal with Irish petitions, and the Archbishop of Canterbury, the Chancellor, the Treasurer and Chief Justice when they needed them, ibid i 272.
[6] " Whether the judges ever actually received the petitions or not, by the eighteenth century they had certainly ceased to do so, and, such are the contradictions between word and fact in our constitution, that they had as certainly begun to try them, whilst the triers had long ceased to do so," Spencer, Municipal Origins 87-88.   [7] Ibid 88 ; Clifford, op. cit. ii 768-769.
[8] Spencer, op. cit. 89 ; it would seem that the occasion for this order was the growing number of estate bills, and that from the first it was confined to them, MSS. of the House of Lords (Hist. MSS. Com.) vi *xxxix ;* this was a useful order as the judges sometimes raised points which had not occurred to the committee of the House, MSS. of the House of Lords vii *xlii.*

by an order made by the House of Lords in 1887.[1] It is in connection with these estate bills that Blackstone mentions a preliminary examination by the judges ; [2] and it would seem that
by 1740 the receivers and triers of petitions had ceased to perform
their original functions, since, in that year, a motion was made
that entries of their appointment should cease to be made in the
Journals.[3] But the motion was lost,[4] and, till 1886, these officials
still continued to be appointed by the House of Lords at the
beginning of every Parliament, in the same form of words and
with the same functions as in the reign of Edward I.[5]

These officials ceased to perform their functions because,
from the fifteenth century onwards, the work formerly done by
them was taken over by committees of the House. In 1399 ten
petitions were referred by the House of Lords to committees
instead of to the triers of petitions.[6] Similar committees on
petitions in the House of Commons are mentioned in 1614 ; [7]
and there are one or two instances in the seventeenth century
in which petitions were referred to committees to see whether
the facts justified the introduction of a bill.[8] But it was not
till the eighteenth century that it became the usual practice to
send petitions for private Acts to a committee to ascertain
whether a prima facie case had been made out for the introduction of a bill.[9] In the eighteenth century both Houses made
use of the committees on petitions for this purpose.[10]

These committees, like the old triers of petitions, exercised
judicial functions. Like them, they must see whether the
petitioner had made out a prima facie case for a bill. As these
petitions multiplied, and as the procedure upon them came to be

---

[1] Clifford, op. cit. ii 769-770.   [2] Comm. ii 345.

[3] Clifford, op. cit. i 273-274.

[4] Parlt. Hist. xi 1015—Lord Hardwicke opposed the motion—" I am inclined,"
he said, " to adhere to all parts of the ancient constitution," ibid 1014 *note*.

[5] Anson, Parliament (5th ed.) 310, 391 n. ; on Queen Victoria's accession
receivers and triers were appointed in the old form of words : " The receivers for
Great Britain and Ireland were ' Messire Nicholas Conyngham Tyndale, chevalier
et chief Justicier de Banc commune ; Messire James Allan Park, chevalier et
Justicier ; Messire William George Adam ecuyer.' For ' petitions de Gascogne et
des autres terres et pays de par la mer et des isles,' the receivers were Baron Abinger
and two others. There was the usual notice ' et ceux qui veulent delivre leur petitions les baillent dedans six jours procheinment en suivant.' The triers of petitions
from Great Britain and Ireland were the Duke of Norfolk and twenty-six other
peers ; from Gascony and places beyond the seas the triers named were the Duke
of Brandon and twenty-three other peers. And it was notified that ' touts eux
ensemble, ou quatre des seigneurs avant-ditz, appellant aux eux le Serjeants de la
Reyne, quant sera besoigne, tiendront leur place en la chambre du Chambellan ',"
Clifford, op. cit. i 274.

[6] Ibid 278-279.   [7] Ibid ii 790.

[8] Ibid.   [9] Ibid.

[10] Ibid 860-861 ; in the earlier part of the century this committee was sometimes
a committee of the whole House, see Parlt. Hist. viii 514 (1726) ; in 1732 Thomas
Lombe's petition for an extension of his patent was referred by the House to a
select committee, ibid 928.

more elaborately regulated by the standing orders of both the Houses, the duties of the committees became more onerous and tended to alter somewhat in character.

As early as 1621 the House of Commons refused to read a bill "because not written sheetwise with wide lines." [1] This was pure form, and it soon became apparent that more important matters of substance needed regulation. Some of the earliest of the standing orders were directed to securing that notification of pending bills was given to those whose interests would be affected by them.[2] Notification was the more necessary since, until 1705, promoters were not obliged to print these bills.[3] Some very precise orders as to the notices to be given on Irish estate bills were made in 1707 ; [4] and in the course of the eighteenth century the increase in the number of inclosure, improvement, drainage, and canal bills made more elaborate orders necessary. These bills

interfered with rights of ownership and occupation extending over wide districts, and it is probable that much hardship and injustice were often occasioned by private statutes of that nature, the full effect of which only became known when it was too late to oppose and hopeless to repeal them.[5]

Therefore in 1774 standing orders were made that notices of inclosure, drainage, and improvement bills should be posted on the church doors in each parish affected, and should be proclaimed at quarter sessions ; that notices of turnpike bills should be advertised in the newspapers ; that the promoters of canal bills should make a specific application to each owner, lessee, and occupier of the land affected, informing them of the bill and asking them whether they assented, dissented, or were neutral ; and that they should deposit plans showing the line of the proposed works.[6]

At the same time the standing orders began to lay down rules as to the contents of bills, with a view to the protection of private or public interests. Thus in 1774 and 1781 orders were made that certain clauses must be inserted in inclosure bills ; [7] and in 1793 the House of Lords, and in 1794 the House of Commons, made orders that certain clauses must be inserted in canal bills.[8] In 1800 the House of Commons made orders as to the financial provisions of turnpike bills ; [9] and

[1] Notestein, Commons Debates 1621 ii 256, v 62.
[2] Clifford, op. cit. ii 760-762 ; cp. House of Lords MSS. (N.S.) vi *xxxix*.
[3] Clifford, op. cit. ii 760 ; Parlt. Hist. xii 643.
[4] Clifford, op. cit. ii 763.   [5] Ibid 763-764.   [6] Ibid 764.
[7] Parlt. Papers 1810 ii 215-219.   [8] Ibid 222-224.
[9] Ibid 220-221 ; cp. Spencer, Municipal Origins 67.

in the same year we may note the beginnings of the movement which resulted in the Lands Clauses Consolidation Acts, for standing orders regulating the provisions as to the purchase of lands in inclosure, road, drainage, paving, dock, or navigation Bills were drawn up.[1]

Thus

by the end of the eighteenth century, both Houses of Parliament had built up a system of standing orders, chiefly controlling the notices to be given of, and the consents to be obtained to, almost every variety of private Bill, together with other preliminaries, such as the deposit of plans and the estimate of costs to be incurred, and to a certain extent controlling the actual contents of the bills.[2]

These standing orders added to the duties of the committees on petitions ; for these committees were made use of, not only to see that the promoters of the bill had made a prima facie case for legislation, but also to see that the requirements of the standing orders had been complied with.[3] In the eighteenth century both these preliminary enquiries were undertaken by these committees. But gradually the committees on petitions restricted their enquiries to the question whether the proposed bill complied with the standing orders.[4] The promoters had only to prove that the standing orders had been complied with, and to make a prima facie case for their bill on the merits. At this stage no adverse evidence on the merits was allowed.[5] If the committee reported that the standing orders had not been complied with, an appeal could be made to the House.[6]

(ii) The second reading of the bill was the stage at which the reasons for passing the bill set out in its preamble were brought before the House. The House, it was thought, was the proper body to judge of the validity of these reasons.[7] There are many instances in the sixteenth and seventeenth centuries in which the parties or their counsel were heard at the bar on this question, not only on the second reading but at later stages.[8] But, since it was for the House to judge of the validity of the reasons for passing the bill set out in the preamble, and its expediency,

committees on private bills used to hold that they could not entertain objections to the general expediency of a measure, and that the sole object of the reference to them was to settle clauses, see that a bill did not go beyond the objects stated by promoters, and that petitioners

---

[1] Spencer, op. cit. 67.   [2] Ibid 68.
[3] Clifford, op. cit. ii 790.   [4] Ibid 790.
[5] Ibid 792.   [6] Ibid 793.
[7] Hence a member opposed to the preamble was disqualified from serving on the committee ; though this disqualification no longer exists, " the principle on which it rested, that preambles were determined by the whole House, and that the powers of committees were limited, remained in full effect until the nineteenth century," ibid ii 863.
[8] Ibid 853-857, 859-860.

whose property and rights were interfered with received adequate protection. If, therefore, opponents wished to call in question the principle of a bill, they were bound to petition against preamble, stating their objections, and praying to be heard by counsel at the bar. They were then heard, if the House thought fit, upon a motion for the second reading, but at this stage no opposition was allowed to particular provisions. Promoters also might then be heard by counsel in defence of the principle. After a second reading petitions against preamble were no longer available.[1]

But such a hearing interrupted public business, and the House was not a good judge of questions which were often as much dependent upon the evidence as to particular circumstances as to considerations of public policy. And so, by the end of the eighteenth century, the whole matter—preamble as well as the clauses of the proposed bill—came to be delegated to the committee on the bill.[2] The last two orders that petitioners against a private bill should be heard at the bar of the House were made in 1824, and neither took effect.[3]

(iii) From the sixteenth century onwards there is evidence that the committees, to whom private bills were sent after the second reading, proceeded judicially, on the evidence of the promoters and the opponents of the bill.[4] In 1562 there is a case in which the House, after hearing counsel at the bar for an opponent, and the case of the promoters of the bill, sent the bill to a committee of twelve persons " to hear the parties and proofs on both sides and then to certify the House." [5] It would seem therefore that, from the first, the proceedings before the committee had an essentially judicial aspect. The House had approved the principle by the second reading, so that the committee's main work was to see that the provisions of the bill gave due weight to the contentions of the promoters and opposers, and gave adequate compensation to the rights of those affected by it. It was necessary therefore for the committee to take evidence and to hear the parties ; and one of the rules as to the competence of witnesses shows the influence of the exclusive rules of evidence applied in the courts. In the House of Commons petitions for a bill must be " signed by the parties who were suitors for it," and in the Lords " by all parties concerned " ; and, till 1844-1845, these persons were disqualified as witnesses on the ground of interest.[6] But though these committees had essentially

---

[1] Clifford, op. cit. ii 863-864.

[2] " Although bills were sometimes opposed on the second reading, for counsel and witnesses to be heard by the House would have been very exceptional at any date between 1700-1735. Indeed, before 1700, the practice of hearing the witnesses and counsel in committee had been well established, and was preferred by the House," Spencer, Municipal Origins 91 ; Clifford, op. cit. ii 860-861.

[3] Ibid 861.   [4] Ibid 850-853.

[5] Ibid ii 853-854—the counsel for the opponent were serjeants Harper and Plowden.

[6] Ibid 870 ; for the parallel common law rule see vol. ix 193-196.

judicial powers they could not administer an oath.[1]   In the Lords,
it is true, a witness could be sworn at the bar of the House ;
and it was sometimes said in the Lords, when the evidence taken
before a House of Commons committee was cited, that " the
inquiry there was a deficient and inferior inquiry because the
usual test had not been applied." [2]   It was not till 1858 [3] that
select committees of the House of Commons on private bills,
and all committees of the House of Lords, were allowed to administer oaths ; and it was not till 1871 that the House of Commons and all its committees were given this power.[4]   On the
other hand, the House of Commons frequently punished for
contempt witnesses who prevaricated or who refused to answer.[5]

The proceedings on the committee stage of the bill were the
most important of all the stages in the passage of a private bill.   It
was at this stage, and at the stage of the committee on the petition
for the bill, that the judicial aspects of this procedure were
the most strongly marked.   There were rules of procedure to be
observed by promoters and opponents of a bill, which were laid
down by the standing orders of both Houses, just as there were
rules of procedure to be observed by plaintiffs and defendants
in the courts.   There was the same need as there was in the
courts to extract the truth from witnesses and documents, and
to use the evidence in such a way that justice was done to all
the parties.   The main difference was and is that the courts,
having ascertained the facts, must apply the rules of law laid
down by the statutes or the cases to the facts so found, and decide
the matter accordingly ;   whilst these committees, having ascertained the facts, must use their notions of justice to determine
the legislative provisions needed to regulate the rights of the
parties.   For though these committees were and are engaged
on a judicial enquiry into many facts and rights, it is a judicial
enquiry which is preliminary, not to a judgment, but to a legislative act ;   and the judges are not experienced lawyers well
acquainted with the rules of evidence, but ordinary members of
Parliament often without any legal training.   For these reasons
it happens that though the judicial aspects of the procedure are
marked, the procedure itself is looser, and the arguments used are
freer and more discursive, than the procedure and the arguments
used in courts who are applying, and not making, law.[6]

---

[1] Clifford, op. cit. ii 887-888 ; the rule was sometimes circumvented by deputing
members who were justices of the peace to examine persons on oath, or witnesses
were ordered to attend the Lord Chief Justice for this purpose, ibid.

[2] Ibid 888.   [3] 21, 22 Victoria c. 78.

[4] 34, 35 Victoria c. 83.   [5] Clifford, op. cit. ii 889.

[6] See the evidence of Mr. Rickards, counsel to the Speaker, given before a House
of Commons committee on Private Bill Legislation, Parlt. Papers 1863 viii 40 ;
cp. also the evidence given before a similar committee in 1847, Parlt. Papers 1847
xii 407.

But, since the judicial aspects of the procedure were well marked, since it was an essential part of that procedure that the truth of many opposing claims must be sifted by the evidence adduced, and that due weight should be given to the claims of those who proved that their rights would be adversely affected by the proposed legislation, it was inevitable that members of the bar should be called upon to appear before these committees on behalf of the parties interested in these bills, and to do for them what they did for their clients in the courts. They were employed to appear before the committees of the two Houses, and to further their clients' causes by taking advantage of their opponents' breach of procedural rules, by examining and cross-examining witnesses, by summing up the evidence, and by putting forward arguments in support of the case which they were retained to advocate. It was inevitable also that the parties interested in these bills should employ, not only members of the bar to advocate these cases, but also other agents to do the work which was done in the courts by attornies and solicitors. But both the character of the tribunal, and the character of the problems which this tribunal was set to solve, caused the barristers employed in this work to develop a somewhat different technique from that of the barristers who practised before the ordinary courts ; and, similarly, the duties of the other agents employed by the parties were different from those of attornies or solicitors. Of the growth, for these reasons, of a special parliamentary bar, and of a set of professional parliamentary agents, I must now speak, in connection with some of the other judicial characteristics of private bill procedure.

Other judicial characteristics of the procedure of private bill legislation.

The substantially judicial character of the procedure of private bill legislation made it inevitable that both in the working of that procedure, and in the machinery employed to work it, other judicial characteristics should be developed. In the first place, the working of that machinery caused the growth of a set of professional parliamentary agents, and a specialized parliamentary bar. In the second place, the machinery used by both Houses shows several interesting analogies to the machinery of the ordinary courts.

(i) We have seen that in the new courts which were newly created or newly organized in the sixteenth century, such as the court of Chancery, the court of Star Chamber, and the court of Requests, the persons who acted as attornies for the parties were members of the clerical staff of these courts.[1] We have seen

---

[1] Vol. vi 454-455.

that in this respect they differed from the courts of common
law ;   for the attornies of the courts of common law, though
officers of the court, were not on the staff of the court.   They
were independent professional men.[1]   It is somewhat remarkable, in view of the close connection of Parliament with the
common law and the common lawyers, that Parliament should
have followed the example of the court of Chancery, and not of
the common law courts, in the provision which it made for the
representation of those who were promoting or opposing private
bills.   Yet so it was.   Just as the six and sixty clerks originally
acted as attornies of the parties to suits in Chancery,[2] so the
clerks of the two Houses acted as parliamentary agents for
the promoters or the opponents of private bills.[3]   When, at the
end of the eighteenth century, the private bill business of the
Houses increased in volume, objections to this system began
to be heard.   In 1810 a committee of the House of Commons
reported against the practice ;   but though clerks in the private
bill office, which was then set up, were not allowed to act as
parliamentary agents, the other clerks of the House still continued
to do so till 1836.   In that year both Houses resolved that their
officers must " elect whether they would retain their offices, confining themselves to their public work, or would retire with a
view to private practice as parliamentary agents. . . . Some
of the officers preferred to retire, and established at Westminster
firms most of which still bear their names." [4]

Thus in Parliament, as in the court of Chancery,[5] the system
of providing the agents needed by suitors from the staff of the
court broke down.   In both cases that system was superseded
by the system, which had always prevailed in the common law
courts, of independent professional agents.   And these independent parliamentary agents, when they made their appearance, resembled the attornies or solicitors, who appeared for
litigants in the courts, in one important respect.   Just as these
attornies and solicitors were regarded as officers of the court to
which they were attached, and so subject to its control,[6] so these
parliamentary agents are subject to the control of the House of
Commons exercised through the Speaker.   They must subscribe
a declaration to the effect that they will be personally responsible
to the Speaker and the House for the observance of its orders

---

[1] Vol. vi 454-455.   [2] Vol. i 421-423 ; vol. vi 455 ; vol. ix 369-370.

[3] " For many centuries the work of soliciting private bills in Parliament was
performed by officers of each House, who took charge of bills on behalf of promoters, saw that the required forms were complied with, made themselves responsible for the fees to which bills were liable, and generally charged a fixed sum
for this service," Clifford, op. cit. ii 878.

[4] Ibid 878-879.   [5] Vol. vi 455 ; vol. ix 369-370.

[6] Vol. vi 435-436.

and of the rules made by the Speaker, and for the payment of fees ; and they are liable to be suspended by the Speaker for misconduct or breach of rules.[1] But in two other respects the rules applicable to them have come to differ from the rules applicable to attornies and solicitors. In the first place, they are allowed to conduct their clients' cases before the committee— counsel have no monopoly of audience.[2] In the second place, they are not required, as a condition of practising, to pass any qualifying examinations—" subject to the rules enforced by the House of Commons, the profession of parliamentary agent remains a perfectly open one." [3]

The parliamentary agent's duties include the preparation of proofs that standing orders have been complied with, the framing of notices, petitions, and memorials as to non-compliance with standing orders, the drafting of bills, and the drafting of all other documents required in the process of promoting or opposing a bill. It is, says Clifford, " a business requiring for its proper discharge great tact and ability, with an exact knowledge of precedents, and of the highly technical and complicated rules embodied in the standing orders and practice of the two Houses." [4] The knowledge possessed by these agents of the practice of the two Houses makes it easier for the officers of the House to conduct its business ; and " if any case of an unusual character arises, they form a body to whom the officers of Parliament can, and frequently do, apply for information and assistance." [5] Having regard to the nature of their business it is easy to see why parliament refuses to allow its members to act as parliamentary agents, or to be members of a firm of parliamentary agents.[6]

These parliamentary agents have thus become a distinct branch of the legal profession. But in many cases they are not the sole agents employed by persons promoting or opposing a bill. Such persons often employ their own solicitors. The solicitor is in immediate touch with his lay client, and possesses local knowledge. He therefore has a more intimate acquaintance than the parliamentary agent with the special facts which the promoters or the opponents of a bill may wish to bring before Parliament ; and, for that reason, he is the better able to collect the information needed by the parliamentary agent in order that he may draft the bill, and the evidence in support of or in opposition to the bill. A witness before a House of

---

[1] Clifford, op. cit. ii 879-880. [2] Ibid 871.
[3] Ibid 881 ; Mr. Rickards, counsel to the Speaker, said in 1863, " any man may become a parliamentary agent. He pays a certain fee, and his name is put down in a book, and then he is a parliamentary agent," Parlt. Papers 1863 viii 41.
[4] Op. cit. ii 879. [5] Ibid 879 n. 3.
[6] Ibid 874.

Commons committee on private bill legislation said:[1] "The parliamentary agent is superior to the country solicitor as to his knowledge of parliamentary proceedings: but you cannot infuse the facts of an intricate case into the mind of a parliamentary agent; he has so many of these cases. . . . Therefore he insists upon having his client at his elbow when the bill is in committee." Thus the solicitor is often an essential assistant to the parliamentary agent.

Though parliamentary agents can conduct their clients' cases before the committee, they usually employ counsel. From an early period counsel have been employed by those who had causes to advocate in Parliament.[2] But, as a general rule, counsel who are members of Parliament cannot appear upon bills before either House.[3] Originally they were employed at many different stages of a bill—at the bar of the House as well as in committee, and at the bar on public, as well as on private, bills.[4] In fact the practice of hearing counsel at the bar lasted longer in the case of public than of private bills. We have seen that the last orders for hearing counsel at the bar on a private bill were made in 1824, and that those orders did not take effect;[5] but as late as 1844 there was a hearing at the bar on a public bill.[6] In the case of private bills, however, the most usual and the most lucrative field of the parliamentary activities of counsel has long been the committees of the two Houses. It is obvious that the technique of advocacy before a committee of laymen must be different from the technique of advocacy before a judge, or before a judge and jury.

It is not surprising, therefore, that just as a special Chancery bar developed, so a special parliamentary bar was gradually formed. It probably began to take shape at the end of the eighteenth century, and attained its full development with the rush of railway bills in the second quarter of the nineteenth century.[7]

---

[1] Parlt. Papers 1863 viii 326—evidence of Mr. Baxter; and another witness said at pp. 256-257 that, since country solicitors know nothing of the standing orders, they go to a parliamentary agent.

[2] Clifford, op. cit. ii 852-859, 871.   [3] Ibid 872-874.

[4] " During this interval of nearly a century (1623-1711), arguments at bar were frequent, and the House of Commons seems to have reserved to itself the right of hearing the arguments of counsel upon private bills, generally before commitment. Sometimes arguments were allowed at other stages, after the report of a committee, and upon the third reading, even after they had been heard upon second reading," ibid 859.

[5] Above 331.   [6] Clifford, op. cit. ii 861.

[7] Clifford, op. cit. ii 871, thinks that the repetition of certain names in the Journals of the sixteenth and seventeenth centuries shows " that advocacy in Parliament even then was limited to certain members of the bar " ; but in 1863 Sir W. Atherton, the attorney-general, said that the parliamentary bar was of comparatively recent origin, and was largely due to the great increase of parliamentary business that came with the introduction of railways, Parlt. Papers 1863 viii 277.

A witness before a parliamentary committee in 1847 pointed out that a leader at the parliamentary bar must have great tact, and great knowledge of practice and precedents.   He must be at home in a tribunal which is very different from that of an ordinary court, because it is a tribunal of laymen—like a court of quarter sessions, it was said, without a chairman [1]—where all sorts of courses could be taken, all kinds of evidence given, and all sorts of observations made.   And from this point of view it was said to be a very bad school for a young barrister, for he earned high fees, little legal knowledge was required, and all sorts of ir-regularities were allowed.[2]   It is clear that proficiency in the art of advocacy before such a tribunal requires a very special training. A witness before a parliamentary committee of 1863 said : [3]

You may put a man of the first ability to the parliamentary bar, and for a year or two he is of very little use. He has to learn the tone and temper of Committees ; he has to learn by experience what he may urge, and what he may not urge ; and it is the keenness of per-ception, the nice judgment, and the talent in taking all the points of his case, which make the leaders of the parliamentary bar.

It is for these reasons that a specialized parliamentary bar has arisen, which, though it is not formally separate from the general body of the bar,[4] is in fact a very separate part of it.

Let us now turn from the branches of the legal profession which play a principal part in the working of the complicated machinery of private bill procedure, to a consideration of some of the other judicial characteristics of that machinery.

(ii) There were four characteristics of the machinery of private bill procedure which closely resembled the machinery of the ordinary courts.

First, the whole of the official staff of the two Houses, like the official staffs of the courts of law and equity,[5] was financed by fees payable to different officials upon different occasions by members or others.[6]   But by far the largest amount of these fees were derived from persons interested in private bills.[7]   The number and amount of those fees, like the number and amount of the fees payable to the officials of the courts of law and equity,

---

[1] Cp. Erskine May's statement in 1863 to the effect that the proceedings before the committee were like a trial by jury without a judge, since there was no one " sufficiently experienced in judicial enquiries to be able to direct the course of proceedings," Parlt. Papers 1863 viii 301.

[2] Ibid 1847 xii 405, 407, 408.

[3] Ibid 1863 viii 314, cited Clifford, op. cit. ii 871-872.

[4] Parlt. Papers 1863 viii 284.   [5] Vol. i 255-256, 424-425, 441.

[6] A list of the fees taken in 1830 will be found in Parlt. Papers 1830 xxx 153-160 ; for the antiquity of the practice see Clifford, op. cit. ii 716-717 ; a list of the fees sanctioned in 1700 and approved again in 1732 will be found in Parlt. Hist. viii 1004-1006 ; in 1621 Noy moved " for a contribution to the Clerkes that have found oute records for us," Notestein, Commons Debates 1621 iii 401.

[7] Above 298-300.

were settled by the usages which prevailed amongst the officials. Hence the number and amount of the fees constantly tended to increase. Old occasions for exacting a fee might cease, but the fee remained; and new occasions for new fees were never let slip. In 1725 a committee of the House of Lords made an enquiry into the fees taken by their officers. The officers produced an old roll of fees, "which they said was their guide in most things; but when any business happened which was not mentioned in this roll, they took such fees as they ' apprehended ' their predecessors had done." But the roll, when inspected, was found to be a most suspicious document, for " erasures were found with alterations of sums to greater amounts plainly shown by different handwriting and fresher ink." The committee thought many of the fees unreasonable, and drew up a new scale of fees.[1] In 1732 a member of the House of Commons called attention to " the extravagant charges and expenses that people are obliged to be at in passing private bills." [2] The Speaker thought that there was not much cause for complaint; [3] but a committee was appointed, and the table of fees sanctioned in 1700 was approved. In later years the officials enlarged the occasions on which fees were charged, and got the House to sanction these additions; [4] and in 1756 the House of Lords followed the practice of the House of Commons, and allowed them to charge multiplied fees on certain classes of bills.[5] Partly under cover of this permission, and partly as we have seen, by enlarging the definition of what bills were private bills for fee-paying purposes,[6] the officials enormously increased their fees, and made it so difficult for anyone but themselves to understand the principle upon which they were levied, that they were in effect arbitrary exactions. Often they were hardly able to understand their own system; for, as in the case of the courts of law,[7]

---

[1] Clifford, op. cit. ii 726.   [2] Parlt. Hist. viii 921.

[3] Ibid 922; he said that he had always been careful to prevent exorbitant fees; but he admitted that officials tended to enlarge them—" I remember some time ago I found that a guinea was usually given to my secretary, upon the giving out the warrant for writs, whereas the old fee was but ten shillings; I therefore ordered expressly that he should not receive any more upon such occasion than the old fee of ten shillings. . . . I likewise have observed that the clerk of committees usually got a guinea, in place of the old fee of 13s. 4d. This also I have endeavoured to rectify."

[4] " Gradually the officers seem to have enlarged on their own authority the table thus settled. In 1732 the House was informed that, no fee being specified for administering the oaths of allegiance and supremacy to persons, with a view to naturalization, their solicitors refused to pay to the clerk assistant and the Black Rod the fees demanded and taken in the Commons. This new charge was authorized; " similarly in 1739, bar fees, similar to the fees charged on the hearing of appeals by the House of Lords, were charged by that House to promoters and opposers employing counsel, Clifford, op. cit. ii 728-729.

[5] Ibid 729; above 299.   [6] Above 300.

[7] See for instance the charge known as damages clear which was abolished in 1665, vol. i 255-256; and the fee collected by the prothonotaries for entering pleas though the work was done by the attorneys for the parties, ibid 258-259.

these fees were often old customary payments made to various officials the original reason for which was lost.[1] A table of fees drawn up for the committee and private bill offices of the House of Commons in 1830, " consisted," says Clifford,[2]

of a great variety of small items, still charged on a system so complicated as not to be easily understood either by the parties who paid or the clerk who collected them. On the second reading of each bill there were eight different charges, imposed originally for the benefit of various officers, from the Speaker to the door-keepers.

Secondly, as in the case of courts of law and equity,[3] many of the officials of the House held their offices by patent, so that they had something in the nature of a freehold interest in them. Like the patent offices in the courts of law and equity, they were often granted in reversion ; and their holders could execute them by deputy. Thus in 1783, while Ashley Cowper was clerk of the Parliaments, George III gave the post to Samuel Strutt, and after him to George Rose ; and in 1795, while George Rose was clerk, the office was granted to his son on his death or resignation. " All these appointments were for life, with a right to nominate all clerks at the table, and to serve by deputy."[4] As in the case of the courts, sinecure offices [5] and saleable offices [6] were not unknown.

Thirdly, as in the case of the courts of law and equity, the vested interests of the holders of these patent offices, and of the other officials paid by fees, helped to delay reform.[7] So, too, when reform came, it at first took the form of gradually substituting the payment of a fixed salary for the right to collect certain fees, without abolishing the fees. The fees remained and were paid over to a special fund—so that the suitors were not profited.[8] This process of substituting payment by fixed salary for payment by fees, and of continuing the fees,

[1] A House of Commons Committee reported in 1847 that the House fees were " so complicated as not easily to be understood either by the clerk who has to collect them or by the parties who have to pay them," Parlt. Papers 1847 xii 353.

[2] History of Private Bill Legislation ii 742-743.

[3] Vol. i 256-262, 424-425, 439, 441.   [4] Clifford, op. cit. ii 739.

[5] Thus " the four out-door clerks were supposed to be in constant attendance on committees, but never in fact attended, and their offices in 1821 had become sinecures," ibid ii 741.

[6] Thus a statute of 1812, 52 George III c. 11 § 15 provided that offices under the Serjeant-at-Arms which had been accustomed to be sold should continue to be sold and the money paid over to the commissioners appointed by the Act ; but the permission to sell these offices given by the Act was revoked by 6 George IV c. 123 § 3.

[7] Vol. i 251 ; Clifford, op. cit. ii 738, where he points out that it appears from an Act of 1812 (52 George III c. 11) that, though twelve years previously the House had attempted to pay the Speaker, the Clerk of the House of Commons, and the Serjeant-at-Arms by fixed salaries instead of fees, yet the Serjeant-at-Arms appointed in 1811 had acquired a vested interest in these fees which the Act was obliged to recognize, so that the full effect of the reform effected in 1812 could not take effect till after this Serjeant-at-Arms had ceased to serve.

[8] Vol. ix 362 ; cp. Clifford, op. cit. ii 739-740 ; 2, 3 William IV c. 105—appropriation of Speaker's fees to the fee fund.

was begun in 1800, and was not complete till 1836.[1] It was not till 1847 that the whole scale of fees was revised.

A comparatively few large fees were substituted for a multitude of small items, and were charged on the principal stages of a bill, with a progressive increase in amount in proportion to proposed capital. The old system of double and treble, and many more sets of fees upon the same bill, by which promoters had so long been harassed, was discontinued.[2]

Fourthly, there were two other minor points in which the system of private bill procedure resembled the procedure of the court of Chancery. First, just as in the seventeenth century payment to the registrar of the court of Chancery could expedite a cause by getting for it a better place on the list,[3] so the payment of extra fees could expedite the ingrossment of a bill, and so hasten this stage in its progression through Parliament.[4] Secondly, just as many of the officials of the court of Chancery made their money out of the profits upon office copies of documents,[5] so, down to 1863, the chief part of the emoluments of the solicitors employed by the promoters or opposers of a private bill came from their profits on copies of the minutes of evidence given each day to the committee. They supplied themselves with these copies at the rate of 2d. a folio and supplied them to the parties at the rate of 8d. or 10d. a folio.[6] As a parliamentary counsel told the committee, " it is the system by which solicitors are paid, not only in this branch of business, but in others too, namely, by these copies which are mere ministerial acts performed by their officers." [7]

On the other hand, till the legislation of the nineteenth century, committees on private bills had no power to award costs against promoters who had subjected an opponent to unreasonable expense in defending his rights, or against opposers who had put forward frivolous objections.[8] Similarly, it was not till 1825 that any provision was made for the taxation of costs.[9]

---

[1] Clifford, op. cit. ii 736-742 ; see 30 George III c. 10—The Speaker ; 39, 40 George III c. 92—Clerk of the House of Commons and Serjeant-at-Arms ; 52 George III c. 11—Clerk of the House of Commons, Serjeant-at-Arms, Housekeeper of the House of Commons, first and second Clerk Assistant to the House of Commons, and deputy Serjeant-at-Arms ; " several officers of the House received fees till the year 1836, when Mr. Hume carried resolutions, founded upon the recommendations of various select committees on which he had served, and the practice was finally discontinued," Clifford, op. cit. 741-742.

[2] Ibid 744.   [3] Vol. i 426.

[4] " It was the duty of the promoters to take the bill to the office for ingrossment, and to pay for the work. The bills were normally ingrossed in the order received, but expedition could be secured by paying an extra fee of two guineas, when all except the longest bills would be copied within twenty-four hours," Spencer, Municipal Origins 76.

[5] Vol. i 441-442.   [6] Parlt. Papers 1863 viii 154.

[7] Ibid.   [8] Clifford, op. cit. ii 812.

[9] Ibid 814 ; 6 George IV c. 123—House of Commons ; 7, 8 George IV c. 64—House of Lords ; further provisions were made by 10, 11 Victoria c. 69 and 12, 13 Victoria c. 78.

Those few illustrations show that the judicial aspects of private bill procedure were a very marked characteristic of that procedure. But the machinery employed to obtain an impartial judgment upon the many questions which demanded a judicial consideration, suffered from many defects. These defects were partly due to the same causes which made the machinery of the courts of justice defective—the system of the payment of officials by fees, the uncertainty and capriciousness of these fees, and patent and sinecure offices. But they were mainly due to the fact that the procedure was as much legislative as judicial. The fact that it was necessary to employ the ordinary machinery of legislation made it necessary to use machinery which was not in all respects well suited to the task of a judicial enquiry. As we shall now see, it was not till the reforms of the nineteenth century that these defects were remedied by measures which strengthened the judicial side of this procedure.

The strengthening of the judicial aspects of private bill legislation.

The three principal defects of this private bill procedure were, first the constitution of the committees on petitions and the committees on bills ; secondly, the absence of proper safeguards, especially in the case of unopposed bills, against clauses detrimental to the interest of the public, or against clauses which made ill-considered changes in the general law ; and, thirdly, the expense and length of the procedure and the uncertainty of its results.

(i) We have seen that the functions both of committees on petitions and committees on bills were predominantly judicial in character.[1] But the constitution of these committees was such that they were very badly equipped for the exercise of judicial functions ; and sometimes they had no desire to exercise their powers judicially. The contrast between them and the modern select committees has been clearly brought out by Mr. Spencer. He says : [2]

The committees to which such petitions for bills, and at a later stage the bills themselves, were referred, in the eighteenth and early nineteenth centuries, bore little resemblance to the private bill committees of to-day. They were not small impartial committees from which all vestiges of local influence have been removed, and before which the proceedings are of at least a quasi-judicial character. The promoters of every private bill were, of course, always careful to procure the services of a member who was willing to undertake to conduct it through the House. It was the practice for this member to be appointed Chairman of the committee which was charged to consider whether a

[1] Above 328, 331.　　　　　[2] Municipal Origins 52-53.

bill ought to be introduced, and he was also Chairman of the committee to which the bill, if ordered, was usually committed for detailed consideration, after the second reading. The Chairman of the committee was not, therefore, the impartial president of a quasi-judicial committee. He was the advocate, or at least the friendly assistant and counsellor, of the promoters. . . . The practice was well established by the beginning of the eighteenth century and continued in the Commons, in spite of complaint, long into the nineteenth.[1]

Both committees on petitions and committees on bills were large and unwieldy bodies.[2] Committees on petitions had small knowledge of the standing orders which, as time went on, were developing into a very technical code ; and they were amenable to local pressure.[3] Committees on bills were often equally unwieldy since, all through the eighteenth century, the practice of giving " voices " to all who liked to attend was growing.[4] Two consequences followed. In the first place, in a bill which aroused great opposition promoters and opponents alike canvassed their friends and brought them down to vote, so that the matter was often decided by persons who had never listened to the arguments or evidence, and knew nothing of the merits of the contentions of the parties. From the seventeenth to the nineteenth century there were plenty of members who were ready thus to oblige their friends. Roger North, at the end of the seventeenth century, noted how the English gentry " were perpetually hunting projects to make their estates richer to themselves without regard to others : some to have wool dear, others corn, and the like.

[1] Mr. Spencer gives, op. cit. 53-54, the following instance of the working of that system in practice : in 1701 Tregonell Luttrell petitioned for an Act to renovate Minehead harbour which his family had constructed in 1616. The petition was referred to a committee of fourteen named members, and " all that served " for the counties of Somerset, Devon, and Cornwall—thus including Luttrell himself who was member for Minehead. The committee having reported in favour of the bill, Luttrell was one of the three members charged to prepare it. The chairman of the committee was " a member of the great west county family in whose interests it was being promoted."

[2] " Substantially the practice throughout the eighteenth century seems to have been that described by the select committee of the Commons in 1825 : Under ' the present system each bill is committed to the member who is charged with its management and such other members as he may choose to name in the House, and the members serving for a particular county (usually the county immediately connected with the object of the bill) and the adjoining counties.' The committees, whether on petitions or bills, were constituted in exactly the same way. Such committees, therefore, were very large, varying in number according to the locality affected by the bill, and thus, according to the number of members for the county or counties directly concerned and for the adjacent counties, from sixty or seventy up to as many as 200," Spencer, op. cit. 55.

[3] Clifford, op. cit. ii 791 ; speaking of committees on petitions, he says that " as constituted by the House, partly by nomination and partly from a ' Speaker's List,' they were an unwieldy body consisting of about 120 members. A committee, almost as numerous, exercised similar functions in the upper House ; and the same proofs had to be repeated before that tribunal at a later period of the Session " ; the Speaker's list was a list of members from counties and divisions of counties, who were added to the committee on bills affecting those or neighbouring counties, ibid ii 828.

[4] Ibid 826, 828-829.

One cannot without the very thing imagine the business that was in all their faces." [1] Earl Grey said in a memorandum which he had prepared for a committee of the House of Lords in 1858,[2] that

thirty years ago the second reading of many private bills (such as the Aire and Calder Navigation) could only be carried by as active a whip as is used for the most keenly disputed party motions, and there were often divisions on such bills in full Houses ; the members notoriously knowing nothing of the merits of the questions so decided. In committees, while their members were unlimited, the proceedings were of the same character.

Matters were no better in the House of Lords :

Agents sometimes thought it hopeless to proceed with bills which were strongly opposed by influential peers, because the latter were able to command a much larger body of friends in the committee than the promoters could have brought there.[3]

In the second place, the proper division of functions between committees on petitions and committees on bills was not always observed. Though it was not the function of the former committees to hear opponents, but only to see if the standing orders had been complied with, and to see that the promoters made out a prima facie case for their bill,[4] hostile members were put up by the opponents of the bill to ask questions and call for evidence which would prejudice the bill.[5] Conversely, standing order objections were often made to committees on bills. " Opponents used to hold back their case on technical grounds till the committee stage, when great cost must have been incurred upon the bill, and incurred perhaps in vain." [6] Owing to the defects of the committees on petitions, an order made in 1825 that such objections should not be raised after a first reading, did not prove an effective cure for this evil. Standing order objections continued to be taken in committees on bills and continued to influence their decisions.[7]

---

[1] Lives of the Norths iii 181, cited vol. vi 623 n. 6.

[2] Parlt. Papers 1863 viii 98 ; Clifford, op. cit. ii 830-831, summing up the evidence given to a House of Commons committee in 1838, says, " committees were so numerous as to be to a great degree irresponsible. Relying on the relative strength of promoters and opponents on particular occasions, objections were often taken and propositions made which would never have been raised before any judicial tribunal. Agents and solicitors in charge of a bill were in constant alarm if their case was much opposed, lest they should be tripped up in any proceeding when they had not a majority of their friends in the room. Canvassing was resorted to generally by the local solicitors or by deputations of promoters, who came to town for the purpose. Sometimes paid canvassers were employed to go round to the houses of members and request their attendance. . . . Even graver scandals were sometimes talked of."

[3] Ibid 827. [4] Above 328-330.

[5] Clifford, op. cit. ii 792. [6] Ibid 793. [7] Ibid.

(ii) Opposed bills were thus sometimes liable to be defeated on wholly inadequate grounds.   On the other hand, unopposed bills were sometimes allowed to slip through the House without any adequate consideration.   On such bills the stage of the committee on petitions was often a farce.   Though at least eight and later five [1] members should have been present, this was rarely insisted on.   Generally only one member attended, and the whole proceeding was purely formal.[2]   The member present merely signed the bill and initialled the clauses.[3]   There was thus no security that the standing orders had been complied with, and no security, therefore, that clauses which, under these standing orders, ought to have been inserted in the bill, were there.   This meant that the interests of the public and of private persons were not properly safeguarded.   There was no adequate security against the insertion in a bill of clauses changing the general law in a manner which was ill-considered, and sometimes unjust.[4]   In 1781 Lord Thurlow animadverted upon the injustice sometimes done to individuals by reason of the rapidity with which private bills were hurried through both Houses, and more especially through the committees of the House of Commons.[5]   Nor, in the case of an unopposed bill, was there any adequate security that such clauses would be discovered in the later stages of the bill.   Clifford says : [6]

It struck acute observers in 1865 that before private bill committees ' the public have no friend,' whose special business it is to protect them, especially in the case of unopposed bills.   When a bill is opposed, opponents ' put themselves in the shoes of the public,' and allege all the public objections which occur to them.

But even this might not be an adequate safeguard.   Canvassing and influence might induce the large committees to which bills were referred to accept clauses without real consideration of their merits or demerits ;   and it was always possible to buy off opponents, in which case Parliament heard nothing of the

---

[1] Clifford, op. cit. ii 843.

[2] Spencer, Municipal Origins 56-57 ; Clifford, op. cit. ii 792.

[3] This was the practice in 1838, and it was no doubt an old-established practice, Spencer, op. cit. 56.

[4] Amendments of the general law ought to have been made by a public Act, but, as Mr. Spencer says, Municipal Origins 49 n. 2, such changes were probably not infrequent in the days when private bills were inadequately supervised ; he cites some later examples from the Report of the Select Committee of the House of Commons in 1846, Evidence at pp. 2, 39-40, 76.

[5] " Many proofs of this evil had come to his knowledge as a member of the other House, not a few in his professional character. . . . He did not recollect the twentieth part of them, but he could not forbear stating a few which had recently challenged his recollection . . . there was a family of the name of Gardiner in Wales which had been stripped of its whole property by the compendious and certain operation of a private bill," Parlt. Hist. xxii 59 ; see ibid 60 for another tale of how a man, too poor to pay counsel, was nearly ruined by a clause in a private bill.

[6] Op. cit. ii 800.

public objections to the bill.[1] It is a significant fact that the committee on Ministers Powers, which reported in 1932, was told that one of the reasons why it was necessary in some modern Acts of Parliament to give ministers powers to remove statutory difficulties in the way of bringing these Acts into force, was the number and variety of private and local Acts of Parliament, containing clauses which might, if unrepealed, have made these modern Acts unworkable in particular districts.[2]

Very many of these two defects in the procedure on private bill legislation were remedied in the course of the nineteenth century.

The earliest reform was made by the House of Lords. In 1800 the House of Lords appointed a paid Lord Chairman of Committees,[3] who exercised a general supervision over the contents of private bills, before they were introduced into either the House of Lords or the House of Commons.[4] The first Lord Chairman appointed under this resolution was Lord Walsingham. But Mr. Spencer has shown that this appointment was simply the formal adoption of a practice followed by the House of Lords for some years past.[5] Lord Walsingham had in fact occupied this position before 1800, and he had had predecessors.[6] The manner in which this office had evolved in the eighteenth century is, in Mr. Spencer's opinion, as follows : [7]

During the eighteenth century we find certain members of the House notable for the regularity of their attendance at the House on all occasions, great or small, normal or extraordinary, and whether the business were legislative or judicial. Not only are this small group always appointed on formal committees, like those on the Privileges of the House, or the Journals, on the committee appointed to draw up the Address in answer to the Speech from the Throne, but, by being almost invariably present, they automatically become members of committees on private bills as well. And of this small group of members we find one usually exercising that one function of a Chairman of Committees (whether of the whole House or of a select committee) of which it is possible to learn anything from the Journals, viz., reporting bills to the House.

The Chairman was assisted by a counsel who was at first probably selected from some of the House of Lords' officials and paid by fees.[8]

Lord Walsingham was succeeded by Lord Shaftesbury in 1814,

[1] Clifford, op. cit. ii 800.
[2] Committee on Ministers Powers (1932) vol. ii Minutes of Evidence 125— evidence of Sir Arthur Robinson, Secretary to the Ministry of Health, and Mr. Maude, Solicitor to the Ministry of Health.
[3] First appointed July 23, 1800, Spencer, Municipal Origins 95.
[4] On the history and position of the Lord Chairman see Mr. Spencer's very able summary in Municipal Origins 95-113.
[5] Ibid 96.   [6] Ibid 98-103.
[7] Ibid 97.   [8] Ibid 105.

and he held the post of Lord Chairman till 1851.[1] The position of the Lord Chairman is clearly described in a book published in 1827 entitled *Practical Instructions on Passing of Private Bills through both Houses of Parliament*.[2] "Lord Shaftesbury," says the author,

is the perpetual Chairman of Committees in the House of Lords. . . . Immediately after the first reading of the bill, the agent and solicitor should wait on his Lordship, and submit to his inspection a printed copy of the bill ; on which occasion he reads it over with them and makes his observations on its various provisions, etc. It is likewise necessary to forward to Lord Shaftesbury three days prior to the sitting of the committee on the bill a printed copy with the blanks filled up, when his Lordship adds to or expunges from it whatever he thinks proper. By adopting the above measures, the parties interested in its welfare are not only spared much time and expense, but have a further advantage of being able to forsee and provide for the objections to which the bill would be liable in the Lords. It is therefore incumbent on persons who wish to forward these measures through Parliament, with as little delay as possible, to pay particular attention to this interview.

As Mr. Spencer points out, so certain was the author of the *Practical Instructions* that the Lord Chairman's views would have been met, before a bill originating in the Commons went before the Committee, that he regards amendments in the Lords as something exceptional.[3] This is still substantially the practice. "The 'filled up' bill which goes to the committee whether of the Lords or Commons, has to-day, as in the days of Lord Walsingham, to run the gauntlet of this official examination." [4]

Thus the Lord Chairman came to be the arbiter of the form and contents of the bill. A guarantee was therefore provided that some regard would be paid to the interests of the public, and to the conformity of the provisions of the bill with the standing orders and with the general rules of law ; and the chance of the success of a wholly unscrupulous opposition was lessened.[5]

Similarly, the House of Lords led the way in so reforming

[1] Spencer, Municipal Origins, 106 ; Clifford, op. cit. ii 798.

[2] Cited Spencer, op. cit. 107-108.   [3] Municipal Origins 110.

[4] " The bill is still submitted to the Chairman. It is read by his counsel who annotates it in ink of one colour, and reread by the Lord Chairman, who makes his comments similarly in ink of another colour. The bill then goes back to the agent, who subsequently returns it with his suggestions for meeting the criticisms made. If these are not satisfactory, the bill goes back again to the agent, and again returns. And this may continue for some time. The 'filled up' bill, therefore, which goes to the committee whether of the Lords or Commons, has to-day, as in the days of Lord Walsingham, to run the gauntlet of this official examination," Spencer, op. cit. 113.

[5] It was not of course wholly got rid of ; but Mr. Spencer thinks that such an opposition only occurred in cases " when a bill threatened political power, financial interest, or aroused local prejudice " ; and that even in such cases it is probable that the views of the Lord Chairman would be upheld in the Lords, Municipal Origins 111-112.

the committees to whom the bill was referred that they became competent judicial tribunals. In 1837 the House ordered that opposed private bills (other than estate bills) should be sent to a select committee of five peers, chosen by a committee of selection, and bound to attend throughout the proceedings. No other peers could take part in the proceedings, and peers who were interested in the bill were exempt from service. Peers were chosen who had as little knowledge as possible of the locality affected by the bill. They were expected to decide, not from their own knowledge, but on the evidence brought before them.[1]

The House of Commons later followed the lead given by the House of Lords. A private bill office was established in 1813, in order to provide for the accuracy and regularity of proceedings on private bills.[2] But the clerks were not competent to make an effective examination;[3] and, though the Chairman of Ways and Means was supposed to supervise them, he had no time to attend to this duty.[4] This defect was to some extent remedied in 1851 by giving him the assistance of the Speaker's counsel. In this way some guarantee was afforded that bills were not in conflict with the standing orders or the general law, and that they did not unduly prejudice private interests.[5] But it was a long time before the Commons could be induced to follow the lead of the Lords, and refer bills to small impartial select committees.[6] In 1844 pressure of business compelled the House to establish such committees for railways bills, and in 1855 for all bills. The number, as in the House of Lords, was fixed at five.[7]

In 1847 the House of Commons substituted two examiners for the committee on petitions.[8] The result was most beneficial. The time of members was saved, at least £100,000 was saved to suitors, and the private business of the House was advanced by about two months.[9] In 1855 the House of Lords agreed to appoint the same two examiners for unopposed bills, and in 1858 for all bills.[10] But appeal lies from them to the standing orders committees of each House on the question whether in any case the standing orders should be dispensed with.[11] In 1864 the House of Commons established a court of referees consisting of the Chairman of Ways and Means, three paid members, and any members of the House who consented to serve, to decide the question whether a petitioner against a bill had a *locus standi*.[12]

[1] Clifford, op. cit. ii 827-828.
[2] Ibid 788-789; cp. Parlt. Papers 1810 ii 201-203.
[3] Clifford, op. cit. ii 798.   [4] Ibid 798-799.
[5] Ibid 799-800.   [6] Ibid 829-841.   [7] Ibid 841-843.
[8] Ibid 794.   [9] Ibid 794-795.
[10] Ibid 795.   [11] Ibid 795-796.
[12] Ibid 806-810; there is a right of appeal from the decision of the court to the committee on the bill, ibid 811.

The reason for this new departure was to get a body which would be able to evolve some clear rules on this important matter.[1]

A further security that private bill legislation does not infringe general legal principles, or the settled policy of the state, is provided by an increase in the strictness of the supervision of government departments. The government departments now watch bills affecting matters within their cognizance, and their criticism sometimes stops bills, and sometimes causes the insertion of amendments.[2] This control is made the more effective by standing orders which require a printed copy of private bills to be deposited with the Home Office, the Local Government Board, and any government department affected by its provisions, and, in certain cases, with the local authorities.[3] Moreover, the government sometimes consults the law officers as to whether it is expedient that opposition should be offered to these bills.[4] We shall see that extensions of the principle of requiring certain groups of clauses to be included in bills of certain types has provided another security against bad drafting and ill-considered changes in the law.[5]

These far-reaching measures of reform have gone far to cure the two main defects in the old procedure of the two Houses—the constitution of committees on petitions and committees on the bill, and the absence of safeguards against ill-considered changes in the law. They have gone far to cure those defects because they have emphasized the judicial aspects of private bill procedure, by providing a machinery which has enabled the essentially judicial problems arising in the consideration of private bills to be judicially considered. We shall now see that the third of the defects of the old procedure—its expense, length, and the uncertainty of its results—has not been and cannot be so completely remedied.

(iii) We have seen that the revision of the system on which fees are charged upon private bills,[6] and the provision for the taxation of costs,[7] have partially mitigated the expensiveness of the old procedure on private bills. But it is still an expensive procedure. The amount of the fees paid to counsel at the parliamentary bar, as compared to the fees paid to counsel in the courts, was noticed by a committee of the House of Commons in 1863.[8] One explanation given was the fact that the sessions of Parliament then lasted a shorter time than the

---

[1] The decisions of the court on *locus standi* questions are reported, and are cited in argument, Clifford, op. cit. ii 809.

[2] Ilbert, Legislative Methods and Forms 91.

[3] Clifford, op. cit. ii 899 ; Erskine May, Parliamentary Practice (13th ed.) 734-735.

[4] Ilbert, op. cit. 91.   [5] Below 384-385.   [6] Above 340.

[7] Above 340.   [8] Parlt. Papers 1863 viii 211-212.

sessions of the courts. But the real explanation is the fact that, since the large amounts at stake render it necessary for promoters and opponents of bills to get the best men to advocate their causes, and since the supply of the best men is always limited, they will always be expensive.[1] No improvement in machinery can change these fundamental facts of human nature.

Similarly, the length of the procedure and the uncertainty of its results have been to some extent mitigated by the reforms of the nineteenth century. The strengthening of the judicial aspects of the procedure has, to a large extent, got rid of the risk that a bill will be defeated by the chance vote of a committee, many of the members of which neither know, nor care to ascertain, the merits of the question upon which they are voting.[2] But there are three causes for the length of the procedure which are inherent in its nature, and can never be wholly cured.

In the first place, if justice is to be done to the arguments for and against a bill the enquiry must in many cases range over a wide field. It is necessary to consider both the rights and interests of the contending parties and more general questions of public policy.[3] The enquiry can never be narrowed down, as in the case of a purely judicial enquiry, to a definite issue between two or more contending parties. We shall see that proposals have been made from time to time that, in order to shorten the proceedings before the committee, some part of the enquiries conducted by the committees of the Houses, should be delegated to some other tribunal.[4] But, as a witness before the House of Commons committee on private bill legislation of 1863 truly said,[5] it would be very difficult to establish any other tribunal. " The case which would have to be provided for is one of a very peculiar character, including mixed questions of public policy and of private interest." A judicial tribunal could not dispose of such issues :

The judicial mind always desires to entertain questions which can be reduced to definite issues. For instance, the very question which is involved in a railway case is the very question which a judge would refuse to try ; he would say, ' you must take this case to arbitration ; I cannot try engineering questions.'

[1] " When the sanction of Parliament is sought for changes in the existing law, usually involving large pecuniary issues, affecting to a greater or less degree the status and welfare of rich and powerful companies or communities, and demanding on all sides the services of skilled witnesses . . . the costs of obtaining or opposing such legislation cannot fail to be heavy. In ordinary litigation, a still more disproportionate outlay has frequently to be faced, when the interests concerned are large, but they seldom approach in magnitude the interests habitually represented in Parliament," Clifford, op. cit. i 260.

[2] Above 342.   [3] Below 350 n. 2.   [4] Below 352-353.
[5] Evidence of W. N. Massey, M.P., Parlt. Papers 1863 viii 87.

It would be equally unsatisfactory to refer such questions to a government department. In practice the question

would be referred to some clerk in the office, or some lawyer who would be hooked on to the department merely for the purpose of preparing reports. Some engineer belonging to the department would have his own views ; he would consider himself armed with authority to determine all these matters, and that power would, I think, be very often abused, and would not result in reports upon which the House could safely rely.

Thus neither a judicial nor an official tribunal would be satisfactory. " It is not so easy a matter as some gentlemen suppose to constitute a tribunal out of doors which will deal satisfactorily with these matters."

In the second place, we have seen that the unprofessional character of the committee before which a bill comes, is another reason why the enquiry is more discursive and more prolonged than a purely judicial enquiry before a court presided over by a professional judge.[1] Partly because the range of the enquiry is wider, and partly because of the character of the tribunal, there can be no such rigid rules as to the admissibility of evidence as there are in a law court. It is inevitable that a lawyer, who regards the procedure exclusively from the judicial point of view, should think that much time is wasted by the admission of unnecessary evidence. The answer is that, as it is not an exclusively judicial procedure, the rules of evidence applied in the courts must be relaxed.[2]

In the third place, the fact that a bill undergoes two separate enquiries before the committees of the two Houses necessarily lengthens the proceedings. As to the advantages of this double enquiry witnesses before the House of Commons committee of 1863 differed.[3] In fact the double enquiry is inevitable because the passing of a private Act of Parliament, being a legislative act, must have the consent of the two Houses. This fact is well

---

[1] Above 337.

[2] This is illustrated by the following questions put to Mr. Rickards, the Speaker's counsel in 1863, and his answers : " Is there not a difference between law making and the administration of the law. In the administration of the law you may perhaps be more precise and vigorous in your rules with regard to evidence than you probably would be in making new law, which is the business of members of Parliament ?—I think that the duty which the House delegates to a select committee on private bills is mainly a judicial duty. But it is partly legislative is it not ?—The object is to obtain the materials for coming to a legislative decision ; but it is in shape and form judicial. The facts are proved by witnesses, just in the same manner as in any trial in the court of Queen's Bench, and it is in proof of those facts that I think unnecessary evidence is allowed, and unnecessary length permitted," Parlt. Papers 1863 viii 40.

[3] Ibid 46—Mr. Rickards thought it generally useless, but Lord Redesdale, ibid 76, was in favour of it ; in 1872 Sir William Harcourt told the House of Commons that " over and over again he had known decisions on private bills reversed by the House of Lords and had never recollected any in which that reversal was not right," Clifford op. cit. ii 911, and see ibid 912-913 for other opinions to the same effect.

brought out by the following question and answer which is contained in the evidence given to the House of Commons committee in 1863 : [1]

Is there in the jurisprudence of this country or of any other country anything the least similar to what happens before the committees of Parliament, namely, that people having been heard and having succeeded in one court are immediately sent to another ?— No, I do not believe that there is any precedent for it in judicial proceedings. I presume that the justification for it is that it is partly a legislative proceeding, and therefore should be participated in by both branches of the Legislature.

That is really the gist of the matter. There is no parallel in the jurisprudence of any other country to the curious blend of the judicial and legislative aspects of private bill procedure ; and it is because these two aspects have been blended that the three causes for the length of the procedure cannot and ought not to be wholly remedied. But this we shall see more clearly when we have examined the legislative aspects of this procedure.

(2) *The legislative aspects of private bill legislation.*

Both in their form and in their effect private Acts of Parliament are legislative measures. Though the many judicial characteristics which they possess have necessitated considerable differences in the process by which they become Acts of Parliament, yet all the main outlines of that process in both Houses are the same as those used for public Acts—first reading, second reading, committee stage, report stage, third reading, and royal assent. In fact, it is because private Acts of Parliament are legislative measures that they have been able to play a very great part in the social, economic, and legal development of the country. They have been the instruments by means of which new social needs have been met, new scientific and mechanical ideas have been tried out, new methods of organizing industry have been made possible, and new legal experiments have been made.[2] By their means it has been possible to make provisions for the varying needs of different localities and different bodies of persons,[3] and to dispense in individual cases with the general rules of law.[4] None of these things could have been done if these private Acts had not been essentially legislative measures. It is for this reason that, as we have seen, many of the objections to the procedure on these bills, based on its length, expense, and uncertainty in its results, fall to the ground. They are in effect objections to the machinery which the Constitution provides for the process of legislation.

[1] Parlt. Papers 1863 viii. 45-46   [2] Below 622-626, 629-630.
[3] Vol. x 188-189.   [4] Below 620-624.

It is for the same reason that neither of the Houses has ever consented to any delegation of its functions to adjudicate upon the policy and contents of private bills. It is true, as we have seen, that they have consented to delegate to others those procedural questions which are purely judicial in character. The powers exercised by the Lord Chairman of Committees in the House of Lords,[1] by the Examiners,[2] and by the Court of Referees [3] are obvious illustrations. But they have never delegated any of their powers to decide, on grounds of public policy, the legislative problems which proposals for this legislation must always raise. Nor would it be right that they should consent to this delegation ; first, because Parliament is the only body which can decide these questions of public policy, and secondly, because it is the only body that can decide impartially between the conflicting interests of private persons or corporate bodies, and of localities.

This truth is demonstrated by the discussions which have taken place, in the course of the nineteenth century, upon many proposals to adopt some new machinery, for the purpose of shortening the length, and diminishing the expense, of the procedure upon private bill legislation. A very short consideration of some of these proposals, and of the successful objections which have been made to them, brings out the essentially legislative character of private bill legislation.

An Act of 1847 provided for the making of a preliminary enquiry by the Commissioners of Woods and Forests, and by the Lords of the Admiralty, in cases of applications for certain classes of bills.[4] But the Act was found to promote injustice —opponents refused to state their case to the inspector who held the inquiry, and went before the committee with the advantage of having learned the case of the promoters ; [5] and it was found that the enquiries were useless because committees refused to be satisfied with the report of a departmental inspector.[6] The Act was repealed,[7] and the discretionary power left to these departments to make enquiries was found to be of little use.[8] In 1858 and 1869 it was proposed that an opposed bill should go to a joint committee of Lords and Commons.[9] But these proposals did not find favour, largely because a powerful body of opinion approved of the separate hearings before each of the Houses.[10] Nor did a proposal made in 1858, that evidence taken in the Lords on private bills should be received in the Commons and *vice versa*, find favour ; [11] or a proposal made

[1] Above 345-346. [2] Above 347. [3] Above 347-348.
[4] 9, 10 Victoria c. 106. [5] Clifford, op. cit. ii 891.
[6] Ibid 892-893. [7] 11, 12 Victoria c. 129.
[8] Clifford, op. cit. ii 892, 896-897. [9] Ibid 909, 910-913.
[10] Above 350 and n. 3. [11] Clifford, op. cit. ii 900-901.

in 1863 that opposed bills passed by the Lords should be dealt with as unopposed in the Commons and *vice versa*.[1] In 1860 Brougham proposed that the jurisdiction of the committees should be superseded by a court of five paid legal members appointed by the Crown, and holding their offices on the same tenure as the judges.[2] But, as bills approved by this court could be opposed in each House, the proceedings before it would merely have added to the length and cost of the proceedings.[3] The objections to this and other projects for a fixed tribunal were brought out by the House of Commons committee on private bill legislation in 1863. Mr. Booth, the Speaker's counsel, then said : [4]

for all open questions, i.e., where the principle of decision cannot be reduced to a law, the committee is, I think, better than a judicial tribunal. Its fluctuating character is not altogether a disadvantage. It varies with, and keeps progress with the times. . . . A judicial tribunal, proceeding strictly on precedent, would be apt to stereotype the policy of a bygone age.

Because the questions raised by private bills are essentially legislative questions, to be decided on grounds of public policy, the Legislature must decide them, and cannot safely leave to any external body the examination of the evidence upon which they must be decided. Because changes in scientific and mechanical knowledge, and changes in social and economic conditions brought about by the application of new scientific and mechanical knowledge, often introduce new questions of public policy, and render obsolete the reasons based on the public policy of an earlier generation, a legislative tribunal unfettered by precedent is a better tribunal than a judicial tribunal which is so fettered. " A judicial tribunal," it was said in 1868,[5]

must aim at consistency, and, from the very nature of its being, always seek to uphold that which it has once decided. Imagine our position if decisions respecting railways had, during the last five and twenty years been left to such a court. The court must either have broken away from its own rules and precedents, in which case it would have lost all weight and character as a judicial tribunal, or it would have lagged behind, and found itself long ago in antagonism to the wants and opinions of the country.

The Legislature, during the last two centuries, has shown that it is well aware of the political importance of this species of legislation. For this reason, it has devoted much attention to the private bills which petitioners for all sorts of *privilegia* have brought before it ; and it has devoted much attention in

---

[1] Clifford, op. cit. ii 910. [2] Ibid 901.
[3] Ibid. [4] Cited ibid 903.
[5] Lord Monk Bretton, 190 Hansard 863, cited Clifford, op. cit. 906-907.

the last century to perfecting the machinery for their proper
consideration. The result of its efforts has been the creation
of an instrument of great flexibility, and of great capacity for
adjudicating justly upon rival claims and conflicting points of
view. Just as in the sphere of mercantile law negotiable instruments were able to help effectively the safe, easy, and rapid circulation of money and credit, because the essence of negotiability
consists of a skilful combination of those parts of the principles
of the law of property and of contract which favour this circulation ; [1] so, in the sphere of constitutional law, the private Act
has been able to help social and economic and legal development,
because it combines the freedom of action of a sovereign Legislature with a semi-judicial procedure, which safeguards the rights
of private persons and the general principles of the law. But
the private Act is essentially legislation, and, because it is essentially legislation, it has, as we shall see in the second part of this
chapter, been a very serviceable instrument for developing the
law.[2] In fact, in the eighteenth century, it went far to mitigate
the effects which would have flowed from the very meagre measures of law reform which were effected by public Acts. All this
we shall see later. At this point we must examine the manner
in which courts have regarded this peculiar and unique kind of
legislation.

(3) *The treatment of this legislation by the courts.*

The fact that private Acts, though legislative in character,
have strongly marked judicial aspects, has influenced their
treatment by the courts. We have seen that the courts have
treated them differently from public Acts in respect of the manner
in which they can be pleaded and proved.[3] We have seen also
that the courts have laid it down that these Acts bind only the
parties to them, and cannot prejudicially affect the rights of
third persons ; [4] and that they have construed strictly the
provisions contained in them which confer benefits upon their
promoters.[5] These are the outstanding contrasts between public
and private Acts which have been established by judicial decisions. At this point we must examine certain other doctrines
which the judicial aspects of these Acts have led the courts at
different periods to lay down concerning them.

The procedure upon a private bill has always brought into
prominence the fact that, over and above the question of public
policy raised by the bill, there may be and generally are many
conflicting interests affected by its proposed provisions. It must

---

[1] Vol. viii 145-146.
[3] Above 290.
[4] Above 296-297.
[2] Below 629-631.
[5] Above 297.

therefore contain provisions for the equitable adjustment of these conflicting interests. The adjustment of these interests contained in the clauses of the Act often represents, in substance if not in form, an agreement sanctioned by the Legislature between the promoters of, and those affected by, the Act. It is for this reason that the courts have been inclined to stress, sometimes too strongly, this element of an agreement *inter partes* contained in private Acts, and to lay down doctrines concerning them which have sometimes failed to give due weight to the fact that they are enactments of a sovereign Legislature. We can see this tendency in doctrines which have been laid down, first as the validity of these Acts, secondly as to the power of the courts to control applications to Parliament for them, and thirdly as to their interpretation. We shall see that these doctrines illustrate this double element in these private Acts— the element of agreement *inter partes* and the legislative element ; and that it is not till modern days that the courts have reached some settled doctrines on these matters which give due weight to both these elements. Let us look at these doctrines from these three points of view.

Validity.

Blackstone, in his later editions,[1] speaking of that variety of private Acts which are known as estate Acts,[2] says that they have " been relieved against when obtained upon fraudulent suggestions," [3] and that they have " been holden to be void if contrary to law and reason." [4] Blackstone does not say that these propositions apply to private Acts other than estate Acts. But in the same paragraph he sets out other characteristics of these Acts which do apply to other private Acts ; and, though the authorities which he cites for the first of the propositions which I have quoted refer only to estate Acts,[5] the authority which he cites for the second of these propositions applies to all private Acts.[6] Blackstone, therefore, leaves it a little uncertain whether or not he thought that these propositions apply only to estate Acts or to other private Acts as well. We shall now see that the first of these propositions has in fact only been applied to estate Acts ; and that the second applies neither to estate Acts nor, *a fortiori*, to any other private Act.

For the proposition that estate Acts have " been relieved against when obtained upon fraudulent suggestions " Blackstone

---

[1] Comm. ii 346.   [2] For these Acts see below 619-621.

[3] This statement appears in the fourth edition.

[4] This statement appears in ninth edition, see Hammond's ed. of Blackstone ii 534 n. 9.

[5] Below 356.   [6] Below 359.

cites two cases. The first is the case of *Richardson v. Hamilton*
decided in 1732. It is not strictly in point, since the Act in
question was not a private Act of Parliament but an Act of the
House of Assembly of Pennsylvania.[1] The second is the case
of *McKenzie v. Stuart* decided in 1754.[2] It is strictly in point,
since in that case the House of Lords did relieve against a provision in an Act obtained upon a fraudulent suggestion. Sir
James McKenzie had got a private Act to enable him to sell an
entailed estate for the payment of certain debts charged on the
estate ; and the amount of these debts was stated in the Act.
It was afterwards discovered that two debts included in the
amount stated in the Act were not charged on the estate, and
were in fact "fictitious and fraudulent." It was held that the
representatives of Sir James and the trustees of the Act must
apply the residue of the money as directed by the Act, after
paying only those debts which were in fact charged on the
estate.[3] The same principle was applied in 1790 in the case of
Biddulph v. Biddulph.[4] In that case a private Act had allowed
a life tenant to sell settled estates, and directed that the money
should be applied in paying off incumbrances, and in repaying
to the tenant for life all the interest then due, and a sum paid
by the tenant for life for the discharge of incumbrances and the
interest thereon. The tenant for life retained all the sums which
he had ever paid as interest since he had come into the possession
of the property, and justified his action by the provisions of the
Act. But it appeared that Parliament was kept in ignorance of
the fact that the rents and profits of the land were sufficient
to keep down the interest upon the incumbrances. Since these
rents and profits ought to have been applied to keep down the
interest, the court held that the tenant for life must account for
the rents and profits which he ought to have so applied, which
amounted to the sum of £7,207, and that that sum must be held
on the trusts declared by the Act.[5]

---

[1] Cruise, Digest v. tit. *Private Act* § 50 p. 23.   [2] Ibid § 51 p. 23.

[3] The argument addressed to the House of Lords, to which the House acceded,
was as follows : " the recital of the debts in the Act was upon information and suggestion of the parties. The enacting part, so far as it directed the discharge of
those incumbrances out of the purchase money, only pursued the recital ; which, if
ill-founded, from the misinformation of the parties, was not conclusive : and though
the appellant by having given his consent to the Act, might be thought concluded ;
yet being drawn into such contract by Sir James McKenzie's misrepresentation of
the true state of the debts, who misled both the remaindermen and the Legislature, he had a right, as against Sir James's representative, to inquire into the reality
of the debts, and application of the purchase money. Nor could a consent, thus
fraudulently obtained, any more stand in the way of the relief he sought, than it
would in the case of an ordinary transaction," Cruise, Digest v. tit. *Private Act* § 50
p. 25.

[4] Ibid § 53 p. 26.

[5] " It being admitted that the said sum of £7207 was received by the said Sir
T. Biddulph for rents and profits of the estates in question of which he was tenant

The principle applied in these cases is substantially the same as that which equity has applied, from the earliest period, to the rules of law, statutory or otherwise. Equity will not allow a rule of law, statutory or otherwise, to be made an instrument of fraud. If therefore a person makes use of a rule of law to obtain for himself an advantage, which equity deems to be fraudulent or otherwise contrary to a conscientious course of dealing, equity will compel that person to use that advantage in accordance with its own ideas of justice. Equity does not deny the validity of the rule of law, statutory or otherwise, but it acts *in personam*, and, admitting the legal title of the person who has obtained the advantage, compels him to use his legal rights in accordance with its principles.[1] This was the manner in which equity dealt with the rules of the common law ; and it is upon this foundation that the leading principles of the law of trusts and of many other equitable doctrines rest. Naturally equity found no difficulty in dealing in the same way with statute law. As Lord Westbury said in the case of *McCormick v. Grogan*,[2]

the Court of Equity has, from a very early period decided that even an Act of Parliament shall not be used as an instrument of fraud ; and if in the machinery of perpetrating a fraud an Act of Parliament intervenes, the Court of Equity, it is true, does not set aside this Act of Parliament, but it fastens on the individual who gets a title under that Act, and imposes upon him a personal obligation, because he applies the Act as an instrument for accomplishing a fraud. In this way the Court of Equity has dealt with the Statute of Frauds, and in this manner, also, it deals with the Statute of Wills.

Lord Westbury, it is true, was referring to the case where a person makes use of the provisions of a public Act to cover some fraud or sharp practice. He was not referring to the case where a person has by fraud or sharp practice procured the passing of a private Act or of particular provisions in it. But obviously the same reasoning applies in both cases. Indeed the latter case is really an *a fortiori* case. Equitable relief in such a case is, to use a phrase of Lord Sumner's, " a perfectly normal exercise of general equitable jurisdiction." [3] But because

for life, and which ought to have been employed in keeping down the interest of the incumbrances affecting the said estates ; and it being admitted that all the expenses of the Act, and all expenses anterior to the money being laid out in land, had been paid ; it was ordered and decreed that the defendant, Sir T. Biddulph, should pay the sum of £7207 into the bank, in the name of the accountant-general, in trust, in the cause, to be laid out in the purchase of lands agreeable to the Act of Parliament," Cruise, Digest v. tit. *Private Act* § 51 p. 28.

[1] See Maitland, Equity 17.   [2] (1869) L.R. 4 H. of L. at p. 97.

[3] " A court of conscience finds a man in the position of an absolute legal owner of a sum of money, which has been bequeathed to him under a valid will, and it declares that, on proof of certain facts relating to the motives and actions of the testator, it will not allow the legal owner to exercise his legal right to do what he will with his own. This seems to be a perfectly normal exercise of general equitable jurisdiction," Blackwell v. Blackwell [1929] A.C. at p. 334.

both the jurisdiction and the principle upon which the exercise of the jurisdiction is based are exclusively equitable, the rule that, in cases of fraud, Acts of Parliament may be relieved against, is unknown to and unrecognized by the common law.[1]

But two points should be noted with regard to the principle upon which this relief is given. In the first place, it is only possible to apply it where the person guilty of the fraud can be treated as a trustee of the property or other benefit which he has acquired by means of it. It is for this reason that it has in practice only been applied to estate Acts. But, if by virtue of a provision in any other private Act, which has been procured by the fraud or sharp practice of a person seeking to take advantage of it, that person has acquired some property or other benefit, there seems no reason why the same principle should not be applied. Obviously, however, it could not be applied unless it was possible to give relief in this way ;[2] and it cannot be applied to the express provisions of a public Act, for, as the Privy Council said in the case of *Labrador Co. v. the Queen*, if such mistakes are made by the Legislature, the Legislature alone is competent to correct them.[3] In the second place, since the grant of this relief is based upon the personal demerits of the person who has procured the Act, it cannot be given merely on account of informalities in the passing of the Act. We have seen that, in the fifteenth century, Fortescue, C. J., was inclined to think that the existence of informalities of this kind did not affect the validity of an Act of Parliament.[4] Apparently in the Scottish courts an idea had prevailed, in the first half of the nineteenth century, that such informalities might affect the validity of a private Act. But in 1842 the House of Lords stated that there was no foundation for such an idea.[5]

---

[1] Stead v. Carey (1845) 1 C.B. 496 at p. 516 *per* Creswell J. ; Waterford, etc., Railway Co. v. Logan (1850) 14 Q.B. 672, where a plea that the plaintiff's Act was obtained by the fraud of the plaintiff and others was overruled.

[2] In the case of the earl of Leicester v. Heydon (1571) Plowden at p. 398, a theory was put forward in argument that an Act of attainder could be disregarded if it could be shown that Parliament had been misinformed ; but the court gave no countenance to it ; and it is clear that the argument was based upon the analogy of Parliament to a court, and of such an Act to the judgment of a court ; but this was a theory which had never been wholly true, and it was at that time definitely obsolete, see vol. ii 434 and n. 4, vol. iv 185-186 ; this passage from Plowden was cited by serjeant Manning *arg.* in Stead v. Carey (1845) 1 C.B. at p. 516, but the court very properly disregarded it ; in fact, unless the equitable principle can be applied by making the person guilty of the fraud a trustee of the property or other advantage he has received, the common law rule, above n. 1, must apply.

[3] " Even if it could be proved that the Legislature was deceived, it would not be competent for a court of law to disregard its enactments. If a mistake has been made, the Legislature alone can correct it . . . the courts of law cannot sit in judgment on the Legislature, but must obey and give effect to its determination," [1893] A.C. at p. 123.

[4] Y.B. 33 Hy. VI Pasch. pl. 8, cited vol. ii 442 n. 3.

[5] " Upon the papers put before us, it does appear that in the course of the argument in the court below, an impression did exist that an Act of Parliament might

For the proposition that estate Acts have " been holden to be void if contrary to law and reason " Blackstone cites Coke's report of *Lord Cromwell's Case*.[1] In that case there had been a discussion whether the Act de Scandalis Magnatum was a private or a public Act. It was held to be a public Act ; but, in the course of their judgment, the judges said that if it was a private Act, and if therefore the court " ought to take it to be such as is alleged, then the said Act was against law and reason and therefore void ; for as it is alleged, those who do not offend shall be punished, and that was *condemnare insontem et demittere reum*." [2] It is clear, in the first place, that this is mere dictum ; and, in the second place, a hypothetical dictum—if the Act was as alleged it would be void for unreasonableness. In the third place, the dictum belongs to the same order of ideas as the dictum in *Bonham's Case* [3] to the effect that " when an Act of Parliament is against common right and reason, or repugnant or impossible to be performed, the common law will controul it, and adjudge such Act to be void." [4] But we have seen that this dictum was based on very little authority,[5] that it was inconsistent with other statements of Coke as to the authority of Parliament, and that it is even more inconsistent with Blackstone's own statements on the same subject.[6] We shall see that the recognition by the courts of the fact that a private Act is, like any other Act, a law made by a sovereign Legislature,[7] has demonstrated the falsity of this proposition.

The power of the courts to control applications to Parliament for private Acts.

There is a considerable amount of authority for the proposition that, just as the court of Chancery could, by means of a common injunction, restrain litigants from bringing an action in the common law courts or any other courts, so it could restrain persons from petitioning Parliament for a private Act. In 1831 Lord Brougham seems to admit that in theory an injunction of this sort was possible, since he points out that, just as the common injunction was not addressed to the common law courts, but to the parties suing there, so this injunction was addressed, not to Parliament, but to the parties who proposed to petition

---

or might not be binding on parties, according as there might or might not be proof that the individual to be affected by it had had notice of the Act while in progress through the two Houses. . . . There is no foundation for such an idea ; but such an impression appears to have existed in Scotland, and I express my clear opinion upon it, that no such erroneous idea may exist in future," Edinburgh and Dalkeith Railway Co. v Wauchope (1842) 8 Cl. and Fin. at p. 720 *per* Lord Cottenham

[1] (1578) 4 Co. Rep. 12b.   [2] At f. 13a.
[3] (1609) 8 Co. Rep. 107.   [4] At f. 118a.
[5] Vol. ii 442-443 ; vol. iv 186-187.
[6] Vol. x 526-527.   [7] Below 362-363.

for a private Act.[1]   In 1850 Lord Cottenham said that in a proper
case the court of Chancery might issue an injunction to prevent
proceedings in Parliament ;   and he pointed out that the issue
of such an injunction would no more interfere with the privileges
of Parliament than the issue of a common injunction interfered
with the jurisdiction of the common law courts.   But he added
that he had difficulty in conceiving what would be a proper case
for its issue.[2]   In 1851 Lord Langdale seemed to think that in a
proper case an injunction to restrain proceedings in Parliament
might issue.[3]   In 1856 Page-Wood, V.C., said that he had not
the slightest doubt that the court had the power to restrain a
person from petitioning Parliament ;   and he pointed out that
Lord Brougham and Lord Cottenham had been of the same
opinion.[4]   In 1870 the Lords Justices again affirmed the proposition that such a jurisdiction existed.[5]   But it was pointed out by
Giffard, L. J., that, though there was abundant authority for the
proposition that such a jurisdiction existed, it had never been
exercised.[6]   In fact, even where the party against whom the
injunction was sought, had contracted, in return for the withdrawal of the plaintiff's opposition to their bill, not to apply for
another Act, the injunction was refused.[7]

[1] " It is quite idle to represent this . . . as an attempt to restrain by injunction
the proceedings of the High Court of Parliament.   This is no injunction to restrain
any proceedings of Parliament, or to restrain any parties who may be called upon
by the authority of Parliament from intervening in such proceedings.   It is simply
an injunction to restrain a partnership now existing under a certain constitution
from doing any act in its corporate capacity with a view to obtain a new modelling
of that constitution," Ware v. Grand Junction Water Co. (1831) 2 Russ. and My.
at p. 483 ; since Lord Brougham was of opinion that the corporation had a right to
take this action he refused to grant an injunction.

[2] " It has been suggested that this Court could not interfere without infringing
upon the privileges of Parliament : so the Courts of Common Law thought at one
time ; and there is as much foundation for the one as for the other supposition.
In both cases, this Court acts upon the person, and not upon the jurisdiction.   In a
proper case, therefore, I have said here and elsewhere that I should not hesitate to
exercise the jurisdiction of this Court by injunction, touching proceedings in Parliament for a private bill or a bill respecting property ; but what would be a proper
case for that purpose it may be very difficult to conceive," Heathcote v. North
Staffordshire Railway Co. (1850) 2 Mac. and G. at p. 109.

[3] Stevens v. South Devon Railway Co. (1851) 13 Beav. at p. 58.

[4] " That the court has power to interfere by injunction to restrain a person from
petitioning Parliament, upon a proper case being made out, I never entertained any
doubt : indeed it would not be possible to entertain the slightest doubt after the
decisions—that of Lord Cottenham not being by any means the first, for Lord
Brougham had expressed himself equally clearly," Lancaster and Carlisle Railway
Co. v. North Western Railway Co. (1856) 2 K. and J. at p. 303.

[5] In re Chatham and Dover Railway Arrangement Act (1870) 5 Ch. App. 671.

[6] " We have the authority of Lord Brougham, Lord Cottenham, Lord
Chelmsford, and the present Lord Chancellor, one and all agreeing that, though
there may be some special cases under which, by the jurisdiction in personam,
an injunction of this description may be granted, yet that in no case which has ever
come before the Court has such an injunction been granted, nor has anyone ventured
to say in what particular case such an injunction would be granted," ibid at p. 682.

[7] Lancaster and Carlisle Railway Co. v. North Western Railway Co. (1856)
2 K. and J. 293.

A principle which the courts have consistently refused to apply is necessarily suspect.   In fact, some of the reasons which the courts have found for refusing to issue an injunction of this kind show that the principle itself is radically unsound.   It is radically unsound because there is no real analogy between the issue of a common injunction to prevent a person from suing in the common law courts, and the issue of an injunction to prevent a person from petitioning Parliament for a private Act.   In the first case the injunction prevented a person from enforcing a right which was given to him by the rules of law.   Because it was a right of this kind the common law courts were obliged to enforce it ; and because they could not take account of equitable considerations, equity was obliged to interpose to prevent an inequitable use of a legal right.   In the second case the application is made, not to a tribunal which is bound by the strict rules of law, but to a tribunal which can take into account, not only the rules of equity, but also considerations of public policy. The reasons, therefore, upon which the issue of a common injunction was justified fail to apply to an application to Parliament.   Both Lord Brougham and Lord Cottenham were aware of this distinction.   Lord Brougham said : [1]

All the arguments used here . . . are still open to the plaintiff before a committee of the House of Commons or House of Lords . . . Is not that the old regular constitutional mode, and is not this a new and irregular mode of proceeding ?

Lord Cottenham said : [2]

The case of Parliament differs widely from that of the Courts of Common Law ; the province of the latter is to enforce legal rights, and the object of the injunction is to prevent an inequitable use of such legal right ; but the ordinary province of Parliament in such bills is to abrogate existing rights, and to create new rights.

It is surprising that neither Lord Brougham nor Lord Cottenham saw that this distinction destroyed the analogy between a jurisdiction to issue a common injunction, and a jurisdiction to restrain a person from petitioning Parliament for a private Act.   But so it was ; and Lord Cottenham was particularly emphatic in insisting upon this analogy.[3]   If, as I think, this analogy is

---

[1] Ware v. Grand Junction Water Co. (1831) 2 Russ. and My. at p. 485.

[2] Heathcote v. North Staffordshire Railway Co. (1850) 2 Mac. and G. at pp. 109-110.

[3] " This Court . . . if it sees a proper case connected with private property or interest, has just the same jurisdiction to restrain a party from petitioning against a bill in Parliament as if he were bringing an action at law, or asserting any other right connected with the enjoyment of the property or interest which he claims. About that there can be no question whatever ; nor could any doubt be raised about it, except by the same confusion of ideas which gave rise to the old discussion between the courts of law and equity . . . which was founded on the supposition that the injunction operated upon the Court and not upon the party," Stockton and Hartlepool Railway Co. v. Leeds and Thirsk and Clarence Railway Cos. (1848) 2 Ph. at p. 671.

destroyed, it would seem to follow that the dicta in favour of this jurisdiction, which are all based on the supposed existence of this analogy, are demonstrably unsound.

Interpretation.

The courts have always been aware that the clauses of a private Act often represent a bargain between the promoters and the opposers of a bill. They have therefore emphasized the contractual element contained in them. Thus Lord Eldon said of these Acts : [1]

I regard them all in the light of contracts made by the Legislature, on behalf of every person interested in anything to be done under them ; and I have no hesitation in asserting that, unless that principle is applied in construing statutes of this description, they become instruments of greater oppression than anything in the whole system of administration under our constitution.

From this premise he deduced the proposition that those to whom powers were given, and upon whom duties were imposed, by these Acts, must act strictly within the limits of those powers, and strictly carry out those duties. This conclusion was emphasized by Lord Macnaghten in 1892.[2] He said :

Where the promoters of a public undertaking have authority from Parliament to interfere with private property on certain terms, any person whose property is interfered with by virtue of that authority has a right to require that the promoters shall comply with the letter of the enactment, so far as it makes provision on his behalf. It is idle for the promoters to say that they have given him all that he can want, or something just as good as that which the Act required them to give, or even something still better, if he only knew his own interest. It is enough for him to show that the thing which is offered is not the thing which the Act said he was to have. It is too late to call for a fresh deal at that stage of the game. Nor is it I think within the province of any tribunal to remodel arrangements sanctioned by Parliament, or relax conditions which the Legislature has thought fit to impose.

On the other hand, as the last sentence in the passage just cited from Lord Macnaghten's speech shows, the courts have always realized that a private Act is a law made by a sovereign Legislature which they must enforce as it stands. In 1853 the court of Exchequer Chamber, reversing a decision of the court of Queen's Bench, held that the court had no power to issue a mandamus to a railway company to compel it to complete its

[1] Blakemore v. Glamorganshire Canal Navigation (1825) 1 My. and K. at p 162.
[2] Herron v. Rathmines and Rathgar Improvement Commissioners [1892] A.C. at pp. 523-524

line, because the words used in the Act were facultative and not imperative.   Jervis, C.J., said : [1]

It is said that a railway Act is a contract on the part of the company to make the line, and that the public are a party to that contract, and will be aggrieved if the contract may be repudiated by the company at any time before it is acted on.   Though commonly so spoken of, railway Acts, in our opinion, are not contracts, and ought not to be construed as such :   they are what they profess to be, and no more ;   they give conditional powers, which, if acted upon, carry with them duties, but which, if not acted upon, are not, either in their nature or by express words, imperative upon the companies to whom they are granted. Courts of justice ought not to depart from the plain meaning of words used in Acts of Parliament :   when they do so they make, but do not construe, the laws.

The true view seems to be that expressed by Lord Watson in the case of *Davis and Sons v. Taff Vale Railway Co.*[2]   He said : [3]

In cases where the provisions of a local and personal Act directly impose mutual obligations upon two persons or companies, such provisions may, in my opinion, be fairly considered as having this analogy to contract, that they must, as between those parties, be construed in precisely the same way as if they had been matter, not of enactment, but of private agreement. . . . But . . . the analogy of contract, for it is nothing more, [cannot] . . . be carried further.   The provisions of a railway Act, even when they impose mutual obligations, differ from private stipulations in this essential respect, that they derive their existence and their force, not from the agreement of the parties, but from the will of the Legislature.   And when provisions of this kind are not limited to the interests of the parties mutually obliged, but impose on one or other or both of them an obligation in favour of third parties, who are sufficiently designated, I am of opinion that the obligation so imposed must operate, as a direct enactment of the Legislature in favour of these parties, and cannot be regarded as a mere stipulation *inter alios*, which they may have an interest but have no title to enforce.

We may, I think, conclude that the courts have held the balance evenly between the contractual and the legislative aspects of a private Act, and have given to each aspect its due weight. Similarly, we have seen that the other distinctions which they have drawn between the manner in which private and public Acts must be interpreted, have emphasized the fact that private Acts are essentially *privilegia*.[4]   It follows, therefore, that the treatment by the courts of these Acts has as faithfully reflected their unique character as the elaborate rules made by Parliament for their enactment.

The length and expense of private bill procedure, which gave rise to many abortive proposals for its reform in the nineteenth

---

[1] York and North Midland Railway Co. v. the Queen (1853) 1 El. and Bl. at p. 864 ; cp. Lee v. Milner (1837) 2 Y. and Coll. at p. 618 *per* Alderson B.
[2] [1895] A.C. 542.   [3] At p. 552.   [4] Above 296-297.

century,[1] are its greatest defects.   During the nineteenth century and later these objections were met by the institution of the
alternative procedure of a Provisional Order made by a government department, and afterwards sanctioned by Parliament by
a Provisional Order Confirmation Act.   Bills to confirm these
Orders are public bills ; [2] but they are treated for some purposes
as if they were private bills.[3]   They " are referred to the Examiners, and any one of the Orders, if opposed, is treated as a private
bill for the purposes of investigation in Committee, the progress
of the public bill being stopped until this investigation is concluded." [4]   This system began with powers given to the inclosure
commissioners in 1845 ; [5]   and, as the powers given to the
executive government were increased, these powers were given
to an increasing number of departments, and their range was
extended.   But because they originate with a government department they are essentially different from private bill legislation.   Under the system of private bill legislation the petitioner
for a *privilegium*, and those who oppose the petition, are brought
face to face, and Parliament adjusts the rights of the parties,
and decides the question of public policy without any intermediary.   Under the provisional order system the government
department is an intermediary ; and

the orders themselves cannot fail to bear the impress of the department's views, which have frequently been revealed in official correspondence already, and are sometimes successive stages in the development
of a policy which the department is seeking to introduce.[6]

In fact this new system is in harmony with that increasing
control over legislation which the executive government has been
acquiring during the latter part of the nineteenth and in the
twentieth centuries—a control which has had, as we shall now
see,[7] an important effect upon the style in which modern statutes
are drafted.   To this question of the drafting of the statutes we
must now turn.

The Drafting of Legislative Proposals

The manner in which legislative proposals have been drafted
at different periods depends partly upon the relations between
the executive and the legislative power in the state, and partly
upon the constitutional machinery by which these legislative

---

[1] Above 349-350, 352-353.   [2] Ilbert, Legislative Methods and Forms 33.
[3] Ibid 92-93.   [4] Clifford, History of Private Bill Legislation i 270.
[5] Ibid ii 677-678 ; see L.Q.R. xxxiv 359-365.
[6] Clifford, op. cit. ii 710 ; cp. L.Q.R. xxxiv 360, and *in re* Morley (1875) L.R.
20 Eq. at pp. 18-19 there cited.
[7] Below 381-383, 386.

proposals are converted into statutes. At all periods the executive government has had a large share in initiating many of these proposals, and therefore its agents have had a large share in drafting them. But from the time when it was recognized that the King in Parliament was the legislative power in the state, it was necessary for these legislative proposals to gain the approval of the two Houses of Parliament ; and therefore they have been liable to be amended in their passage through Parliament. Moreover, since private members of the two Houses have, except in respect of money bills,[1] the same power to make these proposals as the executive government ; and since petitioners for private Acts are able to set in motion the machinery of legislation ; legislative proposals may be drafted not by the agents of the executive government, but by private members or by petitioners for private Acts. It is for this reason that the manner in which legislative proposals have been drafted at different periods is closely related to the comparative strength and activity of the executive government on the one hand, and of the private members of the two Houses, or of the two Houses themselves, on the other hand. When the executive government is strong and active it will have the largest share in drafting legislative proposals, and it will be able to exercise a considerable control over the proposals made by private members, and by petitioners for private Acts. When it is relatively weak it will still take a large share in this work ; for it must draft finance Acts, and other Acts which are necessary for the conduct of the daily work of government. But its work will be shared with those private members and with those petitioners for private Acts, who can persuade Parliament to endorse their legislative proposals.

If we look at the history of the drafting of legislative proposals from this point of view, we can discern four main periods. First, the earliest period, before Parliament had substituted the procedure of legislation by bill for the older procedure of legislation by petition. Secondly, the period of the sixteenth and seventeenth centuries. During the sixteenth century the executive definitely dominated the Legislature, but during the seventeenth century the Legislature was gradually becoming stronger than the executive. Thirdly, the period of the eighteenth century, when the Legislature was definitely stronger than the executive. Fourthly, the latest phase, when the executive, through the working of the system of cabinet government,

---

[1] Money bills cannot be initiated in the House of Lords, vol. x 586-587, 618; vol. vi 250-251 ; and in the House of Commons a proposal for the raising or spending of money must emanate from a minister of the Crown, Hatsell iii 142, citing the standing order of June 11 1713 ; Anson, Parliament (5th ed.) 284 ; vol. x 587.

recovered its strength, and has been able to assert an increasing control over the Legislature for so long as it can command a majority in the House of Commons.

(I) *The earliest phase.*

When the Crown enacted statutes on the petition of Parliament, the drafting of legislative proposals was the work of the King's council.[1] It drew the statutes which were initiated by the petitions of Parliament; and, naturally, the judges and others learned in the law had a principal share in drafting them.[2] In 1305, in a case which turned on the construction of cap. 2 of the statute of Westminster II, Hengham, C.J., said to counsel, " do not gloss the statute; we know it better than you do, because we made it ";[3] and there is evidence from Edward III's reign that the judges had a considerable share in the making of statutes,[4] and that the House of Commons acquiesced in this state of affairs.[5] But we have seen that, early in the fifteenth century, the Commons found that the statutes, thus drafted on their petitions, did not faithfully carry out their wishes; that they therefore applied the practice, which had been used by the King and by private petitioners, of introducing bills in which the text of the enactment was contained; and that to these bills the King either gave or refused his consent.[6] It is obvious that this change, besides emphasizing the legislative authority of Parliament, deprived the executive government of its complete monopoly of the work of drafting statutes.

If we look at the drafting of the statutes of this earliest period, and compare it with the drafting of the statutes at later periods, we shall see that it had considerable merits. The statutes were concisely and clearly drawn, and do not seem to have given rise to many difficulties of construction. This is due not only to the fact that they were drafted by the best lawyers of the day, but also to the fact that the prevailing style of legal draftsmanship was good. Since at all periods the lawyers, whether employed by the government or by private members or by petitioners to Parliament, have had a large share in the drafting of statutes, the style in which they are drafted will be affected by the prevailing style of legal draftsmanship. If we look at any set of mediæval conveyances of this period we shall find that they are far more concise and more intelligible than the conveyances of the succeeding periods in the history of the law.

---

[1] Vol. ii 308, 435, 438-439.   [2] Ibid 308 and n. 5.
[3] Y.B. 33-35 Ed. I (R.S.) 83.
[4] R.P. ii 131, 15 Edward III no. 42, cited vol. ii 308 and n. 5.
[5] R.P. ii 139, 17 Edward III no. 23, cited vol. ii 438 n. 4.
[6] Vol. ii 439-440.

Similarly, we have seen that both Coke and Hale praised the pleaders of the fourteenth century, because, by comparison with later periods, they possessed the virtues of conciseness and clearness.[1] Coke, in fact, made almost exactly the same comparison between the older statutes and the statutes of his own day, as he made between the pleadings and conveyances of the fourteenth century and of later centuries. He said [2] that in his day most questions arose, " not upon any of the rules of the common law," but upon badly drawn conveyances and wills, and

upon Acts of Parliament, overladen with provisoes and additions, and many times on a sudden penn'd and corrected by men of none or very little judgment in the law ;

and he pointed out that

if Acts of Parliament were after the old fashion penn'd and by such only as perfectly knew what the common law was before the making of any Act of Parliament concerning that matter, as also how far forth former statutes had provided remedy for former mischiefs and defects discovered by experience ; then should very few questions in law arise, and the learned should not so often and so much perplex their heads to make attonement and peace by construction of law between insensible and disagreeing words, sentences, and provisoes, as they now do.

We shall see that Hardwicke was substantially of the same opinion as Coke ; [3] and, as Clifford says,[4] " there was something to be said in principle for a system by which, after the will of Parliament was expressed, it was put by experts into precise statutory form." But owing partly to the different conditions in which many statutes were drafted after the substitution of the system of legislating by bill for the system of legislating by petition, and partly to the emergence of a different style of legal draftsmanship, many of the statutes of the following period are, as Coke said, inferior in draftsmanship to the statutes of the mediæval period.

(2) The sixteenth and seventeenth centuries.

We have seen that, throughout the sixteenth century, the King acting through his council was the predominant partner in the state ; and that he was therefore able to maintain the initiative in Parliament.[5] It follows that he and his council had the largest share in the drafting of the many important statutes, by means of which the transition from mediæval to modern conditions was effected.   There is evidence that Henry VIII himself

[1] Co. Litt. 304b, and Hale, Hist. Com. Law (6th ed.) 198-199, cited vol. iii 641 n. 4 ; Hale, op. cit. 211-212, cited vol. iii 642.

[2] Preface to Part ii of his Reports.   [3] Below 374.
[4] History of Private Bill Legislation i 326.   [5] Vol. iv 88-90, 180

helped to settle the drafting of some of the important statutes of his reign ;[1] and probably Elizabeth exercised a real control, if not over the phrasing, at any rate over the contents of the important statutes passed in her reign.[2] Probably these Acts were drafted by the judges and other lawyers employed by the Crown, under the supervision of the ministers of the Crown and the privy councillors.[3] At the same time the Crown was conscious of the usefulness of free discussion upon the legislative proposals which it placed before Parliament ;[4] and there is no doubt that these discussions had some influence upon the contents of these statutes. We have seen that the contents of the statute of Uses were shaped by the necessity of overcoming a strong opposition in Parliament to the King's legislative proposals ;[5] and there is other evidence that some of the provisos and additions to the statutes, which Coke criticized, were the work of independent members of Parliament.[6] Moreover, it is probable that some of the more important public statutes were drafted by committees of the House, upon which both privy councillors, servants of the Crown, and private members sat.[7] Thus Miss Leonard tells us that the statute of 1597, upon which the administration of the poor law long rested, was framed by a large committee of the House of Commons which met in the Middle Temple Hall.[8] Probably other statutes, more especially statutes which dealt with particular places and particular trades, or statutes which dealt with difficulties encountered by the justices of the peace in their conduct of the local government, were framed either by their proposers or by committees of the House ;[9] and, from the first, private bills were drawn by their promoters.[10]

---

[1] Henry VIII himself settled the preamble to the Statute of Appeals, 24 Henry VIII c. 12, vol. i 589 n. 6 ; he himself introduced into the House of Commons a statute as to vagabonds, 27 Henry VIII c. 25, Ilbert, Legislative Methods and Forms 77-78 ; for the interest which he took in the legislative proposals as to uses see vol. iv 450-461 ; for the large share taken by Thomas Cromwell in the preparation of legislative proposals see ibid 96-97.

[2] Hakewill, The Manner how Statutes are Enacted in Parliament chap. i sect. 1 tells us that " a Bill hath been sent to the Speaker, signed by the hand of Queen Elizabeth, with special commandment to be expedited ; but that is a rare case and very extraordinarie : yet such was her majesties favour to Sir Thomas Perrot in a Bill for his restitution in bloud, as it appeareth by the Clerks Journall 35 Eliz. 26 Martii."

[3] Vol. iv 97.   [4] Ibid 90-91.   [5] Ibid 450-461.

[6] Dasent, Acts of the Privy Council ii 193-195, and Porter's Case (1593) 1 Co. Rep. at f. 24b, cited vol. iv 98 n. 8.   [7] Ibid 97.

[8] " The law for the relief of the poor was a new Bill framed by the committee after many other Bills had been considered, and seems to have been accepted at once by the House. This committee was an enormous committee and the number of bills considered by it was altogether exceptional, and it is to the meetings of its members in the Middle Temple Hall that we owe the making of a workable Poor Law and all its lasting effects on English social life," Early History of English Poor Relief 79 ; cp. vol. iv 397.

[9] Ibid 181.   [10] Clifford, op. cit. i 287-288 ; cp. vol. ii 439

Thus in the sixteenth century, though the executive government, through the agency of judges and lawyers whom it employed, had the largest share in the drafting of statutes, it had
ceased to be responsible for the drafting of all the legislative
proposals which found their way on to the statute book.   It
might accept provisos and additions penned by other persons ;
and it was not responsible for the drafting of other legislative
proposals which were made by private members or by petitioners
for private Acts.   The situation at the beginning of the seventeenth century is accurately summed up by Hakewill in his
Tract entitled *The Manner how Statutes are Enacted in Parliament
by Passing of Bills.*   He says : [1]

" Publique Bills are usually drawn by such of the House (with the
advice of lawyers) as of themselves are earnestly inclined to the effecting of some publick good, which requireth the assistance of some
new law, which being fair written in paper with wide lines, they
are either by some Member of the House publickly presented to the
Speaker in the House, with some short speech setting forth the need-
fulness of a Law in that behalf, or are delivered in private to the Speaker,
or the Clerk of the Parliament, to be presented to the House at some
time convenient. . . . Many times upon the motion of someone of the
House (wishing a Law were made for provision to be had in such a case)
a Committee is purposely appointed by the House to draw a Bill to that
effect ; which being done, one of them presents it to the Speaker.   This
is usual in cases of great moment and difficulty.   The Bill for Subsidies is
usually drawn by some of the Kings Councell, after the substance thereof,
for the numbers of Subsidies and fifteans to be granted and the times
of payment is first agreed in the House.   The preamble thereof con-
taineth the clauses of the grant, which is usually drawn by some principal
member of the House, being a selected Committee [2] for that purpose.
Bills for the Revival, Repeal or continuance of Statutes, are usually
drawn by Lawyers, being members of the House, appointed thereunto
by the House, upon some motion to that purpose made, which is usual
at the beginning of every Parliament.   Private Bills are usually drawn
by Councillors at Law, not being of the House, and sometimes by those
of the House (and that for their fees) which howsoever it hath been
held by some to be lawful, yet it cannot be but very inconvenient
seeing they are afterwards to be Judges in the same cause." [3]

The tendencies, which were making for increased variegation
in the draftsmanship of the statutes, were very much accentuated

---

[1] Chap. i § 1 ; Hakewill's account is borne out by Notestein's edition of the
Commons Debates in 1621 ; thus committees were appointed to draw bills, ii 93
(a subsidy bill), iii 151, and it was said, ii 66, that " it was an ancient order that
if any make motion that is liked, it is committed to have a bill drawn " ; on
one occasion, ii 210, Coke produced a bill which he had drawn ; on another, v 286,
Coke and others were ordered to draw a bill ; on another, iii 294, the lawyers, as
directed by the House, drew bills of grace.

[2] The word " committee " is here used in its old sense of a person to whom a
duty is delegated, see vol. iv 99 n. 3.

[3] This view prevailed ; and at the present day members of Parliament cannot
practice as parliamentary agents or as counsel before committees of either House,
Erskine May, Parliamentary Practice (13th ed.) 693 ; Clifford, op. cit. 872-874 ;
above 334-337.

when, in the course of the seventeenth century, the initiative
in legislation passed from the Crown to Parliament. No doubt
some Acts continued to be drawn by government officials.[1]
Money bills must always have been so drawn ; and the judges
continued to be consulted and to be utilized as draftsmen. " In
the period after the Restoration," says Ilbert,[2]

the judges, who at that time assisted the House of Lords, not only in
their judicial but in their legislative business, and habitually attended
the sittings of the House for that purpose, appear to have been occasionally employed by the House as draftsmen of bills or clauses. Sometimes the heads of a bill were agreed to by the House, and a direction
was given either to the judges generally or to particular judges to prepare a bill. In other cases a judge would attend a grand committee
of the House as a kind of assessor, and do such drafting work as was
required.

Sir Leoline Jenkins, Dean of the Arches, judge of the court of
Admiralty, and the most distinguished civilian of his day,[3]
helped Lord Nottingham and Lord North to draft the statute of
Frauds ; [4] and in 1704 two bills relating to Scotland, which did
not become law, were drafted by the judges by order of the House
of Lords.[5] But very many of the most important constitutional
statutes of the seventeenth century were drawn by or under the
instructions of the leaders of the Parliamentary opposition.
Coke had a large share in drafting the Petition of Right ; [6] and
the leaders of the Parliamentary opposition were responsible for
the drafting of the legislation of the Long Parliament, and the
Habeas Corpus Amendment Act.[7] Moreover, the weakening of
the control of the executive government must have given more
opportunities to private members to get through the Houses the
bills proposed and drawn by them.

Thus the style in which statutes were drawn became more
and more variegated. The result was increased difficulty in
interpreting them, and sometimes in ascertaining their relations
to one another. And since, during this period, the style of legal
draftsmanship, which was used in the drawing of pleadings,
conveyances, and other documents, was tending to become more
verbose, the statutes which these lawyers drew exhibited the
same quality ; and so the difficulties of understanding and applying the growing body of statute law were increased. We shall

---

[1] In S.P. Dom. 1703-1704 39 there is a direction by Nottingham to the attorney-
general to draw a clause to be inserted in an Irish Act of Parliament.

[2] Legislative Methods and Forms 78.

[3] Vol. xii 647-661.   [4] Vol. vi 384.

[5] MSS. of the House of Lords (Hist. MSS. Com.) vi nos. 2069, 2070.

[6] Vol. v 452, 453-454.

[7] Stephen said in his evidence to the select committee of the House of Commons
on Acts of Parliament that the Habeas Corpus Amendment Act was " abominably
drawn," Parlt. Papers 1875 viii 266 ; this is perhaps too severe—the Act has carried
out very well the intentions of its framers.

now see that all these tendencies were aggravated in the eighteenth century.

(3) *The eighteenth century.*

Fitz-James Stephen said to a House of Commons Committee in
1875 that he was of opinion that " there is some degree of conflict between the independence of Parliament on the one hand,
and the symmetry of legislation on the other." [1]   There is no
doubt that this statement is true.   History shows that those
periods in which Parliament has had a large amount of independence, and the executive a small amount of control, have been
periods in which the statute book has shown the greatest lack
of symmetry.   In the eighteenth century the executive government was relatively weak.   It was obliged to pass revenue Acts,
mutiny Acts, and other Acts which were necessary to the conduct
of the executive government at home ; and the problems which
resulted from the wars and diplomacy of the eighteenth century,
and from the expansion of England in the East and the West,
compelled it to initiate much important legislation.   Much of
this work was done by the law officers of the Crown. [2]   But the
whole field of local government was left very largely to the
localities themselves, or to those justices of the peace in the
House of Commons who interested themselves in the various
problems which arose in that field. [3]   That is one reason why
private and local Acts were so numerous in this century. [4]   And
though such emergencies as the rebellion of 1745 might lead to
important domestic legislation initiated by the government, [5] for
the most part the initiation of legislation for the purpose of effecting reforms in the law was left to individual peers or members
of the House of Commons.   It is a significant fact that many
measures passed in this century, and in the first half of the
following century, are known by the names of their proposers—
Sir John Barnard's Act, [6] Gilbert's Act, [7] Hardwicke's Marriage
Act, [8] Jervis's Act, [9] Lord St. Leonard's Act, [10] Locke King's Act, [11]
are a few out of many examples.   The result was that statutes had
many different parents.   They might be initiated by government

---

[1] Parlt. Papers 1875 viii 257.

[2] In 1775 there was a scene in the House of Lords because Shelburne said that,
as the bills of last session relating to America were disowned by the law officers,
they must have been drawn by Lord Mansfield ; this was denied passionately by
Lord Mansfield, who said that the law officers had not denied that they had had a
hand in the bills, Parlt. Hist. xviii 281-283 ; obviously, the law officers were expected to draft or to assist in drafting government bills.

[3] Vol. x 242.   [4] Vol. x 188-189; above 323-324.   [5] Vol. x 78-81.

[6] 7 George II c. 8.   [7] 22 George III c. 83.

[8] 26 George II c. 33.   [9] 11, 12 Victoria c. 43.

[10] 22, 23 Victoria c. 35.   [11] 17, 18 Victoria c. 113.

departments,[1] or they might be initiated by distinguished members of either House,[2] or, in the case of local Acts, they might be initiated by members who knew the needs of their particular locality. The manner in which Lord Chesterfield's Act for the reform of the Calendar was drafted illustrates the care taken by the authors of some of these Acts. "This Bill," said Lord Macclesfield in moving the second reading,[3]

was, under his lordship's directions, drawn, and most of the tables prepared, by Mr. Davall, a barrister of the Middle Temple, whose skill in astronomy as well as in his profession, rendered him extremely capable of accurately performing that work ; which was likewise carefully examined and approved of, by . . . Mr. Folkes, president of the Royal Society, and Dr. Bradley his majesty's astronomer at Greenwich ; the latter of whom did himself compose the three general tables, which your lordships find towards the end of the printed copy. . . . As to the Bill itself, no endeavours have been wanting to make it as complete, and as free from objections of all kinds, as possible.

This is the reason why there is a large amount of individuality in the statutes of the eighteenth century. Each statute was, to a large extent, a law by itself. Unless it was necessary to repeal a statute or to amend a statute, the new statute was simply added to the existing mass of statutes new and old ; and it was left to the judges to work it into the existing fabric of the common and statute law. The fact that each new statute was regarded as an individual whole, and not as a unit in the general body of enacted law, is shown by the manner in which the same provisions were repeated over and over again in public, local, and private Acts, with such variations in phraseology as seemed good to their individual draftsmen. Consolidation Acts, which repeal and reinact a series of older Acts and Acts amending those Acts, are rare phenomena in the eighteenth century.[4] In

[1] Thus Sir James Marriott, in the case of The Columbus (1789) Collect. Jurid. i at p. 103, said of an Act of 1787 (27 George III c. 5) regulating trade with America, that " it is not very astonishing, if one considers where such bills are fabricated, by solicitors of boards or their clerks, that there should be so glaring a defect in this important Act " ; this had been the practice throughout the eighteenth century ; thus Mr. Hughes, Studies in Administration and Finance 200, tells us that it was the regular practice of the salt commissioners to submit to the treasury draft clauses to deal with abuses ; but that members whose districts were affected by these proposals were put on the committees, so that an adequate scrutiny was ensured, ibid 232-233,—a course more especially necessary as the treasury control over the House was weak, ibid 234-236; these departmental proposals for legislation were generally drafted by their official legal advisers, see ibid 221 ; for these official legal advisers see vol. xii 11-13.

[2] In 1750 Thomas Pitt introduced a bill limiting the time for soldiers to serve in the army ; it is clear that he drew it himself, since he told the House that in drawing it he had taken the advice of some of the most experienced officers in the army, and had taken care to adopt their suggestions, Parlt. Hist. xiv 729-730.

[3] Parlt. Hist. xiv 991.

[4] For some attempts at consolidation in the matter of highways and turnpikes see vol. x 172, 209; other instances of consolidating Acts are 12 Anne St. 2 c. 23, 13 George II c. 24, and 17 George II c. 5, which consolidated the laws as to rogues and vagabonds ; 2 George II c. 20 which consolidated the statutes relating to the raising and training of the militia.

fact, the idea that some measure of symmetry in the arrangement and contents of the statutes should be attempted, seems to have occurred only occasionally to the Legislature. This mental attitude is illustrated by the fact that several statutes of this century contain provisions upon the most heterogeneous topics. One illustration is an Act of 1744.[1] The title of this Act runs as follows :

An Act to continue the several laws therein mentioned for preventing theft and rapine on the Northern borders of England ; for the more effectual punishing wicked and evil disposed persons going armed in disguise, and doing injuries and violences to the persons and properties of his Majesty's subjects, and for the more speedy bringing of the offenders to justice ; for continuing two clauses to prevent the cutting or breaking down the bank of any river or sea bank, and to prevent the malicious cutting of hop binds ; and for the more effectual punishment of persons maliciously setting on fire any mine, pit, or delph of coal, or cannel coal ; and of persons unlawfully hunting or taking any red or fallow deer in forests or chaces, or beating or wounding the keepers or other officers in forests, chaces, or parks ; and for granting a liberty to carry sugars of the growth, produce, or manufacture of any of his Majesty's sugar colonies in America, from the said colonies directly to foreign parts in ships built in Great Britain, and navigated according to law ; and to explain two Acts relating to the prosecution of offenders for embeziling naval stores or stores of war ; and to prevent the retailing of wine within either of the Universities in that part of Great Britain called England, without licence.

The drafting of these Acts often left much to be desired. It is true that the Acts drafted by departments of government, and Acts drafted by eminent lawyers like Lord Hardwicke, accomplished the purposes of their framers. But in very many cases the drafting of the statutes made them difficult to read and to construe. We have seen that both in Parliament and the courts it was " an age of technicalities " ; [2] and for that reason the length and verbiage of legal documents tended to increase. Moreover, when conveyancers were paid according to the length of their conveyances, and when conveyancers were employed to draft Acts, they naturally used the same style which they found it profitable to employ in the drafting of their conveyances.[3]

[1] 17 George II c. 40 ; for other examples see 22 George II c. 46 ; 4 George III c. 12, and the examples cited in Reports of Committees of the House of Commons xiv 35 n. (g) (1796) ; there is a tradition that a clause allowing the Warden of Wadham College, Oxford, to marry was smuggled into a canal Act ; this is not true; permission was given to the Warden to marry by a personal Act of 1806, 46 George III c. 147 ; by that date the practice of passing these hotchpot Acts had been abandoned, see Reports of Committees of the House of Commons xiv 35 ; but at an earlier date it would have been a not incredible tale.

[2] Vol. x 533.

[3] Robert Lowe said, in his evidence to a Select Committee of the House of Commons in 1875, that bills were drawn " upon the precedents of conveyancers, and it having been thought desirable, for certain reasons which I need not mention, to make conveyances as long as possible, the old Acts of Parliament were drawn upon that principle," Parlt. Papers 1875 viii 341.

The result was that the statute book became not only so heterogeneous and so uncorrelated, but also so bulky, that, by the middle of the eighteenth century, it was becoming unmanageable.

In 1756 Lord Hardwicke pointed out the existence of these defects in the statute law. He said : [1]

We have it from the highest authority, that, in the multitude of counsellors there is safety ; but we in this nation may from experience say, that in the multitude of legislators there is confusion ; for our statute books are increased to such an enormous size, that they confound every man who is obliged to look into them ; and this is plainly owing to a great change which has, by degrees, crept into our constitution. In old times almost all the laws which were designed to be public Acts, and to continue as the standing laws of this kingdom, were first moved for, drawn up, and passed, in this House, where we have the learned judges always attending, and ready to give us their advice and assistance. From their knowledge and experiences they must be allowed to be the best able to tell, whether any grievance complained of proceeds from a non-execution of the laws in being, and whether it be of such a nature as may be redressed by a new law. In the former case, a new law must always be unnecessary, and in the latter it must be ridiculous. . . . But this method seems now to be quite altered : every member of the other House takes upon him to be a legislator, and almost every new law is first drawn up and passed in the other House, so that we have little else to do, especially towards the end of the session, but to read over and consent to the new laws they have made : nay some of them are sent up so late in the session that we have hardly time to read them over, and consider whether we shall consent or not, which is remarkably the case with respect to the Bill now under consideration (the militia bill). . . . But this is far from being the only inconvenience : the other House by their being so numerous, and by their being destitute of the advice and assistance of the judges, are too apt to pass laws, which are either unnecessary or ridiculous, and almost every law they pass stands in need of some new law for explaining and amending it : and we in this House either through complaisance, or through want of time, are but too apt to give our consent, often without any amendment. By this means it is that our statute books have of late years increased to such an enormous size, that no lawyer, not even one of the longest and most extensive practice, can pretend to be master of all the statutes that relate to any one case that comes before him ; and this evil goes on increasing so much, every year, that it is high time for this House to begin to put a stop to it, by resolving not to pass any Bill, for introducing a new and standing law, that comes up from the other House, unless it comes up so early in the session as to leave us sufficient time to take the advice and assistance of the judges upon it, and to consider every clause of it maturely.

Hardwicke was looking back either to the mediæval period when the judges had had a large share in the drafting of laws,[2] or to the period of the sixteenth century when most laws were framed by the servants of the Crown, who could take the advice

---

[1] Parlt. Hist. xv 724 seqq. ; the alternative version of the speech, ibid 724-739, does not contain this passage ; but his speech on the Habeas Corpus Bill 1758, below 375 n. 2, shows that the passage cited represents his views.

[2] Above 366.

of the judges.[1] He induced the House of Lords to act upon his views in 1758. In that year the House had before it a bill extending the Habeas Corpus Act of 1679. It first consulted the judges as to the existing law, and as to the effect of the proposed bill. On receiving their answers it rejected the bill, and ordered the judges to draft a new bill.[2] But the periods to which Hardwicke was looking back were gone beyond recall. Neither the executive government, nor *a fortiori* the judges, could then hope to resume that control over legislation, and therefore over the drafting of legislation, which they had once had.[3] Matters were allowed to drift. The results were summed up by Bentham in his tract entitled *Nomography or the Art of Inditing Laws*,[4] which was based on various manuscripts written between 1811 and 1831. The defects which it points out are substantially the same as those which had been pointed out by the House of Commons Committee of 1796.[5]

Bentham first set out the " imperfections of the first order." He found them to be ambiguity, obscurity which " is ambiguity taken at its maximum," and over-bulkiness.[6] He then sets out seven " imperfections of the second order " ; and, since these are to a large extent well-founded criticisms upon the mode in which the eighteenth-century statutes were drafted, I quote his words. He says : [7]

The imperfections of the second order, of which a mass of law considered in respect of its form is susceptible, may be thus enumerated :

   1. *Unsteadiness in respect of expression*—When for the designation of the same import, divers words or phrases are employed.

   2. *Unsteadiness in respect of import*—When to the same word or phrase, divers imports are attached in different places.

   3. *Redundancy*—When of any number of words employed in connexion with each other, the whole or any part might without prejudice to the sense . . . be simply omitted, or others in less number be inserted in the room of them . . .

---

[1] Above 367-368.

[2] For this episode see vol. ix 119-121 ; Lord Hardwicke's notes of his speech which he made on this occasion run as follows : " It is also a bill for alteration of the law particularly mixed with and relating to the course of proceedings in the great Courts at Westminster. Scarce an instance of passing such a bill without asking the opinions of the judges, not whether it is fit upon political reasons to pass such a bill—that is a legislative consideration—but to inform your lordships in law Peculiar privilege and advantage of this House that the twelve judges attend here by the King's writ. Have more than once known bills, sent up from the other House, which have appeared very plausible there, have been found upon the better lights, produced by this House, to be in the highest degree improper and inexecutable, even to the conviction of the original framers of them," P.C. Yorke, Life of Hardwicke iii 12, citing Hardwicke MSS. 530 f. 37.

[3] It is only in respect of Estate Bills (which are now very rare), below 627, that the judges are called upon to report to the House of Lords, Clifford, op. cit. ii 769-770.

[4] Works (Bowring's ed.) iii 231-283.   [5] Above 309 n. 2.

[6] Works iii at pp. 239-240.   [7] At p. 240.

4. *Longwindedness*—When a portion of legislative matter, the elements of which are in such sort connected with each other, that to comprehend in a complete and correct manner any one part, the mind finds itself under the necessity of retaining within its grasp the whole, is drawn out to such a length as to be liable to overpower the retentive faculty of the mind on which the obligation of taking cognizance of it is imposed.

5. *Entanglement*—When propositions distinct in themselves are forced together in one grammatical sentence, and in this state carried on together throughout the course of it.

6. *Nakedness in respect of helps to intellection*—especially if in respect of such as are in general use :—such as division into parts of moderate length—designation of those parts by concise titles and figures of arithmetic expressive of numbers, for indication of such respective parts—and reference by titles and numbers as above, instead of by general description of their contents.[1]

7. *Disorderliness*—1. In respect of the arrangement given to the several matters—whether by including under one and the same name, and thence under the same treatment, matters which, in respect of the diversity of their nature, require each a different treatment ;—2. By placing at a distance from each other those which for facility, and clearness, and correctness of intellection, ought to stand contiguous to each other, or near at least to each other : or contiguous or near those which ought to be at a distance ;—or, 3. By giving to this or that article the precedence over this or that other, which for clearness or facility of intellection, ought to have been placed before it.

His conclusion is that

the English lawyer, more especially in his character of parliamentary composer, would, if he were not the most crafty, be the most inept and unintelligent, as well as unintelligible of scribblers. Yet no bell-man's verses, no metrical effusion of an advertising oil-shop, were ever so much below the level of genuine poetry, as . . . taken for all in all, are the productions of an official statute-drawer below the level of the plainest common sense.[2]

Bentham's criticism upon the draftsmanship of the statutes was thoroughly well justified ; and in his tract he makes some acute suggestions as to the remedies which ought to be applied. But his suggestions were mainly directed to the improvement of the literary style of the draftsman.   In this matter, as in others, he was so convinced that a principal cause for the evils which he denounced was the knavery or folly of the lawyers, that he never looked deeper, and searched for more substantial causes. In this matter, as in others, his neglect of history caused his diagnosis of the evils to be remedied to be superficial.   He failed to see that the principal cause for these evils was the excessive individuality of the statutes passed by the Legislature ; and that it was this individuality which prevented co-ordination between

---

[1] Some of these defects were remedied by Brougham's Act, 13, 14 Victoria c. 21 §§ 2 and 3.
[2] At p. 242.

them in respect of either their form or their substance, and caused an immense amount of repetition in statutes in which many similar provisions were necessary. We shall now see that the great increase in the bulk and complexity of the statute law, which was caused partly by the industrial revolution and the accompanying changes in economic social and intellectual conditions, and partly by the constitutional and political changes following upon the Reform Act of 1832, at length led statesmen to realize the need for mitigating the principal cause for these evils, by taking measures to produce co-ordination and to reduce repetition.

(4) The latest phase.

In 1838 Arthur Symonds of the Board of Trade wrote an important letter to C. P. Thomson, then President of the Board of Trade, upon the methods of drafting bills public and private.[1] He pointed out that " during the last 250 years our statute law has been a topic of ridicule and sarcasm " ; and that its composition had incurred the censure of " statesmen, judges, lawyers, wits, poets, and public writers of all kinds." [2] He found the main reason for this state of affairs to be the fact that " the Legislature, acting in its own behalf, is not provided with any officers by whose assistance it can give expression to its laws after its own manner." [3] He pointed out that in the mediæval period the judges drafted the Acts passed by Parliament ; and that that practice had been abandoned in favour of " the present practice of propounding the law in the very terms in which it is to be passed." [4] The present practice, he said, suffered from defects different from, but no less serious than, the defects of the older practice.

If the judges sometimes failed to give effect to the real intention of the Legislature (or perverted it), the modern system also fails in another way to make the new law and the old in accordance, and to give to one and the other as part of the same system, that consistency both in spirit and form, which is so necessary for facilitating the understanding of it both by the judges and the people.[5]

The result was that,

at present each Act of Parliament (with few exceptions) is an isolated performance, framed upon no principle, and pieced on very imperfectly to the law to which it belongs. It seldom corresponds with other Acts of the same session in style, or in structure, or in the uniform presence or absence of necessary provisions.[6]

---

[1] Parlt. Papers 1837-1838 xliv 3-18.
[2] Ibid 5, and App. xii pp. 76-77.   [3] Ibid 6.
[4] Ibid.   [5] Ibid.   [6] Ibid 19.

He pointed out that in the case of the customs laws this general superintendence had been provided, with the result that amendments were easily incorporated, and the whole body of these laws was in a consolidated state.[1] The principal need, therefore, was the provision of some machinery by which a certain measure of co-ordination could be introduced into the style and language used by the draftsmen of statutes.

Another need, he pointed out, was the enactment of general Acts, dealing with classes of incidental matter which were common to many particular Acts.[2] No less than thirty-five topics were enumerated by him as fit to be made the subjects of general Acts. Among them were such topics as the summary procedure before the justices, the limitation of actions against persons acting in pursuance of statutes, the constitution of companies, the interpretation of words in ordinary use.[3] The adoption of this plan would, he pointed out, diminish the length of statutes ; and it would get rid of another objection which had been caused by the want of these general Acts.

Under the present system it often happens that the merely incidental proceedings of another Act, under a totally different name, and for a totally different purpose are to be referred to. The Act is repealed—the principal and secondary matters together, without regard to the use which has been made of the secondary matter in some other Act.[4]

There can be no doubt that this last objection added considerably to the obscurity of the statute law, and made it very difficult for lawyers and impossible for laymen to ascertain its provisions. A curious illustration of these effects of this manner of legislating was given by FitzJames Stephen to the Select Committee on Acts of Parliament in 1875. He said : [5]

[1] " The course of proceeding has been the following : In the first instance Mr. Hume was employed to consolidate in some 10 Acts, a body of law extending in its unconsolidated state to 400 or more. Even since that, he has been charged with the preparation of an Edition for the use of the Officers of Customs ; to which he appends extracts from any other Statutes which concern those Officers ; and also an index and notes to each law, marking the alterations made in them by other Statutes. All laws which are introduced for the amendment of the Customs Laws (proper), are prepared by him ; and his method of writing these is such that any alteration can be made, either by the insertion of new matter, or by striking out a few words and substituting others, and so on, without altering the structure of his original Acts. The consequence is that practically the Customs Laws are always in a consolidated state," Parlt. Papers 1837-1838 xliv 68.
[2] " An Act of Parliament often consists of many things, which though related to its subject . . . yet have not necessarily a place in it, but which being of a general nature, and applicable in common to many special laws, should be the subject of a distinct law ; to be referred to in such special cases," ibid 51.
[3] Ibid 53-54.
[4] Ibid 52.
[5] Ibid 1875 viii 268 ; for an account of this important committee of 1875 see Sir William Graham-Harrison, Journal of Soc. of Public Teachers of Law 1935 11.

In the year 1773 when the government first appointed a Governor-General in Council [for India], it was considered very important that arrangements should be made for bringing them to justice if they were guilty of oppression, and there were previous statutes about oppression which were still in force. These statutes made no provision about obtaining evidence upon the spot. Consequently clauses were inserted in the Regulating Act which say that if the Governor-General or any member of the Council misconducts himself, then any person who is aggrieved by him may call upon the Supreme Court at Calcutta to take evidence, and that has to be copied and transmitted to the Queen's Bench, and you may read that evidence in England. That was before any provision had been made for taking evidence by Commission abroad. When from the growth of the Colonial system it became increasingly necessary to take evidence abroad, it was enacted that the Regulating Act should to that extent apply to the Colonies ; then that it should apply to Scotland, and then that it should apply to Ireland, and then that it should apply to civil cases, it having been altogether for criminal cases originally. The consequence is, that if you want to take out a Commission for the examination of a man in Australia about a bill of exchange, you have to do so by virtue of an Act which applied to India in criminal cases, and if you repealed that Act you would cut away the root of one branch of the law of evidence.

It is clear that such anomalies as these would be avoided by the use of general Acts for secondary purposes which could be incorporated into any Act into which it was found desirable to incorporate them. The second great need, therefore, was the provision of a set of general Acts which would both shorten and simplify the general body of the statute law.

Other suggestions were made by Symonds for effecting improvements in the drafting of statutes and for making their contents more easily accessible ; and many of them have been subsequently adopted.[1] But, from the point of view of the history of the measures taken to improve the drafting of legislative proposals in the nineteenth century, these two proposals have proved to be the most fruitful. I shall therefore deal with the history of this matter in the nineteenth century under these two heads. I shall describe first the introduction of the measure of co-ordination which has had the largest effect in improving the form of the statute book ; and, secondly, the provision of general Acts, and the new manner of legislating by reference to them.

[1] Thus he suggested that the statutes should have marginal notes to their sections, tables of contents, short titles, that sentences should be shortened, that sections should be divided into clauses and paragraphs, Parlt. Papers 1837-1838 xliv 8 ; he also laid down the principle that " each statute should, like a pleading on any other composition, be framed according to principles suited to the purposes which it is intended to serve," and that, " it might be a very good composition and yet unsuited for passing through the ordeal of Parliament," ibid ; these principles are now generally accepted, see Ilbert, Legislative Methods and Forms 237-270 ; below 383.

The introduction of a measure of co-ordination.

During the first thirty to forty years of the nineteenth century, the eighteenth-century view that it was the primary business of the executive government to administer, and not to initiate projects of legislation which were unconnected with its duties of administration, still persisted.[1]   Anson says :[2]

There is no instance before 1830 of a Ministry retiring because it was beaten on a question of legislation, or even of taxation. So late as 1841 Macaulay maintained in the House of Commons, speaking as a Cabinet Minister, that a Government was not bound to resign because it ' could not carry legislative changes, except in particular cases, where they were convinced that without such and such a law, they could not carry on the public service.' Legislation which ministers might need for administrative purposes was the only sort of legislation about which, in the opinion of the Melbourne Cabinet, a Government need feel sensitive.

In these circumstances the characteristic of extreme individualism which marked the preparation and drafting of statutes in the eighteenth century still persisted.   Much legislation was initiated by private members who employed their own draftsmen. The Petitions of Right Act[3] originated with Sir William Bovill when he was a private member, and the bill was drawn by Archibald who afterwards became a judge.[4]   Since the different government departments employed their own draftsmen,[5] there was much diversity in the style of government bills.   Sometimes they were drawn by officials in the office.   James Stephen, who was under-secretary for the Colonies, drew the Slave Trade Act of 1824.[6]   Sometimes they were drawn by lawyers employed by the government.[7]   The famous conveyancer, Brodie,[8] who was mainly responsible for parts of the first three reports of the Real Property Commissioners,[9] drew the Fines and Recoveries Act.   That Act is a model of drafting—but his work on the Commission and on this Act cost him several years' labour, and left him so little time to attend to his practice that for a time he lost nearly all of it.[10]

It is under the younger Pitt's administration that we can see the first signs of a movement which will lead ultimately to

[1] Ilbert, op. cit. 82.   [2] The Crown Pt. i (3rd ed.) 132.

[3] 23, 24 Victoria c. 34.

[4] Parlt. Papers 1875 viii 385—evidence of Archibald J.

[5] Ibid 279—evidence of Mr. Reilly ; 340—evidence of Robert Lowe.

[6] Stephen, H.C.L. iii 256 ; cp. Leslie Stephen, Life of Stephen 47.

[7] Robert Lowe, Parlt. Papers 1875 viii 340, said that as much as £800 had been paid for a single bill.

[8] For some account of him see Law Rev. (1854-1855) xxi 348-354.

[9] The part of the first Report dealing with fines and recoveries, the part of the second Report dealing with the probate of wills and taking out administration in cases of terms of years, and the part of the third Report dealing with copyhold and ancient demesne, ibid 351.

[10] Ibid 353.

a measure of co-ordination in the drafting of statutes.   A Mr. William Harrison, who described himself as parliamentary counsel to the treasury, and before him a Mr. Lowndes, were employed by Pitt to draft many government bills.[1] Harrison told a committee of the House of Commons in 1833 that he drew all government bills for the treasury, and also for other departments.   He said that he had drawn foreign office bills for carrying into execution treaties of peace and other purposes ; that he had drawn militia and military bills for the home office ; church bills for the ecclesiastical commissioners ; and that he sometimes drew or settled revenue bills.   He continued to do this work till 1837.   In 1837 his duties seem to have been assumed by the counsel employed by the home office, since that office was responsible for the more important legislative measures of the government.[2]   That office also, in conjunction with the law officers, exercised an oversight over bills introduced by private members ;[3] and since the Lord Chairman of committees in the House of Lords supervised private bills,[4] it is clear that the tendency was in the direction of instituting some control over proposals for legislation.   In fact, shortly after the middle of the nineteenth century, the responsibility of the executive government for legislation, and therefore its control over it, were assuming their modern dimensions.   About the year 1855 Sir Charles Wood said :

When I was first in Parliament, twenty-seven years ago, the functions of Government were chiefly executive.   Changes in our laws were proposed by independent members, and carried, not as party questions, by their combined action on both sides.   Now, when an independent member brings forward a subject, it is not to propose himself a measure, but to call to it the attention of the Government.[5]

The counsel employed by the home office in 1837 was Mr. Bethune, and he was succeeded first by Mr. Coulson and then by Sir Henry Thring.   But till 1869 the home office counsel, though he drew the more important government bills, had no monopoly.

---

[1] See Ilbert, op. cit. 80-82, citing Harrison's evidence given in 1833 to a committee on House of Commons offices and fees.
[2] Ibid 83.
[3] Mr. Bouverie, sometime Chairman of Committees in the House of Commons, said in 1875 : " The old fashioned check upon these defects was the lynx eyes of the Home Secretary and the law officers of the Crown.   When I first became a member of the House of Commons, the Home Secretary, though not a lawyer, was a man of very great ability, and of a legal turn of mind ; I refer to Sir James Graham ; he was supported by very powerful law officers, and they used . . . to look after the wording of independent members' bills ; and when it was required, assuming the object of a bill was one which was accepted by the House and the Government, they gave their assistance, either outside the House or in the House itself to putting it into reasonable and proper shape," Parlt. Papers 1875 viii 374.
[4] Above 345-346.
[5] Cited Ilbert, op. cit. 82.

Other departments still employed their own draftsmen.[1] But by 1869 the control of the executive government was so well established, that the time was ripe for making a further change, which would make that control more effective. That change was made by Robert Lowe, then Chancellor of the Exchequer. He revived in an entirely new form the office of parliamentary counsel to the treasury.[2] The duties of this new official were

to settle all such departmental bills, and draw all such other Government bills (except Scotch and Irish bills) as he might be required by the Treasury to settle and draw. . . . On the requisition of the Treasury he was to advise on all cases arising on bills or Acts drawn by him, and to report in special cases referred to him by the Treasury on bills brought in by private members.[3]

Sir Henry Thring, who had filled the office of counsel to the home office, was appointed to this new office.

The nature of the change was explained by Sir Henry Thring in 1875 to the select committee of the House of Commons on Acts of Parliament.[4] He told the committee that as home office counsel he drew the bills of the Prime Minister for the time being, and any other bills which he could find time for ; and that he advised the home office on all subjects connected with legislation, including private members' bills if he was asked his opinion upon them. He said that the duties of his old office of home office counsel and his new office of parliamentary counsel were of the same character.

The difference was this, that when I was Home Office counsel I had no assistance except that of mere copying clerks, and I was bound to draw Home Office bills only, and such other bills as I could find time to draw. In fact I drew all the Home Office bills, and any Cabinet bills which were of great importance, and which I could find time to draw. When my office was changed, I was made a Treasury Officer ; was provided permanently with the assistance of a barrister, Mr. Jenkyns, and was allowed to call in the further aid of young draftsmen to work under my superintendence. On the other hand my duties were greatly extended, and I was required to draw by myself or my deputies, every Government bill.

Though for a short time after the establishment of the new office some departments continued to employ their own draftsmen,[5] they gradually ceased to do so, " and now all Government bills, except Scotch and Irish bills, and subject to a few other unimportant exceptions, are prepared by or under the responsibility of the parliamentary counsel's office." [6]

The effects of the establishment of this office upon the drafts-

---

[1] Below n. 5. [2] Ilbert, op. cit. 84.
[3] Ibid 84-85. [4] Parlt. Papers 1875 viii 352.
[5] Ibid 340-341—Robert Lowe's evidence; Ilbert, op. cit. 86. [6] Ibid.

manship of Acts of Parliament have been most salutary ; [1] and
its salutary effects have been the more far-reaching because it
was instituted at a time when the day of the private member
was almost over, owing to the increasing demands made by the
government on the time of Parliament. Of these effects the
four following are perhaps the most important. In the first
place, it has provided a machinery of co-ordination which makes
for the elimination of discordant legislative proposals, and the
reconciliation of the conflicting views of different departments.[2]
And this machinery is the more effective because the parliamentary counsel, " like his predecessor the home office counsel,
is not merely a draftsman, but is expected to give advice, when
requested, on any matter involving, or likely to involve, legislation." [3] In the second place, it has been instrumental in
evolving a technique of draftsmanship, suited to bills which have
to face the ordeal of criticism by a large assembly, many of whom
are hostile to the measure. That technique is necessarily different
from the technique of the pleader or conveyancer. The draftsman of these bills is dealing in very many cases, not with law,
but with administrative machinery. He is dealing, not with a
limited number of contingencies which may happen under an
existing set of legal rules, but with the unknown effects which
may result from a new and untried set of legal rules. He needs
more vision, more " constructive imagination " than a draftsman
of conveyances. In addition he must, in the matter both of
style and substance, " study the idiosyncrasies of Parliament
much as a *nisi prius* barrister has to study the idiosyncrasies of
a common jury." [4] In the third place, the improvement in the
style and the increase in the uniformity of the statute law, which
was noted by the committee on Acts of Parliament in 1875,[5] has
made it much easier to produce those measures of consolidation,
which have enormously simplified the statute law.[6] In the fourth
place, these improvements have had their reactions not only,
as was prophesied in 1837,[7] upon the law of the colonies, and upon
the rules and regulations made by the authorities of the local
government; but also upon that mass of rules, orders, and regulations made by the government departments under statutory
authority, which is as characteristic a feature of the late nineteenth and twentieth centuries as private and local Acts were of
the eighteenth century.[8]

[1] With this view Sir William Graham-Harrison agrees, and he gives reasons
why its effects have not done more to improve the statute book between 1875 and
the present day, Journal of the Soc. of Public Teachers of Law 1835 41-45.

[2] Ilbert, op. cit. 219.   [3] Ibid.
[4] Ibid 238-242.   [5] Parlt. Papers 1875 viii 216.
[6] Above 315-316.   [7] Parlt. Papers 1837-1838 xliv 61.

[8] These rules, orders, and regulations are generally drawn in the department to
which the statutory authority has been given ; the Committee on Ministers' Powers

As we shall now see, all these salutary effects of the institution of the office of parliamentary counsel to the treasury have
been materially helped by the rise and growth of a system of
general Acts, and of legislation by reference to them.

General Acts and legislation by reference to them.

We have seen that the policy of these general Acts was foreshadowed in the eighteenth century, by those standing orders of
the two Houses which required that certain clauses should be
inserted in inclosure, turnpike, canal, and improvement Acts.[1]
This policy was very greatly extended in the course of the nineteenth century, and was applied not only to private, but also to
public Acts.   In 1845 the Companies Clauses Act,[2] the Lands
Clauses Act,[3] and the Railway Clauses Act [4] were drawn by
Mr. Booth, counsel to the Speaker, in order to consolidate provisions usually contained in special Acts relating to the formation of companies, the taking of land, and the construction of
railways.[5]   In 1848 Jervis's Act consolidated the provisions as
to the procedure to be employed by magistrates in their petty
sessions, in cases where special Acts gave them jurisdiction over
minor offences.[6]   In 1850 Brougham's Act,[7] now superseded by
the much more comprehensive Interpretation Act, 1889,[8] contained rules for the interpretation of certain words used in Acts
of Parliament.   The Public Authorities Protection Act, 1893,[9]
superseded the need for expressly stating in Acts, which gave
powers to Public Authorities, the procedural advantages which
those Authorities were to have, if actions were brought against
them for acts done in the exercise of these powers.[10]   The Army
Act [11] contains a code of military law, and renders it unnecessary
to re-enact every year a lengthy Mutiny Act.   The clauses of the
Conveyancing Act, 1881,[12] and of the Settled Land Acts, 1882-
1890,[13] which made it unnecessary to set out at length covenants

---

(1932), Cmd. 4060, said at pp. 49-50 that the drafting was uneven, and some of it
not very good ; the Committee pointed out that one way of securing improvement
was to increase the staff of the parliamentary counsel's office, and hand over the duty
of drafting these rules, orders, and regulations to that office.

[1] Above 329-330.   [2] 8, 9 Victoria c. 16.
[3] Ibid c. 18.   [4] Ibid c. 20.
[5] Ilbert, op. cit. 261 ; it is pointed out, ibid n. 1, that this system " has been
subsequently extended to the subjects of Towns Improvements, Police, Waterworks,
Gasworks, Harbours, Docks and Piers, Markets and Fairs, Cemeteries, Commissioners, and Electric Lighting."

[6] 11, 12 Victoria c. 43.   [7] 13, 14 Victoria c. 21 § 4.
[8] 52, 53 Victoria c. 63.   [9] 56, 57 Victoria c. 61.
[10] Vol. x 157.
[11] 42, 43 Victoria c. 33, re-enacted with amendments 44, 45 Victoria c. 58.
[12] 44, 45 Victoria c. 41 §§ 7, 18.
[13] 45, 46 Victoria c. 38 ; 53, 54 Victoria c. 69.

for title or special powers given to mortgagors or mortgagees or to tenants for life, are illustrations of the same policy.

There can be no doubt that the pursuance of this policy of passing general Acts, and legislating by reference to them, has diminished the length, and added to the uniformity and the precision of the provisions of the statute law. Unfortunately the same praise cannot be given to another form of legislation by reference, which became very common in the later years of the nineteenth century.[1] The Legislature, instead of stating its commands clearly and explicitly, stated them by the indirect method of referring to the clauses of another Act. The complexity and obscurity caused by this mode of legislating, were sometimes increased by a proviso that the earlier Act was to apply so far as it was consistent with the later Act ; and sometimes they were still further increased by a proviso that a clause imported from the earlier Act was to be amended in transit. The following example from § 2 (1) (c) of the Finance Act of 1894 is a good instance of this vicious form of legislation by reference : [2]

Property passing on the death of the deceased shall be deemed to include . . . property which would be required on the death of the deceased to be included in an account under section thirty-eight of the Customs and Inland Revenue Act 1881, as amended by section eleven of the Customs and Inland Revenue Act 1889, if those sections were herein enacted and extended to real property and personal property, and the words " voluntary " and " voluntarily " and a reference to a ' volunteer ' were omitted therefrom.

This manner of legislating resulted, as Jessel, M.R., justly said, in the manufacture of a " Chinese puzzle." [3] The reason for resorting to it is the desire to shorten Acts in order to facilitate their passage through Parliament.[4] The longer the Act the greater the opportunity for amendments, and the less the chance of getting it passed. " What shall it profit me," said Robert Lowe, " if I make a very beautiful bill if I by so doing prevent myself from carrying it." [5]

In fact this difficulty in passing Acts is one part of the price which must be paid for the benefit of the independent criticism of Parliament. Another part of the price is the risk that an

---

[1] For an account of the different classes of referential legislation—good and bad—see Graham-Harrison, Journal of the Soc. of Public Teachers of Law 1935, 25-29.

[2] 57, 58 Victoria c. 30.

[3] " A Chinese puzzle is the only expression I can make use of as describing the mode in which Acts of Parliament are enacted as regards amendment," Parlt. Papers 1875 viii 318.

[4] The committee on Acts of Parliament said in 1875 that this method of legislating was on the increase, and that " the only justification offered for it is the difficulty of getting the bill through committee without such references," ibid 216.

[5] Ibid 349.

Act may be rendered obscure by ill-considered amendments. No doubt amendments may improve an Act; but there is no doubt that they often injure it materially.[1] Yet another part of the price is the extreme detail with which many of the older Acts treated what were really minor points of administration. We have seen that in some cases it has been possible to remedy this defect by means of general Acts.[2] But it is not possible to apply this remedy in the case of a wholly new legislative enterprise such as the National Insurance Act, 1911.[3] In such cases, and in other cases where special and technical details are involved, this defect has been to a large extent remedied by the delegation of powers to ministers to make statutory rules and orders upon such matters. Such delegation was encouraged by Sir Henry Thring and his successors in the office of parliamentary counsel to the treasury;[4] and in 1930 Sir William Graham-Harrison, who then held that office, told the Ministers Powers Committee that his twenty-seven years' experience of the work of getting legislation through Parliament had convinced him that

it would be impossible to produce the amount and kind of legislation which Parliament desires to pass, and which the people of this country are supposed to want, if it became necessary to insert in the Acts of Parliament themselves any considerable portion of what is now left to delegated legislation.[5]

That committee in its report indorsed this opinion, but with the proviso that safeguards ought to be provided for the maintenance both of the legislative supremacy of Parliament, and of that judicial control upon which the principle of the Rule of Law ultimately depends.[6] Similarly the evil of ill-considered amendments is to some extent mitigated by that increase of the control of the executive over Parliament, and its assumption of responsibility for all important legislative proposals, which has made the institution of a parliamentary counsel so effective an instrument for the improvement of the draftsmanship of the statutes.[7] No doubt these changes involve the sacrifice of some part of that independence which Parliament enjoyed in the eighteenth and earlier part of the nineteenth centuries. This is

[1] Thus in 1875 Sir Henry Thring said, " the Public Schools Bill was altered by a member in Select Committee; he put in an organic amendment which we were obliged to accept, and it rendered the Act obscure throughout; that is not a solitary instance," Parlt. Papers 1875 viii 366; on this question see Graham-Harrison, Journal of the Soc. of Teachers of Law 1935, 29-31, who is inclined to think that, at the present day, " too large a share of the imperfections in bills is charged to the process of amendment."

[2] Above 384.   [3] 1, 2 George V c. 55.

[4] Report of Ministers Powers Committee (1932) Cmd. 4060 at p. 24.

[5] Ministers Powers Committee, Memoranda and Minutes of Evidence vol. ii 35.

[6] Report of Ministers Powers Committee (1932) Cmd. 4060 at pp. 65-70, 113-117.

[7] Above 381, 383.

not the place to discuss the question whether or not it has been worth while to make this sacrifice. Here we are only concerned with the drafting of the statutes ; and there can be no doubt as to the enormous improvements in their drafting which these changes have effected.

In relating the history of the formalities of legislation it has been necessary to say something of the developments which had taken place in the centuries preceding the eighteenth century, and of the developments which have taken place in the centuries which have succeeded it. It is necessary to know something of the earlier history of the classification and publication of the statutes, of the process of making statutes, and of the manner in which legislative proposals were drafted, if we would understand the system which the eighteenth century inherited. Without some knowledge of that system, it is impossible to understand the effects upon the statute book of the eighteenth century of that weakness of the executive, and that jealousy felt by Parliament of the slightest infringement of its legislative authority, which were the legacies of the Revolution Settlement. The combined effect of these two causes was to leave the statute book in a chaotic condition, which was not effectively remedied till the latter half of the nineteenth century. But since the numerous projects of reform, which were put forward in the nineteenth century, are intimately related to, and therefore shed much light upon, eighteenth-century conditions, I thought it best to carry the history of this subject down to modern times, and to sketch briefly the progress of the reforms which were necessitated by the exigency of modern conditions, and rendered possible by the strengthening of the executive, and its increased control over Parliament. We must now turn back to the eighteenth century and examine the contribution made by the eighteenth-century statutes to the development of English law.

II

THE CONTRIBUTION OF THE EIGHTEENTH-CENTURY STATUTES TO LEGAL DEVELOPMENT

The two topics which occupy the largest place in the statute law of the eighteenth century are public law and commerce and industry. With the first of these topics I have dealt in the preceding chapter. With the second of these topics I shall deal in the first place in this chapter. There are no statutes of sufficient importance on other branches of the law to deserve a separate treatment, except the Act of 1705-1706 " for the amendment of the law and the better advancement of justice." [1]   I shall, in the second place, say something of this Act ; and, in the third place, describe shortly a few of the more important of the statutes which made small changes in, or additions to, various branches of English law.   Lastly, I shall say something of the contribution to legal development made by that large output of private Acts of Parliament, which did much to supplement the comparatively small amount of public legislation upon all branches of private, and many branches of public or semi-public, law.

Commerce and Industry

During the greater part of the eighteenth century the commercial and industrial policy which had been adopted at the Revolution continued to be followed.   We have seen that before the Revolution two different lines of commercial and industrial policy were advocated by the two political parties which divided the state.   Both parties agreed that commerce and industry must be so ordered that national defence was provided for, and therefore that the policy of the Navigation Acts must be maintained.   Both parties agreed that some protection must be given to the agricultural and manufacturing industries.   But whilst the Tory party was inclined to favour a large volume of foreign trade which would raise the revenue derived from the customs, and so lighten the burdens upon the land, the Whig party wished at all costs to encourage native industries—both the manufacturing and the agricultural industries, and to prohibit branches of foreign trade which interfered with the industrial development of the country.[2]   We have seen that the views of the Whigs triumphed at the Revolution ; [3] and that the commercial clauses of the treaty of Utrecht, which were intended to give effect to the views of their opponents, were rejected.[4]   The result was that these ideas of the Whigs inspired the commercial and industrial policy of the state till nearly the end of the eighteenth century.   It is the working out of these ideas, by means of a legislative regulation of all branches of commerce and industry, which gave rise to the economic system which is generally known as " The Mercantile System."

Broadly speaking, all parties were agreed in following an economic policy which in their opinion would make for the increase of the power and welfare of the state ; and to this

---

[1] 4, 5 Anne c. 16.   [2] Vol. vi 339-340.
[3] Ibid 341.   [4] Vol. x 47.

policy the term "Mercantile System" is often applied.[1] This economic policy was very different from that pursued by the mediæval state ; for in the Middle Ages economic dealings were regarded rather as a series of personal relationships than as a mere exchange of commodities, with the result that the ideal aimed at was a moral ideal—honest manufacture, a just price, a fair wage, a reasonable profit.[2] But even in the Middle Ages we can see some approach to the economic ideas which underlay the mercantile system in the legislation which regulated foreign trade.[3] In the sixteenth century the rise of the territorial state, which accentuated national rivalries in many fields, and the changes in economic ideas which accompanied the growth of commerce and the more elaborate organization of industry, gave a greater extension and a greater precision to this system.[4] But the constitutional changes which marked the transition from the Tudor to the Stuart dynasty, and the transition from the Stuart dynasty to the constitutional régime of their successors, caused differences both in the measures taken to secure the power and welfare of the state, and in the administrative machinery employed ; and the changes in the nature of the economic problems of these different periods, and differences of opinion as to the best methods of solving them, caused other differences in the details of these measures.[5]

Therefore the mercantile system does not represent a completely fixed set of economic ideas and expedients. As Mr. Lipson says : [6] " The fact that the term (Mercantile System) was not used by sixteenth or seventeenth century writers warns us against the attempt to give formal shape and substance to what was largely nebulous and opportunist." But after the Revolution, when the views of the Whigs as to the best policy to pursue in order to secure the power and welfare of the state prevailed, it becomes much more possible to give a definite meaning to the phrase "Mercantile System." It becomes more definitely a system, as it comes to be identified with the commercial and industrial policy pursued by the Whig party. Though, as we have seen, there was a considerable measure of agreement between the two parties as to the policy to be pursued, the Whigs laid the greatest emphasis on the need for fostering all branches of native industry.[7] The state must be economically

---

[1] Cunningham, Growth of English Industry and Commerce (4th ed.) ii 16-24 ; Lipson, Economic History of England iii 1 ; vol. iv 316-317.
[2] Vol. ii 468 and n. 4.   [3] Vol. ii 472.
[4] Vol. iv 316-319.   [5] Cunningham, op. cit. ii 20-24.
[6] Economic History of England iii 1 ; Mr. Lipson says, ibid n. 2, " I have not noticed any use of the term in the sixteenth or seventeenth century literature, and if not unknown it was at least extremely rare."
[7] Above 388.

" self-sufficient." [1] This means " that a community must normally produce its own requirements in the shape of food and
manufactured goods, and in so far as it exchanged its commodities for those of other countries it must keep the carrying
trade in its own hands." And so " the Corn Laws, the Protection
of Industry, and the Navigation Acts constitute the three pillars "
of that system.[2]

The political measures taken by the Whigs to develop the
commerce and industry of the country were helped by scientific
discoveries and by the progress of mechanical inventions. In
the agricultural industry new modes of husbandry increased the
productiveness of the land, new modes of breeding improved the
quality of sheep and cattle, and new machinery, such as Jethro
Tull's invention of the drill-plough, gave facilities for improved
cultivation.[3] In the manufacturing industries new machines and
new processes revolutionized the conditions of production. It was
these new machines and new processes which were destined to
have the most profound effects not only upon the economic,[4]
but also upon the political and social life, of the country.[5] A
few facts and dates will show that the foundations for this trans-
formation were being laid in this century. The fly-shuttle
invented by Kay in 1735, the water frame invented by Arkwright
in 1769, the spinning jenny patented by Hargreaves in 1770,
Crompton's mule invented in 1779, the power loom invented by
Cartwright in 1785, and the invention of cylinder printing in the
same year, revolutionized the cotton industry. The invention of
smelting iron by coal, which came into general use between 1740
and 1750, and the application of the steam engine to blast fur-
naces in 1788, revolutionized the iron industry. The application
of the steam engine first to the draining of mines, then to the
working of the new textile and other machinery, and later as a
means of locomotion, transformed the whole industrial system
of the country.[6] All these discoveries and inventions gave a
powerful impulse to the organization of all branches of industry—
agricultural and manufacturing—on a capitalistic basis.

Three consequences followed : In the first place, the capit-

---

[1] " Broadly speaking, Mercantilism denoted the pursuit of economic power in
the sense of economic self-sufficiency," Lipson, op. cit. iii 1.

[2] Ibid 1-2.

[3] " The developments of the seventeenth century paved the way for . . . Jethro
Tull . . . inventor of a drill plough, Townshend cultivator of turnips, Bakewell
scientific breeder of cattle, and Coke the type of the spirited landowner. As in the
parallel case of the ' Industrial Revolution,' the ground was already prepared for
the series of changes which are now designated as the ' Agrarian Revolution,' "
Lipson, op. cit. ii 377-378 ; cp. Cunningham, op. cit. ii 545-552.

[4] Below 464-466.   [5] Below 466-501.

[6] Hammond, The Skilled Labourer 49-53 ; Toynbee, The Industrial Revolution 90-91 ; Lecky, History of England vii 267-269, 272-273, 276-279.

alists, who controlled industry, demanded more and more insistently the abolition of the mediæval restrictions and the mediæval machinery which aimed at securing honest manufacture, a just price, reasonable profit, and a fair wage. These demands had begun to be made in the seventeenth century.[1] As Mr. Tawney has said, it was a natural result of the experience of these capitalists

that, without the formal enunciation of any theory of freedom of contract, they should throw their weight against the traditional restrictions, resent the attempts made by preachers and popular movements to apply doctrines of charity and good conscience to the impersonal mechanism of large scale transactions, and seek to bring the law more closely into conformity with their economic practices.[2]

In the eighteenth century these ideas were still more widely held,[3] and were reflected both in new legislation, and in the manner in which older statutes were interpreted.[4] Some attempts, it is true, were made to secure some of the mediæval ideals in a few trades—more especially the ideal of honest manufacture.[5] But, for the most part, prices, profits, and wages were left to be adjusted by the economic forces of supply and demand.[6] The wealth of the nation was pursued with too little regard to justice to the economically weak,[7] and too little regard to the nation's health.[8] Secondly, and consequently, both in the agricultural and in the manufacturing industries, the small independent owner and the small independent handicraftsman tend to disappear.[9] The workers tend to become simply wage earners. Since these wage earners had ceased to be protected by the old laws which regulated wages and prices, they were obliged to fend for themselves. Hence we begin to see the growth of the modern relations of capital and labour, and the beginnings of combinations amongst masters and men.[10] Sometimes these combinations amongst the men took the form of trade unions formed for the more effective conduct of industrial disputes;[11] and sometimes they took the form of friendly societies formed for the improvement of the physical condition of the workers.[12] In the third place, the tendency of economic theory to justify the increasing freedom of action, which commercial men were demanding, increased in strength. We have seen that at the end of the seventeenth century, economists were arguing that laws which were opposed to the general course or custom of trade could never be effective, and did more harm than good, and that many matters

[1] Vol. vi 356-360.
[2] Tawney's ed. of Wilson's Discourse on Usury 135.
[3] Lipson, Economic History of England iii 265.
[4] Below 419-421, 468, 469-472.
[5] Below 418, 421-424.
[6] Vol. x 165-168; below 466-469, 471-472.
[7] Below 499.
[8] Below 500-501.
[9] Below 453, 462.
[10] Below 475-498.
[11] Below 486-491, 494-496.
[12] Below 492-494.

were governed by natural laws which the laws of the state were powerless to modify.[1]   This manner of reasoning gathered weight all through the eighteenth century, and gained an increasing measure of acceptance from statesmen.[2]   It culminated in 1776 in Adam Smith's famous book on *The Wealth of Nations*.[3]

Adam Smith isolated the economic point of view, and treated economics, not as a means to the promotion of the power and welfare of the state, but as a special body of knowledge, subject to special laws of its own.   " It was," says Cunningham,[4] " his main achievement to treat national wealth as separable from other elements in political life, and in this way he defined the scope of the scientific study of Economics."   Moreover he settled for many years to come the basic principles of that study.   Those principles were an insistence upon the paramount importance of securing to the individual the protection of his property and the freedom of his action, and the recognition of the fact that the wealth and prosperity of society is best secured by giving free play to the efforts of the individual to better his condition.   Thus, speaking of the bounty given on the export of corn when the price was below a certain figure,[5] he denies that this bounty and the other laws regulating the corn trade had had anything to do with the increase in the prosperity of the country which had taken place in the eighteenth century :

That security which the laws in Great Britain give to every man that he shall enjoy the fruits of his own labour, is alone sufficient to make any country flourish, notwithstanding these and twenty other absurd regulations of commerce ;   and this security was perfected by the revolution, much about the same time that the bounty was established. The natural effort of every individual to better his own condition, when suffered to exert itself with freedom and security, is so powerful a principle, that it is alone, and without any assistance, not only capable of carrying on the society to wealth and prosperity, but of surmounting a hundred impertinent obstructions with which the folly of human laws too often incumbers its operations ;   though the effect of these obstructions is always more or less either to encroach upon its freedom, or to diminish its security.   In Great Britain industry is perfectly secure ; and though it is far from being perfectly free, it is as free or freer than in any other part of Europe.[6]

---

[1] Vol. vi 357-359.

[2] It was said in the House of Commons in 1748 that, " in general we may conclude, that when proper laws are made, and executed, for preventing unlawful combinations, the labouring or working men will in a course of years underwork one another, till they reduce their wages to a bare scanty subsistence, and the masters will undersell one another, till they are reduced to a bare living profit ;   consequently all people of business must necessarily, in a course of years, become as frugal and as industrious as it is possible for them to be in that country where they live," Parlt. Hist. xiv 141-142.

[3] For Adam Smith and his book see below 507-512.

[4] Growth of English Industry and Commerce ii 594.

[5] Below 452, 457-458.   [6] Wealth of Nations (Cannan's ed.) ii 42-43.

As Toynbee says,[1] the "two conceptions which are woven into every argument of *The Wealth of Nations*" are "the belief in the supreme value of individual liberty, and the conviction that man's self-love is God's providence, that the individual in pursuing his own interest is promoting the welfare of all." But we shall see that Adam Smith was prepared to admit that both these assumptions might and should on occasion be modified, if it could be shown that it was in the interest of the state that they should be modified;[2] and that he recognized that the second of these assumptions was subject to very considerable limitations.[3]

The ready acceptance which was accorded to some of Adam Smith's theories was due partly "to the fact that he gave articulate expression to ideas, towards which the leaders of industry had long been feeling their way";[4] partly to practical modifications which he admitted must be made to the generality of his theories;[5] and partly to the fact that political and economic causes were sapping the foundations of the particular version of the mercantilist creed which had been accepted all through the century. The American Declaration of Independence, the removal of the commercial disabilities of Ireland by statutes of 1779 and 1780, and the evident advantage of entering into commercial treaties with the United States, created a new political situation which made it necessary to reconsider, and to adapt to this new situation, some of the main articles of this creed.[6] At the same time the enormous growth of English industries, which was rendered possible by the introduction of mechanical improvements, made it unnecessary to give them the amount of protection which they had needed when they were as yet in their infancy.[7] It was therefore possible for Pitt in 1786 to revert to the Tory policy, which had been defeated at the Revolution and in 1713,[8] and, by his commercial treaty[9] with France, to recreate a branch of foreign trade which had been almost non-existent since the Revolution;[10] and in 1797 to make

---

[1] Industrial Revolution 11.   [2] Below 399, 515-516.   [3] Below 515-516.
[4] Lipson, Economic History of England iii 264-265.   [5] Below 514.
[6] Cunningham, Industry and Commerce ii 583-584, 589, 593.
[7] Ibid ii 602; Pitt said in 1787 that "the simple question . . . was, whether, if the situation of the two countries was changed in its relative aspect—if it was true that at the Treaty of Utrecht we had but little to send to France, and that we had now much to send them—that our manufacturers were so confessedly superior as to dread no competition, and greatly to counterbalance the natural produce of France, we ought not to enter into the Treaty," Parlt. Hist. xxvi 389.
[8] Above 388.
[9] For the text of the treaty see Parlt. Hist. xxvi 234-254.
[10] Adam Smith said, "Those mutual restraints have put an end to almost all fair commerce between the two nations, and smugglers are now the principal importers either of British goods into France, or of French goods into Great Britain," Wealth of Nations (Cannan's ed.) i 438.

a commercial treaty with the United States, which *inter alia* modified the Navigation Acts in their favour.[1]

This change in economic policy may have owed something to Adam Smith's arguments. It is certain that Pitt had studied and admired his work. But Mr. Lipson [2] is probably right in thinking that the commercial treaty with France was due rather to practical considerations based on the actual conditions of English commerce and industry, than to Adam Smith's arguments in favour of giving a greater freedom to trade.

The real cause of the change was not any theoretical demonstration of the benefits of free trade, but the confidence which English industrial interests now felt in their ability to meet foreign competition. When confidence in the natural protection afforded by superior efficiency was lacking, the manufacturers showed their former disinclination to dispense with legal protection ; and the teachings of Adam Smith then failed to evoke any response among them. In short, the beginnings of the free trade movement in England were dictated by practical considerations, in which abstract doctrines of economic freedom did not have the influence commonly assigned to them.[3]

It is not till the following period, when the industrial revolution had made still further progress, and when political and economic speculation had come, very much more completely than it ever came in the eighteenth century, under the influence of *a priori* theorists, that the abstract economic doctrines of Adam Smith and his successors and followers began to exert a decisive, and, from many points of view, an unfortunate, influence on the policy of the state.[4] It was not till then that these abstract economic theories, based on the assumptions made by Adam Smith, were preached as absolute truths without any of those modifications and limitations which Adam Smith himself admitted.[5]

These were the main ideas and tendencies which influenced the commercial and industrial legislation of the eighteenth century. I shall consider the manner in which the Legislature endeavoured to give expression to them under the following heads : National Defence ; the Manufacturing Industries and Colonial and Foreign Trade ; Agriculture ; the New Organization of Industry and its Effects ; the Growth of Combinations of Masters and Men ; Adam Smith and the growing Influence of Economic Theory.

---

[1] 37 George III c. 97 ; below 503.

[2] Economic History of England iii 114-116.

[3] Ibid 166 ; the truth of this is clear from the way in which Pitt stated his case, see above 393 n. 7 ; and he pointed out that " the manufacturers, who were in general not a little watchful of their interests . . . had taken no alarm," Parlt. Hist. xxvi 382.

[4] Below 517-518.

[5] Toynbee, The Industrial Revolution 1-10 ; below 515-516.

I. *National Defence.*

We have seen that the manner in which practical effect was given to the general principles which underlay the mercantile system necessarily varied with changes in economic conditions ; and that the question how effect should be given to these principles necessarily caused differences of opinion.[1] One illustration of these facts is the change in the views of economists at the end of the sixteenth century as to the best method of obtaining a stock of gold and silver, in order that the government might be able to get a supply of the commodities needed for national defence.[2] Though Adam Smith is at great pains to refute the popular notion that wealth consists in money or in gold and silver,[3] there is plenty of evidence to prove that, whatever " popular notions " may have been, the economic writers of the seventeenth century did not share this delusion.[4] We have seen that in the seventeenth century it was realized that legislation which attempted to forbid the export of money or the precious metals was a mistake ; and that the wiser policy was so to regulate trade that there was a balance in favour of this country, which must be liquidated in money.[5]

At the same time these writers attached considerable importance to the possession of an adequate store of the precious metals ; and one school—the bullionist school—attached such importance to the maintenance of this store that they wished to prevent the East India Company from exporting them, although such export was necessary to the conduct of their trade.[6] But the Act of 1663 permitted the export of foreign coin or bullion,[7] and so " closed a chapter in a famous controversy." [8] Nevertheless, although the views of the bullionist school did not prevail, there is no doubt that economists continued to attach importance to the possession of an adequate stock of the precious metals because they were the sinews of war. Mr. Lipson says : [9]

[1] Above 388, 393-394.   [2] Vol. iv 331-332.

[3] " I thought it necessary, though at the hazard of being tedious, to examine at full length this popular notion that wealth consists in money, or in gold and silver. Money in common language . . . frequently signifies wealth ; and that ambiguity of expression has rendered this popular notion so familiar to us, that even they who are convinced of its absurdity, are very apt to forget their own principles, and in the course of their reasonings to take it for granted as a certain and undeniable truth," Wealth of Nations (ed. Cannan) i 415-416.

[4] Lipson, Economic History of England iii 62-67.

[5] Vol. iv 332 ; vol. vi 340 ; below 396 ; as Adam Smith says, Wealth of Nations (Cannan's ed.) i 401, " the attention of government was turned away from guarding against the exportation of gold and silver, to watch over the balance of trade, as the only cause which could occasion any augmentation or diminution of these metals."

[6] Vol. vi 340 ; Lipson, op. cit. iii 72-73.

[7] 15 Charles II c. 7 § 9 ; vol vi 340.   [8] Lipson, op. cit. iii 73.

[9] Op. cit. iii 67 ; as Hume said of money in his Essays (ed. 1768) i 317, " 'tis none of the wheels of trades : 'tis the oil which renders the motion of the wheels more

There is no question that mercantilists attached importance to the precious metals primarily as an instrument of war : this is what they meant when they spoke of treasure as a " pillar " of "national power." It provided the ready means to buy arms and victuals and shipping ; to hire men in place of the old feudal levies ; and, in short, to make " just and honourable wars, offensive and defensive " (to quote a proclamation of 1661).

But as foreign trade increased, and as instruments of credit became more extensively used, there was the less need to stress this reason for the maintenance of a stock of the precious metals [1] —though it was still necessary to maintain an adequate supply as a basis of credit,[2] and a constant supply to avoid price fluctuations.[3] As Adam Smith said,[4] " a prince, anxious to maintain his dominions at all times in the state in which he can most easily defend them, ought, upon this account, to guard not only against that excessive multiplication of paper money which ruins the very banks which issue it, but even against that multiplication of it which enables them to fill the greater part of the circulation of the country with it." But it came to be thought that this object could best be secured by securing a favourable balance of trade ; and we shall see that the securing of this balance became, as Mr. Lipson has said,[5] " the corner stone of the mercantilist theory of foreign commerce." We shall see,[6] however, that it was not the sole foundation of that theory ; so that, in spite of Hume's [7] and Adam Smith's [8] successful exposure of some of the fallacies involved in the reasoning of those who considered that the state of the balance of trade was an infallible index to the prosperity or poverty of the country, it may be maintained that this theory of foreign commerce had certain justifications which later political economists ignored.

smooth and easy. If we consider any one kingdom by itself, 'tis evident, that the greater or less plenty of money is of no consequence . . . 'Tis only the *public* which draws any advantage from the greater plenty of money ; and that only in its wars and negotiations with foreign states."

[1] Lipson, op. cit. iii 68 ; Wealth of Nations (Cannan's ed.) i 407-409 ; as Adam Smith truly says it is in barbarous countries, where manufactures are to a large extent non-existent, that the ruler must " accumulate a treasure as the only resource against such emergencies," ibid i 412 ; Hume suggested, Essays i 320, that if a bank, like the bank of Amsterdam, locked up the money it received and put none of it into circulation, this store of money " lying ready at command would be a great convenience in times of public danger and distress."

[2] Lipson, op. cit. iii 68-69.   [3] Ibid 69-70.

[4] Wealth of Nations (Cannan's ed.) i 304.

[5] Lipson, op. cit. iii 85 ; " the conception of ' a well ordered trade ' dominated the thought of the seventeenth century, as it had done the later Middle Ages ; and writers still continued to speak of the ' right ordering ' and the ' right management ' of our trade—but the end in view has now become primarily the realization of a favourable balance," ibid 86-87 ; Wealth of Nations (Cannan's ed.) i 399.

[6] Below 409-411.

[7] Hume said, Essays i 350, that " this apprehension of the wrong balance of trade appears of such a nature, that it discovers itself, whenever one is out of humour with the ministry, or is in low spirits."

[8] Below 459-462.

The securing of a favourable balance of trade was relied upon to secure the prosperity of the country, and therefore *inter alia* to secure the means for providing for national defence. But it was by no means the only means relied upon. In addition, other commercial and industrial measures, very similar in kind to those adopted in the latter part of the seventeenth century,[1] were taken with the direct object of providing for national defence. In the first place, the production of munitions of war was encouraged. In the second place, measures were taken to encourage recruitment for the navy and, more occasionally, for the army, and to ensure an adequate supply of seamen and shipping.

(1) *The encouragement of the production of munitions of war.*

In the first place, measures were taken to secure an adequate supply of the raw materials needed for the manufacture of munitions of war ; and, in the second place, measures were taken to encourage the manufacture of munitions.

(i) We have seen that the charters of the East India Company provided that the company should import a certain quantity of saltpetre and sell it to the government at a fixed price.[2] This obligation was recited in the Finance Act of 1702, which provided for the proportions in which it should be furnished by the two East India Companies, and for its fulfilment by their successor the United Company.[3] The power reserved to the Crown in 1660,[4] to prohibit the transport of gunpowder and of arms and ammunition, was expressly conferred upon the Crown in 1756 by an Act which empowered it to stop the export or carriage coastwise of saltpetre, gunpowder, and any sort of arms or ammunition.[5] Much more numerous were the Acts which provided for the supply of naval stores. The long series of these eighteenth-century statutes begins in 1704. In that year an Act was passed for encouragement of the production of naval stores in the American colonies.[6] The preamble to the statute states clearly the views held during the eighteenth century as to the importance of getting a native supply of these stores ; and it illustrates the manner in which the measures taken with this object were linked up with the other commercial objects which the adherents of the mercantile system had in view, i.e. the encouragement of the shipping industry, the securing of a favourable balance of trade, the position of the colonies in the economic system, and the encouragement of native industries.

---

[1] Vol. vi 314-319.
[2] Ibid 314 n. 14.
[3] 1 Anne St. 1 c. 6 §§ 137 and 138.
[4] 12 Charles II c. 4 § 12.
[5] 29 George II c. 16.
[6] 3, 4 Anne c. 10.

Because it is thus an index to ideas which inspired the Legislature all through the century, I shall cite it in full.   It runs as follows :

Whereas the Royal Navy, and the Navigation of England, wherein, under God, the wealth, safety and strength of this kingdom is so much concerned, depends on the due supply of stores necessary for the same, which being now brought in mostly from foreign parts, in foreign shipping, at exorbitant and arbitrary rates, to the great prejudice and discouragement of the trade and navigation of this kingdom, may be provided in a more certain and beneficial manner from her Majesty's own Dominions : And whereas her Majesty's Colonies and Dominions in America were at first settled and are still maintained and protected at a great expense of the treasure of this kingdom, with a design to render them as useful as may be to England, and the labour and industry of the people there, profitable to themselves : And in regard the said Colonies and Plantations, by the vast tracts of land therein, lying near the sea, and upon navigable rivers, may commodiously afford great quantities of all sorts of naval stores, if due encouragement be given for carrying on so great and advantageous an undertaking, which will likewise tend, not only to the further imployment and increase of English shipping and seamen, but also to the enlarging, in a great measure, the trade and vent of the woollen and other manufactures and commodities of this kingdom, and of other her Majesty's Dominions, in exchange for such naval stores, which are now purchased from foreign countries with money or bullion.

For these reasons the Act gave bounties upon the importation of tar, pitch, rozin, turpentine, hemp, masts, yards, and bowsprits.[1] The commissioners of the navy were given a right to pre-empt these stores on importation,[2] and measures were taken for the preservation of timber in the American colonies which was fit for these purposes.[3] It was also provided that the bounties should be payable only if these stores were imported in English ships manned as required by the Navigation Acts.[4]

The Act was continued by an Act passed in 1713 ; and by that Act bounties were given on naval stores from Scotland.[5] Further provisions to the same effect were made in 1721.[6] By this Act lumber was allowed to be imported free of duty,[7] provision was made for securing that the quality of the tar upon which the bounty was payable should be satisfactory,[8] and new provisions were made for the preservation of pine trees in the American colonies which were fit for masting the navy.[9] These Acts were continued with small variations in 1729 ;[10] and Acts giving bounties on the importation of certain naval stores were

---

[1] 3, 4 Anne c. 10 § 2.   [2] § 5.   [3] §§ 6 and 7.   [4] §§ 1 and 8.
[5] 12 Anne St. 1 c. 9 § 2 ; in 1719 permission was given for the importation of timber from Germany, paying the same duties as timber imported from Norway, 6 George I c. 15 § 2.   [6] 8 George I c. 12.
[7] § 2 ; in 1765 it was enacted that lumber could be exported to Ireland, the Madeiras, the Azores, and any part of Europe south of Cape Finisterre, but not to any other part of Europe except Great Britain, 5 George III c. 45 § 22.
[8] § 4.   [9] §§ 5 and 6.   [10] 2 George II c. 35.

passed or continued in 1752,[1] 1759,[2] 1764,[3] 1765,[4] 1766,[5] 1771,[6] 1779,[7] 1785 [8] and 1786.[9]

Another commodity which was very essential for the manufacture of munitions of war was iron. Until the process of smelting iron with coal was perfected,[10] Great Britain was largely dependent on foreign supplies, which came principally from Sweden, and later in the century from Russia.[11] But Parliament saw that it was dangerous to depend on foreign countries for the supply of so essential a mineral. Moreover, money must be sent out of the kingdom to pay for the iron imported ; and it was alleged by the iron-masters that, owing to the low wages prevailing abroad, they could not meet foreign competition.[12] It was for these reasons that in 1750 the duties on the import of pig and bar iron from the colonies were taken off.[13] In 1764 [14] it was provided that iron should be an enumerated commodity, and therefore should not be shipped to any part of Europe except Great Britain. The same provision had been made with respect to copper ore in 1735.[15] But though the policy of these Acts as to iron was sound, their success in accomplishing their objects was so moderate that they did not diminish seriously the trade with Sweden and Russia.[16]

We have seen that Adam Smith defended the policy of the Navigation Acts on the ground that " defence is of much more importance than opulence." [17] On this principle he considered that these bounties on the import of these commodities might be justified ; [18] and we shall see that he admits that, on the same principle, the encouragement given by means of bounties to certain manufactures,[19] and to the fishing industry,[20] could also be justified.

(ii) In the second place, measures were taken to encourage the manufacture of munitions. In 1731 an Act was passed to encourage the manufacture of British sail cloth.[21] Undressed flax was to be imported free of duty.[22] If foreign sail-cloth was

[1] 25 George II c. 35.
[2] 31 George II c. 35 § 3.
[3] 4 George III c. 11 § 3.
[4] 5 George III c. 45 § 1.
[5] 6 George III c. 44 § 3.
[6] 11 George III c. 41 § 1.
[7] 19 George III c. 22 § 1.
[8] 25 George III c. 69 §§ 8 and 9.
[9] 26 George III c. 53 § 1 ; for a list of the bounties given on these and other commodities see Adam Smith, Wealth of Nations (Cannan's ed.) ii 143-146.
[10] Above 390. [11] Lipson, op. cit. ii 160-161. [12] Ibid 161-162.
[13] 23 George II c. 29 § 1 ; this Act allowed importation only into London, but importation into all British ports was allowed in 1757, 30 George II c. 16 § 1.
[14] 4 George III c. 15 § 28. [15] 8 George I c. 18 § 22.
[16] Lipson, op. cit. ii 162.
[17] Wealth of Nations (Cannan's ed.) i 429 ; see vol. vi 318 n. 6 for Adam Smith's approval of these Acts.
[18] He expresses this view in his first two editions, but not so clearly in the third edition, Wealth of Nations (Cannan's ed.) ii 19 n. 10.
[19] Below 400. [20] Below 406-407.
[21] 4 George II c. 27. [22] § 1.

re-exported there was to be no drawback of the duty paid on importation.[1] A bounty was given on the export of British sail-cloth.[2] In 1736 it was provided that both foreign and British sail-cloth should be stamped in order that its origin might be apparent; [3] and that every ship built in Great Britain or the Plantations should " upon her first setting out or being first navigated at sea, have or be furnished with one full and compleat set of sails made up of sail cloth manufactured in Great Britain." [4] This Act was amended and continued in 1746; [5] it was further amended in 1793; [6] and it was made perpetual in 1805.[7] In 1731 a bounty was given on the exportation of gunpowder manufactured in Great Britain, because the duties payable on saltpetre had made it so dear that export had declined, and British subjects had been buying in foreign markets.[8] The Act was continued in 1764,[9] 1772,[10] 1778,[11] and 1786.[12] It expired in 1792. In 1766 a bounty was given on the export of British made cordage,[13] which was continued by later Acts, and expired in 1800.[14]

It should be noted that Adam Smith did not condemn bounties given in order to encourage manufactures necessary for national defence, just as in the earlier edition of his book he did not condemn bounties on those natural products which were needed for the manufacture of munitions of war.[15] " If," he said,[16]

any particular manufacture was necessary for the defence of the society, it might not always be prudent to depend upon our neighbours for the supply ; and if such manufacture could not otherwise be supported at home, it might not be unreasonable that all other branches of industry should be taxed in order to support it. The bounties upon the exportation of British-made sail cloth and British-made gunpowder, may, perhaps, both be vindicated upon this principle.

In fact we shall see that the policy of encouraging many native industries by protective duties and otherwise was a principal reason why, at the end of the century, British manufactures had so developed that so large a measure of protection was ceasing to be necessary, either on the ground that they were essential in the interests of national defence, or on the ground that they could not stand without such protection against foreign competition.[17]

[1] § 3.   [2] § 4.   [3] 9 George II c. 37 §§ 2 and 3.
[4] § 4 ; cp. 19 George II c. 27 § 11.   [5] 19 George II c. 27.
[6] 33 George III c. 49 § 1.   [7] 45 George III c. 68 § 2.
[8] 4 George II c. 29.   [9] 4 George III c. 11 § 2.
[10] 12 George III c. 56 § 1.   [11] 18 George III c. 45 § 1.
[12] 26 George III c. 53 § 2.   [13] 6 George III c. 45.
[14] 36 George III c. 108 § 4.   [15] Above 399 n. 18.
[16] Wealth of Nations (Cannan's ed.) ii 23.   [17] Below 438, 461.

(2) *Measures taken to encourage recruitment for the navy and the army, and to ensure an adequate supply of seamen and shipping.*

These measures are very similar in character to those taken in the latter half of the seventeenth century.[1] An Act of 1703 [2] provided that the authorities who administered the poor law should have power to bind pauper boys as apprentices to the masters or owners of sea-going ships.[3] The masters of these ships were obliged to take these apprentices; [4] but it was provided that they should not be liable to be pressed into the navy till the age of eighteen; [5] and that those who voluntarily bound themselves apprentices to the sea service were not to be liable to be pressed for three years.[6] If at the age of eighteen, or after three years, these apprentices were impressed into or voluntarily entered the navy, their masters were to be entitled to their wages.[7] Enlarged powers were given to the Admiralty commissioners to nominate disabled seamen and their dependents, and the widows and children of seamen killed in the service, to Greenwhich hospital.[8] In the same year the clause in the Navigation Acts, which provided that the master and three-fourths of the crew must be British subjects,[9] was modified for the duration of the war—only the master and half the crew were required to be British subjects.[10] A register of seamen willing to enter the navy had been established in 1696, and seamen had been encouraged to register by the gift of a bounty of 40s. a year and other privileges.[11] This Act had been amended in 1697.[12] It was proposed in 1703-1704 to make a compulsory register of all seamen. A bill creating this register passed the House of Lords in that year, but was dropped in the Commons; [13] and a similar proposal, made in 1707-1708, failed to become law.[14] It was found that the Acts of 1696 and 1697 " had not had the good effects which were intended thereby," and they were repealed in 1710.[15] In 1704 power was given to press into the army " such able bodied men as have not any lawful calling or

---

[1] Vol. vi 314-316.   [2] 2, 3 Anne c. 6.

[3] § 1.   [4] § 8.   [5] § 4.

[6] § 15 ; but as this section was used to enable fully qualified seamen to escape impressment it was provided in 1705 that only apprentices under eighteen years of age should be able to claim the three years' exemption, 4, 5 Anne c. 19 § 17 (R.C. c. 6).

[7] 2, 3 Anne c. 6 § 17.

[8] § 19 ; several statutes imposed a duty of 6d. per month on all seamen for the upkeep of Greenwich hospital, 7, 8 William III c. 21 § 10 ; 8, 9 William III c. 23 § 6 ; 10 Anne c. 17 § 1 ; 2 George II c. 7 § 1 ; 18 George II c. 31 § 1.

[9] Vol. vi 317 ; above 84 ; below 407.

[10] 2, 3 Anne c. 19 § 8 (R.C. c. 13).

[11] 7, 8 William III c. 21.   [12] 8, 9 William III c. 23.

[13] MSS. of the House of Lords (N.S.) v no. 1986.

[14] Ibid vii no. 2431.   [15] 9 Anne c. 21 § 64.

employment or visible means for their maintenance." [1]   But it was found that the power of impressment into the army and navy, given by the Legislature by this and earlier Acts, was so large that it was necessary to give harvesters, certified to be needed during hay and corn harvest, exemption from June to September.[2] In 1705 it was provided that landsmen, liable to be impressed into the army under the Act of 1704, could be pressed into the navy.[3]   Another device used to attract recruits appears in an Act of 1703. Certain classes of insolvent debtors imprisoned for debt were to be released if they would serve or procure another person to serve in the army or the navy ; [4] and in 1705 it was provided that no seaman should be arrested for a debt not exceeding the sum of £20.[5]   In 1707 provision was made for division of the produce of ships captured from the enemy amongst the officers and crew of the captor, and for the payment of a bounty of £5 per head for every man on board the captured ship.[6] In 1713 discharged officers and soldiers were allowed to set up trades although they had not served an apprenticeship, or, if they had been apprenticed, had not served the full time of their apprenticeship.[7]   Moreover, such soldiers who set up trades were freed for three years from liability to be imprisoned, or from liability to have their stocks or tools distrained upon, for any debt due at the time when they were enlisted.[8]

These statutes of Anne's reign were caused by the exigencies of the war with France ; and similar provisions were made in the course of some of the other wars of the eighteenth century. In 1746 the Navigation Acts were modified for the duration of the war by allowing naval stores to be purchased for the navy, although they had been brought into the country in neutral ships.[9]   In 1779 certain enumerated goods were allowed to be imported in British built ships which had been sold to foreigners.[10]   In 1776 and 1777 the Navigation Acts were modified in a manner similar to that in which they had been modified in 1703—three-fourths of the seamen navigating British ships might be foreigners.[11] In 1772, in order to conserve oak timber for the navy, the East India Company was prohibited from building in Great Britain any new ships for the service of the company until the total tonnage of its fleet was reduced to 45,000 tons.[12]   But the Act specially provided that it could build in India or the American colonies.[13]   In 1744 it was provided that vagabonds could be

---

[1] 3, 4 Anne c. 11 § 1 (R.C. c. 10).   [2] § 10.
[3] 4, 5 Anne c. 19 § 13 (R.C. c. 6).   [4] 2, 3 Anne c. 16 (R.C. c. 10).
[5] 4, 5 Anne c. 19 § 15 (R.C. c. 6).   [6] 6 Anne c. 13 §§ 6-8 (R.C. c. 65).
[7] 12 Anne c. 13 § 1 (R.C. c. 14).   [8] § 6.
[9] 19 George II c. 36.   [10] 19 George III c. 28.
[11] 16 George III c. 20 ; 17 George III c. 34.
[12] 12 George III c. 54 § 1.   [13] § 3.

sent to serve in the army or navy.[1] In 1744, 1778, and 1779 special provisions were made for recruiting the army and navy ;[2] and in 1728 and 1758 Acts were passed for the punctual payment of seaman's wages, for enabling them more easily to remit the same for the support of their wives and families, and for preventing "frauds and abuses attending such payments."[3] In 1779 the protection from impressment given to certain seafaring men under the Acts of Anne and later Acts was suspended.[4] In 1740 and 1744 provisions similar to those made in 1707 were made as to prizes captured by the King's ships ;[5] and in 1749 an Act similar to the Act of 1713, was passed to permit discharged soldiers and sailors to set up trades in any town or place, notwithstanding Elizabeth's statute of apprenticeship.[6] In 1747 provision was made for the establishment of a hospital for seamen disabled in the merchant service, or for the widows or children of those who were killed in that service.[7]

In other directions efforts were made to render navigation more safe. Statutes provided for the erection of lighthouses, landmarks, and buoys.[8] A large number of local Acts provided for the improvement of harbours.[9] Provision was made for a more complete survey of parts of the coasts of Great Britain and Ireland.[10] Several statutes offered a reward for discovering a method of finding longitude at sea,[11] which in 1763 was to be paid to John Harrison if his method proved to be satisfactory.[12]

Some of these Acts are very slightly connected with commerce and industry ; but they all illustrate the close relation which the provisions made by the Legislature for recruiting the army and navy necessarily had both to many different trades and industries and social relations, and to some of the rules of industrial and commercial law. They illustrate the fact that the exigencies of national defence, and especially the needs of the navy, were paramount considerations with the Legislature. Just as the prerogative of the Crown to impress seafaring men was maintained and justified on this ground,[13] though it was hard to

[1] 17 George II c. 5 § 9.
[2] Ibid 15 ; 18 George III c. 53 ; 19 George III c. 10.
[3] 1 George II St. 2 cc. 9 and 14 ; 31 George II c. 10.
[4] 19 George III c. 75 § 1.
[5] 13 George II c. 4 ; 17 George II c. 34.
[6] 22 George II c. 44 ; above 402.   [7] 20 George II c. 38.
[8] 4, 5 Anne c. 20, 8 Anne c. 17 (the Eddystone) ; 3 George II c. 36 (the Skerries) ; 6 George III c. 31 (lighthouses at the mouth of the Humber) ; 16 George III c. 61 (lights, buoys and landmarks for the port of Chester).
[9] See Cunningham, English Industry and Commerce ii 489.
[10] Ibid ; 14 George II c. 39.
[11] 12 Anne St. 2 c. 15 ; 26 George II c. 25 ; 2 George III c. 18.
[12] 3 George III c. 14 ; rewards were offered for further discoveries in 1765, 5 George III c. 11, and in 1770, 10 George III c. 34 ; new provisions were made in 1774, 14 George III c. 66 § 2 ; see W. Bowden, Industrial Society in England 32.
[13] Vol. x 381-382.

reconcile with the principle of the liberty of the subject,[1] so even the Navigation Acts and many other rules of law, statutory and otherwise, were relaxed or suspended, whenever the needs of national defence rendered a relaxation or suspension expedient. But the provisions made by such Acts as these were for the most part temporary. As in the preceding period, the two permanent sets of measures of a commercial kind, which were passed in the interests of national defence, were the encouragement given the fishing industry, and the provisions of the Navigation Acts.

The fishing industry.—We have seen that the Navigation Acts, and other Acts of the latter part of the seventeenth century, had encouraged the fishing industry in various ways, because it provided a school for seamen.[2] The same policy was pursued all through the eighteenth century. Certain kinds of fish could not be imported if caught by or bought or received from any foreigner.[3] Salted or dried fish allowed to be imported in foreign ships paid an import duty from which British ships, manned as required by the Navigation Acts, were free.[4] Salt needed for the curing of fish was freed from excise duties if bought in England, and from import duties if bought abroad.[5] Bounties were given to the exporters of certain kinds of fish,[6] and to the builders of certain types of vessels used in the fishing industry.[7] Exemption from impressment for the navy was given to persons engaged in the whale fishery.[8] In the case of the Newfoundland fishery, rules were made as to the employment of fishermen;[9] and since the whole object of thus subsidizing the fishing industry was to provide trained seamen for the navy, penalties were imposed on those who conveyed seamen from the island of Newfoundland to the mainland without the consent of the governor.[10] In pursuance of the same policy, considerable encouragement was given to the fisheries of the American colonies, by the refusal of the Legislature to place fish in the

---

[1] This fact is illustrated by Voltaire's story of the boatman who had been contrasting the liberties of Englishmen with the tyranny under which the French lived, and whom he found next day in prison—having been arrested by a press gang, cited Morley, Voltaire, 78-79.

[2] Vol. vi 315-316 ; 15 Charles II c. 7 §§ 16, 17 ; 18 Charles II c. 2 § 2.

[3] 1 George I St. 2 c. 18 §§ 1, 3 10 ; 9 George II c. 33, § 1 ; 26 George III c. 81 § 43.

[4] 15 Charles II c. 7 § 16. These duties were payable till 1787, 27 George III c. 13 § 1 ; for the requirements of the Navigation Acts as to the manning of ships see vol. vi 317 ; below 407.

[5] 5 George I c. 18 § 1 ; cp. 8 George I c. 4 ; 11 George I c. 30 § 41 ; 19 George III c. 52.

[6] 5 George I c. 18 § 6 ; 25 George III c. 58 § 1 ; 26 George II c. 81 § 16.

[7] 11 George III c. 31 ; 11 George III c. 38 § 5 ; 15 George III c. 31 §§ 1, 3, 21 ; 19 George III c. 26 § 1 ; 25 George III c. 65 § 1 ; 26 George III c. 50 ; 32 George III c. 22 § 5.

[8] 11 George III c. 38 § 19 ; 32 George III c. 22 § 5.

[9] 15 George III c. 31 §§ 13-18.   [10] § 12.

list of enumerated commodities.[1] This policy was successful.
Adam Smith tells us that the New England fishing was " before
the late disturbances one of the most important in the world " ;
and that there was an extensive trade in fish between North
America and Spain, Portugal, and the Mediterranean.[2]

As in the preceding period, it was considered that the fishing
industry ought to be organized in order that it might be better
able to compete with the Dutch and other rivals.   But neither
the companies formed for this purpose in the seventeenth century, nor the company which was formed in 1750 had any success.
The Royal Fishery Company formed in 1692 failed in 1703,
probably, Professor Scott thinks, because its capital was too
small to enable it to compete with the Dutch.[3]   The Greenland
Company, formed in 1692 to organize the whaling industry,[4]
was not a success, and the trade was thrown open in 1701,[5]
though the company continued its business till 1720.[6]   In 1750
the Society of the Free British Fishery was incorporated by
statute for a term of twenty-one years, for the conduct of the
British white herring fishery.[7]   Its capital was to be £500,000.[8]
For a period of fourteen years the government promised to pay
3 per cent. to the stockholders.[9]   Within eighteen months the
company must spend at least £100,000 on the fisheries.[10]   Bounties
were payable to the company as well as to other persons in respect
of vessels built by them for the use of the fisheries.[11]   Persons
who subscribed £10,000 in particular cities, towns, or ports could
trade as " the Fishing Chamber " of that city, town, or port.
They were to send their accounts to the company in London,
and their members were to be entitled to the government 3 per
cent. on the stock invested.[12]   The company was empowered to
make by-laws for the regulation of the industry.[13]   The Act
establishing the company was several times amended,[14] and in
1765 the government allowance of 3 per cent. was extended for
a further term of four years.[15]   But though the capital of the
company was fully subscribed, and though several fishing
chambers were set up at different ports, it was not a success.[16]

[1] " To increase the shipping and naval power of Great Britain, by the extension
of the fisheries of our colonies, is an object which the legislature seems to have had
almost constantly in view," Adam Smith, Wealth of Nations (Cannan's ed.) ii 79 ;
for the enumerated and non-enumerated commodities see vol. vi 317-318 ; above
84, 85-86.
[2] Wealth of Nations ii 79.   [3] Scott, Joint Stock Companies ii 374-376.
[4] Vol. vi 315.   [5] 1 Anne St. 1 c. 16.
[6] Scott, op. cit. ii 379.   [7] 23 George II c. 24.
[8] § 4.   [9] § 6.   [10] § 7.
[11] §§ 11-15.   [12] § 18.   [13] § 2.
[14] 26 George II c. 9 ;   28 George II c. 14 ;   30 George II c. 30.
[15] 5 George III c. 22.
[16] Cunningham, Industry and Commerce, ii 483-484 ;   Adam Smith, Wealth of
Nations (Cannan's ed.) ii 23, said that " the usual effect of such bounties is to encourage rash undertakers to adventure in a business which they do not understand,

Adam Smith tells us that, when he wrote (1776) the white herring fishery was " entirely or almost entirely carried on by private adventurers." [1]

Mr. Lipson is probably right in thinking that

English enterprise might have contested more resolutely Dutch supremacy in the North-Sea fisheries, had not English capital been largely diverted into other channels, in particular the woollen industry, coal mining, and the Indian and Levant trades.[2]

But the efforts to promote the industry were not wholly without effect. England retained the red herring trade,[3] and at the end of the seventeenth century the Newfoundland fisheries employed about 140 ships and 5000 men.[4] It is clear therefore that though the economic history of the fishing industry was chequered, the industry was able to contribute to national defence by supplying a large number of trained seamen.

In addition to these provisions for the encouragement of the fishing industry, the Legislature made provision for its conduct. Nets having too fine a mesh, and the sale of undersized fish, were prohibited.[5] In 1757 [6] the Corporation of London, in succession to the Company of Fishermen of the River Thames,[7] was given jurisdiction to regulate fishing on the Thames and Medway. In 1761 it was provided that any one could exercise the trade of a fishmonger in London, and elaborate rules were made for the conveyance and sale of fish.[8]

Adam Smith criticized the amount of the bounties granted to herring busses,[9] but he did not entirely condemn them :

Though the tonnage bounties to those fisheries do not contribute to the opulence of the nation, it may perhaps be thought that they contribute to its defence, by augmenting the number of its sailors and shipping. This, it may be alleged, may sometimes be done by means of such bounties at a much smaller expense, than by keeping up a great

and what they loose by their own negligence and ignorance, more than compensates all that they can gain by the utmost liberality of government " ; and that " almost all those different companies . . . lost either the whole, or the greater part of their capitals " ; on the other hand, it is difficult to believe that they did not help to keep up the numbers of able seamen—which was the main object of the government.

[1] Adam Smith, Wealth of Nations (Cannan's ed.) ii 23.

[2] Economic History of England iii 152.

[3] " Partly because the fish had to be brought fresh on shore, which the Dutch were unable to do since their coast was too remote, and partly because the fish was smoked with wood which in this country was plentiful," ibid.

[4] Ibid.

[5] 1 George I St. 2 c. 18 §§ 4-8, cp. 22 George II c. 49 § 21 ; 29 George II c. 39 § 14.

[6] 30 George II c. 21.

[7] Powers had been given to this company in 1710, 9 Anne c. 26, to regulate fishing in the Thames and Medway, but since 1727 it had ceased to act.

[8] 2 George III c. 15.

[9] Wealth of Nations (Cannan's ed.) ii 19-22.

standing navy, if I may use such an expression, in the same way as a standing army.[1]

In fact Adam Smith, though he criticized the details of some of these Acts, could not logically condemn their policy, for he approved the pursuit of the same policy through the agency of the Navigation Acts,[2] some of the clauses of which attempted to carry it out by a stimulation of the fishing industry.[3] With the bearing of these Acts upon national defence I can deal very shortly, since I have already said something of them from this point of view.

The Navigation Acts.—We have seen that these Acts aimed at two principal objects—the encouragement of British shipping,[4] and the preservation of the colonial markets for Great Britain in such a way that the commercial interests both of the colonies and of Great Britain were secured.[5] With the second of these objects I shall deal in the ensuing section. At this point it is only necessary to say that the legislation enacted in the preceding period, in order to secure the first of these objects, was maintained all through the eighteenth century.[6] A few necessary modifications were made in 1786 [7] and 1787 [8] owing to the recognition of the independence of the United States,[9] and to the new constitutional arrangements in Ireland ; [10] and from time to time the demands of the navy occasioned temporary Acts which relaxed the rules as to the proportion of British seamen by whom ships must be manned.[11] Subject only to such trivial and temporary modifications as these, the provisions of these Acts were rigidly enforced. It is only at the very end of this period that they were in any way relaxed.[12] Their effect was that no goods could be imported into Great Britain from countries in Asia, Africa, or America, and no commodity grown, produced, or manufactured in Europe could be imported into the colonies, except in ships built in Great Britain, Ireland, or the colonies, the master and three-fourths of the mariners of which were British.[13] Goods of foreign growth, production, or manufacture could be imported only from the countries where they were

---

[1] Wealth of Nations (Cannan's ed.) ii 19 ; in the first two editions this argument in favour of bounties was put more strongly.

[2] Vol. vi 318 n. 6 ; above 399 ; below 515 .   [3] Below 408.

[4] Vol. vi 316-319.   [5] Ibid 320-323 ; above 85-88.

[6] 12 Charles II c. 18 ; 14 Charles II c. 11 § 5 ; 15 Charles II c. 7 ; 7, 8 William III c. 22 ; 9 William III c. 42.

[7] 26 George III c. 60.   [8] 27 George III c. 19.

[9] Above 394.   [10] Above 31-32.

[11] See e.g. 2, 3 Anne c. 19 (R.C. c. 13), above 401, 402 ; 21 George III cc. 26, 27.

[12] Below 503.

[13] Vol. vi 317-318 ; for the stimulus which this gave to colonial shipbuilding see ibid 322 ; the fact that colonial shipbuilding had been thus stimulated tended to make some of the other provisions of these Acts more irksome to the colonists, above 88, 104.

grown, produced, or manufactured.[1]   No goods could be carried
from one colony to another except in ships built and manned as
required by the Act.[2]   Certain fish could only be imported into
Great Britain in ships so built and manned ; and duties were
imposed on salted and dried fish imported in ships otherwise
built and manned.[3]   In 1773 it was enacted that no foreigner
could purchase a share in a British ship without the consent in
writing of the owner or the owners of three-fourths in value of the
ship.[4]

This policy, which aimed at encouraging British shipping
by securing for it the largest share in the carrying trade, was
assisted by the system of drawbacks.   In very many cases
merchants, upon exporting a commodity, were, in the case of
commodities produced at home, allowed to draw back any excise
or duty imposed upon it, and, in the case of foreign commodities
imported, the duties imposed on importation.[5]   We have seen
that, till 1763, the same drawbacks were allowed on the exportation to the colonies, so that till 1763 " many different sorts
of foreign goods might have been bought cheaper in the plantations than in the mother country ; and some may still." [6]   It
is clear, as Adam Smith says, that these drawbacks were granted
for the encouragement of the carrying trade.   His suggestion
that the motive of granting them was also to bring gold and
silver into the country [7] is less probable.   Here, as elsewhere,
he takes far too narrow a view of the objects aimed at by the
supporters of the mercantile system.[8]   If, by means of the
Navigation Acts, they aimed at encouraging British shipping
in the interests of national defence, by giving to English ships
a large share in the carrying trade, they sought to accomplish
an object of which Adam Smith himself approved ;[9] so that his
statement that the carrying trade " deserves no preference " [10] is
inconsistent with his approval of the policy of the Navigation
Acts.

---

[1] Vol. vi 317 ; for some modifications of this provision see Lipson, Economic
History of England iii 125 ; 14 George II c. 36 § 1.

[2] Vol. vi 318.

[3] 15 Charles II c. 7 §§ 16, 17 ; these provisions were enlarged and made more
stringent in 1715, 1 George I St. 2, c. 18, §§ 1 and 2 ; in 1736, 9 George II c. 33 § 1 ;
and in 1786, 26 George III c. 81 § 43.

[4] 13 George III c. 26.

[5] Adam Smith, Wealth of Nations (ed. Cannan) ii 1-2 ; below 413.

[6] Ibid ii 84-85 ; 4 George III c. 15 ; above 87-88.

[7] " Drawbacks were, perhaps, originally granted for the encouragement of
the carrying trade, which, as the freight of the ships is frequently paid by foreigners
in money, was supposed to be peculiarly fitted for bringing gold and silver into the
country.   But though the carrying trade certainly deserves no peculiar encouragement, though the motive of the institution was, perhaps, abundantly foolish, the
institution itself seems reasonable enough," Wealth of Nations ii 5.

[8] Below 459-462.   [9] Above 399.   [10] Wealth of Nations ii 5.

We have seen that the purely economic effects of the Navigation Acts were not so beneficial as some of their advocates maintained,[1] It would seem that the monopoly of colonial trade thereby gained was gained at the expense of the loss of much of the trade to the Baltic, which was consequently secured by the Dutch,[2] and the consequent rise in price of timber and other requisites for shipbuilding which came from Scandinavia.[3] But in the eighteenth century these losses were, to a large extent, made good by the expansion of the British colonies and settlements in the East and in the West. It is true that British trade was, as Adam Smith said, diverted into a channel different from that in which it would otherwise have flowed,[4] and to a trade which was the less profitable because it was to countries more distant than the neighbouring countries of Europe.[5] But this disadvantage was offset by the fact that this channel of colonial trade was a constantly expanding channel ; [6] and, whatever may be said of the adverse economic effects which flowed immediately from the policy of the Navigation Acts, there is no doubt that their main justification was not economic but political. " The argument in favour of the Navigation Act," as Mr. Lipson has said,[7] was then and continued to be " primarily political " ; and we have seen that the validity of the political argument was endorsed by Adam Smith.[8] It is true that Adam Smith admits that even in Charles II's reign, before the Navigation Acts had produced their full effects, the English navy was superior to that of the Dutch.[9] But there is no doubt that those Acts did tend to the increase of shipping and sailors.[10] Whether or not this great increase would have taken place without the protection of these Acts it is not possible to say. But it is a significant fact that Adam Smith, who was the greatest critic of that mercantile system of which the Navigation Acts were an integral part, and the greatest advocate of freedom of trade, should have ascribed that increase, in part at least, to

---

[1] Vol. vi 318.

[2] Lipson, Economic History of England iii 130-131.

[3] Ibid iii 131-132, 133-134.

[4] " Since the establishment of the Act of Navigation the colony trade has been continually increasing, while many other branches of foreign trade, particularly of that to other parts of Europe, have been continually decaying. Our manufactures for foreign sale, instead of being suited, as before the Act of Navigation, to the neighbouring market of Europe, or to the more distant one of the countries which lie round the Mediterranean Sea, have, the greater part of them, been accommodated to the still more distant one of the colonies, to the market in which they have the monopoly, rather than to that in which they have many competitors," Wealth of Nations ii 97-98.

[5] Ibid ii 101-102 ; below 436.   [6] Below 435, 437.

[7] Economic History of England iii 136.

[8] Vol. vi 318 n. 6 ; above 399.

[9] Wealth of Nations (Cannan's ed.) ii 92, cited Lipson, op. cit. iii 137.

[10] Ibid, citing Anderson, Origin of Commerce (ed. 1764) ii 110.

those Acts. It is at least arguable that the monopoly of the expanding colonial trade, which they secured to British ships and sailors, together with the commercial legislation on other topics designed to increase Great Britain's sea-power, helped to give Great Britain that command of the sea without which she could never have gained her colonial empire.

In this matter indeed Captain Mahan would seem to agree with Adam Smith. He points out that the action of a government may influence the sea-power of its people in peace and in war.[1] In peace

the government by its policy can favour the natural growth of a people's industries and its tendencies to seek adventure and gain by way of the sea ; or it can try to develop such industries and such sea going bent, when they do not naturally exist ; or, on the other hand, the government may by mistaken action check and fetter the progress which the people left to themselves would make. In any one of these ways the influence of the government will be felt, making or marring the sea power of the country in the matter of peaceful commerce ; upon which alone, it cannot be too often insisted, a thoroughly strong navy can be based.

In war the government can maintain a navy of a strength adequate to protect the commerce of the country. But

more important even than the size of the navy is the question of the institutions [of government], favoring a healthful spirit and activity, and providing for rapid development in time of war by an adequate reserve of men and ships. . . . Undoubtedly under this second head of warlike preparation must come the maintenance of suitable naval stations, in those distant parts of the world to which the armed shipping must follow the peaceful vessels of commerce.

The colonies provided these naval bases, and they, as the history of the eighteenth century shows, " afforded the surest means of supporting abroad the sea-power of a country."

If, therefore, it is true that both the territorial and the consequent economic expansion of Great Britain in the eighteenth century are due to the success of the measures taken to make her the greatest sea-power in the world, the commercial expedients adopted with this end in view can be justified even upon strictly economic grounds—provided that a sufficiently long view is taken of the results achieved in this century, and also a point of view sufficiently broad to include the political, military, and naval aspects of the question as well as the purely economic aspects. The legislation which we have been considering aimed at obtaining a supply of ships and men and material : the legislation which we are now about to consider aimed at increasing the productive powers of the whole empire, and of so regulating

[1] The Influence of Sea Power upon History 82-83.

trade amongst its own members and with foreign nations that the health and wealth, and therefore the strength, of its different parts was developed. Captain Mahan has said that "the key to much of the history, as well as of the policy, of nations bordering upon the sea" is to be found in three things: "production, with the necessity of exchanging products, shipping, whereby the exchange is carried on, and colonies, which facilitate and enlarge the operations of shipping and tend to protect it by multiplying points of safety."[1] With the encouragement of shipping I have already dealt. We shall now see that the encouragement to shipping given by those clauses of the Navigation Acts which aimed directly at effecting that object, was assisted by clauses of the Acts which aimed at giving to Great Britain a monopoly of the colonial market. We shall see also that these provisions of these Acts, and a great mass of other legislation, were directed to the encouragement of the production of manufactured goods and raw material, and to the provision of markets for these goods and this material at home, in the colonies, and in foreign countries. All this legislation was directed to secure the objects aimed at by the mercantile system—the predominance of Great Britain's sea-power in the interests of national defence and of commerce, and her commercial and economic predominance. We shall see that, to a large extent, it succeeded in effecting these objects.

II. *The Manufacturing Industries and Colonial and Foreign Trade.*

Adam Smith was right when he said that the discovery of America and of the passage to the East Indies by the Cape of Good Hope had raised the mercantile system "to a degree of splendour and glory which it could never otherwise have attained to."[2] It was, he pointed out, the object of that system to enrich the nation "rather by the industry of the towns than by that of the country,"[3] rather by manufactures and trade than by agriculture. In consequence of those discoveries

the commercial towns of Europe, instead of being the manufacturers and carriers for but a very small part of the world . . . have now become the manufacturers for the numerous and thriving cultivators of America, and the carriers, and in some respects the manufacturers too, for almost all the different nations of Asia, Africa, and America.[4]

This policy pursued by the upholders of the mercantile system was approved by Hume. He pointed out that it increased the riches and therefore the power of the state. He says:[5]

---

[1] The Influence of Sea Power upon History 28.
[2] Wealth of Nations (Cannan's ed.) ii 125. [3] Ibid.
[4] Ibid ii 125-126. [5] Essays (ed. 1768) i 294-295.

Everything in the world is purchased by labour; and our passions are the only causes of labour.   When a nation abounds in manufactures and mechanic arts, the proprietors of land, as well as the farmers, study agriculture as a science, and redouble their industry and attention. The superfluity which arises from their labour is not lost; but is exchanged with the manufacturers for those commodities which man's luxury now makes them covet.   By this means, land furnishes a great deal more of the necessaries of life, than what suffices for those who cultivate it.   In times of peace and tranquility, this superfluity goes to the maintenance of manufacturers,[1] and the improvers of liberal arts. But 'tis easy for the public to convert many of these manufacturers into soldiers, and maintain them by that superfluity, which arises from the labour of the farmers. . . . And to consider the matter abstractedly, manufacturers increase the power of the state only as they store up so much labour, and that of a kind to which the public can lay claim, without depriving anyone of the necessaries of life.   The more labour, therefore, is employed beyond mere necessaries, the more powerful is any state; since the persons engaged in that labour may easily be converted to the public service. . . . Thus the greatness of the sovereign and the happiness of the state are in a great measure united with regard to trade and manufactures.   'Tis a violent method, and in most cases impracticable, to oblige the labourer to toil, in order to raise from the land more than what subsists himself and family.   Furnish him with manufactures and commodities, and he will do it of himself.

For these reasons, therefore, the principal object of the mercantile system was to encourage native manufactures, and to encourage the sale of those manufactures.   It was with this object in view that colonial industry and commerce were regulated and organized, and that foreign trade was encouraged. The attainment of these objects, and more especially the encouragement of native manufactures and the organization of colonial industry and commerce, gave rise to a large amount of legislation.   I propose to examine both the legislation, and other measures taken to promote native manufacturing industries, to regulate and organize colonial industry and commerce, and to encourage foreign trade.

The promotion of native manufacturing industries.

The measures taken for this purpose were, first, fiscal expedients; secondly, measures taken to secure the quality of British manufactured articles; thirdly, the grant of patents of monopoly and other rewards to inventors of new processes; fourthly, the prohibition of the export of newly discovered machines and processes, and of the emigration of skilled artisans.

(1) *Fiscal expedients.*

As in the preceding period, these expedients took several different forms.   By means of duties the importation of competing foreign manufactured goods was discouraged.   On the

---

[1] The term manufacturer is used in the sense of artisan, below 462-463.

other hand, native manufactures were encouraged by remissions of duties on their export, and on the import of raw material,[1] and by the prohibition of exporting certain kinds of raw material. Occasionally also native manufactures were still further encouraged by bounties. Both native trade with foreign countries, and the carrying trade, were encouraged by drawbacks of customs duties imposed on imported goods which were subsequently exported. Adam Smith thus sums up the position as it existed when he published his book in 1776 : [2]

The greater part of the ancient duties which had been imposed upon the exportation of the goods of home produce and manufacture, have either been lightened or taken away altogether. In most cases they have been taken away. Bounties have even been given upon the exportation of some of them. Drawbacks too, sometimes of the whole, and, in most cases, of a part of the duties which are paid upon the importation of foreign goods, have .been granted upon their exportation. . . . This growing favour of exportation, and discouragement of importation, have suffered only a few exceptions, which chiefly concern the materials of some manufactures. These, our merchants and manufacturers are willing should come as cheap as possible to themselves, and as dear as possible to their rivals and competitors in other countries. Foreign materials are, upon this account, sometimes allowed to be imported duty free ; Spanish wool, for example, flax, and raw linen yarn. The exportation of the materials of home produce, and of those which are the particular produce of our colonies has sometimes been prohibited, and sometimes subjected to higher duties. The exportation of English wool has been prohibited. That of beaver skins, of beaver wool, and of gum Senaga has been subjected to higher duties.

A glance at the statute book will show us the elaborate manner in which this policy was applied to different industries.

At the beginning of the eighteenth century the wool industry was still the most important of all the English industries. The export of wool from England continued to be forbidden [3] under such severe laws that Adam Smith said that " like the laws of Draco they may be said to be all written in blood " ; [4] and the

---

[1] In 1756 it was said in the House of Commons that, " from our general practice as well as from common sense, we may with regard to our imports lay down these rules, that foreign materials, which cannot be produced in our own country in sufficient quantities, ought not to be subjected to any tax, or a bounty ought to be given upon the exportation of the manufacture, equal to the tax upon the material ; that foreign materials which can be produced in sufficient quantities within our own dominions, may be subjected to a tax upon importation, or a bounty ought to be given upon their home production ; that foreign materials, improved by any sort of manufacture, ought to be taxed in proportion to their improvement ; and that all sorts of foreign goods, completely manufactured, may be taxed upon importation, and ought to be highly taxed if not prohibited, when they are such as interfere with any of our home manufactures," Parlt. Hist. xv 671-672.

[2] Wealth of Nations (Cannan's ed.) ii 364-365.

[3] For the earlier legislation see vol. vi 328-329.

[4] Wealth of Nations (Cannan's ed.) ii 146 ; see ibid ii 146-149 for a detailed account of the methods adopted by these Acts to make this prohibition effective ; cp. Bl. Comm. iv 154 ; there was a similar prohibition on the export of fuller's earth as it was necessary in the process of wool manufacture, Wealth of Nations ii 153.

statutes relating to this matter were consolidated in 1788.[1] At the same time the export of wool from Ireland except to England and Wales, and all export of Irish woollen manufactures, were forbidden.[2] In 1721 export duties on all goods manufactured in Great Britain were taken off.[3] It is true that a large number of articles were excepted.[4] But, as Adam Smith pointed out, with the exception of horses, they were all " either materials of manufacture, or incomplete manufactures (which may be considered as materials for still further manufacture), or instruments of trade." [5] In 1739 [6] and 1753 [7] the import of woollen yarn from Ireland duty free was permitted. At the beginning of George I's reign the popularity of printed calico seemed to threaten the wool industry; [8] and so in 1720 the wearing of any printed, painted, stained, or dyed calico in any garment was forbidden,[9] and the use of any such stuff in any bed, chair, cushion, window curtain, or other household stuff, was forbidden, except for exportation.[10] This Act was modified in 1736 so as to permit the use of such stuff made of linen yarn and cotton wool, provided the warp was made of linen yarn.[11] In 1765 provision was made for the import of coarse calico goods by the East India Company for the African trade; [12] and we shall see that in 1774 cotton goods made of cotton spun in Great Britain were permitted to be sold and used.[13] Though the statutes forbidding the export of wool were objected to by the graziers, and though they were extensively evaded by the " owlers " or wool smugglers, they remained in force in order that the woollen manufacturers might be able to get their materials cheap, and in order that foreign manufacturers might be deprived of English wool.[14] As Mr. Lipson says, these laws were defended both on economic and on political grounds. If we manufactured all our wool we should be able to secure the markets of the world; and if we prevented France from getting it we should cripple the manu-

---

[1] 28 George III c. 38.

[2] 10, 11 William III c. 10 §§ 1-12; 3 George I c. 21.

[3] 8 George I c. 15 § 7. [4] § 8.

[5] Wealth of Nations (Cannan's ed.) ii 155.

[6] 12 George II c. 21. [7] 26 George II cc. 8 and 11.

[8] For the controversy on this subject see Lipson's Economic History of England iii 42-44.

[9] 7 George I St. 1 c. 7 § 1.

[10] § 2; Mr. Lipson, op. cit. iii 44, points out that the Act did not materially benefit the woollen manufacturers—" The Indian textiles which were excluded from the English market were now shipped off in great quantities to the West Indies, so that the consumption of English woollen goods in the plantations was proportionately diminished."

[11] 9 George II c. 4; see Lipson, op. cit. iii 44; the Act was due to the agitation of the Manchester manufactures of printed fustians.

[12] 5 George III c. 30. [13] Below 416.

[14] Lipson, op. cit. iii 23-34.

factures of our national enemy.[1] In spite of the fact that the
Acts were extensively evaded by the smugglers, they had some
success. In the opinion of Adam Smith they did help the manufacturers by lowering the price of the raw material.[2]

We have seen that in 1663 foreigners had been encouraged
to set up the manufacture of linen.[3] The encouragement thus
afforded was taken advantage of by the Huguenots at the end of
the century.[4] They did much to develop the industry ; and it
was further encouraged by a bounty on export.[5] Moreover, in
1756, in spite of the protests of the spinners,[6] the justice of
which was endorsed by Adam Smith,[7] the duties on foreign yarn imported were removed in the interest of the linen manufacturers ;[8]
and bounties were given on the import of hemp and flax from the
British colonies in America,[9] and on the import of hemp from
Ireland.[10] Foreign linen paid an import duty,[11] and an Act of
1745 forbade the wearing of French cambric.[12] The silk, like
the linen industry, owed much to the Huguenot immigration at
the end of the seventeenth century.[13] We have seen that at the
end of that century the native product had got protection from
the competition of silks from Turkey, Persia, India, and China.[14]
This protection was continued and increased by the legislation
of the eighteenth century. In 1709 the consumption of silk and
mohair yarn was encouraged by compelling the use of these
materials in the manufacture of buttons and button holes ;[15] and
the penalties for the infringement of this Act were increased by
Acts of 1717[16] and 1720.[17] In 1721[18] and 1724[19] a bounty was
given on the export of certain silk manufactures, and in 1769

---

[1] Economic History of England iii 29-30 ; cp. Wealth of Nations (Cannan's ed.) ii 149-150.

[2] Ibid i 230, ii 150 ; and Adam Smith is forced to admit, ibid ii 152, that the low price had not materially affected the quantity or quality of the wool produced—though on his own general principles it ought to have affected the quantity of the annual product.

[3] Vol. vi 330 ; 15 Charles II c. 15.   [4] Lipson, op. cit. ii 110.

[5] 29 George II c. 15 ; 10 George III c. 38 ; 19 George III c. 27 ; 21 George III c. 40 ; an English Linen Company was incorporated in 1763 with a capital of £100,000, 4 George III c. 37.

[6] Lipson, op. cit. ii 111-112.

[7] Wealth of Nations (Cannan's ed.) ii 142-143.

[8] 29 George II c. 15.   [9] 4 George III c. 26.

[10] 19 George III c. 37 ; Wealth of Nations (Cannan's ed.) ii 144, 145.

[11] Wealth of Nations ii 143 ; as usual the duties on French linen were higher than those on the linen from other foreign countries, Lipson, op. cit. ii 112 n. 1.

[12] 18 George II c. 36 ; 21 George II c. 26 ; 32 George II c. 32 ; 7 George III c. 43.

[13] Lipson, op. cit. ii 101.   [14] Vol. vi 330.

[15] 8 Anne c. 6 (R.C. c. 1) ; the reasons given in the preamble are first that this manufacture employed great numbers of persons, and, secondly, that the silk was bought in Turkey which consumed large quantities of English woollen manufactures.

[16] 4 George I c. 7.   [17] 7 George I St. 1 c. 12.

[18] 8 George I c. 15 § 1.   [19] 11 George I c. 29 § 2.

a bounty was given on the import of colonial raw silk.[1] In 1765 the duties on the import of foreign raw silk were lowered,[2] and a drawback was allowed on the export of raw silk to Ireland.[3] In 1763, 1765, and 1766 the import of certain foreign silk manufactures was prohibited.[4] We have seen that the use of stuff made of a mixture of linen and cotton was permitted in 1736.[5] In 1774 Parliament was persuaded by Arkwright to repeal the prohibition imposed by certain Acts on the wearing and use of calico, and to allow the wearing or use of stuff " wholly made of cotton spun in Great Britain when printed, stained, painted or dyed with any colour or colours." [6] In 1781 a bounty was granted on British cotton goods printed or stained in Great Britain ; [7] and in 1783 a drawback on the duties on soap and starch was given when these materials were used in the manufacture of flax and cotton.[8] In 1779 the duties on the export from Great Britain of cotton wool produced in the British colonies in America were taken off.[9]

The dyeing industry was a subsidiary industry to these textile industries. It was encouraged in 1707 [10] by the imposition of a duty on cloth exported undyed, and by the grant of a bounty in 1748 [11] on the import of colonial indigo. The statute of 1721, which freed from export duty goods manufactured in Great Britain, also freed from import duty many of the materials for dyeing, but imposed a small duty on their export.[12] In 1713 [13] and 1726 [14] the Navigation Acts were relaxed so that a supply of cochineal from Spain might be obtained ; and a similar relaxation was made in 1752 in order that the dyeing industry might get a supply of gum senega.[15]

Many other manufactures were protected in the same way as the textile manufactures. Tanners paid only a small export duty, and got a drawback of the excise duties on the export of tanned leather.[16] Leather manufactures could be exported duty free, and on export the whole of the excise duties was drawn back.[17] Raw hides from the colonies and Ireland,[18] seal skins,[19]

---

[1] 9 George III c. 38.　　　[2] 5 George III c. 29 § 2.　　　[3] § 4.
[4] 3 George III c. 21 ; 5 George III c. 48 ; 6 George III c. 28.
[5] Above 414.　　　[6] 14 George III c. 72 § 2 ; Lipson, op. cit. ii 96-97.
[7] 21 George III c. 40.　　[8] 23 George III c. 77.
[9] 19 George III c. 53.
[10] 6 Anne c. 8 (R.C. c. 43) ; 3 George I c. 7 § 1.
[11] 21 George II c. 30.
[12] Wealth of Nations (Cannan's ed.) ii 155 ; 8 George I c. 15 § 11.
[13] 12 Anne St. 1 c. 18 § 3.
[14] 13 George I c. 25 ; 2 George II c. 28 ; 7 George II c. 18.
[15] 25 George II c. 32 ; Wealth of Nations ii 155-156 ; below 442.
[16] Wealth of Nations (Cannan's ed.) ii 153 ; 9 Anne c. 6 § 4.
[17] Ibid 11 § 39 ; 10 Anne c. 26 §§ 5 and 6 ; 12 Anne St. 2 c. 9 §§ 64 and 65.
[18] 9 George III c. 39 ; 32 George III c. 36 § 2.
[19] 15 George III c. 31 § 10.

and goat skins [1] could be imported duty free; and, when the price exceeded a certain level, oak bark could also be imported on payment of a small duty.[2] A supply of raw hides was assured by putting those produced in the colonies in the list of enumerated commodities.[3] "Even the horns of cattle are prohibited to be exported; and the two insignificant trades of the horner and comb-maker enjoy, in this respect, a monopoly against the graziers."[4] In 1721 and 1764 the duties on the import of beaver skins were reduced; and by the latter Act the duty on the export of these skins was raised.[5] In 1784 the hatters were protected by a prohibition of the export of British hare and coney skins, and it was also provided that these skins should not be dyed in order that they might not be made useless to the hatters.[6] We have seen that in 1732 the hatters had secured protection against colonial competition.[7] Though the exportation of certain kinds of metals was allowed, the exportation of brass and gun metal was forbidden.[8] On the other hand, brass manufactures could be exported duty free.[9] The rope manufacturers were encouraged by the grant of a bounty on the import of hemp from the American colonies.[10] Duties protected the manufactures of glass,[11] verdigris,[12] and wall-paper;[13] and the import of gold and silver lace [14] and foreign manufactured gloves was forbidden.[15] On the other hand, since the heavy duties on imported earthenware had led to extensive smuggling, the duty was lowered.[16] For the same reason it was necessary to lower in 1774[17] the large duty which, in 1765,[18] had been imposed on the export of gum senega or gum arabic. This duty had been imposed in 1765 when Great Britain had, by the treaty of Paris, got the exclusive right to trade with Senegal which France had previously enjoyed.[19] Partly because coal was a raw material of manufacture heavy duties were imposed on its export.[20]

---

[1] 15 George III c. 35; 31 George III c. 43 § 7.
[2] 12 George III c. 50 §§ 2 and 3.
[3] Wealth of Nations i 232-233.   [4] Ibid ii 154; 7 James I c. 14 § 4.
[5] Wealth of Nations ii 156-157; 8 George I c. 15 § 13; 4 George III c. 9 § 2.
[6] 24 George III St. 2 c. 21.
[7] 5 George II c. 22, above 86.
[8] Wealth of Nations ii 154; 5, 6 William and Mary c. 17; 9, 10 William III c. 26 § 19; 30 George III c. 4—export of tin to countries beyond the Cape of Good Hope.
[9] 8 George I c. 15.
[10] 4 George III c. 26; 26 George III c. 53 § 12; Wealth of Nations ii 144.
[11] 27 George III c. 28—duties were imposed on glass imported from France to countervail the internal duties imposed on manufacture, and a drawback was allowed on English glass exported.
[12] 21 George III c. 32.   [13] 32 George III c. 54.
[14] 15 George II c. 20 § 7.   [15] 6 George III c. 19.
[16] 15 George III c. 37.   [17] 14 George III c. 10.
[18] 5 George III c. 37.
[19] Wealth of Nations ii 156; above 64.   [20] Ibid 157.

These are some of the many statutes which attempted, not without success, to stimulate British industries by fiscal expedients. That they attained this measure of success is due not only to the skilful and careful manner in which this policy was carried out by their provisions and constantly adjusted and readjusted to meet the shifting needs of the day, but also to the fact that, simultaneously, the Legislature took other well-conceived measures directed to the same object.

(2) *Measures taken to secure the quality of British manufactured articles.*

We have seen that, at the end of the seventeenth century, economic opinion favoured a greater freedom of trade, and a relaxation of those mediæval restrictions which the Tudor and Stuart legislation had adapted to the industrial and commercial needs of their day.[1] This current of opinion gathered force all through the eighteenth century. In 1751 it was said that a large part of the laws regulating trade and manufacture ought to be repealed—

many as being grown out of use, and scarce ever put in execution but on malicious and frivolous prosecutions ; others entirely local ; others, though perhaps well calculated for the times in which they were made, yet now become prejudicial to trade in its present state ; others quite useless.[2]

Dean Tucker, as Mr. Lipson points out,[3] anticipated Adam Smith's doctrine that since " man's self-love is God's providence," [4] competition could be trusted to secure honest manufacture.[5]

But in the eighteenth century the Legislature rightly refused to trust entirely to the beneficent effects of unrestricted competition. The preamble to a statute of 1765,[6] which deals with the manufacture of woollen cloth in Yorkshire, recites that previous statutes have been ineffectual to suppress various frauds, abuses, and deceits,

which tend very much to the debasing, under-valuing, and discrediting of the said manufacture both at home and in foreign parts beyond the seas, where great part thereof hath been usually vended ;

and it proceeds to provide machinery to remedy these abuses.[7] Some regulation was necessary. The problem was to make regulations which would allow the greater freedom which the

---

[1] Vol. vi 355-360.
[2] Lipson, Economic History of England iii 326, citing House of Commons Journals xxvi 292.
[3] Ibid iii 327.   [4] Above 393.
[5] Wealth of Nations (Cannan's ed.) i 131, cited below 419.
[6] 5 George III c. 51.   [7] Below 423.

capitalistic organization of trade demanded, and yet be sufficient to guard against " the frauds, abuses, and deceits " which would destroy the reputation of British goods. And the solution of the problem was the more difficult seeing that the ground was cumbered by much mechanism and many rules which came from past ages, the industrial and commercial problems of which were very different from those of the eighteenth century.

Amongst these decadent institutions were the mediæval privileges which some of the boroughs still possessed of restricting the right to trade to those who were members of a gild and freemen of the borough.[1] These privileges, because they ran counter to the growing feeling in favour of freedom of trade, found little countenance amongst the judges, whose bias had always been in favour of freedom of trade.[2] Adam Smith disapproved of these privileges. He said : [3]

The real and effectual discipline which is exercised over a workman is not that of his corporation, but that of his customers. It is the fear of losing their employment which restrains his frauds and corrects his negligence.

But we have seen that they nevertheless survived in some places till the Municipal Corporations Act 1835.[4]

Another more modern institution was the system of apprenticeship which had been established by Elizabeth's statute of 1562-1563. This statute made a seven years' training necessary for those who wished to " set up, occupy, or exercise any craft mystery or occupation now used or occupied within the realm of England or Wales." [5] The statute had had a somewhat chequered career. Blackstone summed up its history with substantial accuracy when he said that it had been " by turns looked upon as a hard law, or a beneficial one, according to the prevailing humour of the times " ; that " attempts had been frequently made for its repeal " ; [6] and that " the resolutions of the courts had in general rather confined than extended the restriction " of the seven years' apprenticeship imposed by it.[7] In fact, during the eighteenth century the statute was regarded with growing disfavour by (i) the courts, and (ii) the Legislature.

(i) As early as 1615 it was said in *Tolley's Case* that the statute did not extend to new trades not mentioned in the

---

[1] Vol. vi 337.

[2] Ibid ; vol. iv 352 ; vol. viii 57-62 ; below 420 ; The Cloth workers of Ipswich Case (1615) God. 252 ; cp. Lipson, op. cit. iii 348-351 ; as Mr. Lipson says, ibid 350, " the uncertainty that existed as to the legal position is shown by the frequency with which counsel's opinion was taken regarding the validity of by-laws to hinder foreigners from trading in the town."

[3] Wealth of Nations (Cannan's ed.) i 131.

[4] Vol. vi 337.

[5] 5 Elizabeth c. 4 §§ 19 and 24 ; vol. iv 341-342.

[6] Comm. i 427.

[7] Ibid 428.

statute.[1] As early as 1674 it was said that if a man had followed
a trade for seven years without interruption as apprentice and
journeyman, he was not liable to be prosecuted for not having
served the whole seven years as an apprentice ; [2] and in 1763
" all the judges of England at a meeting lately resolved that
if any man as a master had exercised and followed any trade
as a master without interruption or impediment for the term of
seven years, he was not liable to be sued or prosecuted upon
the Statute of the 5th of Eliz." [3] It was held in 1689 that an
employer of workmen must be a qualified man ; [4] but the
dissenting opinion of Dolben, J., represents the trend of opinion
in the following century.[5] It was held in 1711 that if a man lived
with another man who had exercised a trade for seven years,
though the latter was not qualified, the former would get a
qualification ; [6] and that a wife who lived with a husband who
exercised a trade for seven years could continue the trade after
his death.[7] It was held in 1756 than an unqualified man could
be a partner with a qualified man, if he did not interfere in the
business.[8] The reasons for the judicial disapproval of the policy
of the statute, which led to these restrictive interpretations, were
clearly expressed by Lord Mansfield at the Lancaster Assizes in
1759.[9] He said :

If none must employ, or be employed, in any branch of trade, but
who have served a limited number of years to that branch, the particular trade will be lodged in few hands, to the danger of the public,
and the liberty of setting up trades, and the foundations of the present
flourishing condition of Manchester will be destroyed. In the infancy
of trade, the Act of Queen Elizabeth might be well calculated for
public weal, but now when it is grown to that perfection we see it, it
might perhaps be of utility to have those laws repealed, as tending to
cramp and tie down that knowledge it was first necessary to obtain by
rule.

(ii) These were also the views held by the Legislature. The
Legislature, though it refused to repeal the statute, was not

---

[1] Calthrop, at p. 9, S.C. 2 Bulstr. at p. 188 ; it was there said that an uphol-
sterer did not come within the statute as that trade was not there mentioned, " and
the intent of this statute was not to extend unto any other trades, but such as required art and skill for the managing of them " ; The King v. Housden (1665)
1 Keble 848—indictment quashed because the trade was not averred to be a trade
when the statute was passed ; these cases were not approved by Holt C.J., R. v.
Paris Slaughter (1700) 1 Ld. Raym. 513 ; it was eventually settled, in accordance
with the opinion of Holt C.J., that if it was averred that the trade was a trade used
when the statute was passed, the question must be left to be determined by the
jury as a matter of fact, see note to R. Kilderby (1669) 1 Wm. Saunders 312.

[2] R. v. Moor and Dibloe, 3 Keble 400.
[3] French v. Adams, 2 Wils. 168.
[4] Hobbs v. Young (1689) 3 Mod. 313.   [5] Ibid at p. 317.
[6] R. v. Morgan (1711) 10 Mod. 70.   [7] Ibid.
[8] R. v. Chase (1756) 2 Wils. K.B. 40 ; S.C. sub. nom. Raynard v. Chase,
1 Burr. 2.
[9] G. E. Daniels, The Early English Cotton Industry 51-52.

in favour of its strict enforcement. In 1702, in answer to a petition of wool combers and weavers, complaining that intruders had come into their trade who had only been apprenticed for a year or two, the House of Commons replied that trade ought to be free, and declined to take any action ; [1] and in 1733 a clause in an Act of 1724, which made a seven years' apprenticeship compulsory on manufacturers of broad cloth in the West Riding of Yorkshire, was repealed. [2] In 1751 a committee of the House of Commons, appointed to enquire into the laws relating to trade and manufactures, reported against the Elizabethan apprenticeship law, and also against the restraints imposed by the bylaws of corporations. [3] Adam Smith agreed with the committee of 1751 in condemning both the system of apprenticeship and, as we have seen, [4] the exclusive privileges of corporations. "The institution of long apprenticeships," he said,

can give no security that insufficient workmanship shall not be frequently exposed to public sale. When this is done it is generally the effect of fraud . . . and the longest apprenticeship can give no security against fraud. [5]

One or two statutes exempted particular trades from the operation of the statutes of apprentices ; [6] and when it was repealed in 1814 [7] it had long been very largely inoperative in practice. [8]

Another method of securing the good quality of manufactured goods was to entrust the duty of supervision to a company of persons exercising the craft. We have seen that the Legislature made frequent use of this device in the sixteenth century ; [9] and in the seventeenth century a very large number of these companies were created, and given large powers to supervise the conduct of many different trades. [10] Thus the right of search

[1] Lipson, Economic History of England iii 287-288

[2] Ibid 289 ; 11 George I c. 24 ; 6 George II c. 37 § 3.

[3] Lipson, op. cit. iii 290, citing House of Commons Journals xxvi 292—" scarce any prosecutions have been carried on upon these statutes, but against such as have excelled in their own trades by force of their own genius, and not against such as have been ignorant in their professions—which is the reverse of the intent of such laws. . . . These obstructions arise partly from the laws above mentioned, and partly from particular franchises and by-laws of corporations. . . . The most useful and beneficial manufactures are principally carried on, and trade most flourishing, in such towns and places as are under no such local disabilities."

[4] Wealth of Nations (Cannan's ed.) i 131, cited above 419.

[5] Ibid 123-124.

[6] 6 George II c. 37, and Lipson, op. cit. iii 289 ; 17 George III cc. 33 and 55 : 49 George III c. 109 § 5 ; the last-mentioned Act repealed the statute of apprenticeship as to the woollen trade, and also the by-laws of corporations which prevented the setting up of such trades.

[7] 54 George III c. 96.   [8] Lipson, op. cit. iii 291-292.   [9] Vol. iv 322.

[10] Lipson, op. cit. iii 331-332, gives a list of thirty-three grants of incorporation to new and old crafts made by James I and Charles I, and, ibid iii 335, a list of seven similar grants made after the Restoration.

given to the Dutch Bay Hall at Colchester was confirmed by statute in 1660; and Colchester's reputation for the manufacture of bays "was attributed to the success of the Hall in maintaining, by the strictest scrutiny, the deserved reputation of its wares."[1] Some use was made of this expedient in the eighteenth century.[2] The Founders' Company appointed searchers as late as 1746.[3] "The Carpenters appointed 'viewers' of buildings during the eighteenth century, until their duties were taken over by district surveyors under the Building Act of 1774. The Tinplate-workers carried out a search as late as 1773."[4] A statute of 1726, passed to regulate the woollen manufacture, expressly saved the privileges of the corporation of clothiers of the city of Worcester;[5] and a statute of 1783 gave the Dyers' Company, and certain persons named in the Act, power to appoint searchers to inspect the dyeing of woollen goods within ten miles of London.[6] In 1773 two companies—one for Birmingham and one for Sheffield—were incorporated to assay and mark silver-plate manufactured in those towns.[7] But, though a few of these companies still exercise certain powers in relation to their trades to-day,[8] this method of supervising the conduct of industry tended to decay in the course of the eighteenth century.[9] As Mr. Lipson says, it "ceased to be a regular and normal practice as the eighteenth century ran its course, though it did not die out completely."[10]

Chronologically, this method of supervision by means of companies of manufacturers, is intermediate between the older methods of control exercised through craft gilds and corporate boroughs and through the working of the statute of apprentices, and the modern methods of control exercised through inspectors appointed by the central or local government. We can see the beginnings of this modern method in the legislation of the eighteenth century. Parliament began to revive tentatively and slowly a method of control which the Stuarts had tried without success to adopt by virtue of their prerogative powers.[11] Let us look at one or two examples.

In 1726[12] regulations were made for the manufacture of wool because, runs the preamble,

---

[1] Lipson, op. cit. iii 337.

[2] In 1702 the Pewterers Co. petitioned for and got increased powers of supervision, S.P. Dom. 1702-1703, 237-239; and similar grants were made to the tanners of Bermondsey, ibid 444, 608-609; in 1703 the Dyers' Company petitioned for increased powers, S.P. Dom. 1703-1704, 358.

[3] Lipson, op. cit. iii 343.   [4] Ibid.

[5] 13 George I c. 23 § 15.   [6] 23 George III c. 15 § 5.

[7] 13 George III c. 52; amended by 24 George III St. 2 c. 20.

[8] E.g. the Fishmongers, the Goldsmiths, the Gun-makers, the Stationers.

[9] Cunningham, Industry and Commerce ii 321-322.

[10] Economic History of England iii 343-344.

[11] Vol. iv 359-360.   [12] 13 George I c. 23.

divers controversies and disputes have arisen between the clothiers and makers of woollen goods and the manufacturers employed by them, concerning the length of the warping bars, and the uncertainty of weights by which wool yarn and other materials used in the manufacturing or making up of woollen goods have been delivered out to the several workmen employed therein.

The Act fixed penalties for the breach of its provisions, and gave the justices the power to issue search warrants to discover breaches of the law. In 1742 [1] an Act was passed to remedy frauds and abuses in the gold and silver lace trade, which had diminished the credit abroad of the English product. Detailed regulations were laid down, and pecuniary penalties were provided for their breach. In particular the weight of silver in silver wire to be used in the making of silver thread was prescribed, and likewise the weight of silver and gold to be used in the making of silver gilt wire.[2] In order to detect frauds it was provided that every bar of silver which was to be used for gilt wire must be weighed in the presence of the officer of excise, and again weighed and marked by him after the gold had been laid on.[3] In 1765 [4] a number of older statutes relating to the manufacture of woollen cloth in Yorkshire were repealed,[5] and new regulations were laid down. The justices of the West Riding, " not being dealers in woollen cloth or occupiers of any fulling mill," were to appoint searchers and measurers of cloth, who were to measure and seal the cloth.[6] They were also to appoint salaried inspectors of fulling mills who were to supervise these mills, and also the searchers and measurers, according to the rules made by the justices at quarter sessions.[7] Not only must the cloth be sealed, but the manufacturer must weave his name and address at the head of each piece of cloth.[8] The inspectors were given power to enter premises if they suspected that any breaches of the Act had been committed.[9] In 1766 [10] penalties were imposed on the fraudulent marking of framework knitted goods. In 1777 a new departure was made.[11] In an Act passed in that year to prevent frauds in the manufactures of combing wool, worsted yarn, and goods made from worsted in the counties of York, Lancaster, and Chester, the manufacturers and the justices were empowered to regulate the conduct of these industries. A meeting of manufacturers was to elect a committee, and the committee was to recommend two or more persons to be licensed by the justices to be inspectors,[12] to whom the committee was to pay a yearly salary.[13] The

---

[1] 15 George II c. 20.
[2] § 2.
[3] § 8.
[4] 5 George III c. 51.
[5] 7 Anne c. 13 ; 11 George I c. 24 ; 7 George II c. 25 ; 14 George II c. 35.
[6] 5 George III c. 51 § 2.
[7] § 7
[8] § 18.
[9] § 8.
[10] 6 George III c. 29.
[11] 17 George III c. 11.
[12] § 1.
[13] § 9.

committee was to appoint a clerk, meet quarterly, and keep minutes of the business done at their meetings.[1] If it neglected its duties the justices could call a general meeting of manufacturers.[2] The inspectors must bring to justice offenders against this and other Acts relating to these industries,[3] and they were given a right of entry into places where the industry was carried on.[4] Expenses were to be met out of a deduction from the drawback on the tax on soap used in these industries.[5] Similar Acts were passed later for the same industries carried on in the county of Suffolk,[6] and in the counties of Bedford, Huntingdon, Northampton, Leicester, Rutland, Lincoln, and the Isle of Ely.[7] In 1785 [8] penalties were imposed on manufacturers who made bad cordage for shipping. The quality of the cordage must be distinguished by marks, and the manufacturer's name must be affixed.[9]

These statutes show that the state, sometimes on its own initiative, and sometimes in alliance with the manufacturers, is beginning to take some direct responsibilty for the quality of manufactured goods. Adam Smith approved of this development, and said that regulations of this kind were much more efficacious to secure the quality of the goods than the old statute of apprenticeship.[10]

(3) *The grant of patents of monopoly and other rewards to the inventors of new processes.*

The enactments and regulations which we have just been considering were directed to maintaining the standard of established manufactures : the enactments and regulations which we must now consider were directed to encouraging improvements in established manufactures or the invention of new manufacturing processes.

We have seen that the foundations of the modern patent law had been laid in 1624 by James I's statute of monopolies.[11] Monopolies were condemned ; and jurisdiction to determine the validity of grants of monopoly was given to the common law courts.[12] But the Crown was given power to grant a patent

---

[1] §§ 2 and 3. [2] § 7. [3] § 10. [4] Ibid.
[5] § 17. [6] 24 George III St. 2 c. 3.
[7] 25 George III c. 40. [8] Ibid c. 56. [9] §§ 3 and 4.
[10] " The sterling mark upon plate, and the stamps upon linen and woollen cloth, give the purchaser much greater security than any statute of apprenticeship," Wealth of Nations i 124.
[11] Vol. iv 353-354 ; 21 James I c. 3 ; the statute in its preamble mentions the King's declaration in print published in 1610 as to the illegality of certain monopolies ; this is a reference to " The Book of Bounty," which is printed by J. W. Gordon, Monopolies by Patent 157-192.
[12] § 2 ; § 4 forbade injunctions against actions on the statute under the penalty of a praemunire ; but this did not prevent equity from granting an injunction to

of monopoly for fourteen years to the true and first inventor
of a manufacture which at the time of the grant was not
known in the realm.[1] It is reasonably clear that the statute
intended to give the common law courts jurisdiction over the
validity of the patents of monopoly permitted by the statute,
just as it gave them jurisdiction over the validity of any other
monopoly. It was assumed by Coke that this was its intention;
and he considered that in this respect the provisions of the
statute were declaratory of the pre-existing law.[2] The correctness of his opinion is borne out by *Bircot's Case* in which the
Exchequer Chamber in 1573 held that a new addition to an old
manufacture, though it made the old manufacture more profitable, was not patentable as a new manufacture.[3] Nevertheless we have seen that, during the seventeenth and the greater
part of the eighteenth centuries, the Council, assisted by the
law officers, and not the courts, exercised jurisdiction in patent
cases.[4] When, in the latter half of the eighteenth century, the
courts took over from the Council the jurisdiction which the
Council had formerly exercised in patent cases, a distinct break
occurred in the development of the law on this subject. Hulme
has pointed out that, for more than a century,

the reported cases are destitute of any decision of importance in
this branch of jurisprudence. . . . At the end of the eighteenth
century the common law judges were left to pick up the threads of the
principles of law without the aid of recent and reliable precedents.[5]

It is for this reason that in 1795 Eyre, C.J., found that "patent
rights are nowhere accurately described in our books."[6] But

prevent a breach of patent right in the exercise of its concurrent jurisdiction ; it
refused at first to do so till the legal right had been established by an action at law,
see Whitchurch v. Hide (1742) 2 Atk. 391 ; but later it did not necessarily insist
on this condition, Hicks v. Raincock (1783) Dick. 647 ; it may be that the prejudice
against patents on the ground that they were monopolies induced equity to insist
that the legal rights must first be established, and that the later decisions represent
the more favourable attitude to patents taken by the courts in the latter part of the
eighteenth century, below 431 ; moreover, § 4 did not affect the common law jurisdiction of the Chancery to determine an action brought by writ of scire facias for the
repeal of a patent, J. W. Gordon, Monopolies by Patent 37-38.

   [1] § 6 ; it was generally recognized that the King had this power at common
law, vol. iv 351 ; Notestein, Commons Debates 1621 iv 131.
   [2] Third Instit. 181, 182-183.   [3] Ibid 184.
   [4] Vol. iv 354 ; vol. vi 331 ; in this and the preceding period the law officers
were sometimes called upon to report upon the invention for which the grant of
a patent was sought, Calendar of Home Office Papers 1760-1765, 9 ; ibid 1766-
1769, 78, 95, 101, 153, 175, 176 ; in the late sixteenth and early seventeenth centuries
the law officers were called on to report on the " conveniency " of grants—a matter
which they often looked at merely " through fiscal spectacles," E. Hughes, Studies
in Administration and Finance 69 ; and they settled the form of the letters patent,
ibid 75-77, though they had not much control over their contents, ibid 80.
   [5] L.Q.R. xiii 318.
   [6] Boulton v. Bull (1795) 2 Hy. Bl. at p. 491 ; as Eyre C.J. says, " Sir Edward
Coke discourses largely, and sometimes not quite intelligently, upon monopolies
in his chapter on monopolies, 3 Inst. 181. But he deals very much in generals,
and says little or nothing of patent rights, as opposed to monopolies," ibid.

the new mechanical developments, which were taking place at the end of the century, were increasing the importance of this branch of the law.[1] Its increased importance coincided both with the change over from the jurisdiction of the Council to the jurisdiction of the courts, and with great changes in in-dustrial conditions. It is not surprising, therefore, that the law laid down by the courts at the end of the century should diverge at certain points from the older law, that its principles should be more precisely defined, and that the origins of some of the most important rules of the modern law should then have emerged. At this point we must consider (i) the change over from the Council to the courts ; and (ii) the new principles laid down by the courts.

(i) *The change over from the Council to the courts.*

In Hulme's opinion this change was due to the proceedings on a petition for the revocation of Dr. James's patent for a fever powder which was presented by Baker in 1752.[2] The Council followed their usual practice of consulting the law officers,[3] and, in accordance with their advice, dismissed the petition. Baker then preferred an indictment against Dr. James for perjury in the affidavit which he had sworn on the hearing of Baker's petition in 1752, and he asked the Council to allow the clerk of the Council to attend the trial and produce the affidavit. The law officers said that the application was un-precedented, that there was no objection to acceding to it, but that the petitioner had no strict legal right to the production of the affidavit. The Council refused to grant Baker's petition. This case, in Hulme's opinion, led to " a reconsideration from a constitutional standpoint of the Council's jurisdiction," [4] and, " as a result, the Council decided, under the advice of the law officers, to divest itself of its functions." [5] Henceforward the Council does not adjudicate upon the validity of patents. It confined itself

strictly to the performance of duties imposed by the defeasance clause in Letters Patent.[6] Its action is practically directed to compelling

---

[1] The number of patents taken out between 1617 and 1760 was smaller than the number of patents taken out in the course of the following twenty-five years, W. Bowden, Industrial Society in England towards the end of the Eighteenth Century 12.

[2] L.Q.R. xxxiii 189-191.

[3] For an instance of a petition for the extension of a patent, which was referred to the law officers, see S.P. Dom. 1703-1704, 373 ; cp. L.Q.R. l 107.

[4] L.Q.R. xxxiii 194.   [5] Ibid.

[6] The ordinary form of defeasance clause runs as follows : " Provided that these our letters patent are on this condition, that if at any time during the said term it be made to appear to us, our heirs or successors, or any six or more of our Privy Council, that this our grant is contrary to law, or preju dicial or inconvenient to our

patentees to take their common law remedy under the threat of revocation in case of refusal.[1]

If Hulme is right in thinking that it was Lord Mansfield who insisted upon the constitutional objections to the exercise of this jurisdiction by the Council,[2] in consequence of which that jurisdiction passed to the courts, he must be regarded as the founder of this, as of many of the other branches of our commercial law. As early as 1787 Buller, J., could say that "many cases upon patents have arisen within our memory."[3]

(ii) The new principles laid down by the courts.

Perhaps the greatest change in patent law, which this transfer from the Council to the courts made, was the new view taken by the courts as to the consideration for the grant of the patent. Under the old practice the consideration for the grant was the introduction into, and working, of a manufacture which was new in Great Britain. Under the new practice the consideration is the written disclosure of the invention contained in the specification.[4] The first instance in which a specification was required occurred in 1711 in the case of Nasmith's patent, but it did not become a usual requirement till about 1734.[5] The result was that the Crown, as Hulme says, "commuted the obligation to work the industry by the substitution of a proviso requiring a formal disclosure of the inventor's secrets."[6] The reason why the courts were able to introduce this new principle into patent law is due to a change in the kind of inventions for which patents were sought.

So long as the monopoly system aimed at the introduction of new industries such as copper, lead, gold and silver mining, or the manufacture of glass, paper, alum, etc. etc., the requisition of a full description would have required a treatise rather than a specification. . . . [7]

subjects in general, or that the said invention is not a new invention as to the public use and exercise thereof within our United Kingdom of Great Britain and Ireland and Isle of Man, or that the said patentee is not the first and true inventor thereof within this realm as aforesaid, then our letters patent shall forthwith determine and be void to all intents and purposes, notwithstanding anything hereinbefore contained," Parlt. Papers 1901 xxiii 162 ; for various conditions inserted in sixteenth and early seventeenth-century patents in order to secure that the patent should be worked and the resulting benefit to the nation secured see D. Seaborne Davies, L.Q.R. 1 100-106.

[1] L.Q.R. xxxiii 193-194. [2] Ibid 194.
[3] Turner v. Winter (1787) 1 T.R. at p. 606. [4] L.Q.R. xiii 318.
[5] D. Seaborne Davies, L.Q.R. 1 87-90 ; but as early as 1664 the need for a clear description of the invention had been stressed, and the suggestion, carried out in Nasmith's case, had been made, that a patent should be only granted conditionally upon the submission of a specification within a certain time, ibid 274.
[6] L.Q.R. xiii 315.
[7] Other projects which were regarded as patentable in the sixteenth and early seventeenth centuries were the right of fishing for bottle-nosed whales on the coasts of Devon and Cornwall, the insuring of horses, and as late as 1778 "one, John Knox, had a patent for a sort of mutual insurance scheme," L.Q.R. 1 96-97—obviously

But when, by a natural development, the system began to be utilized by inventors working more or less on the same lines for the same objects, the latter for their own protection draughted their applications with a view of distinguishing their processes from those of their immediate predecessors, and of ensuring priority against all subsequent applicants.[1] Hence, while the recitals of the sixteenth century deal almost exclusively with suggestions of the advantages which would accrue to the State from the possession of certain industries, or with statements respecting steps taken by the applicants to qualify themselves for the monopoly, those of a later date not infrequently deal with the technical nature of the proposed improvement. These recitals, therefore, while forming no part of the consideration of the grant, are undoubtedly the precursors of the modern patent specification. . . . About the year 1730 the form of a proviso voiding the grant in case of the non-filing a specification was substituted. Still the practice of requiring a specification cannot be said to have been recognized as essential to the validity of a grant prior to the middle of the eighteenth century.[2]

As we might expect, it was long an unsettled question what information should be included in the specification.[3]

It was this change in the character of inventions for which patents were sought—a change reflected in the wording of the patent—which made it possible for Lord Mansfield, in 1778, to lay it down, in the case of *Liardet v. Johnson*,[4] that the consideration for the patent was not the undertaking to instruct the public by the working of the invention, but the disclosure of the invention in the specification. He said in his address to the jury in that case:[5]

There are three grounds that must be made out to your satisfaction: the first is . . . that the defendant did use that which the plaintiff claims to be his invention. If he did use it, the next point is . . . whether the invention was new or old . . . The third point is whether the specification is such as instructs others to make it. For the condition of giving encouragement is this: that you must specify upon record your invention in such a way as shall teach an artist, when your term is out, to make it—and to make it as well as you by your directions.

By the end of the century this principle was accepted as the settled law.[6] As Hulme says, it followed from this new doctrine

nothing in the nature of a specification was possible in such cases; moreover, the need for the grantee to make a full disclosure to the Crown was got over by the use of non-obstante clauses in patents, L.Q.R. l 263.

[1] See ibid 90-93 for a discussion and general approval of this view; its truth is borne out by the fact that, even in the early seventeenth century, something like a specification in the form of models of the invention was produced when it was important to describe accurately the nature of the invention, ibid 268-270, 271-272.

[2] Ibid xiii 317.

[3] Ibid l 90; for a discussion of the origin of the specification, and the reasons for requiring it, see ibid 90-95.

[4] Ibid xviii 283-287; probably the first case in which this doctrine was laid down was the case of Brand's patent in 1771, L.Q.R. xxxiii 192; Brand's case is referred to by Buller J. in Turner v. Winter (1787) 1 T.R. at p. 608.

[5] L.Q.R. xviii 285.

[6] Turner v. Winter (1787) 1 T.R. 602; Boulton v. Bull (1795) 2 Hy. Bl. at p. 477 *per* Rooke J.; S.C. sub. nom. Hornblower v. Boulton (1799) 8 T.R. at p. 100 *per* Grose J.; cp. Harmer v. Plane (1807) 14 Ves. at p. 132 *per* Lord Eldon.

that a change took place in the law as to when an invention could be considered as possessing sufficient novelty to support the grant of a patent. Under the old practice the test of novelty was whether or not the invention had already been used and worked in the realm. Under the new practice the test was whether in any form a prior disclosure had been made.[1] If, for instance, the invention had already been described in any book published in the realm, the disclosure in the specification was no consideration for the grant, and the patent was void. In Hulme's opinion the economic effects of this new doctrine have not been wholly satisfactory.[2]

The second change made in the old law was the abolition of the old rule, laid down by Coke,[3] that a new addition to an existing manufacture was not patentable. In 1776, in the case of *Morris v. Branson*,[4] Lord Mansfield held that such an addition was patentable. In his opinion if such an objection were held to be valid " it would go to repeal almost every patent that ever was granted."[5] In fact the change in the kind of invention for which patents were sought—a change which, as we have seen, was the reason for the introduction of the specification [6]—made this change in the law necessary.

Thirdly, the discussion of cases before the courts led to the elucidation of what is and what is not an invention which can be made the subject matter of the grant of a patent. In 1795 it was pointed out that an abstract principle could not be the subject matter of a patent.[7] A patent was given " not for a principle, but for a process,"[8] so that till the new principle had been embodied in a new process " in a condition to act and to produce effects in any art, trade, mystery, or manual

---

[1] L.Q.R. xiii 318 ; xviii 287-288.

[2] " (1) It attaches an undue importance to the patent specification, the value of which is mainly contingent upon successful working. The valuable consideration which the inventor brings in return for the monopoly is the expenditure of personal effort and capital. This obligation should never have been allowed to disappear from patent law. (2) Under the old law the inventor could claim the whole of the difference between the state of the Art as he found it and the state of the Art as he proposed to reconstitute it ; but, with systems of Examination for Novelty, founded upon Lord Mansfield's doctrine, the inventor is debarred from incorporating in his claims unused public knowledge. The further Examination is pushed, the further the patent claim is attenuated," L.Q.R. xxxiii 194-195.

[3] Third Instit. 184.

[4] This case is referred to in the judgment of Buller J. in the case of Boulton v. Bull (1795) 2 Hy. Bl. at p. 489.

[5] 2 Hy. Bl. at pp. 488-489 *per* Buller J. ; ibid at p. 491 *per* Eyre C.J.

[6] Above 427-428.

[7] " The very statement of what a principle is, proves it not to be a ground for a patent. It is the very first ground and rule for arts and sciences, or in other words the elements and rudiments of them. A patent must be for some new production from those elements, and not for the elements themselves," Boulton v. Bull (1795) 2 Hy. Bl. at p. 485 *per* Buller J.

[8] Ibid at p. 496 *per* Eyre C.J.

occupation," [1] there was nothing which could be the subject matter of a patent.

It is on the basis of the statute of 1624, as interpreted first by the Council and afterwards by the courts, that the modern patent law rests to-day. Both periods in the history of the law have contributed something to the final result. The fact that the definition of the phrase " true and first inventor " includes the importer of a new industry from abroad, as well as the discoverer of a wholly new industry or process,[2] and the fact that the patent is good though it has been anticipated by an inventor who has not published his discovery,[3] are directly derived from the statute of 1624, the common law on which it is based, and the interpretations put upon it. The later period, as we have seen, added new principles and rules based upon current practice, and a more detailed analysis of what could be the subject matter of a patent. As we have seen,[4] the proviso in the statute that the invention must not be " contrary to law nor mischievous to the state by raising prices of commodities at home, or hurt of trade, or generally inconvenient," has been variously interpreted as men's notions of public policy have changed with changes in industrial organization and economic theory. The idea held in the sixteenth and early seventeenth centuries that an invention was " inconvenient " if it threw men out of work,[5] naturally found no favour in the eighteenth century;[6] for it was wholly contrary to the freedom which the leaders of industry were demanding and obtaining.[7] and to the efforts to increase the productiveness of native industry which was the main object of the mercantile system.

In fact all parties in the state agreed that it was in the interests of the state to encourage new inventions which would " imploy great numbers of our poor, keep our money at home, and increase the profitable trade carried on by the exportation of our own manufactures." [8] The commercial advantages of

[1] 2 Hy. Bl. at p. 495 *per* Eyre C.J.

[2] Edgeberry v. Stephens (1688 ?) Salk. 447 ; L.Q.R. xxxiii 71-72.

[3] Dolland's Case (1758) L.Q.R. xxxiii 191-192 ; Buller J. said of this case: " The objection to Dolland's patent was, that he was not the inventor of the new method of making object glasses, but that Dr. Hall had made the same discovery before him. But it was holden that as Dr. Hall had confined it to his closet, and the public were not acquainted with it, Dolland was to be considered as the inventor," Boulton v. Bull (1795) 2 Hy. Bl. at p. 470.

[4] Vol. iv 354.

[5] Coke, Third Instit. 184 ; vol. iv 354 n. 7.

[6] In 1738 it was said in a debate in the House of Commons that " it is undeniable that every improvement, which, by diminishing the number of hands required in a manufacture, reduces the price of a commodity, ought to meet with encouragement in this House," Parlt. Hist. x 798 ; cp. Halsbury, Laws of England (1st Ed.) xxii 152.

[7] Below 463, 466-469, 471-472.

[8] Preamble to 5 George II c. 8—the Act for giving a recompense to Sir Thomas Lombe.

encouraging inventors by the grant of patent rights were recognized by the courts [1]—they had by that time quite got over their prejudice against patents, which had been due to the early association of patent rights with pernicious monopolies ; and both the Crown and the Legislature were prepared to add to this encouragement by giving them special privileges. In 1700 the Crown, on the advice of the Commissioners for Trade, made a grant to Crommelin, a French refugee, in order to establish the manufacture of linen in Ireland.[2] In 1732 Parliament made a special grant of £14,000 to Sir Thomas Lombe because he had " with the utmost difficulty and hazard and at very great expense, discovered the art of making and working the three capital engines made use of by the Italians to make their organzine silk." [3] Lombe had been granted a patent in 1718, but the time taken to build the factory, to set up the engines, and to overcome the difficulties arising from the King of Sardinia's prohibition of the export of raw silk, had prevented him from being able to reap the benefit of the patent. In 1762 [4] an Act was passed to pay John Harrison a reward of £5,000 in return for a disclosure of his invention of an instrument or watch for the discovery of longitude at sea. In 1773 [5] an Act was passed " to incorporate certain persons therein named, and their successors, with proper powers for the purpose of establishing one or more glass manufactories within the kingdom of Great Britain ; and for the more effectually supporting and conducting the same upon an improved plan, in a peculiar manner, calculated for the casting of huge plate glass." In 1775 [6] James Watt's patent for " certain steam engines commonly called fire engines " was extended. In 1787 [7] it was enacted that the inventors, designers, and printers of patterns for the printing of linens, cottons, calicos, and muslins should have the sole right of printing them for a period of two months. We shall see that inventors sometimes got special privileges by private Acts of Parliament.[8]

---

[1] " The advantages to the public from improvements of this kind, are beyond all calculation important to a commercial country, and the ingenuity of artists who turn their thoughts towards such improvements is in itself deserving of encouragement," Boulton v. Bull (1795) 2 Hy. Bl. at p. 494 *per* Eyre C.J. ; this was the general view, but Lord Kenyon C.J. in Hornblower v. Boulton (1799) 8 T.R. at p. 98 said, " I am not one of those who greatly favour patents ; for though in many instances, and particularly in this, the public are benefited by them, yet . . . I think that great oppression is practised on inferior mechanics by those who are more opulent."

[2] House of Commons Journals xiii 299—a grant of £800 a year for ten years was made to Crommelin, and interest on £10,000 to be advanced by Crommelin and his friends ; the £800 was to be received and issued by the trustees appointed by the King to inspect the employment of the £10,000.

[3] 5 George II c. 8, Preamble. [4] 3 George III c. 14.

[5] 13 George III c. 38.

[6] 15 George III c. 61 ; in the same year a similar Act was passed (c. 52) extending a patent for making porcelain.

[7] 27 George III c. 38. [8] Below 625

During the latter part of the seventeenth and in the eighteenth centuries the administration of the law as to the grant of patents, and these special provisions made from time to time by the Legislature, were successful in encouraging British industries. Mr. Lipson has pointed out that "the inventions of the late eighteenth century were the outcome of a long series of industrial experiments," and that "the Industrial Revolution constituted no sudden breach with the existing order, but was part of a continuous movement which had already made marked advance."[1] Tucker, in the middle of the eighteenth century, catalogues and describes the large number of new machines which had been invented in many different branches of industry ;[2] and Adam Smith testifies to the beneficial effects which they had in promoting British trade. "The demand of the North of Europe," he says,[3] "for the manufactures of Great Britain has been increasing from year to year for some time past."

(4) *The prohibition of the export of newly discovered machines and processes, and of the emigration of skilled artisans.*

Since the encouragement of improved machines and processes was directed to the increased productiveness of British industries, which would give British manufacturers an advantage over their foreign rivals, it followed that measures must be taken to prevent foreigners from profiting by them. Writers of the latter part of the seventeenth and early eighteenth centuries had complained of the injury caused to British trade by the emigration of skilled artisans, and by the export of machinery ;[4] and we have seen that in 1695-1696 the export of knitting frames had been forbidden.[5] This policy was continued during the eighteenth century. In 1719[6] penalties were imposed upon persons who should

contract with, entice, endeavour to persuade or solicit any manufacturer or artificer of or in wool, iron, steel, brass or any other metal, clockmaker, watch maker, or any other artificer or manufacturer of Great Britain to go out of this kingdom into any foreign country ;[7]

and upon artificers who, having gone into a foreign country, "to use or exercise or teach any of the said trades or manufactures to foreigners," did not return within six months after warning given to them.[8] In 1750[9] this Act was extended to artificers

[1] Economic History of England iii 53 ; lists of inventions for which patents were granted will be found in the Calendars of Home Office Papers 1760-1772.
[2] Lipson, op. cit. iii 54-55, citing Tucker, Instructions (ed. 1757) 20-21.
[3] Wealth of Nations (ed. Cannan) ii 107.
[4] Lipson, Economic History of England iii 47-49.
[5] Vol. vi 330 ; 7, 8 William III c. 20 § 3.
[6] 5 George I c. 27.
[7] § 1.
[8] § 3.
[9] 23 George II c. 13.

in mohair, cotton, or silk, and the penalties for persuading them and the artificers mentioned in the Act of 1719 to go out of the kingdom were increased.[1] Penalties were also imposed by this Act on the exportation of tools used in the wool or silk manufactures ; [2] and in 1774 [3] the prohibition of export was extended to tools used in the cotton and linen manufactures. In 1782 [4] penalties were imposed on persons who persuaded artificers in the industry of printing cottons, muslins, or linens, or of making of machinery for such printing, to go out of the kingdom,[5] or who exported blocks, plates, or tools used in this industry.[6] In 1785 a similar Act was passed with reference to the iron and steel industry.[7] This legislation was supplemented by diplomatic action. In 1700 the Commissioners for Trade reported that measures had been taken to prevent the establishment of a woollen factory at Sade near the Groyne, and also the establishment of a similar factory in Sweden.[8]

These statutes, and more especially the statutes which forbade the emigration of artificers, were condemned by Adam Smith.[9] No doubt, as he said, the restraints on artificers were contrary " to the boasted liberty of the subject " ; but, like the power of the Crown to impress sailors,[10] they can be defended on the ground that they were necessary to preserve the benefits of these inventions to British subjects. Eighteenth-century statesmen were not so wedded to abstract principles that they could not modify them when it appeared to be clearly in the national interest so to do. Nor is it at all clear that the interests of the artificer [11] and the consumer [12] were, as Adam Smith alleges,

---

[1] § 1.   [2] § 3.

[3] 14 George III c. 71 ; modified by 15 George III c. 5, and enforced by increased penalties by 21 George III c. 37.

[4] 22 George III c. 60.   [5] § 1.   [6] § 3.

[7] 25 George III c. 67 ; amended by 26 George III c. 89.

[8] House of Commons Journals xiii 298-299 ; for the care taken to enforce this legislation prohibiting artificers from going abroad see Calendar of Home Office Papers 1760-1765, 417, 571, 605-606, 613 ; ibid 1766-1769, 33, 61, 68-69, 156-157, 309 ; ibid 1773-1775, 177, 414 ; W. Bowden, Industrial Society in England 129-134.

[9] " It is unnecessary, I imagine, to observe, how contrary such regulations are to the boasted liberty of the subject, of which we affect to be so very jealous ; but which, in this case, is so plainly sacrificed to the futile interests of our merchants and manufacturers," Wealth of Nations (Cannan's ed.) ii 158.

[10] Vol. x 381-382.

[11] " Though . . . by imposing the necessity of a long apprenticeship in all trades, they endeavour . . . to confine the knowledge of their respective employments to as small a number as possible ; they are unwilling . . . that any part of this small number should go abroad to instruct foreigners," Wealth of Nations ii 159.

[12] " Consumption is the sole end and purpose of all production ; and the interest of the producer should be attended to, only so far as it may be necessary for promoting that of the consumer. . . . But in the mercantile system the interest of the consumer is almost constantly sacrified to that of the producer ; and it seems to consider production, and not consumption, as the ultimate end and object of all industry and commerce," ibid.

sacrificed to " the futile interests of our merchants and manu-facturers." If these regulations helped to maintain the superiority of British goods, and so to increase British trade, they promoted employment, and thus, indirectly, benefited consumers of many different kinds. We have seen that Adam Smith himself ad-mitted that the demand for the manufactures of Great Britain had been increasing.[1] Of course it may be said that trade would have expanded more quickly without these restraints—but that is pure assumption. The truth is that the eighteenth-century statesmen were wise enough to see that the pursuit of a policy which would give foreign nations the benefit of British inventions, and so enable them to compete with our own, though it might cheapen the goods and so appear to be to the interest of the consumer, was in reality contrary to his interest, since it might diminish employment and leave him unable to purchase anything.

These were the principal expedients used to encourage native manufacturing industries. The manner in which they were used testifies to the immense pains taken by the Commis-sioners of Trade and by the Legislature to consider the needs of many various industries. It is true that, at the end of the century the Commissioners of Trade had ceased to perform any useful functions, and aroused the satire of Burke. But the two thousand three hundred volumes of their reports showed that they had once taken a considerable share in guiding the commercial policy of the state;[2] and both the mass and character of the statutes which I have been describing, testify to the readiness of the Legislature to consider and reconsider the new problems and new needs of commerce and industry as a whole, and of many different industries. Its efforts were crowned by a large measure of success. It is generally admitted that between the end of the seventeenth century and the end of the eighteenth century British industry had expanded enormously.[3] We shall now see that this enormous expansion was to a large extent due to the manner in which this policy of encouraging native manufactures was co-ordinated with the organization of colonial trade, and the regulation of foreign trade.

The organization of Colonial Trade.

We have seen that the Acts of Trade attempted to regulate the commerce of the colonies and India in such a way that it strengthened the navy and the mercantile marine, and promoted the interests of British manufacturers; and that, subject to

---

[1] Above 432. [2] Above 72.
[3] Vol. vi 341; Cunningham, Industry and Commerce ii 602; see a letter in the Calendar of Home Office Papers, 1773-1775, 416.

the attainment of these objects, these Acts endeavoured to encourage the economic development of the colonies.[1] We have seen that, though the general principles underlying these Acts were maintained all through the eighteenth century, they were constantly being added to and modified, so that in the course of that century they had come to be an elaborate code.[2] There is no doubt that the objects aimed at by the Acts of Trade were to a large extent attained. Both the carrying trade and the industries of Great Britain expanded enormously during the eighteenth century ; and the colonies themselves developed so rapidly that they became in effect political societies, which were ripe for a larger measure of independence than Great Britain was prepared to concede to them.[3] Moreover the success of the East India Company, and its rise to political power, was beneficial to the shipping industry, and made England the most important market for Indian goods.

There were two reasons why the possession of these colonial markets, which were secured for Great Britain by the Acts of Trade, were an enormous stimulus to British industry and commerce. In the first place, they were not liable to be disturbed by hostile tariffs. " As in our own day, one argument for a colonial empire was expressly based on the contention that most of the neighbouring nations in Europe, by prohibiting or discouraging our manufactures, make it necessary that all proper encouragement should be given towards the increasing our colonies." [4] In the second place, they were a rapidly expanding market. Burke, in his speech on conciliation with America,[5] pointed out that in 1704 the value of English exports to America, the West Indies, and Africa was £569,930, and that in 1772 the value of these exports was £6,022,132. These figures, he said, showed that the value of the colonial trade in 1772 was nearly equal to the whole of the export trade of England in 1704.[6] The stimulus given to British industry and commerce by the Acts of Trade was so great that, when their working was dislocated by the American war of independence, British industry and commerce had attained so great a predominance that it found itself able to adjust itself to the new conditions. Both the new situation created by the emergence of the United States, and the changes in the industrial conditions of the United Kingdom,[7] showed that the time was ripe for a modification of economic

---

[1] Above 84-88. [2] Above 85-86. [3] Above 105-106, 126-128.
[4] Lipson, Economic History of England iii 186, citing House of Commons Journals xxv 850.
[5] Works (Bohn's ed.) i 458-459.
[6] This substantially agrees with the figures from the custom house ledger printed by Mr. Lipson, op. cit. ii 189 ; below 437.
[7] Below 462 seqq.

policy. In fact we have seen that some time before the American war of independence both political and commercial conditions showed that the Acts of Trade needed to be revised.[1] They had outlived their usefulness in their old form ; and it was because they had come to be unsuited to these new conditions that Adam Smith's attack upon the Acts, and the economic theory which underlay them, met with a large measure of acceptance.

Adam Smith maintained that the monopoly of colonial trade, which all European countries endeavoured to retain, was a mistake. That monopoly gave " a relative rather than an absolute advantage," [2] that is, it gave an advantage to the country which enjoyed it, not by increasing its industry and produce, but by depressing those of its neighbours. Also the British monopoly led to the withdrawal of foreign capital which had been or would have been employed in the colonial trade.[3] That trade could therefore draw only on British capital. The result was that, though the colonial trade increased, foreign trade with other parts of Europe diminished.[4] British manufactures were accommodated to the needs of colonial rather than of European customers.[5] If the colonial trade had been left open Great Britain would have retained a large share of that trade, and retained much more of her foreign trade.[6] Moreover, since British capital was not sufficient for the rapidly expanding colonial trade, the rate of profit was high, and that tended to make British goods dearer.[7] To the argument that the colonial trade was a more advantageous trade to Great Britain than any other, Adam Smith replied that the returns of a trade carried on with a neighbouring country are more rapid than those of a trade carried on with a distant country ; that a direct trade was more profitable than the round-about trade which was caused by the obligation of the colonies to send the enumerated commodities to Great Britain ; and that a foreign trade of consumption was more beneficial to British industry than a carrying trade.[8] Finally, Adam Smith pointed out that it was impolitic for a country to drive all its trade into one channel. " The whole system of her industry and commerce has thereby been rendered less secure ; the whole state of her body politic less healthful, than it otherwise would have been." [9] He sums up his argument in the following passage : [10]

---

[1] Above 105-106.   [2] Wealth of Nations (Cannan's ed.) ii 95.
[3] Ibid 96-97.   [4] Ibid 97.
[5] Ibid 97-98.   [6] Ibid 99.
[7] Ibid 99-100 ; " our merchants frequently complain of the high wages of British labour as the cause of their manufactures being undersold in foreign markets ; but they are silent about the high profits of stock. . . . The high profits of British stock, however, may contribute towards raising the price of British manufactures in many cases as much, and in some perhaps more, than the high wages of British labour," ibid 100.
[8] Ibid 101-105.   [9] Ibid 105.   [10] Ibid 108.

The monopoly of the colony trade, so far as it has turned towards that trade a greater proportion of the capital of Great Britain than what would otherwise have gone to it, has in all cases turned it, from a foreign trade of consumption with a neighbouring, into one with a more distant country ; in many cases, from a direct foreign trade of consumption, into a round-about one; and in some cases, from all foreign trade of consumption, into a carrying trade. It has in all cases, therefore, turned it, from a direction in which it would have maintained a greater quantity of productive labour, into one, in which it can maintain a much smaller quantity. By suiting, besides, to one particular market only, so great a part of the industry and commerce of Great Britain, it has rendered the whole state of that industry more precarious and less secure, than if their produce had been accommodated to a greater variety of markets.

Adam Smith's criticisms rest to a large extent upon a series of hypotheses. Nor do the facts altogether bear out his speculations. Burke denied that the " American trade was an unnatural protuberance that has drawn the juices from the rest of the body " ; and he denied that it had caused a decline in foreign trade. He pointed out that while the colonial trade had multiplied twelve-fold between 1704 and 1772, foreign trade had multiplied three-fold—" our general trade has been greatly augmented, and augmented more or less in almost every part to which it ever extended." [1] It is, I think certain that if Great Britain had not had the colonial market, if France had conquered Great Britain in America, British trade as a whole would not have expanded so rapidly. It could not have made the great strides which it actually made if it had only had the European markets. In fact Adam Smith admitted that this was so.

The new market and the new employment which are opened by the colony trade, are of much greater extent than that portion of the old market and of the old employment which is lost by the monopoly. The new produce and the new capital which has been created, if one may say so, by the colony trade, maintains in Great Britain a greater quantity of productive labour, than what can have been thrown out of employment by the revulsion of capital from other trades of which the returns are more frequent.[2]

But then he hastened to add that the great advantages of the colonial trade were not because of, but in spite of the monopoly. Whether or not this hypothesis can be justified it is impossible

---

[1] " But it will be said, is not this American trade an unnatural protuberance, that has drawn the juices from the rest of the body ? The reverse. It is the very food that has nourished every other part into its present magnitude. Our general trade has been greatly augmented, and augmented more or less in almost every part to which it ever extended ; but with this material difference, that of the six millions which in the beginning of the century constituted the whole mass of our export commerce, the colony trade was but one-twelfth part ; it is now (as a part of sixteen millions) considerably more than a third of the whole," Works (Bohn's ed.) i 459 ; cp. the figures of the export trade given by Mr. Lipson, op. cit. ii 186, which bear out Burke's facts.

[2] Wealth of Nations ii 109.

to say. What can be said is that during the existence of this
monopoly, the colonial trade had so stimulated the productive
capacity of Great Britain that the time had come when she was
able to relax it. But it by no means follows that that capacity
would have been so rapidly stimulated if it had not had the
protection which the monopoly of the colonial trade afforded. No
great producing and manufacturing country has ever been able
to dispense with some measure of judicious protection in the
early stages of its career. It is only when it has made good its
position that the amount of the protection which it needs can be
diminished, and its character modified.

Though both political and economic causes had shown that
the protective system of the Acts of Trade needed modification
in the second half of the eighteenth century, it does not follow
that their results had not been beneficial at any earlier period.
But it is clear that, when the American war of independence
broke out, they had outlived much of their usefulness. Adam
Smith admits that the stoppage of the American trade had not
affected British trade so seriously as, according to his theories,
it might have been expected to affect it.[1] He ascribes this
fact partly to certain " transitory and accidental causes," and
partly, as we have seen, to the fact that the demand of the
North of Europe for British manufactures had been increasing
for some years past.[2] We may fairly ask would British manufactures have made sufficient progress to give rise to this demand
if they had not been stimulated by the protection given by the
Acts of Trade ? However that may be, it is I think clear that
the legislation which was passed to regulate the economic
consequences of Great Britain's acquisition of large territories in
the Eastern and Western worlds, had given to Great Britain an
industrial and a commercial position amongst the nations of the
world that she had never before possessed. We shall now see
that this new position naturally reacted upon the character and
extent of her foreign trade.

The Regulation of Foreign Trade.

We have seen that during the sixteenth and seventeenth
centuries foreign trade was controlled by companies, either
regulated or joint stock, which had been given, by charter or
by Act of Parliament, exclusive rights to trade, and other privileges.[3] Trade with European countries and with Africa and
Asiatic countries was to a large extent regulated by these companies. It was during the eighteenth century that a growing

[1] Wealth of Nations ii 107.   [2] Above 432.
[3] Vol. iv 319-321 ; vol viii 199-202, 209-211.

movement in favour of free trade caused the decline of these companies. There was therefore the more need for direct legislation to regulate foreign trade in such a way as to satisfy the needs of the native manufacturer and the merchant. It was a difficult task because the chance that foreign states might impose hostile tariffs, or prohibit British goods, in answer to similar measures taken by Great Britain, was always present. But in spite of the element of precariousness which was thus introduced into foreign trade, it was constantly expanding [1]—a sure proof that the policy pursued in relation, not only to foreign trade, but also to native industry and colonial trade, was on the whole a wise policy. I shall deal with this subject under the three following heads : (i) the decline of the commercial companies ; (ii) the statutory regulation of foreign trade ; (iii) the expansion of foreign trade.

(i) *The decline of the commercial companies.*

The movement in favour of greater freedom of trade, which is apparent in the seventeenth century,[2] was inspired partly by jealousy of the exclusive privileges and dislike of financial exactions of the commercial companies which regulated foreign trade,[3] and partly by the provincial centres of trade which disliked the domination of London.[4] This movement gained, as we have seen,[5] great impetus at the Revolution, and it was making way all through the eighteenth century. The result was that foreign trade, first to European countries and later to Africa and India, was freed from the control of these companies. The diplomatic work which they had done in the countries to which they traded was gradually taken over by the diplomatic agents and consuls appointed by the state ; [6] and the regulations which they made for the control of trade either lapsed or were superseded by the provisions of Acts of Parliament. Let us look at one or two instances of these developments.

The Company of Merchant Adventurers regulated the sale abroad of English cloth and other commodities.[7] Its exclusive powers came to an end when an Act of 1689 threw open the cloth-trade.[8] It survived, however, as a company, and carried on an extensive business at Hamburg, where it continued to hold a privileged position, till the French occupied Hamburg in 1807.[9] As Mr. Lipson has pointed out, it was able to survive because

---

[1] Below 444.   [2] Vol. vi 334, 336, 357-358.
[3] Lipson, Economic History of England ii 244-248.
[4] Ibid 252-261.   [5] Vol. vi 334.
[6] The Levant Company paid expenses of its agents in Turkey till 1803, Cunningham, Industry and Commerce ii 252.
[7] Lipson, op. cit. i 488-498 ; ii 196-269.
[8] 1 William and Mary St. 1 c. 32 § 12.   [9] Lipson, op. cit. ii 267-268.

" its members enjoyed one advantage of which no Act of Parliament could deprive them—their corporate knowledge and experience of trade." [1]   The Eastland Company,[2] which traded to the Baltic, secured a saving of its privileges in the Act of 1689 ; [3] but before that date it had ceased to be an exclusive company, since in 1672 trade to Sweden, Denmark, and Norway had been thrown open,[4] and the company had been compelled to admit all comers on payment of a fine of forty shillings.[5]   In 1764 Anderson said that it existed "in name only, which it seems they still keep up by continuing to elect their annual officers." [6]   Similarly, the membership of the Russian Company [7] was practically thrown open when the entrance fee was reduced in 1698 from £50 to £5.[8]   In 1741 it was allowed to import Persian commodities in exchange for British manufactures exported to Persia ; [9] and in 1750 it was allowed to import Persian raw silk from Russian ports in exchange for British manufactures exported to Russia.[10] We have seen that it continued to exist as a trading company till the end of the eighteenth century.[11]   The Levant Company [12] had a similar history.   It was admitted that some regulation of the trade with Turkey was needed ; [13] but a considerable concession was made to the advocates for a freer trade by a relaxation of the conditions of membership which was made in 1753.[14] The company, as thus reformed, continued to exist till 1825.[15]

On the other hand, the conditions of trade with countries outside Europe gave the companies formed to trade with them a longer life.   The African Company [16] and the Hudson Bay Company [17] were active in the eighteenth century.   The East India Company retained its exclusive trading privileges,[18] and from time to time Acts were passed to make the path of the interloper more

---

[1] Lipson, op. cit. 267.   [2] Ibid ii 315-326.

[3] 1 William and Mary St. 1 c. 32 § 13 ; the privileges of the Levant Co., the Russia Co., and the African Co. were also saved by this statute.

[4] 25 Charles II c. 7 § 5.   [5] § 6.

[6] Origins of Commerce (ed. 1764) i 420, cited Lipson, op. cit. ii 326.

[7] Ibid 326-334.   [8] 10 William III c. 6 § 2 ; vol. viii 209.

[9] 14 George II c. 36.   [10] 23 George II c. 34.

[11] Vol. viii 210 n. 3.   [12] Lipson, op. cit. ii 335-352.

[13] The position was very fairly stated by the Duke of Bedford in the debate on the Levant Trade Bill in 1744—" I know, my lords, how general the opinion is that trade ought to be free : that it will find its own channel : and that it will prosper best when you leave it to its natural course.   But this, like most other general rules, has some exceptions : there are some branches of foreign commerce that must be kept under regulations ; and that the Turkey trade is one of these, we may be convinced by the success of the French Turkey trade, which has always been kept under very many and very strict regulations," Parlt. Hist. xiii 953.

[14] 26 George II c. 18 ; the fee on admission was reduced to £20, and applicants need not be " mere merchants," or, if residing within twenty miles of London, be free of the City, § 1.

[15] Lipson, op. cit. ii 352.   [16] Ibid 352-360 ; above 64.

[17] Lipson, op. cit. ii 360-362 ; vol. viii 210.   [18] Above 147-148.

difficult.[1] But we have seen that as the East India Company came to be the paramount power in India, its commercial came to be of much less importance than its political activities.[2] Adam Smith justly criticized some of the unfortunate results of the attempt of the company to combine these two sets of activities ; [3] but his praise of some of the actions of the councils of Madras and Calcutta shows that some of the servants of the company were beginning to realize its new situation, and that, in co-partnership with the state, they were learning to rule the sub-continent which they were conquering for it.[4] But the exclusive privileges of these companies were coming to be more and more unsuited to the new conditions of commerce, and they therefore aroused an increasing opposition. The African company was dissolved in 1821,[5] and the East India Company lost its exclusive trading privileges in India in 1813, and in China in 1833.[6] We have seen that the Hudson's Bay Company, though it has lost its exclusive rights to trade, still exists and carries on business.[7]

These companies had, by the end of the eighteenth century, come to be merely survivals of a past phase in the history of the regulation of foreign trade. They had once played a great part in the development of that trade. But as in the case of the Acts of Trade,[8] so in the case of these companies, modern conditions were making a relaxation of the old restrictions necessary. We should not, however, forget that they once performed great services to the state. Much of what Mr. Lipson has said of the usefulness of the Company of Merchant Adventurers applies to many of these companies. He says : [9]

It is true that the Company placed restrictions on its membership ; but most professions nowadays insist upon qualifications which in

---

[1] See e.g. 7 George I St. I c. 21 § 1 ; 13 George II c. 18 ; cp. 9 George I c. 26 which was passed to prevent British subjects from subscribing to the East India Co. which was being formed in the Austrian Netherlands, see above 149 ; 13 George I c. 8 which was passed to enable the South Sea Co., with the licence of the East India Co., to ship negroes, within the limits of trade of the East India Co., to Buenos Ayres.

[2] Above 213-214.

[3] " If the trading spirit of the English East India Company renders them very bad sovereigns ; the spirit of sovereignty seems to have rendered them equally bad traders. While they were traders only they managed their trade successfully, and were able to pay from their profits a moderate dividend. . . . Since they became sovereigns, with a revenue which, it is said, was originally more than three millions sterling, they have been obliged to beg the extraordinary assistance of the government in order to avoid immediate bankruptcy," Wealth of Nations (Cannan's ed.) ii 304 ; cp. ibid 136-137.

[4] " In war and negociation the councils of Madras and Calcutta have upon several occasions conducted themselves with a resolution and decisive wisdom which would have done honour to the senate of Rome in the best days of that Republic," ibid ii 140.

[5] 1, 2 George IV c. 28 ; above 64.

[6] Above 214.

[7] Vol. viii 210 ; Lipson, op. cit. ii 362.

[8] Above 105-106.

[9] Economic History of England ii 268-269.

practice limit the numbers admitted to their ranks, and the merchants of the sixteenth and seventeenth centuries regarded commerce in the light of a profession.   It is true that the Company regulated trade ; but now that the "rationalization of industry" is becoming general, price cutting and the glutting of markets, with their attendant reactions on wages and employment, hardly appear as unmixed good. . . . The position of the Merchant Adventurers, as a whole, must be viewed in relation to the traditional framework of society in earlier centuries, and not by reference to standards from which we are already beginning to depart.

(ii) *The statutory regulation of foreign trade.*

The regulation of foreign trade by means of customs duties was a difficult matter for three reasons.   In the first place, a measure of protection desired by one industry was often contrary to the interests of another industry.   Thus in 1744 a demand by the linen manufacturers for additional duties on foreign linen was opposed by other manufacturers, who pointed out that the additional duties might provoke retaliation, and would in any case diminish the market for their wares, since less linen would be imported.[1]   In the second place, this regulation needed constant readjustment to meet the constantly altering conditions of trade.   A statute passed in 1719[2] recites that the woollen manufacturers of France had much increased ; that these manufactures were imported into Turkey in return for raw silk which was shipped to Marseilles ;   that much of this silk was shipped to Italy, and thence imported to Great Britain, to the discouragement of the woollen manufactures of Great Britain and the encouragement of those of France ;   and the British trade to Turkey was thereby lessened.   The Act therefore provided that raw silk should only be imported directly from Turkish ports.   In the same year another Act removed the prohibition of the import of German timber in consequence of the increased demand for timber.[3]   In 1752, in order to help the industries of printing silks, linens, and calicos, gum senega was allowed to be imported from any part of Europe.[4]   In 1774 the duty on raisins was lowered in order to encourage their importation.[5]   In 1786 the export of certain wool cards and spinner's cards was permitted.[6]   In 1720 the export trade in foreign goods was encouraged by extending the time within which the duties paid on importation could be drawn back.[7]   In several cases normal restrictions on import were relaxed in time of war in order to ensure a supply of goods.[8]   In 1783 the recognition of the in-

---

[1] Lipson, op. cit. iii 20-21.   [2] 6 George I c. 14.
[3] Ibid c. 15.   [4] 25 George II c. 32.
[5] 14 George III c. 74.   [6] 26 George III c. 76.
[7] 7 George I St. 1 c. 21 § 10.
[8] E.g. 13 George I c. 25—cochineal ; 2 George II c. 18—cochineal and indigo.

dependence of the United States raised so many problems that the executive was given power to make regulations.[1] In the third place, it was necessary to provide against the effect of retaliatory measures taken by foreign countries. A good illustration is to be found in the case of Flemish bone lace. Its import was prohibited in 1662, 1693, and 1698.[2] The result was that the import of English woollen manufactures into the Netherlands was prohibited. Since the value of the bone lace imported was only £30,000, whereas the value of the woollen manufactures was some £160,000, it was obviously necessary to repeal the prohibition on the import of bone-lace.[3] In 1700 these Acts were repealed conditionally upon the repeal of the prohibition of English woollen manufactures; [4] and they were unconditionally repealed in 1706.[5]

These are a few instances from the mass of statutes passed to settle the problems which the regulation of foreign trade entailed. That this constant supervision by the Legislature, acting under pressure both from its own subjects and from foreign nations, was not wholly unsuccessful can be seen from the increase in foreign trade which, as we shall now see, took place in the course of the eighteenth century.

(iii) *The expansion of foreign trade.*

The expansion of foreign trade was hindered first by hostile tariffs, and secondly by wars. First, in the seventeenth century Sweden, in order to encourage her own industries, laid a duty of over 50 per cent on English woollen manufactures; [6] and the tariff war with France at the end of the seventeenth and in the eighteenth centuries " put an end to almost all fair commerce between the two nations "; with the result that smugglers were " the principal importers either of British goods into France, or of French goods into Great Britain." [7] But some compensation was found in conclusion in 1703 of the Methuen Treaty with Portugal, by which Portuguese wines paid only two-thirds of the duties paid on French wines, and English woollen goods were allowed to be imported into Portugal.[8] In the first half of the eighteenth century this treaty enabled Great Britain to carry on an extensive trade with Portugal and her principal colony Brazil.[9] It was not till the end of the century that the

---

[1] 23 George III c. 39.
[2] Vol. viii 329 ; 14 Charles II c. 13 ; 4 William and Mary c. 10 ; 9 William III c. 9.
[3] Lipson, op. cit. iii 19.
[4] 11, 12 William III c. 11 ; vol. viii 325-326.
[5] 5, 6 Anne c. 17. [6] Lipson, op. cit. iii 295.
[7] Adam Smith, Wealth of Nations (Cannan's ed.) i 438.
[8] Ibid ii 47-48 ; Lipson, op. cit. iii 112. [9] Ibid.

trade with Portugal grew less profitable, and that it was found to be advantageous to make a treaty of commerce with France.[1] Secondly, the wars of the eighteenth century caused periods of inflation and prosperity, followed by periods of depression and unemployment.   Thus the fact that George I was an enemy of Sweden had serious results on the West of England cloth trade.[2]

The War of the Spanish Succession created, while it lasted, a fictitious prosperity owing to the demand for manufactures and foodstuffs to meet the needs of our armies abroad, and the requirements of countries whose tillage and industries were interrupted by the war.   The real situation was, however, disclosed when the period of inflation was ended, and the workhouse made its appearance as the permanent legacy of the war.[3]

The Seven Years' War had serious effects on the carrying trade ; [4] and the American war of independence caused great distress in the manufacturing districts.[5]   But, in spite of these hindrances, foreign trade continued to expand.   In 1700 the value of goods exported was £6,477,402, and the value of goods imported was £5,970,175.   In 1774 the value of goods exported was £15,916,343, and the value of goods imported was £13,275,599.[6]

The very considerable success achieved by the mercantile system in encouraging British manufactures, in so manipulating the commercial relations of Great Britain with India and the colonies that the trade of all these three partners in the British Empire expanded, and in securing the expansion of foreign trade, was marked by the rapid expansion of mercantile and maritime law.   We shall see in the following chapter and in the Second Part of this Book that it was during this period that the principles of the modern law were developed by the judges of the courts of law and equity, and more especially by Lord Mansfield. Naturally these developments were reflected in the statutes. A rapid glance at one or two of the statutes which deal with topics of commercial and maritime law will show us that this industrial and commercial expansion was setting new problems to the Legislature.

Wars and hostile tariffs were two causes which made the fortunes of traders precarious, and led to periods of depression which caused much unemployment and many bankruptcies.[7] Another cause which had the same result was " the phenomenon of the trade cycle." [8]   Defoe [9] explains how some sudden accident

---

[1] Lipson, op. cit. 113-114 ; below 502-503.   [2] Lipson, op. cit. 297.
[3] Ibid ; vol. x 176 n. 4.   [4] Lipson, op. cit. 298.   [5] Ibid 298-299.
[6] See Mr. Lipson's statistics, Economic History of England ii 189.
[7] Below 445, n. 7 ; Lipson, op. cit. iii 297-299.   [8] Ibid 299.
[9] A Plan of English Commerce (ed. 1728) 257-258, cited ibid iii 299-300.

in trade causes an unusual demand for goods ; how the manufacturer proceeds to expand his business with the result that the
market is glutted ; and how, when the unusual demand is satisfied, " he falls into the mire." In these circumstances it was
inevitable that there should be some legislation on the topic of
bankruptcy.[1] The bankrupt had ceased to be regarded as necessarily a criminal.[2] It had come to be realized that since " trade
cannot be carried on without mutual credits, the contracting
of debts is not only justifiable but necessary " ; so that " if by
accidental calamities, as by the loss of a ship in a tempest, the
failure of brother traders, or by the non-payment of persons
out of trade, a merchant or trader becomes incapable of dis-
charging his own debts, it is his misfortune and not his fault." [3]
But since it was the exigencies of trade which necessitated
some change in and elaboration of the law, it was still only to
traders that the law of bankruptcy was applied. The laws of
England, says Blackstone, " are cautious of encouraging prodigality and extravagance by indulgence to debtors ; and therefore they allow the benefit of the laws of bankruptcy to none but
actual traders." [4] It was because the exigencies of trade had
compelled the Legislature to adopt this new attitude towards
bankrupts that it was the topic of mercantile law which produced
the largest crop of statutes ; and it was for the same reason that
many of these statutes are long and elaborate.

An Act of 1705 [5] provided that a bankrupt who did not surrender, or who refused to submit to examination, or who did not
make a full disclosure of his effects, should, on conviction, be
guilty of felony without benefit of clergy.[6] On the other hand,
if he surrendered and made over his property he was entitled to
his discharge,[7] and, if his estate realized enough to pay his
creditor 8s. in the £, to an allowance of 5 per cent. on the amount
of his estate,[8] provided that the commissioners gave a certificate
to this effect.[9] But a bankrupt who had advanced his children
on marriage to the amount of £100 or upwards was entitled to
no benefit, unless at the time of the advance he was able to pay
his creditors in full ; [10] nor was he entitled to any benefit if he
had lost more than £5 in any one day or more than £100 in the
twelve months before he became bankrupt.[11] When there had

---

[1] For the early history of this branch of the law see vol. viii 229-245.
[2] Ibid viii 236-237 ; Bl. Comm. ii 471.   [3] Ibid 474.
[4] Ibid 473 ; vol. viii 237.
[5] 4, 5 Anne c. 17 (R.C. c. 4).   [6] § I.
[7] § 8 ; Lord Hardwicke in *ex parte* Burton (1744) I Atk. at p. 255 said that
this provision was unique, that it was " temporary at first, and never intended to be
a perpetual law, but was made in consideration of two long wars which had been
very detrimental to traders, and rendered them incapable of paying their creditors."
[8] § 8 ; if the estate did not amount to 8s. in the £ the bankrupt was only entitled to such an allowance as the commissioners might make to him, § 9.
[9] § 20.   [10] § 13.   [11] § 16.

been mutual credits between the bankrupt and his debtors the commissioners could adjust the account, and the debtor was only to be liable to pay the balance.[1] Powers were given to the commissioners to summon before them persons who could give evidence as to the circumstances of the bankruptcy.[2] It was provided that the commissioners were not to eat or drink at the expense of the bankrupt's estate.[3]

In 1706 [4] the concealment or embezzling of goods by a bankrupt was made felony without benefit of clergy,[5] and it was provided that a bankrupt should not be entitled to his discharge unless four-fifths in number and value of the creditors consented.[6] It was provided that the creditors should choose assignees to whom the bankrupt's estate was to be assigned.[7] They were to keep accounts of dealings with the estate,[8] and were empowered to compound with the bankrupt's debtors.[9] In order to prevent the fraudulent and malicious issue of commissions of bankruptcy, it was provided that a commission was not to be issued unless at the suit of a creditor who was owed £100 or more, and the creditor must give a bond to the Lord Chancellor to prove his debt, and to prove that the person against whom the commission was taken out was a bankrupt.[10] This Act [11] and an Act of 1711 [12] made some small changes in the persons who were subject to the law of bankruptcy.[13] The Act of 1711 also provided that the discharge of a bankrupt was not to discharge his partners.[14] Further penalties on frauds committed by bankrupts were imposed in 1718,[15] and in 1719 [16] provision was made for the release of bankrupts from prison after they had got their certificates of discharge. In 1720 it was provided that creditors could prove for debts which would become due at a future date.[17]

In 1732 a codifying Act was passed which fixed the law till the end of this century.[18] Under this statute various frauds committed by bankrupts, such as " the bankrupt's neglect of surrendering himself to his creditors ; his nonconformity to

---

[1] § 12.   [2] §§ 3-5.   [3] § 21.   [4] 6 Anne c. 22.   [5] § 1.

[6] § 2 ; securities given by a bankrupt to a creditor to induce him to consent were declared to be void, § 3.

[7] § 4.   [8] § 4.   [9] § 6.   [10] § 7.   [11] § 8.

[12] 10 Anne c. 15 (R.C. c. 25).

[13] Ibid § 1 (R.C. c. 25) repealed 21 James I c. 19 § 2, which provided that certain persons should be capable of being made bankrupt, and defined certain acts of bankruptcy.

[14] § 3.   [15] 5 George I c. 24.   [16] 6 George I c. 22.

[17] 7 George I St. 1 c. 31 ; similarly if commissions of bankruptcy issued against persons who had borrowed money on bottomry or respondentia or against underwriters, the lenders or the assured were allowed to claim though the ship was not lost, and if the loss occurred, they were allowed to prove their debts, 19 George II c. 32 § 2.

[18] 5 George II c. 30 ; for an account of the law of bankruptcy under this Act see Bl. Comm. ii 475-488.

the directions of the several statutes; his concealing and im-
bezzling his effects to the value of £20; and his withholding
any books or writings with intent to defraud his creditors"—
were made felonies without benefit of clergy.[1] We have seen
that it was after and in consequence of this Act that the control
over the jurisdiction in bankruptcy exercised by the commissioners passed to the Lord Chancellor.[2] We have seen also
that the manner in which the jurisdiction of the commissioners
and the Lord Chancellor was exercised came to be very unsatisfactory.[3] But it is the provisions of this Act which were the
foundation of the modern law of bankruptcy which was created
by the statutes of the nineteenth century.[4]

Another topic which was the occasion of a number of
statutes was insurance. The number of persons conducting
this business who had failed,[5] was the reason why the Legislature in 1719 attempted to put the business of marine insurance,
which was then the most important kind of insurance,[6] upon
a better footing. In that year the Crown was empowered to
create two corporations for the conduct of the business of
marine insurance, and for the conduct of the business of lending
money on bottomry.[7] Though private persons alone or in
partnership could conduct these businesses, no other corporation for these purposes was to be created.[8] These corporations
were prohibited from lending their funds to the Crown except on
the security of branches of the revenue appropriated by Parliament to the payment of the loan.[9] If they wrongfully refused
to pay the money to the assured they were made liable to pay
double damages [10]—a liability which was taken away in 1721.[11]

[1] 5 George II c. 30 § 1; Bl. Comm. iv 156; in 1759 it was provided that prisoners charged in execution for debt who did not, on demand, give up their real and
personal estate for the benefit of their creditors were liable to be transported for
seven years, 32 George II c. 28 § 17; Bl. Comm. iv 156; apparently this did not
apply to stocks, shares or other choses in action, below 524, 599-600.

[2] Vol. i 470-471. [3] Ibid 471-473.

[4] 5 George II c. 30, and all other Acts relating to bankrupts were repealed in
1825 by 6 George IV c. 16 § 1; this is an Act of 136 sections, and it begins the modern
series of bankruptcy Acts.

[5] " Before the establishment of the two joint stock companies for insurance in
London, a list, it is said, was laid before the attorney-general of one hundred and
fifty private insurers who had failed in the course of a few years," Adam Smith,
Wealth of Nations (Cannan's ed.) ii 248.

[6] Vol. viii 273, 294; 7 Anne c. 16, which prohibited wagers on contingencies
relating to the war, and insurances for the payment of money on the like contingencies,
provided that the Act was not to affect insurances on ships or cargoes or bottomry
bonds.

[7] 6 George I c. 18; §§ 18-22 of that Act are the clauses which attempted to
suppress bubble companies—hence the Act is generally known as the Bubble Act,
vol. viii 220-221; for the contract of bottomry see ibid viii 261-263; for the connection of this contract with the contract of marine insurance see ibid viii 477.

[8] § 12.

[9] § 29—" on which a credit of loan is or shall be granted by Parliament."

[10] § 4.   [11] 8 George I c. 15 § 25.

In pursuance of this Act the Crown created the Royal Exchange Assurance Company and the London Assurance Company. In 1746 insurances on British ships or goods " interest or no interest," or by way of gaming or wagering,[1] or without benefit of salvage, were made void ; [2] and reassurances were made void unless the assurer was insolvent, became a bankrupt, or died.[3] Money lent on bottomry on ships trading to the East Indies could be lent only on the ship or cargo ; the lender was to have the benefit of salvage, and he alone was to be allowed to insure the money he had lent. No borrower of money on bottomry could recover on any insurance more than the value of his interest in the ship, exclusive of the money so borrowed. If the value of his interest was not equal to the sum borrowed he was personally liable to the lender for so much of the amount as he had not laid out on the ship or cargo, although the ship and cargo were lost.[4] A prohibition imposed in 1752 [5] on insurances on foreign ships bound to the East Indies was repealed in 1758.[6] In 1788 there was legislation as to the form of policies of insurance, marine or otherwise.[7] In 1774 the topic of life insurance attracted the attention of the Legislature.[8] Insurances on the lives of persons in whom, or on other events in which, the insurer had no insurable interest, or by way of wagering or gaming, were declared to be void.[9] The name of the insured must be inserted in the policy,[10] and only the amount or value of the interest of the insured in the life or event could be recovered.[11]

Other branches of commercial and maritime law also attracted the attention of the Legislature. Two Acts of 1734 [12] and 1786 [13] were passed to limit the liability of shipowners for the loss of merchandize without the default of the owners. Shipowners were only to be liable up to the value of the ship and freight due to the ship on that voyage ; and it was provided that a bill in equity could be exhibited to ascertain the amount of the loss and the value of the ship and freight. They were not to be liable for loss or damage by fire, and the shippers must declare the value of any gold, silver, watches, or precious

[1] For gaming and wagering contracts, and the connection of these contracts with the contract of insurance see vol. xii 539.

[2] 19 George II c. 37 § 1 ; except in the case of insurances on privateers or on ships or goods from the Spanish or Portuguese possessions, §§ 2 and 3 ; Bl. Comm. ii 460.

[3] 19 George II c. 37 § 4 ; Bl. Comm. ii 460-461.

[4] § 5 ; Bl. Comm. ii 458.   [5] 25 George II c. 26.

[6] 31 George II c. 27 ; the Act of 1752 had been strongly opposed on the ground that it drove away a profitable trade from this country, Parlt. Hist. xiv 1232-1233.

[7] 28 George III c. 56, which repealed 25 George III c. 44.

[8] 14 George III c. 48 ; Bl. Comm. ii 459-460.

[9] 14 George III c. 48 § 1.   [10] § 2.   [11] § 3.

[12] 7 George II c. 15.   [13] 26 George III c. 86.

stones shipped by them. In 1782 ransom contracts were declared to be illegal.[1]

An Act of 1767 was passed to prevent the practice of splitting the stock of companies, and of making temporary conveyances of it, for the purpose of multiplying votes " immediately before the time of declaring a dividend, of choosing directors, or of deciding any other important question." [2] It also regulated the procedure to be followed in declaring dividends.[3] In 1734 an Act, generally known as Sir John Barnard's Act, was passed " to prevent the infamous practice of stock jobbing." [4] It provided that contracts under which any premium was to be paid " for liberty to put upon or to deliver, receive, accept, or refuse any public or joint stock," and all wagers and contracts " in the nature of putts and refusals " on the price of stock, were to be void,[5] and those concerned in making them were to be liable to a penalty of £500 [6] Agreements to pay differences in case of the non-delivery or non-acceptance of stock were also declared to be void,[7] unless there was a genuine contract to sell or buy stock and a failure to pay for or to deliver the stock.[8] Penalties were also imposed on the sale of stock of which the vendor was not possessed of or entitled to.[9] All contracts for the purchase and sale of stock must be entered in a broker's book.[10] An Act of 1775 made void promissory notes and inland bills of exchange for a less sum than 20/- ; [11] and an Act of 1777 [12] required promissory notes and inland bills of exchange for over 20/- and under £5 to specify the names and addresses of the payees ; to be payable within twenty-one days, after which time they were not to be negotiable ; and to have the signature of the promisor or drawer attested.[13] For the future all such notes and bills were to be payable on demand.[14]

Though it must be admitted that, as compared with the legislation of the nineteenth century, the output of legislation on commercial law is not impressive, yet it is sufficient to illustrate the fact that commerce was expanding, and that, in consequence, the principles of modern commercial law were being rapidly developed.

The expansion of industry and commerce, at which the mercantile system aimed, had thus been attained. Its success was due partly to the working out of the legislative policy which has just been described ; partly, as Adam Smith recognized,

---

[1] 22 George III c. 25 ; for these contracts see vol. xii 534-535, 693.
[2] 7 George III c. 48 § 1.   [3] § 3.   [4] 7 George II c. 8.
[5] § 1.   [6] § 4.   [7] § 5.
[8] §§ 6 and 7.   [9] § 8.   [10] § 9.
[11] 15 George III c. 52.   [12] 17 George III c. 30.
[13] § 1.   [14] § 3.

to the fact that the constitutional character of the English government, home and colonial,[1] and the rule of law, gave a large measure of freedom and security to individuals,[2] and ensured a continuity in policy which was not found in the despotically ruled countries of the Continent; partly to the fact that the British government was an economical government;[3] and partly to the fact that that system aimed at fostering all branches of industry—the agricultural no less than the industrial and commercial. Adam Smith, indeed, sometimes contrasts the outlook of the merchants and master manufacturers with that of the country gentlemen and farmers—to the disadvantage of the former.[4] He speaks as if public-spirited country gentlemen and the farmers were imposed upon by the astute merchants and master manufacturers who were merely seeking their own profit.[5] And the moral he draws is that the proposals of the merchants for the regulation of commerce ought always to be regarded with suspicion because " it comes from an order of men whose interest is never exactly the same with that of the public, who have generally an interest to deceive and even to oppress the public, and who accordingly have, upon many occasions, both deceived and oppressed it." [6] This picture is, to say the least, overdrawn. It is clear that the merchants and country gentlemen worked together in Parliament; and it is obvious that, unless the country gentlemen had agreed with the commercial and industrial policy of the legislation proposed by the merchants, that legislation could never have gained the consent of a Parliament in which the influence of the landed gentry was overwhelming.[7] The truth is, the merchants and the

[1] Wealth of Nations (Cannan's ed.) i 328, ii 76, 78, 86-87.

[2] Adam Smith assigns as the causes which assisted the development of trade with the colonies, the general liberty of trade " superior to what it is in any other country," the liberty of exporting domestic manufactures, and the complete freedom of internal trade—" but above all, that equal and impartial administration of justice which renders the rights of the meanest British subject respectable to the greatest, and which, by securing to every man the fruits of his own industry, gives the greatest and most effectual encouragement to every sort of industry," ibid ii 110-111.

[3] Above 276-278; Adam Smith, op. cit. i 327-328, complained of the profusion of the government, and said that " England has never been blessed with a very parsimonious government "; but, ibid ii 383, he said that " the inconveniences which are in some degree inseparable from taxes upon consumable commodities, fall as light upon the people of Great Britain as upon those of any other country of which the government is nearly as expensive. Our state is not perfect, and might be mended; but it is as good or better than that of most of our neighbours "; and, ibid ii 389, he said that " the French system of taxation was in every respect inferior to the British."

[4] Ibid i 249-250, 400-401, 426.

[5] " It is by this superior knowledge of their own interest that they have frequently imposed on his generosity, and persuaded him to give up both his own interest and that of the public, from a very simple and honest conviction, that their interest, and not his, was the interest of the public," ibid i 249.

[6] Ibid 250.   [7] Vol. x 558, 566, 582.

landed gentry worked together, because the merchants realized
that improvements in agriculture and the prosperity of the
agricultural industry were conditions precedent to the prosperity
of industry and commerce, just as the landed gentry realized
that improvements in manufactures and the expansion of trade
were conditions precedent to improvements in agriculture and
the prosperity of the agricultural industry. And, thus working together, they achieved results which neither could have
achieved alone—as Horatio Walpole pointed out in the House of
Commons in 1743.[1] Indeed, Adam Smith, in spite of his condemnation of the astute and crafty merchants, admits that when
a merchant turned a country gentleman he was " the best of all
improvers." [2] We shall now see that the policy pursued with
regard to agriculture was closely co-ordinated with the policy
pursued with respect to industry and commerce, and that it had
a like measure of success.

III. *Agriculture.*

The policy which, at the end of the seventeenth century,
had been adopted by the Legislature with regard to agriculture,
was in substance adhered to during the eighteenth century. The
characteristic features of that policy can be summed up as
follows : [3] First, the Legislature, subject to prohibitions in years
of famine,[4] allowed the free export of grain, and encouraged

[1] " A member of this House, thus enlightened by enquiry, and whose judgment
is not diverted from its natural rectitude, by the impulse of any private consideration,
may judge of any commercial debate with less danger of error or partiality than the
merchants whose knowledge or probity I do not intend to depreciate, when I declare
my fears, that they may sometimes confound general maxims of trade with the
opinion of particular branches, and sometimes mistake their own gain for
the interest of the public. The interest of the merchants ought indeed always to
be considered in this House ; but then it ought to be regarded only in subordination
to that of the whole community," Parlt. Hist. xii 25 ; Dr. Scott, Joint Stock Companies i 443, 444, cited vol. viii 213, has pointed out that the success of many of the
early joint stock companies was due to the existence of a non-mercantile element
amongst their directors.

[2] Wealth of Nations (Cannan's ed.) i 382-383—" A merchant is commonly a
bold, a country gentleman a timid, undertaker. . . . Whoever has had the fortune
to live in a mercantile town situated in an unimproved country, must have frequently
observed how much more spirited the operations of merchants were in this way,
than those of mere country gentlemen."

[3] Vol. vi 342-343 ; at p. 343 I have misstated the effect of the Act of 1670 and
not given a quite adequate account of the later legislation. The Act of 1670 (22
Charles II c. 13) allowed the free export of grain on payment of export duties ;
these duties were removed by Acts of 1689 and 1699 (1 William and Mary St. 1
c. 12 ; 11, 12 William III c. 20) ; so that the export of grain was free at all times,
and also earned a bounty when the price was low ; the bounty system was inaugurated in 1672 (25 Charles II c. 1 § 31), lapsed in 1681, and was re-introduced
in 1689 ; see Mr. Lipson's clear account of this legislation, Economic History of
England ii 451-454.

[4] See vol. vi 343 n. 7, and Lipson, op. cit. ii 452, for some of these prohibitions in
the late seventeenth and eighteenth centuries ; Mr. Lipson points out that from
1765 export was almost continuously prohibited ; see 5 George III c. 32 ; 6 George
III c. 5.

its export by a bounty when the price fell below a certain level. It imposed high import duties when the price fell below a certain level, and provided for the diminution of these duties as the price increased. Secondly, it facilitated the inclosures made with the object of getting rid of the common field system of cultivation and the cultivation of commons and waste land.[1] Thirdly, as the result of these measures, there was a tendency to organize farming on a capitalistic basis, with the result that the large farmer tended to crowd out the small man.[2] In relating the history of the manner in which this policy was developed in the eighteenth century I shall consider first the growth of the large and the decay of the small farmer; secondly, the progress of inclosure and its effects; and thirdly, the encouragement given to the farmer by the corn laws.

(1) *The growth of the large and the decay of the small farmer.*

Improvements in cultivation began to be heard of after the Restoration.[3] It was said by the Commissioners of Trade and Plantations in 1702 that, since 1670, land had been much improved by the sowing of clover and grass seeds;[4] and the use of roots and artificial grasses began to be used by progressive farmers in the eighteenth century.[5] These practices were both profitable to the farmer and an enormous gain to the nation as a whole. Mr. Lipson says:[6]

They saved the necessity of leaving one-third of the land fallow every year, and the change from a barren fallow to fallow crops provided the means for keeping cattle alive in the winter. This made fresh meat available throughout the year, whereas hitherto the nation had subsisted in the winter on salted meat; and the substitution of fresh for salted meat was responsible, in fact, for the decline in the death rate and the consequent growth of population.

Moreover, they conduced to the maintenance of law and order; for they diminished the risks of times of scarcity which produced riots and disorders.[7] It was the large farmers who were able to make the improvements in cultivation which enabled England to feed the greatly increased population which accompanied the expansion of her industry and commerce, and enabled her to stand the strain of the Napoleonic wars. Naturally large farms were favoured by the economists. Adam Smith considered that landowners great and small were in the best position to make improvements, but that " after small pro-

---

[1] Vol. vi 344-345.   [2] Ibid 345-346.   [3] Lipson, op. cit. ii 373.
[4] Ibid, citing House of Lords MSS. 1702-1704, at p. 70.
[5] Ibid 374.   [6] Ibid.
[7] For riots so caused see Calendar of Home Office Papers 1766-1769, 82-83, 342; ibid 1770-1772, 486-488; ibid 1773-1775, 8-9, 17.

prietors rich and great farmers were in every country the principal improvers "; [1] that an improved farm was to agriculture
what an improved machine was to industry; [2] and that the
diminution of cottagers and small occupiers was "the immediate
forerunner of improvement." [3]

The small farmer was defended by some; [4] and Adam Smith
admitted that the decline in their number had caused a rise
in the price of pigs and poultry.[5] In fact both economically
and socially he played an important part in the state. Economically, because "it is now more generally recognized that the
most appropriate unit of production depends largely on whether
the nature of the produce demands concentration of capital or
intensive application of labour." [6] Socially, because these small
farmers were an independent and industrious class; and the
possibility of getting a small farm "served as an agricultural
ladder to give a spur to the industry of the ambitious labourer." [7]
Nevertheless there is no doubt that the number of small farmers
was declining throughout the eighteenth and early nineteenth
centuries.[8] The agricultural industry, like other industries,[9] was
tending rapidly to become organized on a capitalistic basis, and
the small independent producer was tending to become a dependent wage earner. These results were attained by the adoption
of the policy of inclosing the common fields and common lands.
It was because that policy was favoured both by the landowners
and the economists that it made such rapid progress in the
last half of the eighteenth and the first half of the nineteenth
century.

(2) *The progress of inclosure and its effects.*

There is no doubt that the open or common field system of
cultivation [10] was open to all sorts of objections. It made improvements impossible unless all the shareholders agreed to
adopt them. It penalized the industrious farmer. It led to
many disputes between neighbours. The livestock and produce
raised on the open fields were inferior to that raised in inclosed

---

[1] Wealth of Nations (Cannan's ed.) i 370—he added " there are more perhaps
in England than in any other European monarchy."

[2] " An improved farm may very justly be regarded in the same light as those useful machines which facilitate and abridge labour, and by means of which an equal
circulating capital can afford a much greater revenue to its employer. An improved
farm is equally advantageous and more durable than any of those machines, frequently requiring no other repairs than the most profitable application of the farmer's
capital employed in cultivating it," ibid 264.

[3] Ibid 225 ; for other opinions to the same effect see Lipson, op. cit. ii 373-374.

[4] See ibid 384-385.   [5] Wealth of Nations i 225.

[6] Lipson, op. cit. ii 384.   [7] Ibid 384.

[8] Ibid 385-386.   [9] Below 462-463.

[10] For this system see vol. ii 56-63.

land.[1] Similarly, it was generally recognized that the large tracts of common land which existed all over England were economically objectionable because they made the cultivation of these tracts of land impossible, and socially objectionable because they encouraged all sorts of squatters and vagrants to settle there, who " eked out a precarious subsistence by breaking hedges, cutting wood, and stealing fowls." [2]

We have seen that during the latter part of the seventeenth century the prejudice against inclosures of the common fields had died down ; [3] and it was generally recognized that, economically, inclosure of the commons was desirable.[4] But it was found to be impossible to induce Parliament to pass comprehensive legislation upon either of these problems. Parliament merely tinkered with them. In 1756 an Act was passed to facilitate inclosure by the consent of lords and tenants of common land for the purpose of planting it with timber. Provision was made for compensating the commoners by a share of the profits of the timber, or by the grant of other land, or by an annuity charged on the lands inclosed or other lands.[5] In 1773 a more elaborate Act was passed for the purpose of improving the common field system of cultivation and of making a more profitable use of the commons.[6] Three-fourths in number and value of the occupiers, with the consent of the rector or tithe owner, were to be allowed to make rules for the cultivation of the common fields, which should be in force for the ensuing six years.[7] They were to appoint field reeves to see that the rules were kept, and assess the occupiers to meet expenses.[8] The rights of cottagers and others to their common rights were saved, unless they agreed in writing to a curtailment of their rights ; [9] and it was further provided that the commons might be inclosed if a majority of the cottagers who had not agreed could be induced to accept an equivalent amount of common to be enjoyed by themselves exclusively.[10] Three-fourths of the occupiers, with the consent of the lord of the manor, might allow balks to be ploughed ; [11] and the lord of the manor, with the consent of three-fourths of the occupiers, might lease a twelfth part of the wastes, the rents to be applied in improving the rest of the waste.[12] Regulations could be made by the lord of the manor and the commoners as

---

[1] Lipson, op. cit. ii 395-397 ; Mr. Lipson points out that improvement was not impossible under the common field system, but that the opportunities for it were restricted ; there was a saying that " severalty makes a good farmer better and a bad one worse."

[2] Ibid 413-414.   [3] Vol. vi 344.   [4] Lipson, op. cit. ii 414-416.

[5] 29 George II c. 36, amended by 31 George II c. 41 ; an earlier Act 1 George I St. 2 c. 48 had been passed to encourage the planting of timber.

[6] 13 George III c. 81.   [7] §§ 1 and 2.

[8] §§ 3 and 4.   [9] § 8.   [10] § 9.

[11] § 11.   [12] § 15.

to the use of the commons.[1] The Act failed to effect its purpose. Probably it was as difficult to secure the assent of three-fourths of the occupiers, the tithe owner, the lord of the manor, and the commoners, as to secure unanimity. It was unfortunate that the Act failed because it was a real attempt to deal fairly with the rights of all persons concerned—lords, shareholders in the common fields, and commoners. The result of this failure on the part of the Legislature to deal comprehensively with the problem was the adoption of another expedient, which was conspicuously unfair to the small shareholders and to the commoners.

This expedient was the private Act of Parliament. We shall see that, from the reign of George II onwards, an enormous number of inclosure Acts were passed.[2] No doubt the object aimed at by these Acts was economically beneficial—the improvement of the food supply of the nation. No doubt these Acts did make for the greater efficiency of all branches of the agricultural industry. But there is also no doubt that they were passed with too little regard for the rights of the small owners and commoners ; and that the elimination of their rights had grave social and economic effects, which, as Mr. Lipson has said, " left behind it a permanent legacy of bitterness." [3]

There were several reasons for this defect. In the first place, we have seen that at this period private bill procedure was very defective.[4] The projects of the promoters of these bills were not submitted to any kind of judicial examination. The result was that the land-owners who promoted them were able to insert in them provisions which made it impossible for the small men to make any effectual protest.[5] Their petitions to Parliament were disregarded ; [6] the standing orders gave them very little protection ; [7] and the commissioners appointed by the bill, who were nominated by the promoters of the bill, had powers of allotment which were often subject to no appeal.[8] In the second place, the legal and Parliamentary expenses of an inclosure bill were heavy ; and on the top of these expenses were the expenses of fencing the inclosed land. " The shares of the poorer inhabitants for these expenses involved many of them in debt and led to their ruin." [9] In the third place, though Parliament was not indifferent to the claims of the small men, as the provisions of the Act of 1773 show ; [10]

---

[1] § 18 ; but it was provided by § 19 that a part of the commons should be set apart for the use of such commoners as did not consent to the regulations.

[2] Below 625.

[3] Economic History of England ii 416 ; this point is clearly brought out by Dr. and Mrs. Hammond in their book on the Village Labourer 1760-1832 ; cp. Cunningham, Industry and Commerce iii 713.

[4] Above 341-345.   [5] Hammond, op. cit. 43-48.

[6] Ibid 48-49, 51-52.   [7] Ibid 44.   [8] Ibid 58-61, 62-64.

[9] Cunningham, Industry and Commerce ii 558.   [10] Above 454.

though it very occasionally intervened to stop a piece of flagrant injustice which the promoters of a private bill proposed to perpetrate;[1] it was naturally prejudiced in favour of the promoters of these bills. Parliament was prejudiced in their favour not so much because they were men of the same class, as because it was ignorant of the claims of the poor men,[2] and because the reasons which the promoters of these bills alleged agreed with the economic ideas which Parliament was trying to promote—their proposals made for the improvement and efficiency of the agricultural industry.

Parliament was unconscious of the grave defects in its private bill procedure, which gave opportunities to unscrupulous promoters of private bills, and prevented it from realizing the grave injustices which were perpetrated by this legislation. If it had taken the trouble, as Arthur Young did, to examine the methods by which its economic policy was carried into effect, and to correct the defects of those methods, it could have pursued the same economic policy much more effectively, because much of the social injustice, and much of the economic evil by which it was accompanied, would have been remedied. Arthur Young, say the Hammonds,[3] " had stumbled on the discovery that in those parishes where the cottagers had been able to keep together a tiny patch of property, they had shown a Spartan determination to refuse the refuge of the Poor Law." This led him to see that his old view that the commons were of no value to these cottagers was wrong, and to realize that inclosure Acts which took this land from the cottagers with a merely illusory compensation had grossly injured the poor.[4] But the new economic theories were beginning to stress the absolute rights

[1] See the account of the rejection of the bill for enclosing Sedgemoor related by Hammond, op. cit. 64-70 ; in this case " the obstacle on which the scheme split was a fraudulent irregularity : the bill submitted for signature to the inhabitants differing seriously (in twenty particulars) from the bill presented to Parliament."

[2] In 1845 Lord Lincoln said that " in nineteen cases out of twenty, committees of this House sitting on private bills neglected the rights of the poor. I do not say they wilfully neglected those rights—far from it : but this I affirm, that they were neglected in consequence of the committees being permitted to remain in ignorance of the claims of the poor man, because by reason of his very poverty he is unable to come up to London for counsel, to produce witnesses, and to urge his claims before a committee of this House," cited Hammond, op. cit. 53.

[3] The Village Labourer 83 ; cp. Cunningham, Industry and Commerce iii 714-715.

[4] He said : " By nineteen out of twenty Inclosure Bills the poor are injured, and some grossly injured. . . . Mr. Forster of Norwich, after giving me an account of twenty inclosures in which he had acted as Commissioner, stated his opinion on their general effect on the poor, and lamented that he had been accessory to the injuring of 2000 poor people, at the rate of twenty families per parish. . . . The poor in these parishes may say, and with truth, ' Parliament may be tender of property : all I know is that I had a cow and an Act of Parliament has taken it from me,' " cited Hammond, op cit. 83-84 ; cp. W. Bowden, Industrial Society in England 242.

of the owners of property, and the economic advantage of allowing them the fullest powers to develop it. This theory was
being maintained as early as 1656;[1] and it gathered weight
during the latter part of the seventeenth and in the eighteenth
centuries.[2] After all, the lords of manors were owners of the
soil of the manors; and if the commons were a social evil, and
prevented the proper cultivation of the soil, an inclosure Act
must be for the benefit both of the landowner and the state. It
is significant that the statute of Elizabeth,[3] which provided that
a cottage must have four acres of land attached to it, fell into
disuse and was repealed in 1775;[4] that Arthur Young's exposure of the injustices inflicted by private inclosure Acts did
not command the assent of the Board of Agriculture;[5] and that
a proposed general inclosure bill, promoted by the Board of
Agriculture, which would have remedied some of the defects
of these private Acts, failed to pass.[6]

Since the industrial and commercial expansion of the country
made it necessary that the system of agriculture should be made
capable of producing a larger quantity of food, a reform of the
common field system of agriculture and a curtailment of common
rights were necessary. But there is no doubt that the failure
of the Legislature to deal with the problem on a national scale,
and its acquiescence in its piecemeal solution by private Acts
promoted by landowners, and passed by means of the defective
private bill procedure machinery then in use, caused much
unnecessary hardship, much social injustice, and produced some
economically unsound results which could easily have been
avoided.

(3) *The encouragement given to the farmers by the corn laws.*

The improvements effected in the agricultural industry,
which the growth of large farms and the process of inclosure
facilitated, were helped forward by the corn laws. Down to
1773 the Legislature adhered to the policy which had been inaugurated in the last years of the seventeenth century.[7] An
Act passed in 1773 provided that when the price of wheat was
at or above 44s. a quarter, no export should be permitted;
and that when its price was at or above 48s. a quarter the duty
on its import should be reduced to 6d.[8] This and other Acts
were repealed in 1791, and were replaced by an elaborate

---

[1] See the opinions of Lee, a minister of the Gospel, in a book entitled " A
Vindication of a Regulated Inclosure," cited Lipson, op. cit. ii 409-410.
[2] Ibid 410-411, 415-416.
[3] 31 Elizabeth c. 7; vol. iv 369; Lipson, op. cit. ii 393-394.
[4] 15 George III c. 32.   [5] Hammond, op. cit. 84-85.
[6] Ibid 75-77.   [7] Above 451-452.
[8] 13 George III c. 43; Lipson, op. cit. ii 452, 462, 464.

consolidation Act containing ninety-four sections.[1]   The Act
regulated the prices of various kinds of grain at or above which
export was prohibited, and under which bounties were payable
on export.[2]   It regulated the sliding scale according to which
import duties were charged as the prices of different kinds of
grain varied.[3]   It provided an elaborate scheme for the ascertainment of the prices of different kinds of grain in different
districts in Great Britain.[4]   It provided for the importation and
warehousing of foreign corn free of duty, and for the conditions
under which it could be taken out of the warehouses for home or
foreign consumption.[5]   It gave power to the Crown by Order in
Council to permit the export of corn and the payment of bounties
notwithstanding the provisions of the Act.[6]

This policy of encouraging the export of corn by bounties
when its price was low was condemned by Adam Smith.   He
contended that the bounty did not achieve the object which it
set out to achieve—the raising of a larger quantity of corn than
would otherwise have been raised ; that it raised the price of corn
at home and cheapened it abroad ; and that it was a heavy burden
on the taxpayer.[7]   Mr. Lipson has shown that Adam Smith's
theoretical objections are not borne out by the facts.[8]   He points
out that the fall in the price of corn, and the growth of the export
trade, show that it did encourage the growing of a larger quantity
of corn than would otherwise have been grown.   That being so,
on Adam Smith's own principle that " defence is of much more
importance than opulence," the bounty can be justified.   In
fact the bounty ensured to the farmer a steady market.   This
steady market encouraged him to improve his methods of cultivation, and to refrain from putting land into grass when the
prices of corn in the home market were low.   " Thus the bounty
helped to give corn producers a greater assurance of steady and
uniform prices, and consumers a better prospect of more regular
supplies." [9]   The conclusion which Mr. Lipson draws from the
corn laws of the eighteenth century is in effect that they accomplished their objects.   " They did not make bread dearer, while
the effect of the bounty was to keep land under the plough which
might otherwise have been laid down to grass." [10]   Thus we may

---

[1] 31 George III c. 30.   [2] §§ 3 and 7.

[3] §§ 15 and 16 ; for attacks on the sliding scale which, it was said, was fixed
so low that it would ruin the farmer, see Parlt. Hist. xxix 98-102.

[4] §§ 31-43, 47-49, 52-57.

[5] §§ 19 and 20 ; for the objections made to these clauses see Parlt. Hist. xxix
161-164 ; it was said that the English farmer would not be able to compete with the
great supplies which would be released from the warehouses when the price of corn
rose.

[6] §§ 14, 92, 93.   [7] Wealth of Nations (Cannan's ed.) ii 8-12.

[8] Op. cit. ii 454-460.   [9] Ibid 458.

[10] Ibid 464 ; but see C. R. Fay, the Corn Laws and Social England 16-27, for
criticisms of the policy of bounties, and of Mr. Lipson's views ; Mr. Fay's criticisms

conclude that both the policy pursued with regard to agriculture, and the policy pursued with regard to industry and commerce,[1] enabled the mercantile system to achieve the results at which it aimed.

Adam Smith, the greatest of the critics of the mercantile system, did scant justice to that body of economic doctrine ; and so long as economic thought was dominated by those doctrines of *laissez faire* which he advocated, so long as the economic principles which were deduced from those doctrines were regarded as dogmas which it was heresy to question, Adam Smith's criticisms were accepted as obvious truths, and the economists who had acted upon the fallacies which he had exposed were treated with considerable contempt by his faithful followers. But now that the fallacies of *laissez faire* and unregulated freedom of trade have been exposed, now that it is apparent that they have had some very evil social and economic effects which the mercantile system to a large extent avoided, it is possible to adopt a more judicial attitude, and to decide more fairly between the merits and defects of the mercantile system, and of the new system of political economy which Adam Smith helped to substitute for it. In fact, if we look at the issues involved in this controversy from an historical point of view, we can see that Adam Smith's criticisms of some of the aspects of that system are open to objections of a kind somewhat similar to those which have been successfully made by Mr. Lipson to his criticisms upon the policy of giving a bounty on the export of grain.

First, Adam Smith does not allege that the mercantilists made the elementary blunder of confusing money with wealth. But he does allege that their anxiety to preserve in the country an adequate stock of the precious metals was misplaced. He says [2] that their arguments

were sophistical in supposing that either to preserve or to augment the quantity of those metals required more the attention of government, than to preserve or augment the quantity of any other useful commodities, which the freedom of trade, without any such attention, never fails to supply in the proper quantity.

Mr. Lipson has pointed out that this is a very debateable proposition. In the eighteenth century gold and silver could not be freely imported from all countries. It followed that some official regulations to secure an adequate supply were necessary. In fact these regulations " have their counterpart in the present day

are based purely on economic considerations (see p. 27), and leave out of account those political considerations, which, in the eighteenth century, were never wholly divorced from the discussion of economic questions.

[1] Above 434, 438, 444.
[2] Wealth of Nations (Cannan's ed.) i 400 ; and see pp. 401-402.

method of raising the bank rate in order to attract gold to this country." Moreover, in the interests of national defence, to secure the stability of prices, and as a foundation for credit, it was necessary to take care that the supply of the precious metals was adequate.[1]

Secondly, if it be true that something more than the ordinary law of supply and demand was needed to secure an adequate stock of the precious metals, there was some justification for the anxiety of the mercantilists to preserve a favourable balance of trade— that is a balance of exports over imports which was payable in money. Both Hume and Adam Smith poured scorn on this theory ; and there is no doubt that many of their criticisms are justified. In so far as this preoccupation with the balance of trade tended to magnify the importance of foreign trade at the expense of domestic trade it was clearly fallacious [2]—but that fallacy had been recognized by many of the mercantilists long before it had been pointed out by Adam Smith.[3] In so far as it taught nations that " their interest consisted in beggaring all their neighbours," [4] it thoroughly deserved Adam Smith's severe censures.[5] But the greatest objection to the theory of the balance of trade was the difficulty of striking the balance. The result was, as Hume [6] and Adam Smith [7] pointed out, that gloomy prophecies based on a supposed unfavourable balance had all been falsified. But, though it was true, as Hume pointed out, that, whether the balance was favourable or unfavourable it was impossible that gold and silver could ever permanently leave the country,[8] it was true that a great and sudden drain of money might " dislocate the economic system, and create

---

[1] Economic History of England iii 67-69.

[2] " The inland or home trade, the most important of all . . . was considered as subsidiary only to foreign trade. It neither brought money into the country, it was said, nor carried any out of it. The country therefore could never become either richer or poorer by means of it, except so far as its prosperity or decay might indirectly influence the state of foreign trade," Wealth of Nations i 401.

[3] Lipson, op. cit. iii 89-90.   [4] Wealth of Nations i 457.

[5] " Each nation has been made to look with an invidious eye upon the prosperity of all the nations with which it trades, and to consider their gain as its own loss. Commerce, which ought naturally to be, among nations, as among individuals, a bond of union and friendship, has become the most fertile source of discord and animosity. The capricious ambition of kings and ministers has not, during the present and the preceding century, been more fatal to the repose of Europe, than the impertinent jealousy of merchants and manufacturers," ibid.

[6] " The writings of Mr. Gee struck the nation with an universal panic, when they saw it plainly demonstrated, by a detail of particulars, that the balance was against them for so considerable a sum as must leave them without a single shilling in five or six years. But luckily, twenty years have since elapsed, with an expensive foreign war ; and yet it is commonly supposed, that money is still more plentiful among us than in any former period. . . . This apprehension of the wrong balance of trade, appears of such a nature, that it discovers itself, whenever one is out of humour with the ministry, or is in low spirits," Essays (ed. 1768), i 350.

[7] Wealth of Nations i 461.   [8] Essays (ed. 1768) i 351-355.

grave social problems with which the governments of the day
were not fitted to cope." [1]   " Hume," as Mr. Lipson says,[2]

demonstrated what would happen in the " long run," and the mercantilists attached importance to " the short run." Both points of
view are correct ; and in this respect it is unfair and misleading to speak
—as it is the common practice—of the " fallacy " of Mercantilism.

Thirdly, Adam Smith complained that the mercantilists
systematically sacrificed the interest of the consumer to that
of the producer.[3] But that is not quite true. Mere cheapness
is of little use to the consumer if the competition of those who
are ready to produce more cheaply deprives him of a market
for his own products, and throws him out of work.[4] The
mercantilists were considering the interest of the consumer
when they tried by protection to provide for producers a market
for their goods ; for these producers were also consumers.
Adam Smith said that " what is prudence in the conduct of
every private family, can scarce be folly in that of a great
kingdom " [5]—from which proposition he drew the moral that
" if a foreign country can supply us with a commodity cheaper
than we ourselves can make it, better buy it of them with some
part of the produce of our own industry, employed in a way
in which we have some advantage." [6] We might equally well
draw the moral that, just as in any private family it is well to
spend money in protecting and educating the children so as
to fit them to fend for themselves, so in a great kingdom it is
well to protect and foster industries till they are strong enough
to compete with full-grown rivals.

In fact, during the period of the seventeenth and the earlier
half of the eighteenth centuries, when England was making
its way towards commercial and industrial greatness, there was
more justification for the mercantilist theories than its later
critics admitted. Adam Smith contrasts what he calls the true
balance of trade with that fallacious balance of trade which the
mercantilists were so anxious to preserve. This true balance,
he said,[7]

is the balance of the annual produce and consumption. If the exchangeable value of the annual produce exceeds that of the annual
consumption, the capital of the society must annually increase in proportion to this excess. The society in this case lives within its revenue,
and what is annually saved out of its revenue, is naturally added to
its capital, and employed so as to increase still further the annual
produce. If the exchangeable value of the annual produce, on the
contrary, fall short of the annual consumption, the capital of the society
must annually decay in proportion to this deficiency. The expense

[1] Lipson, Economic History of England iii 98.   [2] Ibid.
[3] Wealth of Nations ii 159, cited above 434 n. 12.   [4] Above 434.
[5] Wealth of Nations i 422.   [6] Ibid.   [7] Ibid i 461.

of the society in this case exceeds its revenue, and necessarily encroaches upon its capital.

The mercantilist would have said that he aimed at securing this true balance of trade ; and that the manner in which he regulated trade was necessary for this purpose. He would have maintained, with some reason, that a comparison between the commercial and industrial position of Great Britain at the beginning of the century, and her position when Adam Smith wrote, showed that he had aimed at and achieved the attainment of this true balance.[1] No doubt at the latter period the success of that system in developing the commerce and industry of Great Britain, and the dislocation of the old colonial system, showed that changes must be made in economic policy. No doubt many of Adam Smith's criticisms were just and timely ; and both his analysis of past and present economic policy, and his suggestion for a new economic policy, were of great value to statesmen.[2] But it is questionable whether that tendency of economic theory, to which he gave classic form, to demand and obtain freedom from all the old restrictions, and to trust to self-interest alone to produce just and harmonious economic relations, was wholly good for the state.[3] No doubt in the changed conditions, which had been brought about largely by the application of the despised mercantile system, Adam Smith's acute and philosophical analysis of the causes which made for the wealth of nations introduced many new points of view. But there was some danger that statesmen might pursue the path to national wealth which he pointed out, without sufficiently considering that some of these paths might not necessarily lead to national health. But with this matter I cannot deal fully till I have considered the new organization of industry and its effects, and the growth of combinations of masters and men. With these two topics I shall deal in the two following sections.

IV. *The New Organization of Industry and its Effects.*

As in the agricultural, so in the manufacturing industries, the main characteristic of the eighteenth century is the growth of the power of capital, and the tendency to organize all industry upon a capitalistic basis. Just as the cottagers and the shareholders in the common fields, tended to sink to the position of agricultural labourers, so the small independent manufacturers tended to sink to the position of wage earners ; and the term manufacturer ceases to denote a person who works with his hands, but the capitalist who has invested his capital in some

---

[1] Cunningham, Industry and Commerce ii 601, cited vol. vi 341.
[2] Below 513-514.   [3] Below 517.

branch of industry, and has organized a business which he conducts by means of his workmen.[1] Obviously the older rules,
which were devised to meet the needs of small businesses, which
were controlled by small independent producers, employing only
a few hands and drawing their customers from local markets,
became more and more inapplicable to large businesses which
were controlled by capitalists, employing many hundreds of
hands, and drawing their customers from all over the world.
We have seen that the beginnings of this new organization of
industry in the sixteenth century had necessitated some departure
from the moral ideals of the mediæval statesman—the securing
of honest manufacture, a just price, a fair wage, and a reasonable
profit.[2] But we have seen that the sixteenth-century legislator,
though he put first the material object of increasing the power
of the state, did not wholly abandon the moral ideals of the
mediæval statesman ; and that many of the sixteenth century
and earlier statutes, which attempted to realize it, were still in
force.[3] We have seen, however, that if this material object was
to be attained, it was necessary to allow more freedom to the
individual ; [4] and that, as industry and commerce expanded,
and came to be more and more organized on a capitalistic basis,
manufacturers and merchants demanded more and more freedom
from the old restrictions, and chafed at the provisions of statutes
which seemed to them to fetter unduly their opportunities to
extend their businesses.[5] We have seen that these demands
were being made by business men and by economists at the end
of the seventeenth century.[6] Naturally they increased in strength
as, during the eighteenth century, the capitalistic organization of
industry became more general.

The course pursued by the Legislature in the eighteenth
century to meet the problems which were caused by the spread
of this new organization of industry, and by the demands of
the capitalists on the one hand and their employés on the other,
was substantially similar to the course which it took with regard
to the problem of safeguarding the consumer by ensuring some
security for honest workmanship.[7] It allowed some of the old
rules to fall into disuse, but it retained others, and it supplemented
those which it retained with new rules adapted to the new industrial and commercial situation. Thus the law of the eighteenth century as to the organization of industry is in a transition
stage. The needs of expanding industries and of an expanding
trade, and the economic theories which were called into existence
by the phenomena of expansion, demanded and obtained an

[1] Hammond, The Town Labourer, 7.   [2] Vol. iv 316-319.
[3] Ibid 319, 325-326.   [4] Ibid 325.   [5] Ibid vi 355-360.
[6] Ibid.   [7] Above 418, 421-424.

increasing freedom from the old restrictions. But, though that freedom was increasing, the Legislature was not prepared to throw overboard all the old restrictions. It was not prepared to leave commercial men entirely free to conduct their businesses as they pleased, and to trust to unrestricted competition to produce harmonious and equitable results. And so we get new laws with regard to prices and wages, and other problems connected with the relations of employers and employer. No doubt, as the century progressed, and as industry and commerce came to be more completely organized on a capitalistic basis, the tendency was in the direction of giving more freedom to the capitalist, and of allowing more scope to unrestricted competition. But in the eighteenth century this tendency was still held in check. It was not till the following period that it gained sufficient strength to sweep away all the old restrictions.

In dealing with the legislation which was caused by the need to make new rules for the organization of industry I shall, in the first place, say something of the growth of capitalism. Secondly, I shall describe the decay of some of the older rules which regulated industry and commerce. Thirdly, I shall deal with the new statutory rules by which some of the older rules were replaced.

(1) *The growth of capitalism.*

Capitalists who employed a large number of hands were known in the seventeenth and earlier centuries. " Large undertakings in the extractive industries, the textile manufactures, and the metal trades, were a recognized feature of the older industrial system." [1] The extent to which industries were organized in this way varied. The wool industry of the West of England was organized on a capitalistic basis in the eighteenth century.[2] The clothier was the capitalist who supervised and directed the manual worker.[3] On the other hand, the woollen industry of the North was in the hands of small working clothiers.[4] " It is this class, the counterpart of the yeomanry in agriculture, which enlisted the unstinted praise of contemporaries, and ever since has been held up to the admiration of posterity." [5] On the other hand, the worsted trade of Yorkshire was from the first organized on a capitalistic basis.[6] This is also true of the cotton and silk industries in the eighteenth century.[7] The coal mining,

---

[1] Lipson, Economic History of England ii 8.   [2] Ibid 11.

[3] Ibid 13-15 ; as Mr. Lipson points out, the clothier was not a manufacturer either in the old or the new sense of the word ; " he was a trading rather than an industrial capitalist. He was primarily concerned with buying and selling—he bought the raw material and he sold the finished product ; the actual details of the manufacture were left to the spinners, weavers, and cloth-finishers."

[4] Ibid 11, 69-71.   [5] Ibid 70.

[6] Ibid 83-84.   [7] Ibid 97, 103-104.

iron, brass, and copper industries needed expensive plants, and for that reason they were also organized on a capitalistic basis.[1]

But though many industries were coming to be organized on this basis, their organization had not, in very many cases, assumed their modern form.   The manufacturing processes were not carried on in a factory under the eye and control of the manufacturer who supplied both the fixed and the circulating capital.   They were carried on in the workers' homes.

Under this domestic system the ownership of capital was divided : the manual workers furnished the fixed capital in the shape of tools and workrooms, and the entrepreneur supplied the circulating capital employed to pay wages and purchase materials.[2]

The wool industry of the West of England was carried on under this system ; and though " factory clothiers " were known in the eighteenth and even in earlier centuries, they were not popular, because they destroyed home industry.[3]   It was the invention of machinery which gave the great impetus to the factory system. Lombe's inventions, which introduced machinery for the manufacture of thrown silk,[4] and Arkwright's machinery for the manufacture of cotton, made factories necessary.[5]   But as yet the factory system was in its initial stages.   Industry was not as yet completely organized on a capitalistic basis, and the factory system was not as yet universally established.

But the organization of industry on a capitalistic basis was making rapid strides during the eighteenth century ;   and towards the end of it the factory system was definitely establishing itself.   Just as the large farmers, who could afford to adopt the latest machinery and improved processes ousted the small farmer,[6] so the new class of manufacturing capitalists ousted the small manufacturers.   These capitalist manufacturers were a new class, quite distinct from merchants and bankers who formed the older aristocracy of trade.   They rose from the ranks of the small manufacturers.   The Hammonds say : [7]

The Industrial Revolution had in one respect an effect exactly contrary to that of the agrarian revolution.   Enclosure eliminated the opportunities of the small man ; the Industrial Revolution threw open the doors to adventure, enterprise, and industry, and the men who pressed in were spinners, weavers, apprentices, anyone who could borrow a little money and was prepared to work like a slave and to live like a slave master.   Many of them came of yeoman stock : Peel, Fielden, Strutt, Wilkinson, Wedgewood, Darby, Crawshaw, and Radcliffe among others.

[1] Lipson, Economic History of England ii 118-119, 162, 176.
[2] Ibid 8.   [3] Ibid 84, 85.   [4] Ibid 103 ;   above 431.
[5] Lipson, op. cit. 103.   [6] Above 390.   [7] The Town Labourer 8.

It was only natural that this new class should seek to free them-selves from the trammels imposed upon the conduct of industry by legislation which was enacted to regulate industrial conditions which were rapidly passing away. But it was also natural that a Legislature which looked at some of the consequences of these new conditions should mistrust the results of giving too much freedom to this new class of employers, and should prefer to adapt some of the old rules to the new conditions. We have seen that Adam Smith had no very high opinion of their honesty or disinterestedness.[1] And so the Legislature, whilst it relaxed or allowed to fall into desuetude some of the older rules which fettered the employers' freedom of action, retained, sometimes in an altered form, some of the old restrictions.

(2) *The decay of some of the older rules which regulated industry and commerce.*

We have seen that, at the end of the seventeenth century, economic opinion was turning against many of the old laws which regulated prices, which gave power to the magistrates to settle rates of wages, which limited the number of apprentices which a master could have, which fixed the kind of commodities which he could manufacture, which defined and extended such offences as forestalling, engrossing, and regrating.[2] We have seen, too, that many of these laws had ceased to be enforced by the justices and the courts of common law;[3] and that the opinion of the Board of Trade and of Parliament was against any attempt to enforce them.[4] Adam Smith says, not quite accurately,[5] that the statutes which enforced the assize of bread were the only survivals left of the old regulations as to the prices of goods.[6] We have seen that the old regulations as to apprenticeship were falling into disuse,[7] and that the old regulations as to the processes of manufacture were being replaced by new legislation designed to ensure honest manufacture.[8] "The popular fear of engrossing and forestalling," says Adam Smith,[9] "may be compared to the popular terrors and suspicion of witchcraft"; and he rightly says that the discouragement of the trade of the middleman, at which the statute of Edward VI dealing with the offences of forestalling, engrossing, and regrating, aimed, "endeavoured to annihilate a trade, of which the free exercise is not only the best palliative of the inconveniences of a dearth, but the best preventative of that calamity."[10] In fact the grow-

---

[1] Wealth of Nations (Cannan's ed.) i 68-69, 143, 400-401, 458 ; above 450.
[2] Vol. vi 356-358.
[3] Vol. x 166-168.
[4] Vol. x 166, 167 ; above 91.
[5] Below 470.
[6] Wealth of Nations (Cannan's ed.) i 144.
[7] Above 419-421.
[8] Above 421-424.
[9] Wealth of Nations ii 35.
[10] Ibid 33-34.

ing elaboration of the machinery of industry and commerce made the middleman a necessary link in its machinery.[1]

Perhaps the most unfortunate result of the decay of these older rules was the abandonment of the machinery set up by the statute of 1563[2] for the rating of wages. Fielding in 1751 said that it was wholly neglected.[3] Adam Smith testifies to its desuetude,[4] and cites Burn to show that there were good reasons for that desuetude.[5] There were several reasons for the decay of these rules. In the first place, the power given to the magistrates to rate wages was discretionary not mandatory. When the strong hand of the Council was removed, the magistrates ceased to make a regular practice of rating wages;[6] and the movement in favour of greater economic freedom confirmed them in the belief that such an exercise of their discretion was economically beneficial.[7] When in 1811 their power to rate wages was held to be an existing power, its discretionary character was emphasized,[8] and the magistrates, in the exercise of their discretion, refused to use it. As we have seen, that case was the preliminary to the repeal, two years later, of the statutes which gave the magistrates this power.[9] In the second place, the statutes of Elizabeth and James I gave no power to the magistrates to order a master to pay to the servant the wages which they had fixed. The master was liable to a penalty if he wrongfully dismissed his servant;[10] but the servant could not, as a rule, get from the justices an order for payment. In the third place, there was one exception to this rule which had a curious origin, and a curious effect on the later history of the view taken of the power to rate wages. A case of 1598,[11] following older precedents based on the older statutes of labourers[12] which had been repealed by the statute of 1563, had laid it down that, if a person was compelled to serve he could bring an action on the statute for his wages, and was not driven to sue by action of debt; so that, if the master was dead, his executor could not defend the action by waging his law. It seems to have been deduced from this rule that, if a person could be compelled to serve in husbandry and so had a remedy

[1] Lipson, op. cit. ii 21-23, 433-440.
[2] 5 Elizabeth c. 4 § 15 ; amended by 1 James I c. 6, which was made perpetual by 16 Charles I c. 4 ; vol. iv 381-382; vol. x 166-167.
[3] Cited Lipson, Economic History of England iii 264.
[4] Wealth of Nations (Cannan's ed.) i 143.
[5] History of the Poor Laws 130.
[6] Vol. iv 382 ; vol. vi 348 ; cp. Lipson, op. cit. iii 261-263.
[7] Above 166 n. 3.
[8] The King v. the Justices of Kent (1811) 14 East 395, at pp. 399-400.
[9] 53 George III c. 40 ; vol. iv 387.   [10] 5 Elizabeth c. 4 § 8.
[11] Watkinson v. Gomersall, Moo. K.B. 698.
[12] Y.BB. 38 Hy. VI, Hil. pl. 4 ; 39 Hy. VI Mich. pl. 24.

under the statute, that remedy might take the form of an application to a magistate for an order against his master to pay.[1] In other words, in the case of labourers in husbandry, the magistrates could not only rate wages, but could make an order to pay them wages. This rule seems to have led to the wholly illogical conclusion, a conclusion which was quite contrary to the provisions of the Acts of Elizabeth and James I, that the magistrates could rate only the wages of persons employed in husbandry. This conclusion was put forward in argument in 1811 and over-ruled.[2] But, in the fourth place, the courts, having regard to the prevailing economic conditions and the current of economic opinion, construed these statutes restrictively. They held that it was only if the hiring was for a year, as prescribed by these statutes, that they applied.[3] This decision ruled out most of the workmen who were employed by the capitalist manufacturer by the week or by the day.

Naturally this current of economic opinion, which was based upon the prevailing economic conditions, was reflected, not only in the practice of the courts, but also in the enactments of the Legislature. Thus an Act of 1761 [4] provided that

no brewer, inn keeper, victualler, or other retailer of strong beer or ale shall at any time hereafter be sued, impleaded, or molested by indictment, information, popular action, or otherwise for advancing or having advanced the price of strong beer or ale in a reasonable degree.

An Act of 1772 [5] repealed all the statutes against badgers, engrossers, forestallers, and regrators. The Act of 1791, which regulated the export and import of corn, repealed the clause of the Act of 1663 which prohibited the buying of corn to sell it again, and the laying of it up in granaries when the price was above a certain figure.[6] An Act of 1761,[7] relating to the London fish trade, which laid down some very detailed regulations as to that trade, and retained some of the old restrictions on the purchase and sale of fish,[8] permitted any person, " although not

---

[1] In The Queen v. London (1702) 3 Salk. 261-262, it was said that " the justices have no power by the Act of 5 Eliza. to order payment of wages to any labourers other than those who are employed in husbandry ; and the reason is, because by virtue of that statute the justices may compel men to work in husbandry ; and therefore it is reasonable that they should enforce payments of their wages" ; cp. R. v. Champion (1691) Carth. 156 ; R. v. Gregory (1699) 2 Salk. 484 ; R. v. Gouch (1702) 2 Ld. Raym 820 ; R. v. Helling (1716) 1 Stra. 8 ; R. v. Inhabitants of Hulcott (1796) 6 T.R. 583 ; the case of Watkinson v. Gomersall, above 467 n. 11, was not a case of a labourer in husbandry who was bound to serve under § 7 of the Act of 1563, but of a maid servant who was bound to serve under § 24.

[2] The King v. the Justices of Kent (1811) 14 East at p. 398 ; cp. Lipson, op. cit. iii 254.

[3] Snape v. Dowse (1685) Comb. 3 ; R. v. Champion (1691) Carth. 156.

[4] 2 George III c. 14 § 1.   [5] 12 George III c. 71 ; below 472.

[6] 31 George III c. 30 § 2.   [7] 2 George III c. 15 § 1.

[8] Above 405-406.

brought up in the trade of a fish monger " to buy and sell fish (subject to the provisions of the Act) in any market in Great Britain.

But though the repeal or desuetude of many of the older laws gave to manufacturers and traders much greater freedom to conduct their businesses than they had ever had before, the Legislature found itself obliged to maintain and strengthen some of the older restrictions and to impose new restrictions.

(3) *The new statutory rules.*

We have seen that in the eighteenth century neither the towns nor the country possessed any adequate police force.[1] Hence it was difficult to deal with a discontent which was sufficiently acute and sufficiently widespread to produce a riot. Therefore the Legislature found it necessary to pass legislation to remove occasions for riots. The Legislature also found it necessary to legislate against the oppressive, fraudulent, or undesirable practices of employers, and against frauds or other criminal acts committed by employés. Let us look at these two classes of statutory rules by which the older rules were replaced.

It was in order to remove occasions for riots that in certain cases the Legislature intervened to fix prices and wages.

In 1709[2] it was recited that the statute attributed to the fifty-first year of Henry III's reign,[3] which regulated the assize of bread, was

expressed in terms so obscure and impracticable in these times that many doubts and difficulties have arisen and daily do arise in the construction thereof; whereby little or no observance hath in many places been made either of the due assize or reasonable price of bread, and covetous and evil disposed persons, taking advantage of the same, have for their own gain and lucre deceived and oppressed her Majesty's subjects, and more especially the poorer sort of people.

The statute therefore empowered the mayors of boroughs or the justices of the peace to fix the price and weight of bread, having regard to the current market prices of grain, meal, or flour.[4] No other bread except that allowed by these authorities could be made or sold.[5] Bakers must mark on their loaves the size and quality of the bread,[6] and penalties were imposed if the bread was made otherwise than in accordance with the regulations laid down by the mayors or justices.[7] In 1758[8] the Act of 1709 and other eighteenth-century statutes were consolidated, and all the older legislation was repealed.[9] The mayor and aldermen of the

---

[1] Vol. x 144. [2] 8 Anne c. 18 (R.C. c. 19).
[3] Printed by the Record Commissioners among the statutes of uncertain date, vol. i 199 ; see vol. ii 222-223.
[4] 8 Anne c. 18 (R.C. c. 19) § 1. [5] § 2. [6] § 3. [7] § 8.
[8] 31 George II c. 29. [9] § 1.

City of London, the mayors of other cities and boroughs, and elsewhere the justices of the peace, were given power to set the assize ;[1] that is they could settle the weight and price of the bread sold within their jurisdiction. The price so set was to be based on the price of grain, meal, or flour in the public markets of the district ;[2] and those who set the assize were to obtain weekly returns of the prices of grain, meal, and flour.[3] Alterations in the price of bread were only to be made when alterations to the amount of 3d. a bushel in the price of grain, meal, or flour occurred.[4] The qualities of the sorts of bread permitted to be baked were to be marked on each loaf ;[5] and penalties were prescribed for bakers who sold at prices higher than those permitted,[6] or who used adulterated flour.[7] The Act was amended from time to time ;[8] but it remained the principal Act till the assize was abolished for London in 1822,[9] and for the rest of England in 1836.[10] Some time before its repeal opinion had come round to Adam Smith's view[11] that competition regulated the price of bread much more efficiently than the assize.[12]

The other commodity in respect of which price regulation survived was fuel. Statutes of Edward VI[13] and Elizabeth's reigns[14] had regulated the price of fuel ; and the latter statute was amended in 1710[15] and 1711.[16] These statutes applied only to wood ; and they apparently remained on the statute book long after they had become obsolete.[17] A statute of 1664 empowered the mayor and aldermen in London, and elsewhere the justices of the peace, to fix the retail price of coals.[18] This statute was made perpetual in 1696,[19] and, in spite of difficulties in administering it,[20] it was amended and extended in its operation in 1744.[21] In 1738[22] the mayor and aldermen of the City of London were empowered to fix the prices of coal imported into London for a year, and rules were made for the weighing and marking of coals.[23] But these Acts fell into disuse and the Act of 1744 was repealed by the Statute Law Revision Act of 1867.[24]

---

[1] § 6.   [2] § 2.   [3] §§ 6-8.   [4] § 16.
[5] § 25.   [6] § 26.   [7] § 29.

[8] 3 George III c. 11 ; 13 George III c. 62 ; 33 George III c. 37 ; 50 George III c. 73.

[9] 3 George IV c. cvi.   [10] 6, 7 William IV c. 37.
[11] Wealth of Nations i 144.   [12] Lipson, op. cit. ii 426-427.

[13] 7 Edward VI c. 7 ; this Act recites that provision was made for fixing the assize by 34, 35 Henry VIII c. 3, and that this was " the same assize that was kept in the time of King Edward the Fourth."

[14] 43 Elizabeth c. 14.   [15] 9 Anne c. 15 (R.C. c. 20).
[16] 10 Anne c. 6 (R.C. c. 5).

[17] 7 Edward VI c. 7, was repealed by 19, 20 Victoria, c. 64 ; 43 Elizabeth c. 14 was repealed by the Statute Law Revision Act 1863 ; and the two Acts of Anne by the Statute Law Revision Act 1867.

[18] 16, 17 Charles II c. 2.   [19] 7, 8 William III c. 36.
[20] Lipson, op. cit. ii 149-150.   [21] 17 George II c. 35.
[22] 11 George II c. 15.   [23] § 8.   [24] 30, 31 Victoria c. 59.

Statutes which aimed at the regulation of wages were more frequently enacted in the eighteenth century than statutes which aimed at the regulation of prices. Though the practice of rating wages under the statutes of Elizabeth and James I was obsolete,[1] the fact that the justices had this power was not wholly forgotten ; and in 1728 it was used by the Gloucestershire justices, who in that year fixed the wages of weavers.[2] At the same time the disorders and riots which accompanied demands for higher wages in particular trades were not without their influence on a Legislature which was conscious of the inadequate means which it possessed of dealing with them. And so, while, as we shall see, it tried to suppress the combinations of workmen which occasioned these tumults,[3] it also tried to remove the occasion for them by attempting to regulate wages in particular trades.

An Act of 1720 [4] recites that the journeymen tailors in London had " entered into combinations to advance their wages to unreasonable prices and lessen their usual hours of work." It declares these combinations to be illegal,[5] and then goes on to prescribe maximum wages and the hours of work for these tailors.[6] The wages were to be recoverable by summary proceedings before two justices of the peace.[7] Quarter sessions were given power to alter these wages and hours of work,[8] and masters who gave, or servants who took, larger wages were made liable to penalties.[9] An Act of 1756 [10] recited that the laws regulating the employment of weavers, and others engaged in the manufacture of wool, were not satisfactorily carried out, by reason *inter alia* " of the want of proper powers to regulate wages." It therefore gave quarter sessions the power to settle annually the wages of weavers and others employed in the woollen manufacture.[11] The clothiers protested against this Act on the grounds that the justices lacked the technical skill necessary to assess wages fairly, that compulsion to pay a fixed rate of wages was repugnant to freedom of contract which was the life of trade, and that such an interference was subversive of the authority of the employer.[12] The employers refused to pay the wages assessed,[13] and induced the Legislature to repeal the Act in the following year.[14]

This repeal was, as Mr. Lipson has said,[15] " almost in the

---

[1] Above 467-468.   [2] Lipson, Economic History of England iii 266.
[3] Below 488-490.
[4] 7 George I St. 1 c. 13 ; amended by 8 George III c. 17.
[5] § 1 ; below 483-484, 488.   [6] § 2.   [7] § 4.   [8] § 5.
[9] § 7.   [10] 29 George II c. 33.
[11] § 1.   [12] Lipson, op. cit. iii 267-269.
[13] Ibid 269.   [14] 30 George II c. 12 § 1.
[15] Op. cit. iii 270 ; " the struggle over the Woollen Cloth Weavers Act of 1756 marks the passage from the old ideas to the new. When in 1776 the . . . woollen operatives of Somerset petitioned against the evil that was being done to their

nature of an economic revolution. . . . The repeal of the Act of 1756 signified that the system of wage assessment was now definitely discarded in the premier industry of the country." It was in effect a surrender to the view later expressed by Adam Smith[1] that "law can never regulate wages properly, though it has often pretended to do so." But as yet the Legislature was not converted to the view that the principle of *laissez faire* was a dogma so universally true that it must be universally applied. It was ready to depart from that principle if it was clearly expedient so to do. In 1770[2] it regulated the wages of coal heavers working on the Thames ; and in 1773[3] power was given to the Lord Mayor in the City of London, and to the justices in Westminster to settle the wages of silk weavers in London and Westminster.[4] Penalties were imposed on masters who gave, and men who took, more or less than these wages ;[5] and on masters who employed men outside the limits of London and Westminster in order to evade the provisions of the Act.[6] In 1792[7] the Act was extended to the weavers of silk mixed with other materials.

Thus, although economic opinion was definitely tending in the direction of *laissez faire*, the Legislature had not quite surrendered to it, and was still ready to regulate both prices and wages if adequate reasons could be produced. But the burden of proof cast upon those who wished for regulation was tending to grow more and more heavy, as the tendencies to adopt a policy of *laissez faire* increased in strength. We shall now see that these tendencies are illustrated by the development of some of the other rules which regulated the actions of masters and the relations of masters and men.

Though, as we have seen, all the statutes passed to penalize the offences of forestalling, engrossing, and regrating were repealed in 1772,[8] the common law rules on these subjects were not repealed till 1844.[9] Blackstone pointed out[10] that those who indulged in these practices were guilty of a common law misdemeanour, and there are instances of prosecutions for these offences in the nineteenth century.[11] Similarly, though the old

accustomed livelihood by the introduction of the spinning-jenny into Shepton-Mallet, the House of Commons, which had two centuries before absolutely prohibited the gigmill, refused even to allow the petition to be received," Webb, History of Trade Unionism 51.

[1] Wealth of Nations (Cannan's ed.) i 79 ; it was said by Lord Sandys in 1744 in a debate on the Levant trade bill that "the price of labour depends chiefly on the price of provisions, and the plenty or scarcity of labourers."

[2] 10 George III c. 53.
[3] 13 George III c. 68.
[4] § 1.
[5] §§ 2 and 3.
[6] § 5.
[7] 32 George III c. 44.
[8] 12 George III c. 71 ; above 468.
[9] 7, 8 Victoria c. 24.
[10] Comm. iv 159.

[11] Stephen H.C.L. iii 201 ; in 1787 the high price of provisions was the cause of a petition from the City of London to the House of Commons to revive these laws ; the petition was ridiculed by Burke and rejected, Parlt. Hist. xxvi 1167-1172.

laws as to apprenticeship were falling into disuse,[1] they were not completely abandoned. Regulations were made as to the treatment of apprentices ;[2] and in order to provide more work for fully qualified men, masters were sometimes prohibited from taking more than a certain number of apprentices.[3] A long series of statutes attempted to compel masters to pay their men's wages in cash, and prohibited all payment " in goods or by way of truck."[4] In 1747 a summary remedy was provided against masters who did not pay their men's wages, and for the settlement of other differences between them.[5] The act provided that

all complaints, differences, and disputes which shall happen or arise between masters and mistresses, and servants in husbandry, who shall be hired for one year or longer, or which shall happen or arise between masters and mistresses, and artficers, handicraftsmen, miners, colliers, keelmen, pitmen, glassmen, potters, and other labourers employed for any certain time or in any other manner shall be heard and determined by one justice or justices of the peace of the county, riding, city, liberty, town corporate or place, where such master or mistress shall inhabit, although no rate or assessment of wages has been made that year by the justices of the peace of the shire, riding, or liberty, or by the mayor, bailiffs, or other head officer where such complaints shall be made, or where such differences and disputes shall arise.[6]

In the preamble to an Act of 1754, which applied the Act of 1747 to tinners within the jurisdiction of the stannary courts, it was said that the Act of 1747 had been found useful and beneficial.[7] On the other hand, a long series of statutes provided various punishments for various misdemeanours of workmen, such as leaving work in breach of contract, assaulting a master, spoiling or embezzling materials.[8]

It is clear that the state was not as yet prepared to abandon all control over the organization of industry. It was not prepared to scrap all the old rules or to abandon all the ideas which inspired those rules ; and it was prepared to make new rules to remedy obvious abuses. At the same time it is quite clear that the current of opinion was setting strongly in favour of giving greater freedom of action to the capitalist employers who were

---

[1] Above 419-421.

[2] 20 George II c. 19 § 3 ; 18 George III c. 47, and 32 George III c. 57 (parish apprentices) ; Bl. Comm. i 426.

[3] 17 George III c. 55 (hatters) ; 28 George III c. 48 (chimney sweepers) ; cp. Hammond, the Town Labourer 293-294 ; similarly the question whether a proposed remission of a duty would or would not increase unemployment was sometimes considered by Parliament, see e.g. Parlt. Hist. xv 686, 690-691.

[4] See e.g. 12 George I c. 34 § 3 ; 13 George II c. 8 § 6 ; 29 George II c. 33 § 3 ; 19 George III c. 49 § 1.

[5] 20 George II c. 19.   [6] § 1.   [7] 27 George II c. 6.

[8] See e.g. 9 George I c. 27 (shoemakers) ; 13 George II c. 8 (wool, linen, fustian, cotton, iron, and leather manufactures) ; 6 George III c. 25 (apprentices) ; 14 George III c. 44.

organizing and expanding industry and commerce.[1] In fact, as the Webbs have pointed out, " the House of Commons was not as yet influenced by any conscious theory of freedom of contract " ; [2] but, under the new conditions which were rapidly prevailing in all branches of industry, " common sense forced the Government to take the easy and obvious step of abolishing the mediæval regulations which industry had outgrown," and so " the workers were left to shift for themselves." [3] But this greater freedom allowed to masters, and to some extent to men, led inevitably to combinations of masters and men, whose aims and activities tended to prevent the regular functioning of the industrial machine, to cause breaches of the laws which regulated industry, and even to threaten the peace of the state.

Henry Fielding was not very far wrong when he asserted that the disuse of the powers of the justices to rate wages was one of the causes " of the late increase of robbers." [4] He pointed out that the proper use of these powers was beneficial both to masters and men, because it kept wages steady—not too high and not too low, and that it was therefore beneficial to the state because it promoted trade.[5] Above all it prevented those disorders which were promoted by the freedom of the workmen to exact what wages they pleased. There was little fear that the justices would use their powers to rate wages oppressively. It was not to be expected that they " would unite in a cruel and flagitious act, by which they would be liable to the condemnation of their own consciences, and to be reproached by the example of all their neighbouring counties." [6] But it was to be expected that if the men were " left to their own discretion to exact what price they please for their labour " that idleness and its concomitant evils would increase.[7] The rating of wages was in fact necessary " in order to execute the intention of the Legislature in compelling the idle to work ; for is it not the same thing to have the liberty of working or not at your own pleasure, and to have the absolute nomination of the price at which you will work ? " [8] The results of this liberty were in fact much the same in Fielding's day as in our own. The men refused to work if they

---

[1] When in 1799 the ribbon workers petitioned that the Act of 1773 relating to the silk weavers, above 472, should be applied to them, a bill to give effect to their wishes, which had passed the House of Commons, was thrown out by the House of Lords ; Lord Loughborough in the debate spoke of the mischievous tendency of the Act of 1773, Hammond, The Skilled Labourer 214.

[2] History of Trade Unionism 53. [3] Ibid 54.

[4] An Enquiry into the Causes of the late Increase of Robbers (1751) 51-61 ; in 1769 Sir John Fielding advocated an Act to give magistrates a clearer authority to settle wages, Calendar of Home Office Papers 1766-1769, 541 ; in 1773 he reported that with the help of the Act for regulating the wages of weavers, above 472, he had made a satisfactory settlement, ibid 1772-1775, 65.

[5] An Enquiry, etc. 56-61. [6] Ibid 58.
[7] Ibid 58, 61. [8] Ibid 61.

could not get " an exorbitant price for their labour." " The habit of exacting on their superiors is grown universal, and the very porters expect to receive more for their work than the salaries of above half the officers of the army amount to." [1] If, on the one hand, the practice of rating wages were re-established, the task of the magistrate would be lightened, for he would be able " to distinguish the corrigible from the incorrigible in idleness " ; for all those who refused to work at the fixed rate " may properly be deemed incorrigibly idle." [2]

We have seen that, at the beginning of the eighteenth century, the dangers inherent in tumultuous combinations of workmen, who wished to improve the conditions of their employment, had become apparent. [3] It was therefore necessary to supplement the scanty statute law and the nebulous rules of the common law as to these combinations. In fact, this was the most serious of all the industrial and commercial problems which the new organization of industry was setting to the Legislature. Its seriousness can be seen from the fact that it was the activity of these combinations which was the chief reason why the Legislature had found it necessary to make the regulations, which have just been described, for the settlement of the relations of masters and men. [4] Therefore the manner in which it dealt with this problem was likely to affect the whole future of the industries which were being organized on this new capitalistic basis. Unfortunately neither the political and social outlook of the Legislature, nor the prevailing trend of economic opinion, were calculated to produce a proper understanding of the nature of the problem, or a just and equitable solution of it. [5]

V. *The Growth of Combinations of Masters and Men.*

From the middle of the fourteenth century onwards there is authority for the principle that all persons ought to be allowed to carry on their trades freely, subject only to any restrictions or regulations which might be imposed by the common law or by statute law. The law, it was said, gave to every man the right to carry on his trade as he pleased, free from arbitrary restrictions not recognized by law, whether those restrictions were imposed by the illegal actions of officials of the local or central government, or by the lawless acts of rivals in trade. [6] This general principle of the common law was quite consistent with the

---

[1] An Enquiry, etc. 61.   [2] Ibid.
[3] Vol. vi 349.   [4] Above 471-472.
[5] As the Webbs say, History of Trade Unionism 54, the attitude of Parliament towards the workmen was, during the greater part of the eighteenth century, " one of pure perplexity quite untouched by the doctrine of freedom of contract."
[6] Below 477-478.

recognition of the need for much legal regulation of many aspects of trade in the interests of the state.[1]   And, since the state considered that it was to its interest to impose many restrictions in order to secure the honest manufacture of goods, skill in the workman, fair prices, fair wages,[2] and many other restrictions, in order to promote foreign trade,[3] this general principle of the common law tended to be comparatively unimportant in practice, as compared with the detailed regulations made by the Legislature.   Occasionally, indeed, it emerges.   It emerged, for instance, at the end of Elizabeth's reign, when the indignation aroused by wholesale grants of monopolies caused the Queen to leave the validity of those grants to be determined by the common law.[4]   But though the principle was always present to the minds of lawyers and statesmen, and though it is assumed as a premise by the Legislature,[5] it was too vague and general a principle to emerge very frequently in the courts.

At the end of the seventeenth and in the eighteenth centuries it was brought into somewhat greater prominence, first by the growth of the capitalistic organization of trade, and secondly by the decadence or abolition of many of the old restrictions on the freedom of trade, and particularly of the rules which regulated prices and wages.[6]   These two allied phenomena led to the growth of combinations of masters and men in particular trades, which were formed to regulate such matters as prices, wages, and hours of work ; and there is no doubt that this general principle of the common law led the lawyers to assert the illegality of these combinations and their activities.   But in the eighteenth century this general principle was again overshadowed by statutes which, in pursuance of the general policy of the state to maintain some regulation of trade in the interests both of masters and men, penalized these combinations in the particular trades in which they had made their appearance.[7]   It was not till the last year of the eighteenth and the first year of the nineteenth century that the growing predominance of the capitalistic organization of trade, and the increase in the number of these combinations owing to the repeal or disuse of older laws passed in the interests of the workmen, induced Parliament to pass the first general Acts, against combinations, first of men and then of masters.[8]   It was not till later in the nineteenth century, and after the growing influence of the doctrine of *laissez faire* preached by the economists had led to the repeal of this legislation against combina-

[1] Below 478-479.
[2] Vol. ii 468-469 ; vol. iv 318-319 ; vol. vi 346-349 ; above 418, 469.
[3] Vol. ii 471-472 ; vol. iv 326 seqq. ; vol. vi 323 seqq. ; above 438.
[4] Vol. iv 348-349.   [5] Below 480, 483-484.
[6] Above 466-468.   [7] Below 488-491.
[8] 39 George II c. 87 ; 39, 40 George III c. 106 ; below 496-498.

tions,[1] that any real stress was laid upon this general principle of the common law. And then, since it proved to be too vague to be satisfactory, it was soon overshadowed by new legislation which has created the modern law as to combinations and trade unions of masters and men.

Those are the conditions in which the law as to combinations of masters and men grew up. I shall consider its development in the eighteenth century under the following three heads: (1) the general theory of the common law and its application to these combinations; (2) the growth of combinations of masters and men and their statutory regulation; (3) the social and economic effects of this statutory regulation of combinations of masters and men.

(1) *The general theory of the common law and its application to combinations of masters and men.*

" At common law," says Sir William Erle,[2] " every person has individually, and the public also have collectively, a right to require that the course of trade should be kept free from unreasonable obstruction." But this freedom allowed to every man engaged in trade " is compatible with countless restraints imposed by law for the benefit of his fellow subjects individually, or of the public generally, or of himself. The right to this freedom for the capitalist and the working man is part of the right to property and personal security, and is subject to analogous restraints." [3] This general theory of the common law that all persons ought to be allowed to carry on their trades freely, subject to any restrictions or regulations which might be imposed by the law, can be traced back to a very early period in our legal history.[4] The principle that trade should be free from arbitrary restraints is implied in the clauses of Magna Carta which relate to the liberty of the subject,[5] and to trade;[6] and the mediæval judges favoured the principle, just as they favoured the principle of freedom of alienation,[7] because they were hostile to all

---

[1] 5 George IV c. 95; 6 George IV c. 129.
[2] The Law Relating to Trade Unions 6; Sir William Erle had been Chief Justice of the Common Pleas; after his retirement he was made chairman of the Commission on Trade Unions which was appointed in 1867; the book was originally written as a memorandum to guide his colleagues on that commission.
[3] Ibid 44.   [4] Ibid 10.
[5] Coke, commenting on § 29 of Magna Carta (§ 39 in the Charter of 1215) which provides that no man is to be disseised of his " liberties," gives as an instance of its infringement, a case where the Merchant Taylors Company had tried by an ordinance to infringe this principle of freedom of trade, Coke, Second Instit. 47.
[6] § 30—as to foreign merchants; vol. x 390.
[7] Vol. iii 85; Coke, commenting on the rule that conditions restricting freedom of alienation are void, says that such a condition is " against trade and traffique and bargaining and contracting between man and man," Co. Litt. 223a.

arbitrary restrictions on personal liberty,[1] or rights of property,[2] for which no legal justification could be shown.   In fact, from the mediæval period onwards, this general theory that trade ought to be free can be traced in judicial decisions and dicta ; it has, at different periods, given rise to rules and doctrines intended to safeguard it ; and, since the acts of combinations of masters and men are generally more dangerous to it than the acts of individuals, the chief, though not the only, means adopted by the common law to safeguard it has been an application of the law of conspiracy.

If we look at the number and character of the mediæval statutes which attempted to realize the moral ideals aimed at by the Legislature—honest manufacture, a just price, a fair wage, a reasonable profit,[3] it would seem at first sight to be difficult to maintain that the common law favoured freedom of trade.   But it is not really difficult to maintain this thesis if we remember that, as Sir William Erle pointed out,[4] the freedom which the common lawyers favoured was freedom from arbitrary restraints not sanctioned by the law, whether those restraints were imposed by the voluntary acts of contracting parties, or were imposed by persons acting without legal authority.   We have seen that in Henry V's reign, Hull, J., was prepared to treat a contract for a very moderate restraint of trade not merely as an illegal contract, but as a criminal offence.[5]   We have seen that in one of the Books of Assizes a case is reported in which a Lombard, who tried to enhance the price of merchandize by spreading false reports, was convicted and fined.[6]   In another of the Books of Assizes, amongst the matters as to which inquiry was to be made by an inquest of office held by the court of King's Bench, were the misdeeds of forestallers of victuals, and of merchants who " by covin and combination between themselves set, from year to year, a certain price on wool for sale in the country, so that none of them will buy or bid more than others in the purchase of wool, beyond the fixed price which they themselves have ordained, to the great impoverishment of the people." [7]   In Edward III's reign the grant to one Peachey of the sole right to sell wine in London was treated as an illegal grant, and his conduct in acting under it was made one of the articles of his impeachment.[8]   Coke com-

---

[1] Vol. ii 562 ; vol. v 348.
[2] Fortescue, De Laudibus c. 36 ; Coke, Second Instit. 63.
[3] Vol. ii 467.   [4] Above 477.
[5] Y.B. 2 Henry V Pasch. pl. 26, cited vol. ii 468 n. 3.
[6] Vol. iv 376 ; 43 Ass. pl. 38.
[7] " Item des marchants que per covin et alliance entre eux d'an en an mettent certein prise sur leins que sont a vendre en pais, issint que nul d'eux achateront ne passeront auters en l'achate de leins oustre le certein prise qu'eux mesmes ont ordeign, a grand enpoverishment de people," etc., 27 Ass. pl. 44 (p. 139).
[8] R.P. 50 Ed. III no. 3, ii 328, cited vol. iv 344 n. 6.

mented upon and emphasized all these mediæval authorities ; [1] and in this, as in other branches of legal doctrine, passed on this mediæval principle into the modern common law.

We have seen that in the sixteenth and seventeenth centuries the crime of conspiracy was enlarged and generalized by the combined efforts of the Star Chamber and the court of King's Bench.[2] It was extended to apply not only to all combinations to do acts which amounted to a crime or a tort, but also to acts which were regarded as illegal because they were contrary to public policy.[3] It is clear from the discussions in the common law courts as to the validity of monopolies, which arose at the beginning of the seventeenth century,[4] that the common law held firmly to the view that restrictions on the freedom of trade were illegal unless they could be justified by a valid local custom, or by some recognized principle of the common law ; and it is clear from the judgment of Parker, C.J., in the case of *Mitchel v. Reynolds* [5] that, at the beginning of the eighteenth century, the courts held exactly the same view. Involuntary restrictions on the freedom of trade were illegal, because they were contrary to public policy, unless they could be justified by a valid local custom or by the common law ; [6] and voluntary restrictions on the freedom of trade, that is contracts in restraint of trade, were likewise illegal because contrary to public policy,[7] unless it could be proved that they were reasonable as between the parties to them [8] and not detrimental to the public.[9] In these circumstances it was inevitable that the courts should hold that combinations of masters which were entered into in order to force down wages or force up prices, or combinations of men which were entered into in order to force up wages or diminish the length of the working day, were indictable conspiracies. These combinations attempted to effect their objects by the pressure of numbers, and so infringed the liberty of masters and men to make what contracts they pleased. The case of *R. v. Starling* [10] was a case in which a combination of masters, to wit the brewers, so to conduct their trade that the King's revenue was impoverished, was held to be a criminal conspiracy, either on the ground that it was a conspiracy to raise prices, or on the ground that it was designed to bring pressure to

---

[1] The Poulterers' Case (1610) 9 Co. Rep. at f. 56b ; the Case of Monopolies (1602) 11 Co. Rep. at ff. 87a, 88a-88b ; cp. the argument of Coke, which was accepted by the court, in the case of Davenant v. Hurdis (1598) Moore, K. B. at pp. 579-580 ; vol. iv 350-353.

[2] Vol. viii 378-379.   [3] Ibid 381-382.   [4] Vol. iv 349-353.

[5] (1711) 1 P. Wms. 181 ; see vol. viii 60-61 for an account of this case.

[6] (1711) 1 P. Wms. at pp. 188-189.

[7] Ibid at p. 192—" all contracts where there is a bare restraint of trade and no more, must be void."

[8] Ibid at pp. 186, 191-192, 193.   [9] Ibid at p. 190.

[10] (1664) 1 Sid. 174 ; S.C. 1 Keb. 650 ; cp. vol. viii 381.

bear on the government.[1] The case of *R. v. Journeymen Tailors of Cambridge*,[2] was a case in which a combination of men refused to work for less than a certain sum per day. The combination was held to be an indictable conspiracy at common law, so that the indictment need not conclude *contra formam statuti*.[3] It was only if a combination was entered into to effect some purpose permitted by law that it could be regarded as lawful. Thus a combination to take legal proceedings to enforce a law which imposed restrictions on the freedom of trade was lawful,[4] and also a combination to petition the King and Parliament to enforce or to alter the law.[5]

In the eighteenth century the principle that a combination of masters or men which interfered with the freedom of trade was a criminal conspiracy, harmonized well with the trend of economic thought which favoured the removal of restraints on the conduct of industry. In the middle of that century there had been considerable disturbance in the cotton trade.[6] Thousands had left work and had entered into combinations to raise wages. They had appointed a committee, established boxes, appointed stewards in every township to collect money to support weavers who had been ordered to strike, and had been guilty of assaulting and abusing weavers who refused to strike. Lord Mansfield, at the autumn assizes at Lancaster in 1758,

---

[1] The latter ground was the ground on which the court relied mainly, (1664) 1 Sid. 174 ; and cp. the account of this case given in the argument in R. v. Thorp (1697) 5 Mod. at p. 224, cited vol.viii 381 n. 6, and in 1 Lev. 126 ; the former ground is hinted at in the report in 1 Keb. 650, where it is said that " the very conspiracy to raise the price of pepper is punishable, or of any other merchandize."

[2] (1721) 8 Mod. 10.

[3] " The omission in not concluding this indictment *contra formam statuti* is not material, because it is for a conspiracy, which is an offence at common law. It is true, the indictment sets forth, that the defendants refused to work under such rates, which were more than enjoined by the statute . . . ; but yet these words will not bring the offence . . . to be within that statute, because it is not the denial to work except for more wages than is allowed by the statute, but it is for a conspiracy to raise their wages for which these defendants are indicted," 8 Mod. at p. 12 ; apart from the statutes, the only ground upon which a conspiracy to raise wages could be indictable was that such a conspiracy interfered with the freedom of trade ; Wright, Law of Criminal Conspiracies 55, says that " it is easy to understand how the established practice that indictments for conspiracy do not conclude *contra formam statuti* even when they are founded on statutes may have led to the impression that the criminality was independent of the statutes " ; but surely it is more natural to suppose that the established practice was founded on the law that conspiracies of this sort were illegal at common law because they interfered with the freedom of trade ; and this was the opinion of Crompton J. in Hilton v. Eckersley (1855) 6 E. and B. at p. 53, cited below 481 n. 5.

[4] " No one seems to have questioned the legality of the 1811-1813 outburst of combinations to prosecute masters who had not served an apprenticeship, or who were employing unapprenticed workmen," Webb, History of Trade Unionism 66 ; combinations for this object were only trying to enforce the law.

[5] For instances of combinations to petition the Privy Council and Parliament which were assumed to be legal, see ibid 65-66.

[6] Daniels, The Early English Cotton Industry 45-46.

adapted his charge to the grand jury to the occasion, and strongly urged to the jury the necessity of suppressing all such combinations and conspiracies on any pretence whatsoever ; gave them an account of all the attempts of the like nature that had been made at different times and in different parts of the kingdom, and told them that an active and vigilant execution of the laws in being, had always been sufficient to suppress such attempts.

He issued a warrant for the arrest of nineteen stewards appointed by the committee, and it was recommended that prosecutions should be instituted against others. In 1783, in the case of *The King v. Eccles and Others*,[1] it was held that a conspiracy to prevent a man carrying on his trade was a criminal offence. In 1796, in the case of *The King v. Mawbey*,[2] Grose, J., said *obiter* that, though an individual workman might insist on a rise in wages, " if several meet for the same purpose it is illegal, and the parties may be indicted for a conspiracy." [3] In 1855, in the case of *Hilton v. Eckersley*,[4] Crompton, J., said that all combinations which fettered the free action of masters and men were " illegal and indictable at common law." [5]

But in 1855 it had become impossible to lay down the law quite as broadly as this, since it had been enacted in 1825 [6] that the act of combining to raise or lower wages, or to affect hours of labour, was no longer to be a criminal offence. Therefore it was not true to say that all combinations of masters or men which fettered their freedom of action were indictable conspiracies. For this reason, in the case of *Hilton v. Eckersley*,[7] Lord Campbell, C.J., and the court of Exchequer Chamber held that, though the agreements entered into by members of these combinations were void, because, being in restraint of trade, they were contrary to public policy, their members had not committed illegal acts of such a kind that their commission in combination amounted to a conspiracy ; [8] and this view of the law has been approved by the

---

[1] 3 Dougl. 337—Lord Mansfield C.J. said at p. 339, " The conspiracy is to prevent Booth from working, the consequence is poverty," and he refused the motion in arrest of judgment.

[2] (1796) 6 T.R. 619.   [3] At p. 636.   [4] 6 E. and B. 47.

[5] " I think that combinations like that disclosed in the pleadings in this case [a combination of masters] were illegal and indictable at common law, as tending directly to impede and interfere with the free course of trade and manufacture. The precedents of indictments for combinations of two or more persons to raise wages, and for other offences of this nature, which were all framed on the common law and not under any of the statutes on the subject, sufficiently show what the common law was in this respect. . . . Combinations of this nature, whether on the part of workmen to increase, or of masters to lower, wages were equally illegal," 6 E. and B. at p. 53.

[6] George IV c. 129.   [7] (1855) 6 E. and B. 47.

[8] Alderson, B., delivering the judgment of the Exchequer Chamber, after holding that the contracts entered into by the combine were void, because they were in restraint of trade, said at p. 75, " we do not mean to say that they are illegal in the sense of being criminal and punishable. The case does not require us : and we think we ought not to express any opinion on that point."

House of Lords.[1]   But it should be observed that Lord Campbell, C. J., the court of Exchequer Chamber, and the House of Lords all adhered to the historic principle that trade ought to be free from all restraints not sanctioned by law, and that therefore agreements which attempted to impose those restraints were void because they were contrary to public policy.

This change in the attitude of the common law is an intelligible change having regard to the changes which had taken place in economic ideas and in the statute law relating to combinations. When *Hilton v. Eckersley* was decided, freedom of contract was supposed to be the panacea for all social ills, and the maintenance of that freedom was even said to be paramount public policy.[2] The Legislature had freed from criminal taint certain combinations to affect wages and other conditions of labour, and had repealed the older statutes which made particular combinations criminal. In these circumstances, it is not surprising to find that eminent lawyers should have denied that the formation of a combination of masters or men which interfered with the freedom of trade had ever been a criminal conspiracy at common law, and have maintained that the formation of these combinations only amounted to a criminal conspiracy if it had been made illegal by statute. This was the view of R. S. Wright (afterwards Wright, J.) in his very able book on *The Law of Criminal Conspiracies*,[3] and of Stephen, J.[4]   But it was not the view of Sir William Erle.   He maintained, as we have seen, that the common law recognized the principle of the freedom of trade subject only to restraints imposed by the law.[5]   It followed that combinations entered into with the intention of depriving persons of that freedom were indictable conspiracies at common law.   The gist of his argument is contained in the following passage from his book:[6]

Every person has a right under the law, as between him and his fellow subjects, to full freedom in disposing of his own labour or his own capital according to his will.   It follows that every other person is subject to the correlative duty arising therefrom and is prohibited from any obstruction to the fullest exercise of this right which can be made compatible with the exercise of similar rights by others.   Every act causing an obstruction to another in the exercise of the right comprised within this description—done, not in the exercise of the actor's

---

[1] Mogul Steamship Co. v. McGregor, Gow & Co. [1892] A.C. at p. 39.

[2] *Per* Jessel M.R. in Printing Co. v. Sampson (1875) L.R. 19 Eq. at p. 465; for some remarks upon this dictum see vol. viii 56.

[3] He says at p. 56 that " there is not sufficient authority for concluding that before the eighteenth century there was supposed to be any rule of common law that combinations for controlling masters or workmen were criminal, except when the combination was for some purpose punishable under a statute expressly directed against such combinations, or were for conduct punishable independently of combination."

[4] H.C.L. iii 209-210, 223-224.   [5] Above 477.

[6] The Law Relating to Trade Unions 12.

own right, but for the purpose of obstruction—would, if damage should be caused thereby to the party obstructed, be a violation of this prohibition ; and the violation of this prohibition by a single person is a wrong, to be remedied either by action or by indictment, as the case may be. It is equally a wrong whether it be done by one or by many—subject to this observation, that a combination of many to do a wrong, in a matter where the public has an interest, is a substantive offence of conspiracy. It is equally a wrong, whether the obstruction be by means of an act unlawful in itself, on the part of the party obstructing, or by means of an act not otherwise unlawful.

In my opinion the authorities prove that historically this is the correct view of the attitude of the common law.

Sir William Erle admits that numerous statutes were passed at different periods to restrain combinations to raise or lower wages ; and he says very truly that " while they were in force they tended to prevent a resort to the common law remedy for conspiracy." [1] On the other hand, Stephen was inclined to infer from the existence of these statutes that " until they were passed the conduct which they punish was not criminal." [2] In my opinion this is not a true inference from their existence for the following reason : When all aspects of trade were carefully regulated by the Legislature, in order to ensure fair wages, fair prices, and good quality in the manufactured article, it is clear that any attempt to vary the provisions made by the Legislature by a combination of masters or men was an illegal act, and that therefore a combination of persons to effect these objects was a criminal conspiracy, whether or not such combinations were directly penalized by the particular statutes. [3] The statutes passed by the Legislature show that that principle was constantly present to its mind. [4] But the statutes by which the Legislature attempted to effect these objects were, as a general rule, statutes which dealt in detail with the regulation of particular trades. They attempted to remedy abuses which had appeared in the conduct of some particular trade ; and the prohibitions which

[1] The Law Relating to Trade Unions 37.
[2] H.C.L. iii 210.   [3] Above 479-480.
[4] Thus the preamble to 12 George I c. 34 presupposes the existence of this principle ; it runs, " Whereas great numbers of weavers . . . have lately formed themselves into unlawful clubs and societies and have presumed contrary to law to enter into combinations and make by-laws or orders " ; there is a similar preamble to 36 George III c. 111 which deals with combinations of workmen employed in the manufacture of paper ; the same assumption is made in the preamble to the general combination Act of 1799, 39 George III c. 81 ; it runs, " Whereas great numbers of journeymen manufacturers and workmen in various parts of this kingdom, have, by unlawful meetings and combinations, endeavoured to obtain advance of their wages, and to effectuate other illegal purposes ; and the laws at present in force against such unlawful conduct have been found to be inadequate to the suppression thereof, whereby it is become necessary that more effectual provision should be made against such unlawful combinations " ; these preambles assume that these combinations are unlawful, and the preamble to 39 George III c. 81 does not say that the statutes referred to have made these combinations illegal —it assumes that they have been passed to enforce an existing rule.

they enact against combinations in that trade are merely a part of the various provisions which they make for its regulation.[1]   For instance, a statute of Edward VI's reign, which penalized combinations of producers to raise the price of victuals, penalized also combinations of workmen to raise their wages.[2]   Similarly, the eighteenth-century statutes, which were directed against combinations of men,[3] were statutes which dealt with particular trades ; and the clauses directed against combinations were part of a larger scheme for the regulation of the particular trade.[4]   I think, therefore, that these statutes, and also the later more general statutes as to combinations, presuppose, as Sir William Erle suggests, the general principle of the common law that trade ought to be free from restraints unless those restraints had been imposed by law ; and that they enforce that principle, first in the case of particular trades, and later in the case of all trades, because it appeared that better provisions for its enforcement were necessary by reason of the prevalence of combinations to raise or lower wages or to alter hours of labour, which infringed it.

During the course of the eighteenth century, many of the old rules directed to securing fair wages, fair prices, and good quality in the manufactured article were rapidly becoming decadent.[5] More and more industry was coming to be organized on a capitalistic basis ; and the capitalists were demanding to be freed from obsolete restrictions.   Wages were coming to be regulated simply by the law of supply and demand.   It is not surprising, therefore, that, as this new organization of industry gained ground, and as the old regulations which protected the workman decayed, combinations of these workmen should be formed in order to compel employers to concede that fair wage which the older legislation had endeavoured to compel them to give.   Nor is it surprising that combinations of employers should also be formed to regulate prices, and to resist the demands of their workmen.   It was these new conditions which produced the rise of the modern trade unions and combinations of masters on the one hand, and, on the other hand, the enactment of more general and more stringent laws against these combinations of masters and men, which were attempting to regulate wages and hours of work.   These general combination laws, which were passed in the last year of the eighteenth and the first year of the nineteenth century,[6] did to a large extent render unnecessary recourse to the

---

[1] Below 491.   [2] 2, 3 Edward VI c. 15.
[3] Before the statute of 1800, 39, 40 George III c. 106, no eighteenth-century statute contained a clause directed against combinations of masters, below 488.
[4] Below 488-491.   [5] Above 419-421, 467-469, 472.
[6] 39 George III c. 81 dealt with combinations of men only ; it was replaced by 39, 40 George III c. 106 ; § 17 of the latter act penalized combinations of masters to reduce wages, to alter hours of labour, or to increase the quantity of work.

common law principle that trade ought to be free. It was not till these and the earlier statutes against combinations were repealed, and replaced by the new legislation of 1824 [1] and 1825,[2] that it was necessary to appeal to it. But, when the appeal was made to this principle, it was called upon to operate in an environment wholly different from that in which it had originated. It had originated at a time when the conduct of all branches of trade was carefully regulated in order to safeguard the interests of masters, of men, and of the state. It was now called upon to settle the disputes which arose under a system of industry wholly organized on a capitalistic system, and dominated by the prevailing economic theory of *laissez faire*. It is not surprising that it failed under these new conditions to settle satisfactorily the relations of capital and labour, and that it was superseded by a wholly new series of statutory regulations which begin in 1871.[3]

But, though for very different reasons, at different periods in our legal history, the principle of the common law that trade ought to be free has been overshadowed by statutory limitations and exemptions, it would be a mistake to suppose that it can be neglected. To some extent in the mediæval period,[4] and to a large extent in the sixteenth and seventeenth centuries,[5] it helped to prevent the imposition upon traders of arbitrary restraints for which no legal authority could be shown. In the eighteenth and early nineteenth centuries it supplied the background of principle which inspired the legislation against combinations of masters and men.[6] Later in the nineteenth century it helped to remedy some of the worst consequences of that permission to combine which the Legislature had, under the influence of the classical economists, granted without adequate consideration, and without any real understanding of the nature of the social and economic problems to which the new conditions of industry had given rise.

But we must turn back to the eighteenth century, and examine the causes of the growth of these combinations of masters and men, and the manner in which they were dealt with by the Legislature, during the period of transition through which the organization of industry was passing in that century. We shall see that it is to this century of transition that we must look for the beginnings of the conditions in which the modern law as to these combinations originated.

[1] 5 George IV c. 95.
[3] Stephen, H.C.L. iii 222-227.
[5] Above 479.

[2] 6 George IV c. 129.
[4] Above 478.
[6] Above 483 and n. 4 ; below 488.

(2) *The growth of combinations of masters and men and their statutory regulation.*

Combinations of masters and men in particular trades originate naturally, and are naturally suspect both by the public at large and by the government ; for, as Adam Smith says,[1] " people of the same trade seldom meet together, even for merriment and diversion, but the conversation ends in a conspiracy against the public, or in some contrivance to raise prices." He added that it was impossible to prevent such meetings by law ; and gave wise counsel when he said that " though the law cannot hinder people of the same trade from sometimes assembling together, it ought to do nothing to facilitate such assemblies ; much less to render them necessary." Unfortunately this wise counsel was not followed. The growth of the capitalistic organization of industry and of the factory system, the partial application which was made by the Legislature of Adam Smith's own theories as to the beneficial effect of unrestricted liberty, and the dangers to life and property and public order which were caused by the activities of combinations of men, produced legislation which succeeded indeed in impeding the growth and activities of those combinations, but not in putting an end to them, because the policy pursued by the Legislature had the effect of rendering them necessary to the workmen.

During the eighteenth century many combinations in different trades were formed.[2] But it was the combinations of men which attracted the most attention. The reason for this phenomenon Adam Smith explains as follows : [3]

We rarely hear of the combinations of masters, though frequently of those of workmen. But whoever imagines, upon this account, that masters rarely combine, is as ignorant of the world as of the subject. Masters are always and everywhere in a sort of tacit, but constant and uniform combination, not to raise the wages of labour above their actual rate. To violate this combination is everywhere a most unpopular action, and a sort of reproach to a master among his neighbours and equals. We seldom, indeed, hear of this combination, because it is the usual, and one may say, the natural state of things which nobody ever hears of. Masters too sometimes enter into particular combinations to sink the wages of labour even below this rate. These are always conducted with the utmost silence and secrecy, till the moment of

[1] Wealth of Nations (Cannan's ed.) i 130.

[2] For combinations of carpenters and cabinet-makers see Walpole, Letters (ed. Toynbee) v 220, 229 ; for a combination of tailors in 1764 and 1768 see Calendar of Home Office Papers 1760-1765, 429-430, ibid 1766-1769, 338 ; for a combination of pit-men in 1765 see ibid 599 ; in 1769 the London and Dublin weavers combined to get higher wages which led to disturbances, ibid 509, 525, 540-541 ; Fielding recommended an Act to give the magistrates further powers to settle wages, ibid 541—a course followed with satisfactory results in 1773, above 474 n. 4 ; Calendar of Home Office Papers 1773-1775 65.

[3] Wealth of Nations (Cannan's ed.) i 68-69.

execution, and when the workmen yield, as they sometimes do, without resistance, though severely felt by them, they are never heard of by other people. Such combinations, however, are frequently resisted by a contrary defensive combination of the workmen; who sometimes too, without any provocation of this kind, combine of their own accord to raise the price of their labour. Their usual pretences [1] are, sometimes the high price of provisions; sometimes the great profit which their masters make by their work. But whether their combinations be offensive or defensive they are always abundantly heard of. In order to bring the point to a speedy decision, they have always recourse to the loudest clamour, and sometimes to the most shocking violence and outrage. They are desperate, and act with the folly and extravagance of desperate men, who must either starve or frighten their masters into an immediate compliance with their demands. The masters upon these occasions are just as clamorous upon the other side, and never cease to call aloud for the assistance of the civil magistrate, and the rigorous execution of those laws which have been enacted with so much severity against the combinations of servants, labourers, and journeymen.

There is no doubt that Adam Smith is right in his assertion that combinations of masters were formed, and in the reasons which he gave for the fact that comparatively little was heard of them.[2] Two instances of combinations of masters are supplied by the coal trade. In 1765 the coal-owners of the Tyne and Wear agreed that no coal-owner should hire another's men, unless the men produced a certificate of leave from their last master.[3] That meant that the men were in effect deprived of their freedom to choose their employment; and for that reason it was probably an illegal combination.[4] In 1773 there was a combination of London publicans to raise the price of beer, which Sir John Fielding considered to be illegal.[5] From the year 1786, and probably earlier, a combination of masters entered into an agreement known as "The Newcastle Vend." This agreement fixed the output of the pits, and the proportion which each pit should supply.[6] There is no doubt that it was an illegal combination because it deprived the parties to it of their freedom to carry on their trade as they pleased.[7]

All these combinations, whether of masters or of men, were illegal, because they were criminal conspiracies by the common

[1] Dr. Cannan points out that the word "pretence" is used here and elsewhere by Adam Smith "without the implication of falsity now attached to it"; and that it means simply something put forward.

[2] See Lipson, Economic History of England iii 396 n. 4; Mr. Lipson also points out that it was difficult for workmen to get a verdict against their employers, because the employers "could transfer the suit to the central courts, and involve their opponents in legal expenses entirely beyond their capacity to support."

[3] Hammond, The Skilled Labourer 13.

[4] Above 481.

[5] Calendar of Home Office Papers, 1773-1775 9, 11-12, 13-14.

[6] Hammond, The Skilled Labourer 24-25.

[7] Proceedings were begun against the members of the "vend" in 1794, but they were dropped, ibid 25 n. 1; there is no doubt about its illegality, above 481.

law.   In the case of *R. v. Hammond and Webb*,[1] which was a case
of an indictment for conspiracy against shoemakers who had
combined to raise their wages, it appeared that the shoemakers
had been encouraged to make their demands by the fact that
some of the masters had given higher wages than were usual in
the trade ; and this fact caused Lord Kenyon, C.J., to say [2]
that " masters should be cautious of conducting themselves in
that way, as they were as liable to an indictment for conspiracy
as the journeymen."   There is, I think, no doubt that this
was a correct statement of the rule of the common law.   Therefore I do not think that Adam Smith is right when he insinuates
that the common law did not treat the masters in the same way as
it treated the men.   But there is no doubt that he is right if he
intended, as he probably did intend, to refer to the statute law.[3]
None of the statutes passed during the eighteenth century to
suppress combinations of men penalized directly a combination
of masters.   It is true that a statute of 1720 [4] imposed a fine
on a master who paid a journeyman tailor higher wages than those
fixed by the Act ; and that a statute of 1725 imposed a penalty
on masters who paid their men in goods " or by way of truck." [5]
It is true that a combination to pay higher wages than those
fixed by the Act, or to pay by way of truck, would therefore be
criminal conspiracies ; but we have seen that such acts were
regarded as a criminal conspiracy at common law and not an
offence under the Acts.[6]   The Acts merely supplied the element
of illegality which was needed to make a combination to do the
things proscribed by them criminal conspiracies at common law.
The only Act which penalized directly a combination, other than
a combination of men, was an Act of 1788 which made it a
criminal offence for more than five persons to combine for the
purpose of purchasing coal for sale, or for making regulations
for carrying on the coal trade.[7]

On the other hand, a series of statutes was passed to suppress combinations of men in different trades.   In 1720 combinations of journeymen tailors in London " for advancing their
wages or for lessening their usual hours of work " were declared
to be illegal, and punishable with imprisonment for a period not
exceeding two months.[8]   Other provisions of the Act fixed the
hours of work and rates of wages,[9] provided for the recovery of

---

[1] (1799) 2 Esp. 719.   [2] At p. 720.
[3] Wealth of Nations i 143-144.   [4] 7 George I St. 1 c. 13 § 7.
[5] 12 George I c. 34 § 4.   [6] Above 480.
[7] 28 George III c. 53 § 2 ; the section recites that coal buyers had formed
themselves into a society which held private meetings, and made regulations for
carrying on the coal trade " which regulations may have a tendency to prevent the
said trade from being free and open."
[8] 7 George I St. 1 c. 13 § 1.
[9] § 2 ; further provisions were made by 8 George III c. 17 §§ 1, 4, 6.

these wages by summary proceedings before justices of the peace,[1] gave power to quarter sessions to alter the rate of wages and hours of work,[2] and prescribed penalties for masters who gave or workmen who took higher wages than those fixed by the Act.[3] In 1725 combinations of wool combers and weavers, of combers of jersey and wool, of frameworker knitters and makers of stockings, were declared to be illegal, and punishable with imprisonment for a period not exceeding three months.[4] Other clauses of the act provided penalties for spoiling work,[5] quitting work in breach of contract,[6] and assaulting or threatening masters.[7] Justices of the peace were given power to enforce the payment of wages,[8] and payment of wages by way of truck was prohibited.[9] In 1749 the provisions of the Act of 1725 as to the combinations of the workmen mentioned in that Act were extended to a number of other industries.[10] The Act also contained provisions dealing with various abuses and frauds committed by workmen in these industries.[11] We have seen that in 1773 provision was made for the regulation of the wages of persons employed in the weaving of silk.[12] Masters or workmen who asked or took more or less wages than those fixed were made liable, the masters to a fine of £50, and the workmen to a fine of 40s. or to imprisonment if the fine were not paid.[13] The same penalties were provided for workmen who entered into combinations to raise wages, and who, for this purpose, persuaded workmen to quit their employers, or who assembled in any numbers beyond ten in order to frame or deliver petitions as to wages, except petitions to quarter sessions.[14] Another clause of the Act prohibited silk weavers from having in their service more than two apprentices.[15] In 1777 combinations of journeymen hatters were penalized,[16] together with various other offences such as spoiling goods or quitting work in breach of contract.[17] The Act also provided that a master must employ one journeyman hatter for every apprentice which he took, provided that a sufficient number of journeymen hatters who had

---

[1] § 4.   [2] § 5.

[3] § 7 ; more stringent provisions were made by 8 George III c. 17 §§ 2 and 7.

[4] 12 George I c. 34 §§ 1 and 8 ; for the history of the tumults which preceded the Act, and led to its enactment, see Lipson, Economic History of England iii 392-395.

[5] § 2.   [6] 2.   [7] § 6.   [8] § 3.   [9] § 4.

[10] 22 George II c. 27 § 12 ; the industries to which the Act of 1725 was extended were : journeymen dyers, journeymen hot pressers, all persons employed in the wool manufacture, journeymen servants, workmen and labourers employed in the making of felts or hats, and in the manufactures of silk, mohair, furs, hemp, flax, linen, cotton, fustian, iron and leather, or any manufactures made up of those materials.

[11] §§ 1, 2, 7.   [12] 13 George III c. 68 ; above 472.

[13] §§ 2 and 3.

[14] § 3 ; this would seem to show that combinations to present petitions to the King or to Parliament were regarded as legal, above 480 and n. 5.

[15] § 7.   [16] 17 George III c. 55 §§ 3 and 4.   [17] § 3.

served as apprentices were available.[1] In 1796 combinations of persons employed in the manufacture of paper were prohibited.[2] The Act also made regulations as to hours of work.[3]

The reasons why these Acts dealt only with combinations of men are obvious. It was much less possible, as Adam Smith pointed out,[4] to keep combinations of a large number of men secret than combinations of a comparatively small number of masters. The manner in which they sought to attain their ends was often the commission of obviously illegal acts such as riots, assaults, murders, and the destruction of property.[5] The action of large numbers of men acting in concert is always dangerous to the peace of the state,[6] and more especially in the eighteenth century, when the police force was hopelessly inadequate.[7] Parliament had learned these truths by bitter experience. Let us look at one or two illustrations taken from a couple of years in the second half of the eighteenth century. In 1767-1768 a bad harvest and a severe winter caused many riotous strikes in London.

Four thousand sailors on board the merchant ships in the Thames mutinied for higher wages, and stopped by force all outward bound ships which were preparing to sail. The watermen of the Thames, the journeymen hatters, the journeymen tailors, the glass grinders, were soon on strike, and during two or three years London witnessed scenes of riot that could hardly have been surpassed in Connaught or the Highlands. At Wapping and Stepney the coal heavers, who were chiefly Irish, were for more than a year at war with the masters of the coal ships. They boarded the ships and compelled the sailors to cease work. They kept guard at every landing place to prevent them from receiving supplies of provisions . . . and fought bloody battles with them in the streets. . . . Riots not less serious were caused by the Spitalfields weavers, who were accustomed during 1767 and the three following years to range the streets disguised and armed, breaking into the shops of weavers who refused to strike, destroying their looms and cutting their work in pieces.[8]

---

[1] § 2.   [2] 36 George III c. 111 §§ 1, 2, 4, 5.
[3] § 3.   [4] Above 486-487.
[5] For cases where these illegal means were employed see Lipson, Economic History of England iii 393, 394-395, 402.
[6] This fact is illustrated by a letter to the earl of Northumberland, with reference to a strike of coal-miners against a combination of masters, which had attempted to alter their conditions of employment, cited Hammond, The Skilled Labourer 14-15. The writer explains that it is impossible to take proceedings under 20 George II c. 19, which empowered a justice to imprison workmen who had misconducted themselves, where there was a general combination of thousands of men—" in the first place it is difficult to be executed as to seizing the men, and even if they should not make a formidable resistance which scarce can be presumed, a few only can be taken . . . so the punishment of probably twenty or forty by a month's confinement in a house of correction, does not carry with it the least appearance of terror, so as to induce the remaining part of so large a number to submit, and those men that should be so confined would be treated as martyrs for the good cause, and be supported and caressed, and at the end of the time brought home in triumph, so no good effect would arise " ; cp. vol. viii 382-384.
[7] Vol. x 144.   [8] Lecky, History of England iii 324-325.

Such events as these made it necessary and right that the Legislature should take these special precautions against combinations of men in those trades in which those precautions had been found to be necessary.

But it should be observed that all these Acts which penalize combinations of men differ, as the Webbs have pointed out,[1] from the later general combination Acts of 1799 and 1800. They were passed primarily to regulate industry; and the clauses dealing with combinations were incidental to this main purpose, which, as we have seen, is contained in the other clauses which all these Acts contain.[2]

It was assumed to be the business of Parliament and the law courts to regulate the conditions of labour; and combinations could, no more than individuals, be permitted to interfere in disputes for which a legal remedy was provided. The object primarily aimed at by the statutes was not the prohibition of combinations, but the fixing of wages, the prevention of embezzlement or damage, the enforcement of the contract of service, and the proper arrangements for apprenticeship.[3]

But in spite of these statutes, combinations of men became more frequent and more permanent as the eighteenth century progressed.[4] The reason was that, under the influence of the capitalistic organization of industry, of the rise of the factory system, and of the new economic doctrines which condemned the old regulations of and restrictions on the conduct of industry, Parliament was gradually ceasing to regulate the relations of masters and men.[5] We have seen that the repeal in 1757 of the Act passed in 1756, which provided for the settlement of the wages of weavers by the justices of the peace, shows that Parliament was exchanging " its policy of mediæval protection for one of administrative nihilism."[6] Therefore the workers were left to shift for themselves. They were obliged to combine in self-defence, so that Parliament had done exactly what Adam Smith had said that it ought not to do;[7] it had rendered these combinations necessary. The result was that they became so numerous and powerful that it was quite impossible to suppress them. The men began to form permanent trade unions, and the masters naturally formed combinations to resist their demands.[8]

It has been proved that we must look for the origins of these

[1] History of Trade Unionism 65.   [2] Above 488-490.
[3] History of Trade Unionism 65.
[4] " The laws against combinations were powerless to check the development of trade unionism. . . . In spite of common law and statute law trade unionism persisted throughout the eighteenth century, and bequeathed its traditions to the unions of the nineteenth century," Lipson, Economic History of England iii 396-397.
[5] Ibid 386-387.
[6] Webb, History of Trade Unionism 51; above 471-472.   [7] Above 486.
[8] For an instance of a union of masters which originated in this way see Lipson, Economic History of England iii 408.

permanent trade unions of men, not to the mediæval gilds, nor to the friendly societies of the seventeenth and eighteenth centuries, but to the fact that the workmen found it necessary to combine in order to secure that protection from oppression which had once been given by the rules of law.[1]

The craft gilds belong to a wholly different order of commercial and political conditions. They were bodies which controlled the industry in the interests of the masters, the men, and the community. As the Webbs point out,[2]

the powers and duties of the medieval gild have been broken up and dispersed. The friendly society and the trade union, the capitalist syndicate and the employers' association, the factory inspector and the poor law relieving officer, the school attendance officer and the municipal officers who look after adulteration and inspect our weights and measures—all these persons and institutions might, with equal justice, be put forward as the successors of the craft gild.

It is true that the journeymen's gilds, which appeared in the fourteenth, fifteenth, and sixteenth centuries, have a distinct resemblance to trade unions of men.[3] They were composed only of workmen ; they were formed to improve the conditions of labour ; and their activities, like the activities of the modern trade unions, were the occasion for the enactment of the earliest combination Act in 1548.[4] But, though these gilds have points of resemblance to the modern trade unions, it is impossible to regard them as their direct ancestors, because they never became permanent, and so had no continuous history. That they never became permanent was due partly to the fact that the state succeeded to a large extent in suppressing them, and partly to the fact that the Legislature still attempted with some success to adjust fairly the relations between masters and men ; but mainly to the fact that at that time the line of cleavage between masters and men was not as yet clear cut. " So long as it was possible for a certain number of journeymen to become masters, a permanent and efficient association was out of the question. The leaders of the journeymen with greater intelligence and capacity than their fellows would constantly be absorbed in the higher grades of fellowship." [5]

Nor is it possible to see in the friendly societies, which sprang up in the seventeenth and eighteenth centuries, the direct ancestors of the trade unions.[6] It is true that these societies

---

[1] Lipson, Economic History of England iii 386-387.
[2] History of Trade Unionism 18-19.
[3] Lipson, Economic History of England i 363-364, iii 388.
[4] 2, 3 Edward VI c. 15 ; vol. iv 382.
[5] Lipson, Economic History of England i 363-364 ; the very different conditions which prevailed in the eighteenth century were the causes which made the rise of the modern trade union possible, ibid ii 55, cited below 495.
[6] See ibid iii 391 for early instances of the formation of these societies.

very often combined the activities of a trade union and a friendly society. Thus the " ostensible purpose " of the west country weavers' unions of the eighteenth century " was to serve as benefit clubs for the relief of the sick " ; [1] and the wool-combers' unions, which in the eighteenth century were spread all over the country, originated in friendly societies.[2] But the law drew a hard and fast line between the friendly society and the trade union. The former was a legal, the latter an illegal, combination. The Legislature tried to suppress the former and to encourage the latter.

In 1793 these friendly societies, which were then very numerous [3] were regulated and given various privileges.[4] Any number of persons were allowed to form a society, to raise a fund for their mutual benefit, and to make rules enforceable by fines.[5] These rules must be approved by quarter sessions, and alterations of the rules must be similarly approved.[6] The societies could appoint officers and committees, and the officers, to whom the money of the society was entrusted, could be required to enter into a bond for the faithful execution of their office.[7] The officers must invest the surplus monies of the society and must render accounts.[8] If they neglected these duties the treasurer or trustees of the society could take proceedings in the court of Chancery.[9] For the conduct of these proceedings no fees were to be payable to any officer of the court, counsel were to be assigned to conduct them, who were to do the work gratuitously, and no stamp duties were to be payable.[10] If an officer of the society died insolvent the society was to have a preferential claim against any money in the hands of his executors.[11] The property of these societies was to be vested in their treasurers or trustees, who could bring and defend actions on their behalf.[12] The purposes of the society must be set forth in their rules.[13] No resolution to dissolve it, so long as any of its purposes could be carried into effect, could be made without the consent of five-sixths of the members, and of all persons then in receipt of benefit ; nor could its funds be distributed amongst its members, otherwise in accordance with its purposes, without the same consents.[14] The justices of the peace were given power to determine summarily and finally disputes between members ; [15] and, if the rules directed that matters in dispute were to be referred to arbitration, the decision of the arbitrator was to be final.[16] Members of such

[1] Lipson, Economic History of England iii 392.   [2] Ibid 398.
[3] " Near the end of the eighteenth century London contained six hundred friendly societies, Sheffield fifty-two, Lancaster eighteen, Carlisle six," Lipson, op. cit. iii 391-392.
[4] 33 George III c. 54.   [5] § 1.   [6] §§ 2 and 3.   [7] § 4.
[8] §§ 6-8.   [9] § 8.   [10] § 9.   [11] § 10.   [12] § 11.
[13] § 12.   [14] § 12.   [15] § 15.   [16] § 16.

societies were not to be removable till they became chargeable
to the parish where they had come to reside ;[1] but neither
residence under this Act, nor the payment of rates by a person
so resident, nor service with such a person, was to confer a settlement.[2]   From the first, therefore, the law had put friendly
societies and other combinations of workmen into two separate
legal categories ; and their separation was emphasized by the
very different manner in which they were treated by the Legislature.   It is for these reasons that friendly societies and trade
unions are quite distinct entities in modern law.

Thus neither the craft gilds, nor the journeymen's gilds,
nor the friendly societies can be regarded as the direct ancestors
of the modern trade unions.   These trade unions were really
new combinations, which originated in the new industrial conditions which were arising in the eighteenth century.   They were
called into existence by the repeal or disuse of the old laws which
regulated the relations of master and workman.   When these
laws were repealed or ceased to be enforced, and when the workmen failed to secure their enforcement the men,

in many instances took the matter into their own hands and endeavoured to secure by trade union regulations, what had once been
prescribed by law.   In this respect, and in this respect only, do we
find any trace of the gild in the trade union.[3]

Since it was the new organization of industry, and the new
economic ideas which came in its train, which created the need
to form these permanent combinations, it is not surprising to find
that they first begin to appear at the close of the seventeenth
century.

In the early years of the eighteenth century we find isolated complaints of combinations 'lately entered into' by the skilled workers
in certain trades.   As the century progresses we watch the gradual
multiplication of these complaints, met by counter-accusations presented
by organized bodies of workmen.   From the middle of the century
the Journals of the House of Commons abound in petitions and counter-
petitions revealing the existence of journeymen's associations in most
of the skilled trades.   And finally, we may infer the wide extension
of the movement from the steady multiplication of the Acts against
combinations in particular industries, and their culmination in the
comprehensive statute of 1799 forbidding all combinations whatsoever.[4]

It was the spread of the capitalistic organization of industry
rather than the factory system which caused, because it created,
the needs for, these permanent trade unions.[5]   But there is no
doubt that the introduction and growth of the factory system
enormously accelerated their progress.   " The massing together

[1] § 17.   [2] §§ 22-24.
[3] Webb, History of Trade Unionism 21.   [4] Ibid 22.   [5] Ibid 26.

in factories of regiments of men all engaged in the same trade facilitated and promoted the formation of journeymen's trade societies." [1]

The causes which made for the growth of these permanent unions of men were gathering strength all through the eighteenth century. Mr. Lipson points out that,[2]

employers and employés were divided by a barrier of wealth and social status. . . . Dean Tucker wrote in a strain which we are more apt to associate with the nineteenth than with the eighteenth century : " as the master is placed so high above the condition of the journeyman, both their conditions approach much nearer to that of planter and slave in our American colonies than might be expected in such a country as England." The master is " tempted by his situation to be proud and over-bearing, to consider his people as the scum of the earth, whom he has a right to squeeze whenever he can." The journeymen are as equally tempted " to get as much wages and to do as little for it as they possibly can," and to look upon their master " as the common enemy with whom no faith is to be kept." The motives to industry, frugality, and sobriety are all subverted by this one consideration, viz. that they shall always be chained to the same oar and never be but journeymen.

But during the first three-quarters of the century these unions appeared chiefly amongst the skilled artisans.

It is not among the farm servants, miners, or general labourers, ill-paid and ill-treated as these often were, that the early trade unions arose. We do not even hear of ephemeral combinations among them, and only very occasionally of transient strikes. The formation of independent associations to resist the will of employers requires the possession of a certain degree of independence and strength of character. Thus we find the earliest trade unions arising among journeymen whose skilled standard of life had been for centuries encouraged and protected by legal or customary regulations as to apprenticeship, and by the limitation of their numbers which the high premiums and other conditions must have involved. It is often assumed that trade unionism arose as a protest against intolerable oppression. This was not so. . . . The tailors of London and Westminster united, at the very beginning of the eighteenth century, not to resist any reduction of their customary earnings, but to wring from their employers, better wages and shorter hours of labour. The few survivors of the hand-wool combers still cherish the tradition of the eighteenth century, when they styled themselves " gentlemen wool combers," refused to drink with other operatives, and were strong enough to give " laws to their masters." The very superior mill-wrights, whose exclusive trade clubs preceded any general organization of the engineering trade, had for " their everyday garb " a " long frock coat and tall hat." And the curriers, hatters, wool staplers, shipwrights, brushmakers, basket-makers, and calico-printers, who furnish prominent instances of eighteenth-century trade unionism, all earned relatively high wages, and long maintained a very effectual resistance to the encroachments of their employers.[3]

[1] Webb, History of Trade Unionism 41.
[2] Economic History of England ij 55.
[3] Webb, History of Trade Unionism 44-45.

But the abolition of the laws which aimed at securing fair wages for the workmen,[1] the decadence of the laws as to apprenticeship which prevented the flooding of the labour market by unskilled labour,[2] the application of Adam Smith's ideas (by which even Burke was deluded) that all attempts to regulate wages and conditions of labour were harmful and useless,[3] and the rapid spread of the factory system, tended to give all classes of labourers a solidarity, which made for the growth of very much larger combinations of men. All the reasons which had induced the Legislature to forbid combinations of men in particular trades [4] applied with greater force to these large combinations which had their affiliations all over England ; and these reasons were reinforced by the fear that these combinations were inspired by French revolutionary principles.[5] "The French Revolution had transformed the minds of the ruling classes, and the Industrial Revolution had convulsed the world of the working classes." [6] These were the causes which led to the passing of the first general combination Act in 1799,[7] and they account for the character of its provisions.

The history of the enactment of this statute is as follows : In April 1799, the master millwrights addressed a petition to the House of Commons, which complained of a dangerous combination amongst their men, and of the inadequacy of the existing laws to suppress its activities, and asked for legislation. A bill was introduced and passed the House of Commons, but it was dropped in the Lords, because a more comprehensive bill dealing with all combinations had been introduced by Pitt. This bill, which was modelled on the Act of 1796 dealing with combinations in the paper trade,[8] became law only twenty-four days after its introduction in the House of Commons.[9] In outline its provisions were as follows :

All contracts made between workmen for obtaining an advance of wages, or decreasing their hours of work, or the quantity

---

[1] Above 491.   [2] Above 419-421.

[3] Hammond, The Town Labourer 196-200, citing Burke, Thoughts and Details on Scarcity (1795).

[4] Above 488-490.

[5] " We have only to recall the key in which Burke himself wrote before 1789 to appreciate the depth of the change in upper class thinking that followed the French Revolution. ' When popular discontents have been very prevalent,' he wrote in 1770, ' it may well be affirmed and supported, that there has been generally something found amiss in the constitution or in the conduct of government. The people have no interest in disorder. When they do wrong it is their error and not their crime.' . . . After the French Revolution the tone was very different. The poorer classes no longer seemed a passive power : they were dreaded as a Leviathan that was fast learning his strength," Hammond, The Town Labourer 93-94.

[6] Ibid 94.   [7] 39 George III c. 81.

[8] 36 George III c. 111 ; above 490.

[9] Hammond, The Town Labourer 115-124 ; Webb, History of Trade Unionism 69-70.

of their work, were declared to be illegal;[1] and the formation of such a contract was made a criminal offence punishable with imprisonment.[2] It was also made a criminal offence for members of such a combination to induce others not to take employment, or to leave their employment, or to hinder masters from hiring what workmen they pleased.[3] Attendance at, or inducing others to attend at, meetings held for the purpose of entering into or maintaining these combinations; or subscribing to, or collecting money from workmen or others for the furtherance of, these combinations, were also made criminal offences.[4] Contributions made for any of the purposes prohibited by the Act were to be divided amongst the subscribers within three months; and, if not so divided, they were to be forfeited.[5] Treasurers and others who had these monies in their hands were compelled to answer on oath to any information preferred against them in a court of equity in the name of the attorney-general.[6] Offenders against the Act could be compelled to give evidence; but if so compelled they were not to be liable to any of the penalties of the Act.[7] Appeals from a conviction could be made to quarter sessions;[8] but its decision was final,[9] and the proceedings were not to be removed into the King's Bench by writ of certiorari.[10] Existing legislation as to combinations of manufacturers or journeymen or workmen, as to the powers of the justices to settle disputes between masters and men, and to settle rates of wages, was not to be affected by the Act;[11] nor was the Act to empower masters to employ men contrary to the provisions of any existing Act.[12]

In the following year many petitions protesting against the Act were presented from all parts of the country. Consequently the whole question was reconsidered;[13] and the result of this reconsideration was the Act of 1800,[14] which repealed the Act of 1799. The main provisions of the Act of 1799 were re-enacted; but there were some important amendments which were due to the numerous petitions which had been presented against it.[15] Offenders were to be tried, not by a single justice, but by two justices;[16] and justices who were masters in the particular trade in reference to which an offence was alleged to be committed, were disabled from acting.[17] Combinations between masters or other persons for reducing wages, altering hours of work, or

---

[1] 39 George III c. 81 § 1.   [2] § 2.   [3] § 3.
[4] §§ 4 and 5.   [5] § 6.   [6] § 7.   [7] § 9.
[8] § 13.   [9] § 14.   [10] § 13.   [11] § 15.   [12] § 16.
[13] Hammond, The Town Labourer 125-126; Webb, History of Trade Unionism 70-71.
[14] 39, 40 George III c. 106.
[15] Stephen is not quite accurate when he says, H.C.L. iii 206-207, that " there was hardly any substantial difference between the two Acts."
[16] § 5.   [17] § 16.

increasing the quantity of work, were made offences : [1] and provision was made for settling disputes between masters and men by arbitration.[2] On the other hand, it was provided that, though masters must not employ workmen contrary to any existing Acts, a justice of the peace could license such employment if the workmen in any trade refused to work for reasonable wages,[3] and in certain other events set out in the Act.[4]

These Acts are, as we have seen, very different in their character from the earlier combination Acts which applied to particular trades. The prohibition of combinations is not part of a general scheme for the regulation of particular industries. It is a general prohibition ; and so far was it from being part of a scheme for the regulation of industry, that the need for this general prohibition was caused by the repeal or decadence of the old regulations, and the failure of Parliament to put any new regulations in their place.[5] In fact these Acts show that Parliament had wholly failed to appreciate the reasons for the rise of these large and permanent combinations of men.[6] Though this legislation, like the earlier legislation, impeded the growth and hampered the activities of these combinations, it did not succeed in suppressing them, and it did succeed in embittering the relations of masters and men. We shall now see that the main reason why Parliament wholly failed to regulate satisfactorily these relations was the influence of the predominant economic doctrine of *laissez faire*, which the masters had deduced from Adam Smith's teaching. That influence prevented Parliament from appreciating the fact that, in addition to the merely negative policy of repealing the old regulations, a positive policy was needed which would have adapted the spirit of the old regulations to the new industrial conditions. In 1703 the coal heavers had petitioned that they might be incorporated under the direction of a governor, rulers, and assistants —pointing out that Elizabeth had incorporated " several inferior bodies of labourers of the like nature to the great ease and good government of the subject." [7] If this policy had been pursued, it would have been very much more possible, through incorporated bodies of workmen, to have regulated the relations of capital and labour peacefully and equitably. Its rejection made a peaceful and equitable solution of these relations impossible.

[1] § 17.   [2] § 18.   [3] § 15.
[4] A refusal " to work for any particular person or persons, or to work with any particular persons," or if the workmen " by refusing to work for any cause whatsoever, or by misconducting themselves when employed to work, in any manner impede or obstruct the ordinary course of any manufacture, trade or business, or endeavour to injure the person or persons carrying on the same."
[5] Above 491.   [6] Above 494-496.
[7] S.P. Dom. 1703-1704, 360.

(3) *The social and economic effects of this statutory regulation of
combinations of masters and men.*

During the greater part of the eighteenth century the Legislature had not abandoned the attempt to settle on an equitable
basis the relations of masters and men.   But, with the spread of
the capitalistic organization of industry, and with the growing
prevalence of the factory system, the economic theory that the
state should interfere as little as possible with industrial relations
had gathered force.   This theory was expressed in classic form in
Adam Smith's book, and his statement gave it enormous impetus.   As interpreted by the manufacturers, who controlled
the Legislature, it taught that all the old regulations which
governed the relations of masters and men should be abolished ;
that the manufacturers should be left to conduct their businesses
as they pleased ;   and that any attempt to regulate wages was
not only ill advised, but as impossible of success as an attempt
to alter one of nature's physical laws.[1]   The surrender of the
Legislature to these views was not only a refusal to attempt to
adjust the relations of masters and men on equitable terms.   It
was also in effect a refusal to attempt to solve the social and
economic problems which the industrial revolution was bringing
in its train.   This refusal, though it enabled the manufacturers
to accumulate wealth, had some very evil social and economic
effects.

In the first place, it tended to convince the working classes
that appeals to the courts and to Parliament were useless.   It
was not till the proceedings which they took in the courts to
enforce the old laws directed to securing a living wage and fair
industrial conditions had failed,[2] it was not till the petitions which
they presented to Parliament to secure the same objects had been
rejected,[3] that the workmen were driven to take other means
to remedy their grievances.   The failure of their appeals to the
courts and to Parliament caused their combinations to gather
size and strength, and to demand, not the enforcement of the

---

[1] " The political economists, in many instances at least, wrote as if an attempt
to alter the rate of wages by combinations of workmen was like an attempt to alter
the weight of the air by tampering with barometers.   It was said that the price of
labour depended, like the price of other commodities, solely upon supply and demand,
that it could not be altered artificially," Stephen, H.C.L. iii 211.

[2] For these appeals to the courts see Webb, History of Trade Unionism 57-60 ;
thus in 1802 the weavers in the West of England combined with the Yorkshire
weavers to appoint an attorney to prosecute employers who infringed the laws relating to their trade—" the result was that Parliament hastily passed an Act, 43
George III c. 136, suspending these statutes in order to put a stop to the prosecutions," ibid 57 ;   similarly prosecutions were instituted for infringements of the
apprenticeship statutes, ibid 59 ;   cp. Cunningham, Industry and Commerce iii
635-636.

[3] See Webb, History of Trade Unionism 52, 53-54, 56-57, 60-61 ;   Cunningham,
Industry and Commerce iii 635-638, 658-660.

old laws, but radical and even revolutionary reforms. Thus, the refusal of the courts and Parliament to act tended to sap that law-abiding instinct, which had been a marked characteristic of the English people during the seventeenth and eighteenth centuries ; [1] for that refusal meant the abandonment of any attempt to submit the relations of masters and men to any effective legal control. The result was that disputes between masters and men were withdrawn from the arbitrament of the law, and left to be decided by the effective forces at the disposal of the contending parties. The fact that it was possible in 1906 to pass a statute which perpetrated the enormous injustice of freeing trade unions of masters or men from liability for torts [2] is, I think, due primarily to the prevalent *laissez faire* doctrines, which induced Parliament, at the end of the eighteenth and the beginning of the nineteenth centuries, to refuse to set up any legal machinery for the equitable adjustment of industrial disputes.

Secondly, and consequently, a new antagonism between the employing class and the workmen sprang up. Capital and labour began to regard one another as enemies. Class war was fomented. [3] This was particularly dangerous at a time when the new democratic theories were gathering strength. Adam Smith had remarked that " the inhabitants of a town, being collected into one place, can easily combine together ; " [4] and there is no doubt that it was the population of Paris and other French towns, which was the moving force behind those democratic theories with which the success of the French Revolution was infecting Europe. [5] In England the growth of old towns and the rise of new urban districts, which the industrial revolution was rapidly creating, made for the spread of democratic theories and the revolutionary proposals which came in their train.

Thirdly, the *laissez faire* attitude which Parliament took up at the bidding of the economists not only prevented a fair settlement of the claims of capital and labour under the new industrial conditions, it made Parliament indifferent to the growth of the enormous social evils, which its refusal to regulate the consequences of the industrial revolution was causing. The growth

---

[1] Thus Cunningham, op. cit. iii 638, speaking of the rejection of the petitions of the weavers against the repeal of the wage clauses of 5 Elizabeth c. 4 §§ 11, 12, 31, vol. iv 382, says, " it is important to observe that in this agitation the weavers were maintaining a strictly conservative attitude ; they asked to have the law of the land put in execution, and they could not but be deeply incensed at the line taken, both by the Legislature and by the magistrates who were charged with the administration of the law."

[2] 6 Edward VII c. 47 § 4 (1)—Trade Disputes Act 1906.

[3] Webb, History of Trade Unionism 73-74.

[4] Wealth of Nations (Cannan's ed.) i 127.

[5] Vol. x 18.

of old towns and the rise of new urban centres were creating new problems of public health and public education, which the un-reformed Parliament disregarded,[1] partly no doubt because the eigteenth-century machinery of local and central government was unequal to dealing with the new problems, but mainly because it considered that the *laissez faire* policy, which they were being taught to consider to be the orthodox attitude in economic questions, was also the orthodox attitude in all other allied social questions.

The failure of Parliament to settle satisfactorily the relations of capital and labour, and the attitude which it adopted to the combinations of masters and men, which, in consequence of this failure were growing in size and strength, were thus largely due to the interpretation put by Parliament on the economic theories which Adam Smith had crystallized. But the inter-pretation put by Parliament on those theories and the inter-pretation put on them by the school of the classical economists who developed them, were by no means identical with the teaching of Adam Smith himself. That teaching had summed up the developments which had taken place in commercial and industrial policy, and in economic theory during the transition period of the eighteenth century. It had stated in a convincing manner an economic theory based on the new commercial and industrial conditions which were beginning to prevail; and, for that reason, it exercised an enormous influence not only on the economic theory of the succeeding age, but also upon the commercial and industrial legislation of that age. Therefore, I must in conclusion say something of Adam Smith and the influence of his economic theories on the commercial and in-dustrial legislation of the end of the eighteenth and the be-ginning of the nineteenth centuries.

VI. *Adam Smith and the growing influence of economic theory.*

We have seen that, as the result of the development of industry and commerce on capitalistic lines, bodies of economic theory, and a distinctively economic point of view, were be-ginning to be developed at the end of the seventeenth century.[2] We have seen also that the economic theories which were being developed under the influence of this point of view were favour-able to the repeal of many of the laws imposing restrictions on the freedom of industry—laws limiting prices, laws fixing the rates of wages, laws as to apprenticeship, laws against engrossing, laws which prohibited the export of bullion, laws which fixed the

[1] Cunningham, Industry and Commerce iii 628-629, 807.
[2] Vol. vi 355-356.

rate of interest.[1] Such laws were condemned either because
they fettered trade, or because they attempted to accomplish
results which, according to these theories, it was naturally impossible for any legislation to accomplish.[2] On one or other
of these grounds greater economic freedom was advocated. At
the same time we have seen that the economic theories which
favoured economic freedom, accepted as axiomatic the mercantilist view that the Legislature should regulate commerce and
industry in such a way that the wealth and power of the state
were increased.[3] Therefore they did not advocate anything
like complete freedom of trade. Protective duties must be
imposed in order to regulate foreign trade in such a way that
British industries and Britain's foreign trade were encouraged.
It is true that Whig and Tory opinions differed as to the manner
in which these results could best be attained [4] but neither party
was in favour of complete freedom of trade, since both parties
agreed that the state must so regulate trade that the power of
the nation was increased.

The views of the Whig party prevailed during the greater
part of the eighteenth century ; and we have seen that their
policy was successful in developing British industry and commerce.[5] On the one hand, the legislative restrictions on freedom
of industry were either repealed, or fell into disuse. We have
seen that debates in Parliament,[6] the records of quarter sessions,[7]
and the views expressed by the Board of Trade,[8] show that
opinion in favour of greater freedom of trade for the manufacturer was growing in strength. On the other hand, colonial
and foreign trade was regulated by a complex mass of statutes,
which was constantly being added to or modified, in order to
ensure the prosperity of the British manufacturer and trader
amidst the constantly shifting commercial conditions of the day.[9]
As the eighteenth century progressed, the capitalist got more
and more freedom to conduct his business as he pleased ; but
he still demanded and obtained protective legislation directed
to maintaining his monopoly of the colonial market, and the
prevention of the competition of foreign manufacturers. Greater
freedom in the conduct of industry, strict regulation of colonial
and foreign trade in order to secure the prosperity of industry,
were the keynotes of the mercantilist system which dominated
the economic practice of the greater part of the eighteenth century.
It was not till the superiority, which the new mechanical inventions had given to British industry, became decisive, that it
was possible for Pitt in 1786 to make a commercial treaty with

[1] Vol. vi 356-358 ; above 391-392.   [2] Vol. vi 357-359.   [3] Ibid 339.
[4] Ibid 339-340 ; above 388.   [5] Above 449-451.
[6] Above 474 n. 1 ; vol. x 166-167.   [7] Ibid.
[8] Above 91.   [9] Above 434-444.

France which reverted to the Tory policy of a freer trade.[1] It was not till after the Old Colonial Empire had been broken up by the recognition of the independence of the United States that the principle of freedom of trade began to get some recognition ; [2] and it was not till 1797 that a relaxation was made in the Navigation Acts by a statute which provided that the produce of the United States could be imported in ships owned and manned by subjects of the United States.[3]

Long before these relaxations of the policy of high protective duties, and of the monopoly given to British ships by the Navigation Acts—relaxations which had been produced mainly by changed industrial and commercial conditions [4]—economic opinion had been moving in the direction of the removal of many of the existing restrictions on trade both domestic and foreign. It was beginning to be thought that trade ought to be free not only from the old legislative restrictions which hampered the manufacturer, but also from the modern restrictions which the Legislatures of different nations had imposed in order to protect and encourage the trade of each particular nation.

This current of opinion is connected with the idea, deduced from Locke's philosophy, that, individuals and societies ought, like the physical universe and the human understanding, to be governed by "natural laws." [5] These natural laws were represented as beneficent, universal, and applicable equally to all peoples. They were thus sharply contrasted with the laws of the state which were in many cases the causes of all kinds of mischief, restricted in their operation, and productive of unfair inequalities. This contrast, which was present to the mind of many political thinkers in the eighteenth century, was epigrammatically expressed by Rousseau in the opening words of his

[1] Lipson, Economic History iii 113-116 ; above 393 ; Shelburne, in 1783, in the speech in which he advocated free trade said, " with more industry, with more enterprise, with more capital than any trading nation upon earth, it ought to be our constant cry, let every market be open, let us meet our rivals fairly and we ask no more," Parlt. Hist. xxiii 410 ; it is not surprising that nations whose commerce was less advanced refused to accede to this demand.

[2] " Lord Shelburne wrote Abbé Morellet in 1783 that the treaties of that year were inspired from beginning to end by ' the great principle of free trade,' and that ' a peace was good in the exact proportion that it recognized that principle,' " Rae, Life of Adam Smith 383 ; in 1783 Lord Shelburne, in the debate on the articles of peace said, " situated as we are between the old world and the new, and between the southern and northern Europe, all that we ought to covet upon earth is free trade and fair equality. . . . It is a principle on which we have had the wisdom to act with respect to our brethren of Ireland ; and if conciliation be our view, why should we not reach out also to America," Parlt. Hist. xxiii 409-410 ; for Shelburne's conversion by Adam Smith to the principles of free trade, see Rae, Life of Adam Smith 153.

[3] 37 George III c. 97 § 1 ; in 1783 fierce opposition had been aroused by proposals to modify the principle of the Navigation Acts in favour of the Americans, Parlt. Hist. xxiii 604-605, 763-764 ; and also by a much more modest proposal in 1785, ibid xxv 274-276.

[4] Above 393-394.   [5] Vol. x 8.

Contrat Social—" Man is born free and everywhere he is in chains." [1] But, as De Tocqueville has pointed out, this contrast between the policy dictated by the laws of nature, and that pursued by the modern state, was emphasized by the French school of *Economists* or *Physiocrats* more thoroughly and more strongly than by the political philosophers. That school did not stop at expounding general abstract theories : they advocated specific reforms based on those theories ; [2] and their advocacy of those reforms led them to construct a system which Adam Smith said was, in spite of its imperfections, " perhaps the nearest approximation to the truth that has yet been published upon the subject of political economy." [3]

In 1793 Lord Lansdowne pointed out to the House of Lords that the " French principles," then generally denounced, had been exported by us to the French by Tucker, the dean of Gloucester, and by Adam Smith.[4] Lord Loughborough replied that in the works of Tucker and Adam Smith " no doctrines inimical to the principles of civil government, the morals or religion of mankind, were contained ; and therefore to trace the errors of the French to these causes was manifestly fallacious." [5] But there is no doubt that Lord Lansdowne was right in his contention that the " French principles," and the theories of free trade held by the Physiocrats and by Adam Smith, had a common ancestor in their appeal to the elusive law of nature ; and there is no doubt also that Bentham's theories were not remotely connected with that same law, disguised so effectually as the principle of utility, that Bentham himself failed to penetrate the disguise.[6] There was thus some reason in the views of those who held that the new economic doctrines were not totally

---

[1] " L'homme est né libre et partout il est dans les fers."

[2] " Les économistes ont eu moins d'éclat dans l'histoire que les philosophes ; moins qu'eux ils ont contribué peutêtre à l'avènement de la Révolution ; je crois pourtant que c'est surtout dans leurs écrits qu'on peut le mieux étudier son vrai naturel. Les philosophes ne sont guère sortis des idées très générales et très abstraites en matière de gouvernement ; les économistes, sans se séparer des théories, sont cependant descendus plus près des faits. Les uns ont dit ce qu'on pouvait imaginer, les autres ont indiqué parfois ce qu'il y avait à faire," L'Ancien Régime et la Révolution 234.

[3] Wealth of Nations (Cannan's ed.) ii 176.

[4] " With respect to French principles, as they have been denominated, those principles had been exported from us to France, and could not be said to have originated among the people of the latter country. The new principles of government, founded on the abolition of the old feudal systems, were originally propagated among us by the dean of Gloucester, Mr. Tucker, and had since been more generally inculcated by Dr. Adam Smith, in his work on the Wealth of Nations, which had been recommended as a book necessary for the information of youth by Mr. Dugald Stewart, in his Elements of the Philosophy of the Human Mind," Parlt. Hist. xxx 329-330, cited Rae, Life of Adam Smith 291.

[5] Parlt. Hist. xxx 334.

[6] Vol. xii 733 ; Dicey, Law and Opinion in England (1st ed.), 143-144, cited vol. ii 603.

unconnected with the French revolutionary ideas.[1] In fact, the movement in the direction of rationalizing the laws and institutions of Europe, by an appeal to *a priori* principles founded on reason or utility or natural law, was giving rise to bodies of political or economic doctrine, and to projects of reform, which varied with the intellectual environment of the writer and the conditions of the society in which he found himself. But, though the doctrines and the projects were diverse, they all belonged intellectually to the same school of thought.

In many respects the principles taught by Adam Smith are identical with those taught by the Physiocrats. It is true that one of their central tenets was rejected by Adam Smith, and never came to be part of accepted economic doctrine. This was the theory that it was only those industries which added to the mass of raw material, such as agriculture or mining, which were really productive, because they alone gave rise to a " produit net," that is something over and above the cost of labour and the interest on capital.[2] But this divergence of view is the exception rather than the rule. In their broad essential outlines their principles are similar ; and it is these principles which were the foundation and starting-point of the reasoning of the English school of classical economists. Thus the idea that the wealth of a nation consists of the annual produce of the nation annually distributed was directly derived from this school ; [3] and the formula " *laissez faire, laissez passer* " was invented by one of its members. That formula expresses the view, at which Adam Smith had arrived independently, that the laws of nature, if left to themselves, would produce ideally just results. It followed that, if the state confined itself to the protection of person and property, if it ceased to impose restrictions on industry and commerce and left individuals free to conduct their businesses as they pleased, the natural desire of each individual to benefit himself would increase the wealth of the nation more quickly and certainly than any of the restrictive laws which

[1] In 1793-1794 Dugald Stewart read his memoir on Adam Smith to the Royal Society of Edinburgh, and he was compelled to abandon his idea of giving a long account of Adam Smith's opinions, because " it was not unusual, even among men of some talents and information, to confound studiously the speculative doctrines of political economy with those discussions concerning the first principles of government, which happened at that time unfortunately to agitate the public mind. The doctrine of Free Trade was itself represented as of a revolutionary tendency," Stewart's Works x 87, cited Rae, Life of Adam Smith 292.

[2] For this theory see Palgrave, Dictionary of Political Economy, *Physiocrats ;* Bagehot, Biographical Studies 266-269 ; Cannan, Introduction to his edition of the Wealth of Nations xxx-xxxiii. Adam Smith says, " that system which represents the produce of land as the sole source of the revenue and wealth of every country has, so far as I know, never been adopted by any nation, and it at present exists only in the speculations of a few men of great learning and ingenuity in France," Wealth of Nations (Cannan's ed.) ii 161.

[3] Cannan, Introd. to Wealth of Nations xxxi-xxxiii.

aimed at producing this result.[1] But if the policy of *laissez faire* produced all the beneficent results claimed for it, and if the object at which the state ought to aim was the increase of the nation's wealth, the state should leave individuals free to produce and distribute as much as they could, and not restrict their activities by laws passed to secure the supposed interests of the state, still less by laws which gave unfair advantages to particular individuals or to corporations.[2] " It is the highest impertinence and presumption in kings and ministers," said Adam Smith, " to pretend to watch over the economy of private people, and to restrain their expence, either by sumptuary laws, or by prohibiting the importation of foreign luxuries. They are themselves always, and without any exception, the greatest spendthrifts in the society." [3] It is not surprising that Adam Smith, though he rejected the central tenet of the Physiocratic school, should say that they had more nearly approximated to the truth than any preceding economic writers.[4]

In the third quarter of the eighteenth century the doctrines of this French school of economists were the largest body of systematic economic theory. But this body of economic theory did not stand alone. During the eighteenth century there had been much scattered economic speculation in England ; and in Scotland this speculation had begun to assume a more systematic and a more scientific form. From the seventeenth century onwards Scotsmen have been great systematizers— remarkable for their " power of reducing human actions to formulæ or principles." [5] This power, due perhaps in the first instance to the dominance of the Calvinistic theology, remained after the leaders of Scottish thought had emancipated themselves from the leading strings of that theology ; and it helped to produce that taste for abstract speculation upon metaphysics, morals, politics, and economics, which is apparent both in the teaching of the Scottish universities and in the writings of eminent

---

[1] Below 513-514.

[2] " The requirements of the State had been the first consideration of seventeenth-century writers, and they had worked back to the funds in the possession of the people from which these requirements could be supplied. Adam Smith approached the subject from the other end. The first object of political economy as he understood it, was ' to provide a plentiful revenue or subsistence for the people,' the second was ' to supply the State or commonwealth with a revenue sufficient for the public services.' He simply discussed the subject of wealth ; its bearing on the condition of the State appeared an afterthought. . . . When the new conception was once clearly grasped it became obvious that interference with any individual, in the way he conducts his business, can scarcely ever be justified on strictly economic grounds, and that costly attempts to foster exotic trades or to stimulate native industries are on the face of it absurd," Cunningham, Growth of English Industry and Commerce ii 593-594, 595.

[3] Wealth of Nations (Cannan's ed.) i 328.　　　　　　[4] Above 504.

[5] Bagehot, Literary Studies ii 247 ; vol. vi 10-11.

Scotsmen of this period. Hutcheson, the professor of moral philosophy at Glasgow when Adam Smith was a student, lectured not only on ethics but also on jurisprudence and civil polity ; and in his lectures on the two latter subjects "a considerable quantity of economic doctrine is scattered." [1] We shall see that the tradition thus attached to this chair influenced Adam Smith when he came to hold it. [2] Hume's Essays on various economic subjects, which were first published in 1752, had criticized prevalent fallacies as to the function of money, and the doctrines held by writers of the mercantilist school as to the balance of trade. [3] In 1767 Sir James Stewart had published what Dr. Cannan calls a great book on political economy. [4] Thus Adam Smith, as a Scotsman and as a student of Glasgow University, was educated in an atmosphere which was favourable to a study of economic theory. That he succeeded in writing a book, of which it was truly said that it "would persuade the present generation and govern the next," [5] was due partly to his own abilities, and partly to the manner in which he made the most of the opportunities which the events of his life gave to him.

Adam Smith was born at Kirkcaldy June 5, 1723. [6] He was a student at Glasgow University between 1737 and 1740. Between 1740 and 1746 he was a Snell exhibitioner of Balliol College, Oxford. Though, like Gibbon, he justly condemned the state of Oxford University, [7] he carried away a knowledge of Greek which was superior to that of his Scotch contemporaries, and, what was more important, a knowledge and an understanding of the English point of view, without which he could never have written a book which was immediately recognized as a classic. [8] After his return to Scotland he lectured at Edinburgh between the years 1748 and 1750. One of these courses of lectures was

---

[1] Cannan, Introd. to Wealth of Nations xxxvi ; for details see ibid xxxvii-xli.
[2] Below 508.   [3] Hume, Essays (ed. 1768) 285-373 ; above 460.
[4] Cannan, Introd. to Wealth of Nations xviii. Its title was, "An Inquiry into the Principles of Political Economy : being an Essay on the Science of Domestic Policy in Free Nations."
[5] "It was Pulteney (one of Adam Smith's pupils) who, in his speech on the suspension of cash payments by the Bank of England in 1797 . . . quoted from some unknown source the memorable saying, which is generally repeated as if it were his own, that Smith 'would persuade the present generation and govern the next,'" Rae, Life of Adam Smith 103.
[6] The best authority for Adam Smith is Rae's Life of Adam Smith ; cp. also Dict. Nat. Biog. and Encyclopædia Britannica ; Bagehot's essay on Adam Smith as a Person, Biographical Studies 247-281, though suggestive, is inaccurate in many details.
[7] "In the university of Oxford, the greater part of the public professors have, for these many years, given up altogether even the pretence of teaching," Wealth of Nations (Cannan's ed.) ii 251 ; on the other hand it is fair to remember that Campbell, comparing the English and Scottish universities, said in 1805 that "if there are greater instances of idleness in English seminaries, there are likewise more astonishing proofs of application," Life of Lord Campbell i 170.
[8] See Bagehot, op. cit. 252-253.

on economics, and in it he advocated those ideas of commercial liberty which he had learned from Hutcheson, and of which he was afterwards to be so great an exponent [1] In 1751 he became professor of Logic at Glasgow ; but in 1752 he exchanged this chair for that of Moral Philosophy. He held this chair till 1764 ; and it was during these years, and in those parts of his lectures on jurisprudence, which he called " Police, Revenue, and Arms," that he laid the foundations of his book on the *Wealth of Nations*.[2]

It was under the head " Police " that he dealt with economic topics. " The name ' police,' " he said, " is French and is originally derived from the Greek πολιτεία, which properly signified the policy of civil government, but now it only means the regulation of the inferior parts of government, viz. cleanliness, security, and cheapness." [3] It was under the head of " cheapness " that Adam Smith lectured on " the opulence of a state," and the notes which we have of his lectures show that he had begun to maintain those principles which were to make his *Wealth of Nations* famous.[4] Some of his ideas he got from Hutcheson's *System of Moral Philosophy*, which no doubt contained the gist of the lectures which he had listened to as a student.[5] Hutcheson had dealt with such topics as the division of labour, value, money, prices, interest, profits, taxation ; and he showed that many of these matters were regulated by natural causes, which cannot be controlled by the Legislature [6]—a point of view which fitted in very well with his insistence on the importance of preserving civil and religious liberty.[7] His teaching made a great impression on Adam Smith.[8] It suggested to him the topics of his lectures on economic subjects,[9] it gave him the idea of investigating the natural causes which determined these

[1] Rae, Life of Adam Smith 36 ; Dugald Stewart cites a paper written by Adam Smith in 1755, in which Smith claimed that, as early as 1749, he had maintained in his lectures that " projectors disturb nature in the course of her operations on human affairs, and it requires no more than to leave her alone and give her fair play in the pursuit of her ends, that she may establish her own designs. . . . Little else is required to carry a state to the highest degree of affluence from the lowest barbarism but peace, easy taxes, and a tolerable administration of justice. All governments which thwart this natural course . . . are unnatural, and to support themselves are obliged to be oppressive and tyrannical," ibid 62-63.

[2] Ibid 61 ; Smith, Wealth of Nations (Cannan's ed.) Introd. xviii-xix ; a copy of the notes of these lectures taken by a student in 1763 has been edited by Cannan ; as Professor Scott says in his lecture on Adam Smith, Proceedings of the British Academy x 451, they show that the fundamental principles embodied in the Wealth of Nations " were being taught in the classroom at Glasgow."

[3] Cited Cannan, Introd. to Wealth of Nations xix.

[4] Ibid xx-xxvii.　　　　　　　　　　　　　　　　[5] Ibid xxxvi.

[6] Ibid xxxvi-xli ; cp. Rae, Life of Adam Smith 14-15.　　　[7] Ibid 13.

[8] In 1787 Smith, in writing to the Principal of Glasgow University to accept the office of Rector to which he had just been elected, spoke of " the abilities and virtues of the never-to-be-forgotten Dr. Hutcheson," ibid 411.

[9] Cannan, Introd. to Wealth of Nations xli.

phenomena, and it gave him that bias in favour of liberty which is strongly marked in all his writings. But to these ideas Adam Smith added others of much greater importance. In the first place, his " belief in the economic beneficence of self-interest," which as Dr. Cannan has said, " permeates the *Wealth of Nations* and has afforded a starting ground for economic speculation ever since," [1] was probably derived, at least in part, from Mandeville.[2]   Smith combined the bias in favour of liberty, which he had learned from Hutcheson, with this belief in the economic beneficence of self-interest, when he said that " in general, if any branch of trade, or any division of labour, be advantageous to the public, the freer and more general the competition, it will always be the more so ; " [3] and that " the natural effort of every individual to better his own condition, when suffered to exert itself with freedom and security, is so powerful a principle, that it is alone, and without any assistance, not only capable of carrying on the society to wealth and prosperity, but of surmounting a hundred impertinent obstructions with which the folly of human laws too often incumbers its operations." [4]   In the second place, his belief in the principle of free trade, and his criticism of the mercantile system, were probably derived from Hume's Essays.   " It seems very likely," says Dr. Cannan,[5] " that the reference in the lectures to Hume's ' essays showing the absurdity of these and other such doctrines ' is to be regarded as an acknowledgment of obligation, and therefore it was Hume, by his Political Discourses on Money and the Balance of Trade in 1752, who first opened Adam Smith's eyes on that subject."

Adam Smith, like other political philosophers or economists, owed intellectual debts to his predecessors and contemporaries ; and it is possible to trace the sources of many of his economic theories. But though he was a student and a critic of other men's theories, though he himself was a great and original exponent of economic theory, he was far from being a mere theorist. It is clear that, though occasionally afflicted with fits of absence of mind which have given occasion to many anecdotes,[6] he was not merely " an awkward Scotch professor, apparently choked with books and absorbed in abstractions ".[7]

---

[1] Cannan, Introd. to Wealth of Nations xli-xlii.

[2] Ibid xliii-xlvi ; Dr. Cannan points out that Smith, twenty years after attending Hutcheson's lectures, criticized him " expressly on the ground that he thought too little of self-love," ibid xlii.

[3] Ibid i 312.   [4] Ibid ii 43.

[5] Introd. to Wealth of Nations xlvi-xlvii.

[6] For some of these anecdotes see Rae, Life of Adam Smith 245-246, 259-260, 329, 330-332 ; Bagehot, Biographical Studies 247-248.

[7] Ibid 247 ; this statement of Bagehot is disproved by Rae ; Mr. Rae, op. cit. 66, says, " a common misconception regarding Smith is that he was as helpless as a child

He took a more active part in the life of his university than any other professor, and acted as college Quæstor or Treasurer from 1758 to 1764.[1] He had many friends amongst the Glasgow merchants ; and one of them was Andrew Cochrane who founded a political economy club in 1743, of which Adam Smith was a member.[2] It is clear that the discussion of such questions as export and import duties, and the advantages and disadvantages of paper money, by practical merchants at such a club, gave him a knowledge of commercial conditions, without which he could not have based his economic theories on the solid foundation of the commercial and industrial facts of his day. As we shall see, it was because Adam Smith, at this and at other periods of his life,[3] never lost sight of the actual concrete facts on which his theories were based, that those theories exercised so great an influence on his own and on succeeding ages. At the same time he was a member of other societies in Glasgow and Edinburgh in which literary and artistic and scientific problems were discussed ; [4] and all this discussion must have helped him both to collect the facts upon which his theories were founded, and to correct, to qualify, and to give precision to his theories.

Adam Smith's lectures at Glasgow made him famous, and it was said that, during the thirteen years that he held his chair, he had converted the leading men at Glasgow to his free trade views.[5] But Smith was not a professor of political economy. He was a professor of moral philosophy, and his economic teaching was only a part of his subject. The first book which he published was a book on a subject which, to modern ideas, was more closely connected with the subject of his chair than jurisprudence or economics. It was entitled a *Theory of Moral Sentiments*, and was published in 1759. It was a very successful book, and at once gave Adam Smith a high place amongst his contemporaries.[6] But its historical importance is due to the fact that it changed the course of Adam Smith's life, and gave him opportunities of a unique kind for the prosecution of his economic studies. Charles Townshend, the stepfather of the young duke of Buccleugh, was so attracted by Adam Smith's book that he offered Adam Smith the post of tutor to the duke on his travels abroad. Smith was to have £300 a year and travelling expenses while abroad, and a pension of £300 a year

in matters of business. . . . This idea of his helplessness in the petty transactions of life arose from observing his occasional fits of absence and his habitual simplicity of character, but his simplicity, nobody denies, was accompanied by exceptional acuteness and practical sagacity, and his fits of absence seem to have been neither so frequent nor so prolonged as they are commonly represented."

[1] Rae, Life of Adam Smith, 66-69.   [2] Ibid 91, 92-93.
[3] Below 514.   [4] Rae, op. cit. 94-96, 107-118, 134-140.
[5] Ibid 60-61.
[6] Ibid 141 ; see Hume's letter of congratulations, ibid 141-144.

for life afterwards. " He was thus to have twice his Glasgow income, and to have it assured till death." [1] Smith accepted this offer, gave up his professorship, and travelled with his pupil in France between the years 1764 and 1766. It was this journey abroad which gave him the opportunity to discuss economic problems with Quesnay, the leader of the Physiocrats, with Turgot, and with many of the other leaders of the French school of economic thought ; and there is no doubt that this discussion inspired important parts of the *Wealth of Nations*, and that it gave him an insight into the strength and weakness of this school, and into the working of French institutions, which he could never have learned from books.[2] It was the pension which was settled upon him for life which enabled him, after his return, to devote all his energies to the writing of his book.

From 1767 to 1773 he lived with his mother at Kirkcaldy, and devoted himself so industriously to the writing of his book that his labours told on his health. In 1773 he thought that he had practically finished it, and went to London with the manuscript. But when he got to London he found that it needed so many additions and alterations that it was not published till 1776. There is no doubt that, just as discussions with the Glasgow merchants, at various literary societies in Glasgow, and with the French economists in Paris, had presented new material and new points of view which he had assimilated and incorporated into his book, so discussions with many of the leading literary men in London at Johnson's Literary Club and elsewhere, showed the need for amplification and modification. Thus, to take one instance, Smith saw much of Benjamin Franklin, whom he had met in Edinburgh in 1759 ; and there is no doubt that it was from Franklin that he got much of that information about the American colonies of which he makes so much use in the *Wealth of Nations*.[3]

---

[1] Rae, Life of Adam Smith, 165.

[2] " When we find that there is no trace of these theories (of the Physiocrats) in the *Lectures* and a great deal in the *Wealth of Nations*, and that in the meantime Adam Smith had been to France and mixed with all the prominent members of the ' sect,' including their master, Quesnay, it is difficult to understand why we should be asked, without any evidence, to refrain from believing that he came under physiocratic influence after and not before or during the Glasgow period," Cannan, Introd. to Wealth of Nations xxx-xxxi ; on the other hand, the influence of the French school must not be exaggerated ; we have seen that Adam Smith had arrived independently at the same conclusions, above 508 n. 1 ; as Professor Scott says, " there is first the main question of similarity in thought ; and, when this is considered in relation to the chief currents of opinion in the eighteenth century, it will be found that it was not so much a question of the indebtedness of Smith to the Physiocrats as of both types of thought having a common source in the Nature-cult of the time," Proceedings of the British Academy x 450.

[3] Rae, op. cit. 264-266 ; J. F. Watson, Annals of Philadelphia i 533, there cited, says, " Dr. Franklin once told Dr. Logan that the celebrated Adam Smith, when writing his *Wealth of Nations*, was in the habit of bringing chapter after chapter

At length the book appeared on March 9, 1776. Its merits were at once recognized by such literary judges as Hume and Gibbon ;[1] Lord North's budgets of 1777 and 1778 adopted ideas taken from it ;[2] in 1779 Smith was consulted by Dundas and the earl of Carlisle on the subject of free trade with Ireland ;[3] and in 1783 he was consulted by Eden on the subject of freedom of trade between Canada and the United States.[4] A second edition appeared in 1778 with some additions and corrections. To the third edition, published in 1784, considerable additions were made.[5] In 1778 Lord North had appointed Adam Smith commissioner of customs in Scotland—an appointment which there is some reason to think was due, not so much to the influence of the duke of Buccleugh and Dundas, as to Lord North's recognition of the value of his book.[6] Now as ever, Smith was always ready to use new information to improve his book. Some of the additions which he made to the third edition are due to the first-hand information which he had got as commissioner of customs,[7] e.g., the account of the working of the bounty system in the Scotch fisheries ;[8] others are due both to this information and to the further reading and reflection which it suggested, e.g., the chapter entitled " Conclusion of the Mercantile System " ; and others to current political discussions, e.g., the account of the chartered companies and especially the detailed account of the East India Company.[9] The fourth and fifth editions published in 1786 and 1789 contain no material alterations.[10] Smith died July 17, 1790, so that the fifth edition was the last published in his life-time.[11]

It may at first sight appear strange that in a history of English Law it should be thought to be necessary to devote so much space to an account of Adam Smith and his book on the *Wealth of Nations*. It is not really strange. Readers of this and of the preceding chapter will realize that this book is the best commentary, not only upon the commercial and industrial

as he composed it to himself, Dr. Price, and others of the *literati ;* then patiently hear their observations and profit by their discussions and criticisms—even sometimes submitting to write whole chapters anew, and even to reverse some of his propositions."

[1] Rae, op. cit. 286-287.   [2] Ibid 294.   [3] Ibid 349-355.

[4] Ibid 383-386.   [5] Cannan, Introd. to Wealth of Nations xiii-xvii.

[6] Rae, op. cit. 320-321 ; on receiving this appointment he offered to give up his pension from the duke of Buccleugh, but he was informed that " the pension was meant to be permanent and unconditional, and that if he were consulting his own honour in offering to give it up, he was not thinking of the honour of Lord Buccleugh," ibid 321. Bagehot, Biographical Studies 262, 275, has given an incorrect account of this episode.

[7] Rae, op. cit. 332-333.   [8] Ibid 363.

[9] Ibid.

[10] Cannan, Introd. to Wealth of Nations xvii-xviii.

[11] This is the edition which is taken by Dr. Cannan as the text of his definitive edition of the Wealth of Nations.

legislation of the eighteenth century, but also upon many aspects of its public law. It is therefore of the first importance to the legal historian of this period, because it gives us not only a lucid account of the most important of the statutes bearing upon industrial and commercial law, and upon many aspects of public law, but also the criticisms of one of the ablest men of the century upon these topics. And they are the criticisms of a man who had derived his knowledge of these statutes and of the law which they added to or amended, not only from books, but also from converse with men whom these statutes or this law affected, and with men who had helped to enact them. There is a very large concrete element in Adam Smith's book, which is due to the manner in which, from his days as a Glasgow professor to the end of his life, he got his materials at first hand from his own experience or from men who had first-hand experience. It is this concrete element which caused his contemporaries at once to accept his book as a book of authority, and makes it so essential an authority for the legal history of this period. And the importance of the book to the legal historian is by no means confined to the light which it throws upon the law of the eighteenth century. Because it inspired the policy of the Legislature, and therefore the contents of the statute book, for very many years afterwards, it is the best guide to an understanding of this legislation.[1] But this aspect of the book is due not only to what I have called its concrete character, but to the nature of the theories by which it was inspired, and in the light of which the mass of concrete facts and statutes and institutions which it details or describes, is interpreted.

We have seen that all through his book Smith is an advocate, first for the liberty of the individual, and, secondly, for the thesis that, inasmuch as " man's self love is God's providence," this liberty, if left to itself, will produce the best economic results.[2] It followed that the wealth of a nation could best be attained, not, as the mercantilists thought, by restrictive legislation directed to secure the prosperity of a particular state at the expense of rival states,[3] but by leaving each individual as free as possible to conduct his own trade in his own way. *Laissez faire*, and the working of natural economic laws would do the rest. It is from this point of view that Smith criticizes all the commercial and industrial laws of his day ; and it is from this point of view that he lays down his celebrated canons of

---

[1] In 1792 Pitt said of Adam Smith's book that, by reason of the author's " extensive knowledge of detail and depth of philosophical research," it furnished " the best solution to every question connected with the history of commerce, or with the systems of political economy," Parlt. Hist. xxix 834.

[2] Above 505-506. [3] Above 460 n. 5.

taxation as a basis for his criticism of existing systems of taxation.[1] But merely abstract theories, economic or otherwise, produce little effect unless they are brought into relation with concrete facts. It is because Adam Smith's theories are based upon and correlated with the facts of his day that they exercised so great an influence upon his contemporaries. Because the theories set forth in the *Wealth of Nations* were the theories of a man who knew the facts and the law, of a man who understood their practical working and could criticize them intelligently, they convinced English statesmen, just as his lectures in Glasgow had convinced the Glasgow merchants.[2]   Like Bentham in the sphere of law, he convinced his contemporaries of the soundness of his theories by the manner in which he applied them in detail to the facts of the system which he was criticizing, and by the practical suggestions which he made as the result of this application of his theories to the facts.[3]

It is this characteristic of Smith's work which differentiates it from the work of the Physiocrats.   Their theories were based upon a series of logical deductions from their ideas as to natural right and natural order.   " This logical method," says Professor Scott,[4] " enabled a system to be constructed, and it was at once the strength and weakness of the school—its strength in giving economic phenomena not only a scientific treatment, but a scientific form, its weakness in the absolute dependence of the latter upon the Nature-cult as they defined it."   From the fallacies which arose from the exclusively logical method of approaching the subject, Adam Smith's knowledge of the political and business worlds of his day saved him, and enabled him to keep his theories in touch with the concrete facts of those worlds.   It was for this reason that his influence on his own contemporaries and on the succeeding generation was so great.[5]

It is this same characteristic of his work which saved him from some of the errors into which his successors and followers fell.   As Cunningham has pointed out,[6] " he dealt with concrete instances and the actual life of a nation.   His disciples followed him in separating out the economic side of human life, but they

---

[1] Wealth of Nations (Cannan's ed.) ii 310-312.   [2] Above 510.

[3] Mill, Dissertations and Discussions i 338, says that Bentham owes his permanent importance to the fact that he was something more than a critic of abuses ; " he made it a point of conscience not to (assail error) until he thought he could plant instead the corresponding truth. . . . He began *de novo*, laid his own foundations deeply and firmly, built up his own structure and bade mankind compare the two."

[4] Proceedings of the British Academy x 450.

[5] " Their extreme reliance on such deductions goes to the root of the criticism by Adam Smith of their doctrine.   It made their system one for the middle of the eighteenth century ; while that of Adam Smith had a broader basis through which it became the inspiration of statesmen in the nineteenth century," ibid 450-451.

[6] Growth of English Industry and Commerce iii 738.

treated it as if it were an independent entity, and not as conditioned by the political circumstances of the community, and
by the personal welfare of the citizens." Thus we have seen
that he approved of the policy of the Navigation Acts ; [1] and
he admitted that bounties on manufactures necessary for the defence of the nation were justifiable.[2] He admitted also that there
were cases in which it might be wise to impose import duties.
For instance, if a tax was imposed on a native commodity, it
was reasonable to impose a similar tax on the same commodities
imported from abroad ; [3] and high duties or prohibitions imposed by foreign states on native commodities might be subjected
to retaliatory taxes, " where there is a probability that they
will procure the repeal of the high duties or prohibitions complained of." [4] He admitted that it was not desirable to repeal
suddenly high duties on, or prohibitions of, foreign products
when those duties or prohibitions had resulted in the establishment of native industries [5]—" were these high duties and
prohibitions taken away all at once, cheaper foreign goods of
the same kind might be poured so fast into the home market,
as to deprive all at once many thousands of our people of their
ordinary employment and means of subsistence. The disorder
which this would occasion might no doubt be very considerable." [6]
He did not condemn the laws which fixed the highest rate of
interest which could be charged for loans of money ; [7] and,
though his views were perhaps shaken by Bentham's arguments
in his *Defence of Usury*, he did not alter his book. [8] Probably
he saw what Bentham and later economists did not see, that
some legislation on this topic is necessary to prevent " the extortion of usury." [9] He defended a law against the issue of
notes for small denominations, although it might " be considered

[1] Wealth of Nations (Cannan's ed.) i 428-429, cited vol. vi 318 n. 6.

[2] Ibid ii 23.   [3] Ibid i 429.

[4] Ibid 432.   [5] Ibid 433.

[6] He adds, however, that the disorder would probably be less than is commonly
imagined, first because manufactures now commonly exported without a bounty
would not be affected, and secondly, because those thrown out of employment would
probably be absorbed in other industries—more especially if the privileges of corporations and the law of settlement were abolished, ibid i 433-435 ; this was one
of the arguments against the proposed commercial treaty with France in 1713,
above 388 ; it would, it was said, destroy our incipient silk and paper manufactures,
and throw thousands out of employment, Parlt. Hist. vi 1211.

[7] Wealth of Nations (Cannan's ed.) i 338-339.

[8] Rae, Life of Adam Smith 422-424. Mr. Rae thinks that " if Smith had lived
to publish another edition of his work, he would have modified his position on the rate
of interest " ; it appears from a letter written by George Wilson to Bentham, which
purported to relate what he had heard from Adam Smith, that Adam Smith had said
that " the *Defence of Usury* was the work of a very superior man, and that tho'
he had given him some hard knocks, it was done in so handsome a way that he
could not complain, and seemed to admit that you were right " ; this does not amount
to a complete surrender to Bentham's views.

[9] Vol. viii 100-101.

as in some respects a violation of natural liberty," on the ground
that " those exertions of the natural liberty of a few individuals,
which might endanger the security of the whole society, are
and ought to be restrained by the laws of all governments ; of
the most free, as well as of the most despotical." [1]

It is perhaps regrettable that Smith did not consider more
fully all the implications of these modifications of his leading
principles, and especially the implications of the principle laid
down in the passage which has just been cited. He had a very
low opinion of the patriotism and the commercial morality of
manufacturers and traders.[2] Manufacturers, he considered, were
always in a tacit combination to depress their workmen ; [3] and
we have seen how he pointed out that whilst they combined
with impunity, workmen who combined were criminally prosecuted.[4] He considered also that these manufacturers and
traders were generally interested in deceiving and oppressing
the public, and that they had " upon many occasions both
deceived and oppressed it." [5] But, if this was so, it followed,
first, that the abolition of all the laws which protected the
workmen could hardly be justified, for it obviously played into
the hands of these crafty and unscrupulous manufacturers ;
and, secondly, that the popular fear of the engrosser and fore-
staller was not a mere superstition comparable to the popular
fear of witchcraft.[6] His view that these crafty manufacturers
had succeeded in deceiving the honest and ignorant country
gentlemen, and so had induced the legislature to fetter trade
in their own selfish interests,[7] can hardly be supported. We
have seen that the country gentlemen were not so simple as he
imagined.[8] There were sometimes other reasons, which out-
weighed the purely economic reasons, for the laws which they
passed. It was necessary to give some initial measure of protection to infant manufactures—as many nations before and since
Adam Smith wrote have discovered ; and he himself admits
that, though the wealth of a neighbouring nation " is advan-

---

[1] Wealth of Nations (Cannan's ed.) i 307.

[2] " The capricious ambition of kings and ministers has not, during the present
and preceding centuries, been more fatal to the repose of Europe than the impertinent jealousy of merchants and manufacturers. The violence and injustice of the
rulers of mankind is an ancient evil, for which, I am afraid, the nature of human
affairs will scarcely admit of a remedy. But the mean rapacity, the monopolizing
spirit of merchants and manufacturers, who neither are, nor ought to be, the rulers of
mankind, though it cannot perhaps be corrected, may very easily be prevented from
disturbing the tranquillity of anybody but themselves," ibid i 457-458 ; above 450.

[3] Ibid 68.   [4] Ibid 68-69, 143-144 ; above 486-487.   [5] Ibid 250.

[6] Ibid ii 35 ; above 466 ; see a letter to Shelburne in 1766 as to the evil effect
of forestalling and ingrossing in raising the prices of corn in Chippenham market
in Calendar of Home Office Papers 1766-1769, 91-92.

[7] Wealth of Nations i 249-250, 400-401, 426-427.

[8] Above 450-451.

tageous in trade," it may be " dangerous in war and politics." [1]
Similarly, the prohibition of the cultivation of tobacco in England,
which he condemns,[2] was an integral part of the price paid to
the colonies for the system of the Acts of Trade.[3] His contention
that the trade in intoxicating liquors should be free because
their cheapness was always a cause "not of drunkenness but of
sobriety," [4] was contradicted by recent experience, which had
led to the passing of Acts which controlled the sale of gin.[5]

That a reconsideration of industrial and commercial policy
was needed, in view of the great changes which were taking place
in industrial and commercial conditions, was obvious ; and
there is no doubt that one of the changes needed was a repeal of
statutes which imposed out-of-date restrictions upon the conduct
of native industries, and that another change was a revision of
statutes which regulated foreign trade, so as to secure greater
freedom of trade. These changes fitted in very well with Adam
Smith's theories as to the beneficent effects which might be
expected to result from leaving traders free to conduct their
business as they pleased ; for those theories obviously led to
the conclusion that the less the state interfered the better.
According to Adam Smith the state " has only three duties to
attend to . . . first, the duty of protecting the society from the
violence and invasion of other independent societies ; secondly,
. . . the duty of establishing an exact administration of justice ;
and, thirdly, the duty of enacting and maintaining certain public
works and certain public institutions which it can never be for
the interest of any individual, or small number of individuals, to
erect and maintain." [6] But thus to restrict the sphere of state
action, at a time of industrial and commercial transition, was
very dangerous. To give manufacturers and traders the power
to conduct their businesses exactly as they pleased at such a time,
was really inconsistent with the opinions which he himself held
as to the commercial morality of those persons—and yet that
was the conclusion to which his theories led, and which, with
a few modifications, he advocated. When, from Adam Smith's
theories, his successors constructed a science of political economy
which was even more rigid and more scientific than that set
forth in the *Wealth of Nations*, and when Parliament surrendered its judgment upon industrial and commercial problems
to the professors of this new science, it augured ill for the future
development of British industry and commerce. The first-fruits

---

[1] " The wealth of a neighbouring nation, though dangerous in war and politics,
is certainly advantageous in trade," Wealth of Nations (Cannan's ed.) i 458.

[2] Ibid 158.   [3] Vol. vi 322.

[4] Wealth of Nations (Cannan's ed.) i 456-457.

[5] Lecky, History of England ii 100-105 ; vol. x 184.

[6] Wealth of Nations (Cannan's ed.) ii 184-185.

of this surrender were the abandonment by Parliament of the attempt to adjust equitably the relations of capital and labour. Its later fruits were the inauguration of a system of one-sided free trade which led to loss of that lead in industry and commerce which Great Britain had secured in the days when the despised mercantilists had worked successfully to secure its predominance.

The *a priori* theories of economics and legislation—theories which in England are associated with the names of Adam Smith and Bentham—had a vast influence upon the legislation of the nineteenth century. They did good service in clearing away much obsolete law which was quite out of harmony with modern conditions. They did good service in bringing to the front new points of view, and new proposals for legislation, which were more in harmony with these conditions. But it is always dangerous for a Legislature, which must deal with the practical problems which changing conditions set to the state, to surrender completely to an *a priori* theory ; and the more logical and more scientific the theory the more dangerous it is to surrender to it, for it is not by logic alone that these problems can be solved. Unregenerate human nature will generally find a way to turn to its own selfish uses the rigid rules which logic dictates. If the Legislature had surrendered as completely to all the proposals of Bentham and all the theories of Austin as it surrendered to the economic proposals and theories of Adam Smith and his successors, the effects upon the English political and legal system would have been as disastrous as the effects of this surrender were upon the industrial and commercial policy of the English state.[1]

All this we shall see in a later chapter. In the period covered by this chapter we can see only the beginnings of the new points of view which, owing to the increasing rapidity of the changes in industrial and commercial conditions, were destined to have a decisive influence upon the industrial and commercial legislation of the following century.

[1] " The school of analytical jurisprudence founded by Austin made English lawyers and statesmen realize the theory of sovereignty more distinctly than they had ever realized it before. But . . . they refused to become its slaves. . . . Austin's Jurisprudence was published in 1832 ; and during the succeeding years of the nineteenth century its influence was great. But the leading principles of responsible government were developed in Canada between 1840 and 1850, and were applied to the other great Dominions long before the end of the nineteenth century," Holdsworth, Lessons from our Legal History 131-132 ; similarly, the reforms in the land law made by the legislation of the nineteenth century, though influenced by Bentham, followed a course very different from that which Bentham would have deduced *a priori* from the principle of utility, see Holdsworth, Historical Introduction to the Land Law, chap. iv.

The Act of 1705-1706 for the Amendment of the Law

We have seen that the course of the political and constitutional history of the seventeenth century had prevented any
extensive law reforms from being undertaken at the time of
the Revolution. Both the political experiments and the legal
reforms of the Commonwealth period had created a fear of any
changes except those which were absolutely necessary.[1] That
attitude persisted throughout the eighteenth century—though it
was tending to weaken to some extent in the two decades before
the outbreak of the French Revolution. It is for this reason, as
we shall see in the following section, that the eighteenth-century
legislation upon various branches of the law and legal doctrine,
though not negligible in bulk, covers very little ground.

The only Act in which any attempt was made to survey the
field of law, and to remedy some of the many defects of its
adjective and substantive rules, is this Act of 1705-1706 " for the
Amendment of the Law and the better Advancement of Justice." [2]
It is probable that the proposal to pass such an Act came from
Somers. On December 15, 1705, a motion was carried in the
House of Lords to appoint a committee " to consider the Act for
preventing frauds and perjuries, and the methods of proceedings
in courts below, the judges to assist " ; and Somers was appointed
its chairman.[3] There were numerous meetings of the committee,
and much discussion with the judges.[4] As a result of these
meetings and these discussions various proposals were made for
legislation. The heads of these proposals were reported to the
House of Lords on January 17, 1706, agreed to by the House,
and the judges were ordered to prepare a bill.[5] The bill was
prepared and read a first time on January 25.[6] It was read a
third time and sent to the Commons on February 4.[7] On March 1
the bill was amended by the Commons, and, as amended, read a
third time.[8] On March 6 some of the Commons' amendments
were agreed to and others were disagreed to by the Lords.[9] On
March 11 the reasons for their disagreement were stated by a
committee of the House,[10] and a conference was held with the
Commons.[11] A complete agreement was not reached,[12] and on
March 18 the Commons resolved to insist on some of their amendments, to make further amendments, and to appoint a committee
to draw up reasons to be given at a conference with the Lords

[1] Vol. vi 411-412, 428-430.   [2] 4, 5 Anne c. 16 (R.C. c. 3).
[3] House of Lords MSS.(N.S.) vi no. 2209.   [4] Ibid.
[5] Ibid ; Lords' Journals xviii 69-70.   [6] Ibid 77.
[7] Ibid 87.   [8] Commons' Journals xv 182-183.
[9] Lords' Journals xviii 140.   [10] Ibid 145-147.
[11] Commons' Journals xv 194.   [12] Ibid.

on the subject-matter of the disputed amendments.[1] The reasons were drawn up on March 19.[2] The two Houses reached an agreement on the same day,[3] and later in the day the royal assent was given to the bill.[4]

The Act deals with several different departments of the law. There are clauses amending the common law system of procedure and pleading and the Chancery system of procedure and pleading. There are clauses amending the land law, the law as to wills, the law as to the action of account, and the law as to the limitation of actions.

Procedure and pleading.

The clauses dealing with this topic are the most numerous group of clauses, and the clauses dealing with common law procedure and pleading are considerably more numerous than those dealing with Chancery procedure and pleading.

Formal defects in writs, processes, and pleadings were not to be ground for a demurrer unless the party demurring specially set down the cause of his demurrer ; [5] and certain defects were specified [6] which, for the future, were not to be taken advantage of except by means of a special demurrer.[7] The effect of this provision was to give the party information of the grounds upon which the demurrer was made, which he would not have had if the demurrer had been general.[8] The statutes of jeofail, by which formal defects were cured in judgments given after verdict,[9] were extended to judgments given on confession, *nihil dicit*, or *non sum informatus*,[10] provided the attorney for the plaintiff duly filed his warrant of attorney when he declared, and the attorney for the defendant duly filed his warrant when he appeared.[11] The defendant or tenant in any action, and the plaintiff in an action of replevin were, with leave of the court, allowed to plead as many separate defences as they should see

---

[1] Commons' Journals xv 196-197.   [2] Ibid 198.
[3] Ibid 199 ; Lords' Journals xviii 161.   [4] Ibid 162.
[5] 4, 5 Anne c. 16 § 1 (R.C. c. 3).
[6] " No advantage or exception shall be taken of or for an immaterial traverse ; or of or for the default of entering pledges upon any bill or declaration ; or of or for the default of alleging the bringing into court any bond, bill, indenture, or other deed whatsoever mentioned in the declaration or other pleading ; or of or for the default of alleging of the bringing into court letters testamentary, or letters of administration ; or of or for the omission of *vi et armis et contra pacem*, or either of them ; or of or for the want of averment of *hoc paratus est verificare* or *hoc paratus est verificare per recordum;* or of or for not alleging *prout patet per recordum* . . . or any other matters of like nature."
[7] For special demurrers see vol. ix 266-267.   [8] Vol. ix 266-267.
[9] For these statutes see vol. iii 650 ; vol. iv 535-536 ; vol. vi 409 ; vol. ix 264 n. 9, 315-316.
[10] 4, 5 Anne c. 16 § 2 (R.C. c. 3).   [11] § 3.

fit.[1] We have seen that this clause was defective in that it did not extend to replications or to any subsequent pleading ; and that the judges restricted the usefulness of the clause by insisting that each plea must state only a single ground of defence.[2] Juries in civil cases[3] were, from henceforth, to be drawn from the bodies of counties, and no challenge for want of hundredors was to be permitted.[4] Rules were made as to cases in which it was necessary that juries should have a view of the land which was the subject-matter of the action, and as to the mode of summoning them.[5] Dilatory pleas, e.g. pleas in abatement or to the jurisdiction of the court, were not to be received unless the party pleading them verified them by affidavit.[6] Payment was to be a good plea to an action of debt brought upon a single bill or a judgment ; and if an action of debt were brought upon a bond, conditioned to be void if a lesser sum be paid at a fixed day or place, payment, though not strictly in accordance with the condition, was to be a good plea.[7] If, pending an action on a bond with a penalty, the defendant paid into court the principal interest and costs, the money so paid in was to operate as a discharge of the bond.[8] As Blackstone points out,[9] this clause and a later statute of 1734[10] had the effect of securing that "what had long been the practice of the courts of equity should also for the future be universally followed in courts of law." In fact, this Act and an earlier Act of 1697[11] may be said to have introduced the courts of law to the distinction between penalties and liquidated damages, which began to be heard of in the eighteenth,[12] and was elaborated in the nineteenth century.[13] The other sections upon this topic deal with the assignment of the bail bonds taken by the sheriff to the plaintiff in the action,[14] the extension of the statutes of jeofail and the provisions of this Act to suits for debts due to the

---

[1] § 4 ; § 5 made provision for the awarding of costs when insufficient pleas had been put forward.

[2] Vol. ix 316-317 ; cp. ibid 425-427.　　　　[3] 4, 5 Anne c. 16 § 7 (R.C. c. 3).

[4] § 6 ; for hundredors, and for the later legislation which entirely abolished the need for hundredors in all actions see vol. i 332.

[5] § 7.　　　　　　　　　　　　　[6] § 11 ; for dilatory pleas see vol. ix 268-269.

[7] § 12.　　　　　　　　　　　　　[8] § 13.

[9] Comm. iii 435 ; the view expressed by Blackstone is in accordance with that expressed by Lord Mansfield C.J. in Bonafous v. Rybot (1763) 3 Burr. at p. 1374 ; for Lord Mansfield's influence on Blackstone, see vol. xii 723.

[10] 7 George II c. 20 ; below 593.

[11] 8, 9 William III c. 11 § 8 ; see Preston v. Dania (1872) L.R. 8 Ex. at p. 21, *per* Bramwell B.

[12] Lowe v. Peers (1768) 4 Burr. at pp. 2228-2229, *per* Lord Mansfield C.J. ; Ponsonby v. Adams (1770) 2 Bro. P.C. 431 ; Rolfe v. Peterson (1772) 2 Bro. P.C. 436 ; Fletcher v. Dyche (1787) 2 T.R. 32 ; vol. xii 519-520.

[13] The starting-points of the modern law are the two cases of Astley v. Weldon (1801) 2 B. and P. 346, and Kemble v. Farren (1829) 6 Bing. 141 ; vol. xii 520.

[14] § 20.

Crown and to all courts of record,[1] and the recovery by the defendant in error of his costs when the writ of error was quashed for defects of form.[2]

These clauses effected some very useful reforms in common law procedure. Two other reforms were proposed which did not, unfortunately, become part of the Act.

The first of these reforms was a proposal that, if a person was likely to be unable to give evidence at a trial because he was about to go beyond the seas, or on account of sickness, the plaintiff or defendant should be able to administer interrogations to him, and that his deposition should be able to be used at the trial in case he was unable to be present.[3] The House of Lords defended this proposal on the following grounds : it would prevent delays which might mean the entire loss of the plaintiff's right, or even if that did not happen, the putting off of the trial till the witness could be present ; and it would prevent " many tedious suits in courts of equity, for, where persons cannot try their causes in due time, by reason the witnesses cannot be present, they will be trying all experiments, rather than lose the testimony of their witnesses." It was also pointed out that the clause was strictly limited to depositions taken after an issue had been reached ; and that these depositions could only be used on the trial of that issue, and then only if the witness was unable to be present.[4]

The Commons objected to the clause mainly because they distrusted all written evidence not taken in open court.[5] They thought that it might lead to abuses, and might tend to make perjury more probable.[6] There was considerable force in these objections. But it is probable that what weighed most with the Commons was their experience of the uselessness of the written evidence elicited by the system in use in the court of Chancery : [7]

[1] § 24 ; this section was extended to writs of mandamus and to informations in the nature of a *quo warranto* by 9 Anne c. 20 § 7.

[2] § 25.   [3] Lords' Journals xviii 69.   [4] Ibid 146.

[5] " When a witness is examined in open court, upon any trial at common law, questions may be asked him upon a cross-examination by the court, the jury . . . or by the counsel at the bar, to sift out the truth of his evidence ; nay, very often the disordered look of an evidence, a faultering in his speech, or such like circumstance may be a guide to the jury as to the credibility of the evidence," Commons' Journals xv 198 ; Blackstone agreed with this view, Comm. iii 373.

[6] " A witness when sworn and examined in the face of the court and country, will be under a greater awe of truth, and more cautious of not forswearing himself, for fear of being detected, and immediately committed by the court for perjury ; in which case the court does at the same time usually direct a prosecution ; whereas depositions (taken in the manner proposed by the clause) may be made by a profligate person, who (intending soon afterwards to go beyond the seas, and to continue out of the kingdom, or pretend sickness, or disability to attend, till after such depositions shall have been made use of upon the trial) may more easily be wrought upon to perjure himself, when he thinks he is without the reach of punishment," Commons' Journals xv 198.   [7] As to this system see vol. ix 353-358.

Upon depositions taken in courts of equity if the witnesses differ as to matters of fact, or the credit of the witnesses is suspected, the courts of equity are so far from relying on such depositions, that they direct issues to be tried at law, in order that the witnesses may be there examined in open court, where the credit of the witnesses will be considered ; but (as it seems to be intended) by this clause, depositions taken at law in all courts, must be allowed as evidence.[1]

The Commons admitted that depositions were allowed in trials at common law, " when such witnesses are out of the kingdom or under a disability to attend, though the witnesses be then living ; "[2] but they thought that this manner of giving evidence ought not to be encouraged, and that therefore this practice should not be extended in the manner proposed by the Lords.[3]

In answer to these objections, it might be said, first, that there was a considerable difference between evidence taken as to a single definite issue, and evidence taken as to all the allegations made in a bill or answer ; and secondly, that in the course of the eighteenth century the growth of Great Britain's oversea possessions made it clear that it was necessary to take measures to give larger powers to secure the evidence of witness out of the jurisdiction. In 1773 the courts were empowered to order the examination of witnesses in India, when a cause of action arising there was to be tried in the courts at Westminster.[4] This power was extended in 1831 to causes of action arising in all colonies,[5] and it was provided that the court might, on the application of the parties, order an examination on interrogatories of witnesses within the jurisdiction.[6] The depositions so taken under this Act could be read at the trial if the witness was beyond the jurisdiction, dead, or unable from some permanent infirmity to attend the trial.[7] It is true that this was a more restricted and a more carefully guarded power than that suggested in 1705-1706. But, probably, the effects of passing the clause then proposed by the Lords would not have been so bad as the Commons anticipated. The evil effects which they anticipated did not follow from the enactment of the statute of 1831.

Though the Commons could make out a good case for the rejection of the Lords' proposal for the reform of the law of evidence, there was much less reason for their failure to assent to the second of these proposals. This was a proposal made by the committee which reported to the House of Lords on January 17, 1706, that

---

[1] Commons' Journals xv 198.
[2] See Fry v. Wood (1737) 1 Atk. 445 ; Comyns, Digest *Testmoigne* C. 4 ; cp. Howard v. Tremaine (1693) 1 Show. K.B. 363 ; Tilley's Case (1704) 1 Salk. 286.
[3] Commons' Journals xv 198.   [4] 13 George III c. 63 § 44.
[5] 1 William IV c. 22 § 1.   [6] § 4.   [7] § 10.

the debts that any defendant hath owing unto him may be attached in execution, in satisfaction for debts and damages recovered against him ; and a day shall be given to the debtor to appear. The court shall give judgment for the plaintiff to recover so much as shall be attached, etc., as in London upon a foreign attachment.[1]

This proposal would have effected a very useful improvement in the law, and might, if it had been further developed, have had other and more considerable beneficial effects. Until 1838 the writs by which a creditor could get execution upon his debtor's property only allowed the tangible property of the debtor to be taken.[2] In 1831-1832 the Common Law Procedure Commissioners said that

the creditor may have execution against all the movable goods of the debtor, but he cannot have execution against the copyhold lands, or more than half the profits of the freehold of the defendant, or against stock in the public funds, or bonds, bills of exchange, or other securities or any debts due to the debtor. . . . The only means which the law at present provides for procuring satisfaction to the creditor, when the debtor's property is of the description before mentioned, is by permitting the arrest and imprisonment of the debtor, until the latter, as a condition of obtaining his liberty, cedes the property for the benefit of the judgment creditor.[3]

It was not till 1838 that a creditor was allowed to take in execution money, bank-notes, negotiable instruments, bonds, specialities, and other securities for money belonging to the debtor.[4] It was not till 1854 that the suggestion made in 1705-1706 was carried out, and that debts due to a judgment debtor were allowed to be attached by means of garnishee proceedings.[5] It is clear that the enormous and unregulated powers allowed by the law to creditors to arrest their debtors, and the manifold abuses consequent upon the existence of these powers,[6] might have been more quickly reformed if the powers of creditors to take their debtor's property in execution had been enlarged. It is true that the proposal made in 1705-1706 was a limited proposal—all that was to be taken in execution was

---

[1] Lords' Journals xviii 70.

[2] Vol. viii 230 ; by the writ of *fieri facias* the debt could be levied from the goods and chattels of the debtor ; by the writ of *levari facias* it could be levied from the goods and profits of the land ; by the writ of elegit the creditor could take and occupy half the land till he had levied the amount due from it ; in the case of Horn v. Horn (1749) Ambler 79 Lord Hardwicke pointed out that stock in the public funds could not be taken on a *fi. fa.*

[3] Parlt. Papers (1831-1832) xxv Pt. i p. 38 ; this was the reason why it was necessary for Dodson and Fogg to arrest Pickwick who had no land or tangible chattels of any value ; it was a master-stroke, when they found that this step was not likely to produce the money, to put further pressure on him by arresting Mrs. Bardell and by sending her to the same prison, see Holdsworth, Charles Dickens as a Legal Historian 142-143.

[4] 1, 2 Victoria c. 110 §§ 12 and 14.

[5] 17, 18 Victoria c. 125 § 61 ; 23, 24 Victoria c. 126 §§ 28-30.

[6] For these abuses see below 595-597.

debts due to a judgment debtor.   But if the principle that a
chose in action could thus be taken had been admitted, it might
well have happened that it would have been sooner extended
to other items of that large and miscellaneous mass of things
which the law classed under the rubric " choses in action."   If
that had happened, the principal reason for permitting these
large powers of arrest would, as the Common Law Procedure
Commissioners pointed out,[1] have disappeared.

The reforms made in the procedure of courts of equity were
much less extensive.   No subpœna or other process to enforce
appearance was to issue till after the bill was filed, except in
cases of bills for injunctions to stay waste or to stay an action
at law.[2]   In order to put a stop to vexatious suits, it was provided that if the plaintiff dismissed his own suit, or if the
defendant got it dismissed for want of prosecution, the defendant
should be entitled to full costs.[3]   In order to diminish expense
it was provided that no copy or abstract of the bill was to go
with the commission to take the defendant's answer, and provision was made for compensating the sworn clerks for the loss
of their fees for copies by giving them the term fees.[4]   Here
again the Lords made another proposal which was not assented
to by the Commons, and did not become part of the Act.   They
proposed that the plaintiff should serve a copy of the bill on the
defendant with the subpœna.[5]   As they pointed out, it would
have given the defendant adequate notice of the cause of action,
it would tend " to prevent the tediousness and impertinence of
bills," and " would contribute to the cure of another very
general and great abuse, in making many persons defendants
unnecessarily and for vexation only."

The land law.

The Act made several small but useful reforms in the land
law.   It got rid of the necessity for the attornment of the tenant
on the grant of manors, rents, reversions, or remainders.[6]   It
provided that the declarations of uses or trusts of fines and
recoveries, made by deeds executed after the levying of the
fine or the suffering of the recovery, were valid [7]—thus clearing
up a doubt raised by the seventh clause of the statute of Frauds,

---

[1] Above 524.   [2] 4, 5 Anne c. 16 § 22 (R.C. c. 3).   [3] § 23.
[4] § 23 ; for the reason for this change and its effect see Barley v. Pearson (1746)
3 Atk. at p. 440 ; the manner in which the vested interests of the officials of the
courts helped to delay reforms is illustrated by a petition of the Six Clerks protesting against taking these term fees from them and giving them to the sworn clerks,
House of Lords MSS. (N.S.) vi no. 2209.
[5] Lords' Journals xviii 146-147.
[6] 4, 5 Anne c. 16 §§ 9 and 10 (R.C. c. 3); for attornment see vol. iii 82, 97, 100,
234.   [7] § 15.

which required creations and declarations of trusts to be proved by writing.[1] A claim or entry was not to avoid the effect of a fine levied with proclamations, or to stop the running of the period of limitation fixed by the statute of 1624, unless, within a year after the making of the entry or claim, an action was begun and prosecuted with effect.[2] Warranties made by tenants for life were to be void, and collateral warranties made by ancestors who had no estate of inheritance in possession were to be void as against their heirs.[3]

Wills.

The law as to the competency of witnesses called to prove a nuncupative will, when the estate exceeded the value of £30, was declared to be the same as that which regulated the competency of witnesses upon trials at law.[4] The jurisdiction to grant probate or letters of administration to the relatives of persons working in the royal dockyards was to belong to the bishop of the diocese, and not to the Prerogative court.[5]

The action of account.

A clause added to the bill by the Commons,[6] effected an improvement in the action of account which had been many times attempted in vain.[7] It extended the scope of the action, and it improved the procedure upon it. The action was to lie against the executors and administrators of guardians, bailiffs, and receivers, and by and against joint tenants and tenants in common and their representatives. The auditors appointed by the court were empowered to administer oaths and examine the parties, and they were to be allowed such remuneration as the court saw fit, which was to be paid by the party on whose side the balance of account appeared to be. This clause did not succeed in reviving the action of account. Blackstone says : [8]

It is found by experience, that the most ready and effectual way to settle these matters of account is by bill in a court of equity, where a discovery may be had on the defendant's oath, without relying merely on the evidence which the plaintiff may be able to produce. Wherefore

---

[1] 29 Charles II c. 3 § 7.

[2] 4, 5 Anne c. 16 § 16 (R.C. c. 3) ; see vol. iii 241.

[3] § 21 ; for collateral warranties see vol. iii 118 n. 1.

[4] 4, 5 Anne c. 16 § 14 (R.C. c. 3).

[5] § 26 ; it was recited that " great trouble and expense is frequently occasioned to the widows and orphans of persons dying intestate to monies or wages due for work done in her Majesty's yards or docks, by disputes happening about the authority of granting probate of the wills and letters of administration of the goods and chattels of such persons" ; this clause was added by the Commons, Commons' Journals xv 182.

[6] Ibid ; 4, 5 Anne c. 16 § 27 (R.C. c. 3) ; for this action see vol. iii 426-428.

[7] Bl. Comm. iii 163.   [8] Comm. iii 163.

actions of account, to compel a man to bring in and settle his accounts, are now very seldom used ; though, when an account is once stated, nothing is more common than an action upon the implied *assumpsit* to pay the balance.

The limitation of actions.

Suits and actions for seamen's wages brought in the court of Admiralty were to be subject to a six years' period of limitation ; [1] but if the plaintiff were an infant, married woman, insane, imprisoned, or beyond the seas, the period was to run from the cesser of the disability.[2] Defendants in such actions, and also in other common law actions set out in the statute,[3] who were beyond the seas when the cause of action arose, could be sued at any time within six years after their return.[4]

The changes made by this Act were by no means far reaching. The fact that it was the most comprehensive of the eighteenth-century statutes for the amendment of the law, is, as we shall now see, an index to the very limited scope of the legislation of this period upon the technical doctrines of various branches of English Law.

Various Branches of the Law

The branches of law with which I propose to deal are : Criminal Law and Procedure ; the Land Law ; Civil Procedure ; Contract and Tort ; and Ecclesiastical Law.

I. Criminal Law and Procedure.

The group of statutes upon this topic is, with the exception of the group of statutes on commerce and industry, the largest group. Starting from the basis of the common law and the existing statute law, the history of which I have related in preceding volumes,[5] the Legislature attempted to adapt this body of principles and rules to the changing conditions of the eighteenth century, by means of a very large number of statutes, all of which were very limited in their scope. These statutes added considerably to the complexity of the law ; and since they were

---

[1] 4, 5 Anne c. 16 § 17 (R.C. c. 3).   [2] § 18.

[3] " Trespass, detinue, actions sur trover, or replevin for taking away goods or cattle, or action of account, or upon the case, or debt grounded upon any lending or contract without specialty, debt for arrearages of rent, or assault, menace, battery, wounding, and imprisonment, or any of them."

[4] § 19.

[5] For the statute law see vol. ii 449-457 ; vol. iv 492-532 ; vol. vi 399-407 ; for the common law doctrines see vol. ii 43-54, 197-199, 256-259, 357-369 ; vol. iii, chap. ii and 597-623 ; vol. v 167-214 ; vol. viii chap. v ; vol. ix 222-245.

accompanied by very few reforms of the many antiquated rules, substantive and adjective, which still survived, it had become clear, at the end of the century, that, though by comparison with continental countries, the English criminal law and procedure had a definite superiority, many reforms in this branch of the law were urgently needed.

Some of the lawyers of this period were well aware of the good and bad features of the law. Sollom Emlyn, who edited Hale's *Pleas of the Crown*,[1] wrote in 1730 a learned Preface to the second edition of the State Trials,[2] in which he sums up its merits and defects in a manner which won praise from Hargrave,[3] who succeeded him as editor of these Trials. He pointed out that English was superior to continental law in the publicity of criminal trials,[4] in the absence of torture,[5] in the safeguarding of the liberty of the subject,[6] in the statutory provisions which defined the offence of high treason and gave procedural advantages to persons accused of this offence.[7] On the other hand he suggested many points in which reform was desirable. He criticized the rule which required unanimity in the jury, and confined them " in one room without meat, drink, fire, or candle " till they reached a unanimous verdict;[8] the rule that all the indictments and other formal proceedings must be in Latin;[9] the misleading form of certain indictments;[10] the refusal of counsel to persons accused of felony;[11] the *peine fort et dure*;[12] the frequency of the death penalty and other defects in the punishments meted out by the law;[13] the oppressions and extortions of gaolers, and the grossly defective manner in

---

[1] Vol. vi 590.   [2] For the State Trials see vol. xii 127-130.

[3] Though Hargrave took exception to some of Emlyn's criticisms on the civil law and the ecclesiastical courts, he says, " the preface is much admired, and certainly deserves great commendation, as well in respect of the learning displayed in it, as on account of the spirit and judgment of most of the remarks, which, in general, do equal credit to the author's humanity and understanding," Pref. to Hargrave's ed. of the State Trials; for Hargrave see vol. xii 410-411.

[4] Vol. iii 620-622; vol. v 176; vol. ix 224.

[5] Vol. v 185-187, 194-195, 493; vol. ix 230.

[6] Ibid 112-119.   [7] Vol. vi 232-234.

[8] See vol. i 347 as to the power of the court to discharge a jury who cannot agree.

[9] Vol. ii 479; below 603.

[10] " As for instance the words *vi et armis* in indictments for writing and publishing libels, and in many other cases, where there is no pretence or colour of truth in them . . . which not only is an absurdity in the nature of the thing, but tends to ensnare the consciences of jurymen; who in giving a general verdict against the defendant, do not always consider whether that part of the indictment be proved. When a juryman gives a general verdict against the defendant, he does in effect declare upon oath, that he believes the entire charge as laid in the indictment to be true; how therefore can he find a man guilty generally, when there is one part of the charge, which he either believes to be false, or at least has no reason to believe to be true ? " For the extreme formality required in indictments see vol. iii 616-620.

[11] Vol. v 192; vol. ix 232, 235.   [12] Vol. i 327.

[13] Below 557-561, 562-564.

which the gaols were managed.[1] We shall see that some of these defects were amended by the Legislature during this period. But others were not amended till the nineteenth and twentieth centuries.[2]

I shall deal with this topic under the following heads : (1) the substantive law ;   (2) procedure ;   (3) punishment ;   (4) the characteristics of the criminal law and procedure of the eighteenth century.

(1) *The substantive law.*

The criminal law is closely connected with many other branches of law, because it is very often necessary to provide that a breach of the rules of these various branches of law shall be a criminal offence, and punished as such. It is closely connected with many aspects of public law. High treason, riot, and seditious libel are obvious illustrations ; and to these can be added the legislation passed to enable the state to fulfil its international obligations, such as the legislation as to ambassadors [3] and the legislation as to foreign enlistment,[4] and also the legislation passed to secure that the House of Commons should be freely chosen by electors, uninfluenced by bribery or corrupt practices.[5] With these aspects of the criminal law I have already dealt. It is closely connected with many aspects of the law as to local government. We have seen that the justices of the peace were given power to punish summarily those many minor offences, which had been created by that large mass of statutes which dealt with such matters as the poor law,[6] the highways,[7] public-houses,[8] and vagrancy.[9] It is closely connected with the legislation as to commerce and industry. We have seen that the numerous statutes on these topics made large additions to the criminal law, and sometimes gave rise to new developments of common law doctrine. Obvious illustrations are the laws which attempted to suppress smuggling,[10] to suppress the export of wool,[11] and the laws which dealt with combinations of workmen.[12] But even after these large groups of statutes, which added to the criminal law, have been eliminated, a considerable residuum remains, which I shall deal with under the following heads : (i) wrongs to property ; (ii) wrongs to the person ; (iii) piracy ; (iv) offences relating to the coinage ;

---

[1] Vol. x 180-183 ; below 567-568.

[2] Thus persons charged with felony were not allowed the help of counsel till 1837, 6, 7 William IV c. 114 § 1 ; the forms of indictments were not materially changed till the Indictments Act 1915, 5, 6 George V c. 90.

[3] Vol. x 370-371.   [4] Ibid 376.   [5] Ibid 573-574.   [6] Ibid 173-177, 211-214.

[7] Ibid 171-172.   [8] Ibid 183-185.   [9] Ibid 177-180.

[10] Above 413-417.   [11] Above 413-414.   [12] Above 488-490, 496-498.

(v) gaming and lotteries ; (vi) the game laws ; (vii) offences
against the machinery of justice ; (viii) miscellaneous.

(i) *Wrongs to property.*

These wrongs can, as Stephen points out,[1] be divided into
two main classes—wrongs which consist in the misappropriation
of property, and wrongs which consist in its destruction or
injury.

Misappropriation. The law as to larceny [2] was developed by
a large number of statutes. One category of these statutes, with
which it is not necessary to deal in detail, was concerned with
taking away benefit of clergy from certain kinds of grand
larceny.[3] Another, and a more important category, added to
the objects of property which could be the subject of larceny.[4]
The rule that there could be no larceny of things which were
annexed to the freehold, gave rise to a large number of statutes
which made certain of these things capable of being the subjects
of larceny. Thus it was enacted in 1731 that stealing lead,
iron bars, gates, or railings fixed to a building, should be felony ; [5]
and a number of statutes made it larceny to steal various fruits,
vegetables, and trees.[6] The rule that there could be no larceny
of animals *ferae naturae* unless " reclaimed or confined " and
useful as food,[7] was, to a large extent, got rid of by statutes
which made it felony to wound, kill or steal deer, to rob warrens,
or to steal fish from rivers or ponds,[8] or to steal dogs.[9] The rule
that wreck, because it was a *res nullius* till the King or other
person having the franchise of wreck seized it, could not be stolen
till it had been so seized,[10] was got rid of by a statute of 1753 which
made it a felony without benefit of clergy to " plunder, steal, take
away or destroy " any goods or merchandise from any ship in
distress or wrecked.[11] The rule that choses in action, " being of
no intrinsic value and not importing any property in *possession*
of the person from whom they are taken," could not be stolen,[12]
was modified in 1729 by a statute which made it felony to steal

---

[1] H.C.L. iii 121.   [2] Vol. iii 360-368.
[3] For the history of benefit of clergy see ibid 294-302.
[4] For the common law on this topic see ibid 367-368.
[5] 4 George II c. 32 ; extended by 21 George III c. 68 to copper, brass, bell-
metal, utensils, or fixtures annexed to buildings ; 25 George II c. 10 made it felony
to enter blacklead mines with intent to steal.
[6] Vol. vi 402 ; 31 George II c. 35 § 5 (madder) ; 6 George III c. 48 (timber,
shrubs, under-wood, plants) ; 13 George III c. 33 (timber).
[7] Bl. Comm. iv 235.
[8] 9 George I c. 22 § 1—usually known as the Waltham Black Act, because it
was directed primarily against a gang of deer stealers in Hampshire known as the
Waltham Blacks, Lecky, History of England ii 113 ; 5 George III c. 14 ; 16 George
III c. 30.
[9] 10 George III c. 18.   [10] Bl. Comm. iv 235.
[11] 26 George II c. 19 § 1.   [12] Bl. Comm. iv 234.

Exchequer orders or tallies, Exchequer bills, South Sea bonds, bank notes, East India bonds, dividend warrants, bills of exchange, navy bills or debentures, goldsmith's notes, or other bonds or warrants, bills or promissory notes.[1] On the other hand, till 1827,[2] it was not a criminal offence to steal the title deeds to land either because they savoured of the realty, or because they were in the nature of choses in action, or because they were regarded as having no value.[3]

It was a common practice among thieves to bargain with the owners of stolen goods for their return to them for a money consideration.[4] To stop this practice, it was enacted in 1717[5] that whoever took money under the pretence of helping the owner to recover his stolen goods should be liable to the same penalties as the thief, unless he caused the thief to be apprehended and brought to trial, and unless he gave evidence against him at the trial. With the same object a statute of 1752 made it an offence to advertise that a reward would be given for the return of stolen goods and that no questions would be asked, or that money paid by a pawnbroker or purchaser of the goods would be repaid.[6] Receiving stolen goods knowing them to be stolen was made a substantive misdemeanour in 1701 ;[7] so that, as the result of this and subsequent statutes, the prosecutor could elect whether to prosecute for this substantive misdemeanour, or to wait till the thief was convicted and prosecute the receiver for being an accessory to the felony.[8] The punishment for receiving stolen lead, iron, and certain other metals was increased in 1756 ;[9] and provision was made for the apprehension and punishment of persons who between sunset and sunrise were found in possession of these metals, and who could not give a satisfactory account of how they came by them.[10] In 1761 receiving goods stolen from a ship in the Thames, knowing them

---

[1] 2 George II c. 25 § 3.   [2] 7, 8 George IV c. 29 § 23.

[3] Bl. Comm iv 234 ; Kenny, Criminal Law 200 ; vol. iii 368.

[4] See a letter from two highwaymen who had robbed Horace Walpole in 1749 printed in Letters of Horace Walpole (ed. Toynbee) Suppl. iii 132-135—they demanded forty guineas, but in fact Walpole got his goods back on the payment of £20.

[5] 4 George I c. 11 § 4.

[6] 25 George II c. 36 § 1 ; Fielding had emphasized the encouragement given to thieves, by the ease with which they were able to dispose of stolen property, in his *Enquiry into the Causes of the late Increase of Robbers*, which had been published in the previous year at pp. 68-69—" if he has made a booty of any value, he is almost sure of seeing it advertised within a day or two, directing him to bring the goods to a certain place, where he is to receive a reward (sometimes the full value of the booty) and no question asked " ; see also *Amelia*, Bk. xi chap. 7 ; B. M. Jones, Henry Fielding, 187-192.

[7] 1 Anne c. 9 ; 5, 6 Anne c. 31 § 6 ; for the career of Jonathan Wild, " the receiver in chief in London of all stolen goods," see Pike, History of Crime ii 256-259 ; Fielding wrote *The History of the Life of the late Mr. Jonathan Wild the Great*, B. M. Jones, Henry Fielding 87-89.

[8] Bl. Comm. iv 132-133.   [9] 29 George II c. 30.   [10] § 3.

to be stolen, was made a substantive felony, whether or not the principal felons had been convicted ;[1] and in 1770 a similar provision was made for cases where persons received jewels, gold or silver plate, or watches, knowing them to be stolen, provided that those articles had been taken as the result of a burglary or a robbery on the highway.[2]

We have seen that an attempt to commit a crime was treated as a misdemeanour.[3] But in the case of robbery it was found desirable to treat such attempts more severely. It was enacted in 1734 [4] that any persons who assaulted another with any offensive weapon, or who, by menaces or in any forcible or violent manner, demanded money or chattels from another person with intent to rob that person, should be guilty of felony. In 1722 it was made a felony knowingly to send an anonymous letter, or a letter signed with a fictitious name, demanding money or other valuable things ;[5] in 1754 the same penalty was provided for the sending of any letter threatening to kill or murder any other persons or to burn their houses ;[6] and in 1757 it was made a misdemeanour to send a letter threatening to accuse another of any crime punishable by death, transportation, or the pillory, with a view or intent to extort money or property from that person.[7]

Until 1757 the obtaining of property by false pretences was not generally a crime. It was only if a person had obtained money or chattels by false tokens or counterfeit letters that he could be made criminally liable.[8] It is true that cheating was a common law misdemeanour ;[9] but this offence was not committed unless the fraud was carried out by some means injurious to the public generally, such as the use of false weights or measures. In 1702 " when A got money from B by pretending that C had sent him for it, Lord Holt grimly asked ' shall we indict a man for making a fool of another,' and bade the prosecutor to have recourse to a civil action." [10] It was enacted in 1757 [11] that a person who knowingly and designedly, by false pretences, obtained from another money or other chattels with intent to cheat or defraud, should be guilty of a misdemeanour. It appears to have been settled, soon after the statute was passed, that the pretence must relate, not to a future, but to a past or a present,

---

[1] 2 George III c. 28 § 12.
[2] 10 George III c. 48 ; further provision was made for the apprehension and punishment of receivers of stolen goods in 1782 by 22 George III c. 58.
[3] Vol. v 201 ; vol. viii 434. [4] 7 George II c. 21.
[5] 9 George I c. 22 § 1. [6] 27 George II c. 15.
[7] 30 George II c. 24 § 1. [8] 33 Henry VIII c. 1 ; vol. iv 514.
[9] Bl. Comm. iv 157.
[10] Kenny, Criminal Law 240, citing R. v. Jones (1704) 2 Ld. Raym. 1013.
[11] 30 George II c. 24 § 1.

fact. The reason given was that if the representation was as to a past or present fact it was impossible to verify its truth, but if it was a representation as to some future transaction, enquiries could be made, so that, if the party was deceived, it was through his own negligence.[1] This Act also made it an offence, punishable on summary conviction, to pawn or to dispose unlawfully of the goods of another person.[2]

We have seen that the crime of larceny by a bailee had been created by statutes of the sixteenth century. In the sixteenth century, this crime was committed, first, if bailees, being servants, embezzled goods the possession of which had been entrusted to them by their masters; and, secondly, if persons to whose possession munitions of war had been entrusted, embezzled them.[3] These statutes thus created two small exceptions to the common law rule that larceny could not be committed by persons to whom possession of chattels had been transferred by their owner. Another modification of the common law rule was made in 1691, when it was enacted that lodgers who stole the furniture of the rooms let to them should be guilty of larceny.[4] In 1742 it was enacted that officers and servants of the Bank of England who embezzled notes, bills, dividend warrants, bonds, deeds, securities or money belonging to the bank, or to other persons who had deposited them with the bank, should be guilty of felony;[5] and in 1754 a similar provision was made for the officers and servants of the South Sea Company.[6] In 1767 it was made a felony for any servant of the Post Office to embezzle or destroy letters and packets containing bank notes, or the securities for money set out in the Act, or to steal such bank notes or securities out of letters or packets.[7] It was also made a felony to destroy a letter after receiving payment for its postage, or to fail to account for money received for postage.[8] We have seen also that a number of statutes made it a criminal offence for employés to spoil material entrusted to them by their masters to work up.[9]

These are all cases where possession had been delivered to servants or bailees by their master or owner. They were not cases where a third person had given the servant possession,

---

[1] See Young v. the King (1789) 3 T.R. at p. 100, per Fielding arg.; Stephen, H.C.L. iii 161; the reason given is not very satisfactory, a better reason is that given by Kenny, Criminal Law 245-246, that "future events are matters of conjecture upon which every person must exercise his own judgment"; in fact the courts were at first by no means clear as to the kind of false pretences which were hit by the statute; in Young v. the King at p. 102 Lord Kenyon C.J. said, "it seems difficult to draw the line, and to say to what cases this statute shall extend"; in this case there was no doubt that the pretence was as to a past fact.

[2] § 3.

[3] Vol. iii 365; vol. iv 501.

[4] 3 William and Mary c. 9 § 5; vol. vi 402.

[5] 15 George II c. 13 § 12.

[6] 24 George II c. 11 § 3.

[7] 7 George III c. 50 § 1.

[8] § 3.

[9] Above 489.

in order that he might transfer it to his master. It was therefore held in *R. v. Bazeley* that where a bank cashier received
from a customer a £100 note, which he forthwith appropriated,
he had committed no crime.[1] Immediately after the decision of
this case the Legislature created the offence of embezzlement,
by enacting that a servant or clerk who, having by virtue of his
employment received money or securities into his possession on
account of his master, embezzled, secreted, or made away with
it or them, should be deemed to have feloniously stolen the same.[2]

We have seen that the crime of forgery had been developed
by the court of Star Chamber; that a statute of 1562-1563 had
made the forgery of certain deeds and documents relating to the
title to real property, chattels real, and annuities, and of obligations, acquittances, or releases, a misdemeanour punishable
by the pillory, loss of ears, imprisonment, and forfeiture, and,
on a second conviction, a felony without benefit of clergy ; [3] and
that, after the abolition of the court of Star Chamber, the courts
of common law, acted on the view, which had emerged in the
earlier part of the seventeenth century, that all manner of
forgeries were common law misdemeanours.[4] There were a
very large number of statutes passed in the eighteenth century
on the subject of forgery, all designed to make the forgery of
certain kinds of documents a felony. Thus in 1724 [5] it was made
felony to forge bank notes or bills with intent to defraud ; and
in 1725 [6] it was made felony without benefit of clergy to forge
with the like intent East India and South Sea bonds, and the
signatures of the accountant-general and certain other officers
of the court of Chancery, and of the cashiers of the Bank of
England, to certain instruments named in the Act. In 1729 [7]
it was made a felony without benefit of clergy to forge with intent
to defraud a deed, will, testament, bond, writing obligatory, bill
of exchange, promissory note, endorsement or assignment of a
bill of exchange or promissory note, an acquittance or receipt
for money or goods. In 1734 [8] acceptances of bills of exchange
and certain other documents were added to the list ; and in
1763,[9] powers of attorney to assign stock. These are only a
few out of the many statutes passed to make forgery a capital
felony. Blackstone says that the result of this series of statutes
was that " there is hardly now a case possible to be conceived,
wherein forgery, that tends to defraud, whether in the name of
a real or fictitious person, is not made a capital crime." [10]

---

[1] (1799) Leach 835, Kenny, Cases on Criminal Law 305.
[2] 39 George III c. 85.   [3] Vol. iv 501-503.
[4] Ibid 503.   [5] 11 George I c. 9 § 6.
[6] 12 George I c. 32 § 9.   [7] 2 George II c. 25 § 1.
[8] 7 George II c. 22.   [9] 4 George III c. 25 § 15.
[10] Comm. iv 250.

Many other statutes were passed to punish offences which are nearly related to forgery. For instance, a statute of 1773 made it a felony without benefit of clergy to make or use, or to cause to be made or used, or to assist in making or using, or knowingly to have the custody or possession of, moulds or instruments for making paper with the words Bank of England visible in the substance of the paper.[1] A statute of 1758 made it a felony without benefit of clergy to personate an officer or seaman in the King's service entitled to wages or prize money, or the representative of such officer or seaman, or to forge any document in order to obtain the money due to the officer or seaman, or, with that object, to take a false oath in order to get probate or letters of administration to his estate.[2] In 1792 it was made an offence punishable with fine or, in default of payment, imprisonment, for a person to give a false character of a servant, or to personate the master or mistress of the servant, or to make certain other false statements as to the servant's service.[3]

Destruction of or injury to property. Very considerable additions were made to the statutes which punished destruction of or injury to property. In many of the Acts which have just been mentioned, which punished various kinds of misappropriation of property, there are clauses which also punish its destruction or injury. Thus the Waltham Black Act of 1722, which dealt with the theft of deer and fish,[4] made it felony without benefit of clergy for persons having their faces blacked, or otherwise disguised, to break the heads of fishponds, to maim cattle, to destroy trees, to fire houses, barns, stacks of corn, hay or wood ;[5] and the Act of 1753, which dealt with stealing from ships in distress or wrecked,[6] also made it felony without benefit of clergy to destroy the goods thereon, or to display false lights in order to endanger a ship.[7] A large number of other Acts dealt with different kinds of damage to property. The following are examples : statutes of 1713, 1717, and 1724 made it felony without benefit of clergy to destroy a ship to the prejudice of the owners or insurers.[8] A statute of 1719 made it felony to assault persons in the street, and wilfully and maliciously to tear, spoil, cut, or deface their clothes [9]— an enactment which was occasioned, Blackstone tells us, " by the insolence of certain weavers and others, who, upon the

[1] 13 George III c. 79 § 1.   [2] 31 George II c. 10 § 24.
[3] 32 George III c. 56.   [4] Above 530.
[5] 9 George I c. 22 § 1.   [6] Above 530.
[7] 26 George II c. 19 § 1 ; see Pike, History of Crime ii 269-271.
[8] 12 Anne St. 2 c. 18 § 5 ; 4 George I c. 12 § 3 ; 11 George I c. 29 § 6 ; Bl. Comm. iv 245.
[9] 6 George I c. 23 § 11.

introduction of some Indian fashions prejudicial to their own manufactures, made it their practice to deface them." [1] The destruction of turnpikes, locks, sluices, and floodgates was dealt with by statutes of 1728,[2] 1735,[3] 1763,[4] and 1767.[5] In 1769 [6] the destruction of mills, of engines for draining mines, of bridges or wagon ways used for conveying minerals, and of fences made for enclosing land by virtue of Acts of Parliament, were made felonies.[7] In 1733 [8] breaking the banks of rivers whereby lands were flooded, and in 1737 [9] setting fire to coal mines, were made felonies without benefit of clergy. In 1766 [10] and 1773 [11] Acts were passed to prevent the destruction of shrubs, roots, plants, and timber. An Act of 1772,[12] which made regulations as to the manufacture, storing, and carriage of gunpowder, and provided penalties for the non-observance of its provisions, was directed to prevent obvious dangers to property.

(ii) *Wrongs to the person.*

We have seen that, in the seventeenth century, the law punished very inadequately wrongs to the person which did not result in death.[13] During the latter part of the seventeenth century Coventry's Act [14] was the only addition to the law made by the Legislature. In 1710 the attempt by Guiscard to assassinate Harley produced an Act which made an attempt to kill, or an assault upon, a privy-councillor while in the execution of his office, a felony without benefit of clergy.[15] In 1722 the Waltham Black Act [16] made it a felony without benefit of clergy to " wilfully and maliciously shoot at any person in any dwelling house or other place " In 1734 an assault with intent to rob was made a felony punishable with transportation for seven years.[17] In 1738 and 1796 penalties were provided for persons who assaulted others in order to hinder the purchase or carriage of corn.[18] The Act of 1753, which dealt with the plundering of a wrecked ship,[19] also made it felony without benefit of clergy

---

[1] Comm. iv 246.
[2] 1 George II St. 2 c. 19 § 1.
[3] 8 George II c. 20.
[4] 4 George III c. 12 § 5.
[5] 7 George III c. 40.
[6] 9 George III c. 29 §§ 1, 2, 3.
[7] In the case of the destruction of mills without benefit of clergy.
[8] 6 George II c. 37 § 5.
[9] 10 George II c. 32 § 6 ; setting fire to gorse and fern in forests and chaces was made punishable by a fine, 28 George II c. 19 § 3.
[10] 6 George III cc. 36 and 48; the first of these Acts was aimed primarily at the protection of nursery gardens and other inclosed ground : the second at the protection of timber and underwood.
[11] 13 George III c. 33.
[12] 12 George III c. 61.
[13] Vol. vi 403.
[14] 22, 23 Charles II c. 1 ; vol. vi 403.
[15] 9 Anne c. 16 § 1.
[16] 9 George I c. 22 § 1.
[17] 7 George II c. 21.
[18] 11 George II c. 22 § 1 ; 36 George III c. 9 § 1.
[19] Above 530.

to beat or wound with intent to kill, or to obstruct the escape of a shipwrecked person.[1] All these Acts dealt only with very special varieties of injuries to the person. " The first Act approaching to generality on this subject was 43 Geo. 3 c. 58, passed in 1803, known from its author as Lord Ellenborough's Act." [2]

(iii) *Piracy.*

We have seen that a statute of 1698-1699, by declaring certain offences to be piracy, introduced the distinction between piracy by statute and piracy *ex jure gentium.*[3] Three statutes passed during this period altered and extended the law as to the former of these two varieties of piracy.[4] An Act of 1717[5] excluded from the benefit of clergy the offences declared to be piracy by the Act of 1698-1699, and provided that persons accused of these offences could be tried in accordance with the statute of 1536.[6] An Act of 1721, after reciting the late increase of piracies, felonies and robberies on the seas, proceeds to declare that the following acts shall be deemed to be piracies : trading with pirates, supplying them with stores or ammunition, fitting out vessels with intent to trade with pirates, consulting or corresponding with pirates, forcibly boarding a merchant ship and destroying her cargo.[7] Ships fitted out to trade with pirates were to be forfeited.[8] Accessories to piracies were to be deemed to be principals and so could be tried, although the principal had not been tried.[9] All persons convicted under this Act were deprived of benefit of clergy.[10] Penalties were provided for masters and seamen of armed merchant ships who did not defend their ships when attacked by pirates.[11] On the other hand, rewards were given to seamen who defended their ships. If a ship was successfully defended, and any of the officers or seamen were wounded or killed, it was provided by a statute of 1670-1671 that they should be entitled to a reward not exceeding two per cent. of the value of the ship and cargo, to be distributed amongst the master, officers and crew, and the widows and children of the slain, as directed by the court of Admiralty ; and it was provided by a statute of 1721 that, in addition to these rewards, seamen who thus defended their ships should be entitled to be admitted into Greenwich hospital in preference to seamen

---

[1] 26 George II c. 19 § 1.   [2] Stephen, H.C.L. iii 113.
[3] 11, 12 William III c. 7 ; vol. vi 400-401.
[4] Bl. Comm. iv 72-73.   [5] 4 George I c. 11 § 7.
[6] 28 Henry VIII c. 15 ; vol. i 550-551.
[7] 8 George I c. 24 § 1.   [8] § 2.   [9] § 3.   [10] § 4.
[11] § 6 ; the penalty was loss of wages and six months' imprisonment ; similar provisions had been made by 22, 23 Charles II c. 11 §§ 2-5.

disabled merely by age.[1] In 1745 it was enacted that subjects who, during a war, committed any hostilities within the jurisdiction of the court of Admiralty against their fellow subjects, by virtue of a commission from the hostile state, or who assisted the enemy in any way upon the sea, should be tried as pirates in the court of Admiralty.[2]

(iv) *Offences relating to the coinage.*

We have seen that a number of new offences relating to the coinage had been created by the legislation of the sixteenth and seventeenth centuries.[3] Several additions were made to this legislation during this period.[4] The most important of these additions was made in 1742.[5] Gilding shillings and sixpences so as to make them resemble guineas and half-guineas, and colouring half-pence or farthings so as to make them pass for shillings and sixpences, were made high treason.[6] Uttering false money knowing it to be false was made punishable with imprisonment, and, on conviction a third time, felony.[7] The counterfeiting of half-pence and farthings was to be punished by imprisonment for two years.[8] This offence was made felony in 1771 ;[9] and in 1797 it was extended so as to include the counterfeiting of all copper coin.[10] In 1771 buying and selling counterfeit copper coin for lower value than its proper denomination was made a felony,[11] and the justices were empowered to search for, seize, and destroy the tools used to make counterfeit copper coin.[12] In 1773 persons to whom gold coin was tendered, which had been diminished otherwise than by reasonable wear, were empowered to deface it.[13] In 1774 the importation of light silver money was prohibited.[14] If silver coin exceeding £5 in

---

[1] 22, 23 Charles II c. 11 § 10 ; 8 George I c. 24 § 5 ; § 7 of the latter Act, in order to prevent seamen from deserting in foreign ports and turning pirates, enacted that masters should not pay more than half the wages due to the seamen at a foreign port, and should retain the rest till the voyage was completed.

[2] 18 George II c. 30 ; the Act was occasioned by a doubt whether these offences did not amount to adhering to the King's enemies, which was high treason, and were therefore outside the jurisdiction conferred on the court of Admiralty to try piracies under 11, 12 William III c. 7 § 8 ; see vol. vi 401.

[3] Vol. iv 498 ; vol. vi 400.   [4] Bl. Comm. iv 89-90, 99-100.
[5] 15 George II c. 28.   [6] § 1.
[7] § 2 ; if a person uttered false money, knowing it to be false, and within ten days uttered more false money to the same or another person, or if, at the time of such uttering, he had about him more false money, he was to be punished as a common utterer of false money, and on a second offence he was to be punished as a felon without benefit of clergy, § 3.

[8] § 6.   [9] 11 George III c. 40 § 1.   [10] 37 George III c. 126 § 1.
[11] 11 George III c. 100 § 2.   [12] § 3.
[13] 13 George III c. 71 § 1 ; if the money was really of proper weight the person who defaced it must receive it in payment ; the justices or the chief official of the town where the tender was made must decide this question, ibid.
[14] 14 George III c. 42 § 1.

value was found on any ship, it was to be seized, and, if proved to be light, it was to be melted down and the produce was to go half to the Crown and half to the prosecutor.

(v) *Gaming and lotteries.*

Blackstone had no doubt that law ought to attempt to prohibit gaming:

Taken in any light, it is an offence of the most alarming nature; tending by necessary consequence to promote public idleness, theft, and debauchery among those of a lower class; and, among persons of a superior rank, it hath frequently been attended with the sudden ruin and desolation of antient and opulent families, an abandoned prostitution of every principle of honour and virtue, and too often hath ended in self murder.[1]

We have seen that the Legislature had already attempted to repress some forms of gaming, partly by means of the criminal law, and partly by refusing to winners the aid of the courts to recover their winnings.[2] A statute of 1664 had imposed penalties upon those who had acquired money or property by fraud in playing at games, had made contracts to pay bets exceeding £100 on the players of games and all securities given for the payment of these bets void, and had made the winner of more than £100 liable to forfeit treble the value of his winnings above that sum.[3] A statute of 1698 had declared lotteries to be public nuisances, and had imposed a penalty on those who held them or took part in them.[4] During the eighteenth century this legislation increased in bulk and in stringency.

In 1708 wagers on any contingency relating to the war were prohibited, and those who made these wagers or who were in any way concerned in making them were to forfeit double the sum for which the wager was laid.[5] In 1710 " an Act for the better preventing of excessive and deceitful gaming " [6] provided as follows : notes, bills, bonds, judgments, mortgages, or other securities or conveyances, given for money won at play or betting on the players, or given for the repayment of money knowingly lent for these purposes, were to be void. If the mortgages or conveyances were of land, or if they encumbered or affected land, the mortgages or conveyances were to enure for the benefit of the person who would have been entitled to the land if the grantor had been dead.[7] A person who had lost £10 at play or in betting on the players at any one sitting, and had paid the

---

[1] Comm. iv 171.
[2] Vol. vi 404.
[3] 16 Charles II c. 7.
[4] 10 William III c. 23 ; vol. vi 404.
[5] 7 Anne c. 16.
[6] 9 Anne c. 14.
[7] § 1 ; all grants made in order to prevent the lands thus devolving on the heir were to be void, ibid.

winner, could, within three months, recover the money from the winner.[1] If the loser did not sue within the three months, any person could sue for treble the value—half to go to the plaintiff and half to the poor.[2] The persons so sued could be compelled to answer to bills brought against them for the discovery of the sums which they had won;[3] and in 1745 it was provided that the court of equity, in which those bills were brought, could decree payment of the money.[4] Persons who won at any one time a sum above the value of £10 were, on conviction, to forfeit five times the sum won, and, if they were proved to have won any sum by means of fraud, they were to be deemed infamous and to suffer the same corporal punishment as in case of perjury.[5] Persons without visible means, who were suspected of supporting themselves by gaming, could be summoned before the justices and ordered to find securities for good behaviour.[6] Assaults committed, or challenges sent, on account of money won at play, were made punishable by forfeiture of chattels and imprisonment for two years.[7]

Statutes of 1710,[8] 1711,[9] 1721,[10] 1722,[11] and 1733[12] were passed to suppress lotteries of various descriptions. But as soon as one variety of lottery was suppressed, another made its appearance. In 1739[13] it was recited that it was doubtful whether certain fraudulent games and lotteries to be determined by the chance of cards or dice, to wit games called ace of hearts, pharaoh, basset, and hazard were caught by these Acts. It was therefore enacted that they should come within these Acts.[14] Penalties were imposed on all persons who were in any way connected with the holding or the preparations for holding these lotteries, or who took part in them.[15] Sales of property by means of lotteries were to entail forfeiture of the property.[16] In 1740 the game of passage, and other games played with dice except back-gammon,[17] and in 1745[18] roulet, were added to the games mentioned in the statute of 1739, and power was given to the court to summon persons to give evidence as to the matters alleged against persons accused of having infringed the provisions of these Acts.[19]

Gaming on horse races was the subject of a statute of 1740.[20]

<hr/>

[1] § 2.

[2] Ibid.

[3] § 3.

[4] 18 George II c. 34 § 3.

[5] 9 Anne c. 14 § 5.

[6] § 6.

[7] § 8; the Act was not to apply to the playing at games in the palaces of St. James or Whitehall when the Queen was residing there, or in any other palaces when the Queen was resident, provided the play was for ready money, § 9.

[8] 9 Anne c. 6 § 56.

[9] 10 Anne c. 26 § 109.

[10] 8 George I c. 2 §§ 36, 37.

[11] 9 George I c. 19 § 4—foreign lotteries.

[12] 6 George II c. 35 § 29.

[13] 12 George II c. 28.

[14] § 2.

[15] §§ 1, 3.

[16] § 4.

[17] 13 George II c. 19 § 9.

[18] 18 George II c. 34 §§ 1, 2.

[19] § 4.

[20] 13 George II c. 19.

The Act laid down conditions under which races were to be run ;[1] and, to check the multiplicity of these races, which gave occasion for much betting and gaming, it was provided that no race should be run for any sum of money, plate, or prize, except at Newmarket or Black Hambleton, or unless the money, plate, or prize was of the value of £50 or upwards ; and penalties were imposed on those who ran or advertised races in contravention of the Act.[2]

Blackstone admits that this legislation had had very little success.[3] This was due, first to the character of the legislation ; and, secondly and chiefly, to the fact that, though it may be possible for a Legislature to regulate, it is impossible for it to suppress wholly certain natural instincts and proclivities of mankind.

First, this legislation, and especially the legislation against lotteries, was not sufficiently general in its scope. Blackstone was right when he said that

particular descriptions will ever be lame and deficient, unless all games of mere chance are at once prohibited ; the inventions of sharpers being swifter than the punishment of the law, which only hunts them from one device to another.[4]

Similarly, though the Legislature prohibited stakes or bets on games, rendered securities given for payment of these stakes or bets void, and enabled a loser who had paid to recover his losses,[5] it did not render all contracts subsidiary to, or leading up to, these gaming or betting contracts void. It was held in the eighteenth century that it was still possible to recover money lent to a person for the purpose of gaming, because it was thought that the Act of Anne avoided only the security and not the debt created by the loan,[6]—a proposition which has given rise to much difference of judicial opinion, and still awaits final determination by the House of Lords.[7] Nor did the Legislature render all of these gaming or betting contracts void. Under the Act of Charles II it was still possible to sue for gaming debts not

---

[1] §§ 1, 3 ; § 3 was in effect repealed by 18 George II c. 34 § 11.

[2] §§ 2, 3, 5 ; for a case on the construction of the clause imposing this £50 limitation see Bidmead v. Gale (1769) 4 Burr. 2432 ; see the reporter's note at p. 2434 to the effect that the decision showed that " the law of Westminster Hall does here happily coincide with the laws of the turf."

[3] " It is the gaming in high life that demands the attention of the magistrate ; a passion to which every valuable consideration is made a sacrifice, and which we seem to have inherited from our ancestors, the ancient Germans ; whom Tacitus describes to have been bewitched with the spirit of play to a most exorbitant degree. . . . One would almost be tempted to think Tacitus was describing a modern Englishman," Comm. iv 171.

[4] Ibid 173.   [5] Above 539-540.

[6] Barjean v. Walmsley (1746) 2 Str. 1249 ; Robinson v. Bland (1760) 1 W. Bl. at p. 260, S.C. 2 Burr. 1077 ; Wettenhall v. Wood (1793) 1 Esp. 18.

[7] See the review of the authorities by Shearman J. in Carlton Hall Club v. Laurence [1929] 2 K.B. at pp. 160-164.

exceeding £100,[1] and under the Act of Anne for gaming debts not exceeding £10.[2] Still less did it render all bets void.[3] Indeed it would have been impossible for the Legislature to have made all bets void without disturbing the machinery of justice. We have seen that the principal means by which a disputed question of fact arising in the court of Chancery was submitted to a jury was by directing a trial in a common law court on a feigned issue—that is, upon a bet upon the truth of the fact in dispute made by the plaintiff and defendant.[4]

But, secondly, the main reason why both this and later legislation has failed to effect its object is the impossibility of wholly suppressing the natural instinct of mankind to gamble and bet. There was considerable truth in Blackstone's remark that it was not so much the laws that were deficient as " ourselves and our magistrates in putting those laws in execution." [5] And the reason is fairly obvious. Betting and gambling, like drinking, if carried to excess produce the worst consequences ; but no sensible person contends that betting, gambling, or drinking are always and necessarily immoral or attended with bad consequences. Hence laws which attempt to suppress them entirely fail, because they run counter to the feelings of average law-abiding citizens. It is impossible to suppress these practices entirely ; and it is impossible so to regulate them that no bad consequences will ever follow from indulgence in them ; but it is possible so to regulate them that excessive indulgence in them is made more difficult. This should be, and to a large extent has been, the object of the Legislature. Moreover, if, as in these cases of gambling and betting and drinking, practices exist which are not *per se* immoral, and are so deeply rooted in man's nature that they cannot be wholly suppressed, it is legitimate for the state to make some profit for itself by permitting their indulgence at a price. The state has long followed this course by taxing alcoholic drinks ; and from 1567 to 1824 it followed the course of permitting lotteries for the benefit of public objects.[6] It is perhaps unfortunate that such lotteries

---

[1] Danvers v. Thistlewaite (1668) 1 Lev. 244 ; Walker v. Walker (1698) 12 Mod. 258.

[2] Bulling v. Frost (1794) 1 Esp. 235 ; and see Moulis v. Owen [1907] 1 K.B. at pp. 763-764 for a discussion of these and similar cases by Fletcher Moulton L.J.

[3] Good v. Elliott (1790) 3 T.R. 693 ; see the judgment of Lord Kenyon C.J. at pp. 704-706, reviewing the authorities.

[4] Vol. ix 357.   [5] Comm. iv 173.

[6] See 4 George IV c. 60 § 19 ; no doubt many frauds were perpetrated in the conduct of the private lotteries which the Legislature tried without success to suppress, above 540 ; Fielding showed up some of these frauds, B. M. Jones, Henry Fielding 43-44, and took the view that the government should give up holding lotteries for public objects, ibid ; this view has prevailed ; but it is clear that a lottery held for public objects and honestly conducted, is very different from a private lottery held for private gain and under conditions in which there is no guarantee that it will be honestly conducted.

were ever abandoned ; for it would be much more possible to suppress gambling of this kind if some lotteries were allowed. And, though no doubt some evils would follow, they would be no worse than the evils which follow from illicit lotteries ; and at least the profits accruing would be devoted to worthy causes.[1]

(vi) The game laws.

We have seen that the main principles underlying the game laws had emerged by the beginning of the eighteenth century.[2] During this century they became, as Blackstone says, "not a little obscure and intricate " ; [3] and they gave rise to a mass of case law.[4] Some of these statutes, it is true, simply made a close time for certain kinds of game ; [5] and to that kind of legislation no objection could be taken. But generally this series of statutes aimed at the definition of the classes who were entitled to kill game, and the sharpening of the law against persons who killed game without a qualification, who had engines for killing game, or game in their possession, or who sold game. The statutes were numerous ; and they were constantly being amended, repealed, and re-enacted in an altered form.[6] The effect of the legislation of this and earlier centuries was thus summed up by Blackstone, who did not love it : [7]

It is in general sufficient to observe, that the *qualifications* for killing game, as they are usually called, or more properly the *exemptions* from the penalties inflicted by the statute law, are 1. the having a freehold estate of £100 *per annum ;* there being fifty times the property required to enable a man to kill a partridge, as to vote for a knight of the shire : 2. A leasehold for ninety-nine years of £150 *per annum :* 3. Being the son and heir apparent of an esquire (a very loose and vague description) or person of superior degree : 4. Being the owner, or keeper of a forest, park, chase, or warren. For unqualified persons transgressing these laws, by killing game, keeping engines for that purpose,

---

[1] As was said in a debate in 1783, and as we now all know, if there was no English lottery " the people would gamble in an Irish, a Dutch, or a French lottery," Parlt. Hist. xxiii 783 ; cp. ibid xxvi 608 seqq. for a debate on the policy of allowing the insurance of lottery tickets ; Fox was right when he said, ibid 610, that since " it was totally impracticable to crush gambling *in toto*, it might be expedient to establish a mode by which the public could reap an advantage from the general passion. But nothing was so clear as that this should be guarded by every possible means against the evils which sprang from small gambling " ; Pitt also took this view, ibid xxix 548.
[2] Vol. vi 403 ; cp. vol. i 107-108, vol. vii 490-495.
[3] " The statutes for preserving the game are many and various, and not a little obscure and intricate ; it being remarked, that on one statute only, 5 Ann. c. 14, there is false grammar in no fewer than six places, besides other mistakes : the occasion of which, or what denomination of persons were probably the penners of these statutes, I shall not at present enquire," Comm. iv 175.
[4] See Burn, Justice of the Peace, Tit. *Game.*
[5] See 2 George III c. 19 ; 36 George III c. 54 ; 39 George III c. 34.
[6] See 5, 6 Anne c. 14 ; 9 Anne c. 25 ; 3 George I c. 11 ; 5 George I c. 15 ; 5 George III c. 14 ; 10 George III c. 19 ; 13 George III c. 80 ; 16 George III c. 30.
[7] Comm. iv 175.

or even having game in their custody, or for persons (however qualified) that kill game, or have it in possession, at unseasonable times of the year, or unseasonable hours of the day or night, on Sundays or on Christmas day,[1] there are various penalties assigned, corporal or pecuniary, by different statutes ; on any one of which, but only on one at a time, the justices may convict in a summary way, or (in most of them) prosecutions may be carried on at the assizes. And, lastly, by statute 28 Geo. II, c. 12, no person, however qualified to *kill*, may make merchandize of this valuable privilege, by *selling* or exposing to sale any game, on pain of like forfeiture as if he had no qualification.

In addition all persons qualified must every year take out a game certificate.[2] In 1828 the penalties for night poaching were increased.[3] A person for a third offence was made liable to transportation for seven years.[4] Powers of arrest were given to owners and keepers ;[5] and if three or more, any one of whom was armed, were found on the land for the purpose of destroying game or rabbits, they were made liable to transportation for fourteen years.[6] All these Acts, except the Act of 1828, were repealed in 1831.[7] The old qualifications for sporting and the prohibition of the sale of game were abolished, and new pecuniary penalties for poaching by day were prescribed.[8]

The best historical summary of this legislation, which has had a continuous history from the Middle Ages to 1832, is that given by Stephen.[9] He says :

A series of statutes extending over 317 years (13 Rich. 2, 1389, to 5 Anne, 1706) erected the right to kill game into the privilege of a class at once artificial and ill defined. The game itself became incapable of being sold. The result of this was that, on the land of an unqualified freeholder, partridges, pheasants, and hares were in an extraordinary position. The owner could not kill them because he was not qualified, and if anyone else did so without the owner's leave he committed a trespass. . . . It was theoretically doubtful whether from 1604 to 1832 anyone could lawfully shoot a pheasant, partridge, or hare whatever qualification he possessed.[10] The penalties by which this privilege was protected were not (except in the case of deer stealers) severe, consisting principally in a moderate money fine, which might, in default of payment, be converted into imprisonment. This system lasted for something over 120 years (1706-1828) when it was sanctioned by an Act (9 Geo. 4 c. 69) which turned night poaching into a serious crime, punishable on a third conviction with transportation. Four years after this the old system was swept away, and a new one was substituted for it, by which the right to game became an incident of the ownership or right to possession (as might be arranged between the owner and occupier) of land, and game itself was allowed to be sold

---

[1] Blackstone is referring to 13 George III c. 80 §§ 1 and 6.
[2] 24 George III St. 2 c. 43 ; 25 George III c. 50.
[3] 9 George IV c. 69. [4] § 1. [5] § 2.
[6] § 9. [7] 1, 2 William IV c. 32.
[8] Stephen, H.C.L. iii 281. [9] Ibid iii 281-282.
[10] It is possible that this was the effect of 1 James I c. 27, see Stephen, H.C.L. iii 279.

like any other produce of the soil, subject to a few restrictions of no interest. Lastly, the severe penalties which had formed the crowning point of the old privilege became the sanction of the new incident of property.

(vii) *Offences against the machinery of justice.*

We have seen that in the Middle Ages the law had come to recognize a considerable number of offences against the machinery of justice. The courts had early assumed power to punish various contempts against themselves or their process ; and in the seventeenth and eighteenth centuries the court of King's Bench assumed the power, formerly exercised by the court of Star Chamber, of punishing summarily contempts against any court.[1] Similarly, the courts punished perversions of the machinery of justice such as rescous, escape, and prison breach ; [2] considerable bodies of law as to these offences had grown up long before the beginning of the eighteenth century ; [3] and in some cases rescues or attempted rescues of prisoners were made substantive felonies.[4] But we have seen that some of these offences, notably forgery, perjury, conspiracy, and deceit, developed into offences which ceased to be regarded as offences necessarily connected with the machinery of justice.[5] Others, such as maintenance, champerty, and embracery have always been regarded as perversions of the machinery of justice ; and they are dealt with by Blackstone in his chapter on this subject. We have seen that the offences of maintenance and champerty have, in the course of their history, somewhat changed their mediæval form, and have developed into important bodies of law.[6] For the most part the law as to these offences against the machinery of justice has been developed by the courts. The mediæval law, added to and elaborated in the sixteenth and seventeenth centuries, formed the bulk of the law as it stood in the eighteenth century. But in one or two cases it was added to by the legislation of the eighteenth century.

In 1692 [7] it was made a felony to personate another as a bail, whereby that other became liable to pay the money recovered in the action. Statutes of 1697 [8] and 1722 [9] provided severe penalties for those who, in the so-called sanctuaries or

---

[1] Vol. iii 390-394.   [2] Ibid 395.   [3] Ibid.

[4] 6 George I c. 23 § 5 ; 8 George II c. 20 § 1 ; 11 George II c. 26 § 2 ; 16 George II c. 31 ; 19 George II c. 34 § 1 ; 24 George II c. 40 § 28 ; 27 George II c. 15.

[5] Vol. iii 395, 400-408 ; for the later history of these offences see vol. iv 501-503, above 534-535 (forgery) ; vol. iv 515-519 (perjury) ; vol. v 203-205, vol. viii 378-397 (conspiracy) ; vol. viii 67-70, 426 (deceit).

[6] Vol. iv 520-521 ; vol. v 201-203 ; vol. viii 397-402.

[7] 4 William and Mary c. 4 § 4.   [8] 8, 9 William III c. 27 § 15.

[9] 9 George I c. 28.

" pretended privileged places," [1] obstructed the service of process, or rescued or concealed or harboured prisoners ; and a statute of 1724 [2] made similar provisions for persons who sheltered themselves from legal process in the hamlets of Stepney or Wapping or elsewhere within the weekly bills of mortality. A series of statutes provided that criminals sentenced to be transported, who escaped before they were sent out of the country, or who returned before the completion of their sentence, and their aiders and abettors, should suffer the death penalty.[3]

(viii) *Miscellaneous.*

We have seen that as early as the end of the seventeenth century there was a growing scepticism amongst the more enlightened as to the existence of witchcraft.[4] Both North, C.J., and Holt, C.J., discountenanced prosecutions for that offence, and generally managed to secure the acquittal of the accused.[5] No doubt it was difficult for an honest Christian to deny the existence of witchcraft.[6] But it was equally clear, as Blackstone says,[7] that

the ridiculous stories that are generally told, and the many impostures and delusions that have been discovered in all ages, are enough to demolish all faith in such a dubious crime. . . . Wherefore it seems the most eligible way to conclude, with an ingenious writer of our own,[8] that in general there has been such a thing as witchcraft ; though one cannot give credit to any particular modern instance of it.

The Legislature, therefore, in 1736, following an example which had been set earlier by Louis XIV,[9] repealed the laws against witchcraft and enacted that, for the future, there should be no further prosecution for " witchcraft, sorcery, inchantment or conjuration." [10] But it also provided that persons who, by means of these arts, pretended to tell fortunes, or to discover lost or stolen property, should be liable to imprisonment for a year and the pillory.[11]

As in the preceding period,[12] the Legislature endeavoured to repress the practice of cursing and swearing, and " the pro-

---

[1] For these sanctuaries see vol. vi 408 n. 4.

[2] 11 George I c. 22.

[3] 4 George I c. 11 § 2 ; 6 George I c. 23 § 6 ; 16 George II c. 15 § 1 ; 8 George III c. 15 ; 24 George III St. 2 c. 56 §§ 4 and 5 ; Bl. Comm. iv 132 ; for transportation see below 568-575.

[4] For the history of witchcraft and the laws against it see vol. iv 507-511.

[5] Vol. vi 518-519, 579 n. 1 ; Lives of the Norths i 166-169.

[6] " To deny the possibility, nay, the actual existence of witchcraft and sorcery, is at once flatly to contradict the revealed word of God in various passages both of the old and new testament," Bl. Comm. iv 60 ; this was the reason why Hale enforced those laws, vol. vi 578-579.

[7] Ibid iv 61.   [8] Addison, The Spectator no. 117.

[9] Bl. Comm. iv 61.   [10] 9 George II c. 5 § 3.

[11] § 4.   [12] Vol. vi 404.

fanation of the Lord's Day vulgarly (but improperly) called sabbath-breaking." [1] In 1746 [2] the existing statutes against profane cursing and swearing were repealed, and a tariff of penalties was provided for various orders of society.[3] Justices of the peace and mayors of towns were authorized and required to convict and fine persons without any further proof who swore in their presence ; [4] and penalties were provided for justices, mayors, constables, and others who neglected to enforce the Act.[5] The Act was to be read four times a year in all parish churches.[6] A certain amount of legislation had been passed which modified the prohibition imposed by the Act of 1677 [7] upon the exercise of ordinary callings on Sunday.[8] An Act of 1781 was passed to deal with the practice of opening places of amusement or entertainment on Sunday evenings, and of holding debates upon texts of Holy Scripture by incompetent persons.[9] Places opened for these purposes on Sunday, for admission to which money was charged, were to be deemed to be disorderly houses, and their keepers were to be liable to pay a fine of £200 for each day that the place was kept open.[10] Other penalties were imposed on their managers, door-keepers, and persons concerned in advertising them.[11]

The need for some measure for the regulation of plays and playhouses had for some time been apparent. During the sixteenth and early seventeenth centuries plays and playhouses had been controlled by the prerogative ; and the prerogative powers of the Crown had been exercised partly through the Privy Council, partly through the powers vested in the Master of the Revels, and partly through the powers vested in the Lord Chamberlain.[12] These prerogative powers were much weakened after the Restoration. The powers of the Master of the Revels were disregarded by the managers of the King's Company and the Duke of York's Company of actors, with the result that the stage was never so licentious. After the Revolution the powers of the Master of the Revels and the Lord

---

[1] Bl. Comm. iv 63.   [2] 19 George II c. 21 § 15.

[3] § 1 ; the tariff was as follows : every day labourer, common soldier, common sailor, and common seaman—1s. ; every other person under the degree of a gentleman—2s. ; every person of or above the degree of a gentleman—5s. ; the fines were doubled for a second offence, and tripled for a third ; persons who did not pay were to be imprisoned, or, in the case of common soldiers and sailors, put in the stocks, §§ 4 and 5.

[4] § 2.   [5] §§ 6 and 7.   [6] § 13.   [7] 29 Charles II c. 7 ; vol. vi 404.

[8] Forty watermen were allowed to ply between Vauxhall and Limehouse on Sunday, 11, 12 William III c. 2 § 13 ; fish carriages were allowed to travel on Sunday, 2 George III c. 15 § 7 ; bakers were allowed to sell bread and cook provisions for their customers between 9 a.m. and 1 p.m., but not to exercise their trade as bakers, 34 George III c. 61.

[9] 21 George III c. 49.   [10] § 1.   [11] §§ 1 and 3.

[12] See Coxe, Memoirs of Sir Robert Walpole i 510-514, for a good account of the manner in which the stage was regulated before the Act of 1737.

Chamberlain were revived ; and owing to their efforts, and to the crusade preached by Jeremy Collier, some improvement was effected.   But this reform did not last long ; and in George I's reign the powers of the Master of the Revels were cut down by a patent granted to Steel, Cibber, and Booth, which allowed them to produce plays without any preliminary licence or revision. It is true that the Lord Chamberlain occasionally exercised his powers, e.g. he forbade the performance of *Polly*—the sequel to *The Beggar's Opera*.   But his powers were not often exercised, with the result that the number of theatres increased, and the moral and political licentiousness of the playwrights was unrestrained.

In 1735 Sir John Barnard brought in a bill to restrain the number of theatres, and to regulate the players.   But though it received considerable support, it was eventually lost because the government wished to insert in it a clause to ratify and enlarge the Lord Chamberlain's power to license plays.[1]   Two years later the government succeeded in passing a bill which contained these powers.   The Act of 1737 [2] imposed regulations as to the licensing of plays, and as to the status of players.   The immediate occasion for passing the Act was the production of two plays by Fielding—*Pasquin* in which bribery at elections was satirized, and the *Historical Register* in which Walpole himself was brought on to the stage under the name of Quidam.[3] The Act, which was very unpopular,[4] provided, in the first place, that no persons should for the future be authorized to act in or produce plays for gain anywhere except in the City of Westminster or in any place in which the King was resident.[5]   In the second place, it provided that a copy of every play must be sent to the Lord Chamberlain, and that the Lord Chamberlain could prohibit the performance of any play or any part thereof.[6] In the third place, an Act of 1713 had provided that all " common players of interludes " should be deemed to be rogues and vagabonds.[7]   The Act of 1737, after reciting that doubts had arisen as to the interpretation of this phrase, enacts that all actors who performed in any play in any place where they had no legal settlement, unless licensed by letters patent or by the Lord Chamberlain, were to be liable to be punished as rogues

---

[1] Parlt. Hist. ix 944-949 ; it appeared that there were then six playhouses in London—the Opera House, the French Playhouse in the Haymarket, and the playhouses in Covent Garden, Drury Lane, Lincoln's Inn Fields, and Goodman's Fields.

[2] 10 George II c. 28 .

[3] B. M. Jones, Henry Fielding, chap. iii ; Colley Cibber said of Fielding that he, " like another Erostratus, set fire to his stage, by writing up to an Act of Parliament to demolish it, ' cited ibid 53.

[4] Ibid 59-60.   [5] 10 George II c. 28 § 5.

[6] §§ 3 and 4.   [7] 12 Anne St. 2 c. 23.

and vagabonds,[1] or to be fined £50.[2] Though the provision confining theatres to Westminster, or to places where the King was resident, was subsequently modified by local Acts,[3] and by an Act of 1788 which gave the magistrates power to license theatrical performances,[4] the provision requiring the Lord Chamberlain's licence is still retained by the Act of 1843,[5] which has replaced this Act of 1737. Apparently the clause of the Act of 1737, which dealt with the liability of actors to be treated as rogues and vagabonds, survived till 1843.

In 1752 the Legislature adopted a suggestion which Fielding had made in 1749 in his charge to the grand jury of Middlesex, that the justices ought to have more control over places of public entertainment.[6] Any place kept for dancing, music, or other public entertainment, other than properly licensed theatrical entertainments, in the cities of London or Westminster or within a radius of twenty miles, must be licensed by quarter sessions.[7] No such place was to open before 5 p.m.[8] The object of this enactment was to diminish the number of the places which had been found to be an incentive to theft and robbery, and so to encourage habits of industry.[9]

The statutes which made quarantine obligatory upon ships which came from infected places, or which had infected persons on board, made it felony without benefit of clergy for the master of a ship to conceal these facts.[10] It was also made felony without benefit of clergy for a person to escape from the lazarets, that is the places where the quarantine was to be performed,[11] or to convey letters or goods from them or from ships under quarantine.[12] Captains who left their ships or allowed other persons to leave them were made liable to fine and imprisonment.[13]

---

[1] 10 George II c. 28 § 1. [2] § 2.

[3] Thus by special Acts Edinburgh, Bath, Norwich, York, Hull, Liverpool, Manchester, Chester, Bristol, Margate, Newcastle-on-Tyne, Glasgow and Birmingham got theatres between the years 1767 and 1807—often in the face of a good deal of opposition, see Parlt. Hist. xviii 632-643 for the opposition in the House of Lords to the Manchester playhouse bill; and ibid xix 198-205 for the successful opposition to the Birmingham playhouse bill.

[4] 28 George III c. 30. [5] 6, 7 Victoria c. 68.

[6] B. M. Jones, Henry Fielding 164-165 ; for an account of this charge see ibid 128-134 ; below 584.

[7] 25 George II c. 36 §§ 2 and 4. [8] § 3.

[9] "Whereas the multitude of places of entertainment for the lower sort of people is another great cause of thefts and robberies, as they are thereby tempted to spend their small substance in riotous pleasures, and in consequence are put on unlawful methods of supplying their wants, and renewing their pleasures," preamble to § 2.

[10] Bl. Comm. iv 161-162 ; 26 George II c. 6 ; amended by 29 George II c. 8 ; 28 George II c. 34.

[11] 26 George II c. 6 § 3. [12] §§ 8 and 18. [13] § 5.

(2) *Procedure*.

In the law of criminal procedure the changes made by the Legislature were few in number and not very important.

The rules as to venue, which the Legislature had begun to modify in the sixteenth century,[1] still existed, but were being whittled away by a growing number of exceptions and modifications, which showed that these rules had altogether outlived their usefulness. These exceptions and modifications took different forms. In some cases, for instance in the case where treason or murder was committed out of the realm, the Legislature provided that the offence could be tried in any county within the realm.[2] In other cases it provided that if a crime was begun in one county and completed in another, the accused could be tried sometimes in the county where the crime had been completed,[3] and sometimes in the county where the crime had been initiated.[4] In some cases, for instance in cases of crimes committed in Wales [5] and certain other crimes,[6] the accused could be tried in the adjacent counties. We have seen that special provision was made for the trial in the King's Bench of crimes committed in India,[7] and of crimes committed by the governors of colonies.[8] But since the general principle that " all offences must be inquired into as well as tried in the county where the fact is committed " [9] was still maintained, the law on this topic tended to become more and more complex and irrational.[10]

In 1747 [11] persons impeached for high treason or misprision of treason were given the same advantages as had been given in 1695-1696, 1702, and 1708 to persons indicted for those offences.[12]

---

[1] Vol. iv 523-524, 530-531.

[2] 33 Henry VIII c. 33 ; 35 Henry VIII c. 2 ; 5, 6 Edward VI c. 11 § 6 ; vol. iv 523-524 ; Bl. Comm. iv 303-304 ; the same provision was made for offences against the Black Act, 9 George I c. 22 § 14, above 530 ; and for the felony of destroying the King's ships, magazines, or stores, 12 George III c. 24 § 2.

[3] 2, 3 Edward VI c. 24 ; vol. iv 530-531.

[4] 2 George II c. 21—if, in the case of murder, the stroke or poisoning was on the sea or out of Great Britain, and the death occurred in Great Britain, or vice versa, the trial was to take place in Great Britain.

[5] 26 Henry VIII c. 6 ; 34, 35 Henry VIII c. 26 §§ 85, 86 ; Bl. Comm. iv 304,

[6] 8 George II c. 20 § 3, 13 George III c. 84 § 42—destruction of turnpikes, 26 George II c. 19 § 8—plundering or stealing from any ship in distress ; Bl. Comm. iv 304.

[7] 13 George III c. 63 ; above 165-168, 208-209.

[8] 11, 12 William III c. 12 ; vol. vi 402 ; above 166.

[9] Bl. Comm. iv 305.

[10] Stephen, H.C.L. i 278, cited vol. iv 531 n. 2 .   [11] 20 George II c. 30.

[12] 7, 8 William III c. 3 ; 1 Anne St. 2 c. 9 § 3 ; 7 Anne c. 21 § 11 ; vol. vi 232-234 ; they were allowed to have a copy of the indictment, a list of witnesses for the Crown, and a copy of the panel of the jury ten days before trial, and to be defended by counsel ; they could compel the attendance of witnesses who were to be sworn ; by the Act of 1702 the prisoner's witnesses were to be sworn on indictments for felony, vol. ix 235.

As Horace Walpole said,[1] it had "hurt everybody at old Lovat's trial, all guilty as he was, to see an old wretch worried by the first lawyers in England, without any assistance but his own unpractised defence." In 1750 the difficulty caused by the strictness of the rules of pleading, in setting out the offence when a person was charged with perjury, was the occasion of an Act which relaxed these rules.[2] In indictments or informations for perjury or subornation of perjury it was to be sufficient to set out the substance of the offence charged, the court before which the oath was taken, together with the proper averments to falsify the matter wherein the perjury was assigned.[3] Judges of assize were empowered to direct persons examined as witnesses before them to be prosecuted, and to assign counsel to the prosecutor.[4] Counsel were to act without fee ; and no court fees were to be payable on such a prosecution.[5]

We have seen that old rules made the hundred liable to compensate a person injured by a crime committed within its borders, unless the hue and cry had been raised, and the criminal had been captured within forty days ;[6] and that the rules as to the liability of the hundred, and as to the mode of enforcing that liability, had been reformed by a statute of 1584-1585.[7] A statute of 1735[8] made further changes in the law on this matter. Persons who wished to make the hundred liable for a robbery, must give a written notice to the constable or other official of the township or parish, near to the place where the robbery was committed.[9] The notice must describe the criminals and state the time and place of the robbery.[10] Within twenty days this notice must be inserted in the *London Gazette*, and security must be given for the payment of costs in case the action failed.[11] No compensation was to be payable if one or more of the criminals were apprehended within forty days after the notice had been inserted in the *London Gazette ;*[12] and actions for compensation must be brought within a period of six months.[13] If damages were recovered the writ of execution was to be served,

---

[1] Letters (Toynbee's ed.) ii 274.   [2] 23 George II c. 11.

[3] §§ 1 and 2 ; "without setting forth the bill, answers, information, indictment, declaration, or any part of any record or proceeding either in law or equity, other than as aforesaid ; and without setting forth the commission or authority of the court, or person or persons before whom the perjury was committed," § 1.

[4] § 3.   [5] Ibid.

[6] Vol. i 294 ; vol. iii 599 ; 13 Edward I St. 2 cc. 1 and 2 ; 28 Edward III c. 11.

[7] 27 Elizabeth c. 13 ; vol. iv 521-522.

[8] 8 George II c. 16 ; earlier statutes had provided for the recovery of damages for special kinds of injury to trees from parishes, townships, or hamlets, 1 George I St. 2 c. 48, 6 George I c. 16, and 29 George II c. 36 § 9 ; in 1722 the Waltham Black Act, which was passed to prevent certain kinds of damage to property, above 530, 535, prescribed conditions for the recovery of damages against the hundred which were similar to those laid down in the Act of 1735, 9 George I c. 22 §§ 7-9.

[9] § 1.   [10] Ibid.   [11] Ibid.

[12] § 3.   [13] § 14.

not on any inhabitant, but on two justices, who were to cause an assessment to be made to pay the damages,[1] and also to reimburse the high constables for the costs which they had incurred in defending the action.[2] If the constables or other officers of the township or parish were negligent in raising the hue and cry after receiving such notice, or after they otherwise knew that a robbery had been committed, they were to be liable to a fine of £5.[3] In actions against the hundred, inhabitants of the hundred were to be admissible witnesses for the hundred.[4] It was enacted in 1749 [5] that no one should be able to recover more than £200 in an action against the hundred, unless at least two persons were together at the time of the robbery and attested the fact of the robbery.

Statutes of 1722 [6] and 1746 [7] provided that in certain cases the secretary of state might issue a proclamation ordering persons to surrender and answer to the charges against them; and that, if they disobeyed, they were to be deemed to have been convicted of a felony without benefit of clergy.

A series of statutes pursued the same policy as that pursued by statutes of William III's reign,[8] and gave rewards to persons who assisted in the discovery, apprehension, or conviction of criminals.[9] Though Beccaria disapproved of this expedient,[10] it was in fact very necessary. There was no efficient machinery for the detection of criminals, and even at the present day, when such machinery exists, this expedient is sometimes resorted to; but, as the case of *R. v. M'Daniel* shows,[11] it sometimes gave rise to very grave abuses. A statute of 1722 [12] gave rewards to persons injured, or to the representatives of persons killed, in apprehending persons who had committed offences against that statute. Other statutes provided that prosecutors should have their costs if there was reasonable cause for the prosecution; and that the judge could, if the prosecutor was poor, give him an allowance for his time and trouble.[13] Similarly, witnesses, who were summoned by writ of subpœna, were " entitled to be paid their charges, with a further allowance (if poor)

---

[1] § 4 ; this clause applied only to actions for robbery ; it was made applicable to all actions against the hundred by 22 George II c. 46 § 34.

[2] 8 George II c. 16 § 7.   [3] § 11.   [4] § 15.

[5] 22 George II c. 24.   [6] 9 George I c. 22 § 4.

[7] 19 George II c. 34 § 2.   [8] Vol. vi 405-406.

[9] 5, 6 Anne c. 31 § 1 ; 8 George II c. 16 § 9 ; 15 George II c. 28 § 7 ; 16 George II c. 15 § 3 ; 8 George III c. 15 ; Bl. Comm. iv 295.

[10] Essay on Crimes and Punishments (Engl. tr.) chap. xxxvi.

[11] (1755) 19 S.T. 746—the prisoners had suborned two persons to commit a robbery, in order that they might get the rewards given for the apprehension of robbers.

[12] 9 George I c. 22 § 12 ; above 530 ; cp. 5, 6 Anne c. 31 § 2.

[13] 25 George II c. 36 §§ 5 and 11 ; 18 George III c. 19 § 1 ; Bl. Comm. iv 362.

for their trouble and loss of time." [1]   Certain statutes provided
that a person who procured the conviction of two others who
had committed the same offence as that of which he was guilty,
should have a pardon, sometimes of all offences except murder
or treason, and sometimes of the like offences of which he was
guilty. [2]   These statutes, which rest upon an idea similar to that
of the old law as to approvement, [3] were supplemented by the
judicial practice of admitting an accomplice to become King's
evidence, on the implied understanding that, if he made a full
disclosure, he would not be prosecuted for that or for any similar
offence. [4]

We have seen that one or two statutes made some modifications in the rules as to the incompetency of certain witnesses
to testify on account of the commission of crimes. [5]

These statutes cover very little ground.   They left untouched most of the archaic rules which the common law had
inherited from the mediæval period, and very many of the rules
which had been added to them in the sixteenth and seventeenth
centuries.   The rules as to the extreme precision required in
indictments, which allowed so many criminals to escape, [6] the
complex rules as to benefit of clergy, [7] the rules as to venue, [8]
the rule which denied counsel to a person indicted for felony, [9]
the appeal of murder, and, with it, the possibility of trial by
battle [5]—all survived.   Similarly, the rules which forbade the

---

[1] Bl. Comm. iv 362 ; 27 George II c. 3 § 3 ; 18 George III c. 9 § 7.

[2] 4, 5 William and Mary c. 8 § 7 (highway robbery) ; 6, 7 William III c. 17
§ 12 (coinage offences) ; 10, 11 William III c. 23 § 5 (burglary, house breaking, and
certain kinds of theft) ; 15 George II c. 28 § 8 (coinage offences) ; 29 George II
c. 30 § 8 (theft of certain metals) ; Bl. Comm. iv 330-331 ; vol. vi 406.

[3] Bl. Comm. iv 330 ; vol. iii 608-609 ; R. v. Rudd (1775) 1 Cowp. at pp. 335-
336, *per* Lord Mansfield C.J.

[4] In the case of R. v. Rudd, 1 Cowp. at p. 339, the judges agreed upon the following statement of the practice : " In cases not within any statute, an accomplice, who
fully and truly discloses the joint guilt of himself and of his companions, and truly
answers all questions that are put to him, and is admitted by the justices of the peace
as a witness against his companions, and who, when called upon, does give evidence accordingly, and appears under all the circumstances of the case, to have
acted a fair and ingenuous part, and to have made a full and true information,
ought not to be prosecuted for his own guilt so disclosed by him, nor, perhaps, for
any other offence of the same kind, which he may accidentally, and without any bad
design have omitted in his confession.   But he cannot by law plead this in bar to
any indictment against him, nor avail himself of it upon his trial ; for it is merely
an equitable claim to the mercy of the Crown from the magistrates' express or implied
promise of indemnity upon certain conditions that have been performed ; " cp.
Bl. Comm. iv 331 ; vol. xii 514.

[5] Vol. ix 193 n. 6 ; that these rules might hamper the administration of justice
is illustrated by a tale told by Horace Walpole—Earl Ferrers, who was later convicted of murder by the House of Lords, prosecuted one Page, a highwayman who
had tried to rob him ; " at the trial Page pleaded that my Lord was excommunicated,
consequently could not give evidence, and got acquitted," Letters (ed. Toynbee)
iv 128.

[6] Vol. iii 617-620.   [7] Ibid 300-302.   [8] Above 550.
[9] Vol. ix 232, 233, 235.   [10] Vol. ii 362-364.

jury on a trial for treason or felony to separate till they had given their verdict, and, after retiring to consider their verdict, forbade them to eat and drink,[1] were probably the reason for the practice of attempting to get a criminal trial, however long, finished in a single day. " The trial of Colonel Townley in 1746," says Mr. Justice Mackinnon,[2]

which would now take at least a week, was all over in a few hours. The trial of Hardy for high treason in 1794 was the first that ever lasted more than one day, and the court seriously considered whether it had any power to adjourn: though it decided that it could, it still sat daily from 8 a.m. until after mid-night.

The trial of Lord George Gordon for high treason in 1781 lasted from 8 a.m. till 5.15 a.m. on the following morning.[3] This practice must often have produced serious miscarriages of justice. Stephen says : [4]

Few judges are able to do justice to a complicated case after a sitting of much more than eight hours, and it is still more unusual for jurymen (quite unaccustomed to sustained attention, which involves a greater physical effort than those who have not tried it might suppose) to be able to attend to what is said, and to deliberate on it to any purpose, after ten hours.

There was considerable truth in Pope's lines : [5]

> Meanwhile declining from the noon of day,
> The sun obliquely shoots his burning ray ;
> The hungry judges soon the sentence sign,
> And wretches hang that jurymen may dine.

Another practice, which must often have caused miscarriages of justice, was the habit of trying prisoners after dinner. The Rev. Martin Madan says that, at the assizes, the effects of the dinner were usually only too apparent when the court reassembled.[6] The noise, crowd, and confusion were, he says, such that it took about an hour before the court could be brought into any kind of order ;

and when this is done drunkenness is too frequently apparent, where it ought of all things to be avoided, I mean in jury-men and witnesses. The heat of the court joined to the fumes of the liquor has laid many an honest jury-man into a calm and profound sleep, and sometimes it has been no small trouble for his fellows to jog him into the verdict—

---

[1] Vol. i 318-319 ; when Blackstone wrote they might, in civil cases, have meat and drink by permission of the judge, Comm. iii 375 ; but not, it would seem, in criminal cases, vol. i 319 n. 3.

[2] Johnson's England ii 307 ; in chapter xxv of this book Mr. Justice Mackinnon has given a very interesting account of the law and lawyers of Johnson's day, see L.Q.R. l 337-353.

[3] 2 Dougl. at p. 592. [4] H.C.L. i 422.

[5] Rape of the Lock, Canto III, lines 19-22 ; I owe this reference to Mr. Justice Mackinnon.

[6] Thoughts on Executive Justice (1785) 142-143.

even when a wretch's life has depended upon the event ! This I myself have seen—as also witnesses, by no means in a proper situation to give their evidence.

But, though the statutory changes in criminal procedure were small, larger and more important changes were made by the judges. We have seen that the changed character of the bench, the growing precision of the rules of evidence, and the growth of a feeling that accused persons ought to be treated with humanity, had changed the whole character of a criminal trial. We have seen that, though prisoners accused of felony were not allowed to be defended by counsel, a practice had grown up of allowing counsel to examine and cross-examine witnesses, and in fact to do everything for the prisoner except address the jury.[1] Stephen, writing in 1882, could say that he did not think that the actual administration of justice, or the course of trials, had altered much since the beginning of George III's reign ; and that, though there had been vast changes in the substantive criminal law, the only change of first-rate importance in the law of criminal procedure was the Act of 1837,[2] which allowed persons accused of felony to be fully defended by counsel—a change which, owing to the practice of allowing counsel to do everything except address the jury, made little difference in the conduct of the trial.[3] Thus, in spite of the survival of many archaic rules, the practice of the courts had made the English law of criminal procedure a branch of the law which, if judged by modern standards, deserved to some extent the qualified eulogium pronounced upon it by Blackstone,[4] and, judged by the standards of other countries in the eighteenth century, wholly deserved it. But Blackstone did not extend this eulogium to the punishments meted out by the law. The archaic rules and ideas, which had survived in this part of the law, could not be corrected, as some of the archaic rules of procedure had been corrected, by the practice of the courts ; and the Legislature, so far from mitigating the evil results of these survivals, had aggravated them. There had been, as Blackstone says,[5] " too scrupulous an adherence to some rules of the antient common law when the reasons have ceased upon which those rules were founded " ; too little care to repeal " such of the old penal laws as are either obsolete or absurd " ; and " too little care and attention in framing and

---

[1] Vol. ix 235.   [2] 6, 7 William IV c. 114 § 1.   [3] H.C.L. i 425.

[4] " Even with us in England, where our crown law is with justice supposed to be more nearly advanced to perfection ; where crimes are more accurately defined, and penalties less uncertain and arbitrary ; where all our accusations are public, and our trials in the face of the world ; where torture is unknown, and every delinquent is judged by his equals, against whom he can form no exception nor even a personal dislike—even here we shall occasionally find room to remark some particulars, that seem to want revision and amendment," Comm. iv 3.

[5] Comm. iv 3-4.

passing new ones." It is true that these strictures applied in
some degree to all parts of the criminal law, substantive and
adjective ; [1] but we shall now see that they applied more
especially to the punishments provided for the breach of law.

(3) *Punishment.*

The law of the eighteenth century provided a great diversity
of punishments for different offences. Blackstone catalogues
them with substantial completeness and accuracy. He says : [2]

Some punishments are capital, which extend to the life of the
offender, and consist generally in being hanged by the neck till dead ;
though in very atrocious crimes other circumstances of terror, pain, or
disgrace are superadded, as in treasons of all kinds, being drawn or
dragged to the place of execution ; in high treason affecting the King's
person or government, embowelling alive, beheading, and quartering ;
and in murder a public dissection. And, in case of any treason committed
by a female, the judgment is to be burned alive. . . . Some punishments consist in exile or banishment, by abjuration of the realm, or
transportation : others in loss of liberty, by perpetual or temporary
imprisonment. Some extend to confiscation, by forfeiture of lands
or movables, or both, or of the profits of lands for life : others induce
a disability of holding offices or employments, being heirs, executors,
and the like. Some, though rarely, occasion a mutilation or dis-
membering, by cutting off the hand or ears : others fix a lasting stigma
on the offender, by slitting the nostrils, or branding in the hand or cheek.
Some are merely pecuniary, by stated or discretionary fines ; and lastly
there are others, that consist principally in their ignominy, though
most of them are mixed with some degree of corporal pain ; and these
are inflicted chiefly for such crimes, as either arise from indigence, or
render even opulence disgraceful. Such as whipping, hard labour in
the house of correction or otherwise, the pillory, the stocks, and the
ducking stool.

This list of punishments comes from all ages in the history
of English law. It contains abundant traces of barbarities
which came very naturally to a primitive society, but which
were a disgrace to a more civilized age. It also contains
penalties suited to feudal ideas, but wholly out of harmony
with the ideas of the eighteenth century. And the punishments
inflicted by the law were not only barbaric and archaic, they
were quite unsystematic ; for they were often inflicted by many
unconnected statutes, which came from all periods in the history
of the law. In most cases there was little or no attempt to
apportion punishment to the magnitude of the crime ; and there
was no attempt to think out any theory as to the objects
at which punishment ought to aim. Let us examine these
characteristics of the punishments known to the English law of
the eighteenth century.

[1] Below 581, 583-586.   [2] Comm. iv 376-377.

First, some of these punishments were or might be disgracefully barbarous. The punishment for treason, which can be read in the records of many trials,[1] dates from about the middle of the thirteenth century. "It attained the full height of its barbarity," says Maitland,[2] "by trying to punish one man for many capital crimes. The famous traitors of Edward I's day, David of Wales and William Wallace, had in the sight of Englishmen committed all crimes against God and man and were to suffer four or five different deaths." That was the reason why petty treason and the treason of counterfeiting the King's money and perhaps his seal was punished only by drawing and hanging.[3] The punishment of death by hanging for all felonies was due to the judicial practice of the thirteenth century. In the eleventh and twelfth centuries

the judges had in this matter discretionary powers larger than those that their successors would wield for many centuries, and the king could favour now one and now another punishment. Such changes could take place easily, because a main idea of the old law had been that by the gravest, the unamendable, crimes a man "forfeited life and member and all that he had."[4]

But in the thirteenth century when the scope of felony was extended to all crimes which were then regarded as serious,[5] when death was awarded as a punishment for all felonies, the way was open for that great extension of capital punishment, which was one of the most barbarous features of the English criminal law ; and we shall see that the efforts made to mitigate this barbarity produced other and much more serious defects in the administration of the law.[6] The punishment of the pillory was essentially barbarous, and wholly capricious. The mob was in effect invited to take a hand. If it sympathized with the criminal the punishment might be negligible : if it did not it might mean that the criminal suffered a lingering and painful death.[7] Blackstone is quite wrong when he says that this punishment consisted principally in its ignominy.

Secondly, some of the consequences of the commission of a felony—consequences which must be reckoned a part of the

---

[1] See e.g. R. v. Cameron (1753) 19 S.T. at pp. 736-738, following precedents of 1485 and 1662.
[2] P. and M. (1st ed.) ii 499.   [3] Ibid n. 3.
[4] Ibid 460.   [5] Vol. ii 357-358.   [6] Below 564.
[7] See the fate of M'Daniel, Berry, Egan, and Salmon narrated in 19 S.T. at pp. 809-810 ; Egan was struck dead and Salmon so dangerously wounded in the head that it was thought impossible that he should recover ; in 1732 two persons were indicted and hanged for the murder of a prisoner in the pillory by pelting him with various missiles, ibid 810 ; in 1780 Burke, alluding to another case of this kind, said that this punishment ought to be abolished, "since it was liable to such violent perversion, as to be rendered not the instrument of reproach and shame, but of death and murder," Parlt. Hist. xxi 390.

punishment—were anachronisms. When felony really meant a breach of the feudal bond, there was some reason for the rule that the felon's land escheated to his lord,[1] and there was some reason for the doctrine that the felon's blood was corrupted, so that no heir born before or after the commission of the felony could claim through him.[2] But, long before the eighteenth century, any reason that this rule had once had had long disappeared—a fact which was sometimes, but not always, realized by the Legislature when it created new treasons and felonies. " And therefore," says Blackstone,[3]

as every other oppressive mark of feodal tenure is now happily worn away in these kingdoms, it is to be hoped that this *corruption of blood*, with all its connected consequences, not only of present escheat, but of future incapacities of inheritance even to the twentieth generation, may in process of time be abolished by Act of Parliament.

As Blackstone points out, the rule that lands were forfeited to the Crown for treason stood upon a very different footing.[4] It is, as he said, " by no means derived from the feodal policy." [5] A man who commits treason has put himself outside the protection of the community, and cannot complain if the community deprives him of the right of owning property ; [6] and, as both Bacon and Blackstone pointed out, forfeiture for treason can be defended on grounds of public policy. A knowledge that treason will ruin not only the traitor but his posterity will do much to restrain ; and, as Bacon said, it is not good for the state that great possessions should " be in discontented races." [7] Similarly, the rule that the Crown was entitled to year, day and waste of a felon's lands, and to the felon's chattels, owed nothing to "feodal policy " ; [8] and it could be defended, though not so convincingly, as forfeiture for treason.

Thirdly, the punishments inflicted were unsystematic, because they were inflicted by many unconnected statutes which came from all periods in the history of the law.[9] Blackstone gives a good illustration of the anomalous results which sometimes ensued.[10] We have seen that some of the Acts which created new treasons and felonies provided that conviction

---

[1] Vol. ii 357-358 ; vol. iii 69. [2] Ibid.
[3] Comm. iv 388. [4] Ibid 382 ; vol. iii 70-71.
[5] Comm. iv 383. [6] Ibid 382.
[7] Ibid ; Bacon, Works vii 633-634, cited vol. vii 201 ; for Charles Yorke's treatise on this subject which takes the same view see vol. xii 362-363.
[8] Comm. iv 385-388 ; vol. iii 69-70, 280, 329-330.
[9] " A slight perusal of the laws by which the measures of vindictive and coercive justice are established, will discover so many disproportions between crimes and punishments, such capricious distinctions of guilt, and such confusion of remissness and severity, as can scarcely be believed to have been produced by public wisdom, sincerely and calmly studious of public happiness," Johnson, The Rambler, no 114.
[10] Comm. iv 389-390.

should not entail attainder and corruption of blood.[1] It was also provided by a statute of 1708 that, after the decease of the then Pretender, attainder for treason should not have the effect of disinheriting the heirs of the traitor, and should not prejudice the right or title of anyone other than the traitor.[2] The operation of this statute was postponed in 1744 till the death of the Pretender's sons.[3] But since there were many felonies, " and those not of the most atrocious kind," to which this legislation did not apply, the absurd result followed that the doctrine of corruption of blood would in course of time be abolished for treason, but would still apply to many felonies.

Fourthly, the influence of the old common law principle, that all felonies were punishable with death, had three consequences which had the worst results on the criminal law. In the first place, larceny of a chattel above the value of twelve pence was grand larceny and punishable with death.[4] The cruelty of this law was so manifest that juries frequently committed " a kind of pious perjury," [5] and either acquitted, or, as Kenny has said, " assessed the value of stolen articles in a humanely depreciatory manner." [6] In the second place, this severity led to a very capricious infliction of punishment. The Crown could not allow the death sentence to be carried out on all petty thieves. But the operation of pardons on condition of transportation or otherwise, coupled with the chance of quashing the indictment for a technical flaw,[7] made it quite uncertain what the punishment would be.[8]

Among so many chances of escaping, the needy and hardened offender overlooks the multitude that suffer ; . . . and, if unexpectedly, the hand of justice overtakes him, he deems himself peculiarly unfortunate, in falling at last a sacrifice to those laws, which long impunity has taught him to contemn.[9]

[1] Above 558.
[2] 7 Anne c. 21 § 10 ; the history of this clause is as follows : it was desired to make a uniform law of treason for England and Scotland, but the Scots did not wish to introduce into Scotland the English rule that estates tail were forfeited (see vol. iii 70 n. 8, vol. iv 500), and the English House of Commons wished to abolish the doctrines of forfeiture and corruption of blood ; but the House of Lords resisted this change ; " at length a compromise was agreed to, which is established by this statute, viz. that the same crimes, and no other, should be treason in Scotland that are so in England ; and that English forfeitures and corruption of blood should take place in Scotland, till the death of the then pretender ; and then cease throughout the whole of Great Britain: the Lords artfully proposing this temporary clause, in the hopes (it is said) that the prudence of succeeding Parliaments would make it perpetual," Bl. Comm. iv 384-385.
[3] 17 George II c. 39 § 3.   [4] Vol. iii 366.
[5] " This, though evidently justifiable and proper, when it only reduces the present nominal value of money to the antient standard, is otherwise a kind of pious perjury, and does not at all excuse our common law in this respect from the imputation of severity, but rather strongly confesses the charge," Bl. Comm. iv 239.
[6] Criminal Law 182.   [7] Above 553.   [8] Below 564, 569.
[9] Bl. Comm. iv 19 ; Madan, Thoughts on Executive Justice, 36-37, tells a story of an old offender who had been condemned to death ; on being asked " how

In the third place, the severity of the common law exercised a perverting influence on the Legislature. It induced the Legislature to punish with death many other offences against property which did not come within the narrow common law definition of larceny, and other acts which in themselves would appear to be almost innocent. As Blackstone pointed out,[1] it was a capital crime to break down the mound of a fish pond whereby the fish escaped, to cut down a cherry tree in an orchard, or to be seen for one month in the company of persons who were known as Egyptians, i.e. gipsies.[2] The extraordinary carelessness and callousness of the Legislature, which made such enactments possible, is illustrated by an anecdote related by Sir William Meredith in his speech on a motion that all clauses in bills creating a capital offence should be agreed to by a committee of the whole House.[3] He said that

he was once passing a committee room, where only one member was holding a committee, with a clerk's boy ; he happened to hear something of hanging ; he immediately had the curiosity to ask what was going forward in that small committee that could merit such a punishment. He was answered that it was an Enclosing Bill, in which a great many poor people were concerned who opposed the bill ; that they feared those people would obstruct the execution of the Act, and therefore this clause was to make it a capital felony in any one who did so.

In 1813 a clause was inserted in committee on the bill for the relief of insolvent debtors, making it an offence punishable with death for an insolvent debtor to give a false account of his property—a clause which Romilly persuaded the House to reject.[4] Blackstone was aware of this carelessness and callousness of the Legislature when he said that

the enacting of penalties, to which a whole nation shall be subject, ought not to be left as a matter of indifference to the passions or

he could venture again on his old practices after so many escapes, Ah Sir, he said, that's the very thing—there are so many chances *for* us, and so few *against* us that I never thought of coming to this—First, said he, there are many chances against being discovered—so many more that we are not taken—and if taken not convicted and if convicted not hanged—that I thought myself very safe, with at least twenty to one in my favour."

[1] Comm. iv 4 ; as Johnson said, The Rambler no. 114, " it has always been the practice, when any particular species of robbery becomes prevalent and common, to endeavour its suppression by capital denunciations. . . By this practice capital inflictions are multiplied, and crimes, very different in their degrees of enormity, are equally subjected to the severest punishment that man has the power of exercising upon man "

[2] 5 Elizabeth c. 20, which created this crime and punished it in this way was repealed by 23 George III c 51.

[3] Cited by Hammond, The Village Labourer 64, from Parlt. Register, Jan 21, 1772.

[4] Memoirs of Sir Samuel Romilly ii 315 ; for this bill which became law, 53 George III c. 102, see below 598.

interests of a few, who upon temporary motives may prefer or support such a bill ; [1]

and when he pointed out that it was

never usual in the House of peers even to read a private bill which may affect the property of an individual, without first referring it to some of the learned judges, and hearing them report thereon. And surely equal precaution is necessary, when laws are to be established, which may affect the property, the liberty, and perhaps even the lives, of thousands.[2]

Fifthly, the Legislature gave little or no consideration to the proper object of punishment. The predominant object of the Legislature was to deter. Hale says : [3]

Regularly the true or at least, the principal end of punishments is to deter men from the breach of laws, so that they may not offend, and so not suffer at all, and the inflicting of punishments in most cases is more for example and to prevent evils, than to punish. When offences grow enormous, frequent, or dangerous to a kingdom or state, destructive or highly pernicious to civil societies, and to the great insecurity and danger of the kingdom and its inhabitants, severe punishments, even death itself, is necessary to be annexed to laws in many cases by the prudence of law-givers, tho' possibly beyond the single demerit of the offence itself simply considered.

This was the predominant principle upon which the Legislature acted in the eighteenth century ; and, though it was beginning to be seen that this severity defeated its own ends, and that punishment should aim also at the amendment of the criminal,[4] these ideas had as yet no great practical effect, partly because it was " easier to extirpate than to amend," [5] and partly because the English state in the eighteenth century lacked the administrative machinery which was necessary to institute and work the kind of punishments which were capable of producing amendment.[6] Thus Fielding held the view that the main object of punishment was to deter [7]—though in practice he sometimes acted on the view that punishment should be also reformative when he dealt gently with first offenders, or refused to imprison for small offences.[8]

It is true that a little had been done to get rid of the more obvious barbarities. The traitor was generally allowed to hang until he was dead,[9] and a woman was generally strangled before she was burned.[10] The punishment of burning alive for female traitors was abolished in 1790.[11] The benefit of clergy, the

[1] Comm. iv 4.
[2] Ibid.
[3] Pleas of the Crown, i 13.
[4] Above 528 ; below 568.
[5] Bl. Comm. iv 17.
[6] Vol. x 182-183.
[7] See B. M. Jones, Henry Fielding, 221-223.
[8] Ibid 223-224.
[9] Bl. Comm. iv 377 ; see R. v. Cameron (1753) 19 S.T. at p. 738.
[10] See Lecky, History of England ii 135-136.
[11] 30 George III c. 48.

facility with which indictments could be quashed for technical flaws, the ease with which pardons, conditional or otherwise, could be got for the less serious felonies, mitigated the common law rule that all felonies were punishable with death. But these devices to diminish the number of cases in which the capital penalty was inflicted had some very serious results upon the criminal law. One of the principles laid down by Beccaria was the principle that the certainty of the punishment was a greater deterrent than its severity.[1] But these devices destroyed, as we have seen, all certainty, and thus destroyed the only justification for this indiscriminate severity. The threat of capital punishment did not deter because the criminal had so many chances of escaping it.[2] But the fact that these expedients were adopted to diminish the severity of the criminal law shows that the public conscience was shocked ; and that was the condition precedent to reform. In fact, from about the middle of the eighteenth century onwards, we can see a steady movement in favour of the reform of the system of punishment. This will be apparent if we look at the criticisms directed to the two commonest punishments inflicted by the common law —death and imprisonment, and at the growth of the system of transporting criminals overseas.

(i) *Death.*—The frequency with which the punishment of death was inflicted aroused the greatest body of criticism ; and a few saw that the publicity with which executions were carried out went far to defeat the lesson which they were intended to convey.

As early as the beginning of the seventeenth century Coke had deplored the frequency with which capital punishment was inflicted, and the fact that that very frequency prevented it from acting as a deterrent.[3]

True it is, that we have found by woful experience, that it is not frequent and often punishment that doth prevent like offences, *Melior est enim Justitia vere praeveniens, quam severe puniens* . . . agreeing with the rule of the Physitian for the safety of the body . . . Those offences are often committed that are often punished : for the frequency of the punishment makes it so familiar as it is not feared.[4]

[1] " Crimes are more effectually prevented by the certainty than the severity of punishment . . . the certainty of a small punishment will make a stronger impression than the fear of one more severe, if attended with the hopes of escaping," An Essay on Crimes and Punishments (Engl. Tr.) chap. xxvii ; this passage is referred to with approval by Blackstone, Comm. iv 17.

[2] Above 559 n. 9.

[3] " What a lamentable case it is to see so many Christian men and women strangled on that cursed tree of the gallows, insomuch as if in a large field a man might see together all the Christians, that but in one year, throughout England come to that untimely and ignominious death, if there were any spark of grace, or charity in him, it would make his heart bleed for pity and compassion," Third Instit. Epilogue.

[4] Ibid

During the eighteenth century this frequency of capital punishment was generally recognized as a scandal, and the laws which freely distributed the punishment of death were often criticized. Horace Walpole deplored " the monthly shambles at Tyburn." [1] Fielding lamented " the many cartloads of our fellow creatures once in six weeks carried to slaughter " at Tyburn.[2] Johnson pointed out that " to equal robbery with murder, is to reduce murder to robbery ; to confound in common minds the gradations of iniquity, and incite the commission of a greater crime to prevent the detection of a less." [3] Goldsmith questioned the right of the state to punish offences against property with death,[4] and pointed out the evil effects of this severity. " When by indiscriminate penal laws a nation beholds the same punishment affixed to dissimilar degrees of guilt, from perceiving no distinction in the penalty, the people are led to lose all sense of distinction in the crime." [5] In fact the law had involved itself in a vicious circle. " The multitude of laws produces new vices, and new vices call for fresh restraints " [6]—restraints which were too often new capital punishments. Blackstone agreed with Johnson and Goldsmith in thinking that theft ought not to be punished with death,[7] and with Coke in lamenting the frequency with which the Legislature imposed this punishment.

It is a melancholy truth, that among the variety of actions which men are daily liable to commit, no less than an hundred and sixty have been declared by Act of Parliament to be felonies without benefit of clergy ; or, in other words, to be worthy of instant death.[8]

And it should be observed that this enumeration did not take account of Private Acts in which capital punishment might sometimes be awarded.[9]

It is true that by no means all the criminals convicted of capital crimes were executed ; and it is true that George III carefully and anxiously considered the cases in which he was

---

[1] " Could the monthly shambles at Tyburn (that scene that shocks humanity, and reproaches our police !) be exchanged for severe labour,—it would reflect honour on a legislature, which ought not to wanton in such punishment of its members as death and banishment, but to extract public utility, even from crimes," Memoirs of the Last Ten Years of George II's Reign i 224 ; cp. Walpole's Letters (ed. Toynbee) iii 88.

[2] An Enquiry into the Causes of the late Increase of Robbers (1751) 127.

[3] The Rambler no. 114.　　　　[4] The Vicar of Wakefield, chap. xxvii.

[5] Ibid.　　　　[6] Ibid.　　　　[7] Comm. iv 9-12, 17-19.

[8] Ibid iv 18 ; Stephen points out, H.C.L. i 470-471, that the number of capital offences on the statute book was no test of its severity, and that a few general enactments would be more severe than a great number of special ones ; but he concludes that, after making all possible allowances of this kind, " the legislation of the eighteenth century in criminal matters was severe to the highest degree, and destitute of any sort of principle or system."

[9] Above 560.

asked to exercise his prerogative of mercy.[1] But all writers
on the criminal law agreed that the effect of too frequent pardons
and reprieves had some very bad consequences. Coke [2] and
Blackstone [3] in this matter agreed substantially with Fielding [4]
and Beccaria.[5] In 1784 the Rev. Martin Madan published a
book entitled *Thoughts on Executive Justice*, in which he maintained this thesis in such unqualified terms,[6] that he provoked
a reply from Romilly,[7] and a criticism from Baron Perryn in
his charge to the grand jury of Surrey.[8] Romilly asserted, and
later Lord Ellenborough denied, that the effect of this book was
temporarily to increase the number of convicts who were executed.[9]
It is perhaps doubtful whether this increase was wholly due
to Madan's book. He was only expounding ideas which Coke,
Fielding, Beccaria, and Blackstone had made familiar ; and
long before the book was published it was clear that the Legislature was not uninfluenced by them. In 1752 it enacted that

[1] Vol. x 415 ; the care taken is shown by the letters addressed to judges to report
on criminal cases, and by their reports, which are calendared in all the volumes of
the Home Office Papers, 1760-1775 ; it should be noted that George III set his face
against any mitigation of the capital penalty in cases of forgery, since it was a particularly dangerous crime in a commercial country, ibid 1766-1769 326.

[2] " Most certain it is that the Word of God hath set down this undisputable
general rule. *Quia non profertur cito contra malos sententia, filii hominum sine
timore ullo perpetrant mala*. And thereupon the rule of law is grounded, *Spes
impunitatis continuum affectum tribuit delinquendi. Et veniae facilitas incentivum
est delinquendi*," Third Instit. 236.

[3] Comm. iv 16-17, 18-19.

[4] " Tho' mercy may appear more amiable in a magistrate, severity is a more
wholesome virtue : nay severity to an individual may perhaps be in the end the
greatest mercy not only to the public in general—but to many individuals, An
Enquiry into the Causes of the late Increase of Robbers (1751) 117-118 ; " pardons
have brought many more to the gallows than they have saved from it," ibid 120.

[5] Below 577.

[6] Thoughts on Executive Justice (1785) 37, 39-41, 46, 64 ; Madan gives instances which show that little care was used in selecting the persons to be pardoned ;
in fact political reasons sometimes exercised a perverting influence ; Thomson,
Secretaries of State 1681-1782 110, tells us that amongst Newcastle's memoranda
is the following note—" Thomas Newman, smuggler in Horsham gaol ; has many
friends in Sussex ; to be released—40 or 50 double votes depend upon this ";
constituencies sometimes put pressure on their members to press for pardons,
Calendar of Home Office Papers, 1766-1769 184 ; but in this case the Crown refused to yield to this pressure, ibid 187-188 ; in 1773 Sir John Fielding deplored
" the impositions which affect the fountain of royal mercy," ibid 1773-1775 11.

[7] Memoirs of Sir Samuel Romilly i 65-66 ; that the unqualified terms in which
Madan maintained his thesis had aroused comment is clear from the tale which
Holliday, Life of Mansfield 186, tells of Mansfield ; at the East Grinstead assizes
there were no prisoners, and Mansfield is said to have remarked to the sheriff,
" Mr. Madan will have a singular pleasure on this occasion, because there is no
condemned prisoner to be reprieved."

[8] He said that if all Madan's recommendations were followed it would make our
laws like the laws of Draco which were written in blood, see the 1785 ed. of Madan's
book where Baron Perryn's criticism is cited and replied to.

[9] Romilly says that in 1783, the year before the book was published, 51 malefactors were executed in London, and that in 1785, the year after it was published,
97 were executed, Memoirs i 65 ; that is not quite so decisive as Romilly thought it,
and Ellenborough may have been, at any rate partially, right.

persons convicted of wilful murder must be executed on the next day but one after sentence had been passed, and that the body was to be anatomized or hung in chains.[1] It is true that the judge might stay the execution;[2] but he was warned that he must always " have regard to the true intent and purpose of this Act." [3]

The public manner in which these frequent capital sentences were carried out helped to demoralize the people. Executions were public till 1868;[4] and, till 1783, the criminals were taken in processions through the streets from Newgate to Tyburn. Samuel Richardson in the eighteenth,[5] and Thackeray in the nineteenth [6] century have recorded the feelings of horror and disgust with which they viewed these spectacles. But the populace regarded them as a fascinating show, and their famil-iarity, though it did not diminish their attractiveness, seems to have taken away all sense of horror or disgust. No doubt some considered that the publicity of the punishment made for edification—this was the opinion of Dr. Johnson,[7] who deplored the abolition of the procession from Newgate to Tyburn.[8] " Sir," he said,[9]

executions are intended to draw spectators. If they do not draw spectators, they don't answer their purpose. The old method was most satisfactory to all parties; the public was gratified by a procession; the criminal was supported by it. Why is all this to be swept away?

Fielding gave some very convincing reasons why all this should be swept away. Apart from its demoralizing effect on the

---

[1] 25 George II c. 37 § 1.
[2] §§ 2 and 5.
[3] § 4.
[4] 31 Victoria c. 24.
[5] In a collection of 173 letters, printed without the author's name—a kind of polite letter writer—no. 160, cited A. Marks, Tyburn Tree, 237-240, describes a public execution; the writer says " the sight has had an extraordinary effect on me, which is more owing to the unexpected oddness of the scene, than the affecting concern which is unavoidable in a thinking person. . . . At the place of execution the scene grew still more shocking; and the clergyman who attended was more the subject of ridicule, than of their serious attention. The Psalm was sung amidst the curses and quarrelling of hundreds of the most abandon'd and profligate of mankind; upon whom (so stupid are they to any sense of decency) all the prepara-tion of the unhappy wretches seems only to serve for subject of a barbarous kind of mirth, altogether inconsistent with humanity."
[6] " I must confess the sight has left on my mind an extraordinary feeling of terror and shame. Forty thousand persons of all ranks and degrees gather together before Newgate at a very early hour; the most part of them give up their natural quiet night's rest in order to partake of this hideous debauchery which is more ex-citing than sleep, or than wine, or the last new ballet, or any other amusement they can have. Pickpocket and peer each is tickled by the sight alike, and has that hidden lust after blood which influences our race," On going to see a man hanged (July, 1840).
[7] Boswell's Life (7th ed. 1811) v 57.
[8] " He said to Sir William Scott (in 1783), ' the age is running mad after innovation; and all the business of the world is to be done in a new way; Tyburn itself is not safe from the fury of innovation '," ibid.
[9] Ibid.

spectators, it went far to deprive the punishment of many of its terrors.   He said : [1]

No hero sees death as the alternative which may attend his undertaking with less terror, nor meets it in the field with more imaginary glory.   The day appointed by law for the thief's shame is the day of glory in his own opinion.   His procession to Tyburn, and his last moments there, are all triumphant ; attended with the compassion of the meek and tender hearted, and with the applause admiration and envy of all the bold and hardened.   His behaviour in his present condition, not the crimes, how atrocious so ever, which brought him to it, are the subject of contemplation.   And if he hath sense enough to temper his boldness with any degree of decency, his death is spoke of by many with honour, by most with pity, and by all with approbation.   How far such an example is from being an object of terror, especially to those for whose use it is principally intended, I leave to the consideration of every rational man. . . .. The great cause of this evil is the frequency of executions : the knowledge of human nature will prove this from reason ; and the different effects which executions produce in the minds of the spectators in the country where they are rare, and in London where they are common, will convince us by experience.   The thief who is hanged to-day hath learnt his intrepidity from the example of his hanged predecessors, as others are now taught to despise death, and to bear it hereafter with boldness from what they see today.

In fact a condemned criminal was in some cases an object of popular interest between the time of his sentence and his execution.[2]   Fielding gave good reasons for thinking that the punishment of death would have a far greater deterrent effect if it were carried out in private.

If the executions were so contrived that few could be present at them, they would be much more shocking and terrible to the crowd without doors than at present, as well as much more dreadful to the criminals themselves, who would thus die in the presence only of their enemies ;   and when the boldest of them would find no cordial to keep up his spirits, nor any breath to flatter his ambition.[3]

Fielding wrote his tract in 1751, but this salutary reform was not made till 1868.[4]

---

[1] An Enquiry into the Causes of the late Increase of Robbers (1751) 121-122 ; cp. Lecky, History of England ii 134-135 ; as Dickens says in A Tale of Two Cities, Bk. ii chap. ii, " the Old Bailey was famous as a kind of deadly inn-yard, from which pale travellers set out continually, in carts and coaches, on a violent passage into the other world."

[2] Thus Horace Walpole tells us that one M'Lean, a highwayman, excited much interest—" the first Sunday after his condemnation, three thousand people went to see him ;   he fainted away twice with the heat of his cell.   You can't conceive the ridiculous rage there is of going to Newgate ;   and the prints that are published of the malefactors, and the memoirs of their lives and deaths set forth with as much parade as—Marshal Turenne's—we have no generals worth making a parallel," Letters (ed. Toynbee) iii 21.

[3] Op. cit. 124.   [4] 31 Victoria c. 24.

(ii) *Imprisonment.*—"The use of imprisonment as a punishment," says Maitland,[1] "more especially if it be imprisonment for a definite period fixed by the sentence, is a sign of advancing civilization." In the twelfth and early thirteenth centuries prisons were used for detention rather than for punishment.[2] Edward I's statutes set the fashion of using imprisonment as a punishment.[3] But "even in these cases the imprisonment was as a general rule but preparatory to a fine. After a year or two years the wrong-doer might make fine; if he had no money, he was detained for a while longer."[4] In fact, in the thirteenth century, fines were not imposed. The imposition of a fine would have been an evasion of Magna Carta, "for an amercement should be affeered, not by royal justices, but by neighbours of the wrong-doer." Fines were not imposed, they were set as the result of a bargain between the Crown and the wrong-doer, on payment of which he was set at liberty.[5] In later law fines, and imprisonments for a definite term, or fines, or imprisonments, were freely imposed by statutes. But just as Magna Carta had provided that amercements should be *salvo contenemento*,[6] so the Bill of Rights provided that fines imposed as a punishment should not be excessive.[7]

From Edward I's reign onwards imprisonment was a usual punishment. But the state of the gaols, right down to the middle of the nineteenth century, made it a peculiarly demoralizing punishment. We have seen that the gaols were self-supporting institutions out of which the gaoler expected to make a profit. No care was taken of the inmates. The sexes were not separated, and the most elementary sanitary precautions were neglected.[8] Gaol fever was rampant, and was sometimes fatal to the judges, barristers, and officers of the courts. At Oxford, in 1577, the chief baron, the sheriff, and about three hundred others died within forty hours, and in 1750 it was so rampant in Newgate that it killed two judges of Assize, the lord mayor, an alderman, and many others.[9] Coke said that "few or none are committed to the common gaol, but

---

[1] P. and M. (1st ed.) ii 514. [2] Ibid 514-515.
[3] Ibid 515 and n. 8. [4] Ibid 515; vol. iii 391.
[5] P. and M. ii 516; Griesley's Case (1588) 8 Co. Rep. at p. 41a; in later law the difference between a fine and an amercement was said to be that "a fine is always imposed and assessed by the Court, but an amercement . . . is assessed by the country," ibid at p. 39a; this case shows that the question when a man should be fined and when amerced, and, if amerced, whether the amercement should be assessed by the court or by his peers, had become the centre of a mass of complex rules.
[6] (1215) § 20; vol. ii 214 n. 6.
[7] "That excessive bail ought not to be required, nor excessive fines imposed; nor cruel and unusual punishments inflicted," 1 William and Mary, Stat. 2 §§ 1, 10.
[8] Vol. x 181-182; Lecky, History of England ii 127-129; vii 327-330.
[9] Lecky, History of England ii 130.

they come out worse than they went in." [1] He added that " few
are committed to the house of correction but they come out
better." [2] But he could not have added this if he had lived in the
eighteenth century. In that century the houses of correction were
as bad as the gaols. Fielding said that of the prisoners which
came before him " the most impudent and flagitious have always
been such as have been before acquainted with the discipline
of Bridewell " ; and that a commitment to Bridewell " tho'
it often causes great horror and lamentation in the novice, is
usually treated with ridicule and contempt by those who have
already been there." [3] In fact magistrates would often not
commit to Bridewell because of the evil effects upon those who
were sent there.[4] Goldsmith did not exaggerate when he said
that the prisons were places which " inclose wretches for the
commission of one crime, and return them, if alive, fitted for
the perpetration of thousands " ; [5] nor did Fielding exaggerate
when he said that the houses of correction were " schools of
vice, seminars of idleness, and common stores of nastiness and
disease." [6] Johnson agreed with these views. " The misery
of gaols," he said, " is not half their evil : they are filled with
every corruption which poverty and wickedness can generate
between them." [7] We have seen that in the last quarter of
the century the public conscience was aroused, largely by the
magnificent work of Howard.[8] Blackstone and others attempted
to reform the prisons ; and Acts were passed for this purpose.[9]
But we have seen that these Acts did not produce all the effects
which their supporters expected.[10] The state of the prisons when
Dickens wrote had in some respects been improved ; but it was
still very bad.[11] It was not till the reform of the administrative
system of the central government in the nineteenth century,
that the state got the necessary machinery for seeing that the
legislation which it passed was carried out. We shall now see
that it was partly the appalling state of the prisons, and partly the
need to provide a suitable punishment for persons whose death
sentences it was thought desirable to commute, which were the
principal causes for the introduction in the eighteenth century
of the punishment of transportation overseas.

(iii) *Transportation.*—Transportation as a punishment for
crime has had a curious history. In the latter part of the seventeenth and in the course of the eighteenth centuries it became

[1] Second Instit. 754.   [2] Ibid.
[3] An Enquiry into the Causes of the late Increase of Robbers (1751) 62.
[4] Ibid.   [5] The Vicar of Wakefield, chap. xxvii.
[6] Op. cit. 63.   [7] The Idler no. 38.
[8] Vol. x 182.   [9] Ibid 182-183.   [10] Ibid 183.
[11] See Holdsworth, Charles Dickens as a Legal Historian 138-140 ; Bowen,
Administration of Justice during the Victorian Period, Essays A.A.L.H. i 544-545.

a very common form of punishment.   It continued to be a form of punishment till, in consequence of the objection of the colonies to receive criminals, it was abolished by Acts passed in 1853 and 1857, and penal servitude or imprisonment with hard labour was substituted for it.[1]

In the twelfth and early thirteenth centuries persons could be forced to abjure the realm ; [2] and Magna Carta recognized exile as a possible punishment after a regular trial and conviction.[3] But at the end of the thirteenth century exile had ceased to be a definite punishment for crime.[4]   It survived only in the case of those criminals who, having taken sanctuary, were forced to abjure the realm ; [5] and we have seen that the institution of sanctuary, and its appendant abjuration, were abolished in 1623-1624.[6]   The result was that it came to be recognized that a subject could not be compelled to leave the realm except by virtue of an Act of Parliament.[7]   On the other hand, it was always possible for the Crown to pardon a criminal, and to attach conditions to its pardon.[8]   Thus the Crown might pardon a criminal on condition that he transported himself over the seas,[9] or on condition that he submitted to be transported and imprisoned overseas.[10]   It is true that a man cannot make a valid contract to submit to be imprisoned ; [11] but it was held in 1839 that this rule did not prevent a criminal from accepting a pardon by virtue of which " his life is spared, but he binds himself to undergo a less severe punishment." [12]   It is on these two bases —direct legislation and conditional pardons—that transportation as a punishment for crime rested.

Legislation began in Elizabeth's reign.   Two Acts of 1593 provided that in certain cases persons who did not conform to the established church should abjure the realm, and that if they

---

[1] Stephen, H.C.L. i 482 ; below 573.   [2] Vol. iii 303-304.
[3] (1215) § 39, cited vol. ii 214 n; 10.   [4] Vol. iii 304.
[5] Ibid 304-306.
[6] Ibid 307 ; 21 James I c. 28 § 7.
[7] Probably the law was so settled in the course of the seventeenth century, Stephen, H.C.L. i 480, L.Q.R. vi 396 ; but in 1621 James I added banishment to Mompesson's sentence, Notestein, Commons' Debates 1621 iv 205, vi 384 ; Hallam C.H. i 358.
[8] Coke, Third Instit. 233 ; Craies, Compulsion of Subjects to Leave the Realm, L.Q.R. vi 404-405 ; Forsyth, Leading Cases 76-77, 460 n. 1.
[9] See R. v. Miller (1772) 2 W. Bl. 797 ; R. v. Aickles (1785) Leach 390 ; cp. L.Q.R. vi 406.
[10] Below 570-571 ; similarly pardons were sometimes granted on condition of service in the navy—" this practice went on throughout the eighteenth century, but in 1771 it was objected to by the Lords of the Admiralty as demoralizing to the ships' crews and as discouraging the voluntary enlistment of better men," L.Q.R. vi 391-392.
[11] " The body of a freeman cannot be made subject to distress or imprisonment by contract but only by judgment," Foster v. Jackson (1616) Hob. at p. 61.
[12] Leonard Watson's Case, 9 Ad. and E. at p. 783.

returned they should suffer as felons without benefit of clergy.[1] A much more important Act of 1597 [2] gave power to the justices in quarter sessions either to banish " out of this realm and all other the dominions thereof," or to send to the galleys for ever, rogues, vagabonds, and sturdy beggars ; and, if they were banished, to convey them at the charges of the county to such parts beyond the seas as the Privy Council should assign. If they returned they were to suffer as felons without benefit of clergy. A somewhat similar expedient was adopted during the eighteenth century to rid the streets of undesirable persons. We have seen that temporary Acts gave power to the justices to enlist incorrigible rogues in the army or navy, and that, on the request of the Privy Council, considerable use was made of this power.[3]

The idea that persons sentenced to death should be sent to people the colonies was mooted in 1611.[4] In 1622 and 1638 there are cases in which reprieved prisoners asked to be transported to Virginia ; [5] and under the Commonwealth pirates, prisoners of war, and Catholic Irish were freely transported.[6] There was no legal warrant for these practices ; but, after the Restoration, a system of transportation was legalized by the device of granting a pardon conditionally upon the prisoners consenting to be transported to the plantations for a term of years.[7] In 1665 Kelyng says [8] that it was lately used,

that for felonies within clergy, if the prisoner desire it, not to give his book, but to procure a conditional pardon from the King, and send them beyond the sea to serve five years in some of the King's plantations, and then to have land there assigned them according to the use in those plantations, for servants after their time expired, with a condition in the pardon to be void if they do not go, or if they return into England during seven years, or after without the King's licence.

[1] 35 Elizabeth c. 1 §§ 2 and 3 (persons who refused to attend church or who attended conventicles) ; c. 2 §§ 8-10 (popish recusants who had little or no property) ; it was not till 1688 that the Toleration Act (1 William and Mary Stat. 1 c. 18 § 4) exempted Protestant non-conformists from the penalties of 35 Elizabeth c. 1 ; cp. L.Q.R. vi 396.
[2] 39 Elizabeth c. 4 § 4.
[3] Vol. x 179 ; L.Q.R. vi 390-391 ; see 17 George II c. 5 § 9 ; difficulties were caused when persons not liable to be thus impressed, were impressed, and by writs of habeas corpus contested their liability to be thus taken ; see Wilmot's Opinions 81 n. (a) ; cp. vol. ix 119-121.
[4] " The first impulse to the sending convicts under sentence of death abroad seems to have been given by Sir Thomas Dale in 1611, who suggested that all offenders out of the common gaols condemned to die should be sent for three years to the colony (Virginia), ' So do the Spaniards people the Indies '," L.Q.R. vi 398.
[5] Ibid.   [6] Ibid 398-399.   [7] Ibid 400.
[8] Kelyng's Reports at p. 45 ; in the directions for justices of the peace made by the judges in 1664 it is ordered that, " such prisoners as are reprieved with intent to be transported, be not sent away as perpetual slaves, but upon indentures between them and particular masters, to serve in our English plantations for seven years, and the three last years thereof, to have wages, that they may have a stock when their time is expired ; and that an account be given thereof, and by whom they are sent, and of their arrivals," ibid 4.

The legality of this system of pardoning felonies, whether clergyable or not, conditionally upon transportation, was recognized by the Habeas Corpus Act of 1679.[1] The Act provided that imprisonment beyond the seas was illegal,[2] but that

if any person or persons lawfully convicted of any felony, shall in open court pray to be transported beyond the seas, and the court shall think fit to leave him or them in prison for that purpose, such person or persons may be transported into any parts beyond the seas.[3]

Both after Monmouth's rebellion and after the Jacobite rising of 1715 there were wholesale transportations of prisoners on conditional pardons.[4]

It will be observed that this system of transportation on conditional pardon depended on the consent of the prisoner, since the Crown by its prerogative cannot, without such consent change or commute a sentence.[5] It was for this reason that transportation on conditional pardon tended to be confused with cases in which persons had contracted to be transported to the colonies under agreements to serve for a term of years. In fact these two very different classes of cases, in which transportation sometimes took place, were sometimes bracketed together by the Legislature. Both the case where a criminal was transported on a conditional pardon, and the case where a person had contracted to serve abroad, were excepted from the clause of the Habeas Corpus Act which prohibited the sending of prisoners out of the country;[6] and the Act of 1717[7] which, as we shall see, made transportation a definite sentence for certain crimes,[8] provided both for transportation on conditional pardon in the case of certain other crimes,[9] and for transportation of unemployed infants, between the ages of fifteen and twenty-one, under contracts to serve in the Plantations for eight years.[10] But, in fact, the element of consent in both these classes of cases was often shadowy. The criminal only consented to transportation in order to save his life; and though these contracts of service rested on consent, in fact the person who thus contracted was often treated in much the same way as the transported convict. Mr. Craies says:[11]

[1] 31 Charles II c. 2 ; cp. Bl. Comm. iv 401.
[2] 31 Charles II c. 2 § 12.   [3] § 14.
[4] L.Q.R. vi 403.   [5] Forsyth, Leading Cases, 463.
[6] " Provided always that nothing in this Act shall extend to give benefit to any person who shall by contract in writing agree with any merchant or owner of any Plantation, or other person whatsoever, to be transported to any parts beyond the seas, and receive earnest upon such agreement, although that afterwards such person shall renounce such contract," 31 Charles II c. 2 § 13.
[7] 4 George I c. 11.   [8] Below 573.
[9] § 1.   [10] § 5.
[11] L.Q.R. vi 397-398.

Transportation under indenture was authorized by the first colonial charter [of Virginia], but was confined to persons contented to go, and the term of bond service to ten years.   But up till 1638, and probably much later, of the hundreds sent to Virginia nearly all were brought in as merchandize to make sale of, and the right to their service, whether under indenture or order of the Crown, was assignable and freely assigned."

There is no doubt that this system led to all sorts of abuses. One abuse, prevalent at Bristol, was exposed by Jeffreys.   It is thus described by Roger North : [1]

There had been an usage among the aldermen and justices of the city (where all persons, even common shop-keepers, more or less trade to the American plantations) to carry over criminals who were pardoned with condition of transportation, and to sell them for money.   This was found to be a good trade ; but, not being content to take such felons as were convicts at their assizes and sessions, which produced but a few, they found out a shorter way which yielded a greater plenty of the commodity.   And that was this.   The mayor and justices, or some of them, usually met at their tolsey (a court house by their exchequer) about noon, which was the meeting of the merchants as at the Exchange in London ; and there they sat and did justice business that was brought before them.   When small rogues and pilferers were taken and brought there, and, upon examination, put under terror of being hanged, in order to which mittimus's were making, some of the diligent officers attending instructed them to pray transportation, as the only way to save them ; and for the most part they did so.   Then no more was done ; but the next alderman in course took one and another as their turns came, sometimes quarrelling whose the last was, and sent them over and sold them.

These iniquitous practices came to the knowledge of Jeffreys. He found that all the aldermen and justices were concerned in it, and " the mayor himself as bad as any." [2]   He compelled the mayor " accoutered with his scarlet and furs " to " go down to the criminal's post at the bar," and ended by taking security of the mayor and aldermen to answer informations.[3]   But interest was made at court, and Jeffreys was induced not to press the prosecutions.   But

the prosecutions depended till the Revolution which made an amnesty ; and the fright only, which was no small one, was all the punishment these juridicial kidnappers underwent ; and the gains acquired by so wicked a trade rested peacefully in their pockets.[4]

Another abuse was the custom of kidnapping persons and " spiriting " them away to the colonies.   In *Designy's Case* in 1682 [5] Designy, a Jamaica merchant, was found guilty of spiriting

---

[1] Lives of the Norths, i 284.   [2] Ibid 285.
[3] Ibid.   [4] Ibid 285-286.
[5] T. Raym. 474 ; North says, Examen 591, that Wilmer, the foreman of the jury which ignored the bill for treason against Lord Shaftesbury, was accused of having kidnapped two young men and sent them to the Plantations.

away " the eldest son of one Turbet who was a scholar at Merchant Taylor's School, and a hopeful youth." In fact so prevalent was this offence that, in the same year, the King issued a proclamation against the practice, and laid down rules as to the conditions under which servants could be engaged and sent over seas.[1]

The power of the Crown to grant a conditional pardon with the consent of the criminal still survives.[2] It was used in the eighteenth century to man the navy,[3] and its use in that century in favour of individuals gave rise to one or two cases which turned on the form and interpretation of these pardons,[4] and on the consequences which ensued if a criminal either did not transport himself according to its terms,[5] or if, having left the country, he returned.[6] It was recognized as an existing prerogative in the nineteenth century ; [7] it was occasionally used in the case of political criminals ; [8] and it was not affected by the Acts of 1853 and 1857 [9] which abolished transportation as a punishment which the court was empowered to award for certain crimes.[10]

The use of transportation as a punishment awarded by the court for certain crimes was introduced by an Act of 1717.[11] Because that Act made transportation a definite punishment which the court could award, it is a turning-point in the history of the punishment of transportation. But, like many other Acts, though it introduced a new principle, it did not quite lose sight of the older principles which had regulated the transportation of persons beyond the seas—whether criminals or not.

The Act of 1717 provided that if persons were convicted of certain felonies within the benefit of clergy, the court might order that, instead of being whipt or burnt in the hand, they should be transported to the American plantations for seven years.[12] If such persons returned before the expiration of this term, they were to be treated as persons convicted of felony without benefit of clergy.[13] These clauses of the Act thus made a new departure in assigning transportation as a definite punishment for certain offences. But two other provisions in the Act recall the old law. First, persons who had been convicted of felony

[1] Tudor and Stuart Proclamations i no. 3737 (Dec. 13, 1682) ; the conditions were : an indenture must be executed by the servant before the magistrate in duplicate ; the clerk of the peace must keep a register of these indentures ; persons over twenty-one might be bound ; persons under twenty-one required the consent of their parents or masters ; persons under fourteen, unless their parents were present, were to be detained on shore for a fortnight at least, for the discovery of abuses.

[2] L.Q.R. vi 397, 405, 407.   [3] Above 569 n. 10.

[4] R. v. Miller (1772) 2 W. Bl. 797.

[5] R. v. Madan (1780) 1 Leach 223 ; R. v. Aickles (1785) 1 Leach 390.

[6] R. v. Madan (1780) 1 Leach 223.

[7] Forsyth, Leading Cases 76-77, 460.   [8] L.Q.R. vi 397, 407.

[9] 16, 17 Victoria c. 99 § 13 ; 20, 21 Victoria c. 3 § 7.

[10] Below 575.   [11] 4 George I c. 11.   [12] § 1.   [13] § 2.

without benefit of clergy, and who had got a conditional pardon, could be ordered by the court to be transported for fourteen years, or such other term as should be contained in the pardon.[1] Secondly, we have seen that infants between the ages of fifteen and twenty could contract to be transported for eight years.[2] These two provisions of the Act were in the nature of survivals of the older law. The important part of the Act was the part which gave the court power to award transportation as a definite sentence. Later Acts made provisions as to contracts for the transportation of felons,[3] as to the apprehension of felons who returned or escaped,[4] and as to the punishment of those who helped them to escape ;[5] and they gave power to the judge to make an order for immediate transportation without waiting for the signification of the King's pleasure.[6]

Transportation having thus been introduced as a definite punishment for certain crimes, it soon became one of the Legislature's most favourite forms of punishment. Stephen says :[7]

In the course of the eighteenth and the early part of the nineteenth century an immense number of Acts were passed by which various terms of transportation, with alternative terms of imprisonment, and powers in some cases alternative and in others cumulative, to order whipping more or less frequently, were allotted to particular offences. This legislation was guided by no sort of principle, and was utterly destitute of any sort of uniformity.[8]

One of the reasons stated in the preamble to the Act of 1717 for its enactment was the great want of servants in his Majesty's colonies and plantations in America.[9] In fact America was the place to which convicts were generally sent till the outbreak of the war of independence. In 1776 an Act was passed which provided that criminals sentenced to transportation should be confined in hulks in the Thames, and used to cleanse the river.[10] The conditions on these hulks were as terrible as those in the prisons of this period, and as demoralizing to their inmates.[11]

---

[1] § 1.   [2] § 5 ; above 571.
[3] 6 George I c. 23.   [4] 16 George II c. 15.   [5] Ibid c. 31.
[6] 8 George III c. 15 ; the former practice on circuit and at the Old Bailey was said in R. v. Beaton (1764) 1 W. Bl. at p. 479 to be as follows : "a sign manual issues signifying the King's intention of either an absolute or conditional pardon, and directing the Justices of Gaol Delivery to bail the prisoner, in order to appear and plead the next general pardon that shall come out ; which they do accordingly, taking his recognizance to perform the conditions of the pardon, if any."
[7] H.C.L. i 480.
[8] For the resulting confusion of the law as to the punishments which might be inflicted in particular cases see ibid i 480-481.
[9] 4 George I c. 11 ; but before this date some of the American colonies had protested against the practice of transporting felons to them, L.Q.R. vi 401.
[10] 16 George III c. 43.
[11] Madan, Thoughts on Executive Justice 74-75 ; Walpole, Letters (ed. Toynbee) xii 331, wrote in 1782 that, "in those colleges, undergraduates in villainy commence Masters of Arts" ; cp. L.Q.R. vi 401 ; see a report on the working of 16 George III c. 43 in House of Commons Journals, April 15, 1778.

In 1779 the system of transportation was resumed, and the Court was given power to order transportation to any place beyond the seas.[1] Under this Act convicts were transported to Africa.[2] In 1784 the Crown was given power to appoint places to which criminals could be transported.[3] In 1786 to 1787 the convict settlement at Botany Bay in Australia was established;[4] and from 1788 to 1853 criminals were transported to Australia.[5] An Act of 1824 [6] consolidated the law as to the powers of the Crown in relation to the transportation of criminals; and it remained the principal Act on this subject till the whole system of transportation was abolished by Acts of 1853 and 1857,[7] which substituted for it the punishment of penal servitude or imprisonment with hard labour. But the Crown can still direct that criminals shall serve their time abroad;[8] and we have seen that it may still send criminals out of the kingdom by means of a conditional pardon to which the criminal has assented.[9]

We have seen that in the latter half of the eighteenth century the many defects in the system of punishments, which were legally possible under the English criminal law, were beginning to attract some public attention.[10] Abroad, Beccaria's famous book had awakened the public conscience to the iniquities perpetrated under the continental codes of criminal procedure, and had turned public attention to a consideration of what was in effect a new subject—the theory or theories which should underlie the infliction of different kinds of punishment, and the qualities which an effective punishment should possess.

Beccaria published his famous *Essay on Crimes and Punishments* in 1764.[11] It had an immediate success. In the Preface to the English translation [12] the translator says :

It is now about eighteen months since the first publication; in which time it hath passed no less than six editions in the original

[1] 19 George III c. 74 § 1.
[2] This is what happened in R. v. Madan (1780) 1 Leach at p. 224 ; for protests against this practice in 1785 on the ground that it meant certain death for the convicts, see Parlt. Hist. xxv 391-392, 430 ; and see a report on this question in House of Commons Journals, May 9, 1785, from which it appears that the difficulties in the way of transportation to Africa were insuperable.
[3] 24 George III Sess. 2 c. 56 § 1.
[4] Lecky, History of England vii 306.
[5] Romilly, Memoirs ii 146, tells us that the system was often worked most unjustly—" in August 1801 forty convicts were transported who had only one year of their term of transportation unexpired at the time of their embarkation, and ten who had only nine months unexpired, though it is a nine months' voyage."
[6] 5 George IV c. 84.
[7] 16, 17 Victoria c. 99 ; 20, 21 Victoria c. 3.   [8] Ibid §§ 3 and 4.
[9] Above 573.   [10] Above 562-566, 568.
[11] For a good short account of Beccaria see Great Jurists of the World (Continental Legal History Series) 505-516.
[12] The copy which I have used is the fourth edition 1785 ; the first edition was published in 1767.

language ; the third of which was printed within six months after its first appearance. It hath been translated into French ; that translation hath also been several times reprinted, and perhaps no book, on any subject, was ever received with more avidity, more generally read, or more universally applauded.

It was true, as the English translator says, that parts of the book were inapplicable to England.[1]   But there were also parts which were very applicable :

The confinement of debtors, the filth and horror of our prisons, the cruelty of jailors, and the extortion of the petty officers of justice, to all which may be added the melancholy reflection, that the number of criminals put to death in England is much greater than in any other part of Europe.

The reason why the book was so successful was the fact that the author tried to rationalize criminal law and procedure, by the application of the same principle that Bentham later applied in much greater detail to all branches of the law. His diagnosis of the state of the law, of the reasons why it had got into this state, and of the manner in which its reform should be approached, anticipate Bentham.   He says : [2]

If we look into history we shall find that laws, which are, or ought to be, conventions between men in a state of freedom, have been for the most part the work of the passions of a few, or the consequences of a fortuitous, or temporary necessity ; not dictated by a cool examiner of human nature, who knew how to collect in one point the actions of a multitude, and had this only end in view, *the greatest happiness of the greatest number*. . . . The art of printing has diffused the knowledge of those philosophical truths, by which the relations between sovereigns and their subjects, and between nations, are discovered. By this knowledge, commerce is animated, and there has sprung up a spirit of emulation and industry, worthy of rational beings. These are the produce of this enlightened age ; but the cruelty of punishments, and the irregularity of proceeding in criminal cases, so principal a part of the legislation, and so much neglected throughout Europe, has hardly ever been called in question. Errors accumulated through centuries, have never yet been exposed by ascending to general principles ; nor has the force of acknowledged truths been ever opposed to the unbounded licentiousness of ill-directed power, which has continually produced so many authorized examples of the most unfeeling barbarity.

And just as he anticipates Bentham by insisting that " greatest happiness of the greatest number " should be the guiding principle of the legislator ; so too he anticipates him by insisting upon the truths, first that " pleasure and pain are the only springs of action in beings endowed with sensibility," [3] and, secondly,

---

[1] " It may be objected, that a treatise of this kind is useless in England, where, from the excellence of our laws and government, no examples of cruelty or oppression are to be found. But it must also be allowed, that much is still wanting to perfect our system of legislation."

[2] Introduction 2-3.   [3] Chap. vi p. 25.

that, since "it is sufficient that the *evil* which a punishment occasions should exceed the *good* expected from the crime," "all severity beyond this is superfluous, and therefore tyrannical." [1]

The book, it has been said, was the outcome of the author's study "of French philosophy and of French rationalism as bearing on existing penal legislation." [2] It had an immediate practical result on the Continent. Catherine II of Russia, Frederick of Prussia, and Leopold of Tuscany abolished the use of torture in their dominions ; [3] and in other states the death penalty was either abolished or restricted to a few crimes. [4] In England the book helped forward the tendency, which had already begun, to reflect upon the deficiencies of the criminal law, and more especially upon its punishments. In fact some of Beccaria's theories had been anticipated, or independently arrived at, by English critics. Of this anticipation two examples will suffice. In the first place, Beccaria insists that " the punishment of a crime cannot be just (that is necessary) if the laws have not endeavoured to prevent that crime by the best means which times and circumstances would allow." [5] This was exactly the point which Fielding had made in 1751. He said : [6]

Nor will the utmost severity to offenders be justifiable unless we take every possible method of preventing the offence. . . . The subject as well as the child should be left without excuse before he is punished : for in that case alone the rod becomes the hand either of the parent or the magistrate.

In the second place, Beccaria insists that the law ought to be so just that it should not be necessary to be constantly invoking the prince's prerogative of pardon :

Clemency is a virtue which belongs to the legislator, and not to the executor of the laws ; a virtue which ought to shine in the code, and not in private judgment. To show mankind, that crimes are sometimes pardoned, and that punishment is not the necessary consequence, is to nourish the flattering hope of impunity, and is the cause of their considering every punishment inflicted as an act of injustice and oppression. The prince in pardoning gives up the public security in favour of an individual, and, by his ill-judged benevolence, proclaims a public act of impunity. [7]

This, as we have seen, is the same argument as that used by Fielding and Madan. [8]

---

[1] Chap. xxvii pp. 99-100.   [2] Great Jurists of the World 506.
[3] Ibid 510.   [4] Ibid 514.
[5] Chap. xxxi p. 132.
[6] An Enquiry into the Causes of the late Increase of Robbers (1751) 126.
[7] Chap. xlvi p. 176.
[8] Above 564; but Blackstone did not agree ; he says, alluding to Beccaria : " pardons (according to some theorists) should be excluded in a perfect legislation, when punishments are mild but certain : for that the clemency of the prince seems

Beccaria made men reflect upon the theory of punishment. Its object he insisted was to prevent crimes, and it should be so adjusted that it deterred others with least possible infliction of pain on the criminal.[1] He concluded his work " with the following general theorem, of considerable utility, though not conformable to custom, the common legislator of nations : that a punishment may not be an act of violence, of one, or of many against a private member of society, it should be public, immediate, and necessary, the least possible in the case given ; proportioned to the crime, and determined by the laws." [2]

If Beccaria's book be compared with Blackstone's remarks on the theory of punishment, it is impossible to doubt that Blackstone owes much to Beccaria. Though Blackstone by no means sees eye to eye with Beccaria on all matters,[3] it is I think clear that it was Beccaria's book which helped Blackstone to crystallize his ideas, and that it was Beccaria's influence which helped to give a more critical tone to his treatment of the English criminal law than to his treatment of any other part of English law. No doubt other influences helped Blackstone to adopt this attitude. We have seen that many had criticized particular aspects of the criminal law.[4] However that may be, there is no doubt that Blackstone does adopt a critical attitude, and does attempt to construct a theory of punishment. Those who still believe in the legend spread by Bentham, that Blackstone was an uncritical optimist who defended all things established,[5] should read the Fourth Book of his Commentaries.[6] He

a tacit disapprobation of the laws. But the exclusion of pardons must necessarily introduce a very dangerous power in the judge or the jury, that of construing the criminal law by the spirit instead of the letter ; or else it must be holden, what no man will seriously avow, that the situation and circumstances of the offender (though they alter not the essence of the crime) ought to make no distinction in the punishment," Comm. iv 397 ; these conclusions would not follow if the judge were given a discretion as to the amount of punishment ; on the other hand, to exclude the power of pardon altogether would be dangerous, since it would be difficult to modify or remit the punishment if new circumstances came to light which made this course just or expedient.

[1] " It is better to prevent crimes than to punish them. This is the fundamental principle of good legislation, which is the art of conducting men to the *maximum* of happiness and to the *minimum* of misery," chap. xli p. 164.

[2] Chap. xlvii pp. 178-179.

[3] Above 577 n. 8 ; Beccaria would give a much smaller place to the punishment of death than either Blackstone or Stephen would allow, cp. Beccaria chap. xxviii with Comm. iv 9-10, and H.C.L. i 478-480 ; nor does Blackstone agree with Beccaria, chap. xxxvi, in condemning the system of giving rewards for the apprehension of criminals ; on the other hand he agrees with Beccaria, chap. xxxiii p. 139, that "if the same punishment be decreed for killing a pheasant as for killing a man, or for forgery, all difference between those crimes will shortly vanish; " cp. Comm. iv 18.

[4] Above 528-529, 559-560, 562-563, 565-566.   [5] Vol. xii 727-729.

[6] It is true that some support is given to Bentham's views by Blackstone's remarks on the benefit of clergy, vol. iii 302, citing Comm. iv 371 ; but, having regard to other parts of Blackstone's treatment of the criminal law, and also to other parts of his Commentaries, I think we may regard these remarks as a rhetorical flourish which is by no means so typical as is sometimes imagined, vol. xii 728-729.

criticized many of the detailed rules of the English criminal law and procedure ; and, what was more important, he put his finger on the two great blots on the English system of punishment —the frequency with which the punishment of death was inflicted, and the horrible state of the prisons.   We have seen that he himself helped to carry a measure of prison reform ; [1] and, after his death, the revelations of Howard made it impossible for the Legislature to shelve this topic.[2]   At the same time there was an attempt to induce the Legislature to take in hand a revision of the laws which inflicted the punishment of death. In 1770 a committee was appointed by the House of Commons " to consider of so much of the criminal law as relates to capital offences." [3]

But though there was much talk of reform in the eighteenth century, and though some useful measures were passed, nothing was done commensurate with the evils which required to be remedied.   The administrative weakness of the government prevented the legislation for the reform of the prisons from producing the effect which Blackstone and others expected from it.[4]   The House of Commons committee on capital punishment, after sitting for two years, only recommended the repeal of eight Acts of Parliament, and that recommendation was not carried into effect.[5]   At the same time the attention devoted to the state of the criminal law, and more especially to the question of punishment, though it resulted in no large measure of reform, was not thrown away.   It prepared the way for the sympathetic consideration of the proposals of Howard and Bentham and Romilly in the following period ; and it ensured priority of consideration for the criminal law, when, in the second quarter of the nineteenth century, the reform of the law began to be taken in hand.   The reasons why, in spite of the admitted defects of the criminal law, no large measures of reform were taken in hand in the eighteenth century, were partly the merits of the English system of criminal law and procedure, partly the manner in which the law had been and was being developed, and partly the characteristics of the public law of the period, of which

---

[1] Vol. x 182-183.

[2] For Howard's great work see Lecky, History of England vii 327-333 ; Webb, Prisons under Local Government, chap. iii.

[3] Journals of the House of Commons xxxiii 27 ; in 1787 a Mr. Minchin moved for a statutory commission to enquire into the defects of the criminal law, Parlt. Hist. xxvi 1056-1058 ; in 1789 Burke described the criminal law as " radically defective," and " in its present state abominable," ibid xxviii 146-147.

[4] Vol. x 183; above 568.

[5] In 1771 it recommended the repeal of four Acts, Journals of the House of Commons xxxiii 365 ; in 1772 a similar committee was re-appointed, ibid xxxiii 442 ; in 1772 it recommended the repeal of four more Acts, ibid xxxiii 612 ; and later, ibid xxxiii 695, a bill was ordered to be brought in to repeal these eight Acts, which does not appear to have become law.

the criminal law is in some of its aspects a part, and by which it must always be largely influenced. Of the outstanding characteristics of the English criminal law which were due to these causes I must in conclusion say a few words.

(4) *The characteristics of the criminal law and procedure of the eighteenth century.*

The outstanding features of the criminal law and criminal procedure of a state are determined by the character, first of the government of that state, to which it must always be very closely related, and secondly of its system of law. The character of the criminal law and criminal procedure of the leading states of Western Europe in the eighteenth century was determined, first by the autocratic character of their governments, and secondly by the manner in which, in the sixteenth century, they had received and developed ideas and principles derived from the civil and canon law.[1] The character of the criminal law and criminal procedure of the common law was determined, first by the constitutional character of the government of the English state, and secondly by the fact that after the fall of the Star Chamber, ideas drawn from the criminal procedure of the civil and canon law had been rejected, and had been replaced by ideas drawn from the mediæval procedure of the common law.[2]

English writers of the eighteenth century, who compared the continental criminal law and procedure with that of the English common law, had no hesitation in praising the system of the common law. And, if we look at the common law system from this point of view, there can be no doubt that their praise was deserved. The history of the criminal law and procedure of these continental states, in which barbarous punishments were frequently inflicted and torture was habitually used, is the most sickening and disgusting topic in the legal history of Western Europe. There is no doubt that Blackstone in the eighteenth century [3] was as well justified as Fortescue in the fifteenth century,[4] in saying that the English criminal law and procedure were nfinitely more humane and more fair to the accused than the continental criminal law and procedure. Though some of the punishments allowed by the law were brutal [5] and many were unreasonably severe,[6] there was a tradition, starting with Magna Carta [7] and confirmed by the Bill of Rights,[8] that they ought to be fixed by the law, and that they ought not to be excessive. It

---

[1] Vol. v 170-176. [2] Ibid 195-196 ; vol. ix 229-236.
[3] Comm. iv 3, cited above 555 n. 4 ; ibid iv 377, cited below 581 n. 1.
[4] De Laudibus, c. 27, cited vol. iii 622 ; vol. v 169.
[5] Above 557. [6] Above 559-560.
[7] Above 567. [8] Above 567 n. 7.

is true that this was an ideal to which the law rarely attained ; but the fact that it was enshrined in documents, which were universally regarded as the most sacred of the title deeds of the constitution, was not without its effect ; at any rate it prevented the deterioration of the law which follows from the practice of leaving the mode of punishment to the discretion of the executive or the judges. This effect was emphasized by Blackstone [1] and Stephen ; [2] and there is no doubt that they are right. Then, too, the fact that trials were public, the fact that the jury decided the issue, and the fact that torture was forbidden, made criminal trials far fairer to the accused than the continental trials even in the seventeenth century ; and when, in the eighteenth century, further privileges were given to accused persons, and the judges conducted the trials with scrupulous fairness to them, the English criminal trial became a model to the nations of Western Europe. [3] It was some of the features of the English criminal procedure that those nations copied when, after the French Revolution, they wished to introduce reforms. [4] It is true that England in the eighteenth century, though she produced some acute criticisms of the existing system, produced no such constructive writer as Beccaria ; but this was due to the fact that there was no such pressing need for radical reform as there was in continental states.

But though the English criminal law and procedure were greatly superior to those of continental states, they were gravely defective. The law was chaotic ; [5] the procedure, though reformed by the judges, was in many respects very faulty ; [6] the punishments were sometimes barbarous, quite unsystematic, and, by reason of their frequent mitigation (caused to a large extent by their undue severity) so uncertain in their operation that they were ineffective to accomplish the only end at which they aimed—deterrence. [7] These grave defects were due mainly to two of the salient features of the eighteenth-century government—first its constitutional character, and secondly and consequently its administrative weakness.

We have seen that both these salient features, and more

---

[1] Blackstone, after setting out the list of punishments, above 556, says, " disgusting as this catalogue may seem, it will afford pleasure to an English reader, and do honour to the English law, to compare it with that shocking apparatus of death and torment, to be met with in the criminal codes of almost every other nation in Europe. And it is moreover one of the glories of our English law, that the species, though not always the quantity or degree, of punishment is *ascertained* for every offence ; and that it is not left in the breast of any judge, nor even of a jury, to alter that judgment, which the law has before-hand ordained, for every subject alike, without respect of persons," Comm. iv 377 ; below 583.

[2] H.C.L. i 478.   [3] Vol. ix 235-236.
[4] Vol. v 493 n. 5   [5] Above 528-529; below 583-584.
[6] Vol. ix 235 ; above 553-556.   [7] Above 557-561.

especially the first, had certain outstanding merits. They gave the subject liberty ;[1] they taught him the arts of government by compelling him to give unpaid service in many different capacities;[2] they gave England a cheap and a solvent government, which secured her economic progress.[3] But they had their corresponding defects ; and in the sphere of criminal law it is their defects which are most obvious. Maitland, speaking of the effect of the rise of Parliament in the thirteenth century upon the development of English law, said,[4] " the supremacy of Parliament may have been worth the price paid for it ; none the less the price was high." So we may say of the criminal law of the eighteenth century—the constitutional character of the English government was worth the price paid for it, but it is answerable for many of the defects in that branch of the law. Let us examine the manner in which these two outstanding features of the eighteenth-century constitution—its constitutional character and its administrative weakness—affected the criminal law.

(i) *Constitutional character.*—Even in the sixteenth century, when the power of the Crown was at its height, and when the criminal jurisdiction of the ordinary courts was supplemented by the elastic criminal jurisdiction of the Star Chamber, no new felonies could be created except by Act of Parliament,[5] and the Star Chamber never dared to interfere in capital cases.[6] Mediæval statutes had effectually precluded the Council and the Star Chamber from exercising jurisdiction in civil cases where the title to freehold was contested, and in criminal cases where the life of the accused was at stake.[7] It is true that the Star Chamber made many salutary additions to the criminal law.[8] It added to and generalized the list of misdemeanours, and it punished severely those who broke the law. It is true that much of this law, and the habit of inflicting these severe punishments, were taken over by the common law courts after the Restoration.[9] But, after the Revolution, the rule that the list of crimes could not be added to or expanded except by the Legislature, long ago established for the felonies,[10] became the rule for all crimes ; and we have seen that the Bill of Rights laid down the rule that " cruel and unusual punishments " ought not to be inflicted.[11] Moreover, after the fall of the Star Chamber, all criminal cases, except the minor cases which fall under the summary jurisdiction of the justices of the peace, were tried by a jury.

---

[1] Above 278. [2] Ibid 275. [3] Ibid 276-278.
[4] Bracton's Note Book i 7, cited vol. ii 289 n. 7.
[5] Vol. i 487. [6] Vol. v 188-189.
[7] Vol. i 488. [8] Vol. v 197-214.
[9] Vol. viii 361-362, 392, 399. [10] Above n. 5.
[11] Above 567.

These characteristics of the criminal law had many beneficial results. In the first place, they ensured that a person could only be made criminally liable for offences defined by the common or statute law, and that he could only be punished in the manner provided by the law.[1] In the second place, it followed that neither the executive nor the judges could expand or modify the law ; and that though the Crown might modify, it could not increase the punishments fixed by the law. In the third place, the fact that the trial was by a jury enabled a certain amount of equity to be administered in individual cases without undue interference with the fixed rules of law. At the same time the control which the judges exercised over the jury, and the respect with which the jury rightly regarded them, was a safeguard against the mistakes which a body of very average citizens was likely to make. In fact trial by jury, as moulded by the judges, approached very nearly to the ideal which Beccaria envisaged for the conduct of criminal trials. He said :[2]

I think it an excellent law which establishes assistants to the principal judge, and those chosen by lot ; for that ignorance, which judges by feelings, is less subject to error, than the knowledge of the laws, which judges by opinion. When the laws are clear and precise, the office of judge is merely to ascertain the fact. If, in examining the proofs of a crime, acuteness and dexterity be required ; if clearness and precision be necessary in summing up the result ; to judge of the result itself, nothing is wanting but plain and ordinary good sense, a less fallacious guide than the knowledge of a judge, accustomed to find guilty, and to reduce all things to an artificial system, borrowed from his studies. Happy is the nation when the knowledge of the law is not a science.

The English system of trial by jury enabled the English system of criminal procedure to combine the advantages of having a scientific system of law, and at the same time of applying that system with a due regard to the justice of particular cases.

But these characteristics of the criminal law had also one very serious disadvantage. No change in or addition to the criminal law could be made except by statute. The result was that to the common law principles which applied to the criminal law in general, or to particular crimes, there was added a mass of statutes which made very many additions, and a few small changes, both in the substantive and in the adjective law. These statutes were hardly ever consolidated, so that a branch of the law which ought to be especially clear was both confused and unsystematic. It was both difficult to know and difficult to apply ; and

[1] In R. v. Collier and Cape (1752) 1 Wils. 332, the defendants were sentenced to a month's imprisonment, to ask pardon of the justice of the peace whom they had insulted, and to advertise the fact in the *Daily Advertiser ;* the court held that all parts of the judgment except the imprisonment were void.

[2] Chap. xiv p. 51.

the old rules and principles which it retained often assorted badly with the changes and additions made by the Legislature.[1] France obtained a code of criminal procedure in 1670.[2] England waited till the nineteenth century for those consolidating Acts which have to some extent supplied the place of a code.

I think that there is no doubt that the advantages to the criminal law which flowed from the constitutional character of the English state out-weighed the disadvantages. But we shall now see that, in so far as this constitutional character produced administrative weakness, the disadvantages out-weighed the advantages.

(ii) *Administrative weakness.*—It was this weakness which was the cause of the greatest blot on the criminal law—its ineffectiveness. The criminal law of the eighteenth century failed adequately to effect its principal object—the protection of life and property; and the administrative weakness which caused this failure had unfortunate effects on the law. In the first place, it rendered ineffective the attempts of the Legislature to reform the law—we have seen that its attempts to reform the prisons were to a large extent unsuccessful.[3] In the second place, when its attempts to suppress particular forms of crime failed, it vainly tried to cure its failures by added severity. This expedient added to the cruelty of the law, but obviously failed to remove the cause for the failures of the Legislature.[4] It also added to the uncertainty of the law, because added severities necessitated a more frequent use of the power to reprieve and pardon.[5] Fielding was correct when he pointed to this administrative weakness as the principal cause of the ineffectiveness of the criminal law, and when he assigned as the cause for this weakness the fact that the administrative machinery of the state had not been adapted to the new social needs and conditions. He said:[6]

It is a common and popular complaint that the Justices of Peace have already too much power. Indeed a very little is too much if it be abused; but, in truth, this complaint proceeds from a mistake of business for power: the business of the Justice is indeed multiplied by a great number of statutes; but I know not of any (the Riot Act perhaps excepted) which hath at all enlarged his power. When a mob of chairmen or servants or a gang of thieves or sharpers are almost too big for the civil authority to suppress, what must be the case in a seditious tumult or a general riot of the people?

The truth was that

the power of the commonalty hath received an immense addition; and the civil power not having increased but decreased in the same proportion, is not able to govern them.

---

[1] For an instance see above 559.   [2] Vol. vi 301 n. 1.
[3] Vol. x 183; above 568.   [4] Above 563.   [5] Above 563-564.
[6] An Enquiry into the Causes of the late Increase of Robbers (1751) xiv.

We have seen that this weakness of the administrative agents of the local government, which Fielding deplores, was aggravated by the weakness of the central government.[1] Neither the central nor the local government possessed any effective machinery for the prevention of crime. They possessed only the most rudimentary machinery for its detection ; [2] and the only means by which riots, and similar forms of organized resistance to the law, could be dealt with, was by calling upon the military to aid the civil power.[3]

We have seen that, in the sphere of local government, this administrative weakness was partially cured, and the machinery of local government was partially adapted to new social needs and conditions, by extra-legal conventions and practices,[4] and by private Acts of Parliament.[5] Though, no doubt, some use was made of extra-legal and illegal practices, the constitutional character of the English government made the use of this expedient to reform the criminal law on any large scale impossible ; [6] and, though watching and lighting Acts, obtained by particular localities, did something to supplement the absence of effective police,[7] those Acts only applied to particular localities. The failure of the criminal law at the beginning of the nineteenth century adequately to protect life and property was notorious. As late as 1837 Lord Bowen could say that " over a considerable portion of England, property was less secure than in any great European country, excepting only Italy and Spain " ; [8] that " footpads lurked in the vicinity of the great manufacturing centres of the north, and robbery with violence and murder itself went often unpunished " ; [9] and that " in the year 1839 there were upwards of five hundred voluntary associations for promoting the apprehension and prosecution of felons—for performing, in fact, by individuals the first duty of a civilized government." [10]

The Industrial Revolution had emphasized and aggravated

---

[1] Vol. x 238. [2] Above 552 ; below n. 10.
[3] Vol. x 646 n. 4. [4] Ibid 220 seqq. [5] Ibid 188 seqq.
[6] Bowen, Administration of Justice during the Victorian Period, Essays A.A.L.H. i 554, gives some illustrations of the use of these practices—" in conformity with the behest of the chief magistrate of one considerable town, the constables seized all vagrants found within their jurisdiction and took them to prison to have their heads shaved, after which operation they were set at liberty and went their ways. The superintendent of police was asked by what right he apprehended them and cut their hair. ' The mayor,' he replied, ' who is a man of few words, says he crops them for cleanliness.' In some rural districts the paid police were in the habit of dispensing altogether with the constitutional formality of a warrant. An officer interrogated on the subject frankly confessed the irregularity, but added that ' he chanced it ' " ; for the doings of a mayor of Deal in 1703 see Webb, Local Government, The Manor and the Borough ii 312-315.
[7] Vol. x 216-218. [8] Bowen, op. cit. 552.
[9] Ibid 553. [10] Ibid 554.

all those defects in the criminal law—-the defects arising from the chaotic character of the law, and the defects arising from the administrative weakness of the local and central government. We shall see in a later chapter that these defects were so notorious that, even before the Reform Act of 1832, some reforms had been made. But we shall see that it was not till the administrative machinery of the state had been overhauled by the reformed Parliament, and made in some measure capable of supplying a government adequate to the needs of a modern industrial state, that the underlying cause of the greatest defects of the criminal law of the eighteenth century was removed.

II. *The Land Law.*

The legislation as to the land law is not bulky. Very few important additions were made and hardly any important changes—Fearne could spend some twenty years in enlarging and revising his great work on Contingent Remainders without any fear that the elaborate doctrines, which the courts were creating and he was expounding, would be drastically changed or wholly abolished by the Legislature.[1]

(1) At the beginning of the eighteenth century a series of Acts were passed which established in Yorkshire and Middlesex registers of conveyances. The project of a register of conveyances or a register of titles had never been wholly lost sight of since it had been mooted by Henry VIII in 1535-1536. We have seen that Henry VIII's bill to establish this register had failed to pass the House of Commons ; and that its place had been taken by a short statute, supplemental to the statute of Uses, for the enrollment of the bargains and sales of those freehold interests in land which the statute of Uses had converted into conveyances.[2] The fact that the obligation to enroll had been evaded by the device of a bargain and sale for a term followed by a release,[3] had called attention to the frauds which were facilitated by the secrecy of conveyancing thus rendered possible. It was for this reason that, in the latter part of the seventeenth century, the project of establishing a register of conveyances or of titles was much considered.[4] No general scheme of registration for the whole country was adopted ; but these discussions were not wholly fruitless, since they resulted in the establishment of registers of conveyances for Yorkshire and Middlesex. In 1703 a register of deeds, conveyances, and wills for the West Riding

---

[1] For Fearne and his book see vol. xii 373-375.
[2] Vol. iv 457-460.
[3] Ibid 460 n. 1 ; vol. vii 360-361.
[4] Vol. vi 532 and n. 9, 594 and n. 2, 610.

of Yorkshire was established.[1] In 1707 a similar register was established for the East Riding and for Kingston-upon-Hull,[2] and in 1708 for Middlesex.[3] The latter Act was initiated by a petition of the justices of the peace and the grand jury of the county.[4] In 1735 a similar register was established for the North Riding of Yorkshire.[5]

The reasons assigned for the establishment of these registers were, first, the difficulty of giving a good title to intending mortgagees and purchasers,[6] and, secondly, the opportunity for the commission of frauds by the execution of "prior and secret conveyances and fraudulent incumbrances."[7] To remedy these evils the Acts provided in effect that all deeds should be adjudged fraudulent and void as against any subsequent purchaser or mortgagee for value, unless a memorial of them was registered before the registration of the memorial of the deed under which the subsequent purchaser or mortgagee claimed; and that judgments, statutes, and recognizances were not to bind the land till they had been registered. The security given by these Acts to mortgagees and purchasers was somewhat diminished by the decision of the court of Chancery that, if a purchaser or mortgagee who registered, had notice of a prior unregistered assurance, he could not in equity gain priority by registering his conveyance. Though he got the legal estate by registering, he must hold it as trustee for the persons of whose interests he had notice.[8] This principle was finally established by Lord Hardwicke in 1747 in the case of *Le Neve v. Le Neve*.[9] Lord Hardwicke pointed out, first that the design of the Act was to secure subsequent purchasers

---

[1] 2, 3 Anne c. 4, amended by 5, 6 Anne c. 18 which required the registration of judgments, statutes and recognizances, except those entered into on account of the Crown; by § 34 of 6 Anne c. 35, the provisions of that Act, which was passed for the East Riding, were applied to the West Riding.

[2] 6 Anne c. 35; cp. House of Lords MSS. (N.S.) vii no. 2471.

[3] 7 Anne c. 20 amended by 25 George II c. 4.

[4] House of Lords MSS. (N.S.) viii no. 2577; the clerks of the enrolment of the court of Chancery put in a petition against the bill on the ground that it would diminish the value of their office in which they had a freehold, ibid, but their claim was disregarded.

[5] 8 George II c. 6.

[6] " Whereas the West Riding of the county of York is the principal place in the North for the cloth manufacture, and most of the traders therein are freeholders, and have frequent occasions to borrow money upon their estates for managing their said trade, but for want of a Register find it difficult to give security to the satisfaction of the money-lenders," 2, 3 Anne c. 4, Preamble.

[7] 6 Anne c. 35, Preamble.

[8] " The enacting clause says, *that every such deed shall be void against any subsequent purchaser or mortgagee*, unless the memorial thereof be registered, etc.; that is, it gives him the legal estate; but it does not say that such subsequent purchase is not left open to any equity which a prior purchaser or incumbrancer may have; for he can be in no danger when he knows of another incumbrance, because he might then have stopped his hand from proceeding," Le Neve v. Le Neve (1747) Amb. at p. 442, *per* Lord Hardwicke.

[9] Amb. 436.

and mortgagees against prior secret conveyances, but that if a person had notice of a prior conveyance it was not, so far as he was concerned, a secret conveyance ;[1] and secondly, that the scheme of the Act was similar to the scheme of the statute of Enrolments, and that it had always been held that a subsequent bargainee was affected by the notice of a prior bargain, although it was not enrolled.[2] He concluded that

the operation of both Acts of Parliament and construction of them is the same ; and it would be a most mischievous thing, if a person taking that advantage of the legal form appointed by an Act of Parliament, might under that protect himself against a person who had a prior equity of which he had notice.[3]

The principle as stated by Lord Hardwicke is not unreasonable ; but the wide extension which the court of Chancery gave to the doctrines of imputed and constructive notice, had the effect, in many cases, of diminishing very seriously the protection afforded by registration which these Acts were intended to give to purchasers and mortgagees.[4]

(2) A number of small but not unimportant changes were made in the law as to landlord and tenant.

We have seen that landlords had been empowered to sell goods distrained for rent if not replevied within five days.[5] Legislation of the first half of the eighteenth century (i) made further improvements in the remedy of distress, and in other remedies open to the landlord, and (ii) gave him new remedies. (i) Creditors who had levied execution were prohibited from removing the goods which they had taken, until they had paid the landlord his rent in arrear to an amount not exceeding one year's rent.[6] If the tenant fraudulently carried off his goods and chattels with intent to prevent the landlord distraining upon them, the landlord, within five days of the carrying off, could seize them as a distress,[7] unless they had been conveyed to a *bona fide* purchaser for value.[8] If a tenant held over after the expiration of his lease, the landlord was empowered to distrain within six months for the arrears of rent due on the expired lease,[9] and the tenant was made liable to pay double the rent due under his lease.[10] He was also to be liable to pay double

---

[1] At p. 442.

[2] " But what had been the construction of this statute ever since ? Why, if a subsequent bargainee has notice of a prior, he is equally affected with that notice as if the prior purchase had been a conveyance by feoffment and livery, etc.," ibid at p. 443.

[3] Ibid.

[4] See e.g. the case of Rolland v. Hart (1871) L.R. 6 Ch. 678.

[5] Vol. vi 397 ; 2 William and Mary c. 5.   [6] 8 Anne c. 14 § 1.

[7] Ibid § 2 ; altered to thirty days by 11 George II c. 19 § 1.

[8] 8 Anne c. 14 § 3 ; 11 George II c. 19 § 2.

[9] 8 Anne c. 14 §§ 6 and 7.   [10] 4 George II c. 28 § 1.

the rent if, after being given notice to quit, he refused to give up possession.[1] The landlord's remedies by distress and by re-entry had come to be fenced about by a mass of technical rules which diminished their efficacy. It was provided that if the rent was really due irregularities in making the distress should not render the landlord a trespasser *ab initio*.[2] Similarly, many delays attended the remedy by re-entry. The landlord must bring ejectment before he could get actual possession, and the lessee would often delay the bringing of such an action by applying to the court of Chancery for a common injunction. It was therefore enacted that the landlord should be able to recover in ejectment if half a year's rent was due ;[3] and the lessee was prevented from applying for a common injunction to stop the action unless he paid the arrears of rent into court and the costs of the suit.[4] (ii). New remedies were given to the landlord. An action of debt was to lie against a tenant for life.[5] The remedy of distress was given for rents seck, chief rents, and rents of assize.[6]   Rent reserved on a demise not under seal was to be recoverable in an action on the case for use and occupation, and the rent so reserved was to be evidence of the quantum of the damages recoverable.[7] If a tenant deserted the premises leaving nothing distrainable thereon, the landlord could apply to two justices of the peace to put him in possession. On his being put into possession the tenant's interest under the lease was to determine.[8]

Renewable leases were often leased out to undertenants. These leases could not be renewed unless the undertenants surrendered their underleases. To obviate the difficulty and delay so caused it was provided that the surrender of the under-leases should not be necessary.[9] It was apparently a common practice for tenants to attorn fraudulently to strangers who claimed to be entitled to the land. The result was that land-lords were turned out of possession, and were put to the difficulty and expense of bringing an action to recover it. It was there-fore enacted that such attornments should be void. For the future, an attornment to be valid must be made in consequence of a judgment, or with the consent of the landlord.[10] Great inconvenience was sometimes caused by tenants who did not give notice to their landlords of declarations in actions of eject-ment which had been served on them, or who refused to enter an

[1] 11 George II c. 19 § 18.   [2] Ibid § 19.
[3] 4 George II c. 28 § 2   [4] § 3.   [5] 8 Anne c. 14 § 4.
[6] 4 George II c. 28 § 5.   [7] 11 George II c. 19 § 14.
[8] Ibid § 16.   [9] 4 George II c. 28 § 6.
[10] 11 George II c. 19 § 11 ; the need to make this enactment is one more illus-tration of the powers possessed by a person who is seised or possessed to affect the position of the rightful owner, see vol. iii 91-92.

appearance in such actions, or to allow their landlords to defend them. It was therefore enacted that if a tenant did not give notice of such a declaration, he should forfeit three years' rack rent of the premises demised.[1]

(3) A small group of statutes was passed to make it possible for persons under various incapacities to deal in certain circumstances with the property vested in them. Statutes of 1708 and 1731 made it possible for infants or lunatics, who were seised or possessed of estates in trust or as mortgagees, with the sanction of the court of Chancery or the court of Exchequer, to make the conveyances of the land desired by the c.q. trust or the mortgagor.[2] In 1756 infants, lunatics, and femes covert were empowered, with the sanction of the court of Chancery or Exchequer, to surrender leases in order to get a renewal thereof.[3] Conversely in 1771 lunatics were empowered to accept surrenders of old leases and to grant renewals.[4] The fines payable for the renewal were, as between the real and personal representatives of the lunatic, to be considered as realty, unless the lunatic was tenant for life of the land, in which case they were to be considered as personalty.[5]

(4) The only statute which made an entirely new addition to the land law was the Charitable Uses Act of 1736.[6] That Act made it impossible to make a gift of land by will to charitable uses. But we shall see that, though the rules made by this Act were new, the principle at the back of them had some affinities with the principle upon which the old law as to gifts in mortmain had come to rest.[7]

The Act provided that no land, or personal estate to be laid out on land, should be given in trust " for the benefit of any charitable uses whatever," except under the following conditions : gifts of land or personal estate (other than stock in the public funds) must be made by deed twelve months at least before the death of the donor, and must be enrolled in the court of Chancery within six months after its execution. Stock in the public funds must be transferred six months before the death of the donor. The gift must take effect in possession immediately, without any power of revocation, or other trust or condition in favour of the donor or persons claiming under him.[8] These provisions were not to apply to the purchase by a charity of any estate in land for full value " paid at or before the making of the conveyance or transfer without fraud or collusion." [9] Gifts in trust for a charity which did not comply with these conditions,

---

[1] 11 George II c. 19 § 12.
[2] 7 Anne c. 19 (infants) ; 4 George II c. 10 (lunatics).
[3] 29 George II c. 31.   [4] 11 George III c. 20 § 1.   [5] § 3.
[6] 9 George II c. 36.   [7] Below 592-593.   [8] § 1.   [9] § 2.

and charges on land or on personalty to be laid out on land on similar trusts, were to be absolutely void.[1] Obviously the effect of these clauses was to make it impossible to leave by will to a charity any land or property defined as land by the Act.

Certain charities were excepted from the operation of the Act ;[2] and in course of time the list of statutory exceptions has tended to grow.[3] But, subject to these exceptions, the Act was strictly enforced, and extensively construed. In 1880 Brett, L.J., summed up the results of a century and a half of this judicial construction. He said :[4]

I cannot but marvel at the great extent to which the construction of this *Mortmain Act* has been carried. It seems to me to have been carried much further than the reason of its enactment suggested or authorized, but the construction has been carried to this length by authorities which are binding on us. . . . Now the authorities seem to me to have gone to this length, that although the devise to a charity is in terms of money only, and although the only thing which by the devise will come to that charity is money, yet if in order to effectuate the devise in favour of that charity it may be necessary to deal with an interest in the land of the testator—the devise is within the *Statute of Mortmain*.

It will be observed that Brett, L.J., speaks of the statute as " the statute of mortmain." Now it is obvious that the legislation against gifts of land in mortmain, and the legislation against gifts of land to charitable uses, differ in respect of the bodies and persons to whom they apply, and in respect of the conditions under which such gifts can be made.[5] The legislation against gifts of land in mortmain applies only to corporations, and prohibits all such gifts, whether *inter vivos* or by will, unless the licence of the Crown has been obtained. The legislation against gifts of land to charitable uses applies to charities, whether or not they are corporate bodies, and prohibits gifts which do not comply with the conditions laid down in the Act of 1736.[6] Nevertheless, although these differences between gifts

---

[1] § 3.

[2] The Universities of Oxford and Cambridge and their colleges, and the colleges of Eton, Winchester, and Westminster, § 4.

[3] See 51, 52 Victoria c. 42 §§ 6 and 7.

[4] Ashworth v. Munn (1880) 15 C.D. at p. 371 ; the following instances of property held to come within the Act, taken from Williams, Executors (9th ed.) ii 907-909, bear out the statement of Brett L.J. : " bequests to charities of money charged on real estate, or of money to arise from the sale of real estate, even though such real estate is partnership property, or the proceeds of growing crops, bequests of terms of years, or of money due on mortgage, or of money secured on turnpike tolls, or of money secured on the poor or county rates. . . . So, when a testator who has given his personal estate to charitable uses, contracts to sell real estate, but the sale is not completed in his life-time, his lien upon the estate for the amount of the purchase money is an interest in land, and the purchase money will not pass by his will to the charity."

[5] For the mortmain legislation see vol. ii 348-349, 375 ; vol. iii 86-87.

[6] Above 590.

in mortmain and gifts to charitable uses are great and obvious, there are affinities between the reasons underlying the legislation against gifts of land in mortmain, and those underlying the legislation against gifts of land to charitable uses, which, from 1736 onwards, have caused the Legislature and the judges to couple them together. " Whereas," runs the preamble to the Act of 1736,[1]

gifts or alienations of lands, tenements, or hereditaments in *Mortmain*, are prohibited or restrained by *Magna Charta*, and divers other wholesome laws, as prejudicial to and against the common utility ; nevertheless this publick mischief has of late greatly increased by many large and improvident alienations or dispositions made by languishing or dying persons, or by other persons, to uses called charitable uses, to take place after their deaths, to the disinherison of the lawful heirs.

Similarly, the consolidating Act of 1888[2] again coupled together, in different Parts of the Act, the topics of gifts of land in mortmain and the gifts of land to charitable uses.

What then are the affinities between the two topics, which have caused both the Legislature and the judges to couple them together ? We have seen that the original reason, which caused the enactment of Edward I's statute of mortmain, was the fact that gifts in mortmain deprived the lord of most of his incidents of tenure.[3] That reason had long been obsolete ; and the recognition of this fact caused the enactment of the statute of 1695-1696, which provided that a licence from the Crown was sufficient to legalize a gift in mortmain, whether or not the land was held in chief of the Crown.[4] But there were other reasons why this legislation against gifts of land in mortmain was still held to be necessary. First, since corporations have not the same unrestricted powers of dealing with their land as individuals, to allow land to be accumulated in their hands, would cause much of the land of the nation to get into the hands of owners who could not put it to the uses which might, in the national interest, be most desirable. Secondly, lands held by a corporation are not so freely alienable as lands held by an individual, and, because a corporation never dies, do not come so frequently into the market. Therefore some of the reasons which make a rule against perpetuities desirable, also make this legislation against gifts of land in mortmain desirable.[5] Thirdly, the unrestricted freedom of alienation *inter vivos* and by will allowed to landowners in England made it possible for a landowner to give all his land to a corporation, and thus totally to disinherit his family. But it is clear

---

[1] 9 George II c. 36. [2] 51, 52 Victoria c. 42.
[3] Vol. ii 348-349. [4] 7, 8 William III c. 37 ; vol. vi 398.
[5] The title of the Act of 1736 is " an Act to restrain the disposition of lands whereby the same become unalienable."

that these three reasons apply equally to gifts of land to charitable uses.[1] Therefore, although the persons or bodies to which these two varieties of legislation apply are different, and although the conditions under which these two classes of gifts are permitted to be made are also different, the reasons for imposing the special conditions fettering an owner's freedom of alienation, which are laid down by these two varieties of legislation, are so similar that the two varieties have not unnaturally come to be classed together.

(5) The different view of a mortgage taken by the courts of law and equity sometimes gave rise to difficulties. Mortgagees brought simultaneously actions of ejectment in the common law courts to get possession, and suits in equity to foreclose. The courts of law had no power to compel mortgagees to accept the money due and stay these actions, so that mortgagors had to go to a court of equity for this purpose, and wait till the cause was heard before they could get relief.[2] It was therefore provided that a court of law, on payment of principal, interest, and costs, should have power to stay the action, and compel the mortgagee to reconvey.[3] Similarly, if a suit were brought to foreclose, the court, on the application of the mortgagor, might make a decree for redemption before the suit had been brought regularly to a hearing.[4] This is an interesting attempt on the part of the Legislature to bring together the divergent principles of law and equity in order to facilitate proceedings for the redemption and foreclosure of mortgages ; and it is not the only attempt by the Legislature to break down the barriers between law and equity. The statute of 1731 made it unnecessary in certain cases for lessees to file a bill in equity to get relief against forfeiture ; [5] and we have seen that the statute of 1705 empowered the courts of law, in actions brought on bonds, to give relief against the penalty of the bond on certain conditions.[6] These statutes show that the Legislature was beginning to move slowly in the direction of making a fusion in certain cases between the principles of law and equity.[7] We shall see in the following chapter that Lord Mansfield attempted to carry this policy of fusion very much further ; but that this attempt was an usurpation of the functions of the Legislature which rightly failed.[8]

[1] This is brought out by the debates on the charitable uses,bill, see Parlt. Hist. ix 1123-1125, 1142-1143, 1144-1145, 1155.
[2] 7 George II c. 20 preamble.   [3] § 1.
[4] § 2 ; this clause was not to apply if the right to redeem or the amount due was contested, or if the title to the equity of redemption was contested by different defendants in the same suit.
[5] 4 George II c. 28 §§ 3 and 4 ; above 589.
[6] 4, 5 Anne c. 16 § 13 ; above 521.   [7] Above 521.
[8] Vol. xii 584-589, 595-601.

(6) It remains only to notice a few miscellaneous enactments. An Act of 1707 provided against the concealment of the death of a *cestui que vie* by a tenant *per autre vie;* [1] and an Act of 1741 provided that when, on an intestacy, an estate *per autre vie* descended to an administrator, it should be applied and distributed as personal estate.[2] An Act of 1752 was passed to explain the Act of 1700,[3] which allowed natural-born subjects to inherit land, in spite of the fact that one of their ancestors, through whom they traced their descent, was an alien. The Act of 1700 was not to entitle any person to inherit, unless the person claiming to inherit was in being and capable of taking the estate at the death of the person who last died seised thereof.[4] If the person entitled and competent to inherit was the daughter of an alien, and the alien afterwards had a son also competent to inherit, the property was to be divested from the daughter and become vested in the son; and similarly, if the alien afterwards had daughters competent to inherit, these daughters were to take as coparceners with their sister.[5] Another Act of 1752 was passed to define the competency of witness to wills.[6] Devisees and legatees were to be competent witnesses but were to lose their benefits under the will.[7] Creditors were to be competent witnesses although the testator's land was charged with the payment of his debts.[8] In 1741 it was enacted common recoveries should be valid, although the lessees for life had not surrendered their leases before the conveyance to the tenant to the præcipe had been made; [9] but it was carefully provided that the Act was not to validate common recoveries made without the consent of the person entitled to the first life estate under the settlement expectant on these leases.[10] The Act also provided that other formal defects in these recoveries should not invalidate them.[11] In 1774 it was enacted that mortgages of land, slaves, or cattle in Ireland [12] or the Plantations, and transfers or assignments thereof, were to be as valid when made and executed in Great Britain as if made and executed in the country where the property was situated; [13] provided that the mortgage was registered in that country.[14] The rate of interest might be that allowed in the country where the property was situated, although it exceeded the rate allowed in England by the statute of 1713.[15]

[1] 6 Anne c. 18 ; for the estate *per autre vie* see vol. iii 123-125.
[2] 14 George II c. 20 § 9 ; vol. iii 124-125.
[3] 12 William III c. 7 ; vol. vi 398. [4] 25 George II c. 39 § 1.
[5] § 2. [6] 25 George II c. 6. [7] § 1. [8] § 2.
[9] 14 George II c. 20 § 1. [10] § 2. [11] §§ 4-6.
[12] Obviously the word " slaves " can only refer to the Plantations ; but grammatically the statute is so worded that it implies that there were slaves in Ireland.
[13] 14 George III c. 79 § 1. [14] § 5.
[15] § 1 ; 12 Anne St. 2 c. 12 ; for this Act see vol. viii 112.

III. Civil Procedure.

We have seen that the power which plaintiffs had to arrest and imprison defendants on mesne process,[1] and the power which judgment creditors had to take the persons of their debtors in execution and to keep them in prison till the debt was paid,[2] gave rise to many abuses ; and we have seen that in the latter half of the seventeenth century the Legislature attempted to remedy some of these abuses.[3] But its efforts met with little success ; and, during the eighteenth century, the largest group of statutes relating to civil procedure deals with this question of arrest and imprisonment on mesne or final process.

In 1725 [4] an Act was passed to prevent frivolous or vexatious arrests on mesne process. No person was to be held to special bail [5] unless the cause of action in a superior court amounted to £10 or upwards, and in an inferior court to 40s. or upwards.[6] If the cause of action was less in amount the plaintiff could not arrest the defendant. He must serve him with a copy of the process, and, if the defendant did not appear within four days of the return of the process, the plaintiff could enter an appearance for him.[7] In all cases an affidavit must be sworn that the cause of action amounted to £10 or 40s. or upwards.[8] In 1779 the £10 limit was substituted for the 40s. limit in the case of inferior courts.[9]

This legislation was no more successful than the earlier legislation in stopping the abuses which arose from the power of plaintiffs to arrest on mesne or final process. " The most substantial trader is liable to be arrested," said Lord Mansfield,[10] " and the mere fact of being arrested is no presumption of insolvency." In 1788 a Mr. Burges, in a speech on a debtor's and creditor's bill, called attention to this defect in the law, and gave some illustrations of the hardship which it caused. He said : [11]

---

[1] Vol. vi 407-408 ; vol. viii 231 ; vol. ix 253. [2] Vol. viii 231-232, 245.
[3] Ibid 234-236. [4] 12 George I c. 29.
[5] For special and common bail see vol. i 220-221 ; and for the abuses to which this system gave rise see vol. ix 253-254.
[6] 12 George I c. 29 § 1.
[7] § 1 ; this provision was extended by 45 George III c. 124 § 3, and 7, 8 George IV c. 71 § 5 ; vol. ix 253.
[8] § 2 ; Dickens in *Pickwick*, chap. xl, gives a vivid picture of the way in which these affidavits were taken, see Holdsworth, Charles Dickens as a Legal Historian, 27-29.
[9] 19 George III c. 70 § 2.
[10] Rose v. Green (1758) 1 Burr. at p. 439 ; Walpole, Letters (ed. Toynbee) xiv 410-411, tells an extraordinary tale of how on one occasion the Primate of Poland, and on another occasion the King of Poland had been arrested.
[11] Parlt. Hist. xxvii 155 ; he pointed out that " the law originally had provided that no process should issue, unless the plaintiff found security for the due, speedy, and effectual prosecution of his demand. This had degenerated into a practice no less iniquitous than generally known. Two obliging gentlemen, John Doe and Richard Roe, were now constantly employed as the standing securities for all

The first grievance which he would mention was the unlimited permission now given to a creditor of arresting a debtor. The process was no more than a loose affidavit of a debt; on which a writ was immediately issued, by which a defendant was arrested, and on which he might be, and often was, imprisoned for a long time, without the existence of a cause of action.

Thus a Mr. Robson was arrested for an imaginary debt of £1,100 and the parties concerned were afterwards convicted at the Old Bailey.[1] A Lieutenant Williams took out a writ to recover £45, and put it into the hands of Laver, a sheriff's officer in Chancery Lane. A few days after, on his calling on the officer, he was himself arrested for a debt of £120 at the suit of one Johnson. Williams objected that he knew no such person and owed no such sum. He was told that if he would withdraw the writ entrusted to Laver these proceedings would be dropped. He refused to do so, and lay in prison 193 days before he could get a supersedeas.[2] The same abuses existed for the same reason at the beginning of the nineteenth century. This fact is proved by the evidence which Mr. Anderton, attorney and secretary to the Metropolitan Law Society, gave to the commissioners appointed to enquire into the courts of common law. He said:[3]

Almost every man's liberty is liable to be invaded, be his means what they may; clergyman, gentleman, merchants, and tradesmen are all alike subject to be torn from their families, at almost any moment, and arrested for debts they do not owe;

and then he gave the following illustration:

A respectable merchant . . . was in April 1826, arrested upon a writ issued by the plaintiff in person for the sum of £60,000 not one sixpence of which he owed; but rather than find bail for so large an amount, and the plaintiff being a man of straw, he submitted to the payment of £100 for his discharge. This having answered so well, he was in the following month again arrested, for £60,000 more, upon which he was discharged by a judge's order upon filing common bail, and no further proceedings were taken in either of the actions. It is true he might have prosecuted the plaintiff for a vexatious arrest, but his doing so would only have increased the expense.

plaintiffs. These persons, ever ready to oppress, were more tardy when called upon for satisfaction. Like the god Baal, they were eating, or drinking, or sleeping, or somehow so much engaged, as never to be forthcoming when a defendant wants them," Parlt. Hist. xxvii 155.

[1] Ibid.

[2] Ibid 156; other similar instances were given by Mr. Burges in 1790, Parlt. Hist. xxviii 381-382.

[3] Parlt. Papers 1831 xx, App. E, p. 220; cp. a case cited by Burges in 1790—one Miller arrested a tradesman for a debt of £700; the tradesman in revenge caused Miller to be arrested for a debt of £40,000 " not one shilling of which he owed "; since the practice was to require bail in double the amount of the debt, and since no one would find bail for £80,000, Miller was imprisoned in the King's Bench prison for six weeks; when he got his release the same debtor had him arrested in an action in the Common Pleas for £20,000, and he was in the Fleet for 191 days before he got released, Parlt. Hist. xxviii 381.

Similarly, the power which creditors had in all cases to take the body of their judgment debtors in execution gave them a weapon which led to even worse abuses.

We have seen that in 1670-1671 and in 1678 [1] Acts had been passed to provide a machinery by which persons imprisoned for debt or on mesne process could get discharged, to compel creditors to pay a weekly sum in support of their imprisoned debtors, to remedy abuses committed by gaolers and their officials, and to see that funds given for the relief of poor prisoners were properly administered. A similar Act was passed in 1702, in favour of debtors who swore that they had no estate worth £10.[2] If these debtors made a full disclosure of their effects, including any debts owing to them which the Act empowered their creditors to collect, the quarter sessions could order their discharge.[3] But the discharge did not put an end to the debt; [4] the Act did not apply to debts over £20; [5] and the debtor must have been in prison six months before he could take advantage of the Act.[6] If he was under forty years of age his discharge was made conditional upon his enlisting in the army or navy; [7] for the preamble to the Act states that it was the fact that many of these poor prisoners were "able and willing to serve her Majesty by sea or land," that was one of the reasons for passing it. The Act applied only to persons imprisoned for debts incurred previously to January 1, 1701.[8]

Many other Acts of a like character were passed during the eighteenth century.[9] The reason assigned for passing them was the same as that assigned by the Act of Anne—many persons who might make useful soldiers or sailors were kept in prison, to which the later Acts added the further reason that skilled artificers, to avoid imprisonment, left the country and taught their trades to foreign nations.[10] Like the Act of Anne, these Acts applied only to debts incurred before the date named in the Act. As Romilly pointed out, they were in effect *ex post facto* laws, "which took away merely because such was the pleasure of the legislature the stipulated effect of contracts entered into under the sanction of the law." [11] But he admitted that the state of

---

[1] 22, 23 Charles II c. 20; 30 Charles II c. 4; vol. viii 235.
[2] 1 Anne St. 1 c. 25 § 2 (R.C. c. 19).   [3] §§ 2 and 11.
[4] § 5; cp. Edgell v. Hayward and Dawe (1746) 3 Atk. 352.
[5] § 13.   [6] § 14.   [7] § 15.   [8] § 2.
[9] See e.g. 11 George I c. 21; 2 George II c. 20; 1 George III c. 17; 9 George III c. 26; 12 George III c. 23; it was said in 1730, with reference to 2 George II c. 20, that "near 6000 persons have been discharged out of the said gaols by virtue of the Act passed in the last session of Parliament for the relief of insolvent debtors; and that 600 of his Majesty's subjects have returned and reaped the benefit of that Act," Parlt. Hist. viii 811.
[10] See the preamble to § 22 of 12 George III c. 23.
[11] Memoirs of Sir Samuel Romilly ii 212.

the law made them necessary.[1]   In fact, their provisions tended to become more elaborate ; and, though each Act applied only to debts incurred before the date fixed by it, they came to be a permanent set of conditions, periodically enacted, by compliance with which persons imprisoned for debt could get their discharge. At length in 1813 [2] the Legislature passed a permanent Act which embodied the provisions generally inserted in these temporary Acts.   That Act created the court for the relief of insolvent debtors, to which prisoners for debt must make their applications for discharge under the conditions set out in the Act.   It was this court, situated in Portugal Street, Lincoln's Inn Fields,[3] which Dickens described so vividly in *Pickwick*.[4]

In addition to these temporary Acts, which were passed to enable debtors to get their discharge, other Acts were passed to alleviate the lot of prisoners who were kept in custody, and also to provide a machinery by which they might, if their creditors consented, secure their release.   An elaborate Act to effect these objects was passed in 1729.[5]   Sheriff's officers were not to carry arrested persons to taverns without their consent or charge them with money spent on drink unless they voluntarily ordered it, or charge them larger fees than the law allowed, or take them to prison till twenty-four hours had elapsed from the time of the arrest.[6] Prisoners were to be allowed to send to any place they pleased for food and bedding.[7]   Gaolers' fees were to be fixed, and the table of fees was to be hung up in every gaol.[8]   The judges were empowered to hear and determine in a summary way complaints of abuses committed by gaolers or their officers.[9]   They were also

---

[1] Memoirs of Sir Samuel Romilly ii 212; in fact they secured the release of many prisoners, above 597 n. 9 ; but on the ground that they gave rise to abuses, they were sometimes opposed ; for instance Lord Thurlow and Lord Mansfield in 1781 opposed one of these bills, Parlt. Hist. xxii 625-628, 628-631 ; Lord Mansfield said, " every Act of Insolvency and the variety of bankrupt laws now in existence, had proceeded from that mistaken compassion ; and it was notorious that there was not a single statute that has not been grossly abused, and which, instead of producing good, had not produced a considerable deal of fraud and villainy," ibid 629 ; in 1780 the House of Lords heard counsel in opposition to one of these bills, ibid xx 1395-1399.

[2] 53 George III c. 102 ; the object of the Act was " to put an end to the legislative practice of having recourse . . . to the . . . occasional insolvent debtors' Acts, passed at uncertain but never at distant periods, which for the time abrogate the law, cancel men's contracts, and turn loose a crowd of insolvent debtors, because they are multiplying so fast that the prisons are hardly capacious enough to hold them," Memoirs of Sir Samuel Romilly ii 314.

[3] See 1, 2 Victoria c. 110 § 28.

[4] Chap. xliii ; Holdsworth, Charles Dickens as a Legal Historian 23-25.

[5] 2 George II c. 22.

[6] § 1 ; the sheriff must take the debtor to prison at or before the return of the writ—otherwise " the sheriff keeps him at his peril in case the creditor is delayed," Planck v. Anderson (1792) 5 T.R. at p. 41, *per* Buller J.; but it would seem from Fielding's description of the doings of Bondum, the bailiff in *Amelia*, that this legislation was not very effective, see B. M. Jones, Henry Fielding 215-216.

[7] 2 George II c. 22 § 3.   [8] § 4.   [9] § 6.

empowered to see that money given on trust for poor prisoners was properly spent.[1]   A prisoner taken in execution for a debt not exceeding £100, could exhibit a petition to the court upon the process of which he had been taken in execution, praying for his discharge.[2]   The petition must show the cause of his imprisonment, and make a full statement of his property.[3]   The creditors must be summoned, and the case heard.[4]   If the debtor swore to the truth of his petition, and assigned to his creditors his property or so much of it as was sufficient to satisfy them, he was to be discharged of his imprisonment, unless the creditors insisted on his continued detention, in which case they must pay a weekly sum of 2s. 4d. to the prisoner.   If that sum was not paid the prisoner was to be discharged.[5]   If there were mutual debts between the creditor and the prisoner one debt could be set off against the other.[6]   The Act was amended in 1730 ;[7] and was superseded by a more elaborate Act in 1759.[8]   This Act required a prisoner who desired to get his discharge, to make out a schedule of his estate and to assign it for the benefit of his creditors.[9]

It should be noted that none of these Acts compelled a prisoner who did not apply for a discharge to deliver up his property. There was nothing to prevent a prisoner, who chose to remain in prison, from continuing to live in prison and from spending his property on his subsistence there.   It is true that some clauses in Acts of 1743 [10] and 1760 [11] attempted to stop this abuse. Prisoners were to be compelled to disclose their estates, make them over to their creditors, and so get their discharge from prison.[12]   But those clauses were thought to give too much power to creditors ; and since a prisoner who refused to disclose, or who concealed property to the amount of £20 or upwards, was to be guilty of felony,[13] there was some justification for this view. It was for this reason that they were repealed in 1762.[14]   The effect of thus reverting to the old law, coupled with the manner in which the prisons were managed,[15] was disastrous.   A select committee of the House of Commons, appointed to enquire into the state of the gaols, said in 1730 that

[1] § 7.   [2] § 8.   [3] § 8.   [4] § 8.   [5] § 9.
[6] § 13.   [7] 3 George II c. 27.   [8] 32 George II c. 28.   [9] § 13.
[10] 16 George II c. 17 ; for this Act see Smith v. Cooke (1746) 3 Atk. 378.
[11] 1 George III c. 17.
[12] 1 George III c. 17 §§ 46-49 ; the preamble to § 46 recites that " many persons who are prisoners for debt too often choose rather to continue in prison, and spend their substance there, than discover and deliver up to their creditors their estates or effects towards satisfying their just debts."
[13] § 46.
[14] 2 George III c. 2 ; the Act recited that " great inconveniences have arisen from such power being given to creditors."
[15] Vol. x 181-182 ; above 567-568.

the prisoners make large presents to the Marshal [of the King's Bench prison] for the liberty of these Rules ; and being under his protection and in his favour, may take houses or lodgings within the Rules, and live in a very easy manner; whilst the poor honest debtor, who hath paid away all his substance, to satisfy his creditor, is a close prisoner within the prison : thus the debtor, who will not pay his creditors, lives at ease ; and he who cannot pay suffers.[1]

This was true throughout the eighteenth century, and, as the pages of Dickens show, in the early part of the nineteenth century.

The fact that all this legislation was necessary to mitigate the evils which flowed from large powers of arrest on mesne or final process, which the law allowed to litigants, is a sufficient condemnation of this system.   Its illogical character was exposed by Dr. Johnson ; [2] and its abuses were exposed in detail in a report made by a committee of the House of Commons in 1792 on imprisonment on mesne process and imprisonment as a mode of execution.[3]   But the system remained unreformed till, in the second quarter of the nineteenth century, the long process of reform began with the abolition of arrest on mesne process.[4]   As we have seen, a principal cause for the long continuance of this system was the limitation of the scope of the writs of *fieri facias* and *elegit* by which the property of a debtor could be taken in execution.   So long as stocks and shares and other choses in action could not be taken in execution, it was necessary to give creditors a weapon by which they could compel their debtors to make a voluntary cession of this property.[5]

The legislation of which I have just given some account, was directed to facilitating the discharge or alleviating the lot of prisoners.   An Act of 1701 was directed to facilitating the rearrest of prisoners who had escaped by collusion with their gaolers or otherwise.[6]   At common law, in addition to the powers given by this Act, plaintiffs and judgment creditors had a right of action against gaolers who allowed their prisoners to escape. The nature of this action and the damages recoverable differed according as the prisoner was arrested on final or on mesne process.   If he was arrested on final process he was a judgment debtor for the amount found due from him.   Therefore

---

[1] Parlt. Hist. viii 809 ; the Rules were the limits around the prison in which the prisoners were allowed to reside ; they were fixed by the Court, and from time to time enlarged, ibid.

[2] " Since poverty is punished among us as a crime, it ought to be treated with the same lenity as other crimes : the offender ought not to languish at the will of him whom he has offended, but to be allowed some appeal to the justice of his country," *The Idler*, no. 22.

[3] House of Commons Journals, April 2, 1792.

[4] See Bowen, Essays, A.A.L.H. i 544.   [5] Above 524.

[6] 1 Anne St. 2 c. 6 ; for an earlier Act see vol. vi 408.

the creditor has a right to the body of his debtor every hour till the debt is paid ; and, if the prisoner escape, may bring an action of debt upon the statute against the sheriff in which he may . . . recover the whole debt.[1]

If he was arrested on mesne process he did not necessarily owe anything.   Therefore

where the prisoner escapes out of custody on mesne process, the creditor cannot bring an action of debt, but is driven to his action upon the case, which is founded on the damage sustained ; and if no damage is sustained, the creditor has no cause of action.[2]

As in the preceding period, some effort was made to prevent suitors from suing in the superior courts of law for trifling sums.[3] Defendants who were sued in inferior courts were in the habit of alleging fictitiously that there was a cause of action against themselves for the sum of £5.   By this device they got actions for very small amounts removed into the superior courts, with the result that plantiffs abandoned their demands rather than incur the expense of an action in these courts.[4]   To remedy this abuse, the judges of the inferior courts were empowered in 1725 to proceed in all actions in which the amount at issue did not exceed £5, though there might be other actions against the same defendants in which the amount at issue exceeded £5.[5]   In 1779 a remedy was provided for the case where persons, served with the process of an inferior court, removed themselves and their effects out of the jurisdiction of that court.   It was enacted that when final judgment had been got in any inferior court of record, and it appeared that the person and effects of the defendant were not to be found within the jurisdiction, the record of the judgment could be moved into a superior court, and execution could be had in any county as upon judgments obtained in the superior courts.[6]   The same Act provided that the bringing of a writ of error to reverse the judgment of an inferior court of record should not, if the damages were under £10, operate to stay execution, unless security was given to prosecute the writ of error with effect, and to pay all damages and costs if the judgment were affirmed.[7]   It was also provided that the like security must be given by defendants who wished to remove any case, in which the amount at issue was under £10, into the superior courts.[8]   We have seen that this legislation was not successful in relieving the pressure of business in the superior courts, by increasing the business of the inferior courts of record.[9]

[1] Planck v. Anderson (1792) 5 T.R. at p. 40, *per* Buller J. ; cp. Bonafous v. Walker (1787), 2 T.R. at pp. 131-133.
[2] Planck v. Anderson at p. 40.
[3] Vol. iv 539 ; vol. vi 409.
[4] 12 George I c. 29 § 3, Preamble.
[5] 12 George I c. 29 § 3.
[6] 19 George III c. 70 § 4.
[7] § 5.
[8] § 6.
[9] Vol. i 191.

Some efforts were made to render the prerogative writ of mandamus, and the information in the nature of a quo warranto,[1] more efficacious remedies. In 1710 it was provided that returns to writs of mandamus must be made immediately; and the pleadings on such a writ were assimilated to the pleadings in an action on the case.[2] Facilities were given for prosecuting informations in the nature of a quo warranto, and power was given to determine the several rights of different persons on one information.[3] If the relator succeeded in his action he was to have his costs, and the intruder was made liable to a fine.[4] In 1772 citizens and freemen of cities and boroughs, who were obliged to enforce their claim to admission by writ of mandamus, were to have their costs against the mayor or other officer who wrongfully refused to admit them.[5] In 1792 the information in the nature of a quo warranto, when brought to establish the right to membership of, or office in, a city or borough, was subjected to a time limitation of six years.[6] Defects in the title of electors to an office or in the title of the person admitting to the office, were not to invalidate the title of the holder, if the electors or person admitting were *de facto* exercising their powers six years before the information was filed.[7]

In 1708 the writ of Quare Impedit was made more useful to patrons of livings. A usurpation during an avoidance was not to turn the patron's title to a mere right, and so prevent him from using a Quare Impedit, and drive him to a writ of right of advowson. Also, if the right to present was vested in coparceners or joint tenants, and it was agreed that they should present by turns, each was to be regarded as seised of his or her separate turn, so that each could sue by Quare Impedit.[8]

In 1741 an attempt was made to prevent plaintiffs from delaying the trial of their causes. If issue were joined, and the plaintiff neglected to take the usual steps to set down the cause for trial, the judge could on motion, after notice given to the plaintiff, give judgment for the defendant as in case of a non-suit.[9] The same Act also provided that no cause, civil or criminal, was to be tried at *nisi prius*, when the defendant lived more than forty miles away, unless he was given ten days' notice of the trial.[10]

---

[1] For the writ of mandamus see vol. i 229; for the writ of quo warranto see ibid 229-230; the writ of quo warranto was superseded in the sixteenth century by the information in the nature of a quo warranto, ibid 230; Bl. Comm. iii 262-263, iv 312.

[2] 9 Anne c. 20 §§ 1 and 2 (R.C. c. 25).   [3] § 4.   [4] § 5.
[5] 12 George III c. 21 § 1.   [6] 32 George III c. 58 § 1.   [7] § 3.
[8] 7 Anne c. 18; the enactment of the statute was due to the case of Shireburne v. Hitch (1708) 1 Bro. P.C. 110. That case showed that a coparcener or joint tenant had some difficulty in asserting his or her right to present in his oɪ her turn, see MSS. of the House of Lords viii nos. 2538, 2578; for the writ of Quare Impedit and the writ of right of advowson see vol. iii 24, 25.
[9] 14 George II c. 17 § 1.   [10] § 4.

In 1718 it was provided that in civil cases (but not in criminal) defects of form in writs of error could be amended ; and that, after verdict, judgment was not to be stayed or reversed " for any defect or fault, either in form or substance, in any bill, writ original or judicial, or for any variance in such writs from the declaration or other proceedings." [1]

In 1730 an Act was passed to regulate the preparation of the lists of jurors, and the manner of summoning, and the mode of impanelling them.[2] The Act also contained regulations as to the taking of " the view " by a jury,[3] and as to the composition of the special jury.[4] In 1751 regulations were made as to the fee payable to special jurymen, which was not to exceed a guinea a head.[5] The provision of the Act of 1705-1706, which dispensed with the necessity for the presence of hundredors on a jury in civil actions,[6] was extended to actions on penal statutes ; [7] and the necessity for the presence of a knight on the jury, if a peer or a lord of Parliament was a party to an action was abolished.[8]

In 1721 [9] changes were made in the method of enrolling recognizances in the nature of a statute staple prescribed by a statute of 1531-1532.[10] If a recognizance were lost or damaged a copy from the roll was to be of the same validity as the original.[11] The manner of getting execution on these recognizances, and the fees payable to the sheriff were also regulated.[12]

I have already mentioned the Act of 1731 [13] which enacted that the writs, proceedings, and records of all courts, central or local, should be written in English, in the hand used for engrossing Acts of Parliament and not in court hand, and without abbreviations.[14] It was specially provided that the statutes of jeofail should extend to these English forms.[15] The Act did not extend to the court of the receipt of the Exchequer ; [16] but in 1733 it was extended to the Welsh courts.[17]

The ground covered by this legislation on civil procedure is not large. Though useful reforms were effected, the bulk of the law on this topic was, as we have seen,[18] created by the courts. In many cases, notably in the case of the legislation as to arrest on

[1] 5 George I c. 13.   [2] 3 George II c. 25 §§ 1-13.   [3] § 14.
[4] §§ 15-19.   [5] 24 George II c. 18 § 2.
[6] 4, 5 Anne c. 16 § 7 (R.C. c. 3) ; above 521.
[7] 24 George II c. 18 § 3.   [8] § 4.   [9] 8 George I c. 25 § 1.
[10] 23 Henry VIII c. 6.   [11] 8 George I c. 25 § 2.   [12] §§ 3-5.
[13] 4 George II c. 26 ; vol. ii 479 ; the mixed jargon of English, Latin, and law French which the lawyers continued sometimes to use was satirized by Fielding in his newspaper, The Champion, Nov. 27, 1739, B. M. Jones, Henry Fielding 42.
[14] 4 George II c. 26 § 1.
[15] § 4 ; for these statutes see vol. iii 650 ; vol. iv 535-536 ; vol. vi 409 ; vol. ix 264 and n. 9, 315-316.
[16] 6 George II c. 6 § 1.
[17] Ibid 14 § 3.   [18] Vol. ix 245-262.

mesne process, as to imprisonment for debt, and as to the juris-diction of the inferior courts, it failed to effect its objects.

IV. *Contract and Tort.*

The development of the law of contract during this period was the work of the courts and not of the Legislature.[1] What legislation there was was directed to regulating, not the general principles of the law of contract, but particular contracts. Thus we have seen that there was legislation as to contracts of in-surance,[2] as to the purchase and sale of stocks and shares,[3] as to gaming contracts,[4] and as to contracts by which young persons engaged to transport themselves overseas.[5] We have seen also that there was some legislation as to apprenticeship,[6] and much legislation as to the relations of masters and servants.[7] The only statute which I propose to notice under this head is a statute of 1777 which was passed " for the registration of grants of life annuities, and for the better protection of infants against such grants." [8]

This statute was passed to regulate, and in the case of infants, to stop, a method by which money could be borrowed at a higher rate of interest than that allowed by the usury laws.[9] The practice was for the borrower to sell an annuity on his own life to the lender for a sum down, which was generally six years' purchase.[10] It is clear that if the borrower died the next day the lender would get nothing. It followed that the lender risked the loss of the principal sum advanced. Because the principal was thus risked the fact that the lender might get more than the legal rate of interest if the borrower lived many years, did not make the contract void under the usury laws. In the case of *Murray v. Harding* [11] it was held that the purchase by a lender of an annuity for the life of the borrower, who was aged thirty-two, at six years' purchase, was not usurious, even though it was made redeemable by the borrower at the end of five years at five and a half years' purchase. Blackstone, J., said : [12]

---

[1] Vol. viii chap. iii.   [2] Above 447-448.
[3] Above 449.   [4] Above 539-541.   [5] Above 571, 574.
[6] Above 421.   [7] Above 471-473, 488-490, 496-498.
[8] 17 George III c. 26 ; for an interesting account of the causes which led to the passing of this Act, and of its effects see Sybil Campbell, Usury and Annuities of the Eighteenth Century, L.Q.R. xliv 473-491

[9] For these laws see vol. viii 100-113 ; it was for this reason that the Act did not apply to annuities which were not granted for this purpose, see 17 George III c. 26 § 8 ; also it did not apply to " any annuity where the sum to be paid does not exceed ten pounds, unless there be more than one such last-mentioned annuity from the same grantor or grantors to or in trust for the same person or persons," ibid.

[10] L.Q.R. xliv 473.   [11] (1773) 2 W. Bl. 859.
[12] At p. 865.

I do not know an instance where the principal is *bona fide* hazarded, that the contract has been held to be usurious. If the price be inadequate to the hazard, it may be an imposition, and under some circumstances relievable in equity, but it cannot be legal usury. In the present case the principal or part of it is clearly in jeopardy for six years together, and the purchaser cannot receive back his principal with legal interest unless the vendor continues to live for eight years.

Naturally much use was made of this expedient by needy borrowers in all ranks of life; and it was for this reason that the statute was passed.[1]

In the case of persons of full age the statute made no attempt to stop these sales of annuities, or to dictate the price at which they could be sold.[2] It attempted, as the modern bills of sale Acts attempt, to secure that members of the public interested should be able to discover what annuities a person had granted, and that the terms of the contract should be intelligible. To effect these objects the Act provided that a memorial of the granting of the annuities therein specified must be inrolled in Chancery, which memorial was to contain the date, parties, witnesses, the sum payable annually, the person for whose life the annuity was granted, and the consideration—otherwise the annuity was to be void.[3] Deeds of annuity must contain the consideration *bona fide* paid, and that consideration must be in money. They must also state by whom the consideration was advanced.[4] If any part of the consideration was returned or not paid, or paid in goods, or retained, the deed of annuity could be cancelled by the court.[5] In the case of infants, the Act provided that contracts made by them for the sale of annuities should be void, notwithstanding any attempt to confirm such sale when they came of age.[6] Procuring or soliciting an infant to grant an annuity, or inducing him not to plead infancy, or to ratify the grant when he came of age, were made misdemeanours.[7] Brokers who negotiated for the grant of these annuities were to be guilty of a misdeamour if they took more than 10s. per cent. commission.[8] The inrollment of these annuities under the Act show that this mode of evading the usury laws was extensively used, in spite of the publicity and expense of registration. It was extensively used because it was " a safe and legal method by which borrowers and lenders,

---

[1] This is made clear by the inrollments under the Act of 1777, L.Q.R. xliv 485-490; naturally Charles James Fox appears—" on the 16th May 1777 the hon'ble Charles James ffox of Saint James Street Westminster in the County of Middlesex obtains £300 from Moses ffernandez of Bury Street in the parish of St. James aforesaid by selling an annuity of £50 payable quarterly for the life of Charles James ffox," ibid 486; in 1772 Horace Walpole wrote, Letters (ed. Toynbee) viii 176, " there are advertized to be sold more annuities of his (Fox's) and his society, to the amount of five hundred thousand pounds a year!"

[2] L.Q.R. xliv 484.   [3] 17 George III c. 26 §§ 1 and 2.

[4] § 3.   [5] § 4.   [6] § 6.   [7] § 6.   [8] § 7.

determined to obtain and provide money at rates above the legal maximum, were able to do so." [1]

The development of the law of tort is even more exclusively the work of the courts than the development of the law of contract. The only important topic in which that development was affected, and not very happily affected by the Legislature, was the topic of liability for damage done by fire. But to understand the legislation on this subject, and its effect on the development of the law, we must recall the manner in which this liability was regulated by the common law.

At all times it has been recognized that fire is a dangerous thing which must be specially carefully guarded. We have seen that, in the Middle Ages, the modern conception of negligence had not emerged; and that the central idea of the mediæval common law was that a man was civilly liable if he had done an act which caused damage to another, provided that that act fell within one of the causes of action provided by the law. [2] He was liable for his act, and therefore he escaped if he could prove that the act causing damage was not his act, e.g. by proving that it was the act of the plaintiff, or the act of God, or the act of some third person. [3] In effect his liability was very similar to the strict liability, imposed by the rule in *Rylands v. Fletcher*, [4] on persons who pursue activities which are lawful, and yet so intrinsically dangerous that they expose their neighbours to extraordinary risks. [5] That being so, the form which the stricter liability for the escape of fire took could not be the application of the rule of strict liability laid down in the case of *Rylands v. Fletcher*; for that rule was the general rule of civil liability. [6] We have seen that it took the form of a rule that a householder was liable for the damage caused by his fire, even though the damage was caused, not by his own act, but by the act of his servants or guests. [7] We have seen that in 1698, in the case of *Turberville v. Stamp*, [8] this mediæval rule was recognized and applied to all fires whether arising in a house or not.

But in 1698 this mediæval rule was beginning to look anomalous. In the first place, the frequency of fires in London and the

---

[1] L.Q.R. xliv 490.　　　　　　[2] Vol. iii 375-377, 379-382; vol. viii 449-450.

[3] Vol. iii 378-379, 380; Professor Winfield in his paper The Myth of Absolute Liability, L.Q.R. xlii 37, questions this view of mediæval civil liability; he admits that, in the cases concerning the escape of fire, the term "negligence" "had not the technical sense which it now bears in the law of torts" (p. 49); and he admits that "it is difficult to say precisely what negligence did mean"; but he "refuses to believe that it meant nothing" (p. 50 n. 5); I should be inclined to maintain that absolute liability was the dominant theory, though here and there we see signs of the manner in which that theory will be later modified.

[4] (1866) L.R. 1 Ex. 265; (1868) L.R. 3 H. of L. 330.

[5] Vol. viii 468.　　　　　　[6] Ibid 469.

[7] Vol. iii 385; vol. viii 469.

[8] Skinner 681; S.C. 1 Salk. 13, Comb. 459, 1 Ld. Raym. 264; vol. viii 474.

suburbs was calling attention to the law on the subject of liability
for damage caused by fires.[1] In the second place, the form of the
action in which the liability for damage caused by fire was asserted
was case ; and it was in connection with actions on the case that
the idea that civil liability was based on negligence, was coming to
be familiar to the lawyers.[2] It was generally alleged that the
defendant had negligently kept his fire whereby damage had
been caused to the plaintiff ; [3] and this tended to make lawyers
and others think that it was anomalous that a man should be
made liable for damage done by a fire which was not occasioned
by his negligence.   In the third place, the new rule of employers' liability, which was being created and applied by Holt,
C.J.,[4] gave sufficient protection against the negligence of servants
acting in the course of their employment, if that negligence
caused damage either by reason of the escape of fire or otherwise.
It was probably for these three reasons that the Legislature in
1707 laid down some new rules as to liability for damage done
by the escape of fire.

The Act of 1707 [5] laid down rules for the prevention of fires
in London and Westminster and places comprised within the
weekly bills of mortality ; [6] it imposed a criminal liability on
servants through whose negligence dwelling-houses or outhouses
were set on fire ; [7] and it made rules for the construction of the
party walls of houses, designed to prevent the spread of fire.[8]
Then it modified materially the common law rule as to the
liability for damage caused by fire originating in houses.   The
clause [9] in which this modification was effected runs as follows :

No action, suit, or process whatsoever, shall be had, maintained,
or prosecuted against any person in whose house or chamber any fire
shall . . . accidentally begin, or any recompense be made by such
person for any damage suffered or occasioned thereby.

The Act of Anne was repealed in 1772,[10] and the Act of 1772 was
repealed in 1774 ; [11] but in 1772 this clause in the Act of Anne was
re-enacted,[12] and in 1774 it was applied not only to fires originating
in buildings, but also to fires (like the fire which was the cause
of action in Turberville v. Stamp) originating " on estates." [13]

---

[1] This is stated in the Preamble to 6 Anne c. 31 (R.C. c. 58) to be the reason for
passing the statute.
[2] Vol. viii 450-453.
[3] In Turberville v. Stamp the form of the writ was " quare negligenter custo-
divit ignem suum in clauso suo, ita quod per flammas blada querentis in quodam
clauso ipsius querentis combusta fuerunt," 1 Salk. 13.
[4] Vol. viii 474-477.   [5] 6 Anne c. 31 (R.C. c. 58).
[6] §§ 1 and 2.   [7] § 3.   [8] § 4.
[9] § 6 ; this clause, which was only to last for three years, was made perpetual
by 10 Anne c. 14 § 1.
[10] 12 George III c. 73 § 46.   [11] 14 George III c. 78 § 101.
[12] 12 George III c. 73 § 37.   [13] 14 George III c. 78 § 86.

The question how this legislation affected the common law liability for damage caused by fire has given rise to some very divergent opinions. First, some thought that it meant that a person was not liable if he negligently kept his fire so that it damaged others. It was thought that the word " accidentally " was used in contra-distinction to the word " wilfully " ; and that it therefore included a fire begun accidentally through the defendant's negligence.[1] Secondly, others have thought that the statute applies only to fires which have been accidentally kindled ; and that the old common law rule still applies to all fires deliberately lighted by the defendant or his servants.[2] Thirdly, the better opinion would seem to be that the words " any fire shall accidentally begin " mean " a fire produced by mere chance or incapable of being traced to any cause," and that it does not include a fire caused by the negligence of the defendant or his servants.[3] The effect of this interpretation is to assimilate to a large extent liability for damage caused by fire to liability for any other acts which cause damage. Bankes, L.J., pointed out, in the case of *Musgrove v. Pandelis*,[4] that a man was liable at common law for damage done by fire originating on his property (1) if it escaped even without his negligence,[5] (2) if it was caused by the negligence of himself or his servants or by his own wilful act, or (3) on the principle of *Rylands v. Fletcher ;* and that the effect of this legislation was to eliminate the first head of liability, and to leave the other two unaffected. So far, therefore, the assimilation is complete. But it would not be quite true to say that liability for damage caused by fire is completely assimilated to liability for other acts which cause damage. Generally a man is liable only for the tortious acts of his servants and sometimes for the tortious acts of an independent contractor. But in the case of damage caused by an escape of fire it is probable that the mediæval rule still applies, and that he is liable for the acts not only of his servants and independent

---

[1] Blackstone, Comm. i 431, says, " now the common law is altered by statute, 6 Ann. c. 31, which ordains that no action shall be maintained against any, in whose house or chamber any fire shall accidentally begin ; for their own loss is sufficient punishment for their own or their servant's carelessness " ; in Viscount Canterbury v. the Queen (1842) 4 S.T. N.S. at p. 775, Lord Lyndhurst seems to approve this view, but, as Lord Lyndhurst admits (at p. 778), this is only dictum.

[2] This view is maintained in Clerk and Lindsell Torts (4th ed.) 436 ; but it would give the statute of Anne very little effect, see Salmond, Torts (7th ed.) 370 ; the concluding remarks of Denman C.J. in Filliter Phippard (1847) 11 Q.B. at p. 358 give some countenance to this theory, but, having regard to the view taken of the effect of the statute of Anne in that case, they are obiter.

[3] Filliter v. Phippard (1847) 11 Q.B. at p. 357.

[4] [1919] 2 K.B. at pp. 46-47.

[5] The weight of authority is in favour of this view, notwithstanding Professor Winfield's remarks in L.Q.R. xlii 46-50 ; see Dr. Stallybrass's note in Salmond, Torts (7th ed.) 369 n. (*d*) ; cp. also Lord Lyndhurst's remarks in Viscount Canterbury v. the Queen (1842) 4 S.T. N.S. at pp. 775-776.

contractors, but also of his guests, his family, and his licensees.[1]

V. *Ecclesiastical Law.*

The most important enactment in the sphere of ecclesiastical law was Lord Hardwicke's Marriage Act,[2] which put an end to the scandal of the Fleet marriages often performed by bogus parsons,[3] and made the clandestine marriages, which figure so largely in eighteenth-century novels, impossible in England.[4] The immediate and the direct cause of the Act was said by the attorney-general to have been a case which had come recently before the House of Lords.

A gentleman had married a lady of family and fortune, had lived several years with her, and had children by her, yet after his death another woman laid claim to him as her husband, by virtue of a marriage solemnized between them before his marriage with the lady, whom he always acknowledged as his wife.[5]

But the Act did not apply to Scotland,[6] and so an easy way of evasion was provided, which provoked a satirical comment from Richard Burn who lived in a border county.[7]   There was an earlier

[1] See Black v. Christ Church Finance Co. [1894] A.C. 48—a case of an independent contractor; as to guests, family, and licensees, they were liable in mediæval law, this liability was recognized in the seventeenth century, Rolle Ab. *Action sur case* B. pls. 3-5, and it has never been taken away.

[2] 26 George II c. 33; vol. x 82; for earlier legislation on the subject of marriage see vol. iv 490-492; vol. vi 410.

[3] "The only qualification these alleged clergymen had was often the mere wearing of a cassock and gown; they performed the cermony at the ' Pen in Hand ' or ' The King's Head,' and they all employed touts to bring them business.   At this time the notorious Dr. Wyatt and Dr. Gaynham conducted a most lucrative practice, and the registers of the latter alone contained more than 2,000 entries in one year," B. M. Jones, Henry Fielding 48; Lord Hardwicke in the case of More v. More (1741) 2 Atk. at p. 158 said, " proctors sometimes stand at the door of the Commons, and solicit persons to take out licences, just in the same manner as runners to Fleet parsons do "; this solicitation of persons to take out licences was known in the early nineteenth century, and was the undoing of Mr. Tony Weller, *Pickwick Papers*, Chap. x; Holdsworth, Charles Dickens as a Legal Historian, 35-36.

[4] Lord Mansfield pointed out in the case of Birt v. Barlow (1779) 1 Dougl. at p. 174 that the clauses of the Act establishing marriage registers were of " infinite utility "; " besides facilitating and ascertaining the evidence of marriages . . . they are of great assistance in the proof of pedigrees, which has become so much more difficult since inquisitions post mortem have been disused, that it is easier to establish one for 500 years back, before the time of Charles II, than for 100 years since his reign."

[5] Parlt. Hist. xv 8.

[6] Compton v. Bearcroft (1769), 2 Hagg. Con. 444 note.

[7] " It is astonishing, and what posterity will never believe, that their forefathers made a law, that people in England should not marry but under such and such circumstances; but if they would go into Scotland, they might marry as they pleased. Insomuch that it became fashionable to take a tour into Scotland to be married; and it was almost a reproach to a young lady to have been married, and not to have been thought worth stealing.   As if it were an honour to a noble family, that the heir can make out his title to the inheritance by virtue of a Scotch marriage,

Act which had made the marriage of a lunatic void.[1] These two Acts laid the foundation of the modern law as to the conditions for the celebration of a valid marriage ; and I shall deal with their provisions in the Second Part of this Book. Here it will be sufficient to cite Blackstone's summary of the conditions necessary for a valid marriage, which were prescribed by the ecclesiastical law and by the statute law in the eighteenth century : [2]

As the law now stands, we may upon the whole collect that no marriage by the temporal law is *ipso facto void*, that is celebrated by a person in orders,—in a parish church or public chapel (or elsewhere, by special dispensation)—in pursuance of banns or licence,—between single persons,—consenting,—of sound mind,—and of the age of twenty-one years ;—or of the age of fourteen in males and twelve in females, with consent of parents or guardians, or without it in case of widow-hood. And no marriage is *voidable* by the ecclesiastical law, after the death of either of the parties ; nor during their lives, unless for the canonical impediments of pre-contract, if that indeed still exists ; of consanguinity ; and of affinity, or corporal imbecility, subsisting previous to their marriage.

Another topic of ecclesiastical law on which there was legislation, both in the eighteenth and in the two preceding centuries, was the topic of simony.[3] The ecclesiastical law and the statute law on this subject had given rise to a complex and not very rational body of law, of the development of which I shall speak in the Second Part of this Book.

The most important series of statutes affecting the Church of England was that which established Queen Anne's Bounty. An Act had been passed in 1703,[4]

for the making more effectual her Majesty's gracious intentions for the augmentation of the maintenance of the poor clergy, by enabling her Majesty to grant in perpetuity the revenues of the first-fruits and tenths, and also for enabling any other persons to make grants for the same purpose.[5]

---

solemnized probably by an ale-house keeper, in a very ridiculous manner ; and that he can be able to boast, tho' not born, yet that he was begotten, on the other side of the Tweed," Burn, History of the Poor Laws 232-233 ; a similar use was made of the Isle of Man and the Channel Isles, Lecky, History of England ii 126 ; Sir W. Wynne in the case of Middleton v. Janverin (1802) 2 Hagg. Con. at p. 448 said that when Hardwicke's Act was passed it was intended to pass a similar Act for Scotland—" but by the Act of Union the state of religion is not to be touched . . . and therefore there was a difficulty in applying the Marriage Act to that country."

　[1] 15 George II c. 30.　　　　　　　　　　　[2] Comm. i 440.
　[3] 12 Anne St. 2 c. 12 § 2 ; 31 Elizabeth c. 6 ; 1 William and Mary c. 16 ; vol. iv 489 ; vol. vi 410 ; Bl. Comm. ii 278-280.
　[4] 2, 3 Anne c. 11 (R.C. c. 20).
　[5] § 3 of the Act contained a proviso that nothing in it was to affect existing in-cumbrances on the fund ; it would seem that this proviso made the value of the Bounty in the first instance very small ; the yearly value of the first-fruits and tenths transferred was £16,567 11s. 5¼d., and the charges on this fund amounted to £11,993 6s. 8d., MSS. of the House of Lords (N.S.) v no. 2008 ; among the incumbrancers were the Duchess of Portsmouth and the Duke of St. Albans.

Pursuant to the power given by this statute the Crown created the corporation of " The Bounty of Queen Anne for the Augmentation of the maintenance of the poor Clergy " ; and throughout the century and later there was legislation as to the duties and powers of the corporation.[1]   In 1714 it was enacted that all rules made by the governors of the corporation for the conduct of its business should, when consented to by the Crown, be as effectual as if contained in the letters patent creating the corporaation.[2]   A few other statutes were passed with the object of improving the position of the clergy.   In 1713 it was enacted that if any rector or vicar nominated a curate to serve in his absence, the bishop, before licensing or admitting him, must settle the yearly sum to be paid by the rector or vicar.   That sum was not to exceed £50 and was not to be less that £20 a year.[3]   Curates who complained that a sufficient stipend had not been assigned to them were given a right to appeal to the bishop.[4]   In 1777, in order to promote the residence of the clergy, facilities were given for borrowing money for the building and repairs of rectories or vicarages on the security of the glebe, tithes, or other profits of the living.[5]

An Act of 1708 was directed to the improvement of the learning of the clergy.[6]   The Act recited that in many places " the provision for the clergy is so mean that the necessary expense of books for the better prosecution of their studies cannot be defrayed by them " ; and that in many places charitable persons had established parochial libraries.   It then made provision for the care of these libraries.   The incumbent must give security for the observance of the orders and rules made by their founders ; [7] and if the library was appropriated to his use he must make a catalogue of it.[8]   On the death of an incumbent the library was to be locked up by the churchwardens.[9] Benefactions to the library must be entered in a register kept for that purpose.[10]   The bishop was given a power to enquire into the state of the library and to make rules and orders.[11]   None of the books were to be alienated without the bishop's consent, and that consent could only be given if the book was a duplicate.[12]

The recognition of the independence of the United States made it obvious that there might be members of the Church of England who owed no allegiance to the Crown.   But, since no person could be ordained priest or deacon unless he had first taken the oath of allegiance, it was difficult to see how a supply of properly ordained persons could be provided for aliens who were members

---

[1] See 5, 6 Anne c. 24 ;   1 George I St. 2 c. 10 ;   3 George I c. 10.
[2] 1 George I St. 2 c. 10 § 3.   [3] 12 Anne St. 2 c. 12 § 1.
[4] Ibid.   [5] 17 George III c. 53, amended by 21 George III c. 66.
[6] 7 Anne c. 14.   [7] § 2.   [8] § 4.
[9] § 6.   [10] § 8.   [11] §§ 3 and 9.   [12] § 10

of the Church of England. To meet this difficulty it was provided that the bishop of London, or any other bishop appointed
by him, might ordain aliens to be priests or deacons, without
requiring them to take the oath of allegiance.[1] Such persons
were not to be capable of exercising their offices within his
Majesty's dominions.[2]

In 1787, in order " to prevent frivolous and vexatious suits
in ecclesiastical courts," it was provided that no suit for defamatory words should be begun, unless it was brought within
six months from the time when the defamatory words were
uttered ; [3] and that no suit should be begun for fornication, or
incontinence, or brawling in church or churchyard, after the
expiration of eight months from the offence.[4] No suit was to
be instituted for fornication after the marriage of the offending
parties.[5]

The Act of William III's reign [6] permitting Quakers to affirm
was made perpetual ; [7] and the remedy for the recovery of tithes
and church rates from Quakers, given by this Act, was extended
to the recovery of any " other rights, dues, or payments belonging to any church or chapel which . . . ought to be paid for
the stipend or maintenance of any minister or curate officiating
in any church or chapel." [8]

We have seen that it was the custom of the Crown, during
the sixteenth, seventeenth, and early eighteenth centuries, to
authorize by letters patent the issue of briefs for the collection
of money for many various charitable purposes.[9] This practice
had given rise to many frauds. It was therefore enacted in
1705 [10] that only so many of these briefs should be issued as were
required by the petitioners, and that they should be printed by
the Queen's printer.[11] They were to be delivered only to the
persons who undertook to collect the money, and these persons
were to give a receipt for them to the Queen's printer, which
receipt was to be registered in the court of Chancery.[12] They
must then cause the briefs to be signed by the trustees named in
the letters patent; and, after signature, send them to the churches
and chapels in the districts mentioned in the letters patent.[13]
The church wardens or chapel wardens were to indorse upon
them the date of their receipt, and hand them over to the priests
or ministers, who were, within two months, to read them before
the sermon.[14] The church or chapel wardens were to collect the
money, indorse the amount on the brief, and hand it over to the

---

[1] 24 George III St. 2 c. 35 § 1.   [2] § 2.
[3] 27 George III c. 44 § 1.   [4] § 2.   [5] Ibid.
[6] 7, 8 William III c. 34 ; vol. vi 200-201.   [7] 1 George I St. 2 c. 6.
[8] § 2.   [9] Vol. iv 306 and n. 7 ; vol. vi 309 and n. 6.
[10] 4, 5 Anne c. 14 (R.C. c. 25).   [11] § 1.
[12] Ibid.   [13] Ibid.   [14] Ibid.

persons who issued the briefs.[1] These persons must keep an account of the briefs issued, of the places to which they were sent, and of the money received, which was to be open to public inspection.[2] The returned brief must be deposited in the court of Chancery, and compared with the number for which the Queen's printer had got a receipt.[3] The persons issuing the briefs were to be liable to a fine of £50 for each brief missing unless they could account for its loss.[4] Provisions were made to prevent the forgery of briefs ; [5] and the persons issuing them must account for the money received to one of the masters in Chancery,[6] who must make a report, which must be confirmed by the court.[7] The practice of " farming and purchasing for a sum of money the charity money that should or might be collected on such briefs " was prohibited.[8]

Though the legislation on these various topics made many minor changes in, and additions to, the fabric of English law, it made no fundamental changes, and no large additions. This phenomenon is partly due to the fact that in the earlier part of the century social and political conditions were comparatively static, and partly to the fact that there was no great demand for reforms in a body of law which, like the constitution founded upon it, was a source of national pride.[9] But, from the middle of the century onwards, social and political conditions were ceasing to be so static ; demands for reform were beginning to be made ; and we have seen that in some branches of the law, more especially in the laws which regulated commerce and industry, considerable changes were made. The fact that no really fundamental changes were made either in these or in any other branches of the law public or private, is, as we shall now see, due mainly to the fact that the need for changes in, and additions to, the law was, to a large extent, met by private bill legislation.

Private Bill Legislation

Under this head I include not only the legislation which is contained in the list of private Acts printed at the end of the public Acts in the collections of the statutes at large, but also that large mass of local and personal Acts which appears sometimes in the lists of public, and sometimes in the lists of private,

---

[1] § 1.   [2] § 2.   [3] Ibid.   [4] Ibid.   [5] § 3.
[6] § 4 ; for a case arising on this section and § 2 see *ex parte* Angel (1741) 2 Atk 162.
[7] § 4.   [8] § 6.   [9] Above 278.

Acts.[1] We have seen that the distinctions drawn between public and private Acts were very technical distinctions, and that these distinctions were drawn in different ways by the courts and by the two Houses of Parliament.[2] An Act might be a private Act from the point of view of the two Houses, but it might be provided in it that it was to be treated as a public Act by the courts.[3] A turnpike Act, for instance, was often a public Act because it was provided that it should be so treated by the courts, and yet, it was a private Act from the point of view of the two Houses, in that it was promoted by private petitioners and fees were payable upon it. Conversely an Act might be a public Act from the point of view of Parliament, and yet be a private Act from the point of view of the courts. An Act of attainder, for instance, was like a public Act in that it did not originate from private petitioners and no fees were payable upon it ; but the principles laid down by the courts as to the distinction between public and private Acts,[4] compelled them to regard it as a private Act, unless it was especially provided in the Act that it should be treated by them as a public Act.[5] In this section I include in the phrase " private bill legislation " all those Acts, whether public or private, which, in the words of Blackstone, lay down no universal rule regarding the whole community, but " are rather exceptions than rules." [6]

From the Middle Ages onwards legislation of this kind has played a large part in the development of English law. During the greater part of the mediæval period the distinction between public and private bill legislation, though it existed in fact, was not yet a formally recognized distinction. We have seen that it was only beginning to be recognized in the latter half of the fifteenth century.[7] In the Middle Ages Acts dealing with particular persons, particular places, and particular trades, were in no way distinct from general Acts. In fact, in the earlier part of the period, particular cases sometimes gave rise to statutes which, after some hesitation, have been received as public and general.[8] But we have seen that during the latter part of the

[1] The chapters of the statutes printed in the lists of public Acts are cited in arabic figures, and the chapters of the statutes printed in the lists of private Acts are cited in roman figures.
[2] Above 294-300.   [3] Above 298.   [4] Above 294-297.
[5] These Acts in Henry VIII's reign are generally listed as private Acts, and the first in the list of the private Acts of the Long Parliament is the Act attainting Strafford ; but Katherine Howard's attainder (33 Henry VIII c. 21) is listed as a public Act ; the practice varies in Mary's and Elizabeth's reigns ; but after the Restoration they are generally listed as public Acts.
[6] Comm. i 85-86.   [7] Above 289.
[8] Vol. ii 301 and nn. 9 and 10 ; see Y.B. 8 Ed. II (S.S.) xiii-xvii for the difficulties which sometimes arose in the courts in the fourteenth century as to whether a particular document cited as a statute was really a statute.

sixteenth and in the seventeenth centuries, the distinction between public and private Acts was beginning to be elaborated
by the courts and by Parliament.[1] It thus begins to be possible
to estimate the effects of the growing mass of personal and local
Acts upon the development of English law. These Acts played
some part in this development in the sixteenth and seventeenth
centuries; and they played a great part in the eighteenth and
nineteenth centuries. We shall see that their main influence was
in the sphere of public and semi-public law; but that they also
had a considerable influence upon several branches of private law.[2]

The long life and continuous influence of this form of legislation is due to three main causes. (1) It is due to the two
leading characteristics which English constitutional law had
inherited from the Middle Ages—(i) the separateness and
autonomy of the organs through which the local,[3] and to some
extent the central,[4] government was administered; and (ii) the
existence of the rule of law.[5] In continental states the rise of
a centralized and absolute monarchy caused these mediæval
characteristics to disappear.[6] In England the autonomy of the
units of government and, to a large extent, the rule of law, were
preserved by the Tudors,[7] and played no small part in frustrating
the scheme of the Stuart kings to refashion the English state
upon the continental model.[8] We have seen that the result of
the Revolution was to make it clear that the prerogative, and
therefore the central government, were subject to a supreme law
which could be changed only by Parliament, and thus to emphasize the autonomy of all the organs of government.[9] The
result was that the needs of these autonomous units could only
be satisfied by the Legislature; so that, in the eighteenth century,
a large sphere was opened for this type of legislation. (2) When
the discoveries of science, by making transit speedy and easy,
began to sap the isolation and individualism of the units of government by creating uniform and standardized modes of life and
thought, the prevailing political and economic ideas emphasized
the importance of this type of legislation. Politically no party
in the state, and least of all the Whigs,[10] wished to see any increase
in the powers of the central government; and economically it
was the age of *laissez faire*.[11] Therefore the only way in which
it was possible to exploit the new discoveries, when their exploitation involved some modification of the law, was to approach

---

[1] Above 292 seqq.   [2] Below 617-626.
[3] Vol. ii 404-405; vol. iv 163-166; vol. vi 59-61; vol. x 188-189.
[4] Ibid 514-518.
[5] Vol. ii 435-436; vol. iv 187-189; vol. v 454, 493; vol. x 647-649.
[6] Vol. iv 172-173, 191-192.   [7] Ibid 208-215.
[8] Vol. vi 62-66.   [9] Vol. x 716-718.
[10] Ibid 420, 454.   [11] Above 503-506.

the Legislature and ask for a private Act. This was the only course open to those who wished to build canals or railways or tramways, to construct gas or water-works, or to create a system of telegraphs and telephones. It is for this reason that in the nineteenth century the demand for private bill legislation enormously increased.[1] (3) In a state in which a very technical body of law was so supreme that it could be modified only by the Legislature, hard cases were bound to occur. The sphere in which equity could give relief had always been limited, and became more and more limited as equity became systematized.[2] The only recourse was to ask the Legislature to modify the law. We shall see that many requests for these modifications were made, especially in the oldest and most technical branch of the law—the law of real property.[3]

These were the main causes for the long life and continuous influence of this form of legislation. But we have seen that, because the causes were substantial and the need was great, an efficient procedure was gradually devised by the two Houses of Parliament for dealing with petitions for private Acts.[4] It was because the two Houses were able to devise a procedure by which they could exercise their sovereign legislative powers under quasi-judicial forms, that they were able to make the necessary modifications of, and additions to, the law, without inflicting injustices upon those whose rights these modifications of, or additions to, the law infringed.[5] Unless a form of procedure had been devised which enabled the two Houses of Parliament to use their legislative powers justly, the large body of public opinion which, in the eighteenth century, was as attached to the dogma of the supremacy of the law as it disliked changes in, or additions to it, would not have acquiesced in these numerous grants of " privileges." In that case these local and private Acts could not have exercised the great and salutary effect which we shall see that they have in fact exercised upon the social, the commercial, the political, the economic, and the legal development of Great Britain.[6]

[1] Between 1800 and 1884 the public Acts number 9,556, and the local, personal and private Acts 18,497, Clifford, History of Private Bill Legislation i 491-492.
[2] This fact is illustrated by applications made by litigants for Acts to confirm decrees made by the court of Chancery ; thus in 1676 there is a private Act, 29, 30 Charles II c. vii, " for confirmation of a decree made in the court of Chancery the four and twentieth day of February, *Anno Regni Regis Caroli secundo vicesimo sexto*, in a cause between Sir Francis Rodes, Baronet, since deceased, and Dame Martha, his wife, plaintiffs, and William Thornton an infant, by Ciprian Thornton his guardian, and John Thornton and the said Ciprian Thornton, defendants, and of several conveyances and assurances made by the said Sir Francis Rodes in pursuance thereof, as well for payment of his debts as for provision for his wife and children."
[3] Below 620.   [4] Above 345-349.
[5] Above 349-351, 353-354.   [6] Below 629, 630-631.

We have seen that the procedure evolved, though in form and spirit it has strong judicial elements, and though these elements have been strengthened in the last century, is essentially legislative in character.[1]   It is because it is essentially legislative in character that its effects have been so great and so salutary. No bounds can be set to the topics with which a sovereign Legislature can concern itself ; and so we find that, on a local and personal stage, this private bill legislation is concerned with topics almost as various as those which are dealt with by public and general statutes.   We see reflected in it the influence of political events ; and its contents illustrate economic changes, and the beginnings of new legal expedients to meet new political and social needs.   If we glance rapidly at this legislation from these points of view, we shall be able to estimate its influence on the development of English law.

From the Middle Ages onwards much political history is reflected in these personal or private Acts.   The constitutional troubles of the reign of Richard II are reflected in statutes passed in 1387-1388 against certain of his judges and other councillors,[2] in the statute of 1397-1398 which repealed this legislation,[3] and in the statute of 1399 which repealed the statute of 1397-1398.[4]   A statute of 1423, which allowed the Duke of Bedford to appear by attorney in all suits, reminds us that he was acting as Protector during the infancy of his nephew Henry VI.[5] Strode's Act passed in 1512[6] is a landmark in the history of the privileges of Parliament ; and the numerous Acts of attainder passed in Henry VIII's reign recall well-known episodes in the political and religious history of the reign.[7]   Similarly, the policy of Mary and its reversal under Elizabeth were the occasion both of Acts of attainder,[8] and of Acts repealing these attainders and restoring the capacity of the heirs of the persons attainted.[9] The beginning of James I's reign was marked by the passing of many private Acts naturalizing the King's Scottish friends.[10] The first of the private Acts passed by the Long Parliament in 1640 was the Act for the attainder of Strafford.[11]   At the beginning of Charles II's reign there are, as we might expect, several

---

[1] Above   .   [2] 11 Richard II cc. 1-6.   [3] 21 Richard II cc. 12, 13.
[4] 1 Henry IV c. 3.   [5] 2 Henry VI c. 3.
[6] 4 Henry VIII c. 8 ; vol. iv 91 and n. 6 ; vol. vi 98.
[7] 14, 15 Henry VIII c. vii (Buckingham) ; 26 Henry VIII c. iii (the Bishop of Rochester) ; c. 5 (Sir Thomas More).
[8] 2, 3 Philip and Mary c. iii—" an Act to confirm the attainder of Henry, Duke of Suffolk, John Gray, Thomas Gray, Thomas Wyatt, James Croft, Peter Carewe, Robert Dudley, Henry Isley, knights, and many others " ; 13 Elizabeth c. 16— " an Act for the confirmation of the attainders of Charles Earl of Westmoreland, Thomas Earl of Northumberland and others."
[9] 1 Mary Sess. 3 c. i ; 1, 2 Philip and Mary c. ii ; 1 Elizabeth cc. i-iv, viii, xii, xvii, xviii ; 5 Elizabeth cc. ix-xix.
[10] 1 James I cc. x-xiii, xv, xvi, xviii-xxiv.   [11] 16 Charles I c. i.

private Acts for the restoration to some of the King's supporters of the lands of which they had been dispossessed.[1] The beginning of William and Mary's reign is marked by private Acts which reversed the attainders of Russell and Sidney,[2] and naturalized Count Schonberg and George, Prince of Denmark.[3] The accession of George I is marked by Acts attainting Bolingbroke[4] and the Duke of Ormond.[5] The bill of pains and penalties passed against Francis Atterbury[6] commemorates the part which he took in the Jacobite conspiracies of the early years of George I's reign; and the rebellion of 1745 is commemorated by an Act attainting thirty-nine persons.[7] The bursting of the South Sea Bubble is marked by an Act which confiscated the estates of principal officers of the company.[8] These few examples show that, down to the middle of the eighteenth century, the local and private Acts form a running commentary upon many important episodes in the history of England.

From the middle of the eighteenth century onwards, the personal and private Acts cease to be so closely connected with important political events. But they have never ceased to be connected with the dealings of the King or his servants with the estates or other property of the Crown. The settlement by the King of a dower or jointure on his Queen,[9] confirmation of grants made by the King to his nobles,[10] exchanges or purchase by the King of estates,[11] are the occasion for many Acts in Henry VIII's reign. In fact, throughout English history, the dealings of the King with his estates have occasioned much legislation;[12] and even after the Crown lands were made over to the nation,[13] many Acts have been necessary to regulate the dealings of the King with land not thus surrendered, and with his private estates.[14]

[1] 12 Charles II cc. iv, vi-ix, xvi; 13 Charles II St. 1 c. iii.

[2] 1 William and Mary Sess. 1 cc. i and ii.

[3] Ibid cc. iii and iv.   [4] 1 George I St. 2 c. 16.

[5] Ibid c. 17.   [6] 9 George I c. 17.

[7] 19 George II c. 26.   [8] 7 George I c. 28.

[9] 1 Henry VIII c. iii, 25 Henry VIII c. vii (Katherine of Aragon); 25 Henry VIII c. iii (Anne Boleyn); 32 Henry VIII c. xii—an Act giving the King power to make a jointure for any future wife he may marry.

[10] 5 Henry VIII cc. i-iii; 26 Henry VIII cc. i and ii.

[11] 6 Henry VIII cc. i and ii; 23 Henry VIII cc. i-viii; 25 Henry VIII cc. viii and xii; 28 Henry VIII cc. xv and xvi; 32 Henry VIII c. xix; 34, 35 Henry VIII c. i; these are a few out of very many instances.

[12] Three instances are—4 James I c. i—" an Act to ensure the house of Theobalds to the Queen with remainder to the King and his heirs "; 12 George I c. vi—" an Act to enable His Majesty to grant the inheritance of certain lands called Bowood Park in the county of Wilts to trustees upon trust for Sir Orlando Bridgman Baronet and his heirs, upon a full consideration to be paid for the same "; 2 Edward VII c. 37—" an Act to make provision with respect to the disposition and management of His Majesty's Osborne Estate in the Isle of Wight."

[13] Vol. x 348.

[14] See Halsbury, Laws of England (2nd ed.) vi 839-857 (Duchy of Lancaster), 858-889 (Duchy of Cornwall), 893-897 (Crown Private Estates).

Other Acts were found to be necessary to give validity to dealings with land [1] or offices [2] by the Crown or its servants, or to enable its servants to compound debts due to the Crown. [3]

Similarly, we get in the sixteenth century Acts which are connected with the estates of the nobility. In Henry VIII's reign there are many Acts passed to confirm the titles of the nobility and others to their estates. [4] Such Acts cured defects of title ; and it was soon found that they could be put to another use. They could be used to give powers which were denied to landowners by the ordinary law of the land. In 1555 a private Act was passed to enable the duke of Norfolk, with the advice of the Lord Chancellor, the earl of Arundel, and the bishop of Ely, to make sales and grants of his land notwithstanding his minority. [5] This was an expedient which was soon seized upon by other landowners either to gain new powers over their lands, or to free themselves from legal doubts arising from the complex settlements which the recognition of the validity of contingent remainders, the statute of Uses, and the rise of new equitable estates, had rendered possible. It was because the law of real property was growing continually more complex that these estate Acts form one of the most numerous classes of private Acts in the sixteenth, seventeenth, and eighteenth centuries. Maitland said of some of the rules of the mediæval common law that what was originally law for the great men became law for all ; [6] and we can say the same thing of these estate Acts—the expedient originally used by the King and the nobility became an expedient used by all the large landowners.

The lists of the private Acts passed in the seventeenth and eighteenth centuries show how extensive a use was made of this expedient. Thus we get Acts to confirm agreements between lords of manors and their copyholders ; [7] Acts to enable

---

[1] E.g. 9 George I c. 32—an Act for confirming articles of agreement between the principal officers of the Ordnance and Thomas Missing Esquire, for exchange of some lands at Plymouth for the service of his Majesty ; 15 George III c. 22—an Act for vesting part of the garden of the society of Lincoln's Inn in the accountant-general of the court of Chancery for the purpose of erecting thereon offices for the accountant-general, and for the register of the said Court.

[2] E.g. 27 George II c. 17—an Act for *inter alia* revesting in the Crown the power of appointing the marshal of the Marshalsea of the court of King's Bench.

[3] E.g. 10 George III c. 12—an Act to enable the Commissioners executing the office of Treasurer of his Majesty's Exchequer, or the Lord High Treasurer for the time being, to compound with William Hill and John Dyer a debt due to the Crown from William Pye, for which they are sureties.

[4] See e.g. 3 Henry VIII c. i ; 4 Henry VIII c. iv ; 24 Henry VIII c. iv ; 28 Henry VIII c. xx.

[5] 2, 3 Philip and Mary c. i.

[6] Maitland, P. and M. ii 272 (1st ed.), speaking of the spread of primogeniture, says that the King's court " here as elsewhere generalized the law of the great folk and made it common law for all free and lawful men."

[7] E.g. 21 James I c. vi ; Acts of 7 James I cc. i and ii confirmed decrees of the Exchequer Chamber and the Duchy Chamber as to the copyholders on two of the royal manors.

landowners to sell their lands for the payment of their debts ; [1]
Acts to enable them to grant leases ; [2] Acts to enable estates to
be partitioned ; [3] Acts to enable infants to acknowledge fines
and suffer recoveries,[4] to make marriage settlements,[5] and to
grant leases ; [6] Acts to discharge settled lands from the uses of
the settlement and to enable the settlor to settle lands in lieu
thereof ; [7] Acts to enable lands to be sold for the discharge of
incumbrances.[8] These are a few examples of the hundreds of
Acts of this kind which were passed from the sixteenth to the
nineteenth century. In fact a very cursory inspection of the
statute book substantiates the truth of Blackstone's account of
these Acts. He says : [9]

Private Acts of Parliament are, especially of late years, become
a very common mode of assurance. For it may sometimes happen,
that by the ingenuity of some, and the blunders of other practitioners,
an estate is most grievously entangled by a multitude of contingent
remainders, resulting trusts, springing uses, executory devises, and the
like artificial contrivances ; . . . so that it is out of the power of
either the courts of law or equity to relieve the owner. Or, it may
sometimes happen, that by the strictness or omissions of family settlements, the tenant of the estate is abridged of some reasonable power,
(as letting leases, making a jointure for a wife, or the like) which power
cannot be given him by the ordinary judges either in common law or
equity. Or it may be necessary, in settling an estate, to secure it
against the claims of infants or other persons under legal disabilities ;
who are not bound by any judgments or decrees of the ordinary courts
of justice. In these, or other cases of the like kind, the transcendent
power of Parliament is called in, to cut the Gordian knot ; and by a
particular law, enacted for this very purpose, to unfetter an estate ;
or to give its tenant reasonable powers ; or to assure it to a purchaser,
against the remote or latent claims of infants or disabled persons, by
settling a proper equivalent in proportion to the interest so barred.

Blackstone was aware of the danger inherent in this legislation—
a danger which, he reminds us, had been pointed out by Clarendon
just after the Restoration of Charles II.[10] But he says that in

---

[1] E.g. 29 Charles II c. vii—" an Act to enable Herbert Awbrey and his trustees
to sell lands for the payment of his debts " ; 22 George II c. xliii.

[2] E.g. 29 Charles II c. vi ; 1 George I St. 2 c. viii ; 20 George II c. xviii.

[3] E.g. 3 George I c. vii. [4] E.g. 7 George I St. 1 c. xvii.

[5] E.g. 9 George I c. i. [6] E.g. 8 George I c. ix.

[7] E.g. 7 George I St. 1 c. xx. [8] Ibid c. xxiv.

[9] Comm. ii 344-345.

[10] " At last it proceeded so far, that, as the noble historian expresses it, every
man had raised an equity in his own imagination, that he thought was entitled to
prevail against any descent, testament, or act of law, and to find relief in Parliament : which occasioned the king at the close of the session to remark, that the
good old rules of law are the best security ; and to wish that men might not have
too much cause to fear, that the settlements which they make of their estates shall
be too easily unsettled when they are dead, by the power of Parliament," Comm.
ii 345 ; that the King's advice was taken, is shown by the fact that the number of
private Acts in the years following the Restoration is not inordinate ; but the
number of private estate bills brought before Parliament at the beginning of the
eighteenth century was the occasion of the standing order by which they were referred
to two judges, above 327.

his day it was obviated by the fact that both Houses, and especially the House of Lords, acted "with great deliberation and caution." The House of Lords usually referred the matter to two judges and acted upon their advice.[1]

Nothing is also done without the consent expressly given, of all parties in being and capable of consent, that have the remotest interest in the matter ; unless such consent shall appear to be perversely and without any reason withheld. . . . And a general saving is constantly added at the close of the bill, of the right and interest of all persons whatsoever ; except those whose consent is so given or purchased, and who are therein particularly named.[2]

Closely akin to these estate Acts are Acts which were passed to settle schemes for the administration of charities, to grant or confirm privileges to the Universities of Oxford and Cambridge and their colleges, or to adjust the difficulties arising in parishes or in ecclesiastical corporations.

From the Tudor period onwards many Acts were passed to enable the charitable intentions of settlors and testators to be carried out. Thus in 1548 an Act was passed, "for the confirmation of a free school erected in the town of Stamford, and for more sure enjoying of the lands given by William Ratcliffe for maintenance of the schoolmaster there."[3] In 1724 an Act was got "for incorporating the executors of the last will and testament of Thomas Guy late of the City of London, and others, in order to the better management and disposition of the charities given by his said last will ; "[4] and in 1748 an Act "for raising money out of an estate in the county of Middlesex given by Lawrence Sheriff for the founding and maintaining a school and almshouses at Rugby in the county of Warwick, to be applied in rebuilding the said school, or purchasing one or more messuage or messuages, together with some ground adjoining thereto, and for the better support of the said charity."[5] The Universities of Oxford and Cambridge got a statutory confirmation of their charters in 1571 ;[6] and in 1719 Cambridge got a private Act, "to enable any corporations within the university or any other persons to sell and convey any messuages and ground to the said university for enlarging their public library."[7] Several of the colleges of Oxford and Cambridge got private Acts which either confirmed their existing status and privileges or the titles to

[1] Since a bill originating in the Commons was always referred to two judges if it got to the Lords, it was found more convenient to originate these bills in the Lords, and this came to be the invariable practice, MSS. of the House of Lords (Hist. MSS. Com.) vi *xxxix* note.

[2] Comm. ii 345 ; as Blackstone points out this general saving was not really necessary, see above 296, 362-363.

[3] 2, 3 Edward VI c. xxi.

[4] 11 George I c. 12.

[5] 21 George II c. xxiii.

[6] 13 Elizabeth c. 29 ; vol. i 168, 174.

[7] 6 George I c. xxxi.

their estates, or granted them new privileges.[1] The affairs of
parishes sometimes gave rise to private Acts. Thus in 1548
two Acts were passed for the union of churches; [2] in 1696 an Act
was passed " to ascertain and settle the payment of the im-
propriate tithes of the parish of St. Lawrence, Old Jury, in
London to the Master and Scholars of Balliol College in Oxford,
and for confirming an award made concerning the same "; [3]
and in the same year another Act was passed " to enable the
parish of St. James, within the Liberty of the City of Westminster,
to raise upon themselves so much money as will discharge
their debt for building their parish church, rector's house, vestry,
and other public works there." [4]   Similarly, the affairs of dioceses
and cathedrals sometimes called for the interference of the
Legislature.   Thus in 1676 an Act was passed, " for the appropri-
ating the rectories of Llaurhayader in Mochnant in the counties of
Denbigh and Montgomery and of Skeviog in the county of Flint
for the repairs of the cathedral church of St. Asaph, and the better
maintenance of the choir there, and also for the uniting of several
rectories *sine cura*, and the vicarages of the same parishes, within
the diocese of St. Asaph aforesaid." [5]   The agitation against
tithes at the beginning of the nineteenth century was the
occasion of the passing of some twelve hundred private Acts
exonerating particular places from tithes or providing for their
commutation. [6]

Just as the long series of estate Acts was rendered necessary
either by the complications of the land law, or by the fact that
the law did not give to landowners the powers needed either
to make the best use of their estates, or to satisfy the claims of
their families or their creditors ; so this series of Acts for the
benefit of charities, or of the universities and colleges, or of
ecclesiastical communities or corporations, was rendered necessary
or desirable by similar defects or uncertainties in the general
rules both of the law of property and of other branches of law.
Other defects in the law were the occasion of other Acts designed
either to effect objects for which the law made no provision, or
to remedy hardships occasioned by its rigidity or technicality.
Of these Acts the following three classes are perhaps the most
important :

First, we have seen that the law made no provision for a
divorce *a vinculo* ; [7] and the Reformation " had stopped up all

---

[1] 1 Mary Sess. 2 c. iii (Merton) ; 1 Elizabeth c. x (Trinity Hall) ; 3 James I
c. ix (Oriel) ; 21 James I c. i (Wadham) ; 1 George I St. 2 c. v (All Souls).

[2] 2, 3 Edward VI cc. ix and xi ; for another Act passed for the same purpose
see 8 George I c. viii.

[3] 7, 8 William III c. xviii.   [4] Ibid c. xvii.

[5] 29, 30 Charles II c. xvi.

[6] Clifford, History of Private Bill Legislation i 266.   [7] Vol. i 623.

loopholes of escape by the old devices and fiction of canonical degrees and alleged precontracts." [1] The only recourse therefore was an Act of Parliament. The Marquis of Northampton was divorced by Act of Parliament in 1551, a marriage he had already contracted was made valid, and the children of that marriage were legitimated. [2] The next instance of a divorce Act was that obtained by Lord Roos, in 1670. In 1666 an Act had been passed to illegitimate a child of Lady Anne Roos; and in 1670 Lord Roos procured an Act allowing him to marry again as if Lady Anne was naturally dead. [3] The Norfolk divorce Act of 1700 was the model of subsequent divorce Acts. [4] From 1551 to 1857 three hundred and thirty-seven such Acts were passed [5] Analogous to these Acts were Acts occasionally passed to legitimate or illegitimate children, [6] to grant a judicial separation, [7] or to annul marriages effected by force or fraud. [8]

Secondly, from the fifteenth century onwards there was a series of Acts making foreigners either denizens or naturalized British subjects. [9] These applications were so frequent that public Acts laid down certain conditions with which those who petitioned for such Acts must comply. Thus an Act of 1609 [10] made it necessary for the petitioner to have received the sacrament, and to take the oaths of allegiance and supremacy. The obligation to receive the sacrament was removed in 1826; [11] but the standing orders of the House of Lords had prescribed other conditions, [12] some of which survive in the conditions prescribed

---

[1] Clifford. History of Private Bill Legislation i 392; in 1853 the Divorce Commissioners said, "the doctrine of indissolubility . . . operated in this country with a rigour unknown in Roman Catholic times; the various fictions and devices in the shape of canonical degrees and alleged precontracts, which thus afforded so many loopholes of escape from its severity, having been each and all put an end to at the Reformation," Parlt. Papers 1852-1853 xl 258.

[2] Clifford, op. cit. i 389-391; this statute was repealed in 1553, 1 Mary St. 2 (not printed), see Clifford, op. cit. i 391 n. 4.

[3] Ibid 394-398.   [4] Ibid 410.   [5] Ibid 451.

[6] Ibid 444; a late instance is the Townshend Peerage Case of 1842, ibid 444-450.

[7] The Countess of Anglesea's Case (1700), ibid 433-436; Lady Ferrers's Case (1757-1758), ibid 436-442.

[8] May Wharton's Case (1690), ibid 398-400; Hannah Knight's Case (1696-1697), ibid 427-431; the Turner-Wakefield Case (1827), ibid 431-432.

[9] The first naturalization Act was passed in 1406, and there was another in 1423, ibid 378-380; vol. ix 76, 89-90.

[10] 7 James I c. 2.   [11] 6 George IV c. 67.

[12] "The first step was a memorial to the Home Secretary, giving his reasons for desiring naturalization, and declaring that he professed the Protestant religion, intended to reside in England, and was well affected to the government and to the British constitution. In corroboration of these statements, letters of recommendation were usual from persons of position able to testify to his orderly life and conduct. These letters, with the petitions, were then communicated to the Alien Office, which for many years kept note of the proceedings of foreigners in this country. If the report from the Alien Office were satisfactory, the Home Secretary signed a certificate to this effect, without the production of which no Naturalization Bill could be read a second time," Clifford, op. cit. i 381-382.

for getting a certificate of naturalization under the naturalization Acts.[1] The Act of Settlement provided that no person naturalized or made a denizen should, unless he were born of English parents, be able to be a privy councillor, a member of either House of Parliament, or a servant of the Crown, or to be the recipient of a grant of lands from the Crown ; [2] and, since this provision was sometimes evaded by the express clauses of private Acts, it was provided in 1714 that every naturalization bill must contain a clause which expressly enacted these incapacities.[3] An Act of 1774 provided that all naturalization bills must contain a clause to the effect that the person naturalized was not entitled to the trading immunities and indulgences of a British subject unless he continued to reside in Great Britain or the Dominions for seven years after the Act had passed.[4]

Thirdly, the extreme technicality of the law sometimes made it necessary to have recourse to a private Act. Thus Acts were necessary to remedy the defective wording of settlements and other conveyances,[5] and even of the clauses in private Acts themselves.[6] In 1609 an Act was passed " for the amending of a writ of entry whereupon a common recovery was had of the inheritance of Sir John Byron, knight, within the county palatine of Lancaster." [7] This Act was passed to remedy a hardship caused by two of the most technical branches of the common law—the law of real property and the law of procedure. How long-lived were some of the technicalities of the law of procedure, which created the necessity for these Acts, is evident from the following two instances. A statute passed in 1421 [8] provided that " writs purchased by the Wardens of Rochester Bridge, or against them, shall not abate by their death or removal." A statute passed in 1832 [9] enabled the Liverpool Marine Assurance Company to sue and be sued in the name of the chairman for the time being, or of any one of the directors of the company.

The numerous branches of law which are included under the rubric Industry and Commerce gave rise to another series of private Acts. It was during the latter part of the eighteenth

---

[1] 7, 8 Victoria c. 66 ; 33 Victoria c. 14 ; 4, 5 George V c. 17 ; cp. vol. ix 90, 91.
[2] 12, 13 William III c. 2 § 3 ; vol. ix 89.
[3] 1 George I St. 2 c. 4 § 2 ; vol. ix 89. [4] 14 George III c. 84.
[5] See e.g. 12 George I c. ix—an Act to rectify a mistake in the settlement made on the marriage of the Honourable George Carpenter Esquire with Elizabeth his now wife.
[6] See e.g. 19 George II c. xi—an Act for rectifying and amending defects in a former Act of Parliament, made in the fifteenth year of the reign of his present Majesty for sale of part of the estate of Edward Bayntun Rolt Esquire ; and for the better and more effectual execution of the trusts of the said former Act.
[7] 7 James I c. xxxix. [8] 9 Henry V St. 1 c. 12.
[9] 2, 3 William IV c. i.

century that Inclosure Acts became common.[1] The earliest Inclosure Act was passed in 1606-1607 ; [2] no other was passed till 1693 ; [3] and in Anne's reign only two Inclosure Acts were passed.[4] Sixteen were passed in George I's reign, two hundred and twenty-six in George II's reign, and three thousand three hundred and sixty in George III's reign.[5] Both in the seventeenth and eighteenth centuries the drainage and improvement of land was encouraged by local and private Acts.[6] We have seen that in the sixteenth and seventeenth centuries both trade and colonization were encouraged by Acts which created or gave enlarged powers to trading companies.[7] Similarly, in the eighteenth, as in earlier centuries,[8] Acts were passed to give enlarged powers to trading corporations,[9] and to the companies which supervised special trades.[10] Sometimes inventors got special Acts to give them a monopoly in the sale of their inventions ; [11] and in one case a stationer was given a copyright for a certain period in a named book.[12]

Closely allied to these Acts, which were passed to foster different branches of industry and commerce, are Acts to provide for various public utilities—Acts to make particular rivers navigable,[13] to preserve and improve particular harbours,[14] to provide particular towns with water,[15] to reconstruct particular

[1] For the common field system of agriculture which these Acts were passed to abolish see vol. ii 56-63.

[2] 4 James I c. 11 ; vol. iv 368 n. 10 ; vol. vi 344.

[3] 4, 5 William and Mary c. xxxi ; this was an Act to confirm an agreement as to inclosure ; it had then become clear that an agreement, though confirmed by the court of Chancery, could not bind a dissentient minority, vol. vi 345.

[4] Clifford, op. cit. i 21.   [5] Ibid and App. B no. 1.

[6] Vol. iv 368 n. 5 ; vol. vi 345 ; Clifford, op. cit. i 10-13 ; 5 Elizabeth c. viii ; 43 Elizabeth c. 11.

[7] Vol. viii 208-211.

[8] Vol. iv 353, 355 ; Lipson, Economic History of England iii 330-336.

[9] See e.g. 6 George I c. 18, which gave power to the Crown to give charters to two marine insurance companies containing various powers and privileges.

[10] 10 George I c. 20—powers given to the College of Physicians to supervise drugs and other materials for medicines ; 18 George II c. 15—the companies of Surgeons and Barbers of London separated and their powers defined ; 9 Anne c. 26—the company of fishermen of the river Thames, the powers of which were handed over to the City of London by 30 George II c. 21, as the company had ceased to act ; 23 George III c. 15 § 5—the Dyers' Company.

[11] See e.g. 15 Charles II c. xii—an Act to enable Edward Marquis of Worcester to receive the benefit and profit of a water-commanding engine by him invented, one-tenth part whereof is appropriated for the benefit of the King's Majesty his heirs and successors ; 23 George II c. xxxii—an Act to secure the profits of a dredging machine to the children of the inventor for a term of years.

[12] 7 George II c. 24—an Act for granting to Samuel Buckley, citizen and stationer of London, the sole liberty of printing and reprinting the Histories of Thuanus with additions and improvements during the time therein limited.

[13] 13 Elizabeth c. 1—for making the Welland navigable ; 21 James I c. 32—the Thames from Bercot to Oxford.

[14] See e.g. 22 George II c. 40—Ramsgate and Sandwich.

[15] See e.g. 35 Elizabeth c. x—Plymouth.

bridges.[1] It was in the second half of the eighteenth century that Acts creating new public utilities began to be common. Their number and variety were immensely increased by the mechanical inventions of the end of the eighteenth and the beginning of the nineteenth centuries. The first Canal Act, promoted by the duke of Bridgewater, was passed in 1762 ; [2] and more than a hundred canal Acts were passed before 1800.[3] The first Railway Act was passed in 1801 ; [4] and in 1843 2,036 miles of railway were open for traffic.[5] During the railway mania of 1845-1847 five hundred and seventy-eight projects for making new railways were sanctioned by Parliament.[6] Tramways came much later. It was not till 1868 that the first Tramway Acts were passed.[7] In the seventeenth and eighteenth centuries several companies for the supply of water to London were authorized.[8] In 1810 the first Act was passed to incorporate a company for the supply of gas ; [9] and " down to 1885 more than one thousand gas bills had passed the Legislature, and of these about sixty apply to the metropolis alone." [10] The first Electric Lighting Acts were obtained by the corporations of Leicester, Liverpool, Blackpool, and Over Darwen in 1879.[11]

We have already seen how large and important a place private bill legislation took in the sphere of local government.[12] It was by means of these local or private Acts that many towns and districts obtained the power to watch, light, cleanse, and pave their streets,[13] and to carry out their duties in relation to vagrants and paupers ; [14] and it was by means of these Acts that *ad hoc* bodies, such as the commissioners of sewers,[15] the turnpike trusts,[16] corporations for the administration of the poor law,[17] and improvement commissioners,[18] were established. As we have seen, these Acts were the principal means by which the semi-mediæval system of local government, which the eighteenth century had inherited, was adapted to the needs of a modern and an industrialized state. Similarly, we have seen that it was by local Acts, creating courts of Conscience or of Request, that the excessive centralization of the administration of justice in civil cases was remedied.[19]

---

[1] See e.g. 43 Elizabeth c. 16—bridges over the Eden near Carlisle.

[2] Clifford, op. cit. i 34-38.

[3] Ibid 41 n. 1—" there was a canal mania in 1791-1794, like the railway mania which broke out on a larger scale in 1845-1846 ; and eighty-one canal and navigation Acts were passed in those four years alone."

[4] Ibid 44-45—horse-power only was contemplated and the users provided their own trucks or carriages ; it was not till 1823 that the Stockton and Darlington Company got power to use steam, ibid 48-49.

[5] Ibid 86	[6] Ibid 87-88.	[7] Ibid 187.
[8] Ibid ii 79-103.	[9] Ibid i 208-209.	[10] Ibid 221.
[11] Ibid 233	[12] Vol. x 188 seqq.	[13] Ibid 191-195.
[14] Ibid 176, 190.	[15] Ibid 199-206.	[16] Ibid 207-211.
[17] Ibid 211-214.	[18] Ibid 214-219.	[19] Vol. i 190-191.

In the latter part of the nineteenth century the amount of private bill legislation did not diminish, but it tended to alter in character. It tended to alter in character because general legislation had, in a large number of cases, provided general remedies, and so obviated the necessity of applying to the Legislature for special Acts. Thus

the Public Health Acts, and more recently the Local Government Act 1858, have invested the Secretary of State, acting on the requisition of the authorities of towns, with large *quasi*-legislative powers, extending to almost every object previously attainable only by Private Acts, and including even the compulsory purchase of lands, subject only to a confirmation of the Provisional Orders by a Public Act of Parliament. This measure has gone very far to supersede private legislation, so far as regards the local management and sanitary regulation of towns, heretofore effected by " Improvement Bills." Still more recently the construction of piers and harbours has been in certain cases made practicable without applying for a Private Bill.[1]

The Act of 1846,[2] which established the new County Courts, put an end to the series of Acts passed to establish in different places courts of Conscience or of Request. The statutes which gave new powers of leasing, selling, or improving settled land to tenants for life,[3] and the statutes which made land equitable assets for the payment of simple contract debts,[4] have enormously diminished the number of those estate Acts which were so numerous in the eighteenth century. The Inclosure Clauses Act of 1801 shortened the form of Inclosure Acts and diminished the expense of passing them;[5] and the general Inclosure Act of 1845[6] rendered it unnecessary to apply for a private Act to get rid of the common field system of agriculture. Similarly, the Act of 1857 which established the Divorce Court,[7] the Naturalization Acts of 1844 and 1870,[8] and the Companies Acts,[9] have rendered

[1] Cited by Lord Redesdale, Parlt. Papers 1863 viii 68, from a paper which G. K. Rickards, the counsel to the Speaker, presented in 1863 to a House of Commons Committee on private bill legislation.

[2] 9, 10 Victoria c. 95 ; vol. i 191.

[3] 19, 20 Victoria c. 120, and 40, 41 Victoria c. 18 (the Settled Estates Acts) ; 45, 46 Victoria c. 38 (the Settled Land Act).

[4] 47 George III Sess. 2 c. 74 ; 11 George IV and 1 William IV c. 47 ; 3, 4 William IV c. 104.

[5] 41 George III c. 109—" an Act for consolidating in an Act certain provisions usually inserted in Acts of inclosure ; and for facilitating the mode of proving the several facts usually required on the passing of such Acts."

[6] 8, 9 Victoria c. 118—under this Act the Commissioners appointed under the Act could authorize inclosures ; but in 1853 the Commissioners were forbidden to enclose without the previous authority of Parliament, 15, 16 Victoria c. 79 § 1.

[7] 20, 21 Victoria c. 85.

[8] 7, 8 Victoria c. 66 ; 33 Victoria c. 14 ; above 624.

[9] Acts passed in 1825, 1834, and 1837 (6 George IV c. 91, 4, 5 William IV c. 94, and 7 William IV and 1 Victoria c. 73) were passed to facilitate the granting of incorporation by letters patent, and thus to make it unnecessary to apply for a private Act, see R. H. Formoy, Historical Foundations of Modern Company Law

unnecessary private Acts to get divorces, to get a grant of naturalization, or to get the benefit of incorporation. A glance at the list of local and private Acts for the year 1900 will show that the main topics of this legislation are now the needs and activities either of cities, boroughs, and other units of the local government, or of industrial, insurance, banking, or public utility companies ; and it will also show that very much is now effected by the provisional order procedure which could formerly have been only effected by a private Act.[1]

It is clear that the vast number of local and private Acts, which, for so many centuries, the Legislature has been adding to the statute book, has affected many branches of English law, public and private. It is in the sphere of public and semi-public law that these Acts have had the most far-reaching effects. The following instances are a few illustrations of their most important effects. First, the Acts which incorporated and gave large powers to those joint stock companies formed to carry on trade overseas, helped forward the expansion of England and of English trade in the Eastern and Western worlds.[2] Secondly, the enormous number of Acts relating to different aspects of local government,[3] and relating to those public utilities which are closely connected with local government, such as the supply of water, light, and road repair,[4] introduced modern ideas as to the proper sphere of state control. Thirdly, the series of Naturalization Acts accustomed statesmen to the idea that a subject could change his allegiance and his state.[5] Fourthly, the series of Acts which were passed to settle schemes for the administration of public charities helped to create the modern law as to charitable trusts.[6] In the sphere of private law the influence of these Acts, if not quite so far-reaching as in the sphere of public law, has not been negligible. They have had large effects on many branches of the law connected with industry and commerce. The long series of Inclosure Acts revolutionized the

---

53-60 ; the modern law begins with the Act of 1844, 7, 8 Victoria c. 110, which made it unnecessary to apply to the Crown for letters patent, or to the Legislature for an Act, by providing that " a company shall automatically be constituted by registration if it furnishes certain information about itself and complies with certain regulations," Formoy, op. cit. 67.

[1] In 1900, 291 local Acts were passed and 1 private Act ; of these local Acts 100 related to the activities of various units of local government, 135 to the activities of various companies, and 59 were confirmations of provisional orders ; for the provisional order procedure see above 364.

[2] Above 36, 44, 139.   [3] Vol. x 188 seqq.
[4] Ibid 191-195, 214-219.   [5] Above 623-624.

[6] " In the Lords' Index to Local and Personal Acts, 1801-1865, there are about 600 statutes relating to almshouses, asylums, charitable and benevolent societies and trusts, hospitals and infirmaries, colleges, schools, universities and museums. The necessity for this class of legislation has been for the most part dispensed with by the Charitable Trusts Acts," Clifford, op. cit. i 451 n. 3.

agricultural industry ; [1] and grants of incorporation and grants of patent rights helped to develop manufacture and domestic and foreign trade.[2] The numerous Estate Acts [3] were necessary appendices to the law of real property, and the divorce Acts [4] to the marriage law.

The permanent effect of this legislation on the development of English law may, I think, be stated in this way : it has supplied a series of experiments in the working of new legislative ideas, which has been of great use in suggesting the lines upon which general legislation should proceed. Just as case law has supplied a storehouse of tried principles and rules upon which the framers of codifying Acts have drawn, so these local and personal Acts have supplied a storehouse of tried legislative expedients from which the framers of general legislation have been able to select the most successful. Let us look at one or two illustrations.

We have seen that the standing orders of the two Houses, which required that certain clauses should be inserted in certain types of bills, were the precursors of those general Acts, such as the Clauses Consolidation Acts of 1845 and later Clauses Acts.[5] These Clauses Acts embody the experience gained by the consideration of private bills as to the proper clauses to insert in bills of different types. We have seen also that local and private Acts establishing bodies of improvement commissioners and poor law corporations, helped the Legislature to pass general legislation as to public health and as to the poor law.[6] The standing orders of the House of Lords as to the conditions with which a person who intended to petition for a Naturalization Act must comply, helped to suggest some of the conditions laid down by the Naturalization Acts of 1844 and 1870.[7] The provisions of the Tithe Commutation Act of 1836 were suggested by the provisions of many local and private Acts.[8] The rules laid down by the House of Lords as to the conditions which must be satisfied before it would consider a divorce bill, had some influence upon the general law laid down in 1857 as to the conditions under which the court can grant a divorce.[9] The provisions of

---

[1] Above 625. [2] Above 405, 424-432. [3] Above 620.
[4] Above 622-623. [5] Above 329-330, 384. [6] Vol. x 211-219.
[7] Above 623-624. [8] Erskine May, Constitutional History iii 219-220.
[9] In 1798 Lord Loughborough L.C. passed a series of rules as to the conditions upon which the House would receive a petition for a Divorce Bill ; *inter alia* the petitioner must have got a sentence in the Ecclesiastical court, and a verdict in an action at law against the adulterer, Parlt. Papers 1852-1853 xl 262-263 ; vol. i 623 ; in 1772 the Speaker had said that it was necessary to insist upon proceedings at the common law, as a condition precedent for getting a divorce Act, because " judgments in the spiritual courts were often obtained in the most collusive manner," Parlt. Hist. xvii 381 ; it is clear from the report of the Divorce Commissioners, that their recommendations as to the conditions upon which husbands and wives could get divorces or judicial separations, were strongly influenced by the practice both of the Ecclesiastical courts and of the House of Lords ; thus, according to the

the Inclosure Clauses Act of 1801, and of the general Inclosure
Act of 1845,[1] were the result of the consideration of the thousands
of Inclosure Acts which had come before Parliament during the
eighteenth and the earlier part of the nineteenth centuries.[2] The
need for the settled Estate Acts of 1856 and 1877, and the powers
given by those Acts to the court of Chancery, were suggested by
the long series of Estate Acts in which relaxations from the
strict rules of the law of real property had been granted.[3]

These few illustrations indicate the nature of the permanent
contribution of these local personal and private Acts to the
development of English law. In the eighteenth century they
made another contribution to the development of the law which
was then almost equally important. It was due largely to these
Acts that, during that century, the courts were able to develop
the principles of law and equity logically and continuously with
the minimum of legislative interference. A period during which
these principles could be thus developed was then essential both
for their firm establishment and their orderly settlement. During
the seventeenth century the development of modern English law
from its mediæval foundations had been begun ; but in that age
of political and constitutional turmoil it had not been able to
proceed very far. The fact that during the eighteenth century
the courts were able to consolidate and to settle the principles of
the modern law; and the fact that they were able to settle the relations of common law and equity,[4] and the sphere of the civilians'
practice,[5] were due largely to the freedom with which they were
able to develop their principles unimpeded by legislative interferences. This freedom from legislative interferences would
hardly have been possible without this system of private bill
legislation. There would have been so many cases in which,
to use the words which Blackstone uses of Estate Acts, it would
have been " out of the power of either the courts of law or equity
to release the owner," that general legislation would have been
demanded. Such legislation might no doubt have conferred
some benefits upon the English legal system. Some of the
reforms of the next age might have been anticipated. But it
would probably have had the effect of preventing the courts
from settling the principles of the modern law upon so logical,
and therefore upon so firm, a basis, as they in fact settled them.
And this was a matter of no small importance for the future
development of English law. If the courts had not had this

practice of Parliament, divorce was generally granted only at the husband's suit—
something more than adultery must be proved by the wife to get a divorce ; and
this distinction was followed in the Act of 1857, see Clifford, op. cit. i 414-418,
423-426.

[1] Above 627.   [2] Above 625.   [3] Above 620.
[4] Vol. xii 583-605.   [5] Ibid 695-702.

opportunity thus to settle the principles of the law and the relations of its different parts, there would have been some danger
that, in the ensuing age of reform, there might have been a
considerable breach in the continuity of its development. We
shall see in the following chapter that the courts used very skilfully the opportunity given to them by this infrequency of general
legislation, which the system of private bill legislation rendered
possible—so skilfully that we shall see in later chapters that the
principles, which they then established, were accepted by the
Legislature as an adequate foundation upon which it could base
the changes in and additions to the law, which it made in the
ensuing period of reform.

INDEX

A